# EMPLOYMENT RIGHTS LEGISL

## (SECOND EDITION)

UNITED KINGDOM
Sweet & Maxwell Ltd
London


AUSTRALIA
Law Book Co. Ltd
Sydney


CANADA AND USA
Carswell
Toronto


NEW ZEALAND
Brookers
Wellington


SINGAPORE AND MALAYSIA
Sweet & Maxwell
Singapore and Kuala Lumpur

# EMPLOYMENT RIGHTS LEGISLATION

## (SECOND EDITION)

Extracted from Divisions A, B, C, D, E, F, G, H and O of *Irish Employment Legislation*, a Thomson Round Hall looseleaf service

EDITED BY
Anthony Kerr M.A., LL.M., B.L.
Statutory Lecturer-in-Law, University College Dublin.

THOMSON ROUND HALL 2006

Published in 2006 by
Thomson Round Hall
43 Fitzwilliam Place
Dublin 2
Ireland


Typeset by
authorserv.com, County Clare


Printed by ColourBooks


10-digit ISBN: 1-85800-466-7
13-digit ISBN: 978-1-85800-466-2
EAN: 9781858004662


A CIP catalogue record for this book is available
from the British Library

# TABLE OF CONTENTS

**NOTE:** As this book has largely been extracted from Divisions A, B, C, D, E, F, G, H and O of the looseleaf work *Irish Employment Legislation*, the page numbers reflect the structure of that work and are not strictly sequential.

[vi]

## APPENDICES

# TERMS OF EMPLOYMENT (INFORMATION) ACT 1994

## (1994 No. 5)

ARRANGEMENT OF SECTIONS

An Act to provide for the implementation of Directive No. 91/533/EEC of 14 **AB.201** October, 1991 of the Council of the European Communities on an Employer's Obligation to Inform Employees of the Conditions Applicable to the Contract or Employment Relationship, to amend the Minimum Notice and Terms of Employment Act 1973, and to provide for related matters.

[5th April, 1994]

GENERAL NOTE

This Act implements the provisions of Council Directive 91/533/EEC on an Employer's Obligation **AB.202** to Inform Employees of the Conditions Applicable to the Contract or Employment Relationship (O.J. L288/32); on which see Clark and Hall, "The Cinderella Directive? Employee Rights to Information about Conditions Applicable to their Contract or Employment Relationship" (1992) 21 I.L.J. 106. The Directive, according to its preamble, is intended to provide employees with "improved protection against possible infringement of their rights" and to create "greater transparency" in the labour market. Employers are required to provide employees with documents notifying them of the "essential aspects" of their contract and special arrangements apply to employees who work abroad for more than one month. The Directive was based on Article 100 of the Treaty of Rome which deals with matters directly affecting the functioning of the common market, despite the U.K. Government disputing the appropriateness of the chosen legal basis because the Directive, in its view also sought to improve the living and working conditions of workers in accordance with the aims of Community social policy.

The scope of the Directive, and in particular Article 2 thereof, was considered by the Court of **AB.203** Justice in Case C-350/99, *Lange v Georg Schuenemann GmbH* [2001] E.C.R. 1–1061. The Court said that the obligation to notify employees concerned "all the aspects of the contract of employment relationship which are, by virtue of their nature, essential elements." Article 2(2) did not reduce the scope of that general requirement and the elements listed therein did not constitute "an exhaustive enumeration of the essential elements referred to in Article 2(1)." Accordingly, apart from the elements mentioned in Article 2(2) of the Directive, any element, which in view of its importance, must be considered an essential element of the contract of which it forms part must be notified to the employee.

Since 1973 Ireland has had legislation on written statements of the main terms of employment, but sections 9 and 10 of the Minimum Notice and Terms of Employment Act 1973 did not go far enough to comply with the provisions of the Directive. Accordingly these sections are repealed and replaced by this Act, which gives effect to the provisions of the Directive in two ways; first, by obliging employers to provide their employees with a written statement of particulars of their terms of employment and to notify them of any changes in those particulars and, secondly, by providing for a system of redress for employees who consider that they have been denied entitlement to information under the terms of the Act.

A–101

**AB.204** The scope of the Act was wider than the previous legislation in the following respects:

(i) It applied to all employees other than those who work less than eight hours a week or had less than four weeks continuous service. The 1973 Act, as amended by the Worker Protection (Regular Part-Time Employees) Act 1991, excluded those who worked less than eight hours a week and had less than 13 weeks' continuous service. By virtue of section 8 of the Protection of Employees (Part-Time Work) Act 2001, this act now applies to all part-time employees.

(ii) The range of employment particulars to be included in the statement required by the Act was more extensive than was required under the 1973 Act.

(iii) The Act introduced a complaints procedure if employees believe that they have failed to secure their full entitlement. The 1973 Act provided merely for the prosecution of employers who failed to meet their statutory obligations.

The Act, like the Directive, stops short of imposing an obligation on employers to provide employees with a written contract of employment. The statement to be provided under section 3 is merely evidence of the terms of the contract (see Browne-Wilkinson J. in *System Floors (UK) v Daniel* [1982] I.C.R. 54 at 58). The issue of the probative value of the notification was considered by the Court of Justice in Case C–253/96 *Kampelmann v Landschaftsverband Westfalen-Lippe* [1997] E.C.R. 1-6907, where the Court ruled that the employer's notification to the employee serves as factual proof of the essential aspects of the employment relationship, enjoying such presumption as to its correctness as would attach in domestic law to any similar document communicated to the employee. However, proof of the essential aspects of the employment relationship did not depend solely on the employer's notification and the employer must be allowed to show that the information in the notification is incorrect. For a detailed analysis of the *Kampelmann* decision see Kenner, (1999) 28 I.L.J. 205.

CITATION

**AB.205** See section 14(1).

COMMENCEMENT

**AB.206** The Act came into operation on May 16, 1994: see S.I. No. 96 of 1994.

STATUTORY INSTRUMENTS

**AB.207** Terms of Employment (Information) Act 1994 (Commencement) Order 1994 (S.I. No. 96 of 1994).
Terms of Employment (Information) (Appeals and Complaints) Regulations 1994 (S.I. No. 244 of 1994).
Terms of Employment (Information) Act 1994 (Section 3(6)) Order 1997 (S.I. No. 4 of 1997).
Terms of Employment (Additional Information) Order 1998 (S.I. No. 49 of 1998).

PARLIAMENTARY DEBATES

**AB.208** 437 *Dáil Debates* Cols. 191–209 (Second Stage)
Select Committee on Enterprise and Economic Strategy (E2 No. 2, January 19, 1994) Cols. 106–152 (Committee Stage)
Select Committee on Enterprise and Economic Strategy (E2 No. 3, February 8, 1994) Cols. 155–188 (Committee Stage resumed)
439 *Dáil Debates* Cols. 594–610 (Report and Final Stages)
139 *Seanad Debates* Cols. 1425–1455 (Second Stage)
139 *Seanad Debates* Cols. 1697–1707 (Committee and Final Stages)

**AB.209** Be it enacted by the Oireachtas as follows:

## Interpretation

**AB.210** **1.**—(1) In this Act—

"the Act of 1973" means the Minimum Notice and Terms of Employment Act 1973;

"the Council Directive" means Council Directive No. 91/533/EEC of 14 October, 1991;

"contract of employment" means—

(a) a contract of service or apprenticeship, and

(b) any other contract whereby an individual agrees with another person, who is carrying on the business of an employment agency within the meaning of the Employment Agency Act 1971, and is

A–102

acting in the course of that business, to do or perform personally any work or service for a third person (whether or not the third person is a party to the contract), whether the contract is express or implied and if express, whether it is oral or in writing;

"employee" means a person who has entered into or works under (or, where the employment has ceased, entered into or worked under) a contract of employment and references, in relation to an employer, to an employee shall be construed as references to an employee employed by that employer; and for the purposes of this Act a person holding office under, or in the service of, the State (including a member of the Garda Síochána or the Defence Forces) or otherwise as a civil servant, within the meaning of the Civil Service Regulation Act 1956, shall be deemed to be an employee employed by the State or Government, as the case may be, and an officer or servant of a local authority for the purposes of the Local Government Act 1941, a harbour authority, [the Health Service Executive] or a vocational education committee shall be deemed to be an employee employed by the authority, [Executive] or committee, as the case may be;

"employer", in relation to an employee, means the person with whom the employee has entered into or for whom the employee works under (or, where the employment has ceased, entered into or worked under) a contract of employment subject to the qualification that the person who under a contract of employment referred to in paragraph (b) of the definition of 'contract of employment' is liable to pay the wages of the individual concerned in respect of the work or service concerned shall be deemed to be the individual's employer;

"the Minister" means the Minister for [Enterprise, Trade and Employment];

"the Tribunal" means the Employment Appeals Tribunal.

(2) A word or expression that is used in this Act and is also used in the Council Directive has, unless the contrary intention appears, the meaning in this Act that it has in the Council Directive.

(3) In this Act—

(a) a reference to any enactment shall, unless the context otherwise requires, be construed as a reference to that enactment as amended, adapted or extended by or under any subsequent enactment including this Act,

(b) a reference to a section is a reference to a section of this Act unless it is indicated that reference to some other enactment is intended,

(c) a reference to a subsection, paragraph or subparagraph is a reference to the subsection, paragraph or subparagraph of the provision in which the reference occurs unless it is indicated that reference to some other provision is intended.

GENERAL NOTE

The definition of "contract of employment" encompasses not only contracts of service and of **AB.211** apprenticeship but also contracts under which workers are supplied by employment agencies. In so extending the coverage of the legislation the Act is in line with section 13 of the Unfair Dismissals

A–103

(Amendment) Act 1993 which similarly extends the protection of that legislation to persons employed through employment agencies. But note the decision of the Labour Court in *Rooney v Diageo Global Supply* [2004] E.L.R. 133, that an agency supplied worker was employed by the client under a contract of employment. On whether a person is employed under a contract of service see *Henry Denny & Sons (Ireland) Ltd v Minister for Social Welfare* [1998] 1 I.R. 34.

**AB.212**    The definition of "employee" was amended by virtue of s.66 of the Health Act 2004. The definition of "the Minister" was amended by virtue of the Enterprise and Employment (Alteration of Name of Department and Title of Minister) Order 1997 (S.I. No. 305 of 1997).

## Exclusions

**AB.213**    **2.**—(1) This Act shall not apply to—

    (a)  employment in which the employee is normally expected to work for the employer for less than 8 hours in a week, or

    (b)  employment in which the employee has been in the continuous service of the employer for less than 1 month.

(2) Where the exclusion of a class or classes of employment from any provision of this Act is justified by objective considerations, the Minister may, after consultation with representatives of employers and of employees within that class or classes of employment, by order declare that that provision shall not apply to that class or those classes of employment and this Act shall have effect in accordance with the provisions of any such order for the time being in force.

(3) The First Schedule to the Act of 1973 shall apply for the purpose of ascertaining for the purposes of this Act the period of service of an employee and whether that service has been continuous with the following modifications and with any other necessary modifications—

    (a)  the reference to 21 hours shall be construed as a reference to 8 hours,

    (b)  the references to an employee shall be construed as references to an employee within the meaning of this Act.

(4) The Minister may by order amend or revoke an order under this section, including an order under this subsection.

GENERAL NOTE

**AB.214**    This section excluded from the operation of the Act employees who were normally expected to work for less than eight hours a week or who have been in continuous service for less than four weeks. The section also contains an enabling provision to allow other classes of employment to be excluded by order from any provision of the Act. As a result of an amendment accepted at Committee Stage in the Dáil, any such exclusion will only be put into effect after consultation with the social partners. It should be noted, however, that the Directive is stated, in Article 1, to apply to every paid employee having a contract or employment relationship defined by and/or governed by the law in force in a Member State" although it is permissible to exclude, in addition to temporary employment relationships of a month or less and employees with a working week not exceeding eight hours, "casual and/or specific" employment relationships where this is "justified by objective considerations". By virtue of s.8 of the Protection of Employees (Part-Time Work) Act 2001, the Act now applies to all part-time employees regardless of the number of hours worked.

## Written statement of terms of employment

**AB.215**    **3.**—(1) An employer shall, not later than 2 months after the commencement of an employee's employment with the employer, give or cause to be given to the employee a statement in writing containing the following particulars of the terms of the employee's employment, that is to say—

    (a)  the full names of the employer and the employee,

(b) the address of the employer in the State or, where appropriate, the address of the principal place of the relevant business of the employer in the State or the registered office (within the meaning of the Companies Act 1963),

(c) the place of work or, where there is no fixed or main place of work, a statement specifying that the employee is required or permitted to work at various places,

(d) the title of the job or nature of the work for which the employee is employed,

(e) the date of commencement of the employee's contract of employment,

(f) in the case of a temporary contract of employment, the expected duration thereof or, if the contract of employment is for a fixed term, the date on which the contract expires,

[(g) the rate or method of calculation of the employee's remuneration and the pay reference period for the purposes of the National Minimum Wage Act, 2000,

(ga) that the employee may, under section 23 of the National Minimum Wage Act, 2000, request from the employer a written statement of the employee's average hourly rate of pay for any pay reference period as provided in that section,]

(h) the length of the intervals between the times at which remuneration is paid, whether a week, a month or any other interval,

(i) any terms or conditions relating to hours of work (including overtime),

(j) any terms or conditions relating to paid leave (other than paid sick leave),

(k) any terms or conditions relating to—

    (i) incapacity for work due to sickness or injury and paid sick leave, and

    (ii) pensions and pension schemes,

(l) the period of notice which the employee is required to give and entitled to receive (whether by or under statute or under the terms of the employee's contract of employment) to determine the employee's contract of employment or, where this cannot be indicated when the information is given, the method for determining such periods of notice,

(m) a reference to any collective agreements which directly affect the terms and conditions of the employee's employment including, where the employer is not a party to such agreements, particulars of the bodies or institutions by whom they were made.

(2) A statement shall be given to an employee under subsection (1) notwithstanding that the employee's employment ends before the end of the period within which the statement is required to be given.

(3) The particulars specified in paragraphs (g), (h), (i), (j), (k) and (l) of the said subsection (1), may be given to the employee in the form of a reference to provisions of statutes or instruments made under statute or of any other laws or of any administrative provisions or collective agreements, governing those particulars which the employee has reasonable opportunities of reading during the course of the employee's employment or which are reasonably accessible to the employee in some other way.

(4) A statement furnished by an employer under subsection (1) shall be signed and dated by or on behalf of the employer.

(5) A copy of the said statement shall be retained by the employer during the period of the employee's employment and for a period of 1 year thereafter.

(6) (a)　The Minister may by order require employers to give or cause to be given to employees within a specified time a statement in writing containing such particulars of the terms of their employment (other than those referred to in subsection (1)) as may be specified in the order and employers shall comply with the provisions of such an order.

　　(b)　The Minister may by order amend or revoke an order under this subsection, including an order under this paragraph.

(7) This section (other than subsection (6)) shall not apply or have effect as respects contracts of employment entered into before the commencement of this Act.

GENERAL NOTE

**AB.216**　　This section specifies the particulars of the terms of employment which an employer must give in writing to an employee. This information must be given not later than two months after the date of commencement of employment. Section 6 deals with the rights of existing employees. Certain of these particulars may be given by the employer through reference to legislation or collective agreements governing those particulars, provided they are reasonably available. Many of these particulars were required to be given under section 9 of the Minimum Notice and Terms of Employment Act 1973, but this section extends the list of particulars to include the name and address of the employer, the place of work, the job title, the expected duration of temporary contracts of employment and a reference to any relevant collective agreements. Paragraphs (g) and (ga) of subsection (1) were inserted by virtue of section 44 of the National Minimum Wage Act 2000.

　　Pursuant to the Terms of Employment (Information) Act 1994 (Section 3(6)) Order 1997 (S.I. No. 4 of 1997), any employer of a child or young person within the meaning of the Protection of Young Persons (Employment) Act 1996 must give or cause to be given, not later than one month after the commencement of employment, a copy of the abstract of the 1996 Act prescribed by section 12 of that Act. Pursuant to the Terms of Employment (Additional Information) Order 1998 (S.I. No. 49 of 1998), art. 3(1), an employer must give or cause to be given, within two months of the commencement of employment, a statement in writing containing particulars of the terms and duration of the rest periods and breaks referred to in sections 11, 12 and 13 of the Organisation of Working Time Act 1997 that are being allowed to the employee and of any other terms and conditions relating to these periods and breaks.

　　This section also requires that the written statement be signed and dated by or on behalf of the employer and that it must be retained for one year after the employee's employment has ceased. In addition to the obligation to provide the particulars as specified herein, there is also the obligation, under section 14 of the Unfair Dismissals Act 1977 (as amended), to give employees a notice in writing setting out the procedure which the employer will observe before and for the purpose of dismissal. Although neither this Act nor the 1977 Act require that the statement specify to whom and in what manner an employee may apply for the purpose of seeking redress of any grievance relating to his or her employment, clause 3.3 of the Industrial Relations Act 1990 (Code of Practice on Grievance and Disciplinary Procedures) (Declaration) Order 2000 (S.I. No. 146 of 2000) provides that a copy of the grievance and disciplinary procedure should be given to all employees "at the commencement of employment".

## Employment outside State

**AB.217**　　**4.**—(1) Where, after the commencement of this Act, an employee is required to work outside the State for a period of not less than 1 month, the employer concerned shall give or cause to be given to the employee, prior to the departure of the employee from the State, a statement under section 3 and there shall be added to the statement the following particulars, that is to say-

A–106

(a) the period of employment outside the State,

(b) the currency in which the employee is to be remunerated in respect of that period,

(c) any benefits in cash or kind for the employee attendant on the employment outside the State,

(d) the terms and conditions, where appropriate, governing the employee's repatriation.

(2) The particulars referred to in paragraphs (b) and (c) of subsection (1) may be given in the form of a reference to provisions of statutes or instruments made under statute or of any other laws or of any administrative provisions or collective agreements, governing such particulars.

GENERAL NOTE

This section deals with employment outside the State and provides that, where employees are **AB.218** assigned to work abroad for a period of not less than one month, an employer must provide the complete written statement required by section 3 before the employees' departure. Furthermore the employer must provide certain supplementary information which includes the period of employment outside the State and the benefits in cash or in kind attendant on that employment.

## Notification of changes

**5.**—(1) Subject to subsection (2), whenever a change is made or occurs in any **AB.219** of the particulars of the statement furnished by an employer under section 3, 4 or 6, the employer shall notify the employee in writing of the nature and date of the change as soon as may be thereafter, but not later than—

(a) 1 month after the change takes effect, or

(b) where the change is consequent on the employee being required to work outside the State for a period of more than 1 month, the time of the employee's departure.

(2) Subsection (1) does not apply in relation to a change occurring in provisions of statutes or instruments made under statute or of any other laws or of any administrative provisions or collective agreements referred to in the statement given under section 3 or 4.

GENERAL NOTE

This section deals with changes in the particulars of the terms of employment and provides that **AB.220** such changes must be notified to the employee in writing within one month after the changes take effect.

## Existing contracts of employment

**6.**—(1) Where, before the commencement of this Act, an employee has entered **AB.221** into a contract of employment with an employer, then, the employer shall, if so requested by the employee, furnish to the employee a statement under section 3 and, if so requested by the employee, there shall be added to the statement the particulars specified in section 4.

(2) An employer shall, within 2 months after the employer has been required to do so under subsection (1), furnish to the employee concerned a written statement in accordance with that subsection.

GENERAL NOTE

This section provides that where an existing employee requires the employer to furnish a written **AB.222** statement of particulars, the employer must do so within two months of the date of the request. It was considered that: "it would not be reasonable or administratively feasible to require employers automatically to furnish a written statement of employment terms of each existing employee on the date of implementation of the Directive." (See the Minister of State at the Department of Enterprise and Employment at 437 *Dáil Debates* Col. 198). Having regard to the provisions of subsection (1) it was the view of the Tribunal in *Murphy v. Tesco Ireland Ltd* TE7/1999 that an essential proof in a case involving a complaint that an employer has contravened section 6 is whether the employee has made a request to the employer for a statement under section 3 and/or 4. The Tribunal went on to say that, although the provisions of subsection (1) refer to a request by an employee, if a third party "be it a shop steward, union official or otherwise" makes a request to an employer "for and on behalf of an employee" then such action by the third party would satisfy the request requirement set out in subsection (1).

Pursuant to the Terms of the Employment (Additional Information) Order 1998 (S.I. No. 49 of 1998), art. 3(2), the employer of an employee who has entered into a contract of employment before March 1, 1998 must, if requested by the employee so to do, give or cause to be given, within two months of the request being made, a statement in writing containing the particulars of the terms and duration of the rest periods and breaks referred to in sections 11, 12 and 13 of the Organisation of Working Time Act 1997 that are being allowed to the employee and of any other terms and conditions relating to these periods and breaks.

## Complaints by employees in relation to contraventions of Act by their employers

AB.223    **7.**—(1) An employee may present a complaint to a rights commissioner that his or her employer has contravened section 3, 4, 5 or 6 in relation to him or her and, if he or she does so, the commissioner shall give the parties an opportunity to be heard by the commissioner and to present to the commissioner any evidence relevant to the complaint, shall give a recommendation in writing in relation to it and shall communicate the recommendation to the parties.

(2) A recommendation of a rights commissioner under subsection (1) shall do one or more of the following:

(a)  declare that the complaint was or, as the case may be, was not well founded,

(b) (i)  confirm all or any of the particulars contained or referred to in any statement furnished by the employer under section 3, 4, 5 or 6, or

    (ii)  alter or add to any such statement for the purpose of correcting any inaccuracy or omission in the statement and the statement as so altered or added to shall be deemed to have been given to the employee by the employer,

(c)  require the employer to give or cause to be given to the employee concerned a written statement containing such particulars as may be specified by the commissioner,

(d)  order the employer to pay to the employee compensation of such amount (if any) as is just and equitable having regard to all the circumstances, but not exceeding 4 weeks remuneration in respect of the employee's employment calculated in accordance with regulations under section 17 of the Unfair Dismissals Act 1977,

and the references in the foregoing paragraphs to an employer shall be construed, in a case where ownership of the business of the employer changes after a contravention to which the complaint relates, as references to the person who, by virtue of the change, becomes entitled to such ownership.

(3) A rights commissioner shall not entertain a complaint under this section if it is presented to the commissioner after the period of 6 months beginning on the date of termination of the employment concerned.

(4) (a) A complaint shall be presented by giving notice thereof in writing to a rights commissioner and the notice shall contain such particulars and be in such form as may be specified from time to time by the Minister.

(b)  A copy of a notice under paragraph (a) shall be given to the other party concerned by the rights commissioner concerned.

(5) Proceedings under this section before a rights commissioner shall be conducted otherwise than in public.

(6) A rights commissioner shall furnish the Tribunal with a copy of any recommendation given by the commissioner under subsection (1).

(7) The Minister may by regulations—

(a)  provide for any matters relating to proceedings under this section that the Minister considers appropriate, and

(b)  amend paragraph (d) of subsection (2) so as to vary the maximum amount of the compensation provided for in that paragraph, and this section shall have effect in accordance with the provisions of any regulations under this paragraph for the time being in force.

GENERAL NOTE

Article 8 of the Directive requires the Member States to provide an enforcement mechanism so that **AB.224** employees can pursue claims by judicial process if they consider they have been wronged by an employer's failure to comply with the obligations imposed. This section provides that an employee may refer a complaint in the first instance to a rights commissioner, who is given power, *inter alia*, to correct any inaccuracies or omissions in the statement of particulars and to award up to four weeks remuneration by way of compensation. In *Archbold v CMC (Ireland) Ltd* TE05/2003, the Tribunal held that money payable under the Act did not "equate to loss of remuneration" but was "in the nature of compensation". Accordingly, the Tribunal was entitled to determine what payment was just and equitable in all the circumstances (not exceeding four weeks remuneration) including whether the claimant was "unduly prejudiced" by the failure of the employer to provide the written statement of terms and conditions of employment. Consequently, in light of s.192A of the Taxes Consolidation Act 1997 (inserted by s.7 of the Finance Act 2004), such awards are exempt from income tax and will not be reckoned in computing total income for the purposes of the Income Tax Acts. The relevant regulations for the computation of remuneration are the Unfair Dismissals (Calculation of Weekly Remuneration) Regulations 1977 (S.I. No. 287 of 1977). The rights commissioner, however, has no power to adjudicate on terms of employment (see 139 *Seanad Debates* Col. 1432). Consequently the rights commissioner has no power to invent particulars of terms of employment which the contract is not required to contain or which have not been agreed (see, on a similar point, the English Court of Appeal in *England v British Telecommunications* [1993] I.C.R. 644).

## Appeals from and enforcement of recommendations of rights commissioners

**8.**—(1) A party concerned may appeal to the Tribunal from a recommenda- **AB.225** tion of a rights commissioner under section 7 and, if the party does so, the Tribunal shall give the parties an opportunity to be heard by it and to present to it any evidence relevant to the appeal, shall make a determination in writing in relation to the appeal affirming, varying or setting aside the recommendation and shall communicate the determination to the parties.

(2) (a) An appeal under this section shall be initiated by the party concerned giving, within 6 weeks of the date on which the recommendation to which it relates was communicated to the party, a notice in writing to the Tribunal containing such particulars (if any) as may be specified in regulations under subsection (3) and stating the intention of the party concerned to appeal against the recommendation.

(b) A copy of a notice under paragraph (a) shall be given by the Tribunal to the other party concerned as soon as may be after the receipt of the notice by the Tribunal.

(3) The Minister may by regulations provide for all or any of the following matters in relation to proceedings before the Tribunal and for anything consequential thereon or incidental or ancillary thereto:

(a) the procedure in relation to all matters concerning the initiation and the hearing by the Tribunal of appeals under this section.

(b) the times and places of hearings of such appeals.

(c) the representation of the parties to such appeals,

(d) the publication and notification of determinations of the Tribunal,

(e) the particulars to be contained in a notice under subsection (2),

(f) the award by the Tribunal of costs and expenses in relation to such appeals and the payment thereof,

(g) the extension by the Tribunal of the time for initiating such appeals.

(4) (a) The Minister may, at the request of the Tribunal, refer a question of law arising in proceedings before it to the High Court for determination by it and the determination of the High Court shall be final and conclusive.

A–109

(b) A party to proceedings before the Tribunal may appeal to the High Court from a determination of the Tribunal on a point of law and the determination of the High Court shall be final and conclusive.

(5) Section 39(17) of the Redundancy Payments Act 1967, shall apply in relation to proceedings before the Tribunal under this Act as it applies to matters referred to it under that section with the substitution in paragraph (e) of the said section 39(17) of "a fine not exceeding £1,000 [€1,269.74]" for "a fine not exceeding twenty pounds [€25.39]".

(6) (a) Where a recommendation of a rights commissioner in relation to a complaint under this Act has not been carried out by the employer concerned in accordance with its terms, the time for bringing an appeal against the recommendation has expired and no such appeal has been brought, the employee concerned may bring the complaint before the Tribunal and the Tribunal shall, without hearing the employer concerned or any evidence (other than in relation to the matters aforesaid), make a determination to the like effect as the recommendation.

(b) The bringing of a complaint before the Tribunal by virtue of this subsection shall be effected by giving to the Tribunal a notice in writing containing such particulars (if any) as may be specified in regulations made for the purposes of subsection (3).

GENERAL NOTE

AB.226    This section provides that either party may appeal to the Employment Appeals Tribunal from a recommendation of a rights commissioner under section 7. Subsection (4) provides for a further appeal on a point of law only to the High Court and also enables the Tribunal to request the Minister to refer a question of law to the High Court. Although the Rules of the Superior Courts do not specifically provide for appeals under this Act, it is suggested that any such appeal be brought by special summons, by analogy with the procedure set out in R.S.C. 1986, Order 105. In the absence of any specific rule of court, any such appeal need only be brought within a reasonable time: *per* McCracken J. in his *ex tempore* ruling in *McGaley v Liebherr Container Cranes Ltd* (2001/234Sp) delivered on October 12, 2001. In the event of an employer not complying with a rights commissioner's recommendation, subsection (6) provides that the matter may be brought before the Tribunal. The procedures to be followed in relation to the submission and hearing of appeals and complaints are prescribed by the Terms of Employment (Information) (Appeals and Complaints) Regulations 1994 (S.I. No. 244 of 1994).

    The circumstances in which the High Court will overturn a decision of a specialist tribunal such as the Employment Appeals Tribunal have been considered in many cases: see for example, *Henry Denny & Sons (Ireland) Ltd v Minister for Social Welfare* [1998] 1 I.R. 34 and in particular the comments of Hamilton C.J. at 37. In considering whether to allow an appeal against a decision of such a tribunal, the High Court must consider whether that body based its decision on an identifiable error of law or on an unsustainable finding of fact. A decision cannot be challenged on the grounds of irrationality if there is any relevant material to support it: see further *Mulcahy v Waterford Leader Partnership Ltd* [2002] E.L.R. 12 (O'Sullivan J.) and *Thompson v Tesco Ireland Ltd* [2003] E.L.R. 21 (Lavan J.). In *National University of Ireland, Cork v Ahern* [2005] 2 I.R. 577, the Supreme Court held that, although findings of fact must be accepted by the High Court on appeal, that court could still examine the basis upon which those facts were found. The relevance or admissibility of the matters relied on in determining the facts were questions of law.

### Enforcement of determinations of Tribunal

AB.227    **9.**—(1) (a) If an employer fails to carry out in accordance with its terms a determination of the Tribunal in relation to a complaint under section 7 within 6 weeks from the date on which the determination is communicated to the parties, the District Court shall, on application to it in that behalf by—

(i)    the employee concerned,

(ii)   the employee's trade union, or

(iii)  the Minister, if the Minister considers it appropriate to make the application having regard to all the circumstances, without hearing the employer or any evidence (other than in relation to the matters aforesaid) make an order directing the employer to carry out the determination in accordance with its terms.

(b) In paragraph (a) the reference to a determination of the Tribunal is a reference to such a determination in relation to which, at the expiration of the time for bringing an appeal against it, no such appeal has been brought, or if such an appeal has been brought it has been abandoned and the reference to the date on which the determination is communicated to the parties shall, in a case where such an appeal is abandoned, be construed as a reference to the date of such abandonment.

(2) The District Court may, in an order under this section, if in all the circumstances it considers it appropriate to do so, where the order relates to the payment of compensation, direct the employer concerned to pay to the employee concerned interest on the compensation at the rate referred to in section 22 of the Courts Act 1981, in respect of the whole or any part

A–110/1

of the period beginning 6 weeks after the date on which the determination of the Tribunal is communicated to the parties and ending on the date of the order.

(3) Proceedings under this section shall be heard by the judge assigned to the district court district in which the employer concerned ordinarily resides or carries on any profession, business or occupation.

GENERAL NOTE

This section provides for enforcement of tribunal determinations by giving the Minister, the employee's trade union or the employee concerned the power to apply to the District Court for an order directing the employer to implement the determination. The District Court judge is also empowered by subsection (2) to award interest on any compensation awarded. The relevant District Court Rules are now to be found in Ord.99B, rr.5 and 6 which were inserted by the District Court (Terms of Employment Information) Rules 2003 (S.I. No. 409 of 2003) reproduced below at AC.501.　AB.228

## Evidence of failure to attend before or give evidence or produce documents to Tribunal

**10.**—A document purporting to be signed by the chairman or a vice-chairman of the Tribunal stating that—　AB.229

(a) a person named in the document was, by a notice under paragraph (c) of section 39(17) of the Redundancy Payments Act 1967, required to attend before the Tribunal on a day and at a time and place specified in the document, to give evidence or produce a document,

(b) a sitting of the Tribunal was held on that day and at that time and place, and

(c) the person did not attend before the Tribunal in pursuance of the notice or, as the case may be, having so attended, refused to give evidence or refused or failed to produce the document,shall, in a prosecution of the person under paragraph (e) of the said section 39(17), be evidence of the matters so stated without further proof.

GENERAL NOTE

This section, which mirrors section 12 of the Unfair Dismissals (Amendment) Act 1993, specifies that a document signed by the chairman or a vice-chairman of the Tribunal, stating details of the alleged offence, shall be admitted as evidence of the matters so stated without further proof.　AB.230

## Laying of orders and regulations before Houses of Oireachtas

**11.**—Every order or regulation made under this Act shall be laid before each House of the Oireachtas as soon as may be after it is made and, if a resolution annulling the order or regulation is passed by either such House within the next 21 days on which that House has sat after the order or regulation is laid before it, the order or regulation shall be annulled accordingly but without prejudice to the validity of anything previously done thereunder.　AB.231

## Expenses of Minister

**12.**—The expenses incurred by the Minister in the administration of this Act shall, to such extent as may be sanctioned by the Minister for Finance, be paid out of moneys provided by the Oireachtas.　AB.232

## Repeals

**13.**—Sections 9 and 10 of the Act of 1973 are hereby repealed.　AB.233

GENERAL NOTE

**AB.234**     This section repeals sections 9 and 10 of the Minimum Notice and Terms of Employment Act 1973. The former section specified the details of the terms of employment to be provided by an employer and the latter provided that an employer who failed to comply could be prosecuted. Both sections have been overtaken by the provisions of sections 3, 7, 8, and 9 of this Act.

## Short title and commencement

**AB.235**     **14.**—(1) This Act may be cited as the Terms of Employment (Information) Act 1994.

(2) This Act shall come into operation on such day as the Minister may appoint by order.

GENERAL NOTE

**AB.236**     Section 1(5) of the Protection of Employees (Part-Time Work) Act 2001 provides that, insofar as the 2001 Act relates to this Act, the two Acts may be cited together as the Terms of Employment (Information) Acts 1994 and 2001. The Terms of Employment (Information) Act 1994 (Commencement) Order 1994 (S.I. No. 96 of 1994) appointed May 16, 1994 as the day on which the Act came into operation. The Directive, however, required transposition by June 30, 1993 at the latest.

# TERMS OF EMPLOYMENT (INFORMATION) (APPEALS AND COMPLAINTS) REGULATIONS, 1994

### (S.I. No. 244 of 1994)

**1.**—(1) These Regulations may be cited as the Terms of Employment (Infor- AC.201 mation) (Appeals and Complaints) Regulations, 1994.

(2) These Regulations shall come into operation on the 2nd day of August, 1994.

**2.** In these Regulations— AC.202

"the Act" means the Terms of Employment (Information) Act 1994 (No. 5 of 1994);

"appeal" means an appeal under section 8(1) of the Act;

"complaint" means a complaint under section 8(6) of the Act;

"the Minister" means the Minister for [Enterprise, Trade and Employment];

"the Tribunal" means the Employment Appeals Tribunal.

**3.** A notice under subsection (2) or (6) of section 8 of the Act shall contain— AC.203

(a) the names, addresses and descriptions of the parties to the proceedings to which the appeal or complaint relates,

(b) the date of the recommendation to which the appeal or complaint, as the case may be, relates and the name of the rights commissioner who made the recommendation, and

(c) a brief outline of the grounds of appeal or complaint, as the case may be.

**4.** An appeal or complaint may be withdrawn by giving a notification in writing AC.204 signifying such withdrawal to the Tribunal.

**5.**—(1) A party to an appeal or complaint under subsection (2) or (6) of section AC.205 8 of the Act who receives a notice thereof shall—

(a) if he or she intends to contest the appeal or be heard by the Tribunal at the hearing of the appeal,

(b) if he or she intends to contest the complaint or be heard by the Tribunal in relation to the matters referred to in section 8(6)(a),

enter an appearance to the appeal or the complaint, as the case may be, by giving notice of appearance to the Tribunal within 14 days (or such longer period as the Tribunal may fix under paragraph (3) of this Regulation) of receipt by him or her of the said notice.

(2) A notice of appearance under this Regulation shall contain a brief outline of the grounds on which the appeal or complaint will be contested by the person entering the appearance.

(3) A party to an appeal or complaint may, before the expiration of the period referred to in paragraph (1) of this Regulation, apply to the Tribunal, by notice in writing given to the Tribunal and containing a brief outline of the grounds for the application, for an extension of that period for entering an appearance to the appeal or complaint, as the case may be, and the Tribunal may, if it is satisfied that there are reasonable grounds for doing so, extend the time aforesaid by such period as it considers appropriate.

**6.** On receipt by the Tribunal of a notification under Regulation 4 of these AC.206 Regulations or of a notice of appearance under Regulation 5 of these Regulations, the Tribunal shall cause a copy of the notice or notification, as the case may be, to be given to the other party concerned.

AC.207 **7.** An error (including an omission) of a formal nature in a determination of the Tribunal may be corrected

    (a) in any case, by the chairman of the Tribunal, and

    (b) in a case in which the determination concerned was made at a time when a vice-chairman was acting as chairman of the Tribunal, by the vice-chairman,

by a certificate signed by him or her.

AC.208 **8.**—(1) The Tribunal shall maintain a register, to be known as the Register of Terms of Employment (Information) Determinations (referred to subsequently in this Regulation as the "Register") and shall cause to be entered in the Register particulars of every determination of the Tribunal under section 8 of the Act.

(2) The Register may be inspected free of charge by any person during normal office hours.

(3) Particulars of any correction made under Regulation 7 of these Regulations shall be entered in the Register.

(4) A copy of an entry in the Register shall be sent to the parties concerned.

AC.209 **9.**—(1) A notice or notification under these Regulations or subsection (2) or (6) of section 8 of the Act may be given by sending it by registered post addressed to the Secretary, Employment Appeals Tribunal, Davitt House, 65A Adelaide Road, Dublin 2, and a notice or notification under these Regulations or a document under paragraph (b) of the said section 8(2) may be given to any other person by sending it by registered post addressed to the person

    (a) in case his or her address is specified correctly in a notice referred to in Regulation 5 of these Regulations, at that address, and

    (b) in any other case

        (i) if the person is a company (within the meaning of the Companies Act, 1963), at its registered office,

        (ii) if the person is not a company (within the meaning aforesaid) at a place where the person resides or carries on a profession, business or occupation.

(2) Any such notice or notification or document aforesaid that is given to a person authorised to receive it by the person to whom it is required to be given by the Act or by these Regulations shall be deemed to have been given to the latter person.

AC.210 **10.** Regulations 10 to 17(2), 19, 20, 20A (inserted by the Redundancy (Employment Appeals Tribunal) Regulations, 1979 (S.I. No. 114 of 1979)), 23, 23A (inserted by the Redundancy (Employment Appeal Tribunal) Regulations, 1979), and 24 of the Redundancy (Redundancy Appeals Tribunal) Regulations, 1968 (S.I. No. 24 of 1968), shall, with any necessary modifications (and, in the case of the said Regulations 20 and 20A, with the modification that a sum awarded by the Tribunal under either of those Regulations shall, in lieu of being paid out of the Fund referred to therein, be paid by the Minister for [Enterprise, Trade and Employment] with the consent of the Minister for Finance) apply in relation to appeals and complaints under section 8 of the Act and proceedings in relation to such appeals or complaints as they apply in relation to appeals provided for by section 39 of the Redundancy Payments Act, 1967 (No. 21 of 1967), and proceedings in relation to such appeals.

General Note

AC.211     These Regulations prescribe the procedures to be followed in relation to the submission and hearing of appeals and complaints before the Employment Appeals Tribunal under the 1994 Act. The title of

A–154

the Minister amended by the Enterprise and Employment (Alteration of Name of Department and Title of Minister) Order 1997 (S.I. No. 305 of 1997). It should be noted that a determination which does not state correctly the name of the employer concerned or any other material particular may, on application to the Tribunal, be amended so as to state correctly the name or other material particular: see section 39(2) of the Organisation of Working Time Act 1997.

# TERMS OF EMPLOYMENT (INFORMATION) ACT 1994 (SECTION 3(6)) ORDER 1997

## (S.I. No. 4 of 1997)

**1.** This Order may be cited as the Terms of Employment (Information) Act 1994 (Section 3(6)) Order 1997.  AC.301

**2.** An employer who employs a child or young person (within the meaning of AC.302 the Protection of Young Persons (Employment) Act 1996 (No. 16 of 1996)), to work for him or her shall, not later than one month after the commencement of the employer's employment, give or cause to be given to the employee a copy of the abstract of the Protection of Young Persons (Employment) Act 1996, prescribed for the purpose of section 12 of that Act.

GENERAL NOTE

This Order provides that employees under the age of 18 be given a copy of the abstract of the AC.303 Protection of Young Persons (Employment) Act 1996 not more than one month after employment commences. The abstract should be in the form specified in the Schedule to the Protection of Young Persons (Employment) (Prescribed Abstract) Regulations 1997 (S.I. No. 3 of 1997): see below, para. FC.301.

# TERMS OF EMPLOYMENT (ADDITIONAL INFORMATION) ORDER 1998

## (S.I. No. 49 of 1998)

**1.** This Order may be cited as the Terms of Employment (Additional Informa- AC.401 tion) Order 1998, and shall come into operation on the 1st day of March, 1998.

**2.** In this Order "the Act" means the Organisation of Working Time Act 1997 AC.402 (No. 20 of 1997).

**3.**—(1) In relation to an employee who has entered into a contract of AC.403 employment after the commencement of this Order, the employee's employer shall, within two months after the employee's commencement of employment with the employer, give or cause to be given to the employee a statement in writing containing particulars of the times and duration of rest periods and breaks referred to in sections 11, 12 and 13 of the Act that are being allowed to the employee and of any other terms and conditions relating to those periods and breaks.

(2) In relation to an employee who has entered into a contract of employ- ment before the commencement of this Order, the employee's employer shall, if requested by the employee to do so, give or cause to be given to the employee, within 2 months of the request being made, a statement in writing containing particulars of the times and duration of the rest periods and breaks referred to in sections 11, 12 and 13 of the Act that are being allowed to the employee and of any other terms and condtions relating to those periods and breaks.

GENERAL NOTE

**AC.404**     This Order provides that, where an employer is required to provide an employee with a written statement of certain particulars of his or her terms of employment, such statement should include details of the times and duration of (and any other terms and conditions relating to) the rest periods and breaks referred to in sections 11, 12 and 13 of the Organisation of Working Time Act 1997 that are being allowed to the employee.


# DISTRICT COURT (TERMS OF EMPLOYMENT INFORMATION) RULES, 2003

## (S.I. No. 409 of 2003)

**AC.501**     1. These rules may be cited as the District Court (Terms of Employment Information) Rules, 2003.

**AC.502**     2. These rules shall come into operation on the 9th day of October, 2003 and shall be read together with all other District Court rules for the time being in force.

**AC.503**     3. Order 99B of the District Court Rules, 1997 (S.1. No. 93 of 1997) shall be amended by the insertion immediately following Order 99B, rule 4 of the following:

    5.    "An application to the Court for an order pursuant to section 9 of the Terms of Employment (Information) Act, 1994 may be made to any sitting of the Court for the court district in which the respondent employer carries on any trade, profession, business or occupation.

    6.    Such application shall be by notice of application in the Form 99B.3, Schedule C and shall be served on the respondent by prepaid registered post not later than seven days before the date of the sitting for which the application is returnable. An order made pursuant to section 9 of the said Act of 1994 on such application shall be in the Form 99B.4, Schedule C".

**AC.504**     4. The Forms numbered 99B.3 and 99B.4 in Schedule 1 hereof shall be added to the Forms in Schedule C of the District Court Rules, 1997 (S.I. No. 93 of 1997).

## Schedule 1

FORM 99B.3

TERMS OF EMPLOYMENT (INFORMATION) ACT, 1994, SECTION 9

NOTICE OF APPLICATION

AC.505

District Court Area of

District No.

......................................................................................................................................................
Applicant
......................................................................................................................................................
Respondent

WHEREAS by determination made in writing pursuant to section 8 of the above-named Act in the matter of an appeal (reference number ......) from the recommendation of a rights commissioner on the complaint of *the above-named applicant * .................... (herein referred to as the "employee") against you the respondent, the Employment Appeals Tribunal determined that .............................................

[*which said determination was communicated to the parties on        and the time for appeal against said determination having expired]
[*and appeal having been brought against said determination, but abandoned on        ]

AND WHEREAS you the respondent have failed to carry out the said determination of the Employment Appeals Tribunal in accordance with its terms.

TAKE NOTICE that I will apply at the sitting of the District Court to be held at
on the        day of        at        am/pm
for an order under section 9 of the aforesaid Act, directing you to comply with the said determination. *[and for an order that you pay interest on the compensation at the rate referred to in section 22 of the Courts Act, 1981, for such period as may be ordered (being not more than the period beginning six weeks after the date on which the said determination of the Employment Appeals Tribunal was communicated or appeal from such determination was abandoned and ending on the date of such order)].

Dated this        day of

Signed........................................................
Solicitor for the Applicant

To.        The above named respondent
Of

To the District Court Clerk,
District Court Office at .......................................

*delete as appropriate

A–157

**AC.506**                                     No. 99B.4

TERMS OF EMPLOYMENT (INFORMATION) ACT, 1994. Section 9 ORDER

District Court Area of                              District No.

...................................................................................................................................................
Applicant
...................................................................................................................................................
Respondent

WHEREAS on the application of the above-named applicant for an order directing the respondent to carry out the determination of the Employment Appeals Tribunal made in writing pursuant to section 8 of the above-named Act in the matter of an appeal (reference number......) from the recommendation of a rights commissioner on the complaint of *the applicant * ................(herein referred to as the "employee") against the respondent,

[*which said determination was communicated to the parties on                and the time for appeal against such determination having expired]
[*and appeal having been brought against such determination, but abandoned on                    ]

And the Court being satisfied that the respondent was duly served with notice of the application

IT IS ORDERED AND DIRECTED that the respondent do forthwith carry out the above-mentioned determination of the said Employment Appeals Tribunal in accordance with the terms of said determination.

[*IT IS FURTHER ORDERED AND DIRECTED that the respondent pay to the employee interest on the compensation at the rate referred to in section 22 of the Courts Act, 1981, for the period of (being not more than the period beginning six weeks after the date herein specified on which the determination of the Employment Appeals Tribunal was communicated to the parties or appeal from such determination was abandoned and ending on the date of this order)].

Dated this            day of

                                   Signed ..............................................
                                        Judge of the District Court
[*delete as appropriate]

GENERAL NOTE

**AC.507**    These Rules amend Ord.99B of the District Court Rules 1997 (S.I. No. 93 of 1997) to allow applications to be made pursuant to s.9 of the Terms of Employment (Information) Act 1994 to any sitting of the court for the court district in which the respondent employer carries on any trade, profession, business or occupation. Such application shall be by notice of application in the Form 99B.3, Sch. C and shall be served on the respondent by prepaid registered post not later than seven days before the date of the sitting for which the application is returnable. An order made pursuant to s.9 of the said Act of 1994 on such application shall be in the Form 99B.4, Sch. C.

# ORGANISATION OF WORKING TIME ACT 1997

## (1997 No. 20)

ARRANGEMENT OF SECTIONS

### PART I

PRELIMINARY AND GENERAL

### PART II

MINIMUM REST PERIODS AND OTHER MATTERS RELATING TO WORKING TIME

### PART III

HOLIDAYS

### PART IV

MISCELLANEOUS

33. Prohibition on double employment.
34. Penalties, proceedings, etc.
35. Codes of practice.
36. Provisions in relation to Protection of Young Persons (Employment) Act 1996.
37. Voidance of certain provisions.
38. [...]
39. Powers of rights commissioner, Employment Appeals Tribunal or Labour Court in certain cases.
40. Alternative means of claiming relief in cases of non-compliance with Part III.
41. [...]

FIRST SCHEDULE

Transitional Provisions in relation to Annual Leave Entitlements

SECOND SCHEDULE

Public Holidays

THIRD SCHEDULE

Entitlement under section 21 in respect of Public Holidays: Exceptions

FOURTH SCHEDULE

Enactments Repealed

FIFTH SCHEDULE

Transitional Provisions in relation to Section 15(1)

SIXTH SCHEDULE

Text of Council Directive [93/104/EC of 23 November 1993 (See para. BA.101, above.)]

**BB.101**    An Act to provide for the implementation of Directive 93/104/EC of 23 November 1993 of the Council of the European Communities concerning certain aspects of the organization of working time, to make provision otherwise in relation to the conditions of employment of employees and the protection of the health and safety of employees, to amend certain enactments relating to employees, to repeal the Conditions of Employments Acts 1936 and 1944, the Holidays (Employees) Acts 1973 and 1991, and certain other enactments and to provide for related matters.

[7th May, 1997]

INTRODUCTION AND GENERAL NOTE

**BB.102**    The purpose of this Act is the transposition into Irish law of Council Directive 93/104/EC of November 23, 1993 concerning certain aspects of the organisation of working time. The 1993 Directive contained a considerable number of exclusions (mainly relating to the various transport sectors and to doctors in training) and derogations, and an amending Directive was adopted in June 2000 (Directive 2000/34/EC) extending protection to non-mobile workers in the excluded sectors and to doctors in training. In addition, sectoral social partnership negotiations at European level took place which produced agreements between the Federation of Transport Workers' Unions and the European Community Shipowners' Association in the maritime transport sector and between the Association of European Airlines, the European Transport Workers' Federation, the European Cockpit Association, the European Regions Airlines Association, and the International Air Carrier Association in the civil aviation sector. The former was adopted by the Council in June 1999 as Directive 99/63/EC, and the latter was adopted in November 2000 as Directive 2000/79/EC. An agreement was also reached between the Community of European Railways and the European Transport Workers' Federation in the railway sector which was adopted in July 2005 as Directive 2005/47/EC. Talks between the Federation of Transport Workers' Unions and the International Road Transport Union, however, broke down in September 1998 forcing the Commission to propose a Directive covering mobile workers in the road transport sector. This was eventually adopted in March 2002 as Directive 2002/15/EC. Self-employed drivers are exempted from the scope of the Directive until March 23, 2009, at which time

B–52

the Commission will either propose their inclusion or their continuing exclusion. The 1993 Directive and the 2000 amending Directive were then consolidated by Directive 2003/88/EC.

The issue of working time has been one of the main focuses of labour market debate both in Ireland and in the rest of Europe, over the past three decades. The number of hours worked by individuals has decreased considerably and this decline is characterised by shorter working weeks, increased paid annual leave and public holidays, earlier retirement, etc. In addition reductions in weekly working time have been high on the collective bargaining agenda for nearly all trade unions not just as a means of improving working conditions but also as a means of job creation.

The working hours of those employed in industrial work and retail distribution used to be regulated, respectively, by the Conditions of Employment Acts 1936 and 1944 and the Shops (Conditions of Employment) Acts 1938 and 1942 which essentially provided for a working week of 48 hours and a nine-hour day. Overtime could not exceed two hours a day, 12 hours per week or 240 hours per year. Ministerial licences, however, could be granted for particular employers and industries derogating from the provisions of the legislation. Many such licences were granted and by the 1980s it had become accepted that the provisions of this legislation were outdated and needed to be reviewed.

In 1984 the then government introduced an Hours of Work Bill which was clearly aimed at **BB.103** expanding the level of employment by reducing working hours and overtime and banning "double jobbing". The Bill proposed that the basic working week would be 40 hours a week, averaged over a 12-week period, with permitted overtime of 40 hours in any period of four consecutive weeks or 100 hours in any period of twelve consecutive weeks. Employers were to be prohibited from employing persons to work hours in excess of those prescribed and employees were to be similarly prohibited from working hours in excess. The Bill did not gain great support amongst employer and trade union bodies and the proposals were abandoned following the change of government in 1987.

The issue appeared back on the legislative agenda when the European Commission, on July 25, 1990, adopted a proposal for a Council Directive on the organisation of certain aspects of working time. Following consultation with the European Parliament, an amended proposal was submitted to the Council on April 23, 1991 and a common position was reached by the Ministers of Social and Labour Affairs at a meeting on June 1, 1993 with all Member States voting in favour with the exception of the United Kingdom, which announced its intention to challenge the legal basis of the proposed directive in the Court of Justice. Nevertheless, the Directive was adopted by the Council at a meeting on November 23, 1993, the United Kingdom abstaining.

The legal basis chosen by the Commission for the Directive was Article 118A of the Treaty which **BB.104** allows qualified majority voting on proposals concerning the health and safety of workers. The U.K. government's view, however, was that there was no reliable evidence linking working time with health and safety and that the proposal related to "working conditions" and therefore should have been adopted on a legal basis which required unanimous voting, such as Article 100 or even Article 235.

The U.K.'s challenge was rejected by the Court of Justice in a decision delivered on November 12, 1996: Case C–84/94, *United Kingdom v Council of the European Union* [1996] E.C.R. I-5755. The U.K. had argued that Article 118A permitted only the adoption of directives which had a "genuine and objective link" to the health and safety of workers and that this interpretation was borne out by the expression "working environment" used in Article 118A which implied that directives based on that provision must be concerned only with physical conditions and risks at the workplace. The court, however, was of the opinion that there was nothing in the wording of Article 118A to indicate that the concept of working environment should be interpreted restrictively and not as embracing "all factors, physical or otherwise, capable of affecting the health and safety of the worker in his working environment, including in particular certain aspects of the organisation of working time."

The decisive factor for the court was the World Health Organisation's definition of "health" as being "a state of complete physical, mental and social well being that does not consist only in the absence of illness or infirmity". Because the court decided that the Directive had as its principal objective the protection of the health and safety of workers, it followed that no Article of the Treaty, other than Article 118A, could have constituted the appropriate legal basis for its adoption.

For a detailed analysis of the court's decision, see Ellis, (1997) 34 C.M.L. Rev. 1049, Kenner "A Distinctive Legal Basis for Social Policy" (1997) 22 E.L. Rev. 579 and Fitzpatrick "Straining the Definition of Health and Safety" (1997) 26 I.L.J. 115. See also O'Mara "The Use of Article 118A of the E.C. Treaty to Achieve Wider Social Goals" [1996] *Commercial Law Practitioner* 276. On the Directive generally see Bercusson, *Working Time in Britain: Towards a European Model* (Institute of Employment Rights, 1994) and Bercusson, *European Labour Law* (1996) pp. 305-347, wherein the important point is made that collective bargaining has received a major stimulus in the Directive, as it could play an important role in setting substantive standards in relation to night work, daily rest breaks and maximum weekly working hours.

The Directive laid down minimum requirements for the organisation of working time. Member **BB.105** States are obliged to take the measures necessary to ensure that every worker is entitled to a minimum daily rest period of 11 consecutive hours per 24-hour period (Art.3), to a rest break where the working day is longer than six hours, the details of which to be determined by the two sides of industry or by national legislation (Art.4), to a minimum uninterrupted rest period of 24 hours in each seven-day period, plus the 11 hours daily rest referred to in Art.3 (Art.5) and to four weeks paid annual leave (Art.7). Furthermore, Art.6 requires Member States to take the measures necessary to ensure that, in keeping with the need to protect the health and safety of workers, the period of weekly working time is determined by the two sides of industry or by national legislation, provided that the average working time for each seven-day period, including overtime, does not exceed 48 hours.

**BB. 106**    Chapter 3 of the Directive contains various requirements concerning night work, shift work and patterns of work. Member States were accordingly obliged to take the measures necessary to ensure that normal hours of work for night workers do not exceed an average of eight in any 24-hour period (Art.8). Night workers must also be entitled to a free health assessment before their assignment and thereafter at regular intervals (Art.9). Finally, where work is organised according to a certain pattern, employers are to take account of the general principle of adapting work to the worker, with a view, in particular, to alleviating monotonous work and work at a pre-determined work-rate, depending on the type of activity and also of health and safety requirements.

**BB. 107**    The Court of Justice has ruled that Art.6(2) fulfils all the conditions necessary for it to have "direct effect": Case C–397/01 *Pfeiffer v Deutsches Rotes Kreuz* [2004] E.C.R. 1-8835. The English Court of Appeal, however, has ruled that Art.7 is not sufficiently clear and precise to have "direct effect": *Gibson v East Riding of Yorkshire District Council* [2002] I.R.L.R. 598. The nature and scope of the right which Art.7 was intended to confer was considered by the Court of Justice in Case C–173/99 *Broadcasting, Entertaining, Cinematographic and Theatre Union (BECTU) v Secretary of State for Trade and Industry* [2001] E.C.R. 1-4881. In *Royal Liver Assurance Ltd v Services Industrial Professional Technical Union DWT* 41/2001, the Labour Court emphasised the Advocate General's conclusion in *BECTU* that the right to paid annual leave constituted "a fundamental social right" which was characterised as an "automatic and unconditional right granted to every worker".

**BB.108**    The 1997 Act, in providing for the transposition of the Directive, other than Articles 8, 9, 10, 11, 12 and 13 which were implemented under the Safety, Health and Welfare at Work Act 1989 where they were not already in force under that Act, repeals the Conditions of Employment Acts 1936 and 1944, the Night Work (Bakeries) Acts 1936 and 1981, the Shops (Conditions of Employment) Acts 1938 and 1942, the Holidays (Employees) Act 1973 and section 4 of the Worker Protection (Regular Part-Time Employees) Act 1991 (the remainder of which was repealed by the Protection of Employees (Part-Time Work) Act 2001). In addition the Act contains provisions concerning the payment of Sunday workers and the use of so-called "zero hours" contracts, neither of which were addressed by the Directive. The relevant health and safety provisions are now to be found in the Safety, Health and Welfare at Work (Night Work and Shift Work) Regulations 2000 (S.I. No. 11 of 2000).

**BB.109**    The activities of doctors in training were effectively brought within the scope of the Act by the European Communities (Organisation of Working Time) (Activities of Doctors in Training) Regulations 2004 (S.I. No. 494 of 2004) reproduced below at BC.1201. Transport workers (other than those performing "mobile road transport activities" and mobile staff in civil aviation) together with offshore workers were effectively brought within the scope of the Act by the Organisation of Working Time (Inclusion of Transport Activities) Regulations 2004 (S.I. No. 817 of 2004) and the Organisation of Working Time (Inclusion of Offshore Work) Regulations 2004 (S.I. No. 819 of 2004), reproduced below at BC.1301 and BC.1401 respectively. The provisions of Directive 2002/15/EC on the organisation of the working time of persons performing mobile road transport activities were transposed by the European Communities (Organisation of Working Time of Persons Performing Mobile Road Transport Activities) Regulations 2005 (S.I. No. 2 of 2005), reproduced below at BC.1501.

**BB.110**    Two specific aspects of the Directive are currently under consideration by the European Commission. The first concerns the reference period for calculating the average maximum weekly working time and the second concerns the option not to apply the maximum weekly working time if the worker gives his or her agreement to carry out such work. The concept of "working time" as interpreted by the Court of Justice is also being considered. See *Commission Communication Document* COM (2003) 843 final.

**BB.111**    The introduction of the 1999 Act was heavily criticised by employer bodies and was opposed by Fianna Fáil principally on the then government's decision not to avail of the individual opt-out clause in the Directive whereby employees could volunteer to work more than the maximum 48 hours a week. It is likely, however, that such a provision would have been a source of disputes involving allegations by workers that they had opted out under duress or that they were victimised because they declined to opt-out. Furthermore the Directive requires detailed monitoring of the use of the individual opt-out and this would obviously have imposed a significant administrative cost burden. In any event, given the flexibility permitted by the Act, the only purpose that would appear to be served by such an opt-out would be to permit high levels of overtime to be worked on an on-going basis. The inclusion of a provision specifically to permit this would appear to be inconsistent with the objective of attempting to ensure that available employment is shared as widely as possible (for a detailed study of the operation of the opt-out in the United Kingdom see Barnard *et al*, (2003) 32 I.L.J. 223). To assuage concerns, however,

B–54

the Bill was amended at Committee Stage in the Dáil to allow for the phased introduction of the 48-hour week over a two year period.

A considerable amount of flexibility can be secured as regards the application of the core provisions of the Act by the negotiation of appropriate collective agreements. In the case of unionised firms this should not present a problem, unless of course working time issues become linked to pay issues: see, for instance, the Labour Court's Recommendation No. 15932 in a dispute between Roadstone and SIPTU where the union had refused to sign an agreement in the transition period unless an arrangement was put in place to protect the workers' future earnings. The Labour Court pointed out the union's claim was presented during a period designed "to facilitate the introduction of the 48 hour week in a manner that would alleviate the impact on employees". Accordingly the court would not consider recommending concession of the claim for protection of earnings, adding that the claim was "contrary to the spirit of the Act". In the case of non-union firms however, those who want to avail of the flexibility will have to devise appropriate consultation and negotiation structures.

The Court of Justice has recognised, however, that the Directive imposes certain limits on the extent to which the rights conferred by the Directive can be derogated from by a collective agreement. In Case C–397/01, *Pfeiffer v Deutsches Rotes Kreuz* [2005] I.R.L.R. 137, the Court was asked whether Art.18(1)(b)(i) was to be construed as requiring consent to be expressly and freely given by each worker individually if the 48-hour maximum period of weekly working time, as laid down by Art.6 of the Directive, is to be validly extended or whether it was sufficient that the relevant worker's contract of employment referred to a collective agreement which permitted such an extension. The Court of Justice confirmed, as indicated in *SIMAP*, that the consent of the individual worker was required and that consent given by trade union representatives, in the context of a collective agreement, was not equivalent to that given by the worker himself or herself. Consequently, the Court ruled that the requirements of Art.18 were not met where the worker's contract of employment merely referred to a collective agreement authorising an extension of maximum weekly working time.

CITATION                                                 **BB.112**
    See section 1(1).

COMMENCEMENT
    The Act was signed by the President on May 7, 1997 and came into operation as follows (see S.I. **BB.113**
No. 392 of 1997):

    (1)   September 30, 1997
         (a)   sections 1 to 8 and 10,
         (b)   section 9 insofar as it relates to the Holidays (Employees) Act 1973 (the 1973 Act) and section 4 of the Worker Protection (Regular Part-Time Employees) Act 1991 (the 1991 Act),
         (c)   section 15(2),
         (d)   sections 17 to 23 and 25 to 41,
         (e)   subsections (8) and (9) of section 24,
         (f)   the First, Second and Third Schedules,
         (g)   the Fourth Schedule insofar as it relates to the 1973 and 1991 Acts,
         (h)   paragraphs 5, 6, 8 and 9 of the Fifth Schedule, and
         (i)   the Sixth Schedule.
    (2)   November 30, 1997
         (a)   subsections (1) to (7) and (10) of section 24, and
         (b)   paragraphs 3, 4 and 7 of the Fifth Schedule.
    (3)   March 1, 1998
         (a)   section 9 insofar as it relates to any enactment other than the 1973 and 1991 Acts,
         (b)   sections 11 to 14 and 16,
         (c)   subsections (1), (3), (4) and (5) of section 15,
         (d)   the Fourth Schedule insofar as it relates to any enactment other than the 1973 and 1991 Acts, and
         (e)   paragraphs 1 and 2 of the Fifth Schedule.

STATUTORY INSTRUMENTS
    Organisation of Working Time Act 1997 (Commencement) Order 1997 (S.I. No. 392 of 1997).   **BB.114**
    Organisation of Working Time (Determination of Pay for Holidays) Regulations 1997 (S.I. No. 475 of 1997).
    Organisation of Working Time (General Exemptions) Regulations 1998 (S.I. No. 21 of 1998).
    Organisation of Working Time (Code of Practice on Compensatory Rest and Related Matters) (Declaration) Order 1998 (S.I. No. 44 of 1998).
    Organisation of Working Time (Exemption of Civil Protection Services) Regulations 1998 (S.I. No. 52 of 1998).

Organisation of Working Time (Breaks at Work for Shop Employees) Regulations 1998 (S.I. No. 57 of 1998).

Organisation of Working Time (Code of Practice on Sunday Working in the Retail Trade and Related Matters (Declaration) Order 1998 (S.I. No. 444 of 1998).

Organisation of Working Time (Public Holidays) Regulations 1999 (S.I. No. 10 of 1999).

Organisation of Working Time (National Day of Mourning) Regulations 2001 (S.I. No. 419 of 2001).

Organisation of Working Time (Records) (Prescribed Form and Exemptions) Regulations 2001 (S.I. No. 475 of 2001).

Organisation of Working Time (Inclusion of Transport Activities) Regulations 2004 (S.I. No. 817 of 2004).

Organisation of Working Time (Inclusion of Offshore Work) Regulations 2004 (S.I. No. 819 of 2004).

GENERAL NOTE

**BB.118**   The Organisation of Working Time Act 1997 (Commencement) Order 1997 (S.I. No. 392 of 1997) appointed September 30, 1997, November 30, 1997 and March 1, 1998 as the dates on which the various provisions of the Act came into operation.

## Interpretation

**BB.119**   **2.**—(1) In this Act—

["the Activities of Doctors in Training Regulations" means the European Communities (Organisation of Working Time) (Activities of Doctors in Training) Regulations 2004 (S.I. No. 494 of 2004);]

"annual leave" shall be construed in accordance with section 19;

"collective agreement" means an agreement by or on behalf of an employer on the one hand, and by or on behalf of a body or bodies representative of the employees to whom the agreement relates on the other hand;

"contract of employment" means

(a)  a contract of service or apprenticeship, and

(b)  any other contract whereby an individual agrees with another person, who is carrying on the business of an employment agency within the meaning of the Employment Agency Act, 1971, and is acting in the course of that business, to do or perform personally any work or service for a third person (whether or not the third person is a party to the contract), whether the contract is express or implied and if express, whether it is oral or in writing;

"the Council Directive" means Council Directive 93/104/EC of 23 November 1993 concerning certain aspects of the organization of working time, the text of which (other than the second sentence of Article 5) is, for convenience of reference, set out in the Sixth Schedule;

"employee" means a person of any age, who has entered into or works under (or, where the employment has ceased, entered into or worked under) a contract of employment and references, in relation to an employer, to an employee shall be construed as references to an employee employed by that employer; and for the purposes of this Act [and the Activities of Doctors in Training Regulations], a person holding office under, or in the service of, the State (including a civil servant within the meaning of the Civil Service Regulation Act, 1956) shall be deemed to be an employee employed by the State or Government, as the case may be, and an officer or servant of a local authority for the purposes of the Local Government Act, 1941, or of a harbour authority, [the Health Service Executive] or vocational

B–56

education committee shall be deemed to be an employee employed by the authority, [the Executive] or committee, as the case may be;

"employer" means in relation to an employee, the person with whom the employee has entered into or for whom the employee works under (or, where the employment has ceased, entered into or worked under) a contract of employment, subject to the qualification that the person who under a contract of employment referred to in paragraph (b) of the definition of "contract of employment" is liable to pay the wages of the individual concerned in respect of the work or service concerned shall be deemed to be the individual's employer;

"employment regulation order" means an order under section 48 of the Industrial Relations Act, 1990;

"lay-off" has the meaning assigned to it by the Redundancy Payments Act, 1967;

"leave year" means a year beginning on any 1st day of April;

"the Minister" means the Minister for [Enterprise, Trade and Employment];

"outworker" means an employee who is employed under a contract of service to do work for his or her employer in the employee's own home or in some other place not under the control or management of the employer, being work that consists of the making of a product or the provision of a service specified by the employer;

"prescribed" means prescribed by regulations made by the Minister under this Act;

"public holiday" shall be construed in accordance with the Second Schedule;

"registered employment agreement" has the meaning assigned to it by section 25 of the Industrial Relations Act, 1946;

"rest period" means any time that is not working time;

"short-time" has the meaning assigned to it by the Redundancy Payments Act, 1967;

"working time" means any time that the employee is

(a) at his or her place of work or at his or her employer's disposal, and

(b) carrying on or performing the activities or duties of his or her work,

and

"work" shall be construed accordingly.

(2) A word or expression that is used in this Act and is also used in the Council Directive has, unless the contrary intention appears, the meaning in this Act that it has in the Council Directive.

(3) In this Act—

(a) a reference to a Part, section or Schedule is a reference to a Part or section of, or a Schedule to, this Act unless it is indicated that reference to some other enactment is intended,

(b) a reference to a subsection, paragraph or subparagraph is a reference to the subsection, paragraph or subparagraph of the provision in which the reference occurs, unless it is indicated that reference to some other provision is intended,

(c) a reference to any enactment shall be construed as a reference to that enactment as amended, adapted or extended by or under any subsequent enactment (including this Act).

GENERAL NOTE

**BB.121**    "the Activities of Doctors in Training Regulations": this definition was inserted by virtue of reg.12 of the European Communities (Organisation of Working Time) (Activities of Doctors in Training) Regulations 2004 (S.I. No. 494 of 2004).

"collective agreement": this definition differs from the definition of collective agreement in s.1(1) of the Anti-Discrimination (Pay) Act 1974 which covered agreements "relating to terms and conditions of employment" which are made "between parties who are or who represent employers and parties who are or represent employees". It also differs somewhat from the definition in s.1(1) of the Protection of Young Persons (Employment) Act 1996 which covers agreements "by or on behalf of an employer on the one hand and by or on behalf of a trade union or trade unions representative of the employees to whom the agreement relates on the other hand".

"contract of employment": as to whether a person is employed under a contract of service see, most recently, *Henry Denny & Sons (Ireland) Ltd v Minister for Social Welfare* [1998] 1 I.R. 34. See also the determinations of the Labour Court in *Maher v Department of Agriculture, Food and Rural Development* DWT 22/2002 and *O'Reilly v Department of Agriculture, Food and Rural Development* DWT 32/2002. In the former a veterinarian was found to be employed under a contract of service whereas in the latter a veterinary inspector was found to be employed under a contract for services. The difference between the two cases lay in the finding that the veterinary inspector was "a free agent with an economic independence of the person engaging the service".The inclusion of a specific reference to persons employed through employment agencies is similar to the provisions of s.13 of the Unfair Dismissals (Amendment) Act 1993, s.1(1) of the Terms of Employment (Information) Act 1994 and section 1(1) of the Protection of Young Persons (Employment) Act 1996. But note the decision of the Labour Court in *Rooney v Diageo Global Supply* [2004] E.L.R. 133, that an agency supplied worker was employed by the client under a contract of employment.

"employee": this definition was amended by virtue of reg.12 of the European Communities (Organisation of Working Time) (Activities of Doctors in Training) Regulations 2004 (S.I. No. 494 of 2004) and by virtue of s.66 of the Health Act 2004.

"employment regulation order": these are orders made by the Labour Court, following the formulation of proposals by a Joint Labour Committee, for the fixing of minimum rates of remuneration and for regulating the conditions of employment of workers covered by the committee. When such proposals are confirmed by the Labour Court they become statutory minimum remuneration and statutory conditions of employment and employers are bound under penalty to pay rates of wages and to grant conditions of employment not less favourable than those prescribed in the order.

"lay-off": section 11(1) of the Redundancy Payments Act 1967, as amended, provides that where an employee's employment ceases by reason of his employer's being unable to provide the work for which the employee was employed to do, and it is reasonable in the circumstances for that employer to believe that the cessation of employment will not be permanent, and the employer gives notice to that effect to the employee prior to the cessation, that cessation of employment shall be regarded as "lay-off".

"the Minister": this definition was amended by virtue of the Enterprise and Employment (Alteration of Name of Department and Title of Minister) Order 1997 (S.I. No. 305 of 1997). By virtue of the Enterprise, Trade and Employment (Delegation of Ministerial Functions) (No. 2) Order 1997 (S.I. No. 330 of 1997), the Minister's powers under the Act have been delegated to the Minister for Labour, Trade and Consumer Affairs.

"registered employment agreement": these are agreements which have been registered with the Labour Court and which, pursuant to section 30 of the Industrial Relations Act 1946, apply to every worker of the class, type or group to which the agreement is expressed to apply, and to his or her employer, notwithstanding that such worker or employer is not a party to the agreement.

"short-time": section 11(2) of the Redundancy Payments Act 1967, as amended, provides that where:

(a)   for any week an employee's remuneration is less than one half of his or her normal weekly remuneration or his or her hours of work are reduced to less than one-half of his or her normal weekly hours;

(b)   the reduction in remuneration or hours of work is caused by a diminution either in the work provided for the employee by his or her employer or in other work of a kind which under his or her contract the employee is required to do;

(c)   it is reasonable in the circumstances for the employer to believe that the diminution in work will not be permanent and the employer gives notice to that effect to the employee prior to the reduction in remuneration or hours of work;

the employee shall be taken to be kept on "short-time" for that week. Similarly section 11(3) of the

1967 Act, as inserted by section 19 of the Redundancy Payments Act 1971, provides that where by reason of a diminution in the work provided for an employee by his or her employer, being work of a kind which under his or her contract the employee is employed to do, the employee's reduced hours of work for any week are less than one-half of his normal weekly hours, the employee shall be taken to be kept on "short-time" for that week.

"working time": it would appear, by the use of the word "and", that both conditions must be satisfied. The definition differs somewhat from that used in the Directive where three conditions are stipulated, namely that the worker must be: (i) working; (ii) at the employer's disposal; and (iii) carrying on his or her activity or duties. The issue of whether the conditions are disjunctive or conjunctive came before the Court of Justice in Case C–303/98, *Sindicato de Medicos de Asistencia Publica (SIMAP) v Conselleria de Sanidad y Consumo de la Generalidad Valenciana* [2000] E.C.R. I-7963.

The Court avoided answering this question explicitly, although the Advocate General in his opinion expressed the view that the conditions were disjunctive. The Court said that the essential question it had to decide was whether time spent "on call" by doctors was to be regarded as working time regardless of whether they were required to be present in the health centre or merely contactable. The Court (in para. 48) said that the "characteristic features" of working time were present in the case of time spent on call by doctors where their presence at the health centre was required. The Court added that "the fact that such doctors are obliged to be present and available at the workplace with a view to providing their professional services means that they are carrying out their duties on that instance" even if "the activity actually performed varies according to the circumstances". The situation was different, however, where doctors were on call "by being contactable at all times without having to be at the health centre" (para. 50). Even though they were at the disposal of their employer, in that they had to be contactable," "in that situation doctors may manage their time with fewer constraints and pursue their own interests". It followed that such on-call time, unless it was linked to the actual provision of primary care services, could not be regarded as working time.

For two excellent commentaries on *SIMAP* see O'Mara "Changing Times? Recent European Developments in Working Time Law" (2001) 8 *Commercial Law Practitioner* 60 and Fairhurst "Interpreting the Working Time Directive" (2001) 30 I.L.J. 236.

The issue of what constitutes "working time" has been further considered by the Court of Justice in Case C–151/02, *Landeshauptstadt Kiel v Jaeger* [2003] E.C.R. I-8399. The Schleswig-Holstein Landes-arbeitsgericht had referred the question of whether time spent "on call" by an employee in a hospital constituted working time "even where the employee is permitted to sleep at times when he is not required to work". The Court of Justice ruled that a period of duty spent by a hospital doctor on call, where the doctor's presence in the hospital was required, must be regarded as constituting in its entirety "working time", even though the person concerned was permitted to rest at their place of work during periods when their services were not required. The Court of Justice said that the decisive factor in considering that time spent "on call" by doctors in the hospital is "working time" is that they are required to be present at the place determined by the employer and to be available to the employer to provide their services immediately in case of need. As these obligations made it impossible for doctors to choose the place where they stay during the waiting periods, they must be regarded as coming within the ambit of the performance of their duties: see, to similar effect, the decision of the Japanese Supreme Court in *Yamagishi v Taisei Building Custodial Services Inc* (2002) 22 I.L.L.R 229.

The conclusions of the Court of Justice in *SIMAP* and *Jaeger* have now been reinforced by the decision in Case C–14/04, *Dellas* [2006] I.R.L.R. 225. The court ruled that there was no "intermediate category" between "working time" and "rest periods" and the fact that on-call duty included some periods of inactivity was completely irrelevant. The intensity of the work done by the worker and his or her output were not among the characteristic elements of the concept of working time. Accordingly, on-call duty performed by a worker where he or she was required to be physically present on the employer's premises had to be regarded in its entirety as working time regardless of the work actually done by the person concerned during that on-call duty.

The issue of whether time spent on "off-the-job training" by statutory apprentices is "working time" came before the Labour Court in *Fitzpatrick v Whelan* DWT36/2005. The court noted that such training was an integral part of the statutory apprenticeship and that during this period the apprentice was "at a place determined by the employer, carrying out the instructions of the employer and fulfilling the employer's obligations under the rules of the scheme". Accordingly, time spent on "off-the-job training" was "working time" for the purposes of this Act.

## Non-application of Act or provisions thereof

**3.**—(1) Subject to subsection (4), this Act shall not apply to a member of the     **BB.122**
Garda Síochána or the Defence Forces.

(2) Subject to subsection (4), Part II shall not apply to—

(a)  a person engaged in—
    (i)  sea fishing,
    (ii)  other work at sea, or
    (iii) the activities of a doctor in training,
(b)  a person—
    (i)  who is employed by a relative and is a member of that relative's household, and
    (ii)  whose place of employment is a private dwelling house or a farm in or on which he or she and the relative reside, or
(c)  a person the duration of whose working time (saving any minimum period of such time that is stipulated by the employer) is determined by himself or herself, whether or not provision for the making of such determination by that person is made by his or her contract of employment.

(3) The Minister may, after consultation with any other Minister of the Government who, in the opinion of the Minister, might be concerned with the matter, by regulations exempt from the application of a specified provision or provisions of this Act persons employed in any specified class or classes of activity—
(a)  involving or connected with the transport (by whatever means) of goods or persons, or
(b)  in the civil protection services where, in the opinion of the Minister and any other Minister of the Government in whom functions stand vested in relation to the service concerned, the inherent nature of the activity is such that, if the provision concerned were to apply to the said person, the efficient operation of the service concerned would be adversely affected.

(4) The Minister may, after consultation with any other Minister of the Government who, in the opinion of the Minister, might be concerned with the matter, by order provide that a specified provision or provisions of this Act or, as the case may be, of Part II shall apply to a specified class or classes of person referred to in subsection (1) or (2) and for so long as such an order remains in force the said provision or provisions shall be construed and have effect in accordance with the order.

(5) The reference in subsection (4) to an order in force shall, as respects such an order that is amended by an order in force under section 7(4), be construed as a reference to the first-mentioned order as so amended.

(6) In this section "relative", in relation to a person, means his or her spouse, father, mother, grandfather, grandmother, step-father, step-mother, son, daughter, grandson, grand-daughter, step-son, step-daughter, brother, sister, half-brother or half-sister.

GENERAL NOTE

**BB.123**  Two sets of regulations have been made pursuant to subsection (3): the Organisation of Working Time (Exemption of Transport Activities) Regulations 1998 (S.I. No. 20 of 1998) (now revoked by S.I. No. 817 of 2004) and the Organisation of Working Time (Exemption of Civil Protection Services) Regulations 1998 (S.I. No. 52 of 1998).

**BB.124**  The latter Regulations prescribe that persons employed in the activities in the civil protection services specified in the Schedule shall also be exempt from the application of sections 11, 12, 13, 15 and 16 of the Act. The specified activities are:

(1)  the activity of a person employed in a prison (including St Patrick's Institution) or place of detention (provided under section 2 of the Prisons Act 1970), being an activity that involves the maintenance of security in that prison or place of detention or the control or care of prisoners and which cannot be carried on within the normal rostering schedules applicable to that prison or place of detention;

(2)  the activity of a person employed by a fire authority (within the meaning of the Fire Services Act 1981) in the position commonly known as retained fire fighter;

(3)   the activity of a person, other than a member of the Garda Síochána, employed as an authorised officer (within the meaning of the Air Navigation and Transport Acts 1950 to 1998, and any enactment amending or extending those Acts);

(4)   the activity of a person employed by Dublin Port Company as a member of its harbour police;

(5)   the activity of a person employed in the Irish Marine Emergency Service, not being an activity of a clerical nature.

It should be noted that, although the Directive does not apply to persons engaged in seafishing, other work at sea or the activities of a doctor in training, the provisions in Part III of the Act dealing with holidays are applied to such persons. For doctors in training, see the European Communities (Organisation of Working Time) (Activities of Doctors in Training) Regulations 2004 (S.I. No. 494 of 2004). In addition the Act avails of the optional derogation permitted by the Directive to exclude from the working time provisions family workers and employees who can determine their own working time.

## Exemptions

**4.** —(1) Without prejudice to section 6, section 11 or 13 or, as appropriate, both   **BB.125** these sections shall not apply, as respects a person employed in shift work, each time he or she changes shift and cannot avail himself or herself of the rest period referred to in section 11 or 13 or, as the case may be, both those sections.

(2) Without prejudice to section 6, sections 11 and 13 shall not apply to a person employed in an activity (other than such activity as may be prescribed) consisting of periods of work spread out over the day.

(3) Subject to subsection (4), the Minister may by regulations exempt from the application of section 11, 12, 13, 16 or 17 any activity referred to in paragraph 2, point 2.1. of Article 17 of the Council Directive, or any specified class or classes of such activity, and regulations under this subsection may, without prejudice to section 6, provide that any such exemption shall not have effect save to the extent that specified conditions are complied with.

(4) Where the Minister proposes to make regulations under subsection (3), the Minister shall consult with such persons as he or she considers to be representative of the employers and employees who, in the opinion of the Minister, are likely to be affected by the proposed regulations.

(5) Without prejudice to section 6, if—

(a)   a collective agreement that for the time being stands approved of by the Labour Court under section 24, or

(b)   a registered employment agreement,

provides that section 11, 12 or 13 shall not apply in relation to the employees to whom the agreement for the time being has effect, or a specified class or classes of such employees, section 11, 12 or 13, as the case may be, shall not apply in relation to those employees or the said class or classes of such employees.

(6) Without prejudice to section 6, an employment regulation order may include one or more provisions providing that section 11, 12 or 13 shall not apply in relation to the employees to whom the order relates or a specified class or classes of such employees.

GENERAL NOTE

This section exempts, from the daily and weekly rest provisions set out in Part II of the Act, an   **BB.126** employee each time he or she changes shift and an employee whose work involves periods of work spread out over the day.

Subsection (3) allows the Minister, while ensuring that compensatory rest is provided, to exempt, following consultations with the social partners, specified sectors set out in Article 17(2) of the Directive from the provisions of the Act regarding daily and weekly rest, rest intervals at work, night working and information on working hours. One set of Regulations have so far been made: Organisation of Working Time (General Exemptions) Regulations 1998 (S.I. No. 21 of 1998). These provide that persons employed in the activities specified in the Schedule shall be exempt from the application of sections 11, 12, 13 and 16 of the Act. The specified activities are:

(1)  an activity in which the employee is regularly required by the employer to travel distances of significant length, either from his or her home to the workplace or from one workplace to another workplace;

(2)  an activity of a security or surveillance nature the purpose of which is to protect persons or property and which requires the continuous presence of the employee at a particular place or places, and, in particular, the activities of a security guard, caretaker or security firm;

(3)  an activity falling within a sector of the economy or in the public service—

    (a)  in which it is foreseeable that the rate at which production or the provision of services, as the case may be, takes place will vary significantly from time to time, or,

    (b)  the nature of which is such that employees are directly involved in ensuring the continuity of production or the provision of services, as the case may be;

    and, in particular, any of the following activities—

    (i)  the provision of services relating to the reception, treatment or care of persons in a residential institution, hospital or similar establishment,

    (ii)  the provision of services at a harbour or airport,

    (iii)  production in the press, radio, television, cinematographic, postal or telecommunications industries,

    (iv)  the provision of ambulance, fire and civil protection services,

    (v)  the production, transmission or distribution of gas, water or electricity,

    (vi)  the collection of household refuse or the operation of an incineration plant,

    (vii)  any industrial activity in which work cannot, by reason of considerations of a technical nature, be interrupted,

    (viii)  research and development,

    (ix)  agriculture,

    (x)  tourism.

**BB.127**     The exemptions do not apply if the employee is not engaged "wholly or mainly" in carrying on or performing the duties of the activity concerned. Nor do they apply if the employee either is a special category night worker within the meaning of s.16(3) of the Act or falls within a class of employee to which a joint labour committee may perform functions under the Industrial Relations Acts 1946 to 2004.

Regulation 4 provides that, if an employee is not entitled, by reason of this exemption, to the rest period and break referred to in ss.11, 12 and 13, the employer must ensure that the employee has available a rest period and break that, in all the circumstances, can reasonably be regarded as equivalent to the aforementioned rest period and break. Regulation 5 further provides that an employer shall not require an employee to whom the exemption applies to work during a shift or other period of work of more than six hours duration without allowing the employee a break "of such duration as the employer determines". In determining the duration of this break the employer must have regard to the need to protect and secure the health, safety and comfort of the employee and to the general principles concerning the prevention and avoidance of risk at the workplace.

Subsection (5) also provides that a collective agreement approved by the Labour Court, a registered employment agreement or an employment regulation order may exempt affected employers and employees from compliance with the provisions dealing with daily and weekly rest and rest intervals, provided that the employees benefit from compensatory rest.

## Employer relieved from complying with certain provisions in certain circumstances

**BB.128**     **5.** Without prejudice to section 6, an employer shall not be obliged to comply with section 11, 12, 13, 16 or 17 where due to exceptional circumstances or an emergency (including an accident or the imminent risk of an accident), the consequences of which could not have been avoided despite the exercise of all due care, or otherwise to the occurrence of unusual and unforeseeable circumstances beyond the employer's control, it would not be practicable for the employer to comply with the section concerned.

GENERAL NOTE

**BB.129**     This section exempts employers from compliance with the working time provisions, without prejudice to the employee's entitlement to compensatory rest, in exceptional or emergency circumstances.

## Compensatory rest periods

**6.**—(1) Any regulations, collective agreement, registered employment agree-  **BB.130**
ment or employment regulation order referred to in section 4 that exempt any
activity from the application of section 11, 12 or 13 or provide that any of these
sections shall not apply in relation to an employee shall include a provision requiring the employer concerned to ensure that the employee concerned has available to
himself or herself such rest period or break as the provision specifies to be equivalent
to the rest period or break, as the case may be, provided for by section 11, 12 or 13.

(2) Where by reason of the operation of subsection (1) or (2) of section 4, or
section 5, an employee is not entitled to the rest period or break referred to in
section 11, 12, or 13 the employer concerned shall—

(a) ensure that the employee has available to himself or herself a rest
period or break, as the case may be, that, in all the circumstances,
can reasonably be regarded as equivalent to the first-mentioned rest
period or break, or

(b) if for reasons that can be objectively justified, it is not possible for the
employer to ensure that the employee has available to himself or
herself such an equivalent rest period or break, otherwise make such
arrangements as respects the employee's conditions of employment as
will compensate the employee in consequence of the operation of
subsection (1) or (2) of section 4, or section 5.

(3) The reference in subsection (2)(b) to the making of arrangements as
respects an employee's conditions of employment does not include a reference
to—

(a) the granting of monetary compensation to the employee, or

(b) the provision of any other material benefit to the employee, other than
the provision of such a benefit as will improve the physical conditions
under which the employee works or the amenities or services available
to the employee while he or she is at work.

General Note

This section provides that, if employees are not entitled to the minimum rest provisions set out in  **BB.131**
sections 11, 12 and 13 because of ministerial regulations, an approved collective agreement or an
employment regulation order, the employer must ensure that the employees have available equivalent
compensatory rest. If, for objective reasons, it is not possible for an employer to ensure that the employees avail of the minimum rest to which they are entitled, then the employer must make such arrangements
as will compensate the employee save that that compensation can not be of monetary or material benefit
but it may take the form of provision of a benefit which improves the physical conditions under which the
employees work or the amenities or services available to the employees while at work.

Pursuant to section 35 of the Act, the Minister requested the Labour Relations Commission to
provide practical guidance as to the steps that may be taken for the purpose of complying with section
6. The resultant Code of Practice on Compensatory Rest Periods was declared to be a Code of Practice
for the purposes of the Act by ministerial order: S.I. No. 44 of 1998. The Commission stated that, as
regards appropriate compensation arrangements, a "common sense approach" should be adopted. It
would be desirable, the Commission said, that employers and employees and/or their representatives
agreed appropriate protection measures and, while it was not feasible to define the appropriate
measures, the concept was regarded as including such measures as:

(i)   enhanced environmental conditions to accommodate regular long periods of attendance at
work;
(ii)  refreshment facilities, recreational and reading material;
(iii) appropriate facilities/amenities such as television, radio and music;
(iv)  alleviating monotonous work or isolation;
(v)   transport to and from work where appropriate.

B–63

Complaints arising under section 6 should be presented to a rights commissioner in accordance with section 27 of the Act.

## Regulations and orders

BB.132    **7.**—(1) The Minister may make regulations prescribing any matter or thing which is referred to in this Act as prescribed or to be prescribed or for the purpose of enabling any provision of this Act to have full effect.

(2) Regulations under this Act may make different provisions in relation to different classes of employees or employers, different areas or otherwise by reference to the different circumstances of the matter.

(3) A regulation or order under this Act may contain such incidental, supplementary and consequential provisions as appear to the Minister to be necessary or expedient.

(4) The Minister may by order amend or revoke an order under this Act (other than an order under section 1(2) but including an order under this subsection).

(5) A regulation or order under this Act (other than an order under section 1(2)) shall be laid before each House of the Oireachtas as soon as may be after it is made and, if a resolution annulling that regulation or order is passed by either such House within the next 21 days on which that House has sat after the regulation or order is laid before it, the regulation or order shall be annulled accordingly, but without prejudice to the validity of anything previously done thereunder.

## Inspectors

BB.133    **8.**—(1) In this section "inspector" means a person appointed under subsection (2).

(2) The Minister may appoint in writing such and so many persons as the Minister sees fit to be inspectors for the purposes of this Act [or the Activities of Doctors in Training Regulations].

(3) An inspector may for the purposes of this Act [or the Activities of Doctors in Training Regulations] do all or any of the following things—

(a) subject to the provisions of this section, enter at all reasonable times any premises or place where he or she has reasonable grounds for supposing that any employee is employed in work or from which he or she has reasonable grounds for supposing the activities that an employee is employed to carry on are directed or controlled (whether generally or as respects particular matters),

(b) make such examination or enquiry as may be necessary for ascertaining whether the provisions of this Act [or the Activities of Doctors in Training Regulations] are complied with in respect of any employee employed in any such premises or place or any employee the activities aforesaid of whom are directed or controlled from any such premises or place,

(c) require the employer of any employee or the representative of such employer to produce to him or her any records which such employer is required to keep and inspect and take copies of entries in such records (including in the case of information in a non-legible form a copy of or an extract from such information in a permanent legible form),

(d) require any person whom he or she has reasonable cause to believe to be or to have been an employee or the employer of any employee to furnish such information as the inspector may reasonably request,

(e) examine with regard to any matters under this Act [or the Activities of Doctors in Training Regulations] any person whom he or she has reasonable cause to believe to be or to have been an employer or employee and require him or her to answer such questions (other than questions tending to incriminate him or her) as the inspector may put relative to those matters and to sign a declaration of the truth of the answers.

(4) An inspector shall not, other than with the consent of the occupier, enter a private dwelling (other than a part of the dwelling used as a place of work) unless he or she has obtained a warrant from the District Court under subsection (7) authorising such entry.

(5) Where an inspector in the exercise of his or her powers under this section is prevented from entering any premises an application may be made under subsection (7) authorising such entry.

(6) An inspector, where he or she considers it necessary to be so accompanied, may be accompanied by a member of the Garda Síochána when exercising any powers conferred on an inspector by this section.

(7) If a judge of the District Court is satisfied on the sworn information of an inspector that there are reasonable grounds for suspecting that information required by an inspector under this section is held on any premises or any part of any premises, the judge may issue a warrant authorising an inspector accompanied by other inspectors or a member of the Garda Síochána, at any time or times within one month from the date of issue of the warrant, on production, if so requested, of the warrant, to enter the premises (if need be by reasonable force) and exercise all or any of the powers conferred on an inspector under subsection (3).

(8) A person who—

(a) obstructs or impedes an inspector in the exercise of any of the powers conferred on an inspector under this section,

(b) refuses to produce any record which an inspector lawfully requires him or her to produce,

(c) produces or causes to be produced or knowingly allows to be produced, to an inspector, any record which is false or misleading in any material respect knowing it to be so false or misleading,

(d) gives to an inspector any information which is false or misleading in any material respect knowing it to be so false or misleading, or

(e) fails or refuses to comply with any lawful requirement of an inspector under subsection (3),

shall be guilty of an offence.

(9) Every inspector shall be furnished by the Minister with a certificate of his or her appointment and, on applying for admission to any premises or place for the purposes of this Act [or the Activities of Doctors in Training Regulations], shall, if requested by a person affected, produce the certificate or a copy thereof to that person.

GENERAL NOTE

This section was amended by virtue of reg.12 of the European Communities (Organisation of Working Time) (Activities of Doctors in Training) Regulations 2004 (S.I. No. 494 of 2004). The High Court has ruled that there is nothing in either the express powers or the purposes for which those powers are conferred which enables them to be construed as including any incidental or consequential power to prepare a report intended for publication of the results of an investigation into alleged breaches by an employer of its obligations under the 1997 Act: *Gama Endustri Tesisleri Imalat Montaj AS v Minister for Enterprise, Trade and Employment*, unreported, High Court, June 14, 2005. Finlay Geoghegan J., however, went on to hold that an inspector must have an implicit or consequential power to pass to the Minister and persons concerned with the civil enforcement procedures information, documents or evidence gathered pursuant to the Inspector's express statutory powers for the purposes of those persons enforcing the obligations imposed by the Act on employers either by way of civil procedures or by prosecuting alleged offences.

## Repeals

**BB.134**   **9.** Each enactment specified in the Fourth Schedule is hereby repealed to the extent specified in the third column of that Schedule.

## Expenses

**BB.135**   **10.** The expenses incurred by the Minister in the administration of this Act shall, to such extent as may be sanctioned by the Minister for Finance, be paid out of moneys provided by the Oireachtas.

PART II

MINIMUM REST PERIODS AND OTHER MATTERS RELATING TO WORKING TIME

## Daily rest period

**BB.136**   **11.** An employee shall be entitled to a rest period of not less than 11 consecutive hours in each period of 24 hours during which he or she works for his or her employer.

GENERAL NOTE

**BB.137**   This section implements Article 3 of the Directive and provides for an entitlement by an employee to a minimum rest period of eleven consecutive hours in each 24 hour period. Employers of persons employed in activities covered by S.I. Nos. 21 and 52 of 1998 are exempted from the provisions of section 11 as are workers employed as a member of travelling or flying personnel by an undertaking which operates transport services for passengers or goods by road, air, or inland waterway (see S.I. No. 817 of 2004).

## Rests and intervals at work

**BB.138**   **12.**—(1) An employer shall not require an employee to work for a period of more than 4 hours and 30 minutes without allowing him or her a break of at least 15 minutes.

(2) An employer shall not require an employee to work for a period of more than 6 hours without allowing him or her a break of at least 30 minutes; such a break may include the break referred to in subsection (1).

(3) The Minister may by regulations provide, as respects a specified class or classes of employee, that the minimum duration of the break to be allowed to such an employee under subsection (2) shall be more than 30 minutes (but not more than 1 hour).

(4) A break allowed to an employee at the end of the working day shall not be regarded as satisfying the requirement contained in subsection (1) or (2).

GENERAL NOTE

This section implements Article 4 of the Directive and provides for an entitlement by employees to **BB.139** a rest break while at work of fifteen minutes in a period of four and a half hours' work and 30 minutes in a period of six hours' work. Subsection (4) provides that breaks at the end of the working day do not satisfy these requirements. In *The Tribune Printing & Publishing Group v Graphical Print & Media Union* [2004] E.L.R. 222, the Labour Court held that an employer was under a positive duty to ensure that employees received their rest breaks: "Merely stating that employees could take rest breaks if they wished and not putting in place proper procedures to ensure that the employee receives those breaks, thus protecting his health and safety, does not discharge that duty." Employers of persons employed in activities covered by S.I. Nos. 21 and 52 are exempted from the provisions of section 12 as are workers employed as a member of travelling or flying personnel by an undertaking which operates transport services for passengers or goods by road, air, or inland waterway (see S.I. No. 817 of 2004). This section was amended at Committee Stage in the Dáil to provide that the 30 minute minimum rest period might be extended to one hour for certain categories of employees. It would appear that this was done to preserve the existing rights of shop workers to a one hour lunch break. Consequently the Organisation of Working Time (Breaks at Work for Shop Employees) Regulations 1998 (S.I. No. 57 of 1998) provide that, in relation to "shop employees" whose hours of work include the hours from 11.30 a.m. to 2.30 p.m., the minimum duration of the break to be allowed under subs.(2) shall be one hour.

Shop employees are defined as employees who work in or about a shop and "shop" is defined as including "any premises in which goods are received direct from customers for cleaning, repairing, altering or laundering", "any wholesale shop" and "any warehouse occupied for the purpose of a retail trade or business, by the person carrying on such retail trade or by a wholesale dealer or merchant for the purposes of the business carried on by him or her in a wholesale shop". The Regulations go on to provide that the word "shop" does not include any premises used "for the purpose of a hotel, the preparation of food or the catering for any persons as respects their requirements in respect of food or drink, or any business carried on pursuant to an intoxicating liquor licence". The Regulations further provide that the expression "retail trade or business" includes the business of a barber or hairdresser, hiring goods otherwise than for use in a trade or business, a pawnbroker and retail sales by auction but does not include the sale of programmes or catalogues at theatres or other places of entertainment.

## Weekly rest periods

**13.**—(1) In this section "daily rest period" means a rest period referred to in **BB.140** section 11.

(2) Subject to subsection (3), an employee shall, in each period of 7 days, be granted a rest period of at least 24 consecutive hours; subject to subsections (4) and (6), the time at which that rest period commences shall be such that that period is immediately preceded by a daily rest period.

(3) An employer may, in lieu of granting to an employee in any period of 7 days the first-mentioned rest period in subsection (2), grant to him or her, in the next following period of 7 days, 2 rest periods each of which shall be

a period of at least 24 consecutive hours and, subject to subsections (4) and (6)—

(a)   if the rest periods so granted are consecutive, the time at which the first of those periods commences shall be such that that period is immediately preceded by a daily rest period, and

(b)   if the rest periods so granted are not consecutive, the time at which each of those periods commences shall be such that each of them is immediately preceded by a daily rest period.

(4) If considerations of a technical nature or related to the conditions under which the work concerned is organised or otherwise of an objective nature would justify the making of such a decision, an employer may decide that the time at which a rest period granted by him or her under subsection (2) or (3) shall commence shall be such that the rest period is not immediately preceded by a daily rest period.

(5) Save as may be otherwise provided in the employee's contract of employment—

(a)   the rest period granted to an employee under subsection (2), or

(b)   one of the rest periods granted to an employee under subsection (3), shall be a Sunday or, if the rest period is of more than 24 hours duration, shall include a Sunday.

(6) The requirement in subsection (2) or paragraph (a) or (b) of subsection (3) as to the time at which a rest period under this section shall commence shall not apply in any case where, by reason of a provision of this Act or an instrument or agreement under, or referred to in, this Act, the employee concerned is not entitled to a daily rest period in the circumstances concerned.

GENERAL NOTE

This section implements Article 5 of the Directive and provides for an entitlement to a weekly rest **BB.141** period of 24 hours which must be in addition to the daily rest period of 11 hours prescribed by section 11. The section adheres to the original text of the Directive, even though the relevant portion of Article 5 was annulled by the Court of Justice, by providing, in subsection (5), that, unless otherwise specified in an employee's contract of employment, the weekly rest period must include Sunday.

Employers of persons employed in activities covered by S.I. Nos. 21 and 52 of 1998 are exempted from the provisions of section 13 as are workers employed as a member of travelling or flying personnel by an undertaking which operates transport services for passengers or goods by road, air, or inland waterway (see S.I. No. 817 of 2004).

## Sunday work: supplemental provisions

**14.**—(1) An employee who is required to work on a Sunday (and the fact of his **BB.142** or her having to work on that day has not otherwise been taken account of in the determination of his or her pay) shall be compensated by his or her employer for being required so to work by the following means, namely—

(a)   by the payment to the employee of an allowance of such an amount as is reasonable having regard to all the circumstances, or

(b)   by otherwise increasing the employee's rate of pay by such an amount as is reasonable having regard to all the circumstances, or

(c)   by granting the employee such paid time off from work as is reasonable having regard to all the circumstances, or

(d)   by a combination of two or more of the means referred to in the preceding paragraphs.

(2) Subsection (3) applies to an employee where the value or the minimum

B–67

value of the compensation to be provided to him or her in respect of his or her being required to work on a Sunday is not specified by a collective agreement.

(3) For the purposes of proceedings under Part IV before a rights commissioner or the Labour Court in relation to a complaint that this section has not been complied with in relation to an employee to whom this subsection applies ("the first-mentioned employee"), the value or the minimum value of the compensation that a collective agreement for the time being specifies shall be provided to a comparable employee in respect of his or her being required to work on a Sunday shall be regarded as the value of compensation to be provided under this section to the first-mentioned employee that is reasonable having regard to all the circumstances:

> Provided that if each of 2 or more collective agreements for the time being specifies the value or the minimum value of the compensation to be provided to a comparable employee to whom the agreement relates in respect of his or her being required to work on a Sunday and the said values or minimum values are not the same whichever of the said values or minimum values is the less shall be regarded, for the purposes aforesaid, as the value of compensation to be provided under this section to the first-mentioned employee that is reasonable having regard to all the circumstances.

(4) Unless the fact of such a value being so specified has come to the notice of the rights commissioner or the Labour Court, as the case may be, it shall be for the person who alleges in proceedings referred to in subsection (3) that a value of compensation of the kind referred to in that subsection is specified by a collective agreement mentioned in that subsection to show that, in fact, such a value is so specified.

(5) In subsection (3) "comparable employee" means an employee who is employed to do, under similar circumstances, identical or similar work in the industry or sector of employment concerned to that which the first-mentioned employee in subsection (3) is employed to do.

(6) References in this section to a value or minimum value of compensation that is specified by a collective agreement shall be construed as including references to a value or minimum value of compensation that may be determined in accordance with a formula or procedures specified by the agreement (being a formula or procedures which, in the case of proceedings referred to in subsection (3) before a rights commissioner or the Labour Court, can be readily applied or followed by the rights commissioner or the Labour Court for the purpose of the proceedings).

GENERAL NOTE

**BB.143**    This section provides that an employee required to work on a Sunday is entitled to a premium payment for the work which may consist of a payment or time off in lieu or a combination of both. The section goes on, in effect, to provide that the Sunday premium is to be set by reference to the going industry rate which will be determined by the Labour Court by looking at collective agreements already in force for comparable workers. The Labour Relations Commission has prepared a Code of Practice for the purposes of this section: see Organisation of Working Time (Code of Practice on Sunday Working in the Retail Trade and Related Matters) (Declaration) Order 1998 (S.I. No. 444 of 1998).

The provisions of section 14 were considered by the Labour Court in *Group 4 Securitas v SIPTU* DWT 6/1999. The union had submitted a claim for an increase on the Sunday premium paid to all employees in unionised employment in the security industry, claiming that it was not "reasonable in all the circumstances" as stated in subsection (1). The Labour Court ruled that, because the employee was paid an allowance for working on Sunday, his pay did take into account the requirement to work on Sunday. The Court did not consider that this section could be used to claim an enhancement of the rate that had previously been agreed.

See also *Campbell Catering Ltd v SIPTU* DWT 35/2000 where the Court, *inter alia*, ruled that section 14 could not be interpreted so as to provide that it should fix a rate of premium payment for part-time employees, which was less than that agreed in respect of full-time employees engaged in identical work in the same employment.

## Weekly Working Hours

**15.**—(1) An employer must not permit an employee to work, in each period of 7 days, more than an average of 48 hours, that is to say an average of 48 hours calculated over a period (hereafter in this section referred to as a "reference period") that does not exceed— **BB.144**

(a)   4 months, or

(b)   6 months—

    (i)   in the case of an employee employed in an activity referred to in paragraph 2, point 2.1. of Article 17 of the Council Directive, or

    (ii)   where due to any matter referred to in section 5, it would not be practicable (if a reference period not exceeding 4 months were to apply in relation to the employee) for the employer to comply with this subsection, or

(c)   such length of time as, in the case of an employee employed in an activity mentioned in subsection (5), is specified in a collective agreement referred to in that subsection.

(2) Subsection (1) shall have effect subject to the Fifth Schedule (which contains transitional provisions in respect of the period of 24 months beginning on the commencement of that Schedule).

(3) The days or months comprising a reference period shall, subject to subsection (4), be consecutive days or months.

(4) A reference period shall not include—

(a)   any period of annual leave granted to the employee concerned in accordance with this Act (save so much of it as exceeds the minimum period of annual leave required by this Act to be granted to the employee),

[(aa) any period during which the employee was absent from work while on parental leave, *force majeure* leave or carer's leave within the meaning of the Carer's Leave Act 2001,]

(b)   any absences from work by the employee concerned authorised under the Maternity Protection [Acts 1994 and 2004], or the Adoptive Leave [Acts 1995 and 2005], or

(c)   any sick leave taken by the employee concerned.

(5) Where an employee is employed in an activity (including an activity referred to in subsection (1)(b)(i))—

(a)   the weekly working hours of which vary on a seasonal basis, or

(b)   as respects which it would not be practicable for the employer concerned to comply with subsection (1) (if a reference period not exceeding 4 or 6 months, as the case may be, were to apply in relation to the employee) because of considerations of a technical nature or related to the conditions under which the work concerned is organised or otherwise of an objective nature,

B–69

then a collective agreement that for the time being has effect in relation to the employee and which stands approved of by the Labour Court under section 24 may specify, for the purposes of subsection (1)(c), a length of time in relation to the employee of more than 4 or 6 months, as the case may be (but not more than 12 months).

GENERAL NOTE

**BB.145** This section implements Article 6 of the Directive and provides that an employer shall not permit an employee to work for more than 48 hours a week. The averaging period, which should only take account of time spent carrying on the activities of work, is:

(i) two months for employees who are night workers (see s.16);

(ii) four months for most employees;

(iii) six months for certain activities and employments, such as agriculture and tourism; or

(iv) up to 12 months for employees covered by a collective agreement approved by the Labour Court under s.24 of the Act.

The 48-hour week came into effect generally on March 1, 1998 but the transitional provisions contained in the Fifth Schedule provide for a phased introduction by March 1, 2000 whereby employees could be permitted to work up to 60 hours in the first year and up to 55 hours in the second. To avail of these provisions the procedures set out in the Fifth Schedule had to be observed, principally that an agreement had been reached between the parties which had been approved by the Labour Court.

In *Barber v RJB Mining UK Ltd* [1999] 2 C.M.L.R. 833, Gage J. held that the equivalent British provision imposed a contractual obligation on an employer to ensure that an employee worked no more than the statutory maximum hours in any given week. Consequently he granted a declaration that, having worked in excess of the statutory maximum in a particular reference period, the plaintiff did not need to work until such time as his working time fell within the statutory limits.

**BB.146** If a collective agreement provided for an average working week of more than 48 hours, the Schedule went on to require that each employee covered was named in the agreement and that he or she had consented in writing to such an agreement being entered into in relation to him or her, the giving of such consent having been preceded by an explanation to the employee in everyday language of the statutory consequence that the giving of such consent would have for him or her. This is consistent with the Court of Justice's ruling in Case C–397/01, *Pfeiffer v Deutsches Rotes Kreuz* [2004] E.C.R. 1-8835, that a worker's consent must be given individually for a derogation from Article 6. The Labour Court, furthermore, could not approve such a collective agreement unless it was satisfied that "it has been concluded in a manner usually employed in determining the pay or other conditions of employment of employees in the employment concerned".

In cases where a trade union, or an excepted body within the meaning of the Trade Union Act 1941, does not stand recognised by the employer concerned for the purpose of negotiations concerning pay or other conditions of employment, the employer could only avail of the transitional provisions if the employee had consented in writing to the application of the transitional provisions and the Labour Court was satisfied that the employee concerned freely gave such consent.

Employers of persons employed in activities covered by S.I. No. 52 of 1998 are exempted from the provisions of s.15.

Paragraph (aa) of subsection (4) was inserted by virtue of s.28 of the Carer's Leave Act 2001.

## Nightly working hours

**BB.147** **16.**—(1) In this section—

"night time" means the period between midnight and 7 a.m. on the following day;

"night work" means work carried out during night time;

"night worker" means an employee—

(a) who normally works at least 3 hours of his or her daily working time during night time, and

(b) the number of hours worked by whom during night time, in each year, equals or exceeds 50 per cent of the total number of hours worked by him or her during that year.

(2) Without prejudice to section 15, an employer shall not permit a night worker, in each period of 24 hours, to work—

(a) in a case where the work done by the worker in that period includes night work and the worker is a special category night worker, more than 8 hours,

(b) in any other case, more than an average of 8 hours, that is to say an average of 8 hours calculated over a period (hereafter in this section referred to as a "reference period") that does not exceed—

    (i) 2 months, or

    (ii) such greater length of time as is specified in a collective agreement that for the time being has effect in relation to that night worker and which stands approved of by the Labour Court under section 24.

(3) In subsection (2) "special category night worker" means a night worker as respects whom an assessment carried out by his or her employer, pursuant to a requirement of regulations under section 28(1) of the Safety, Health and Welfare at Work Act, 1989, in relation to the risks attaching to the work that the night worker is employed to do indicates that that work involves special hazards or a heavy physical or mental strain.

(4) The days or months comprising a reference period shall, subject to subsection (5), be consecutive days or months.

(5) A reference period shall not include—

(a) any rest period granted to the employee concerned under section 13(2) (save so much of it as exceeds 24 hours),

(b) any rest periods granted to the employee concerned under section 13(3) (save so much of each of those periods as exceeds 24 hours),

(c) any period of annual leave granted to the employee concerned in accordance with this Act (save so much of it as exceeds the minimum period of annual leave required by this Act to be granted to the employee),

[(cc) any period during which the employee was absent from work while on parental leave, *force majeure* leave or carer's leave within the meaning of the Carer's Leave Act 2001,]

(d) any absences from work by the employee concerned authorised under the Maternity Protection [Acts 1994 and 2004], or the Adoptive Leave [Acts 1995 and 2005], or

(e) any sick leave taken by the employee concerned.

GENERAL NOTE

This section implements Article 8 of the Directive and provides definitions of "night time", "night work", "night worker" and "special category night worker". Note the decision of Kerr J. of the Northern Ireland High Court in *R v Attorney General for Northern Ireland, ex p. Burns* [1999] I.R.L.R. 315 that the definition of "night worker" could not be confined to someone who worked night shifts exclusively or even predominantly. Consequently the applicant, who spent one week of each three-week cycle working from 9 p.m. to 7 a.m., Sunday to Friday, was deemed to be a "night worker" for the purposes of the Directive.

In accordance with the provisions of Article 8, the section provides that where a night worker is not a special category night worker, the employer must ensure that the employee does not work more than an average of eight hours per night or 48 hours per week averaged over a two month period. A collective agreement, which must be approved by the Labour Court, may extend the period over which the night working is averaged.

Employers of persons employed in activities covered by S.I. Nos. 21 and 52 of 1998 are exempted from the provisions of s.16 as are workers employed as a member of travelling or flying personnel by an undertaking which operates transport services for passengers or goods by road, air, or inland waterway (see S.I. No. 817 of 2004).

**BB.148**

Paragraph (cc) of subs.(5) was inserted by virtue of s.28 of the Carer's Leave Act 2001.

## Provision of information in relation to working time

BB.149   **17.**—(1) If neither the contract of employment of the employee concerned nor any employment regulation order, registered employment agreement or collective agreement that has effect in relation to the employee specifies the normal or regular starting and finishing times of work of an employee, the employee's employer shall notify the employee, subject to subsection (3), at least 24 hours before the first day or, as the case may be, the day, in each week that he or she proposes to require the employee to work, of the times at which the employee will normally be required to start and finish work on each day, or, as the case may be, the day or days concerned, of that week.

(2) If the hours for which an employee is required to work for his or her employer in a week include such hours as the employer may from time to time decide (in this subsection referred to as "additional hours"), the employer shall notify the employee, subject to subsection (3), at least 24 hours before the first day or, as the case may be, the day, in that week on which he or she proposes to require the employee to work all or, as the case may be, any of the additional hours, of the times at which the employee will be required to start and finish working the additional hours on each day, or, as the case may be, the day or days concerned, of that week.

(3) If during the period of 24 hours before the first-mentioned or, as the case may be, the second-mentioned day in subsection (1) or (2), the employee has not been required to do work for the employer, the time at which the employee shall be notified of the matters referred to in subsection (1) or (2), as the case may be, shall be not later than before the last period of 24 hours, preceding the said first or second-mentioned day, in which he or she has been required to do work for the employer.

(4) A notification to an employee, in accordance with this section, of the matters referred to in subsection (1) or (2), as the case may be, shall not prejudice the right of the employer concerned, subject to the provisions of this Act, to require the employee to start or finish work or, as the case may be, to work the additional hours referred to in subsection (2) at times other than those specified in the notification if circumstances, which could not reasonably have been foreseen, arise that justify the employer in requiring the employee to start or finish work or, as the case may be, to work the said additional hours at those times.

(5) It shall be a sufficient notification to an employee of the matters referred to in subsection (1) or (2) for the employer concerned to post a notice of the matters in a conspicuous position in the place of the employee's employment.

General Note

BB.150   This section provides that an employee shall be entitled to be notified in advance of the hours which the employer will require the employee to work, subject to unforeseeable circumstances justifying a change in the notified times. This section was amended at Committee Stage in the Dáil to clarify that notice must be given on Thursday evening of the following Monday morning's work. The Labour Court has held that the section requires an employer to give an employee at least 24 hours notice of overtime working: see *Anglo Irish Beef Processors v SIPTU* DWT 19/2000.

## Provision in relation to zero hours working practices

BB.151   **18.**—(1) This section applies to an employee whose contract of employment operates to require the employee to make himself or herself available to work for the employer in a week—

    (a)   a certain number of hours ("the contract hours"), or

    (b)   as and when the employer requires him or her to do so, or

    (c)   both a certain number of hours and otherwise as and when the employer requires him or her to do so,

and the said requirement is not one that is held to arise by virtue only of the fact, if such be the case, of the employer having engaged the employee to do work of a casual nature for him or her on occasions prior to the said week (whether or not the number of those occasions or the circumstances otherwise touching the said engagement of the employee are such as to give rise to a reasonable expectation on his or her part that he or she would be required by the employer to do work for the employer in the said week).

(2) If an employer does not require an employee to whom this section applies to work for the employer in a week referred to in subsection (1)—

    (a)   in a case falling within paragraph (a) of that subsection, at least 25 per cent of the contract hours, or

    (b)   in a case falling within paragraph (b) or (c) of that subsection where work of the type which the employee is required to make himself or herself available to do has been done for the employer in that week, at least 25 per cent of the hours for which such work has been done in that week,

then the employee shall, subject to the provisions of this section, be entitled—

        (i)   in case the employee has not been required to work for the employer at all in that week, to be paid by the employer the pay he or she would have received if he or she had worked for the employer in that week whichever of the following is less, namely

(I)   the percentage of hours referred to in paragraph (a) or (b), as the case may be, or

(II)  15 hours,

or

(ii)  in case the employee has been required to work for the employer in that week less than the percentage of hours referred to in paragraph (a) or (b), as the case may be (and that percentage of hours is less than 15 hours), to have his or her pay for that week calculated on the basis that he or she worked for the employer in that week the percentage of hours referred to in paragraph (a) or (b), as the case may be.

(3) Subsection (2) shall not apply—

(a) if the fact that the employee concerned was not required to work in the week in question the percentage of hours referred to in paragraph (a) or (b) of that subsection, as the case may be—

(i)   constituted a lay-off or a case of the employee being kept on short-time for that week, or

(ii)  was due to exceptional circumstances or an emergency (including an accident or the imminent risk of an accident), the consequences of which could not have been avoided despite the exercise of all due care, or otherwise to the occurrence of unusual and unforeseeable circumstances beyond the employer's control, or

(b) if the employee concerned would not have been available, due to illness or for any other reason, to work for the employer in that week the said percentage of hours.

(4) The reference in subsection (2)(b) to the hours for which work of the type referred to in that provision has been done in the week concerned shall be construed as a reference to the number of hours of such work done in that week by another employee of the employer concerned or, in case that employer has required 2 or more employees to do such work for him or her in that week and the number of hours of such work done by each of them in that week is not identical, whichever number of hours of such work done by one of those employees in that week is the greatest.

(5) References in this section to an employee being required to make himself or herself available to do work for the employer shall not be construed as including references to the employee being required to be on call, that is to say to make himself or herself available to deal with any emergencies or other events or occurrences which may or may not occur.

(6) Nothing in this section shall affect the operation of a contract of employment that entitles the employee to be paid wages by the employer by reason, alone, of the employee making himself or herself available to do, at the times and place concerned, the work concerned.

GENERAL NOTE

This section applies to what are known as "zero hour contracts" or "zero hours working practices". **BB.152** These refer to arrangements where an employee is either asked to be available for work, without the guarantee of work, or where an employee is informed that there will be work available on a specified day or days. In effect the section provides that, in the event of an employer failing to require an employee to work at least 25 per cent of the time the employee is required by his or her contract of employment to be available to work for the employer, the employee will be entitled to payment for 25 per cent of the contract hours or 15 hours whichever is less. An amendment was passed at Committee Stage in the Dáil to ensure that there would be no entitlement to this minimum payment if there was only an "expectation" that employment would be given. The provisions only apply when the employee is notified in advance of being required to work or where the contract of employment operates to require the employee to be available for work. So if the employee's contract of employment operates to require the employee to be available for 40 hours in a week, he or she will be entitled to a minimum payment of ten hours even if not required to work that week. Similarly if an employee is asked to be available over a four week period and is not called into work, that employee will be entitled to a minimum payment of 15 hours or 25 per cent of the number of hours worked by another employee doing such work and for such number of hours as the "zero hours" employee would or could have done had he or she been called into work.

**BB.153**     This section was considered by the Labour Court in DWT1/1998 (a dispute between *Ocean Manpower Ltd* and the *Marine Port and General Workers' Union*). The agreement between the union and the company required the employees (casual dockers) to remain available for work during defined periods. They were also required to report to the company's premises at a specified time for the purpose of being allocated work and failure to so report could be the subject of disciplinary proceedings. Although the court found that these obligations might not be "rigidly enforced" by the company, they remained part of the agreement and were a requirement in the employees' contracts of employment. Accordingly the court was satisfied that section 18 applied.

The court rejected, however, the union's contention that the "floor payment" to which its members were entitled should be calculated by reference to the number of hours over which they were required to make themselves available to the employer. It seemed clear to the court that the "floor payment" provided by section 18(2) "should be calculated by reference to the number of hours which the employee may be required to work in a week and not to the number of hours over which they are required to be available to undertake that work". As the agreement provided that normal working hours were to be from 0800 hours to 1700 hours for a five-day week,the Rights Commissioner's calculation of a floor payment of 10 hours, or 3/4 hours in the case of a 39 hour week, was correct. The Rights Commissioner was also correct in stipulating that, where an employee does not present himself or herself for work on any day or days of the week, the entitlement should be reduced by 20 per cent or multiples of 20 per cent as the case may be. The Labour Court added that, where an employee works on any day or days of the week, no entitlement under section 18 arises once the basic entitlement has been exceeded. This decision is reported at [1998] E.L.R. 299.

Part III

Holidays

## Entitlement to annual leave

**BB.154**     **19.**—(1) Subject to the First Schedule (which contains transitional provisions in respect of the leave years 1996 to 1998), an employee shall be entitled to paid annual leave (in this Act referred to as "annual leave") equal to—

    (a) 4 working weeks in a leave year in which he or she works at least 1,365 hours (unless it is a leave year in which he or she changes employment),

    (b) one-third of a working week for each month in the leave year in which he or she works at least 117 hours, or

    (c) 8 per cent of the hours he or she works in a leave year (but subject to a maximum of 4 working weeks):

Provided that if more than one of the preceding paragraphs is applicable in the case concerned and the period of annual leave of the employee, determined in accordance with each of those paragraphs, is not identical, the annual leave to which the employee shall be entitled shall be equal to whichever of those periods is the greater.

(2) A day which would be regarded as a day of annual leave shall, if the employee concerned is ill on that day and furnishes to his or her employer a certificate of a registered medical practitioner in respect of his or her illness, not be regarded, for the purposes of this Act, as a day of annual leave.

(3) The annual leave of an employee who works 8 or more months in a leave year shall, subject to the provisions of any employment regulation order, registered employment agreement, collective agreement or any

B–74

agreement between the employee and his or her employer, include an unbroken period of 2 weeks.

(4) Notwithstanding subsection (2) or any other provision of this Act but without prejudice to the employee's entitlements under subsection (1), the reference in subsection (3) to an unbroken period of 2 weeks includes a reference to such a period that includes one or more public holidays or days on which the employee concerned is ill.

(5) An employee shall, for the purposes of subsection (1), be regarded as having worked on a day of annual leave the hours he or she would have worked on that day had it not been a day of annual leave.

(6) References in this section to a working week shall be construed as references to the number of days that the employee concerned usually works in a week.

GENERAL NOTE

This section implements Article 7 of the Directive and sets out the three mechanisms for earning **BB.155** an entitlement to annual leave. These mechanisms are similar to those that applied under the Holidays (Employees) Act 1973, as amended by section 4 of the Worker Protection (Regular Part-Time Employees) Act 1991, while allowing for the increase in holiday entitlement from three weeks to four weeks, or from 6 per cent to 8 per cent of time worked for part-time employees. Although the expression "working week" is not defined in the Act, the Labour Court has ruled that it can only be construed as referring to the number of days or hours encompassing each work cycle: *Irish Ferries v Seamen's Union of Ireland DWT* 35/2001. In this case the claimants worked under an annualised hours contract by which they were required to work 2,016 hours per year. They were rostered for work for over a continuous seven day period starting on Wednesday in each week and ending on the Tuesday of the following week. They were then rostered off duty for the next following seven days. Their annual leave entitlement was calculated by the company as being 168 hours paid leave (14 days by 12 hours) which was equivalent to 8.33 per cent of the hours worked. The union, however, contended that they effectively only received two weeks paid holidays per year. Both the rights commissioner and, on appeal, the Labour Court rejected the union's claim. The Court said that the entitlement to annual leave must correspond to the amount of time which the employee would normally be required to work in each work cycle. Here the claimants were required to work fourteen 12-hour days (or 168 hours) over each four week period, hence their entitlement had been correctly calculated.

The new four-week entitlement, however, did not come into effect until April 1999. Up to then the First Schedule set out transitional arrangements giving entitlement on a phased basis. For the leave year beginning April 1997, there were 16 days of leave; for the leave year beginning April 1998, 18 days; and for the leave year beginning April 1999, 20 days.

There has been a statutory entitlement to annual leave since 1936, when the Conditions of Employment Act prescribed a minimum legally enforceable entitlement to six consecutive days paid annual leave for "industrial employees". The Shops (Conditions of Employment) Act 1938 extended a similar annual leave entitlement to employees in the retail and wholesale trades and in hotels, licensed premises and restaurants. The relevant provisions of the 1936 and 1938 Acts were repealed by the Holidays (Employees) Act 1939 which gave an entitlement to seven consecutive days paid annual leave to the majority of employees with an annual wage of £350 [€444.41] or less, irrespective of the type of employment. The main category of employees outside the scope of the 1939 legislation were agricultural workers and it was not until the Agricultural Workers (Holidays) Act 1950 that these employees enjoyed the benefit of statutory paid annual leave.

The Holidays (Employees) Act 1961 increased the minimum legally enforceable annual leave **BB.156** entitlement to 14 consecutive days annual leave and abolished the £350 annual wages ceiling to eligibility provided under the 1939 Act. A minimum hours threshold of 1,600 hours was provided instead. The Agricultural Workers (Holidays) Act 1961 gave 12 days annual leave to agricultural workers.

The Holidays (Employees) Act 1973 repealed the two Acts of 1961 and extended the annual leave entitlement to three working weeks and reduced the minimum hours threshold for eligibility to 1,400 hours per leave year. The Worker Protection (Regular Part-Time Employees) Act 1991 extended the scope of the 1973 Act to regular part-time employees, *i.e.* employees not previously covered by the

1973 Act who had at least 13 weeks continuous service and who were normally expected to work at least eight hours a week.

According to the Department of Enterprise and Employment's Discussion Paper on Holidays Legislation (1994) the statutory minimum entitlement to annual leave "is based on the notion that in our society a certain amount of paid time-off should be available to every individual employee" (page 26). In *Cementation Skanska v Carroll* DWT38/2003, the Labour Court said that the "obligation to provide annual leave is imposed for health and safety reasons" and acknowledged that the right to leave had been characterised "as a fundamental social right in European law". Statutory annual leave was intended to set a realistic basic entitlement while allowing a negotiated element on top of this by agreement between the parties. Although the term "paid annual leave" is not defined in the Act, the Labour Court has ruled that it is "a term of common usage in industrial relations and is well understood as meaning a period of rest and relaxation during which a worker is paid his or her normal wages without any obligation to work or provide any service to the employer": *Royal Liver Assurance Ltd v Services Industrial Professional Technical Union* DWT 41/2001. See, to similar effect, the decision of the Court of Justice in Joined Cases C–131/04 and C–257/04, *Robinson-Steele v RD Retail Services Ltd* [2006] I.R.L.R. 386.

### Times and pay for annual leave

**BB.157** **20.**—(1) The times at which annual leave is granted to an employee shall be determined by his or her employer having regard to work requirements and subject—

(a) to the employer taking into account-

(i) the need for the employee to reconcile work and any family responsibilities,

(ii) the opportunities for rest and recreation available to the employee,

(b) to the employer having consulted the employee or the trade union (if any) of which he or she is a member, not later than 1 month before the day on which the annual leave or, as the case may be, the portion thereof concerned is due to commence, and

(c) to the leave being granted within the leave year to which it relates or, with the consent of the employee, within the 6 months thereafter.

(2) The pay in respect of an employee's annual leave shall-

(a) be paid to the employee in advance of his or her taking the leave,

(b) be at the normal weekly rate or, as the case may be, at a rate which is proportionate to the normal weekly rate, and

(c) in a case in which board or lodging or, as the case may be, both board and lodging constitute part of the employee's remuneration, include compensation, calculated at the prescribed rate, for any such board or lodging as will not be received by the employee whilst on annual leave.

(3) Nothing in this section shall prevent an employer and employee from entering into arrangements that are more favourable to the employee with regard to the times of, and the pay in respect of, his or her annual leave.

(4) In this section "normal weekly rate" means the normal weekly rate of the employee concerned's pay determined in accordance with regulations made by the Minister for the purposes of this section.

GENERAL NOTE

**BB.158** This section sets out the criteria which apply to the times at which annual leave should be granted and to the arrangement whereby an employee will be paid for this leave. Although the times at which annual leave is granted are to be determined by the employer, the employer must take into account not only the opportunities for rest and recreation available to the employee but also the need for the employee "to reconcile work and any family responsibilities". In addition the employer must consult with the employee or the trade union of which he or she is a member not later than one month before the day on which the annual leave (or portion thereof) is due to commence. The purpose of subsection (1)(c), *per* Lavan J. in *Royal Liver Assurance Ltd v Macken* [2002] 4 I.R. 427, is "to enable flexibility so the employer may reconcile the needs of his business with the rights of an employee". The learned judge went on to point out that the "express language" of the paragraph suggested that the consent of the employee was "a condition precedent to the ability of the employer to extend the leave year by an additional six months". The Court of Justice has ruled that Art.7 of the Directive precludes the replacement, by an allowance in lieu, of untaken days of annual leave because the possibility of financial compensation in respect of annual leave carried over would create an incentive not to take leave or to encourage employees not to do so: see Case C–124/05 *Federatie Nederlandse Vakbeweging v Staat der Nederlanden* [2006] I.R.L.R. 561.

The "normal weekly rate of pay" is determined in accordance with the provisions of the Organisation of Working Time (Determination of Pay for Holidays) Regulations 1997 (S.I. No. 475 of 1997). Regulation 3(2) provides that if the employee's pay is calculated wholly by reference to a time rate or a fixed rate or salary or any other rate that does not vary in relation to the work done, the normal weekly rate of pay shall be:

"the sum (including any regular bonus or allowance the amount of which does not vary in relation to the work done by the employee but excluding any pay for overtime) that is paid in respect of the normal weekly working hours last worked by the employee before the annual leave (or the portion thereof concerned) commences".

If the employee's pay is not calculated wholly by reference to any of the matters referred to in paragraph 2 of Regulation 3, the normal weekly rate of pay shall be the sum that is equal to the average weekly pay (excluding any pay for overtime) of the employee calculated over the period of 13 weeks last worked before the annual leave (or the portion thereof concerned) commences. Overtime was similarly excluded under the 1973 Act, yet on many occasions the Labour Court has recommended that where "regular rostered overtime" is worked it should be reflected in holiday pay: see LCR 7135 (CIE); LCR 7318 (Dublin Voluntary Hospitals); LCR 7365 (Waterford Crystal Ltd); LCR 9273 (Ergas Ltd); LCR 10155 (Eason  LCR 10390 (St Vincent's Hospital); LCR 10494 (Donnelly Mirrors Ltd); LCR 10794 (Deansgrange Joint Burial Board); and, most recently, LCR 18118 (Banagher Concrete).

## Entitlement in respect of public holidays

**21.**—(1) Subject to the provisions of this section, an employee shall, in respect **BB.159** of a public holiday, be entitled to whichever one of the following his or her employer determines, namely—

  (a)  a paid day off on that day,

  (b)  a paid day off within a month of that day,

  (c)  an additional day of annual leave,

  (d)  an additional day's pay:

Provided that if the day on which the public holiday falls is a day on which the employee would, apart from this subsection, be entitled to a paid day off this subsection shall have effect as if paragraph (a) were omitted therefrom.

(2) An employee may, not later than 21 days before the public holiday concerned, request his or her employer to make, as respects the employee, a determination under subsection (1) in relation to a particular public holiday and notify the employee of that determination at least 14 days before that holiday.

(3) If an employer fails to comply with a request under subsection (2), he or she shall be deemed to have determined that the entitlement of the employee concerned under subsection (1) shall be to a paid day off on the public holiday concerned or, in a case to which the proviso to subsection (1) applies, to an additional day's pay.

(4) Subsection (1) shall not apply, as respects a particular public holiday, to an employee (not being an employee who is a whole-time employee) unless he or she has worked for the employer concerned at least 40 hours during the period of 5 weeks ending on the day before that public holiday.

(5) Subsection (1) shall not apply, as respects a particular public holiday, to an employee who is, other than on the commencement of this section, absent from work immediately before that public holiday in any of the cases specified in the Third Schedule.

(6) For the avoidance of doubt, the reference in the proviso to subsection (1) to a day on which the employee is entitled to a paid day off includes a reference to any day on which he or she is not required to work, the pay to which he or she is entitled in respect of a week or other period being regarded, for this purpose, as receivable by him or her in respect of the day or days in that period on which he or she is not required to work as well as the day or days in that period on which he or she is required to work.

GENERAL NOTE

This section sets out the criteria which shall apply to public holiday entitlements. The qualifying **BB.160** period is that at least 40 hours work during the five weeks before the public holiday will be required. The section was amended at Committee Stage in the Dáil to ensure that an employee will be entitled to a public holiday even though that employee is not rostered to work a public holiday.

There are, at present, nine "public holidays", as set out in the Second Schedule, although celebration of the Millenium, December 31, 1999 was designated a special public holiday: see Organisation of Working Time (Public Holiday) Regulations 1999 (S.I. No. 10 of 1999). See also the Organisation of Working Time (National Day of Mourning) Regulations 2001 (S.I. No. 419 of 2001) which appointed Friday September 14, 2001, to be a day of National Mourning as a mark of respect for the victims of the attacks in the United States of America on September 11, 2001. "Public holidays" should not be confused with "bank holidays". For instance, Good Friday is a bank holiday but not a public holiday.

The concept of a "bank holiday" originated with the Bank Holidays Act 1871 which, as amended by the Holidays Extension Act 1873, provided that Easter Monday, Whit Monday, the first Monday in August and St Stephen's Day (December 26) would be "bank holidays". Prior to 1871 the only holidays generally observed were Good Friday and Christmas Day (both of which appear to have been common law holidays). The holidays referred to in the 1871 Act related specifically to banks, the reasons being mainly of a technical nature. Banks were subject to compulsory duties which could only be relaxed by legislation and, accordingly, section 1 of the 1871 Act provided that Bills of Exchange and promissory notes which were due and payable on a bank holiday should be payable on the next following day. Similarly section 3 provided that "no person shall be compellable to make any payments or to do any act upon such bank holidays which he could not be compellable to do or make on Christmas Day or Good Friday". The Bank Holiday (Ireland) Act 1903 established St Patrick's Day (March 17) as an additional bank holiday in Ireland. The 1871, 1875 and 1903 Acts were ultimately repealed by the Central Bank Act 1989 which, Good Friday apart, assigned as "bank holidays" the "public holidays" designated by the 1973 Act.

**BB.161**     The first specific statutory designation of "public holidays" occurred in the Conditions of Employment Act 1936, which specified as public holidays Easter Monday, Whit Monday, the first Monday in August, Christmas Day, St Stephen's Day and St Patrick's Day (although the concept of "public holiday" as distinct from a "bank holiday" first appears in the Public Holidays Act 1924). The 1936 Act provided for leave or financial compensation for employees in respect of each of the six public holidays. The provisions were repeated in the Holidays (Employees) Acts 1939 and 1961 and no change was mooted until 1965 when the Minister for Transport and Power (Erskine Childers T.D.) established a Commission of Inquiry into Public Holidays and Bank Holidays under the Chairmanship of Gabriel Hogan B.L. (Chairman of Irish Steel Holdings Ltd). The impetus for this inquiry appears to have arisen from the Minister's interest in promoting the development of tourism and relieving the congestion in transport and accommodation. Amongst its recommendations were that the Whit public holiday should be moved from Whit Monday to the first Monday in June, that New Year's Day should be a bank, but not a public, holiday and that a new public holiday might appropriately be placed in either late October or early November. The last recommendation had been supported both by the Irish Congress of Trade Unions and Bord Failte, the latter advocating the introduction of an additional public holiday in order to provide a stimulus towards extending the holiday season with consequent benefit to hoteliers and transport concerns.

The change in the Whit holiday recommended by the Commission of Inquiry was effected by the Holidays (Employees) Act 1973, under which Act three further public holidays were designated in 1974, 1977 and 1994 (namely New Year's Day, the last Monday in October and the first Monday in May).

**BB.162**     In its 1994 *Discussion Paper on Holidays Legislation* the Department of Enterprise and Employment stated there were a number of criteria which were central to any examination of the case for a change in the date of an existing public holiday or for an increase in the number of public holidays. These were:

(a)    the cultural or social significance of the date,

(b)    how the date fits in with the spread of public holidays on the calendar, and

(c)    the scope the date provides for recreational purposes.

New Year's Day is observed as a public holiday in all the E.U. member states. Its designation as a public holiday here marked Ireland's entry to the E.E.C. Although within six days of St Stephen's Day, the placing of this holiday, as noted in the 1994 Discussion Paper, facilitates those who wish to take a long break over Christmas.

St Patrick's Day is the national day, having counterparts in other E.U. countries (such as Bastille Day in France), and provides an essential focus for national identity. As such it has immense symbolic significance, but the Department perceived two main disadvantages to the holiday. The first is that it may occur within as little as five days of the range of possible dates of Easter. The second is that the recreational value of the holiday is limited when it occurs midweek. Consequently the Department sought views on whether the public holiday should be moved to the Monday or Friday nearest the actual feast day.

Easter Monday is a long standing public holiday and is designated as such in most E.U. member states. Easter Monday is a movable holiday and its date depends on the date of Easter. This date gave rise to many disputes in the early days of Christianity which were resolved, to a large extent, by a decree of the First Ecumenical Council at Nicaea in 325 AD which prescribed that Easter would fall on the first Sunday after the first full moon after the Spring Equinox (March 21). This provided, in effect, that Easter will always fall between March 22 and April 25.

It might be noted that some attempts have been made to secure agreement to a fixed Easter day **BB.163** since at least 1582 (when Pope Gregory XIII introduced his solar calendar) and in 1928 the U.K. Parliament passed the Easter Act which provided that Easter would fall on the first Sunday after the second Saturday in April. The Act contained a provision, however, that it would only come into force in the event of an Order in Council passed by both Houses of Parliament. No such order has ever been placed before Parliament and the Act, therefore, has never come into force.

The first Monday in May was designated in commemoration of the centenary of the first Irish Trade Union Congress. It is of course very close to May Day which has been a traditional springtime festival since pagan times. The formal connection between May Day and workers rights dates from 1889 when the Socialist International was founded at a Congress in Paris and designated May Day as International Labour Day. In 1955 Pope Pius XII declared May Day to be the feast of St Joseph the Worker.

The first Mondays in June and August are the two summer public holidays, the former associated historically with the religious feast of Pentecost and the latter with the beginning of the traditional annual holidays of employees in industrial and manual employment. In addition, "for reasons connected with tourist traffic between the two countries", they are set on dates separate from the two U.K. summer public holidays (last Monday in May and last Monday in August). The Department did seek views, however, as to whether the June holiday might be moved to a date later in the month to allow for better spacing between the various holidays.

The designation of the last Monday in October was intended to provide a holiday break midway **BB.164** through the then 20–21 week gap between the August and Christmas public holidays. It is also associated with the old Celtic festival of Samhain (in Christian terms Hallowe'en). One disadvantage as to the timing is that the recreational benefits are diminished by the inclement weather and shorter daylight hours. The Department sought views as to whether it should be moved to a date earlier in the month.

Christmas Day and St Stephen's Day fall on consecutive days and together provide a break for social and family activities at Christmas time. The latter is a public holiday in most E.U. member states.The Department concluded in its 1994 Discussion Paper (page 39) that the existing arrangements for public holidays left no major gaps in the calendar which might support the argument in favour of a further holiday. Nor did the Department feel there was a clear case for a further public holiday based on a date of important social or cultural significance other than Good Friday (page 51). It would appear that, in light of the responses received by the Department, it was felt that there was insufficient consensus to warrant any change in the timing of the various public holidays. During the 2002 General Election the Labour Party pledged to provide two extra public holidays and used an online poll at its website to establish when people would like them. Midsummer's Day (June 21) topped the poll at 28 per cent closely followed by St Brigid's Day (February 1) at 27 per cent. Other suggested dates included National Commemoration Day (July 7), the Feast of the Assumption (August 15) and Europe Day (May 9).

## Public holidays: supplemental provisions

**22.**—(1) The rate—                                                                                              **BB.165**

(a)  at which an employee is paid in respect of a day off under section 21, and

(b)  of an employee's additional day's pay under that section,

shall be such rate as is determined in accordance with regulations made by the Minister for the purposes of that section.

(2) For the purposes of section 21, time off granted to an employee under that section or section 19 shall be regarded as time worked by the employee.

General Note

**BB.166**     This section provides that the mechanism for calculating the rate of pay for a public holiday shall be set out in Regulations, in this case the Organisation of Working Time (Determination of Pay for Holidays) Regulations 1997 (S.I. No. 475 of 1997). Regulation 5 provides that, if the employee's pay is calculated wholly by reference to a time rate or a fixed rate or salary or any other rate that does not vary in relation to the work done, the relevant rate in respect of a public holiday is the sum equal to the sum (including any regular bonus or allowance the amount of which does not vary in relation to the work done by the employee but excluding any pay for overtime) paid to the employee in respect of the normal daily hours last worked before that public holiday. If the employee's pay is not calculated by reference to any of the above matters, the relevant rate in respect of a public holiday is the sum that is equal to the average daily pay (excluding any pay for overtime) of the employee calculated over the period of 13 weeks last worked before the public holiday. An employee who is not rostered to work a public holiday is entitled to a sum equal to one-fifth of the above sums: see *Cadbury Ireland Ltd v. SIPTU* [1999] E.L.R. 202. Specific provision is also made in Regulation 6 for certain categories of job-sharer for whom the relevant rate is the sum that is equal to one-tenth of the sum (including any regular bonus or allowance the amount of which does not vary in relation to the work done by the employee but excluding any pay for overtime) that is paid in respect of the last two weeks of normal working hours worked by the employee before the public holiday.

**BB.167**     Prior to 1986 a problem had arisen as to whether an employer was obliged to pay an employee who was sick on a public holiday or whether the employer could merely top up the employee's social welfare entitlements. Section 10 of the Social Welfare Act 1986 provided that an employee was not entitled to disability benefit for day on which he or she was being paid by the employer in respect of holiday leave. This provision is now found in section 31(3)(f) of the Social Welfare (Consolidation) Act 1993.

## Compensation on cesser of employment

**BB.168**     **23.**—(1) Where—

(a)  an employee ceases to be employed, and

(b)  the whole or any portion of the annual leave in respect of the current leave year or, in case the cesser of employment occurs during the first half of that year, in respect of that year, the previous leave year or both those years, remains to be granted to the employee,

the employee shall, as compensation for the loss of that annual leave, be paid by his or her employer an amount equal to the pay, calculated at the normal weekly rate or, as the case may be, at a rate proportionate to the normal weekly rate, that he or she would have received had he or she been granted that annual leave.

(2) Where—

(a)  an employee ceases to be employed during the week ending on the day before a public holiday, and

(b)  the employee has worked for his or her employer during the 4 weeks preceding that week,

the employee shall, as compensation for the loss of his or her entitlements under section 21 in respect of the said public holiday, be paid by his or her employer an amount equal to an additional day's pay calculated at the appropriate daily rate.

(3) If an employee ceases to be employed by reason of his or her death, any compensation payable under this section shall be paid to the personal representative of the employee.

(4) Where compensation is payable under subsection (2), the employee concerned shall, for the purpose of Chapter 9 of Part II of the Social Welfare (Consolidation) Act, 1993 (which relates to unemployment benefit) and Chapter 2 of Part III of that Act (which relates to unemployment assistance), be regarded as not having been, on the public holiday concerned, in the employment of the employer concerned.

(5) In this section "appropriate daily rate" and "normal weekly rate" mean, respectively, the appropriate daily rate of the employee concerned's pay and the normal weekly rate of the employee concerned's pay determined in accordance with regulations made by the Minister for the purposes of this section.

GENERAL NOTE

This section provides that an employee, or his or her personal representative, is entitled to the **BB.169** payment of any holidays or public holiday compensation owing at the time of cesser of employment. The "appropriate daily rate" and "normal weekly rate" are computed in accordance with the Organisation of Working Time (Determination of Pay for Holidays) Regulations 1997 (S.I. No. 475 of 1997).

The provisions of subsection (2) were considered by the Labour Court in *Gazboro Ltd v Building and Allied Trades' Union* DWT 16/1999. In this case the union claimed that its members, who were let go on Friday, December 18, 1998, were entitled to payment for Christmas Day and St Stephen's Day. The Labour Court said that two questions of interpretation arose for its determination:

1. what period constitutes "the week ending on the day before" the public holiday for the purpose of applying subsection (2); and
2. is an employee who receives an additional day's pay under subsection (2) deemed to have worked on that day?

In the Labour Court's opinion, the week ending at midnight on December 24, 1998 commenced at midnight on December 18, 1998. Since the employees worked for the employer during the four weeks preceding that week, they were entitled to compensation of an amount equal to an additional day's pay in respect of Christmas Day. It followed that, because the week ending on December 25 commenced at midnight on December 19, the employees had no entitlement in respect of St Stephen's Day, since they ceased to be employed on December 18. The Labour Court rejected the Union's contention that, because the employees were entitled to be paid an extra day's pay in respect of Christmas Day, they should be deemed to have worked an extra day, thus bringing their termination date within the week ending on the day before St Stephen's Day. The Labour Court's reasoning was as follows:

> "Section 22(2) of the Act provides that time off granted to an employee under section 21 in respect of the public holiday is to be regarded as time worked for the purpose of that section. In this case the claimants are not entitled to time off under section 21 in respect of the 25th of December but to compensation in an amount equal to an additional day's pay under section 23(2)."

PART IV

MISCELLANEOUS

## Approval of collective agreements by Labour Court

**24.**—(1) In this section "collective agreement" means a collective agreement **BB.170** referred to in section 4, 15 or 16 or paragraph 4(a) of the First Schedule [or in regulation 9(4) or 10(2) of the Activities of Doctors in Training Regulations].

(2) On an application being made in that behalf by any of the parties thereto, the Labour Court may, subject to the provisions of this section, approve of a collective agreement.

(3) On receipt of an application under this section, the Labour Court shall consult such representatives of employees and employers as it considers to have an interest in the matters to which the collective agreement, the subject of the application, relates.

(4) The Labour Court shall not approve of a collective agreement unless the following conditions are fulfilled as respects that agreement, namely—

(a) in the case of a collective agreement referred to in section 4, 15 or 16 [or regulation 9(4) or 10(2) of the Activities of Doctors in Training Regulations], the Labour Court is satisfied that it is appropriate to approve of the agreement having regard to the provisions of the Council Directive permitting the entry into collective agreements for the purposes concerned,

(b) the agreement has been concluded in a manner usually employed in determining the pay or other conditions of employment of employees in the employment concerned,

(c) the body which negotiated the agreement on behalf of the employees

B–81

concerned is the holder of a negotiation licence under the Trade Union Act, 1941, or is an excepted body within the meaning of that Act which is sufficiently representative of the employees concerned,

(d)   the agreement is in such form as appears to the Labour Court to be suitable for the purposes of the agreement being approved of under this section.

(5) Where the Labour Court is not satisfied that the condition referred to in paragraph (a) or (d) of subsection (4) is fulfilled in relation to a collective agreement, the subject of an application under subsection (2) (but is satisfied that the other conditions referred to in that subsection are fulfilled in relation to the agreement), it may request the parties to the agreement to vary the agreement in such manner as will result in the said condition being fulfilled and if those parties agree so to vary the agreement and vary it, accordingly, the Labour Court shall approve of the agreement as so varied.

(6) Where a collective agreement which has been approved of under this section is subsequently varied by the parties thereto, any of the said parties may apply to the Labour Court to have the agreement, as so varied, approved of by the Labour Court under this section and the provisions of this section shall apply to such an application as they apply to an application under subsection (2).

(7) The Labour Court may withdraw its approval of a collective agreement under this section where it is satisfied that there are substantial grounds for so doing.

(8) The Labour Court shall determine the procedures to be followed by a person in making an application under subsection (2) or (6), by the Labour Court in considering any such application or otherwise performing any of its functions under this section and by persons generally in relation to matters falling to be dealt with under this section.

(9) The Labour Court shall publish, in such manner as it thinks fit, particulars of the procedures referred to in subsection (8).

(10) The Labour Court shall establish and maintain a register of collective agreements standing approved of by it under this section and such a register shall be made available for inspection by members of the public at all reasonable times.

GENERAL NOTE

**BB.171**    This section, as amended by regulation 12 of the European Communities (Organisation of Working Time) (Activities of Doctors in Training) Regulations 2004 (S.I. No. 494 of 2004), empowers the Labour Court to approve "collective agreements" which have been concluded to vary the basic terms of the Act concerning working time. The Court must be satisfied, before approving the agreement, that it accords with the Directive, that it has been concluded in the manner usually employed in determining the pay or other conditions of the employees concerned and that the body negotiating the agreement is representative of the employees concerned.

There is no prescribed format for agreements but the Labour Court has published a Guide to its functions and procedures (November 1997) in which sample outline agreements are included. By the end of 2003 the Labour Court had approved a total of 193 collective agreements, dealing with the transitional weekly limits, the 12 month averaging period and rest arrangements, which were expressed to apply to some 112,878 workers.

## Records

**BB.172**    **25.**—(1) An employer shall keep, at the premises or place where his or her employee works or, if the employee works at two or more premises or places, the premises or place from which the activities that the employee is employed to carry on are principally directed or controlled, such records, in such form, if any, as may be prescribed, as will show whether the provisions of this Act [and, where applicable, the Activities of Doctors in Training Regulations] are being complied with in relation to the employee and those records shall be retained by the employer for at least 3 years from the date of their making.

(2) The Minister may by regulations exempt from the application of subsection (1) any specified class or classes of employer and regulations under this subsection may provide that any such exemption shall not have effect save to the extent that specified conditions are complied with.

(3) An employer who, without reasonable cause, fails to comply with subsection (1) shall be guilty of an offence.

(4) Without prejudice to subsection (3), where an employer fails to keep records under subsection (1) in respect of his or her compliance with a particular provision of this Act [or the Activities of Doctors in Training Regulations] in relation to an employee, the onus of proving, in proceedings before a rights commissioner or the Labour Court, that the said provision was complied with in relation to the employee shall lie on the employer.

GENERAL NOTE

This section, as amended by the European Communities (Organisation of Working Time) (Activ- **BB.173** ities of Doctors in Training) Regulations 2004 (S.I. No. 494 of 2004), requires an employer to keep records for at least three years to show compliance with the Act. This section was amended at Committee Stage in the Dáil to allow the Minister to exempt employers from this obligation. The relevant Regulations are the Organisation of Working Time (Records) (Prescribed Form and Exemptions) Regulations 2001 (S.I. No. 473 of 2001) which came into operation on November 1, 2001; reproduced at BC.1101. Regulation 11(5) of S.I. No. 494 of 2004 provides that the 2001 Regulations do not apply to an employer of doctors in training. The importance of maintaining records is highlighted by the Labour Court's decision in *Feeney v Baquiran* [2004] E.L.R. 304.

### Refusal by an employee to co-operate with employer in breaching Act

**26.**—(1) An employer shall not penalise an employee for having in good faith **BB.174** opposed by lawful means an act which is unlawful under this Act [or the Activities of Doctors in Training Regulations].

(2) If a penalisation of an employee, in contravention of subsection (1), constitutes a dismissal of the employee within the meaning of the Unfair Dismissals Acts, 1977 to [2001], relief may not be granted to the employee in respect of that penalisation both under this Part and under those Acts.

GENERAL NOTE

This section, as amended by the European Communities (Organisation of Working Time) (Activ- **BB.175** ities of Doctors in Training) Regulations 2004 (S.I. No. 494 of 2004), provides that an employee who refuses to co-operate with an employer in breaching the Act shall not be penalised by the employer. The Labour Court has ruled that, in order to make out a complaint of penalisation under subs.(1), it is necessary for the complainant "to establish a causal link between her activities in seeking to have s.19 of the Act applied by the respondent and some detriment which she suffered in her employment". Moreover the activities alleged to have given rise to the detriment suffered must relate to the complainant having opposed an act which was unlawful under the 1997 Act: see *University College Cork v Keohane* DWT 47/2001. The section also provides against the possibility of double relief.

### Complaints to rights commissioner

**27.**—(1) In this section "relevant provision" means— **BB.176**

(a)  any of the following sections, namely, section 6(2), sections 11 to 23, or section 26,

[(aa) any of the following regulations of the Activities of Doctors in Training Regulations namely, regulations 5 to 10,]

(b)  the provision referred to in section 6(1) of regulations, a collective agreement, registered employment agreement or employment regulation order referred to in that section, or

(c)  paragraph 9 of the Fifth Schedule.

(2) An employee or any trade union of which the employee is a member, with the consent of the employee, may present a complaint to a rights commissioner that the employee's employer has contravened a relevant provision in relation to the employee and, if the employee or such a trade union does so, the commissioner shall give the parties an opportunity to be heard by the commissioner and to present to the commissioner any evidence relevant to the complaint, shall give a decision in writing in relation to it and shall communicate the decision to the parties.

(3) A decision of a rights commissioner under subsection (2) shall do one or more of the following:

(a) declare that the complaint was or, as the case may be, was not well founded,

(b) require the employer to comply with the relevant provision,

(c) require the employer to pay to the employee compensation of such amount (if any) as is just and equitable having regard to all the circumstances, but not exceeding 2 years remuneration in respect of the employee's employment,

and the references in the foregoing paragraphs to an employer shall be construed, in a case where ownership of the business of the employer changes after the contravention to which the complaint relates occurred, as references to the person who, by virtue of the change, becomes entitled to such ownership.

(4) A rights commissioner shall not entertain a complaint under this section if it is presented to the commissioner after the expiration of the period of 6 months beginning on the date of the contravention to which the complaint relates.

(5) Notwithstanding subsection (4), a rights commissioner may entertain a complaint under this section presented to him or her after the expiration of the period referred to in subsection (4) (but not later than 12 months after such expiration) if he or she is satisfied that the failure to present the complaint within that period was due to reasonable cause.

(6) A complaint shall be presented by giving notice thereof in writing to a rights commissioner and the notice shall contain such particulars and be in such form as may be specified from time to time by the Minister.

(7) A copy of a notice under subsection (6) shall be given to the other party concerned by the rights commissioner concerned.

(8) Proceedings under this section before a rights commissioner shall be conducted otherwise than in public.

(9) A rights commissioner shall furnish the Labour Court with a copy of each decision given by the commissioner under subsection (2).

(10) The Minister may by regulations provide for any matters relating to proceedings under this section that the Minister considers appropriate.

GENERAL NOTE

BB.177    This section, as amended by the European Communities (Organisation of Working Time) (Activities of Doctors in Training) Regulations 2004 (S.I. No. 494 of 2004), provides that an employee or an employee's trade union may make a complaint to a rights commissioner who shall investigate the complaint and make a decision. The complaint must be presented within six months of the alleged contravention of the Act unless the commissioner is satisfied that failure to present the complaint within that period was due to reasonable cause. The power to extend the time-limit was fully considered by the Labour Court in *Cementation Skanska v Carroll* DWT38/2003. It was the court's view that:

"[I]n considering if reasonable cause exists, it is for the claimant to show that there are reasons which both explain the delay and afford an excuse for the delay. The explanation must be reasonable, that is to say it must make sense, be agreeable to reason and not be irrational or absurd. In the context in which the expression reasonable cause appears in statute it suggests an objective standard, but it must be applied to the facts and circumstances known to the claimant at the material time. The claimant's failure to present the claim within the six-month time limit must have been due to the reasonable cause relied upon. Hence there must be a causal link between the circumstances cited and the delay and the claimant should satisfy the Court, as a matter of probability, that had those circumstances not been present he would have initiated the claim in time."

The Court went on to say that the length of the delay should also be taken into account. A short delay might only require "a slight explanation" whereas a long delay might require "more cogent reasons". Even where "reasonable cause" was shown, the court determined that it should still consider if it was appropriate in the circumstances to exercise its discretion in favour of granting an extension of time. Here the court said that it should consider if the employer has suffered prejudice by the delay and whether the claimant has a good arguable case.

In *Campbell Catering Ltd v SIPTU* DWT 35/2000 the Labour Court did not accept that the wording of subs.(2) restricted a trade union to making a complaint on behalf of a single employee affected by the subject matter of the complaint. The Court said that, while the subsection referred to "an employee", this did not prevent a trade union from presenting more than one complaint, each identical in form and content, where the alleged infringement affected a multiplicity of employees. The circumstances in which compensation under subs.(3)(c) should be awarded in addition to outstanding holiday entitlements were considered by the Labour Court in *Kennedy's Café Bar Ltd v A Worker* DWT 26/2000 and *Cementation Skanska v Carroll* DWT38/2003. In the latter case, the Labour Court said that, given the requirements of Art.7 of the Working Time Directive, an award of compensation for loss of annual leave "need not be limited to the value of the lost holidays". The court recognised that, where the right to annual leave is infringed, the redress provided "should not only compensate for economic loss sustained but must provide a real deterrent against future infractions". In *Feeney v Baquiran* [2004] E.L.R. 304, the Labour Court said that similar considerations applied in computing compensation for contravention of ss.12 and 15 of the Act. See also *Goode Concrete Ltd v Munro* DWT1 /2005. In awarding compensation, the rights commissioner and the Labour Court must make it clear whether the award is or is not "in respect of remuneration including arrears of remuneration", otherwise it may not be regarded as being exempt from income tax: see s.192A of the Taxes Consolidation Act 1997 (inserted by s.7 of the Finance Act 2004).

The issue of from when time begins to run under subs.(4) has now been definitively considered by the High Court in *Royal Liver Assurance Ltd v Macken* [2002] 4 I.R. 427. The Labour Court (DWT 41/2001) had held, as regards both annual and public holiday entitlements, that an infringement of the Act could not occur while the opportunity to lawfully comply still subsisted. Consequently, having regard to the provisions of s.20 (1)(c), an infringement of those provisions could only occur six months after the end of the leave year in question. On appeal, Lavan J. said that nowhere in the Labour Court's decision was the question of whether the employer had sought the employees' consent to the extension of the leave year, as required by s.20(1)(c), "considered or even referred to". Therefore, insofar as the Labour Court found that the operative date for the purposes of the six-month time-limit in subs.(4) was six months after the expiry of the leave year, it erred in law.

The judgment of the High Court leaves unclear the date from which the six-month period commences as Lavan J. was not convinced that time necessarily ran from the last day of the leave year in question. As regards the employees' entitlements in respect of public holidays, Lavan J. was emphatic that, despite the provisions of s.21(1), "the infringement would arise on the date of the public holiday itself". In *Singh & Singh Ltd v Guatam* DWT44/2005, the Labour Court, having regard to Lavan J.'s decision, said that, where an employer fails to provide an employee with the requisite amount of paid annual leave, the contravention of the Act occurs at the end of the leave year to which the leave relates. Where employment ceases during a leave year an employer is required to pay the employee compensation for any outstanding annual leave. Failure to do so constituted a contravention of the Act which occurred on the day on which the employment terminated.

## Appeals from and enforcement of recommendations of rights commissioner

**28.**—(1) A party concerned may appeal to the Labour Court from a decision **BB.178** of a rights commissioner under section 27 and, if the party does so, the Labour Court shall give the parties an opportunity to be heard by it and to present to it any evidence relevant to the appeal, shall make a determination in writing in relation to the appeal affirming, varying or setting aside the decision and shall communicate the determination to the parties.

(2) An appeal under this section shall be initiated by the party concerned giving, within 6 weeks of the date on which the decision to which it relates was communicated to the party, a notice in writing to the Labour Court containing

such particulars as are determined by the Labour Court under subsection (4) and stating the intention of the party concerned to appeal against the decision.

(3) A copy of a notice under subsection (2) shall be given by the Labour Court to the other party concerned as soon as may be after the receipt of the notice by the Labour Court.

(4) The following matters, or the procedures to be followed in relation to them, shall be determined by the Labour Court, namely—

    (a)   the procedure in relation to all matters concerning the initiation and the hearing by the Labour Court of appeals under this section,

    (b)   the times and places of hearings of such appeals,

    (c)   the representation of the parties to such appeals,

    (d)   the publication and notification of determinations of the Labour Court,

    (e)   the particulars to be contained in a notice under subsection (2),

    (f)   any matters consequential on, or incidental to, the foregoing matters.

(5) The Minister may, at the request of the Labour Court, refer a question of law arising in proceedings before it under this section to the High Court for determination by the High Court and the determination of that Court shall be final and conclusive.

(6) A party to proceedings before the Labour Court under this section may appeal to the High Court from a determination of the Labour Court on a point of law and the determination of the High Court shall be final and conclusive.

(7) Section 39(17) of the Redundancy Payments Act 1967, shall apply in relation to proceedings before the Labour Court under this Part as it applies to matters referred to the Employment Appeals Tribunal under that section with—

    (a)   the substitution in that provision of references to the Labour Court for references to the Tribunal,

    (b)   the deletion in paragraph (d) of that provision of "registered", and

    (c)   the substitution in paragraph (e) of that provision of "a fine not exceeding £1,500 [€1,904.61]" for "a fine not exceeding twenty pounds [€25.39]".

(8) Where a decision of a rights commissioner in relation to a complaint under this Act has not been carried out by the employer concerned in accordance with its terms, the time for bringing an appeal against the decision has expired and no such appeal has been brought, [the employee concerned may bring the complaint] before the Labour Court and the Labour Court shall, without hearing the employer concerned or any evidence (other than in relation to the matters aforesaid), make a determination to the like effect as the decision.

(9) The bringing of a complaint before the Labour Court under subsection (8) shall be effected by giving to the Labour Court a notice in writing containing such particulars (if any) as may be determined by the Labour Court.

(10) The Labour Court shall publish, in such manner as it thinks fit, particulars of any determination made by it under paragraphs (a), (b), (c), (e) and (f) of subsection (4) (not being a determination as respects a particular appeal under this section) and subsection (9).

GENERAL NOTE

**BB.179**    The words in square brackets in subs.(8) were substituted by virtue of s.19(2)(a) of the Protection of Employees (Fixed-Term Work) Act 2003.

This section provides than an appeal lies from a decision of a rights commissioner under s.27 to the Labour Court with a further right of appeal on a point of law only to the High Court. Although the Rules of the Superior Courts do not specifically provide for appeals under this Act, it is suggested that any such appeal be brought either by special summons or by notice of motion, by analogy with the procedures set out in R.S.C. 1986, Orders 105 and 106 respectively. In the absence of any specific rule of court, any such appeal need only be brought within a reasonable time: *per* McCracken J. in his *ex tempore* ruling in *McGaley v Liebherr Container Cranes Ltd* (2001/234Sp) delivered on October 12, 2001.

The circumstances in which the High Court will overturn a decision of a specialist tribunal such as the Labour Court have been considered in many cases: see for example, *Henry Denny & Sons (Ireland) Ltd v Minister for Social Welfare* [1998] 1 I.R. 34 and in particular the comments of Hamilton C.J. at 37. In considering whether to allow an appeal against a decision of such a tribunal, the High Court must consider whether that body based its decision on an identifiable error of law or on an unsustainable finding of fact. A decision cannot be challenged on the grounds of irrationality if there is any relevant material to support it: see further *Mulcahy v Waterford Leader Partnership Ltd* [2002] E.L.R. 12 (O'Sullivan J.) and *Thompson v Tesco Ireland Ltd* [2003] E.L.R. 21 (Lavan J.). In *National University of Ireland, Cork v Ahern* [2005] 2 I.R. 577, the Supreme Court held that, although findings of fact must be accepted by the High Court on appeal, that court could still examine the basis upon which those facts were found. The relevance or admissibility of the matters relied on in determining the facts were questions of law.

The Labour Court's first determination under the Act (DWT1/1998) concerned a dispute between casual dockers represented by the Marine Port and General Workers' Union and Ocean Manpower Ltd over payment for public holidays and zero-hours working practices. The union claimed that the workers in question should receive public holiday pay calculated by reference to a formula in a collective agreement more favourable than that laid down by the Organisation of Working Time (Determination of Pay of Holidays) Regulations 1997 (S.I. No. 475 of 1997). In this regard the union relied on Article 7 of these Regulations. In the Labour Court's opinion that Article "merely restates the established principle of employment law that where an entitlement is created by statute, it is to be regarded as a minimum entitlement which can be improved upon by agreement". This did not mean, however, that "any enhanced terms so provided are recoverable by the enforcement procedures established by the Act".

The Labour Court concluded that, even if a collective agreement provided a valid and subsisting **BB.180** entitlement "in industrial relation terms" over and above that created by the Act, the Act did not allow the Rights Commissioner, or the Labour Court on appeal, "to substitute the terms of an agreement for those of the Regulations in deciding if a relevant provision of the Act has been contravened". As the company had properly applied the Regulations in calculating pay due to the complainants in respect of public holidays, the Right Commissioner's decision that the complaint was not well founded was affirmed. However, the complaint on the zero hours working practices was upheld. This decision is reported at [1998] E.L.R. 299.

## Enforcement of determinations of Labour Court

**29.**—(1) If an employer fails to carry out in accordance with its terms a **BB.181** determination of the Labour Court in relation to a complaint under section 27 within 6 weeks from the date on which the determination is communicated to the parties, the Circuit Court shall, on application to it in that behalf by—

(a) the employee concerned,

(b) with the consent of the employee, any trade union of which the employee is a member, or

(c) the Minister, if the Minister considers it appropriate to make the application having regard to all the circumstances,without hearing the employer or any evidence (other than in relation to the matters aforesaid) make an order directing the employer to carry out the determination in accordance with its terms.

(2) The reference in subsection (1) to a determination of the Labour Court is a reference to such a determination in relation to which, at the expiration of the time for bringing an appeal against it, no such appeal has been brought, or if such an appeal has been brought it has been abandoned and the references to the date on which the determination is communicated to the parties shall, in a case where such an appeal is abandoned, be construed as a reference to the date of such abandonment.

(3) The Circuit Court may, in an order under this section, if in all the circumstances it considers it appropriate to do so, where the order relates to the payment of compensation, direct the employer concerned to pay to the employee concerned interest on the compensation at the rate referred to in section 22 of the Courts Act 1981 in respect of the whole or any part

of the period beginning 6 weeks after the date on which the determination of the Labour Court is communicated to the parties and ending on the date of the order.

(4) An application under this section to the Circuit Court shall be made to the judge of the Circuit Court for the circuit in which the employer concerned ordinarily resides or carries on any profession, business or occupation.

GENERAL NOTE

This section provides that the Labour Court's determination can be enforced by the employee, the employee's trade union or the Minister in the Circuit Court without the employer or any evidence, other than in relation to non-implementation, being heard. The procedure for applications to the Circuit Court is set out in the Circuit Court Rules 2001 (S.I. No. 510 of 2001) Order 57, rule 4. **BB.182**

## Evidence of failure to attend before or give evidence or produce documents to Labour Court

**30.** A document purporting to be signed by the chairman or the registrar of the Labour Court stating that— **BB.183**

(a) a person named in the document was, by a notice under paragraph (c) of section 39(17) of the Redundancy Payments Act, 1967 (as adapted by section 28(7)) required to attend before the Labour Court on a day and at a time and place specified in the document, to give evidence or produce a document,

(b) a sitting of the Labour Court was held on that day and at that time and place, and

(c) the person did not attend before the Labour Court in pursuance of the notice or, as the case may be, having so attended, refused to give evidence or refused or failed to produce the document,shall, in a prosecution of the person under paragraph (e) of the said section 39(17) (as so adapted) be evidence of the matters so stated without further proof.

GENERAL NOTE

This section concerns evidence in relation to prosecution of a person for failure to attend before the Labour Court or refusal to give evidence or produce documents. **BB.184**

## References to rights commissioner by Minister

**31.** Where— **BB.185**

(a) it appears to the Minister that an employer is not complying with a relevant provision (within the meaning of section 27) in relation to a particular employee,

(b) a complaint under section 27, in relation to the matter, has not been presented to a rights commissioner by that employee or any trade union of which he or she is a member, and

(c) the circumstances touching the matter are, in the opinion of the Minister, such as to make it unreasonable to expect the employee or any trade union of which he or she is a member to present such a complaint,

the Minister may present a complaint in relation to the matter to a rights commissioner and a complaint so presented shall be dealt with, and the provisions of this Part shall, with any necessary modifications, apply to the complaint, as if it were a complaint presented by the employee concerned under section 27.

**BB.186**     This section allows the Minister to go to a rights commissioner on behalf of an employee where it would be unreasonable to expect the employee to pursue the complaint.

## Provisions in relation to outworkers who are employees

**BB.187**     **32.**—(1) An employer who employs any outworkers shall keep, in the prescribed form, a register in which he or she shall cause to be entered prescribed particulars in respect of each such worker for the time being employed by him or her.

(2) The Minister may, by regulations, prohibit an employer from employing outworkers to do a specified class or classes of work unless the employer complies with specified conditions in respect of the employment of the outworkers to do the said work.

(3) An employer who—

(a)   fails to comply with subsection (1), or

(b)   fails to comply with any condition specified in regulations under subsection (2) in respect of the employment by him or her of an outworker to do work of a class specified in such regulations,shall be guilty of an offence.

General Note
**BB.188**     This section obliges employers who employ "outworkers" to keep a register of same. Outworker is defined in section 1 of the Act as an employee employed to do work for the employer in the employee's own home or in some other place not under the control or management of the employer.

## Prohibition on double employment

**BB.189**     **33.**—(1) An employer shall not employ an employee to do any work in a relevant period during which the employee has done work for another employer, except where the aggregate of the periods for which such an employee does work for each of such employers respectively in that relevant period does not exceed the period for which that employee could, lawfully under this Act [or the Activities of Doctors in Training Regulations], be employed to do work for one employer in that relevant period.

(2) In subsection (1) "relevant period" means a period of—

(a)   24 hours,

(b)   7 days, or

(c)   12 months.

(3) Whenever an employer employs an employee in contravention of subsection (1), the employer and the employee shall each be guilty of an offence.

(4) Where an employer is prosecuted for an offence under this section it shall be a good defence for him or her to prove—

(a)   that he or she neither knew nor could by reasonable enquiry have known that the employee concerned had done work for any other employer in the period of 24 hours, 7 days or 12 months, as the case may be, in respect of which the prosecution is brought, or

(b)   that he or she neither knew nor could by reasonable enquiry have known that the aggregate of the periods for which the employee concerned did work in the said period of 24 hours, 7 days or 12 months, as the case may be, exceeded the period for which he or she could lawfully be employed to do work for one employer in the said period of 24 hours, 7 days or 12 months, as the case may be.

GENERAL NOTE

This section, as amended by the European Communities (Organisation of Working Time) (Activ- **BB.190** ities of Doctors in Training) Regulations 2004 (S.I. No. 494 of 2004), prohibits double employment where the aggregate total of hours worked exceeds what is permitted by the provisions of the Act and the Regulations.

## Penalties, proceedings, etc.

**34.**—(1) A person guilty of an offence under this Act shall be liable on **BB.191** summary conviction to a fine not exceeding £1,500 [€1,904.61].

(2) Where an offence under this Act is committed by a body corporate and is proved to have been committed with the consent or connivance of, or to be attributable to any neglect on the part of, a person being a director, manager, secretary or other officer of that body corporate, or a person who was purporting to act in that capacity, that person shall also be guilty of an offence and be liable to be proceeded against and punished as if he or she were guilty of the first-mentioned offence.

(3) If the contravention in respect of which a person is convicted of an offence under this Act is continued after the conviction, the person shall be guilty of a further offence on every day on which the contravention continues and for each such offence the person shall be liable, on summary conviction, to a fine not exceeding £500 [€634.87].

(4) Proceedings for an offence under section 8 or a further offence, in relation to such an offence, under subsection (3) may be brought and prosecuted by the Minister.

(5) Notwithstanding section 10(4) of the Petty Sessions (Ireland) Act, 1851, proceedings for an offence under this Act may be instituted within 12 months from the date of the offence.

## Codes of practice

**35.**—(1) In this section— **BB.192**
  "code of practice" means, in relation to a section of this Act, a code that provides practical guidance as to the steps that may be taken for the purposes of complying with the section;
  "the Commission" means the Labour Relations Commission.

(2) The Commission may and, at the request of the Minister, shall, prepare a code of practice for the purposes of any section of this Act (other than section 6(2)) or, in the case of a request by the Minister, a section of this Act (other than section 6(2)) specified in the request.

(3) The Commission, after consultation with the National Authority for Occupational Safety and Health, shall prepare a code of practice for the purposes of section 6(2).

(4) In preparing a code of practice referred to in subsection (2) or (3), the Commission shall invite such organisations representative of employers, such organisations representative of employees, and such other bodies, as the Commission considers appropriate to make submissions, whether orally or in writing, to it in relation to the proposed code of practice and shall have regard to any such submissions made to it, in response to the invitation, by such organisations or bodies.

(5) The Commission shall submit a copy of a code of practice prepared by it under this section to the Minister who may—

(a) by order declare the code (which shall be scheduled to the order) to be a code of practice, or

(b) make such modifications to the code as he or she considers appropriate and declare the code as so modified (which shall be scheduled to the order) to be a code of practice,

for the purposes of the section or sections concerned of this Act.

(6) The Minister may, at the request of the Commission or of his or her own volition after consultation with the Commission, by order—

(a) amend or revoke a code of practice, the subject of an order under subsection (5) or this subsection (and the code of practice shall, in case it is amended by the order, be scheduled, in its amended form, to the order), and

(b) declare, accordingly, the code of practice, as appropriate—

(i) to be no longer a code of practice, or

(ii) in its form as amended by the order, to be a code of practice,

for the purposes of the section or sections concerned of this Act,

and

(c) revoke, as the case may be, the order concerned under subsection (5) or the previous order concerned under this subsection.

(7) A failure by a person to observe a code of practice under this section shall not of itself render that person liable to any civil or criminal proceedings.

(8) In any proceedings under this Act before a court, the Labour Court or a rights commissioner, a code of practice for the time being declared under subsection (5) or (6) to be a code of practice for the purposes of one or more sections of this Act shall be admissible in evidence and any provision of the code which appears to the court, the Labour Court or rights commissioner, as the case may be, to be relevant to any question arising in the proceedings shall be taken into account by it, him or her in determining that question.

GENERAL NOTE

**BB.193** The Labour Relations Commission was established under section 24 of the Industrial Relations Act 1990: see Labour Relations Commission (Establishment) Order 1991 (S.I. No.7 of 1991). The Commission has general responsibility for promoting the improvement of industrial relations and has prepared a Code of Practice on Compensatory Rest (see S.I. No. 44 of 1998) and a Code of Practice on Sunday Working in the Retail Trade (see S.I. No. 444 of 1998).

## Provisions in relation to Protection of Young Persons (Employment) Act, 1996

**BB.194** **36.**—(1) In this section "the Act of 1996" means the Protection of Young Persons (Employment) Act, 1996.

(2) Nothing in the preceding sections of this Act shall prejudice the provisions of the Act of 1996.

(3) The obligation of an employer under section 15 of the Act of 1996 to keep the records referred to in that section at the place where the young person or child concerned is employed shall, if the young person or child is employed by the employer at 2 or more places, be construed as an obligation to keep the said records at the place from which the activities that the young person or child is employed to carry on are principally directed or controlled.

(4) [amending section 22 of the 1996 Act].

## Voidance of certain provisions

**37.** Save as expressly provided otherwise in this Act [or the Activities of **BB.195** Doctors in Training Regulations], a provision in an agreement (whether a contract of employment or not and whether made before or after the commencement [or coming into operation] of the provision concerned of this Act [or the Activities of Doctors in Training Regulations]) shall be void in so far as it purports to exclude or limit the application of, or is inconsistent with, any provision of this Act [or the Activities of Doctors in Training Regulations].

GENERAL NOTE

In *Kvaerner Cementation (Ireland) Ltd v Treacy* DWT 7/2001 the Labour Court ruled that a **BB.196** provision in a contract which provided that the hourly rate of pay included a fixed amount to cover all paid annual leave and public holidays for the period of the contract was not consistent with the results envisaged by the Act and was thus void by the operation of this section. See also, to similar effect, *Wolf Security v O'Donnell* [2001] E.L.R. 136 and *Prime News Ltd v Patchell* DWT 7/2002. In *O'Briens Cabs & Courier Services Ltd v Martin* DWT 40/2005, the Labour Court stated that the provisions of the Act laid an onus on the employer to ensure that the employee received the requisite period of paid leave and that this could not be offset by an agreement between them to grant extra pay to cover holiday entitlements which the employee might or might not decide to take in the future. The court held that "any agreement or arrangement, the likely practical effect of which is that employees will not take holidays, is inconsistent with the result envisaged by the Directive, which is to protect the health and safety of workers and must be regarded as inconsistent with the Act". The court therefore ruled that the practice of "paying in lieu of time off in respect of annual leave" was rendered void by the combined effect of this section and Art.7(2) of Directive 93/104/EC. The Court of Justice has ruled that the prohibition in Art.7(2) was intended to ensure that an employee is entitled to "actual rest" with a view to ensuring effective protection of his or her health and safety. In Joined Cases C–131/04 and C–257/04, *Robinson-Steele v RD Retail Services Ltd* [2006] I.R.L.R. 386, the Court of Justice condemned a regime whereby payments for minimum annual leave were staggered over the corresponding annual period of work and paid together with the remuneration for work done, rather than in the form of a payment in respect of a specific period during which the employee actually takes leave. The Court said that this practice could lead to situations in which the minimum period of paid annual leave was, in effect, replaced by an allowance in lieu. This section was amended by virtue of reg.12 of the European Communities (Organisation of Working Time) (Activities of Doctors in Training) Regulations 2004 (S.I. No. 494 of 2004).

## Amendment of section 51 of Safety, Health and Welfare at Work Act, 1989

**38.** [...]

GENERAL NOTE

This section was repealed by s.4 of the Safety, Health and Welfare at Work Act 2005.    **BB.197**

## Powers of rights commissioner, Employment Appeals Tribunal or Labour Court in certain cases

**39.**—(1) In this section "relevant authority" means a rights commissioner, the    **BB.198**
Employment Appeals Tribunal or the Labour Court.

(2) A decision (by whatever name called) of a relevant authority under this Act or an enactment [or statutory instrument] referred to in the Table to this subsection that does not state correctly the name of the employer concerned or any other material particular may, on application being made in that behalf to the authority by any party concerned, be amended by the authority so as to state correctly the name of the employer concerned or the other material particular.

TABLE

Adoptive Leave Act, 1995
Maternity Protection Act, 1994
Minimum Notice and Terms of Employment Acts, 1973 to 2001
[National Minimum Wage Act, 2000
Parental Leave Act, 1998]
Payment of Wages Act, 1991
Protection of Employees (Employers' Insolvency) Acts, 1984 to [2004]
Protection of Young Persons (Employment) Act, 1996
Redundancy Payments Acts, 1967 to [2003]
Terms of Employment (Information) Act, 1994
Unfair Dismissals Acts, 1977 to 2001
[Protection of Persons Reporting Child Abuse Act 1998
European Communities (Protection of Employment) Regulations
    2000 (S.I. No. 488 of 2000)
Carer's Leave Act 2001
Protection of Employees (Part-Time Work) Act 2001
European Communities (Protection of Employees on the
    Transfer of Undertakings) Regulations 2003 (S.I. No. 131 of 2003)
Protection of Employees (Fixed-Term Work) Act 2003]

(3) The power of a relevant authority under subsection (2) shall not be exercised if it would result in a person who was not given an opportunity to be heard in the proceedings on foot of which the decision concerned was given becoming the subject of any requirement or direction contained in the decision.

(4) If an employee wishes to pursue against a person a claim for relief in respect of any matter under an enactment [or statutory instrument] referred to in subsection (2), or the Table thereto, and has already instituted proceedings under that enactment [or statutory instrument] in respect of that matter, being proceedings in which the said person has not been given an opportunity to be heard and—

(a) the fact of the said person not having been given an opportunity to be heard in those proceedings was due to the respondent's name in those proceedings or any other particular necessary to identify the respondent having been incorrectly stated in the notice or other process by which the proceedings were instituted, and

(b) the said misstatement was due to inadvertence,

then the employee may apply to whichever relevant authority would hear such proceedings in the first instance for leave to institute proceedings against the said

B–91

person ("the proposed respondent") in respect of the matter concerned under the said enactment [or statutory instrument] and that relevant authority may grant such leave to the employee notwithstanding that the time specified under the said enactment within which such proceedings may be instituted has expired:

Provided that that relevant authority shall not grant such leave to that employee if it is of opinion that to do so would result in an injustice being done to the proposed respondent.

(5) References in subsection (4) to the institution of proceedings in respect of any matter under an enactment [or statutory instrument] referred to in subsection (2), or the Table thereto, shall be construed as including references to the presentation of a complaint, or the referral of a dispute, in respect of the said matter, to the relevant authority concerned.

**BB.199** GENERAL NOTE

This section provides for a solution to the difficulties encountered with the enforcement of decisions where details relating to an employer are incorrectly set out. The two Acts in square brackets in the Table in subsection (2) were inserted by virtue of section 45 of the National Minimum Wage Act 2000. The other legislation in square brackets were inserted by virtue of section 19(2) of the Protection of Employees (Fixed-Term Work) Act 2003 which also inserted the words "or statutory instrument" into subsections (2), (4) and (5).

## Alternative means of claiming relief in cases of non-compliance with Part III

**BB.200**    **40.**—(1) As respects a failure to comply with any provision of Part III in relation to an employee, the employee or, with the consent of the employee, any trade union of which the employee is a member may, in lieu of presenting a complaint in respect of such a failure under section 27, include in proceedings to be instituted by him or her or it in respect of any matter under an enactment referred to in the Table to section 39(2) a claim for relief in respect of such a failure and where such a claim is included the following provisions shall have effect:

(a)  subject to the provisions of this section, the provisions of the said enactment (hereafter in this section referred to as "the relevant enactment") shall, with any necessary modifications, apply in like respects to the said claim (hereafter in this section referred to as "the holidays claim") and the procedures to be followed in respect of it (including procedures in respect of appeals) as they apply to the proceedings otherwise under the enactment,

(b)  the relevant authority that hears the said proceedings may grant the same relief in respect of the holidays claim as a rights commissioner may grant under section 27(3) in respect of such a claim and in so far as the grant of such relief consists of or includes the making of a requirement on the employer concerned to pay compensation to the employee the limit specified in section 27(3) in relation to compensation under that provision shall, in lieu of any limit specified in the relevant enactment in relation to compensation that may be required to be paid under that enactment, apply in relation to such compensation.

(2) Notwithstanding subsection (1)(a)—

(a)  any provision of the relevant enactment requiring proceedings under that enactment to be instituted within a specified period shall not apply to such proceedings in so far, but only in so far, as they relate to the holidays claim,

(b)  subsections (4) and (5) of section 27 shall apply to the hearing of the holidays claim by the relevant authority concerned as they apply to the hearing of a complaint under section 27 by a rights commissioner.

(3) In this section "relevant authority" has the same meaning as it has in section 39.

(4) References in this section to the institution of proceedings in respect of any matter under an enactment referred to in the Table to section 39(2) shall be construed in accordance with subsection (5) of section 39.

GENERAL NOTE

This section was added at Committee Stage in the Dáil to ensure that holiday entitlements may be claimed at the same time as entitlements under other enactments such as the Minimum Notice or the Unfair Dismissals legislation.                                                                   BB.201

## Increase of penalties under certain enactments

**41.** [...]                                                                                                          BB.202

GENERAL NOTE

This section was repealed by s.4 of the Safety, Health and Welfare at Work Act 2005.            BB.203

Section 19                                      FIRST SCHEDULE

TRANSITIONAL PROVISIONS IN RELATION TO ANNUAL LEAVE ENTITLEMENT

[...]                                                                                                               BB.204

Section 2                                      SECOND SCHEDULE

PUBLIC HOLIDAYS

1. Each of the following days shall, subject to the subsequent provisions of this Schedule, be a   BB.206
public holiday for the purposes of this Act:
   (a)   Christmas Day,
   (b)   St. Stephen's Day,
   (c)   St. Patrick's Day,
   (d)   Easter Monday, the first Monday in May, the first Monday in June and the first Monday in August,
   (e)   the last Monday in October,
   (f)   the 1st day of January,
   (g)   any other day or days prescribed for the purposes of this paragraph.
2. The Minister may by regulations vary paragraph 1 by substituting for any day referred to in that paragraph another day.
3. An employer may, for the purpose of fulfilling any relevant obligation imposed on him or her by this Act, treat as a public holiday, in lieu of a public holiday aforesaid, either—
   (a)   the Church holiday falling in the same year immediately before the public holiday, or
   (b)   the Church holiday falling in the same year immediately after the public holiday or, if the public holiday is a day which is a public holiday by virtue of paragraph 1(b), the 6th day of January next following,by giving to the employee concerned notice of his or her intention to do so not less than 14 days before the Church holiday (where that holiday is before the public holiday) or before the public holiday (where that holiday is before the Church holiday or, as the case may be, the said 6th day of January).
4. Each of the following days shall be a Church holiday for the purposes of paragraph 3:          BB.207
   (a)   the 6th day of January, except when falling on a Sunday,
   (b)   Ascension Thursday,
   (c)   the Feast of Corpus Christi,
   (d)   the 15th day of August, except when falling on a Sunday,
   (e)   the 1st day of November, except when falling on a Sunday,
   (f)   the 8th day of December, except when falling on a Sunday,
   (g)   any other day or days prescribed for the purposes of this paragraph.
5. The Minister may by regulations vary paragraph 4 by deleting from that paragraph any day or by substituting, for any day referred to therein, another day.6. A notice under paragraph 3 may be given by delivering a copy of the notice to the employee concerned or by posting a copy of the notice in a conspicuous position in the place of the employee's employment.

ENTITLEMENT UNDER SECTION 21 IN RESPECT OF PUBLIC HOLIDAYS: EXCEPTIONS

**BB.208**    Each of the following are the cases mentioned in section 21(5) of absence by the employee concerned from work immediately before the relevant public holiday:

1. such an absence, in excess of 52 consecutive weeks, by reason of an injury sustained by the employee in an occupational accident (within the meaning of Chapter 10 of Part II of the Social Welfare (Consolidation) Act, 1993),

2. such an absence, in excess of 26 consecutive weeks, by reason of an injury sustained by the employee in any accident (not being an accident referred to in paragraph 1) or by reason of any disease from which the employee suffers or suffered,

3. such an absence, in excess of 13 consecutive weeks, caused by any reason not referred to in paragraph 1 or 2 but being an absence authorised by the employer, including a lay-off,

4. such an absence by reason of a strike in the business or industry in which the employee is employed.

FOURTH SCHEDULE

ENACTMENTS REPEALED

**BB.209**

| Number and year (1) | Short title (2) | Extent of repeal (3) |
|---|---|---|
| No. 2 of 1936 | Conditions of Employment Act, 1936. | The whole Act. |
| No. 42 of 1936 | Night Work (Bakeries) Act, 1936. | The whole Act. |
| No. 4 of 1938 | Shops (Conditions of Employment) Act, 1938. | The whole Act. |
| No. 2 of 1942 | Shops (Conditions of Employment) (Amendment) Act, 1942. | The whole Act. |
| No. 12 of 1944 | Conditions of Employment Act, 1944. | The whole Act. |
| No. 25 of 1973 | Holidays (Employees) Act, 1973. | The whole Act. |
| No. 6 of 1981 | Night Work (Bakeries) (Amendment) Act, 1981. | The whole Act. |
| No. 5 of 1991 | Worker Protection (Regular Part-Time Employees) Act, 1991. | Section 4 |

**Section 15(2)**                    FIFTH SCHEDULE

TRANSITIONAL PROVISIONS IN RELATION TO SECTION 15(1)

**BB.210**    [...]

**BB.220**                        SIXTH SCHEDULE

TEXT OF COUNCIL DIRECTIVE (See para. BA.101, above.)

# ORGANISATION OF WORKING TIME (DETERMINATION OF PAY FOR HOLIDAYS) REGULATIONS, 1997

## (S.I. No. 475 of 1997)

*Citation and commencement*

**1.** These Regulations may be cited as the Organisation of Working Time (Determination of Pay for Holidays) Regulations, 1997, and shall come into operation on the 8th day of December, 1997. BC.101

*Interpretation*

**2.**—(1) In these Regulations "the Act" means the Organisation of Working Time Act, 1997 (No. 20 of 1997). BC.102

(2) References in these Regulations to a sum paid to an employee in respect of time worked by him or her shall, where appropriate (and, in particular, in a case of the employer's insolvency), be construed as including references to a sum that is liable to be paid to the employee in respect of time worked by him or her and references to an employee's pay shall be construed accordingly.

*Normal weekly rate of pay*

**3.**—(1) The normal weekly rate of an employee's pay, for the purposes of sections 20 and 23 of the Act (hereafter in this Regulation referred to as the "relevant sections"), shall be determined in accordance with the following provisions of this Regulation. BC.103

(2) If the employee concerned's pay is calculated wholly by reference to a time rate or a fixed rate or salary or any other rate that does not vary in relation to the work done by him or her, the normal weekly rate of his or her pay, for the purposes of the relevant sections, shall be the sum (including any regular bonus or allowance the amount of which does not vary in relation to the work done by the employee but excluding any pay for overtime) that is paid in respect of the normal weekly working hours last worked by the employee before the annual leave (or the portion thereof concerned) commences or, as the case may be, the cesser of employment occurs. BC.104

(3) If the employee concerned's pay is not calculated wholly by reference to any of the matters referred to in paragraph (2) of this Regulation, the normal weekly rate of his or her pay, for the purposes of the relevant sections, shall be the sum that is equal to the average weekly pay (excluding any pay for overtime) of the employee calculated over— BC.105

   (a) the period of 13 weeks ending immediately before the annual leave (or the portion thereof concerned) commences or, as the case may be, the cesser of employment occurs, or

   (b) if no time was worked by the employee during that period, over the period of 13 weeks ending on the day on which time was last worked by the employee before the annual leave (or the portion thereof concerned) commences or, as the case may be, the cesser of employment occurs.

*Appropriate daily rate of pay ("the relevant rate")*

**4.** The following, namely— BC.106

   (a) the rate at which an employee is paid in respect of a day off under section 21 of the Act,

   (b) the rate of an employee's additional day's pay under that section,

and

   (c) the appropriate daily rate of the employee's pay for the purposes of section

Irish Employment Legislation

23 of the Act, (each of which is referred to hereafter in these Regulations as "the relevant rate") shall be determined in accordance with the subsequent provisions of these Regulations.

*Relevant rate for employees (other than certain categories of job sharer)*

**BC.107**    **5.**—(1) If the employee concerned works or is normally required to work during any part of the day which is a public holiday, then—

(a) in case the employee's pay is calculated wholly by reference to any of the matters referred to in Regulation 3(2) of these Regulations, the relevant rate in respect of that public holiday shall be the sum that is equal to the sum (including any regular bonus or allowance the amount of which does not vary in relation to the work done by the employee but excluding any pay for overtime) paid to the employee in respect of the normal daily hours last worked by him or her before that public holiday,

(b) in any other case, the relevant rate in respect of that public holiday shall be the sum that is equal to the average daily pay (excluding any pay for overtime) of the employee calculated over—

(i)   the period of 13 weeks ending immediately before that public holiday,

or

(ii) if no time was worked by the employee during that period, the period of 13 weeks ending on the day on which time was last worked by the employee before that public holiday.

(2) If the employee concerned (not being an employee to whom paragraphs (a), (b) and (c) of Regulation 6 of these Regulations apply) does not work on a day which is a public holiday, then—

(a) in the case the employee's pay is calculated wholly by reference to any of the matters referred to in Regulation 3(2) of these Regulations, the relevant rate in respect of that public holiday shall be the sum that is equal to one-fifth of the sum (including any regular bonus or allowance the amount of which does not vary in relation to the work done by the employee but excluding any pay for overtime) paid in respect of the normal weekly hours last worked by the employee before that public holiday,

(b) in any other case, the relevant rate in respect of that public holiday shall be the sum that is equal to one-fifth of the average weekly pay (excluding any pay for overtime) of the employee calculated over—

(i)   the period of 13 weeks ending 1 immediately before that public holiday, or

(ii)  if no time was worked by the employee during that period, the period of 13 weeks ending on the day on which time was last worked by the employee before that public holiday. Provided that the relevant rate to which the employee concerned shall be entitled under this paragraph in respect of a public holiday shall not exceed the relevant rate to which he or she would be entitled in respect of that holiday if subparagraph (a) or (b), as the case may be, of paragraph (1) of this Regulation were to apply to him or her.

*Relevant rate for certain categories of job sharer*

**BC.108**    **6.** If—

(a) the employee concerned does not work or is not normally required to work on a day which is a public holiday,

and

(b) he or she is required to work half the time required to be worked by a whole time employee of the employer, being an employee employed to do work that is identical or similar to that which the employee concerned is employed to do,

and

(c)   the pay of the employee concerned is calculated wholly by reference to any of the matters referred to in Regulation 3(2) of these Regulations, then the relevant rate in respect of that public holiday shall be the sum that is equal to one-tenth of the sum (including any regular bonus or allowance the amount of which does not vary in relation to the work done by the employee but excluding any pay for overtime) that is paid in respect of the last 2 weeks of normal working hours worked by the employee before that public holiday:

Provided that the relevant rate to which the employee concerned shall be entitled under this Regulation in respect of a public holiday shall not exceed a sum that is equal to one-half of the relevant rate to which he or she would be entitled in respect of that holiday if Regulation 5(1)(a) of these Regulations were to apply to him or her.

## Saving

**7.** Nothing in these Regulations shall prevent an employer and employee from entering into arrangements that are more favourable to the employee with regard to the pay in respect of a public holiday.     **BC.109**

GENERAL NOTE

The purpose of these Regulations is to set out the method for calculating, for the purposes of the     **BC.110** 1997 Act, both the normal weekly rate of an employee's pay (ss.20 and 23) and the appropriate daily rate of an employee's pay (s.22).

Where an employee receives both salary and commission, must account be taken of the latter when calculating annual leave and public holiday entitlements? The question was fully considered by the Labour Court in *Hidden Hearing Ltd v Smart* [2005] E.L.R. 367. The complainant contended that, since his pay varied depending on the amount of commission which he earned, his holiday pay should have been calculated in accordance with reg.3(3). The employer, however, contended that reg.3(3) could not apply because the complainant's pay was calculated by reference to one of the matters referred to in reg.3(2), namely a rate which did not vary in relation to the work done by the employee. The Labour Court was of the view that the underlying object of the requirement to provide paid annual leave was to afford employees opportunities for rest and relaxation and to reconcile the requirements of work and family responsibilities. The Labour Court said that it was difficult to envisage how these objectives could be fulfilled "if a worker could be made to suffer a significant reduction in his or her income while on holidays". The requirement to provide paid annual leave had to be interpreted as meaning that "a worker is entitled to receive the same pay in respect of holidays as he or she would have received (less overtime) had they been working normally during the period of the leave". Since commission payments constituted the major portion of the complainant's normal pay, the Labour Court concluded that these Regulations could not be interpreted in a way which would completely exclude these emoluments in calculating holiday pay. The Labour Court noted that reg.3(2) made no mention of the "amount" of work done (in contrast to s.221 of the Employment Rights Act 1996 in Britain). Consequently, reg.3(2) had a broader meaning and comprehended situations where the pay is determined by the quality of the work produced and by the success of that work in generating revenue for the employer. Since the complainant's pay varied by reference to the quality or success of his work, reg.3(2) was not applicable and consequently his holiday pay should have been calculated on the formula prescribed by reg.3(3).

What do the expressions "normal daily hours" and "normal weekly hours" in regs.5(1)(a) and (2)(a) mean in the case of an employee whose hours are irregular? Take the case of a part-time shop assistant who works three days each week for four hours, seven hours, and seven hours on Wednesdays, Saturdays, and Sundays, respectively, and who occasionally works on public holidays. Regulation 5(1)(a) provides the formula for when the employee works on the public holiday and reg.5(2)(a) provides for when the employee does not.

If the latter, the employee's entitlement is a sum equal to one-fifth of his or her "normal weekly hours" prior to the public holiday. Although the word "normal" is not defined, in this case it could only be considered to be 18 hours, which are the core hours worked each week: see *Moriarty's Supervalu v A Worker* DWT 17/1999. Where the employee works on a public holiday, however, his or her entitlement is to an extra payment of the hours worked on the day before the public holiday, *i.e.* in the example given above, seven hours if the public holiday falls on a Monday, Tuesday, or Wednesday, or four hours if it falls on Thursday or Friday: see *Moriarty's Supervalu*, above. In that case the Labour Court said that, "as a matter of plain language", those hours would constitute an employee's "normal daily hours" for the purpose of applying reg.5(1)(a).

# ORGANISATION OF WORKING TIME (GENERAL EXEMPTIONS) REGULATIONS, 1998

## (S.I. No. 21 of 1998)

*Citation and commencement*

BC.301　**1.** These Regulations may be cited as the Organisation of Working Time (General Exemptions) Regulations, 1998, and shall come into operation on the 1st day of March, 1998.

*Definitions*

BC.302　**2.** In these Regulations—
"the Act" means the Organisation of Working Time Act, 1997 (No. 20 of 1997),
"the exemption" means the exemption provided for by Regulation 3(1) of these Regulations.

*Exemption*

BC.303　**3.** —(1) Without prejudice to Regulations 4 and 5 of these Regulations and subject to the subsequent provisions of this Regulation, each of the activities specified in the Schedule to these Regulations is hereby exempted from the application of sections 11, 12, 13 and 16 of the Act.

(2) exemption shall not, as respects a particular employee, apply in relation to–
(a) section 11, 12, 13 or 16 of the Act if the employee—
　(i) is not engaged wholly or mainly in carrying on or performing the duties of the activity concerned,
　(ii) is exempted from the application of that section by virtue of regulations under section 3(3) of the Act, or
　(iii) falls within a class of employee in relation to which a joint labour committee (within the meaning of the Industrial Relations Acts, 1946 to [2004]) may perform functions under those Acts,
or
　(b)　section 16 of the Act if the employee is a special category night worker within the meaning of subsection (3) of the said section 16.

(3) The exemption shall not apply, as respects a particular employee, if and for so long as the employer does not comply with Regulation 5 of these Regulations in relation to him or her.

## Compensatory rest periods

**4.** If an employee is not entitled, by reason of the exemption, to the rest period **BC.304** and break referred to in sections 11, 12 and 13 of the Act, the employer shall ensure that the employee has available to himself or herself a rest period and break that, in all the circumstances, can reasonably be regarded as equivalent to the first-mentioned rest period and break.

## Duty of employer with respect to the health and safety of employee

**5.**—(1) An employer shall not require an employee to whom the exemption **BC.305** applies to work during a shift or other period of work (being a shift or other such period that is of more than 6 hours duration) without allowing him or her a break of such duration as the employer determines.

(2) In determining the duration of a break referred to in paragraph (1) of this Regulation, the employer shall have due regard to the need to protect and secure the health, safety and comfort of the employee and to the general principle concerning the prevention and avoidance of risk in the workplace.

## Saving

**6.** Nothing in Regulation 4 or 5 of these Regulations shall prejudice a provision **BC.306** or provisions of a more beneficial kind to the employee concerned which is or are contained in—

    (a)   a collective agreement referred to in section 4(5) of the Act,

    (b)   a registered employment agreement, or

    (c).  an employment regulation order.

SCHEDULE

**1.** An activity in which the employee is regularly required by the employer to travel distances of **BC.307** significant length, either from his or her home to the workplace or from one workplace to another workplace [including offshore work].

**2.** An activity of a security or surveillance nature the purpose of which is to protect persons or **BC.308** property and which requires the continuous presence of the employee at a particular place or places, and, in particular, the activities of a security guard, caretaker or security firm.

**3.** An activity falling within a sector of the economy or in the public service— **BC.309**

    (a)   in which it is foreseeable that the rate at which production or the provision of services as the case may be, takes place will vary significantly from time to time,

or

    (b)   the nature of which is such that employees are directly involved in ensuring the continuity of production or the provision of services, as the case may be,

and, in particular, any of the following activities—

        (i)   the provision of services relating to the reception. treatment or care of persons in a residential institution, hospital or similar establishment,

        (ii)   the provision of services at a harbour or airport,

        (iii)  production in the press, radio, television, cinematographic, postal or telecommunications industries,

        (iv)  the provision of ambulance, fire and civil protection services,

        (v)   the production, transmission or distribution of gas, water or electricity,

        (vi)  the collection of household refuse or the operation of an incineration plant,

        (vii) any industrial activity in which work cannot, by reason of considerations of a technical nature, be interrupted,

        (viii) research and development,

        (ix)  agriculture,

        (x)   tourism,

        (xi)  workers concerned with the carriage of passengers on regular urban transport services,

        (xii) in the case of persons working in railway transport—

            (I)   whose activities are intermittent;

B–105

(II)   who spend their working time on board trains; or

(III)  whose activities are linked to transport timetables and to ensuring the continuity and regularity of traffic.]

GENERAL NOTE

BC.310    These Regulations, as amended by S.I. Nos. 817 and 819 of 2004, prescribe that persons employed in the activities specified in the Schedule to these Regulations shall be exempt from the application of ss.11, 12, 13 and 16 of the 1997 Act.

Even where an employer is exempted under these Regulations, the Labour Court will still determine that discussions take place as to how rest periods can be implemented for the employees concerned. The Code of Practice on Compensatory Rest Periods (S.I. No. 44 of 1998) should be used as a guide in those discussions. See *Bord na Mona v SIPTU* DWT11/1999. The scope of the Regulations was considered by O'Sullivan J. in *Coastal Line Container Terminal Ltd v Services Industrial Professional Technical Union* [2000] E.L.R. 1. The learned High Court judge held that the Regulations were clearly intended to apply to dock or airport workers when they referred, in para.3(b)(ii) of the Schedule, to those engaged "in the provision of services at a harbour or airport". Consequently the Labour Court had been correct in determining that terminal operatives driving cranes and other such equipment for the purpose of loading or unloading vessels at a facility operated by the company at Dublin Port were not employed in a transport activity and thus were covered by these Regulations.

# ORGANISATION OF WORKING TIME (CODE OF PRACTICE ON COMPENSATORY REST AND RELATED MATTERS) (DECLARATION) ORDER, 1998

## (S.I. No. 44 of 1998)

### Citation

BC.401    **1.** This Order may be cited as the Organisation of Working Time (Code of Practice on Compensatory Rest and Related Matters) (Declaration) Order, 1998.

### Code of Practice

BC.402    **2.** The code of practice set out in the Schedule to this Order is hereby declared to be a code of practice for the purposes of section 6 of the Organisation of Working Time Act, 1997 (No. 20 of 1997), so much of the other provisions of Part 1 of that Act as relate to that section and so much of Parts II and IV of that Act as relate to that section.

SCHEDULE

ORGANISATION OF WORKING TIME ACT, 1997 CODE OF PRACTICE ON COMPENSATORY REST PERIODS AND RELATED MATTERS

CONTENTS

1.   Labour Relations Commission
2.   Introduction
3.   General Principles of Arrangements for Equivalent Compensatory Rest and Appropriate Protection
4.   Complaints Procedure
5.   Appeals
6.   Enforcement of Decisions of the Rights Commissioner/Determinations of the Labour Court
7.   Annex Exempted Activities

1. LABOUR RELATIONS COMMISSION

**1.** The Labour Relations Commission has prepared this Code of Practice on Compen- **BC.403** satory Rest in accordance with the provisions of s.35 of the Organisation of Working Time Act, 1997. When preparing the Code of Practice the Commission held meetings and

consultations with the Irish Business and EmployersÇÇ Confederation, the Irish Congress of Trade Unions, the Labour Court, the Department of Enterprise, Trade and Employment and the Irish Co-Operative Organisation Society.

2. In accordance with section 35(3) of the Act the Commission has also consulted the National Authority of Occupational Safety and Health in the preparation of this Code.

3. The Commission has taken account of the views expressed by these organisations to the fullest extent possible in preparing this Code.

4. The Code is designed to assist employers, employees and their representatives in observing the 1997 Act generally as regards compensatory rest. It gives guidance, in particular, on arrangements that may be put in place to comply with the compensatory rest provisions which apply where, because of exemptions or collective agreements of emergencies or unforeseeable circumstances, employees cannot avail themselves of the rest or break periods provided for in sections 11, 12 or 13 of the Act.

5. While failure on the part of any person to observe the Code will not, in itself, render that person liable to civil or criminal proceedings, the Code shall be admissible in evidence before a Court, the Labour Court or a Rights Commissioner in proceedings under the Organisation of Working Time Act 1997.

## 2. Introduction

Note

This section of the Code gives a general description of some of the provisions of the Organisation of **BC.404** Working Time Act 1997 and is not a legal interpretation.

## *The Organisation of Working Time Act, 1997*

1. The terms of the EU Directive on Working Time, (Council Directive 93/104/EC of 23 November, 1993), have been transposed into Irish law by means of the Organisation of Working Time Act, 1997 and Regulations made under the Safety, Health and Welfare at Work Act, 1989.

2. The Organisation of Working Time Act, 1997 became law on 7 May, 1997. Section 35 of that Act provides for a Code of Practice that provides practical guidance as to the steps that may be taken for the purposes of complying with any section of the Act. The Commencement Order bringing the Act into operation, on a phased basis, was signed on 24 September, 1997. Under the Commencement Order, section 35 of the Act, inter alia, came into operation on 30 September, 1997. The provisions on rest and working ours are effective from 1 March, 1998.

3. The Minister for Labour, Trade and Consumer Affairs, under section 35 of the 1997 Act, asked the Labour Relations Commission to prepare a Code of Practice for the purposes of section 6 of the Act. As section 35(3) of the Act provides that the Commission, after consultation with the National Authority for Occupational Safety and Health, shall prepare a Code of Practice for the Purposes of section 6(2), this Code is prepared under section 35(2) for the purposes of section 6(1) and under section 35(3) for the purposes of section 6(2). Under the Commencement Order, section 6 of the Act came into operation on 30 September, 1997.

4. The Organisation of Working Time Act, 1997 sets out statutory rights for employees in respect of rest, maximum working-time and holidays. In summary, the key provisions of the Act on minimum rest and maximum working time are as follows:

> maximum average net weekly working time of 48 hours;
> a daily rest break of 11 consecutive hours;rest breaks while at work;
> a weekly rest break of 24 consecutive hours;
> maximum average night working of 8 hours;
> maximum hours of work for night workers engaged in work involving special hazards or a heavy physical or mental strain - an absolute limit of hours in a 24 hour period.

5. 48 hour working week comes into effect, generally, on 1 March, 1998. However, the Act contains transitional provisions. These provide that employees may work up to 60 hours per week from 1 March, 1998 to 28 February, 1999 and up to 55 hours per week from 1 March, 1999 to 29 February, 2000. The 48 hour week comes into effect in respect of all employees covered by the Act on 1 March, 2000. To work the maximum permitted hours during 1998 and 1999 an agreement must be reached between the parties which is approved of by the Labour Court. The Fifth Schedule to the Act details the procedures to be observed in implementing the transitional provisions (see also *Guide to the Labour Court's Functions and Procedures* for the purposes of the Act).

Irish Employment Legislation

6. The specific provisions of the Act relating to rest times may be varied in certain circumstances—

by Regulations,

through legally binding collective agreements made under the Act and approved by the Labour Court,

through registered employment agreements,

through employment regulation orders, or

as otherwise provided under the Act (e.g. emergencies, unforeseeable circumstances, certain shift changes, split shifts).

7. The circumstances in which the rest times and averaging periods for weekly working hours may be varied are as follows:—

## (I) Section 6(1) of the Act provides for circumstances:

Where Regulations[1] exempt certain activities from the rest breaks, daily and weekly rest periods set out in sections 11, 12 and 13 of the 1997 Act.

Where collective agreements providing for a similar exemption have been concluded by the parties and approved by the Labour Court. (Registered Employment Agreements and Employment Regulation Orders may also provide for the variation of rest periods, but not of working time provisions.)

**In every case at (1) above where statutory rest times are varied the employer concerned must ensure that equivalent compensatory rest is made available to the employee.**

## (II) Section 6(2) of the Act provides for circumstances:

Where shift workers who change shift and cannot avail themselves of the rest period are exempted (in respect of the daily and weekly rest periods).

Where persons employed in activities consisting of periods of work spread out over the day are exempted (in respect of the daily and weekly rest periods).

Where employers are exempted from the obligation to provide daily and weekly rest periods and rest breaks as provided for in sections 11, 1.2 and 13 of the Act due to exceptional circumstances or an emergency, including an accident or the imminent risk of an accident, or otherwise the occurrence of unusual and unforeseeable circumstances beyond the employer's control.

**Where statutory rest times are varied in any of the circumstances mentioned at (II) above the employer must ensure that the employee has available to himself or herself**

**(i) equivalent compensatory rest**

**or**

**(ii) where this is not possible for objective reasons, appropriate protection.**

NOTE

**BC.405**    While circumstances relating to shift changeover come within the scope of the exemption included in the legislation, shift working is subject to the provisions in the Act providing for rest and maximum working time.

NOTE

1. See Annex to this Code-General Exemptions Regulations (S.I. No. 21 of 1998)

## 3. GENERAL PRINCIPLES OF AND ARRANGEMENTS FOR EQUIVALENT COMPENSATORY REST AND APPROPRIATE PROTECTION

### General

**BC.406**    1. Appropriate rest breaks from work are vital to the health and safety of workers and are of importance in the efficient and effective operation of the workplace. While the Organisation of Working Time Act, 1997 specifies minimum rest breaks employers may provide longer breaks.

### Compensatory Rest Timescale (Section 6(1) and 6(2) of the Act)

2. Exempted employees who miss out on their statutory rest entitlements should receive equivalent

compensatory rest as soon as possible after the statutory rest has been missed out on. It is most important for employers to make rest time available to employees to allow them to recuperate from long periods of work without adequate rest. The Organisation of Working Time Act, 1997 and the EU Directive on Working Time do not specify any timeframes within which compensatory rest must be made available. However, when determining when compensatory rest is to be given, an employer should always have regard to the circumstances pertaining in the individual place of employment and to the health and safety requirements for adequate rest. In this context, it is important that the compensatory rest for rest breaks at work and for daily rest breaks, in particular, be provided as soon as possible and, generally, in an adjacent time frame.

3. While it is not possible to provide extensive examples of the various situations that may arise in the many diverse employments, the following four examples may typify some work situations which may give rise to a need to grant compensatory rest.

EXAMPLE 1

An exempted employee works Monday to Friday 9 a.m. to 5.30 p.m. He/she works in an industry which cannot be interrupted on technical grounds (an exempted activity) [1]. For 2 weeks per month that employee is "on call" for maintenance work. On Wednesday night he/she is called out to perform emergency repair work. The call out commences at 8.30 p.m. and finishes at 11.30 p.m. The employee's entitlement to 11 hours consecutive rest is interrupted. Prior to the call out the employee had received 3 hours rest and after the call out he/she received 9.5 hours rest. In total the employee received 12.5 hours rest, therefore no further entitlement to rest arises as an exemption applies (see sections 2(7)(1) and 2(7)(11) of this Code).

If no exemption applied then the employee is entitled to the full 11 consecutive hours rest from the end of the call out.

EXAMPLE 2

Under an exemption provided for in a collective agreement approved of by the Labour Court an employee is permitted to work 14 consecutive 8 hour days. In those circumstances the employee, in respect of that period, has a minimum entitlement of 2 periods of 24 hours compensatory rest plus 2 periods of 11 consecutive hours daily rest. The employee is given 3 consecutive periods of 24 hours off immediately after the 14 consecutive working days. This goes beyond the requirement to give 2 periods of 24 hours compensatory rest preceded by the relevant daily rest requirement and is, therefore, acceptable.

EXAMPLE 3

An employee is entitled to a break of at least 15 minutes after working for 41/2 hours. If an exemption applies the taking of the break may be delayed but compensatory rest should be provided. In this circumstance the employee is given a later break of 15 minutes or breaks totalling 15 minutes by way of compensatory rest before the end of the day. No further compensatory rest is required.

EXAMPLE 4

An exempted employee works a three cycle rotating shift pattern:
  Week 1 8 a.m. – 4 p.m.
  Week 2 4 p.m. – 12 a.m.
  Week 3 12 a.m. – 8 a.m.

NOTE

1. See Annex to this Code-General Exemptions Regulations (S.I. No. 21 of 1998)    **BC.407**

In a 5 over 7 day roster no changeover provides for less than 48 hours rest. Therefore, no entitlement to compensatory rest arises. In a 6 over 7 day roster, however, the changeover between week 2 and week 3 provides only for 24 hours rest. In this circumstance, the exempted employee is entitled to compensatory rest of 11 consecutive hours.

GENERAL COMMENTS ON COMPENSATORY REST

The 11 consecutive hour interval between shifts is required for reasons of health and safety to ensure that employees have a minimum period of sleep. From a health and safety point of view, it is dangerous for employees to miss out on a minimum number of hours sleep and then report for work.

Irish Employment Legislation

Therefore, when any variation of the 11 consecutive hours statutory rest is permitted under the Act, the employer should ensure that the health and safety requirements for adequate compensatory rest are sufficient in the circumstances pertaining in that employment. This is equally applicable to the weekly rest provision. Consideration should also be given to such issues as distance from home and employment in order to ensure that adequate rest is obtained.

NOTE

**BC.408** Typically in industry call-out arrangements provide for 8 hours consecutive rest before returning to work. Such arrangements will, where an exemption is applicable, continue to be acceptable provided that the compensatory rest requirements are fulfilled.

Where variation of the weekly statutory rest periods is permitted under the 1997 Act the employer concerned should have regard to the circumstances pertaining in that employment and to the health and safety requirements for adequate rest for his/her employees.

## *Appropriate Protection*

**BC.409** 4. If for reasons that can be objectively justified, it is not possible for an employer to ensure that an employee has available to himself or herself the equivalent rest period or break set out in section 6(1) of the 1997 Act, the employer must make such arrangements as respects the employee's conditions of employment as will compensate the employee.

While neither "arrangements as respects the employee's conditions of employment as will compensate the employee" nor "appropriate protection" are defined in, respectively, the Act and the Directive the Act specifies that these concepts do not include:

(i) the granting of monetary compensation to the employee

or

(ii) the provision of any other material benefit to the employee, other than the provision of such a benefit as will improve the physical conditions under which the employee works or the amenities or services available to the employee while he or she is at work.

A common sense approach should be adopted by employers and employees in such situations which takes account of the circumstances existing in the employment and has regard to the safety, health and well being of employees. It would be desirable that employers and employees and/or their representatives agree appropriate protection measures as respects an employee's conditions of employment.

While it is not feasible to define such appropriate protection/conditions of employment measures, the concept might include measures which provide for, in addition to normal health and safety requirements:

(i) enhanced environmental conditions to ccommodate regular long periods of attendance at work;

(ii) refreshment facilities, recreational and reading material;

(iii) appropriate facilities/amenities such as television, radio and music;

(iv) alleviating monotonous work or isolation;

(v) transport to and from work where appropriate.

NOTE

**BC.410** **The measures listed are not exhaustive and are for illustrative purposes only. Employers should consider other measures which might be more relevant to their circumstances.**

## *4. Complaints procedure*

**BC.411** 1. The Organisation of Working Time Act, 1997 sets out a complaints procedure for dealing with the various complaints that may arise under the Act. While the procedure deals with general complaints concerning various entitlements, for the purposes of this Code the procedure concerns itself with complaints about the working hours, rest periods, compensatory rest and appropriate protection issues. For example, an employee may complain that he or she had not received an equivalent rest period or that he or she is not satisfied with the compensatory (or appropriate protection) arrangements provided.

## *Who can make a complaint?*

2. An employee or any trade union of which the employee is a member, with the consent of the

employee, may present a complaint. The Minister for Labour, Trade and Consumer Affairs may also present a complaint if it is apparent that an employer is not complying with a provision and where the employee/trade union has not done so and the Minister is of the opinion that the circumstances are such as to make it unreasonable to expect the employee/trade union to present such a complaint.

## *How is a complaint presented and processed?*

3. Complaints arising under section 6 of the 1997 Act should be presented in the first instance to a Rights Commissioner. A complaint must be made within six months of the date of the alleged contravention by the employer. However, a complaint which is presented not later than twelve months after the six months time limit may be investigated if the Rights Commissioner is satisfied that the delay was due to reasonable cause. A complaint should be in writing and should contain the requisite particulars.

4. The Rights Commissioner must give the employer a copy of the complaint. The Rights Commissioner must hear the parties and allow relevant evidence to be presented. The investigation of a complaint will be held in private. The Rights Commissioner must furnish the Labour Court with a copy of each decision given under the 1997 Act.

5. The Rights Commissioner in making a decision shall do one or more of the following:
    (a) declare that the complaint was, or, as the case may be, was not well founded,
    (b) require the employer to comply with the relevant provisions,
    (c) require the employer to pay compensation of such amount (if any) as is just and equitable having regard to all the circumstances, up to a maximum of two years' remuneration.

NOTE

Queries relating to complaints and procedures should be forwarded in writing to the Rights **BC.412** Commissioner Service, Labour Relations Commission, Tom Johnson House, Haddington Road, Dublin 4 - telephone (01) 6609662.

## 5. APPEALS

1. Either party may appeal a decision of a Rights Commissioner to the Labour Court. The appeal **BC.413** must be made within 6 weeks of the date on which the decision was communicated to the party. The notice of appeal should be submitted to the Labour Court on the relevant form, which is available from the Court.

2. The Labour Court must give a copy of the notice of appeal to the other party. The Labour Court shall give the parties an opportunity to be heard and to present relevant evidence to it. It will make a determination in writing affirming, varying or setting aside the decision. The Court must communicate that determination to the parties.

NOTE

The procedure on appeals is laid down by the Labour Court. Details of these procedures can **BC.414** be obtained from the Labour Court, Tom Johnson House, Haddington Road, Dublin 4 – (01)6608444.

## 6. ENFORCEMENT OF DECISIONS OF THE RIGHTS COMMISSIONER/DETERMINATIONS OF THE LABOUR COURT

1. An employee may bring a complaint to the Labour Court where an employer has not imple- **BC.415** mented a decision of the Rights Commissioner under the Act or has not appealed a decision within the requisite time. The Labour Court shall make a determination to the like effect as the original decision without hearing the employer concerned. The complaint must be brought by the employee not later than six weeks after the time limit for making an appeal has expired. Complaints of the non-implementation of Rights Commissioners' decisions under the Act should be submitted to the Labour Court on the relevant form, which is available from the Court. The Labour Court shall publish particulars of its determinations in such manner as it thinks fit.

2. The Minister, at the request of the Labour Court, may refer a question of law arising in proceedings before it, concerning appeals from the enforcement of recommendations of a Rights

Irish Employment Legislation

Commissioner, for determination by the High Court. The determination of the High Court shall be final and conclusive.

3. A party to proceedings may appeal to the High Court from a determination of the Labour Court on a point of law. The determination of the High Court shall be final and conclusive.

4. Where a determination of the Labour Court has not been implemented, within six weeks from the date on which the determination is communicated to the parties, the Circuit Court, on application to it by an employee, trade union or the Minister, shall, without hearing the employer or any evidence, make an order directing the employer to carry out the determination in accordance with its terms.

5. The Circuit Court, if it deems it appropriate to do so, may direct the employer to pay interest on the compensation in respect of any period commencing 6 weeks following the communication of the Labour Court's determination to the parties and ending on the date of the order.

6. The application to the Circuit Court will be in the Circuit where the employer usually resides or carries out the business.

ANNEX

*Exempted activities*

*General exemptions*

BC.416    The Organisation of Working Time (General Exemptions) Regulations, 1998 (S.I. No. 21 of 1998) prescribe, in accordance with Section 4(3) of the Organisation of Working Time Act, 1997, that persons employed in the following activities shall be exempt from the application of sections 11, 12 and 13 of the Act which deal respectively with daily rest, rests and intervals at work and weekly rest:

1. An activity in which the employee is regularly required by the employer to travel distances of significant length, either from his or her home to the workplace or from one workplace to another workplace.

2. An activity of a security or surveillance nature the purpose of which is to protect persons or property and which requires the continuous presence of the employee at a particular place or places, and, in particular, the activities of a security guard, caretaker or security firm.

3. An activity falling within a sector of the economy or in the public service—
   (a) in which it is foreseeable that the rate at which production or the provision of services, as the case may be, takes place will vary significantly from time to time, or
   (b) the nature of which is such that employees are directly involved in ensuring the continuity of production or the provision of services, as the case may be, and, in particular, any of the following activities—
      (i)    the provision of services relating to the reception, treatment or care of persons in a residential institution, hospital or similar establishment,
      (ii)   the provision of services at a harbour or airport,
      (iii)  production in the press, radio, television, cinematographic, postal or telecommunications industries,
      (iv)   the provision of ambulance, fire and civil protection services,
      (v)    the production, transmission or distribution of gas, water or electricity,
      (vi)   the collection of household refuse or the operation of an incineration plant,
      (vii)  any industrial activity in which work cannot, by reason of considerations of a technical nature, be interrupted,
      (viii) research and development,
      (ix)   agriculture,
      (x)    tourism.

NOTES

*Exceptions*

BC.417    Regulation 3 of the Regulations provides that the exemption shall not, as respects a particular employee, apply

B–112

(a) in relation to sections 11, 12 and 13 of the Act if the employee—
    (i) is not engaged wholly or mainly in carrying on or performing the duties of the activity concerned,
    (ii) is exempted from the application of that section by virtue of regulations under section 3(3) of the Act,
    or
    (iii) falls within a class of employee in relation to which a joint labour committee (within the meaning of the Industrial Relations Acts, 1946 to 1990) may perform functions under those Acts,
or
(b) if and for so long as the employer does not comply with Regulation 5 of the Regulations in relation to him or her.

## Compensatory rest periods

Regulation 4 of these Regulations provides that if an employee is not entitled, by reason of this exemption, to the rest period and break referred to in sections 11, 12 and 13 of the Act, the employer shall ensure that the employee has available to himself or herself a rest period and break that, in all the circumstances, can reasonably be regarded as equivalent to the first-mentioned rest period and break.

## Duty of employer with respect to the health and safety of employee

Regulation 5 of the Regulations provides that:

(1) an employer shall not require an employee to whom the exemption applies to work during a shift or other period of work (being a shift or other such period that is of more than 6 hours duration) without allowing him or her a break of such duration as the employer determines.

(2) in determining the duration of such a break, the employer shall have due regard to the need to protect and secure the health, safety and comfort of the employee and the general principle concerning the prevention and avoidance of risk in the workplace.

## More beneficial arrangements

Regulation 6 of the Regulations provides that nothing in the Regulations shall prejudice a provision or provisions of a more beneficial kind to the employee concerned which is or are contained in—
    (a) a collective agreement referred to in section 4(5) of the Act,
    (b) a registered employment agreement,
    or
    (c) an employment regulation order.

## Exemption of transport activities

The Organisation of Working Time (Exemption of Transport Activities) Regulations, 1998 (S.I. No. 20 of 1998) prescribe, in accordance with Section 3(3) of the Organisation of Working Time Act, 1997, that persons employed in a transport activity as follows shall be exempt from the application, inter alia, of sections 11, 12 and 13 of the Act dealing respectively with daily rest, rests and intervals at work and weekly rest:

1. An activity consisting of, or connected with, the operation of any vehicle, train, vessel, aircraft or other means of transport (whether of goods or persons) other than any activity of a person holding a position of an administrative, managerial or clerical nature that is not directly related to the operation of such a means of transport.

2. An activity that is carried on—
    (a) for the purpose of the transport timetable, that is to say an activity that is carried on for the purpose of ensuring the continuity or regularity of any service which provides a means of transport referred to in paragraph 1 above, or
    (b) for the purpose of ensuring the safety of such a means of transport, other than any activity of a person holding a position of an administrative, managerial or clerical nature that is not directly related to the doing of the things required to be done for either such purpose.

3. In paragraph 1 "vessel" includes any vessel used to navigate inland waters (including any lake).

NOTE—COMPENSATORY REST PERIODS

**BC.418**     It should be noted that an employer is not obliged to ensure that an employee engaged in these activities has available to himself or herself equivalent compensatory rest. However, Regulation 3 of these Regulations provides that the exemption shall not apply as respects a particular employee if he or she is not engaged wholly or mainly in carrying on or performing the duties of the activity.

GENERAL NOTE

**BC.419**     Under section 35(3) of the 1997 Act, the Labour Relations Commission is required, having consulted with the National Authority for Occupational Safety and Health, to prepare a code of practice for the purposes of section 6(2) of the Act and to submit same to the Minister for Labour, Trade and Consumer Affairs, being the Minister for State to whom functions in this matter have been delegated by the Enterprise, Trade and Employment (Delegation of Ministerial Functions) (No. 2) Order 1997 (S.I. No. 33 of 1997). By this Order the Minister declared the code to be a code of practice for the purposes of section 6 of the 1997 Act.

# ORGANISATION OF WORKING TIME (EXEMPTION OF CIVIL PROTECTION SERVICES) REGULATIONS, 1998

## (S.I. No. 52 of 1998)

*Citation and commencement*

**BC.501**     **1.** These Regulations may be cited as the Organisation of Working Time(-Exemption of Civil Protection Services) Regulations, 1998, and shall come into operation on the 1st day of March, 1998.

*Definitions*

**BC.502**     **2.** In these Regulations—

"fire authority" has the same meaning as it has in the Fire Services Act, 1981 (No. 30 of 1981);

"place of detention" means a place of detention provided under section 2 of the Prisons Act, 1970 (No. 11 of 1970),

"prison" includes Saint Patrick's Institution (within the meaning of the Criminal Justice Act, 1960 (No. 27 of 1960)).

*Exemption*

**BC.503**     **3.** The persons employed in each of the classes of activity specified in the Schedule to these Regulations are, as respects the carrying out of the duties involved in that activity, hereby exempted from the application of sections 11, 12, 13, 15 and 16 of the Organisation of Working Time Act, 1997 (No. 20 of 1997).

SCHEDULE

**BC.504**     1. The activity of a person employed in a prison or place of detention, being an activity that involves the maintenance of security in that prison or place of detention or the control or care of prisoners and which cannot be carried on within the normal rostering schedules applicable to that prison or place of detention.

2. The activity of a person employed by a fire authority in the position commonly known as retained fire fighter.

3. The activity of a person, other than a member of the Garda Síochána, employed as an authorised officer (within the meaning of the Air Navigation and Transport Acts, 1950 to 1988, and any enactment amending or extending those Acts).

4. The activity of a person employed by Dublin Port Company as a member of its harbour police.

5. The activity of a person employed in the Irish Marine Emergency Service, not being an activity of a clerical nature.

GENERAL NOTE

Section 3 of the 1997 Act enables the exemption, from the application of one or more provisions of that Act, of persons employed in any class or classes of activity in the civil protection services where, in the opinion of the Minister for Enterprise, Trade and Employment (the Minister) and any other Minister in whom functions stand vested in relation to the service concerned, the inherent nature of the activity is such that, if the provision concerned were to apply to the said person, the efficient operation of the service concerned would be adversely affected. In consequence of the Minister, the Minister for Justice, Equality and Law Reform, the Minister for the Environment and Local Government, the Minister for Public Enterprise and the Minister for the Marine and Natural Resources having formed such an opinion, these Regulations prescribe that persons employed in the activities in the civil protection services specified in the Schedule shall be exempt from the application of sections 11, 12, 13, 15 and 16 of the 1997 Act. **BC.505**

# ORGANISATION OF WORKING TIME (BREAKS AT WORK FOR SHOP EMPLOYEES) REGULATIONS, 1998

## (S.I. No. 57 of 1998)

*Citation and commencement*

**1.** These Regulations may be cited as the Organisation of Working Time (Breaks at Work for Shop Employees) Regulations, 1998, and shall come into operation on the 1st day of March, 1998. **BC.601**

*Definitions*

**2.** In these Regulations— **BC.602**

"the Act" means the Organisation of Working Time Act, 1997 (No. 20 of 1997);

"retail trade or business" includes the business of—

(a) a barber or hairdresser,

(b) hiring goods otherwise than for use in a trade or business,

(c) a pawnbroker,

(d) retail sales by auction, but does not include the sale of programmes or catalogues at theatres or other places of entertainment;

"shop" includes-

(a) any premises which any retail trade or business is carried on,

(b) any premises in which goods are received direct from customers for cleaning, repairing, altering or laundering

(c) any wholesale shop,

(d) any warehouse occupied—

(i) for the purpose of a retail trade or business, by the person carrying on such retail trade or business, or

(ii) by a wholesale dealer or merchant for the purposes of the business carried on by him or her in a wholesale shop,

but does not include—

(i) so much (if any) of a premises referred to in a preceding provision of this definition as is not used for any purposes aforesaid or, in the case of a wholesale shop, is not used for the purposes mentioned in the definition of "wholesale shop" in this Regulation,

(ii) any premises used for, or so much (if any) of a premises referred to In a preceding provision of this definition as is used for, the purpose of—

(I) a hotel,

(II) the preparation of food or the catering for any persons as respects their requirements in respect of food or drink, or

(III) any business carried on pursuant to an intoxicating liquor licence;

"shop employee" means an employee who does shop work;

"shop work" means work in or about a shop;

"wholesale shop" means any premises occupied by a wholesale dealer or merchant where goods are kept for sale wholesale to customers resorting to the premises.

*One hour break for certain shop employees*

BC.603    3. In relation to the following class of employee, namely, an employee—

(a) who is a shop employee, and

(b) whose hours of work as such an employee include the hours from 11.30 a.m. to 2.30 p.m., the minimum duration of the break to be allowed by the employer under section 12(2) of the Act to him or her shall be one hour and that break shall, unless its commencement between those hours would result in section 12(4) of the Act not being complied with, commence between the hours aforesaid.

GENERAL NOTE

BC.604    These Regulations provide that shop employees whose hours of work include the period from 11.30 a.m. to 2.30 p.m. shall, after six hours work, be allowed a break of one hour which must commence between these hours, provided such commencement would not result in the break occurring at the end of the working day.

## ORGANISATION OF WORKING TIME (CODE OF PRACTICE ON SUNDAY WORKING IN THE RETAIL TRADE AND RELATED MATTERS) (DECLARATION) ORDER, 1998

### (S.I. No. 444 of 1998)

*Citation*

BC.701    **1.** This Order may be cited as the Organisation of Working Time (Code of Practice on Sunday Working in the Retail Trade and Related Matters) (Declaration) Order, 1998.

*Code of Practice*

BC.702    **2.** The code of practice set out in the Schedule to this Order is hereby declared to be a code of practice for the purposes of section 14 of the Organisation of Working Time Act, 1997 (No. 20 of 1997), and so much of Part IV of that Act as relates to that section.

SCHEDULE

ORGANISATION OF WORKING TIME ACT, 1997

CODE OF PRACTICE

ON

SUNDAY WORKING IN THE RETAIL TRADE

NOTE

This Code of Practice is not a legal interpretation of the Act **BC.703**

CONTENTS

1. INTRODUCTION

1. The Minister for Labour, Trade and Consumer Affairs, requested the Labour Relations Commis- **BC.704** sion, pursuant to section 35(2) of the Organisation of Working Time Act 1997 and in relation to the Sunday work supplemental provisions of section 14 of the Act, to prepare a Code of Practice on Sunday Working in the Retail Trade.

2. The Labour Relations Commission has prepared this Code of Practice on Sunday Working in the Retail Trade in accordance with the provisions of section 35(2) of the Organisation of Working Time Act 1997. When preparing the Code of Practice the Commission sought submissions from the Irish Business and Employers Confederation, the Irish Congress of Trade Unions, the Union of Retail Bar and Administrative Workers (MANDATE) and the Services Industrial Professional Technical Union.

3. The Commission has taken account of the views expressed by these organisations to the fullest extent possible in preparing this Code.

4. The Code is designed to assist employers, employees and their representatives in observing the 1997 Act as regards Sunday working in the retail trade. It gives guidance, in particular, on arrangements that may be put in place to comply with the supplemental provisions of section 14 of the Act.

5. While failure on the part of any person to observe the Code will not, in itself, render that person liable to civil or criminal proceedings, the Code shall be admissible in evidence before a Court, the Labour Court or a Rights Commissioner in proceedings under the Organisation of Working Time Act 1997.

2. SUPPLEMENTAL PROVISIONS OF SECTION 14 OF THE ORGANISATION OF WORKING TIME ACT, 1997 — SUNDAY WORK

NOTE

This section of the code gives a general description of some of the supplemental provisions of **BC.705** section 14 of the Organisation of Working Time Act 1997 and is not a legal interpretation.

1. The terms of the EU Directive on Working Time, (Council Directive 93/104/EC of 23 November 1993), were transposed into Irish law by means of the Organisation of Working Time Act. 1997 and Regulations made under the Safety, Health and Welfare at Work Act, 1989.

2. Section 14 of the Organisation of Working Time Act, 1997 sets out statutory rights for employees in respect of Sunday working. Any employee who is required to work on a Sunday

B–117

and, his or her having to work on that day has not been taken account of in the determination of pay, shall be compensated as follows:

by the payment to the employee of a reasonable allowance having regard to all the circumstancesorby increasing the employee's rate of pay by a reasonable amount having regard to all the circumstances

or

by granting the employee reasonable paid time off from work having regard to all the circumstances

or

by a combination of two or more of the above means.

3. GENERAL PRINCIPLES OF COMPENSATORY ARRANGEMENTS FOR SUNDAY WORKING IN THE RETAIL TRADE

## 1. General

**BC.706**     The retail trade consists of many varied groups of businesses such as drapery, grocery, hardware or fast food, operating in diverse business environments. The purpose of this Code is to ensure that best practices are operated by all employers for those employees who service that sector of industry through Sunday working. Sunday hours of work and rostering arrangements have a significant impact on the quality of life of workers as well as being important to the efficient operation of the enterprise. Therefore, they should be subject to discussion and consultation between the Employer and the relevant trade union(s) representing employees or between the employer and the employees who are affected by Sunday trading, in circumstances where employees are not unionised.

2. The following is a general guide to all employers and their employees on the type of compensatory arrangement's that should apply for Sunday working. While the compensatory arrangements listed are set out for general guidance only, employers may provide enhanced compensatory arrangements to suit particular business environments. Minimum compensatory requirements are set out at section 14 of the Organisation of Working Time Act, 1997.

## 3. Guidelines on compensatory arrangements for Sunday working

3.1 Where a collective agreement of the type implied in section 14 of the Organisation of Working Time Act, 1997 exists between an employer and a trade union(s) representing employees or between an employer and employees who are not unionised, this should not be altered, except through the standard negotiating mechanisms.

3.2 In the absence of a collective agreement, best practice should be set by reference to compensation arrangements provided for in a collective agreement applying to comparable employees in the (retail) sector.

3.3 All new agreements being entered into should be negotiated between the employer and the relevant trade union(s) representing employees, based on a consensus approach. In circumstances where employees are not unionised the agreement should be negotiated between the employer and the employees who are affected by Sunday trading. Agreements should take account of the following:

In accordance with provisions of the Organisation of Working Time Act 1997 a premium payment will apply to Sunday working. Section 14 of the Act specifies the means by which the premium should be granted. The nature and value of this premium rate should be negotiated and agreed between the employer and the trade union(s) representing employees or between the employer and the employees who are affected by Sunday trading, in circumstances where employees are not unionised.

Existing employees should have the option to volunteer to opt into working patterns, which include Sundays on a rota basis and form part of a regular working week (*i.e.* being required to work no more than 5 days out of 7).

Newly recruited employees may be contracted to work Sundays as part of a regular rostered working pattern.

Employees who have a minimum of two years' service on a Sunday working contract should have the opportunity to seek to opt out of Sunday working, for urgent family or personal reasons, giving adequate notice to the employer.

B–118

Meal breaks on Sundays should be standardised in line with the other working days of the week.

All employees should have the opportunity of volunteering to work on the peak Sunday trading days prior to Christmas, in addition to their normal working week. In these circumstances length of service will not be the overriding criterion for selection for Sunday working.

NOTE

The Labour Relations Commission will provide assistance to employers and trade union(s) repre- **BC.707** senting employees and to employers and their employees who are not unionised, in the negotiation of collective agreements on compensatory arrangements of the kind specified in section 14 of the Organisation of Working Time Act, 1997.

Requests for such assistance should be forwarded in writing to the Labour Relations Commission, Tom Johnson House, Haddington Road, Dublin 4 – telephone 6609662 (01 area) and 1890 220227 (outside 01 area), fax (01) 6685069.

### 4. COMPLAINTS PROCEDURE

1. The Organisation of Working Time Act, 1997 sets out a complaints procedure for dealing with **BC.708** the various complaints that may arise under the Act. While the procedure deals with general complaints concerning various entitlements, for the purposes of this Code the procedure concerns itself with complaints about Sunday working in the retail sector.

### *Who can make a complaint?*

2. An employee or any trade union of which the employee is a member, with the consent of the employee, may present a complaint. The Minister for Labour, Trade and Consumer Affairs may also present a complaint if it is apparent that an employer is not complying with a provision and, where the employee trade union has not done so and, the Minister is of the opinion that the circumstances are such as to make it unreasonable to expect the employee trade union to present such a complaint.

### *How is a complaint presented and processed?*

3. Complaints arising under section 14 of the 1997 Act, should be presented in the first instance to a Rights Commissioner. A complaint must be made within six months of the date of the alleged contravention by the employer. However, a complaint which is presented not later than twelve months after the six months time limit may be investigated if the Rights Commissioner is satisfied that the delay was due to reasonable cause. A complaint should be in writing and should contain the requisite particulars.

4. The Rights Commissioner must give the employer a copy of the complaint. The Rights Commissioner must hear the parties and allow relevant evidence to be presented. The investigation of a complaint will be held in private. The Rights Commissioner must furnish the Labour Court with a copy of each decision given under the 1997 Act.

5. The Rights Commissioner in making a decision shall do one or more of the following:
   (a)   declare that the complaint was, or, as the case may be, was not well founded,
   (b)   require the employer to comply with the relevant provision(s),
   (c)   require the employer to pay compensation of such amount (if any) as is just and equitable having regard to all the circumstances, up to a maximum of two years' remuneration.

NOTE

Queries relating to complaints and procedures should be forwarded in writing to the Rights **BC.709** Commissioner Service. Labour Relations Commission, Tom Johnson House, Haddington Road, Dublin 4 – telephone 6609662 (01 area) and 1890 220227 outside (01 area), fax (01) 6685069.

### 5. APPEALS

1. Either party may appeal a decision of a Rights Commissioner to the Labour Court. The appeal **BC.710** must be made within 6 weeks of the date on which the decision was communicated to the party. The notice of appeal should be submitted to the Labour Court in writing.

2. The Labour Court must give a copy of the notice of appeal to the other party. The Labour Court shall give the parties an opportunity to be heard and to present relevant evidence to it. It will make a determination in writing affirming, varying or setting aside the decision. The Court must communicate that determination to the parties.

NOTE

**BC.711** The procedure on appeals is laid down by the Labour Court. Details of these procedures can be obtained from the Labour Court, Tom Johnson House, Haddington Road, Dublin 4 – telephone 6608444 (01 area) and 1890 220228 – (outside 01 area).

## 6. ENFORCEMENT OF DECISIONS OF THE RIGHTS COMMISSIONER/DETERMINATIONS OF THE LABOUR COURT

**BC.712** 1. An employee may bring a complaint to the Labour Court where an employer has not implemented a decision of the Rights Commissioner under the Act or has not appealed a decision within the requisite time. The Labour Court shall make a determination to the like effect as the original decision without hearing the employer concerned. The complaint must be brought by the employee not later than six weeks after the time limit for making an appeal has expired. Complaints of the non-implementation of Rights Commissioners' decisions under the Act should be submitted to the Labour Court. The Labour Court shall publish particulars of its determinations in such manner as it thinks fit.

2. The Minister, at the request of the Labour Court, may refer a question of law arising in proceedings before it, concerning appeals from the enforcement of decisions of a Rights Commissioner, for determination by the High Court. The determination of the High Court shall be final and conclusive.

3. A party to proceedings may appeal to the High Court from a determination of the Labour Court on a point of law. The determination of the High Court shall be final and conclusive.

4. Where a determination of the Labour Court has not been implemented, within six weeks from the date on which the determination is communicated to the parties, the Circuit Court, on application to it, by an employee, trade union or the Minister, shall, without hearing the employer or any evidence, make an order directing the employer to carry out the determination in accordance with its terms.

5. The Circuit Court, if it deems it appropriate to do so, may direct the employer to pay interest on the compensation in respect of any period commencing 6 weeks following the communication of the Labour Court's determination to the parties and ending on the date of the order.

6. The application to the Circuit Court will be in the Circuit where the employer usually resides or carries out the business.

GENERAL NOTE

**BC.713** Under section 35(2) of the 1997 Act, the Labour Relations Commission is required, having been so requested by the Minister for Labour, Trade and Consumer Affairs, being the Minister of State to whom functions in this matter have been delegated by the Enterprise, Trade and Employment (Delegation of Ministerial Functions) (No. 2) Order 1997 (S.I. No. 33 of 1997), to prepare a code of practice for the purposes of any section of the 1997 Act (other than section 6(2) : on which see S.I. No. 44 of 1998). The Minister requested the Commission to prepare a code of practice for the purposes of section 14 and the code of practice so prepared and submitted to the Minister is declared, by this Order, to be a code of practice for the purposes of section 14 of the 1997 Act and so much of Part IV of that Act as relates to that section.

The Code of Practice seeks to balance the rights of existing employees to opt in or out of Sunday working while new staff "may be contracted" to work Sundays as part of a regular rostered working pattern. The standard premium in the retail sector for Sunday work is double time for existing staff on a voluntary basis and time-and-a-half for new staff as part of a roster, with Christmas Sundays at higher premium again: see *Industrial Relations News* No. 46 (3 December 1998), pp. 14–15 outlining trade union concerns at the lack of protection for staff obliged to work on Sundays.

# CIRCUIT COURT RULES 2001

## (S.I. No. 510 of 2001)

ORDER 57

## Rule 4 Organisation of Working Time Act 1997

**1.** In this Order "the Act" means the Organisation of Working Time Act 1997    BC.851
(No. 20 of 1997), "a determination of the Labour Court" shall be interpreted
having regard to the provisions of section 29(2) of the Act and "the Minister"
means the Minister for Enterprise, Trade and Employment.

**2.** All applications under section 29 of the Act by way of claim for enforcement    BC.852
of determinations of the Labour Court by the Minister or by the employee
concerned or, with the consent of the employee, by any trade union of which
the employee is a member shall be made by way of Motion on Notice in accordance with Form 36D of the Schedule of Forms annexed hereto with such amendments as are appropriate which shall set out the grounds upon which the Applicant
relies for the reliefs sought and which shall have annexed thereto:

   (a)   the original determination of the Labour Court or a certified copy of same,
certified by the plaintiff employee or his trade union or on behalf of the
Minister as being a true copy of the determination received from the
Labour Court and sought to be enforced and shall state the date on
which the determination of the Labour Court was communicated to the
plaintiff.

**3.** Applications shall be brought in the County where the employer concerned    BC.853
ordinarily resides or carries on any profession, business or occupation.

**4.** Notice of every application shall be given to the employer or employers in    BC.854
question and to the Labour Court by serving notice of the proceedings (including
the Notice of Motion and grounding Affidavits, if any) no later than 10 days prior
to the return date specified in the Notice of Motion, in the case of the employer or
employers personally in accordance with the provisions of Order 11 of these
Rules, or by leaving a true copy of same at the employer's residence or place
of business or by pre-paid registered post to the employer's residence or place of
business and, in the case of the Labour Court, by leaving a true copy of same at the
Labour Court.

**5.** Save by special leave of the Court, all applications under section 29 of the    BC.855
Act shall be heard upon oral evidence or as may be determined by the Court.

**6.** The Court may make such Order as to costs as may be appropriate including    BC.856
an Order measuring the costs.

**7.** The Registrar of the Labour Court shall have the right of access to all the    BC.857
information contained on the file kept in the Office of the County Registrar in
respect of each application and shall be entitled upon request to receive a copy of
any written Judgment delivered by the Judge relating thereto.

BC.858

FORM 36D

## AN CHÚIRT CHUARDA

## THE CIRCUIT COURT

CIRCUIT          COUNTY OF

## IN THE MATTER OF THE ORGANISATION OF WORKING TIME ACT, 1997

## NOTICE OF MOTION FOR RELIEF UNDER SECTION 29 OF THE ORGANISATION OF WORKING TIME ACT, 1997

BETWEEN

..............................................................Plaintiff

AND

..............................................................Defendant

Take notice that application will be made to the Court on the or the next opportunity thereafter for the following reliefs:
[Here insert details of the relief sought by way of enforcement.]
And further take notice that the said application will be grounded upon:

1.  [here insert grounds upon which the Applicant is relying for the reliefs sought to include all the facts relevant to the alleged failure to carry out the decisions or determinations and whether or not an appeal has been brought from the decisions or determinations and, if no such appeal has been brought, that the time for appeal has elapsed and, if such appeal has been brought, the date upon which Notice of Appeal was given and evidence of abandonment thereof.]

2.  [here insert basis of jurisdiction]

3.  [here insert name, address and description of the Plaintiff]

4.  [here insert the date on which the determination of the Labour Court was communicated to the Applicant]

5.  [The following documents must be annexed to this Notice of Motion namely the original determination of the Labour Court or a certified copy of the same, certified by the Applicant employee or his trade union or on behalf of the Minister as being a true copy of the determination received from the Labour Court and sought to be enforced.]

Dated the        day of

Signed....................................................
Plaintiff/Solicitor for the Plaintiff

To: ...................................
     The Defendant/Solicitor for the Defendant

And

To: The Labour Court

And

To: The County Registrar

B–122

GENERAL NOTE

This rule sets out the procedure for applications to the Circuit Court pursuant to section 29 of the **BC.859**
1997 Act.

# SAFETY, HEALTH AND WELFARE AT WORK (NIGHT WORK AND SHIFT WORK) REGULATIONS, 2000

## (S.I. No. 11 of 2000)

## Citation

**1.** These Regulations may be cited as the Safety, Health and Welfare at Work BC.1001 (Night Work and Shift Work) Regulations, 2000.

## Revocation

**2.** The Safety, Health and Welfare at Work (Night Work and Shift Work) BC.1002 Regulations, 1998 (S.I. No. 485 of 1998) are hereby revoked.

## Interpretation

**3.**—(1) In these Regulations—                                                                        BC.1003

"Principal Act" means the Safety, Health and Welfare at Work Act, 1989 (No. 7 of 1989);

"1997 Act" means the Organisation of Working Time Act, 1997 (No. 20 of 1997);

"Directive" means Council Directive 93/104/EC of 23 November, 1993 concerning certain aspects of the Organisation of working time;

"night work" and "night worker" have the same meaning as they have in the 1997 Act;

"Principal Regulations" means the Safety, Health and Welfare at Work (General Application) Regulations, 1993 (S.I. No. 44 of 1993);

["Activities of Doctors in Training Regulations" means the European Communities (Organisation of Working Time) (Activities of Doctors in Training) Regulations 2004 (S.I. No. 494 of 2004)].

(2) A word or expression that is used in these Regulations and is also used in the Directive has, unless the contrary intention appears, the meaning in these Regulations that it has in the Directive.

(3) In those Regulations a reference to a paragraph is a reference to a paragraph of the Regulation in which the reference occurs, unless it is indicated that reference to some other Regulation is intended.

## Application

**4.**—(1) These Regulations shall apply to—                                                            BC.1004

(a) an employee and employer to whom the 1997 Act [or the Activities of Doctors in Training Regulations apply], and

(b) a self-employed person as they apply to an employer and as if that self-employed person was an employer and his or her own employee,

(2) The provisions of these Regulations are in addition to, and not in substitution for, Part II of the Principal Regulations.

## General duty with respect to night workers and shift workers

**5.** It shall be the duty of every employer—                                                           BC.1005

(a) to take such steps as, having regard to the nature of the work concerned, are appropriate for the protection of the safety and health of an employee who is a night worker or a shift worker,

(b) in taking steps to comply with Regulation 8 of the Principal Regulations, to have regard to his or her duty under paragraph (a).

## Risk assessment

**6.**—(1) For the purposes of section 16(2)(a) of the 1997 Act [and Regulation BC.1006

B–125

10(2)(a) of the Activities of Doctors in Training Regulations], it shall be the duty of an employer to carry out an assessment in relation to the risks, being risks to the safety and health of the employee concerned, that attach to the work that a night worker is employed to do so as to determine whether that work involves special hazards or a heavy physical or mental strain.

(2) An assessment referred to in paragraph (1) shall take into account the specific effects and hazards of night work.

(3) In determining for the purposes of this Regulation whether particular work involves special hazards or a heavy physical or mental strain, regard shall be had to the assessment of risks at the place of work concerned referred to in section 12(3) of the Principal Act and Regulation 10 of the Principal Regulations.

## Health assessment and transfer to day work

BC.1007    **7.**—(1) It shall be the duty of an employer—

(a)  before he or she employs a person as a night worker, and

(b)  at regular intervals during the period that that person is employed as such a worker, to make available to that person, free of charge, an assessment in relation to the effects, if any, on the health of that person by reason of his or her being employed as such a worker.

(2) Such assessment—

(a)  shall be carried out by a registered medical practitioner or a person acting under his or her supervision,

(b)  if the employee has such an entitlement, may be made available to the employee by informing him or her of his or her entitlement to have such an assessment carried out by the State, free of charge, and facilitating the employee in his or her availing himself or herself of that entitlement.

(3) The person who carries out an assessment referred to in paragraph (1) shall—

(a)  endeavour to detect if the health of the employee concerned is being or will be adversely affected by reason of the fact that he or she performs or will perform night work,

(b)  on the completion of the assessment, inform the employer and employee concerned of his or her opinion as to whether the employee is fit or unfit to perform the night work concerned and, if that opinion is that the employee is unfit to perform that night work by reason only of the particular conditions under which that work is performed, of his or her opinion of what changes in those conditions could be made that would result in his or her being able to consider the employee fit to perform that work.

(4) Neither a registered medical practitioner nor a person acting under his or her supervision shall disclose:

(a)  the clinical details of the assessment referred to in paragraph (1) to any person other than the employee concerned or an occupational medical adviser,

or

(b)  the results of such an assessment to any person other than the employee and employer concerned.

(5) If a night worker becomes ill or otherwise exhibits symptoms of ill-health, and that illness or those symptoms is or are recognised as being connected with the fact that he or she performs night work, the employer shall, whenever possible, assign duties to the worker to perform that do not involve his or her performing any night work and to which he or she is suited.

(6) References in paragraphs (2), (3) and (4) to the employee shall be construed

as including references to the person proposed to be employed as the night worker concerned.

GENERAL NOTE

These Regulations, as amended by the European Communities (Organisation of Working Time) **BC.1008** (Activities of Doctors in Training) Regulations 2004 (S.I. No. 494 of 2004), revoke and replace the Safety, Health and Welfare at Work (Night Work and Shift Work) Regulations 1998 (S.I. No. 485 of 1998) and give effect, in respect of night workers and shift workers, to the health and safety provisions of Art.9 of Council Directive 93/104/EC. They require employers to carry out, for the purposes of the maximum hours of night working permitted under s.16(2) of the Organisation of Working Time Act 1997, an assessment of health and safety risks attaching to the work of night workers whom they employ with a view to determining whether that work involves special hazards or a heavy physical or mental strain. The Regulations also require employers, whose night workers become ill or exhibit symptoms of ill-health as a result of performing night work, to re-assign such workers to daywork whenever possible. Apparently there was some possible confusion as regards the application of the provisions of reg.6 of the 1998 Regulations to night workers and these Regulations seek to avoid that (see reg.7).

# ORGANISATION OF WORKING TIME (RECORDS) (PRESCRIBED FORM AND EXEMPTIONS) REGULATIONS 2001

### (S.I. No. 473 of 2001)

## Citation and commencement

**1.** These Regulations may be cited as the Organisation of Working Time **BC.1101** (Records) (Prescribed Form and Exemptions) Regulations, 2001, and shall come into operation on the 1$^{st}$ day of November 2001.

## Interpretation

**2.**—(1) In these Regulations—                                                                   **BC.1102**

"the Act" means the Organisation of Working Time Act, 1997 (No. 20 of 1997), and

"inspector" means an inspector within the meaning of section 8 of the Act.

(2) A reference in these Regulations to a section is a reference to a section of the Act unless it is indicated that reference to some other enactment is intended.

(3) A reference in these Regulations to a Regulation or the Schedule is to a Regulation of, or the Schedule to, these Regulations unless it is indicated that a reference to some other enactment is intended.

(4) A reference in these Regulations to a paragraph or subparagraph is to a paragraph or subparagraph of the provision in which the reference occurs, unless it is indicated that a reference to some other provision is intended.

## Form of records under section 25(1)

**3.** The records required to be kept under section 25(1) shall contain the **BC.1103** following particulars and documents—

(a) the name and address of each employee concerned, the number known as the [Personal Public Service] number that has been assigned to him or her and a brief statement (which may be by reference to any form of job description or classification used by the employer concerned) of his or her duties as an employee,

(b) a copy, as appropriate, of the statement provided to each employee concerned in accordance with the provisions of the Terms of Employment (Information) Act, 1994 (No. 5 of 1994), or any order or regulation made under that Act, that relates to him or her,

(c)   (i) the days and total hours worked in each week by each employee concerned,

   (ii) any days and hours of leave in each week granted by way of annual leave or in respect of a public holiday to each employee concerned and the payment made to each employee in respect of that leave,

   (iii) any additional day's pay referred to in section 21(1)(d) provided in each week to each employee concerned, and

(d) a copy of a written record of a notification issued to an employee concerned in relation to any of the matters provided for in section 17 (including a copy of a notice posted in the manner referred to in subsection 5 of that section),

and shall generally be in such form as will enable an inspector to understand the particulars contained in them without difficulty.

BC.1104   **4.**—(1) Where no clocking in facilities are in place in a work place a form to record the days and hours worked in each week by each employee shall be kept by the employer in the form set out in the Schedule entitled Form OWT 1 or in a form substantially to like effect.

(2) Notwithstanding the obligation to keep records imposed on the employer by paragraph (1), where the employer and employee agree, an employee may—

(a) complete the Form OWT 1, as set out in the Schedule or a form substantially to like effect, and

(b) present the completed form to his or her employer for counter-signature and retention by the employer in accordance with paragraph (1).

(3) The Form OWT 1 should be made available at all reasonable times for inspection by an inspector.

## Exemption from section 25(1)

BC.1105   **5.**—(1) For the purposes of these Regulations and subject to paragraph (2), the following classes of employer are exempt, by virtue of section 25(2), from the obligation to keep records of rest breaks—

(a) employers who have electronic record-keeping facilities such as flexi-time or clocking-in facilities, and

(b) employers who have manual as opposed to electronic record-keeping facilities and who are required to keep records in accordance with Regulation 4.

(2) The exemption under paragraph (1) shall only apply to an employer if he or she complies with the following conditions—

(a) the employer notifies in writing each employee of the rest periods and breaks referred to in sections 11, 12 and 13 or, in case of the non-application of one or more of those sections (by virtue of regulations referred to in section 4(3), a collective agreement or a registered employment agreement referred to in section 4(5), or an employment regulation order referred to in section 4(6)) of the terms of such regulations, collective agreement, registered employment agreement or employment regulation order and, in particular, of the requirement contained in section 6(1),

(b) the employer puts in place, and notifies in writing each employee of procedures whereby an employee may notify in writing the employer of any rest period or break referred to in sections 11, 12 and 13 of the Act to which such employee is entitled and was not able to avail himself or herself of on a particular occasion and the reason for not availing of such rest period or break,

and

(c)  the employer keeps—

(i)  a record of having notified each employee of the matters provided for in paragraph (a),

(ii)  a record of having notified each employee of the procedures provided for in paragraph (b), and

(iii) records of all notifications made to him or her by each employee in accordance with those procedures.

(3) A notification made to an employer by an employee under paragraph 2(b) shall be made within 1 week of the day on which the rest period referred to in that paragraph became due to, but was not availed of by, the employee. Where such notification is duly made the employer, having regard to the circumstances pertaining to the work of the employee and to the employee's health and safety interests, shall, as soon as possible, make available to the employee such rest period or break as is equivalent to the rest period or break which had been due to, but had not been availed of by, the employee. Failure by an employee to avail of such equivalent rest period or break offered by an employer shall not constitute a breach on the part of the employer under the Act or these Regulations.

## Form of records under Regulation 5

**6.** Any record that an employer is required to keep under Regulation 5 shall **BC.1106** contain like particulars to those specified in Regulation 3(a) and shall generally be in such form as will enable an inspector to understand the particulars contained in it without difficulty.

7. An employer who fails to keep records under these Regulations shall be guilty of an offence and shall be liable on summary conviction to a fine not exceeding €1,900 (£1,496.37).

**BC.1107**                                  SCHEDULE

                                                                    FORM OWT1

                                ORGANISATION OF WORKING TIME ACT, 1997


AN ROINN FIONTAR TRADÁLA AGUS FOSTAÍOCHTA—DEPARTMENT OF
                     ENTERPRISE, TRADE AND EMPLOYMENT
                     PLEASE COMPLETE THIS FORM IN BLOCK CAPITALS


                                                FIGURES                    LETTER·

EMPLOYER'S PAYE REGISTERED NUMBER


BUSINESS NAME OF EMPLOYER        _____

BUSINESS ADDRESS                 _____

                                 _____


                                                FIGURES          LETTERS
EMPLOYEE'S [PERSONAL PUBLIC
SERVICE (PPS)] NUMBER


SURNAME _____      FIRST NAME _____


* NUMBER OF HOURS WORKED BY EMPLOYEE PER DAY AND PER WEEK


|                       |                       |                       |                       |
| --------------------- | --------------------- | --------------------- | --------------------- |
| WEEK COMMENCING: AND ENDING: | WEEK COMMENCING: AND ENDING: | WEEK COMMENCING: AND ENDING: | WEEK COMMENCING: AND ENDING: |
| MONDAY        : | MONDAY        : | MONDAY        : | MONDAY        : |
| TUESDAY       : | TUESDAY       : | TUESDAY       : | TUESDAY       : |
| WEDNESDAY   : | WEDNESDAY   : | WEDNESDAY   : | WEDNESDAY   : |
| THURSDAY    : | THURSDAY    : | THURSDAY    : | THURSDAY    : |
| FRIDAY        : | FRIDAY        : | FRIDAY        : | FRIDAY        : |
| SATURDAY    : | SATURDAY    : | SATURDAY    : | SATURDAY    : |
| SUNDAY       : | SUNDAY       : | SUNDAY       : | SUNDAY       : |
| WEEKLY TOTAL: | WEEKLY TOTAL : | WEEKLY TOTAL : | WEEKLY TOTAL : |


I DECLARE THAT THE ABOVE INFORMATION IN RELATION TO DAILY AND
WEEKLY HOURS WORKED IS CORRECT


SIGNATURE OF EMPLOYER: _____


SIGNATURE OF EMPLOYEE: _____


* NUMBER OF HOURS WORKED EXCLUDES MEAL BREAKS AND REST BREAKS


B–130

GENERAL NOTE

The main purpose of these Regulations is to require employers to keep: **BC.1108**

    (a) a record of the number of hours worked by employees (excluding meals and rest breaks) on a daily and weekly basis;

    (b) a record of leave granted to employee in each week by way of annual leave or in respect of

    (c) a public holiday and payment made in respect of that leave;

    (d) a weekly record of the notification of the starting and finishing times of employees.

The Regulations also require that an employer keep a copy of the statement provided to each employee under the provisions of the Terms of Employment (Information) Act 1994.

The Regulations also provide for exemptions subject to certain conditions, in relation to the keeping by employers of records of rest breaks and rest periods of employees under the 1997 Act.

# EUROPEAN COMMUNITIES (ORGANISATION OF WORKING TIME) (ACTIVITIES OF DOCTORS IN TRAINING) REGULATIONS 2004

## S.I. No. 494 of 2004

### Citation and commencement

**1.** (1) These Regulations may be cited as the European Communities (Organi- **BC.1201** sation of Working Time) (Activities of Doctors in Training) Regulations 2004.

(2) These Regulations shall come into operation on 1 August 2004.

### Interpretation

**2.** (1) In these Regulations— **BC.1202**

"1997 Act" means the Organisation of Working Time Act 1997 (No. 20 of 1997);

"activities of a doctor in training" means the activities of a registered medical practitioner other than the activities of:

    (a)  a hospital consultant,

    (b)  a consultant psychiatrist, whether in hospital practice, practice in the community or both, and

    (c)  any other person, not being a person in hospital practice or psychiatric practice, who is entitled to be registered in the Register of Medical Specialists under section 31 of the Medical Practitioners Act 1978 and who, in the performance of his or her duties as a registered medical practitioner, works without supervision in professional matters by any other person;

"consultant psychiatrist" means a registered medical practitioner who, by reason of his or her training, skill and experience in the specialty of psychiatry, is consulted by registered medical practitioners in relation to that specialty;

"Directive" means Directive 93/104/EC1 or Directive 2000/34/EC2, as the context admits or requires, and a reference to the Directives is a reference to each of them;

"Directive 93/104/EC" means Directive 93/104/EC of the Council of 23 November 1999 concerning certain aspects of the organisation of working time as amended by Directive 2000/34/EC;

"Directive 2000/34/EC" means Directive 2000/34/EC of the European Parliament and of the Council of 22 June 2000 amending Council Directive 93/104/EC concerning certain aspects of the organisation of working time to cover sectors and activities excluded from that Directive;

"employee" means an employee within the meaning of section 2(1) of the 1997 Act who is engaged in the activities of a doctor in training and references, in relation to an employer, to an employee shall be construed as references to an employee employed by that employer;

"hospital consultant" means a register ed medical practitioner in hospital practice who, by reason of his or her training, skill and experience in a particular specialty, is consulted by registered medical practitioners in relation to that specialty;

"Minister" means the Minister for Health and Children;

"registered medical practitioner" has the meaning assigned to it by section 2 of the Medical Practitioners Act 1978;

"rest period" means any period which is not working time;

"working time" means any period during which an employee is working, at the employer's disposal and carrying out the activity or duties of his or her work, including on-call duty performed by an employee where he or she is required to be physically present at his or her place of work, and

"work" shall be construed accordingly.

(2) A word or expression that is used in both these Regulations and the 1997 Act has, unless the contrary intention appears, the meaning in these Regulations that it has in the 1997 Act.

(3) A word or expression that is used in both these Regulations and the Directives has, unless the contrary intention appears, the meaning in these Regulations that it has in the Directives.

(4) In these Regulations —

(a) a reference to a Regulation or a Schedule is a reference to a Regulation of, or a Schedule to, these Regulations unless it is indicated that reference to some other Regulations is intended,

(b) a reference to a paragraph or subparagraph is a reference to the paragraph or subparagraph of the provision in which the reference occurs, unless it is indicated that reference to some other provision is intended,

(c) a reference to a section is a reference to a section of the 1997 Act unless it is indicated that a reference to some other enactment is intended,

(d) a reference to any enactment shall be construed as a reference to that enactment as amended, adapted or extended by or under any subsequent enactment.

### Scope

**BC.1203**   **3.** These Regulations apply to the activities of doctors in training.

### Exemptions

**BC.1204**   **4.** (1) Subject to Regulation 5,

(a)  Regulation 6 shall not apply in relation to a shift worker when he or she changes shift and cannot take a daily rest period between the end of one shift and the start of the next one; and

(b) Regulation 8 shall not apply to a shift worker when he or she changes shift and cannot take a weekly rest period between the end of one shift and the start of the next one.

(2) In paragraph (1) of this Regulation:

"shift work" means any method of organising work in shifts whereby employees succeed each other at the same work stations according to a certain pattern, including a rotating pattern, and which may be continuous or discontinuous, entailing the need for employees to work at different times over a given period of days or weeks; and

"shift worker" means any employee whose work schedule is part of shift work.

(3) Subject to Regulation 5, an employer shall not be obliged to comply with Regulations 6, 7 and 8 where due to exceptional circumstances or an emergency (including an accident or the imminent risk of an accident), the consequences of which could not have been avoided despite the exercise of all due care, or otherwise due to the occurrence of unusual and unforeseeable circumstances beyond the employer's control, it would not be practicable for the employer to comply with the Regulation concerned.

## Compensatory rest

**5.** Where the application of any provision of these Regulations is excluded by BC.1205 Regulation 4 and an employee is accordingly required by his or her employer to work during a period which would otherwise be a rest period or a break, the employer shall:

(a) ensure that the employee has available to himself or herself a rest period or break, as the case may be, that in all the circumstances can reasonably be regarded as equivalent to the first-mentioned rest period or break, or

(b) if, in exceptional cases in which it is not possible for the employer, for reasons that can be objectively justified, to grant the employee such an equivalent rest period or break,

the employer shall otherwise afford him or her such protection as may be appropriate in order to safeguard his or her health and safety.

## Daily rest

**6.** An employee is entitled to a rest period of not less than 11 consecutive hours BC.1206 in each period of 24 hours during which he or she works for his or her employer.

## Breaks

**7.** (1) An employer shall not require an employee to work for a period of more BC.1207 than 4 hours and 30 minutes without allowing him or her a break of at least 15 minutes.

(2) An employer shall not require an employee to work for a period of more than 6 hours without allowing him or her a break of at least 30 minutes; such a break may include the break referred to in paragraph (1).

(3) A break allowed to an employee at the end of the working day shall not be regarded as satisfying the requirement contained in paragraph (1) or (2).

**Weekly rest**

BC.1208   **8.** (1) In this Regulation "daily rest period" means a rest period referred to in Regulation 6.

(2) Subject to paragraph (3), an employee shall, in each period of 7 days, be granted a rest period of at least 24 consecutive hours and subject to paragraphs (4) and (5), the time at which that rest period commences shall be such that that period is immediately preceded by a daily rest period.

(3) An employer may, in lieu of granting to an employee in any period of 7 days the first-mentioned rest period in paragraph (2), grant to him or her, in the next following period of 7 days, two rest periods each of which shall be a period of at least 24 consecutive hours and, subject to paragraphs (4) and (5)—

   (a) if the rest periods so granted are consecutive, the time at which the first of those periods commences shall be such that that period is immediately preceded by a daily rest period, and

   (b) if the rest periods so granted are not consecutive, the time at which each of those periods commences shall be such that each of them is immediately preceded by a daily rest period.

(4) If considerations of a technical nature or related to the conditions under which the work concerned is organised or otherwise of an objective nature would justify the making of such a decision, an employer may decide that the time at which a rest period granted by him or her under paragraph (2) or (3) shall commence shall be such that the rest period is not immediately preceded by a daily rest period.

(5) The requirement in paragraph (2) or subparagraph (a) or (b) of paragraph (3) as to the time at which a rest period under this Regulation shall commence shall not apply in any case where, by reason of a provision of these Regulations the employee concerned is not entitled to a daily rest period in the circumstances concerned.

**Maximum weekly working time**

BC.1209   **9.** (1) An employer shall not permit an employee to work, in each period of 7 days more than an average of

   (a) 58 hours, during the period 1 August 2004 to 31 July 2007;

   (b) 56 hours, during the period 1 August 2007 to 31 July 2009; and

   (c) 48 hours, from 1 August 2009 onwards

calculated over a period (hereafter in this Regulation referred to as a "reference period").

(2) Subject to paragraph (3), the reference period referred to in paragraph (1) is:

   (a) for the period from 1 August 2004 to 31 July 2007, 12 months and;

   (b) with effect from 1 August 2007, 6 months or such length of time as may be specified in any agreement made under paragraph (4).

(3) Where an employee has worked for his employer for less  than the

reference period that would otherwise apply under paragraph (2), the reference period applicable is the period that has elapsed since the employee started work for his or her employer.

(4) A collective agreement that for the time being has effect in relation to an employee and which stands approved of by the Labour Court under section 24 of the 1997 Act may, for objective or technical reasons or reasons concerning the organisation of work, modify the application of paragraph (2)(b) in relation to that employee by the substitution for the reference to 6 months of a different period, being a period not exceeding 12 months.

(5) The days or months comprising a reference period shall, subject to paragraph (6), be consecutive days or months.

(6) A reference period shall not include—

(a) any period of annual leave granted to the employee concerned in accordance with the 1997 Act (save so much of it as exceeds the minimum period of annual leave required by that Act to be granted to the employee),

(b) any period during which the employee was absent from work while on parental leave, *force majeure* leave or carer's leave within the meaning of the Carer's Leave Act 2001,

(c) any absences from work by the employee concerned authorised under the Maternity Protection [Acts 1994 and 2004] or the Adoptive Leave [Acts 1995 and 2005], or

(d) any sick leave taken by the employee concerned.

## Nightly working hours

**10.** (1) In this Regulation—                                                    BC.1210

"night time" means the period between midnight and 7a.m. on the following day;

"night work" means work carried out during night time;

"night worker" means an employee—

(a) who normally works at least 3 hours of his or her daily working time during night time, and

(b) the number of hours worked by whom during night time, in each year, equals or exceeds 50 per cent. of the total number of hours worked by him or her during that year;

"special category night worker" means a night worker as respects whom an assessment carried out by his or her employer pursuant to Regulation 6 of the Safety, Health and Welfare at Work (Night Work and Shift Work) Regulations 2000 in relation to the risks attaching to the work that the night worker is employed to do indicates that that work involves special hazards or a heavy physical or mental strain.

(2) Without prejudice to Regulation 9, an employer shall not permit a night worker, in each period of 24 hours, to work—

(a) in a case where the work done by the employee in that period includes night work and the employee is a special category night worker, more than 8 hours,

(b) in any other case, more than an average of 8 hours, that is to say an average of 8 hours calculated over a period (hereafter in this Regulation referred to as a "reference period") that does not exceed—

(i)   2 months, or

(ii)  such greater length of time as is specified in a collective agreement that for the time being has effect in relation to that night worker and which stands approved of by the Labour Court under section 24 of the 1997 Act.

(3) The days or months comprising a reference period shall, subject to paragraph (4), be consecutive days or months.

(4) A reference period shall not include—

(a)  any rest period granted to the employee concerned under Regulation 8(2) (save so much of it as exceeds 24 hours),

(b)  any rest periods granted to the employee concerned under Regulation 8(3) (save so much of each of those periods as exceeds 24 hours),

(c)  any period of annual leave granted to the employee concerned in accordance with the 1997 Act (save so much of it as exceeds the minimum period of annual leave required by that Act to be granted to the employee),

(d)  any period during which the employee was absent from work while on parental leave, *force majeure* leave or carer's leave within the meaning of the Carer's Leave Act 2001,

(e)  any absences from work by the employee concerned authorised under the Maternity Protection [Acts 1994 and 2004] or the Adoptive Leave [Acts 1995 and 2005], or

(f)  any sick leave taken by the employee concerned.

## Records

**BC.1211**    **11.** (1) [Amending section 25 of the 1997 Act]

(2) The records to be maintained under section 25(1) shall, in the case of an employee to whom these Regulations apply, contain the following particulars and documents:

(a)  the name of each employee concerned, the number known as the Personal Public Services (PPS) number that has been assigned to him or her and a brief statement (which may be by reference to any form of job description or classification used by the employer concerned but which, in any event, should include his or her medical specialty and stage of training) of his or her duties as an employee; and

(b)  a copy, as appropriate, of the statement provided to each employee concerned in accordance with the provisions of the Terms of Employment (Information) Act 1994 (No. 4 of 1994), or any order or regulation made under that Act, that relates to him or her,

(c)  in the case of each employee, his or her normal schedule of, and actual,

(i)   daily hours of work and rest,

(ii)  rest breaks,

(iii) hours of night work,

(iv)  weekly hours of work and rest,

(v)   hours on-call on-site,

      (vi) hours on-call off-site,

      (vii) periods of release from the activities or duties of his or her work for the purpose of engaging in training activities including study and examination leave; and

(d) in the case of each employee,

      (i) any days and hours of leave in each week granted by way of annual leave or in respect of a public holiday to each employee concerned and the payment made to each employee in respect of that leave,

      (ii) any additional day's pay referred to in section 21(1)(d) of the 1997 Act; and those records shall be retained for at least three years from the date of their making.

(3) Each record under paragraph (1) shall generally be in such form as will enable an inspector understand the particulars contained therein without difficulty.

(4) An employer shall, on request, make available:

(a) to an employee a copy of records required to be kept under this Regulation which relate to that employee,

and

(b) to the Minister a copy of records required to be kept under this Regulation provided that in the case of information in a non-legible form, a copy of the information or of extracts from it in permanent legible form shall be made available to an employee or the Minister, as the case may be.

(5) The Organisation of Working Time (Records) (Prescribed Form and Exemptions) Regulations 2001 (S.I. No. 473 of 2001) shall not apply to the employer of an employee to whom these Regulations apply.

## Other Amendments to the 1997 Act

**12.** [Amending sections 2, 8, 24, 26, 27, 33 and 37 of the 1997 Act].    BC.1212

## Amendment of the Safety, Health and Welfare at Work (Night Work and Shift Work) Regulations 2000

**13.** [...]    BC.1213

GENERAL NOTE

These Regulations, which came into operation on August 1, 2004, implement those provisions of Directive 2000/34/EC which bring the activities of doctors in training within the scope of Directive 93/104/EC (itself implemented by the Organisation of Working Time Act 1997). The Regulations prescribe maximum hours of work and minimum hours of rest for those persons engaged in the activities of doctors in training. Between August 1, 2004 and July 31, 2007, an employer cannot require such persons to work for more than 58 hours a week averaged over a 12 month reference period. Between August 1, 2007 and July 31, 2009 an employer cannot require such persons to work for more than 56 hours a week averaged over a 6 month reference period. A 48 hour average working week is due to be introduced from August 1, 2009. It should be noted that the Minister for Health and Children has not sought to apply a derogation whereby individual doctors in training could opt-out of the Directive's requirement.

The Regulations also amend certain provisions of the 1997 Act and the Safety, Health and Welfare at Work (Night-Work and Shift Work) Regulations 2000 (S.I. No. 11 of 2000) to apply them to the activities of doctors in training. It would appear that the postgraduate medical training bodies have agreed training principles which will be phased in and will underpin future rosters. These principles can be used by employers in the discussions on rosters at national and local level. These agreed training principles are available on the Department of Health and Children's website www.dohc.ie. According to a report in *The Irish Times* (September 10, 2004), the introduction of new rosters to allow for the required reduction in working hours will lead to major reductions in services for patients and increased waiting lists unless "significant resources" are provided by the Department.

Section 27 of the Medical Practitioners Act 1978 defines "registered medical practitioner" as follows: a person whose name is entered on the General Register of Medical Practitioners established under s.26 of the 1978 Act.

# ORGANISATION OF WORKING TIME (INCLUSION OF TRANSPORT ACTIVITIES) REGULATIONS 2004

## (S.I. No. 817 of 2004)

1. These Regulations may be cited as the Organisation of Working Time BC.1301 (Inclusion of Transport Activities) Regulations 2004 and shall come into effect on 1 January 2005.

2. In these Regulations— BC.1302

"the Act" means the Organisation of Working Time Act 1997 (No 20 of 1997);

"the Directive" means Council Directive 93/104/EC of 23 November 1993 as amended by Directive 2000/34/EC of the European Parliament and of the Council of 22 June 2000.

3. A word or expression which is used in these Regulations and which is also BC.1303 used in the Directive has, unless the context otherwise requires, the same meaning in these Regulations as it has in the Directive.

4. These Regulations shall not apply to: BC.1304

   (a) persons performing mobile road transport activities as defined in Directive 2003/15/EC of the European Parliament and of the Council of 11 March 2002, and

   (b) mobile staff in civil aviation as defined in the Annex to Council Directive 2000/79/EC of 27 November 2000.

5. The Organisation of Working Time (Exemption of Transport Activities) BC.1305 Regulations 1998 (S.I. No. 20 of 1998) are revoked.

6. Mobile Workers are exempted from the application of sections 11, 12, 13 BC.1306 and 16 of the Act.

7. If a mobile worker is not entitled, by reason of an exemption under Regula- BC.1307 tion 6, to the rest period and break referred to in sections 11, 12, and 13 of the Act, the employer shall ensure that such a mobile worker has available to himself or herself a rest period and break that, in all the circumstances, can reasonably be regarded as adequate rest.

8. [Amending S.I. No. 21 of 1998] BC.1308

9. These Regulations shall apply without prejudice to any legislation that offers BC.1309 a greater level of protection to workers.

GENERAL NOTE

These Regulations transpose the provisions of Council Directive Parliament and Council Directive BC.1310 2000/34/EC of June 22, 2000 concerning certain aspects of the organisation of working time in relation to transport workers other than; (a) workers performing mobile road transport activities as provided for in Directive 2002/15/EC, and (b) mobile staff in civil aviation as defined in the Annex to Directive 2000/79/EC of November 27, 2000.

The effect of the transposition of Directive 2000/34/EC is to apply the maximum average working week of 48 hours to mobile and non-mobile transport workers covered by that Directive.

In addition, these Regulations prescribe that persons employed in the activities specified in regs 6 and 8 of these Regulations shall be exempt from the application of ss.11, 12, and 13 of the Organisation of Working Time Act 1997, which deal respectively with daily rest, rests and intervals at work and weekly rest, subject to being granted adequate rest or equivalent compensatory rest. Such persons shall also be exempt from the application of s.16 of that Act which deals with nightly working hours.

# ORGANISATION OF WORKING TIME (INCLUSION OF OFFSHORE WORK) REGULATIONS 2004

## (S.I. No. 819 of 2004)

**BC.1401**   1. These Regulations may be cited as the Organisation of Working Time (Inclusion of Offshore Work) Regulations 2004 and shall come into effect on 1 January 2005.

**BC.1402**   2. In these Regulations—

"the Act" means the Organisation of Working Time Act 1997 (No. 20 of 1997);

"the Directive" means Council Directive 93/104/EC of 23 November 1993 as amended by Directive 2000/34/EC of the European Parliament and of the Council of 22 June 2000.

**BC.1403**   3. A word or expression which is used in these Regulations and which is also used in the Directive has, unless the context otherwise requires, the same meaning in these Regulations as it has in the Directive.

**BC.1404**   4. Subject to Regulation 5, Part II of the Act shall apply to employees engaged in offshore work.

**BC.1405**   5. [Amending S.I. No. 21 of 1998]

**BC.1406**   6. These Regulations shall apply without prejudice to any legislation that offers a greater level of protection to workers.

GENERAL NOTE

**BC.1407**   These Regulations transpose the provisions of Parliament and Council Directive 2000/34/EC of June 22, 2000 concerning certain aspects of the organisation of working time in relation to offshore work which means work performed mainly on, or from, offshore installations (including drilling rigs), directly or indirectly in connection with the exploration, extraction or exploitation of mineral resource, including hydrocarbons, and diving in connection with such activities, whether performed from an offshore installation or a vessel.

The effect of the transposition of Directive 2000/34/EC is to apply the maximum average working week of 48 hours to offshore workers covered by that Directive.

In addition, these Regulations prescribe that persons employed on offshore work shall be exempt from the application of ss.11, 12, 13 and 16 of the Organisation of Working Time Act 1997, which deal respectively with daily rest, rests and intervals at work, weekly rest and maximum nightly working hours subject to being granted adequate rest or equivalent compensatory rest.

# EUROPEAN COMMUNITIES (ORGANISATION OF WORKING TIME OF PERSONS PERFORMING MOBILE ROAD TRANSPORT ACTIVITIES) REGULATIONS 2005

## (S.I. No. 2 of 2005)

1. (1) These Regulations may be cited as the European Communities (Organi- **BC.1501** sation of Working Time of Persons Performing Mobile Road Transport Activities) Regulations 2005.

(2) These Regulations come into operation on 2 January 2006.

2. (1) In these Regulations— **BC.1502**

"the Council Regulation of 1985" means Council Regulation (EEC) No. 3820/85 of 20 December 19852 as amended;

"the Directive of 2002" means Directive 2002/15/EC of the European Parliament and of the Council of 11 March 2002;

"AETR" means the European agreement concerning the work of crews of vehicles engaged in international road transport done at Geneva on 1 July 1970 as amended;

"Authorised Officer" means a transport officer appointed by the Minister pursuant to section 15 of the Road Transport Act, 1986 (No. 16 of 1986), any officer of Customs and Excise or any member of the Garda Síochána;

"collective agreement" means an agreement by or on behalf of an employer on the one hand, and by or on behalf of a body or bodies representative of the employees to whom the agreement relates on the other hand.

"contract of employment" means—

(a) a contract of service or apprenticeship,

(b) any other contract whereby an individual agrees with another person, who is carrying on the business of an employment agency within the meaning of the Employment Agency Act 1971, and is acting in the course of that business, to do or perform personally any work of service for a third person (whether or not the third person is a party to the contract), and

whether the contract is express or implied and if express, whether it is oral or in writing;

"employee" means a person of any age, who has entered into or works under (or, where the employment has ceased, entered into or worked under) a contract of employment and references, in relation to an employer, to an employee shall be construed as references to an employee, employed by that employer.

"employer" means in relation to an employee, the person with whom the employee has entered into or for whom the employee works under (or, where the employment has ceased, entered into or worked under) a contract of employment, subject to the qualification that the person who under a contract of employment referred to in subparagraph (b) of the definition of "contract of employment" is liable to pay the wages of the individual concerned in respect of the work or service concerned shall be deemed to be the individual's employer;

"employment" in relation to a worker, means employment under his or her contract of employment, and "employed" shall be construed accordingly;

"employment regulation order" means an order under section 48 of the Industrial Relations Act, 1990 (No. 19 of 1990);

"Minister" means the Minister for Transport;

"mobile worker" shall mean any worker forming part of the travelling staff, including trainees and apprentices, who is in the service of an undertaking which operates transport services for passengers or goods by road for hire or reward or on its own account;

"motor vehicle" has the meaning assigned to it by Article 1(2)(a) of the Council Regulation of 1985;

"night time" means in respect of motor vehicles used for carrying goods the period between 00.00 hours and 04.00 hours and in respect of motor vehicles used for carrying passengers the period between 01.00 hours and 05.00 hours;

"night work" shall mean any work performed during night time;

"period of availability" means a period during which the mobile worker is not required to remain at his or her workstation, but is required to be available to answer any calls to start or resume driving or to carry out other work, including but not limited to periods during which the mobile worker is accompanying a vehicle being transported by a ferry or by a train as well as periods of waiting at frontiers and those due to traffic prohibitions;

"person performing mobile road transport activities" shall mean any mobile worker or self-employed driver who performs such activities;

"reference period" means the period for calculation of the average maximum weekly working time;

"registered employment agreement" has the meaning assigned to it by section 25 of the Industrial Relations Act 1946 (No. 26 of 1946);

"self-employed driver" means anyone whose main occupation is to transport passengers or goods by road for hire or reward within the meaning of Community legislation under cover of a Community licence or any other professional authorisation to carry out such transport, who is entitled to work for himself and who is not tied to an employer by a contract of employment or by any other type of working hierarchical relationship, who is free to organise the relevant working activities, whose income depends directly on the profits made and who has the freedom, individually or through a co-operation between self-employed drivers, to have commercial relations with several customers;

"week" means the period between 00.00 hours on Monday and 24.00 hours on Sunday;

"worker" means an individual who has entered into or works under (or, where employment has ceased, worked under)—

    (a)  a contract of employment, or

    (b)  any other contract whether express or implied and if express, whether it is oral or in writing, whereby the individual undertakes to do or perform personally any work or services for another party to the contract,

and any reference to a worker's contract shall be construed accordingly;

"working time" means the time from the beginning to the end of work during which the mobile worker is at his or her workstation, at the disposal of his or her employer and exercising his or her functions or activities, being:

    (a)  time devoted to all road transport activities, including, in particular—

        (i)   driving;

    (ii)   loading and unloading;

    (iii)  assisting passengers boarding and disembarking from the vehicle;

    (iv)  cleaning and technical maintenance;

    (v)   all other work intended to ensure the safety of the vehicle, its cargo and passengers or to fulfil the legal or regulatory obligations directly linked to the specific transport operation under way, including monitoring of loading and unloading and dealing with administrative formalities with police, customs, immigration officers and others; or

  (b)  time during which the mobile worker cannot dispose freely of his or her time and is required to be at his or her workstation, ready to take up normal work, with certain tasks associated with being on duty, in particular during periods awaiting loading or unloading where their foreseeable duration is not known in advance, that is to say either before departure or just before the actual start of the period in question, or under collective agreements or employment regulation orders or registered employment agreements;

"workstation" means:

  (a)  the location of the main place of business of the undertaking for which the person performing mobile transport activities carries out duties, together with its various subsidiary places of business, regardless of whether they are located in the same place as its head office or its main place of business;

  (b)  the vehicle which the person performing mobile road transport activities uses when he or she carries out duties; or

  (c)  any other place in which activities connected with transport are carried out.

(2) A word or expression that is used in these Regulations and is also used in the Directive of 2002 has, unless the contrary intention appears, the meaning in these Regulations that it has in the Directive of 2002.

(3) (a) A reference in these Regulations to a Regulation is to a Regulation of these Regulations, unless it is indicated that reference to some other Regulations is intended.

  (b)  A reference in these Regulations to a paragraph or subparagraph is to the paragraph or subparagraph of the provision in which the reference occurs, unless it is indicated that reference to some other provision is intended.

3. (1) These Regulations apply to mobile workers who are employed by, or who **BC.1503** do work for, undertakings established in a Member State of the European Union, and to whom paragraph (2) or (3) of this Regulation applies.

(2) This paragraph applies to mobile workers who in the course of that employment or work drive, or travel in, vehicles—

  (a)  which fall within the meaning of 'vehicles' in Article 1 of the Council Regulation of 1985;

(b) which are not referred to in Article 4 of the Council Regulation of 1985; and

(c) in respect of which exemption from provisions of the Council Regulation of 1985 has not been granted by the Minister.

(3) This paragraph applies to mobile workers, to whom paragraph (2) of this Regulation does not apply, who in the course of that employment or work drive, or travel in, vehicles—

(a) which fall within the meaning of a "vehicle" in Article 1 of the AETR; (b) which are not referred to in Article 2(2)(b) of the AETR; and (c) which are performing international transport.

(4) These Regulations do not apply to—

(a) self-employed drivers, or

(b) any worker who does work which is included in the calculation of working time—

(i) where the reference period is shorter than 26 weeks, on fewer than 11 days in a reference period applicable to that worker, or

(ii) in any other case on fewer than 16 days in a reference period applicable to that worker.

**BC.1504**     4. Nothing in these Regulations shall prejudice a provision or provisions of a more beneficial kind to the employee concerned which is or are contained in—

(a) a collective agreement,

(b) a registered employment agreement, or

(c) an employment regulation order.

**BC.1505**     5. (1) Subject to paragraph (2) of this Regulation, the working time, including overtime, of a mobile worker shall not exceed 60 hours in a week.

(2) In any reference period which is applicable to his or her case, a mobile worker's working time shall not exceed an average of 48 hours for each week.

(3) The reference periods which apply in the case of a mobile worker shall be—

(a) where a collective agreement or an employment regulation order or registered employment agreement provides for the application of this Regulation in relation to successive periods of 17 weeks, each such period,

(b) in a case where—

(i) there is no such provision, and

(ii) the employer gives written notice to the mobile worker in writing that he or she intends to apply this subparagraph,

any period of 17 weeks in the course of the worker's employment, or

(c) in any other case, the period ending at midnight between Sunday 30th April 2006 and Monday 1st May 2006 and thereafter, in each year, the successive periods beginning at midnight at the beginning of the Monday which falls on, or is the first Monday after, a date in column 1 below and ending at midnight at the beginning of the Monday which falls on, or is the first Monday after, the date on the same line in column 2 below.

(4) The reference period may be extended in relation to particular mobile

| Column 1 (beginning) | Column 2 (end) |
| --- | --- |
| 1st January | 1st May |
| 1st May | 1st September |
| 1st September | 1st January |

workers or a specified class or classes of mobile workers for objective or technical reasons or reasons concerning the organisation of work, by a collective agreement or a registered employment agreement or an employment regulation order, by the substitution for 17 weeks of a period not exceeding 26 weeks in the application of paragraphs (2) and (3)(a) of this Regulation.

(5) A mobile worker's average weekly working time during a reference period shall be determined according to the formula—

$$(A + B) \div C$$

where—

A is the aggregate number of hours comprised in the mobile worker's working time during the course of the reference period;

B is the number of excluded hours during the reference period; and

C is the number of weeks in the reference period.

(6) In paragraph (5) of this Regulation, "excluded hours" means hours comprised in—

(a) any period of annual leave taken by the mobile worker in accordance with the Act of 1997 (save so much of it as exceeds the minimum period of annual leave required by the Act of 1997 to be granted to the mobile worker);

(b) any absences from work by the mobile worker concerned authorised under the Maternity Protection Act 1994 (No. 34 of 1994) or the Adoptive Leave Act 1995 (No. 2 of 1995) or the Parental Leave Act 1998 (No. 30 of 1998) or the Carer's Leave Act 2001 (No. 19 of 2001); and

(c) any period of sick leave taken by the mobile worker.

(7) For the purposes of paragraph (5) of this Regulation, the number of hours in a whole day shall be eight and the number of hours in a whole week shall be forty-eight. (8) An employer shall ensure that the limits specified above are complied with in the case of each mobile worker employed by him.

6. The times of breaks, rests and periods of availability shall not be included in **BC.1506** the calculation of working time.

7. (1) A period shall not be treated as a period of availability unless the mobile **BC.1507** worker knows before the start of the relevant period about that period of availability and its reasonably foreseeable duration.

(2) The time spent by a mobile worker, who is working as part of a team, travelling in, but not driving, a moving vehicle as part of that team shall be a period of availability for that mobile worker.

(3) Subject to paragraph (4) of this Regulation a period of availability shall not include a period of rest or a break.

(4) A period of availability may include a break taken by a mobile worker during waiting time or time which is not devoted to driving by the mobile worker and is spent in a moving vehicle, a ferry or a train.

**BC.1508**   8. (1) No mobile worker shall work for more than six hours without a break.

(2) Where a mobile worker's working time exceeds six hours but does not exceed nine hours, the worker shall be entitled to a break lasting at least 30 minutes and interrupting that time.

(3) Where a mobile worker's working time exceeds nine hours, the worker shall be entitled to a break lasting at least 45 minutes and interrupting that period.

(4) Each break may be made up of separate periods of not less than 15 minutes each.

(5) An employer shall ensure that this Regulation is complied with in the case of each mobile worker employed by him.

**BC.1509**   9. (1) In the application of these Regulations, the provisions of the Council Regulation of 1985 relating to daily and weekly rest shall apply to the driver of the vehicle or a person carried in the vehicle in order to be available for driving.

(2) An employer shall ensure that this Regulation is complied with.

**BC.1510**   10. (1) The working time of a mobile worker, who performs night work in any period of 24 hours, shall not exceed 10 hours during that period.

(2) The period of 10 hours may be extended in relation to particular mobile workers or a specified class or classes of mobile workers for objective or technical reasons or reasons concerning the organisation of work, by a collective agreement or an employment regulation order or a registered employment agreement.

(3) Compensation for night work shall not be given to a mobile worker in any manner which is liable to endanger road safety.

(4) An employer shall ensure that the limit specified in paragraph (1) of this Regulation, or extended in accordance with paragraph (2) of this Regulation, is complied with in the case of each mobile worker employed by him.

**BC.1511**   11. An employer of mobile workers shall notify each worker of the provisions of these Regulations and the provisions of any collective agreement or employment regulation order or registered employment agreement which is capable of application to that worker.

**BC.1512**   12. An employer of a mobile worker shall:

    (a) request from each mobile worker details of any time worked by that worker for another employer;

    (b) include time worked for another employer in the calculation of the mobile worker's working time;

    (c) keep records which are adequate to show whether the requirements of these Regulations are being complied with in the case of each mobile worker employed by him to whom they apply;

    (d) retain such records for at least two years after the end of the period covered by those records;

    (e) provide, at the request of a mobile worker, a copy of the record of hours worked by that worker;

(f) provide to an authorised officer copies of such records relating to mobile workers as the officer may require;

(g) provide to a mobile worker or authorised officer copies of such documentary evidence in the employer's possession as may be requested by the worker or officer in relation to records provided to him in accordance with paragraph (e) or (f) of this Regulation.

13. A mobile worker shall, at the request of his or her employer under Regula- **BC.1513** tion 12(a), notify his or her employer in writing of time worked by the worker for another employer for inclusion in the calculation of the mobile worker's working time.

14. (1) This Regulation applies in any case where an individual ("the agency **BC.1514** worker") is supplied by a person ("the agent") to do the work of a mobile worker for another ("the principal") under a contract or other arrangements made between the agent and the principal but—

(a) is not, as respects that work, a worker, because of the absence of a worker's contract between the individual and the agent or the principal, and

(b) is not a party to a contract under which he or she undertakes to do the work for another party to the contract whose status is, by virtue of the contract, that of a client or customer or any profession or business undertaking carried on by the individual.

(2) In a case where this Regulation applies, the other provisions of these Regulations shall have effect as if there were a contract for the doing of the work by the agency worker made between the agency worker and—

(a) whichever of the agent and the principal is responsible for paying the agency worker in respect of the work, or

(b) if neither the agent nor the principal is so responsible, whichever of them pays the agency worker in respect of the work,

as if that person were the agency worker's employer.

15. (1) This Regulation applies in any case where an individual, who is not a **BC.1515** self-employed driver, drives a vehicle described in Regulation 3(2) or Regulation 3(3) for the purpose of a trade or business carried on by him.

(2) Where this Regulation applies—

(a) subject to subparagraph (b) of this paragraph, the other provisions of these Regulations shall have effect as if—

(i) the individual were a mobile worker, and

(ii) the individual were the employer of that mobile worker;

(b) Regulations 10, 11(a) and (e) and 12 shall not have effect.

(3) This Regulation shall not apply in any case where Regulation 14 applies.

16. These Regulations shall apply without prejudice to any legislation that **BC.1516** offers a greater level of protection to workers.

17. An authorised officer appointed appointed by the Minister pursuant to **BC.1517** section 15 of the Road Transport Act, 1986 (No. 16 of 1986) is an authorised officer for the purposes of enforcing these Regulations and may exercise any of the powers conferred on an authorised officer under section 16 of the said Act for the purposes of enforcing these Regulations.

**BC.1518**    18. (1) Any person who fails to comply with these Regulations shall be guilty of an offence.

(2) A person guilty of an offence under these Regulations shall be liable on summary conviction to a fine not exceeding €5,000 or imprisonment for a term not exceeding 6 months or both.

(3) Where an offence under these Regulations is committed by a body corporate and is proved to have been committed with the consent or connivance of, or to be attributable to any neglect on the part of, a person being a director, manager, secretary or other officer of that body corporate, or a person who was purporting to act in that capacity, that person shall also be guilty of an offence and be liable to be proceeded against and punished as if he or she were guilty of the first-mentioned offence.

(4) If the contravention in respect of which a person is convicted of an offence under these Regulations is continued after the conviction, the person shall be guilty of a further offence on every day on which the contravention continues and for each such offence the person shall be liable, on summary conviction, to a fine not exceeding €1,000.

(5) Proceedings for an offence under these Regulations including a further offence under paragraph (4) of this Regulation may be brought and prosecuted by the Minister.

(6) Notwithstanding section 10(4) of the Petty Sessions (Ireland) Act, 1851, proceedings for an offence under these Regulations may be instituted within 24 months from the date of the offence.

GENERAL NOTE

**BC.1519**    These regulations transpose the provisions of Directive 2002/15/EC of the European Parliament and of the Council of 11 March 2002 on the organisation of the working time of persons performing mobile road transport activities.

The effect of the transposition of Directive 2002/15/EC is to apply the maximum average working week of 48 hours to mobile road transport workers covered by that Directive. The Regulations also prescribe that the working time of such mobile road transport workers must not exceed 60 hours in any single week and contain provisions concerning minimum breaks and the amount of night work that can be performed.

# MATERNITY PROTECTION ACT 1994

## (1994 No. 34)

### ARRANGEMENT OF SECTIONS

### PART I

### PART II

### PART III

#### LEAVE TO PROTECT HEALTH AND SAFETY OF PREGNANT EMPLOYEES, ETC.

### PART IV

#### EMPLOYMENT PROTECTION

C–51

25. Provisions regarding periods of probation, training and apprenticeship.
26. General right to return to work on expiry of protective leave.
27. Right to suitable alternative work in certain circumstances on return to work.
28. Notification of intention to return to work.
29. Postponement of return to work.

PART V

RESOLUTION OF DISPUTES

30. Reference of disputes to which Part V applies.
31. Procedure for referral of disputes to rights commissioner.
32. Redress.
33. Appeal from decision of rights commissioner.
33A Burden of proof.
34. Appeal to High Court on point of law.
35. Service of documents.
36. Provisions relating to winding up and bankruptcy.
37. Enforcement of decisions and determinations.

PART VI

AMENDMENTS AND APPLICATION OF OTHER ENACTMENTS

38. Amendments relating to unfair dismissal.
39. Amendment of Schedule 3 to Redundancy Payments Act, 1967.
40. Provisions applying where employee not permitted to return to work.
41. Protection of employee's rights on insolvency of employer.

**CB.101** An Act to implement Council Directive 92/85/EEC of 19 October 1992 on the introduction of measures to encourage improvements in the safety and health at work of pregnant workers and workers who have recently given birth or are breastfeeding, to re-enact with amendments the provisions of the Maternity Protection of Employees Acts, 1981 and 1991, to entitle a male employee to leave in certain cases where the mother of his child dies, to extend as a consequence of the above-mentioned provisions the protection against unfair dismissals conferred by the Unfair Dismissals Act, 1977, and to provide for related matters.

[27th December, 1994]

INTRODUCTION AND GENERAL NOTE

**CB.102** It has long been recognised that, to ensure full implementation of the equality principle in the employment field, measures must be developed which enable women, and indeed men, to reconcile occupational and family obligations. Macfarlane put it well when she wrote, in (1983) 5 DULJ (N.S.) at p. 187, that it was "futile to make laws to ensure the equal treatment of women in all forms of employment if, as soon as they might choose to exercise their option of motherhood, their rights evaporate". Consequently in 1981 the Maternity Protection of Employees Act was enacted which provided for a minimum period of fourteen weeks maternity leave, with an optional four weeks additional leave, as well as important safeguards for employment rights during such leave. These rights could only be exercised by the mother but, in Case 184/83, *Hofmann v Barmer Ersatzkasse* [1984] E.C.R. 3047, the Court of Justice of the European Communities held that maternity leave fell within the scope of Article 2(3) of Council Directive 76/207/EEC: [1976] O.J. L39/40, which leaves Member States with a discretion as to the social measures which they adopt in order to guarantee the protection of women in connection with pregnancy and maternity-and that such leave could legitimately be reserved to the mother without violating the principle of equal treatment laid down in the Directive. In Case C–411/96, *Boyle v Equal Opportunities Commission* [1998] E.C.R. 1-6401, the

Court of Justice emphasised that maternity leave was intended, first, to protect a woman's biological condition during and after pregnancy and, secondly, to protect the special relationship between a woman and a child over the period which followed pregnancy and childbirth.

The leave was unpaid but qualifying employees were entitled to maternity benefit under the social **CB.103** welfare legislation. In Case C–342/93, *Gillespie v Northern Health and Social Services Board* [1996] E.C.R. 1-475, the Court of Justice ruled that the principle of equal pay, laid down in Article 119 of the EEC Treaty and set out in detail in Council Directive 75/117/EEC: [1975] O.J. L45/19, neither required that women continue to receive full pay during maternity leave nor laid down specific criteria for determining the amount of benefit payable to them during that period, provided that the amount was not set so low as to jeopardise the purpose of maternity leave. It should be noted, however, that Council Directive 92/85/EEC: [1992] O.J. L348/1 (the Pregnant Workers Directive), which provides for payment of an "adequate" allowance to workers on maternity leave, was not in force at the relevant time.

This Act provides for the implementation of the employment rights provisions in the Pregnant Workers Directive. In Case C–438/99, *Melgar v Ayuntamiento de los Barros [2001]* I.R.L.R. 848, the Court of Justice ruled that Article 10 of the Directive was sufficiently clear, precise and unconditional to be directly effective. This Directive also involved significant social welfare and health and safety measures implemented, respectively, by the European Communities (Social Welfare) Regulations 1995 (S.I. No. 25 of 1995) and now the Safety, Health and Welfare at Work (Pregnant Employees etc.) Regulations (S.I. No. 218 of 2000). This Act, consequently, repeals and re-enacts with amendments the 1981 Act (as amended by the Worker Protection (Regular Part-Time Employees) Act 1991). The Minister for Equality and Law Reform (446 *Dáil Debates* Col. 889) thought it would be "more helpful to employers and employees" to proceed this way rather than to draw up legislation which merely amended the 1981 Act.

The existing minimum 14 week period of maternity leave (and the optional four weeks additional **CB.104** leave) were preserved but were extended to 18 and eight weeks respectively with effect from February 8, 2001: see Maternity Protection Act 1994 (Extension of Periods of Leave) Order 2001 (S.I. No. 29 of 2001). That Order has now been revoked and its provisions have been incorporated into ss.13 and 14 of the Act by virtue of ss.4 and 5 of the Maternity Protection (Amendment) Act 2004. Those periods have now been extended with effect from March 1, 2006 to 22 and 12 weeks (rising to 26 and 16 weeks with effect from March 1, 2007): see Maternity Protection Act 1994 (Extension of Periods of Leave) Order 2006 (S.I. 51 of 2006). Certain difficulties had arisen, however, with the complex procedural requirements for the exercise, in particular, of the right to return to work (see *Ivory v Skiline Ltd* [1988] I.R. 399) and the opportunity was taken to improve this aspect of the legislation. The Act, in line with the requirements of the Directive, introduced a number of important new provisions particularly in regard to the granting of "health and safety" leave (see Part III of the Act) and various important amendments were made to the Unfair Dismissals legislation. The Act has now been extensively amended by the Maternity Protection (Amendment) Act 2004, the purpose of which was to give effect to the recommendations made by the Working Group on the Review and Improvement of the Maternity Protection Legislation which was set up in accordance with commitments in the national social partnership agreement known as the *Programme for Prosperity and Fairness.*

CITATION

See section 1(1). The collective citation is now the Maternity Protection Acts 1994 and 2004.     **CB.105**

COMMENCEMENT

The Act came into operation on January 30, 1995: see S.I. No. 16 of 1995. The amendments made **CB.106** by the Maternity Protection (Amendment) Act 2004 came into operation on October 18, 2004: see S.I. No. 652 of 2004.

STATUTORY INSTRUMENTS

Maternity Protection Act 1994 (Commencement) Order 1995 (S.I. No. 16 of 1995).     **CB.107**

Maternity Protection (Disputes and Appeals) Regulations 1995 (S.I. No. 17 of 1995).

Maternity Protection (Time off for Ante-Natal and Post-Natal Care) Regulations 1995 (S.I. No. 18 of 1995).

Maternity Protection (Health and Safety Leave Certification) Regulations 1995 (S.I. No. 19 of 1995).

Maternity Protection (Health and Safety Leave Remuneration) Regulations 1995 (S.I. No. 20 of 1995).

Maternity Protection (Maximum Compensation) Regulations 1999 (S.I. No. 134 of 1999).

Maternity Protection (Time Off for Ante-Natal Classes) Regulations 2004 (S.I. No. 653 of 2004).

C–53

Maternity Protection (Protection of Mothers who are Breastfeeding) Regulations 2004 (S.I. No. 654 of 2004).

Maternity Protection (Postponement of Leave) Regulations 2004 (S.I. No. 655 of 2004).

Maternity Protection Act 1994 (Extension of Periods of Leave) Order 2006 (S.I. No. 51 of 2006).

PARLIAMENTARY DEBATES

**CB.108**    446 *Dáil Debates* Cols 888–893 (Second Stage)

446 *Dáil Debates* Cols 1032–1072 (Second Stage resumed)

446 *Dáil Debates* Cols 1198–1219 (Second Stage resumed)

Select Committee on Social Affairs S3 No. 1 Cols 3–13 (Committee Stage)

447 *Dáil Debates* Cols 628–629 (Report and Final Stages)

141 *Seanad Debates* Cols 1243–1266 (Second Stage)

141 *Seanad Debates* Cols 1266–1271 (Committee and Final Stages)

**CB.109**    Be it enacted by the Oireachtas as follows:

PART I

PRELIMINARY AND GENERAL

## Short title and commencement

**CB.110**    **1.**—(1) This Act may be cited as the Maternity Protection Act, 1994.

(2) This Act shall come into operation on such day as may be fixed by order made by the Minister, and different days may be so fixed for different provisions and for different purposes.

GENERAL NOTE

**CB.111**    The Act came into operation on January 30, 1995: Maternity Protection Act 1994 (Commencement) Order 1995 (S.I. No. 16 of 1995). The collective citation is now the Maternity Protection Acts 1994 and 2004: see s.27(3) of the Maternity Protection (Amendment) Act 2004.

## Interpretation

**CB.112**    **2.**—(1) In this Act—

"the 1977 Act" means the Unfair Dismissals Act, 1977;

"the 1981 Act" means the Maternity Protection of Employees Act, 1981;

"the 1989 Act" means the Safety, Health and Welfare at Work Act, 1989;

"the 1992 Directive" means Council Directive 92/85/EEC of 19 October 1992 on the introduction of measures to encourage improvements in the safety and health at work of pregnant workers and workers who have recently given birth or are breastfeeding;

"additional maternity leave" has the meaning assigned by section 14;

"associated employer" has the meaning assigned by section 27(3);

"the Authority" means the [Health and Safety Authority];

"confinement" and "the date of confinement" have the meanings respectively assigned to them by [section 51 of the Social Welfare (Consolidation) Act 2005];

"contract of employment" means, subject to subsection (2)—

(a)  a contract of service or apprenticeship, or

"maternity leave" has the meaning assigned by section 8;

"the Minister" means the Minister for [Justice, Equality and Law Reform];

"pregnant employee" means an employee who is pregnant and who has informed her employer of her condition;

"successor" has the meaning assigned by section 26(1);

"the Tribunal" means the Employment Appeals Tribunal.

(2) For the purposes of this Act—

(a) a person holding office under, or in the service of, the State (including a member of the Garda Síochána or the Defence Forces) or otherwise as a civil servant, within the meaning of the Civil Service Regulation Act, 1956, shall be deemed to be an employee employed by the State or Government, as the case may be, under a contract of service;

(b) an officer or servant of a local authority for the purposes of the Local Government Act, 1941, a harbour authority, [the Health Service Executive] or a vocational education committee shall be deemed to be an employee employed by the authority, [the Executive] or committee, as the case may be, under a contract of service; and

(c) in relation to an employee whose contract of employment falls (or, where the employment has ceased, fell) within paragraph (b) of the definition of "contract of employment" in subsection (1), the person who is liable to pay the employee's wages shall be deemed to be the employer.

(3) Subject to subsections (1) and (2), expressions used in this Act have the same meaning as in the 1992 Directive.

(4) In this Act, a reference to a Part or section is to a Part or section of this Act, unless it is indicated that reference to some other enactment is intended.

(5) In this Act a reference to a subsection or paragraph is to the subsection or paragraph of the provision in which the reference occurs, unless it is indicated that reference to some other provision is intended.

(6) In this Act a reference to an enactment includes a reference to that enactment as amended by any other enactment, including this Act.

GENERAL NOTE

"the 1977 Act": this Act was amended by the Unfair Dismissals (Amendment) Act 1993.  **CB.113**

"the 1989 Act": this Act was repealed by the Safety, Health and Welfare at Work Act 2005.

"the Authority": this definition was amended by virtue of s.32(1)(a) of the Safety, Health and Welfare at Work Act 2005.

"confinement" and "date of confinement": s.51(1)(a) of the 2005 Act defines "confinement" as "labour resulting in the issue of a living child, or labour after 24 weeks of pregnancy resulting in the issue of a child whether alive or dead". Section 51(1)(b) goes on to provide that references to the "date of confinement" should be taken as referring, "where labour begun on one day results in the issue of a child on another day, to the date of the issue of the child or, if a woman is confined with twins or a greater number of children, to the date of the issue of the last child."

"contract of employment": as to whether a person is employed under a contract of service see *Henry Denny & Sons (Ireland) Ltd v Minister for Social Welfare* [1998] 1 I.R. 34. The inclusion of a specific reference to persons employed through employment agencies is similar to the provisions of s.13 of the Unfair Dismissals (Amendment) Act 1993, s.1(1) of the Terms of Employment (Information) Act 1994 and s.2(1) of the Organisation of Working Time Act 1997. But note the decision of the Labour Court in *Rooney v Diageo Global Supply* [2004] E.L.R. 133 that an agency supplied worker was employed by the client under a contract of employment.

"the Minister": this definition was amended by virtue of the Equality and Law Reform (Transfer of Departmental Administrative and Ministerial Functions) Order 1997 (S.I. No. 297

of 1997) and the Justice (Alteration of Name of Department and Title of Minister) Order 1997 (S.I. No. 298 of 1997).

## Orders and regulations

**CB.114**   **3.** —(1) The Minister may, in relation to any provision of this Act relating to notification (or confirmation of notification), by order vary any such provision.

(2) An order under this Act may contain such consequential, supplementary and ancillary provisions, including any provisions modifying any provision of this Act, as the Minister considers necessary or expedient.

(3) Any power under this Act to make an order includes power to amend or revoke an order made in the exercise of that power.

(4) Where an order is proposed to be made under this Act, other than an order under section 1, a draft of the order shall be laid before both Houses of the Oireachtas, and the order shall not be made until a resolution approving the draft has been passed by each such House.

(5) Every regulation made under this Act shall be laid before each House of the Oireachtas as soon as practicable after it is made and, if a resolution annulling the regulation is passed by either such House within the next twenty-one days on which the House has sat after the regulation is laid before it, the regulation shall be annulled accordingly, but without prejudice to the validity of anything previously done under the regulation.

## Voidance or modification of certain provisions in agreements

**CB.115**   **4.** —(1) A provision in any agreement shall be void in so far as it purports to exclude or limit the application of any provision of this Act or is inconsistent with any provision of this Act.

(2) A provision in any agreement which is or becomes less favourable in relation to an employee than a similar or corresponding entitlement conferred on the employee by this Act shall be deemed to be so modified as to be not less favourable.

(3) Nothing in this Act shall be construed as prohibiting any agreement from containing any provision more favourable to an employee than any provision in Parts II to VI.

(4) References in this section to an agreement are to any agreement, whether a contract of employment or not, and whether made before or after the commencement of this Act.

## Expenses

**CB.116**   **5.** Any expenses incurred by the Minister or the Minister for [Enterprise, Trade and Employment] in the administration of this Act shall, to such extent as may be sanctioned by the Minister for Finance, be paid out of moneys provided by the Oireachtas.

GENERAL NOTE

**CB.117**   The title of Minister for Enterprise and Employment was amended by virtue of the Enterprise and Employment (Alteration of Name of Department and Title of Minister) Order 1997 (S.I. No. 305 of 1997).

## Repeal of 1981 Act, as amended

**CB.118**   **6.** —(1)The Maternity Protection of Employees Acts, 1981 and 1991 (which are replaced by the provisions of this Act) are hereby repealed.

C–56

(2) The repeal by this Act of the Maternity Protection of Employees Acts, 1981 and 1991 does not affect the construction of any reference in any other Act which defines "employee" or "employer" or any other expression by reference to those Acts (or the 1981 Act alone).

(3) [*Amending the Social Welfare (Consolidation) Act 1993*]

(4) In so far as any order or regulation made, notification given or other thing done under an enactment repealed by this Act could have been made, given or done under a corresponding provision of this Act, it shall have effect as if so made, given or done.

(5) Where a period of time specified in any enactment repealed by this Act is current at the commencement of this Act, this Act shall have effect as if the corresponding provision thereof had been in force when that period began to run.

PART II

MATERNITY LEAVE

## Interpretation of Part II

**7.**—(1) In this Part "the minimum period of maternity leave" has the meaning assigned by section 8.  CB.119

(2) References in this Part to an employee are references to a female employee only.

(3) References in this Part to a pregnant employee include, as respects any time before the expiry of her maternity leave, an employee who was pregnant immediately before that leave began.

## Entitlement to maternity leave

**8.**—[(1) Subject to this Part, a pregnant employee shall be entitled to leave, to  CB.120 be known (and referred to in this Act) as "maternity leave", from her employment for a period (in this Part referred to as "the minimum period of maternity leave") of not less than—

(a)  [22] consecutive weeks, or

(b)  [22] weeks part of which is postponed in accordance with sections 14B,

as may be appropriate.

(2) The Minister may by order, made with the consent of the Minister for Social and Family Affairs and the consent of the Minister for Finance, amend subsection (1) and section 13(2) so as to extend the period mentioned in each of those subsections.]

GENERAL NOTE

Article 8 of the Pregnant Workers Directive provides in paragraph (1) that Member States are to  CB.121 take the necessary measures to ensure that workers are entitled to a "continuous period of maternity leave of at least 14 weeks allocated before and/or after confinement in accordance with national legislation and/or practice".

This section was substituted by virtue of s.2 of the Maternity Protection (Amendment) Act 2004 and incorporates the extension of maternity leave from 14 to 18 weeks effected by the Maternity Protection Act 1994 (Extension of Periods of Leave) Order 2001 (S.I. No. 29 of 2001), which Order is revoked by s.26 of the 2004 Act. The extension of maternity leave from 18 to 22 weeks was effected by the Maternity Protection Act 1994 (Extension of Periods of Leave) Order 2006 (S.I. No. 51 of 2006).

C–56/1

## Notification to employer

CB.122    **9.**—(1) Entitlement to the minimum period of maternity leave shall be subject to a pregnant employee—

(a) having, as soon as reasonably practicable but not later than four weeks before the commencement of maternity leave, notified in writing her employer (or caused her employer to be so notified) of her intention to take maternity leave; and

(b) having, at the time of the notification, given to her employer or produced for her employer's inspection a medical or other appropriate certificate confirming the pregnancy and specifying the expected week of confinement.

(2) A notification under this section may be revoked by a further notification in writing by the employee concerned to her employer.

GENERAL NOTE

CB.123    The Employment Appeals Tribunal consistently took the view that the statutory entitlement to take maternity leave, conferred by the very similarly worded s.9 of the 1981 Act, was dependent on strict compliance with its provisions and that failure to comply could not be excused by reason of the employee's ignorance of the statutory requirements. See, for example, *O'Flaherty v Coughlan* P8/1983.

## Allocation of minimum period of maternity leave

CB.124    **10.**—(1) Subject to subsection (2) and sections 11 to 13, the minimum period of maternity leave shall commence on such day as the employee selects, being not later than [four] weeks before the end of the expected week of confinement, and shall end on such day as she selects, being not earlier than [four] weeks after the end of the expected week of confinement.

(2) Where an employee is employed under a contract for a fixed term and that term expires before the day which, apart from this subsection, would be the last day of her maternity leave, then—

(a) notwithstanding any other provision in this Part, the last day of her maternity leave shall be the day on which the term expires; and

(b) nothing in this Part shall affect the termination of the employee's contract of employment on that day.

GENERAL NOTE

CB.125    Article 8(2) of the Pregnant Workers Directive provides that the maternity leave stipulated in paragraph (1) "must include compulsory maternity leave of at least two weeks allocated before and/or after confinement in accordance with national legislation and/or practice". The substitution in subs.(1) of two weeks for four weeks in respect of the compulsory period of pre-confinement maternity leave was effected by virtue of s.3 of the Maternity Protection (Amendment) Act 2004.

## Variation in allocation of minimum period of maternity leave

CB.126    **11.**—(1) Where it is certified by a registered medical practitioner or otherwise to the satisfaction of the Minister and the Minister for [Social and Family Affairs] that, for an employee specified in the certificate, the minimum period of maternity leave should for a medical reason so specified commence on a date so specified, and the certificate is produced for inspection by the employer concerned within such period as may be prescribed by regulations made by the Minister under this section, the minimum period of maternity leave for that employee shall commence on the date so specified.

(2) Where a certificate under this section is issued and the requirement in subsection (1) relating to the production of the certificate for the employer's inspection is complied with, the employee specified in the certificate—

    (a)    shall be taken to have informed her employer of her pregnancy (if she had not previously done so); and

    (b)    shall be deemed to have complied also with section 9(1)(a).

GENERAL NOTE

The title of the Minister for Social Welfare was amended by virtue of the Social Welfare (Alteration **CB.127** of Name of Department and Title of Minister) Order 1997 (S.I. No. 307 of 1997) and the Social, Community and Family Affairs (Alteration of Name of Department and Title of Minister) Order 2002 (S.I. No. 310 of 2002).

## Extension of maternity leave

**12.**—(1) Where the date of confinement of a pregnant employee occurs in a **CB.128** week after the expected week of confinement, the minimum period of maternity leave shall be extended by such number of consecutive weeks (subject to a maximum of four consecutive weeks) after the week in which the date of confinement occurs as ensures compliance with section 10.

(2) Where the minimum period of maternity leave is proposed to be extended under this section, the employee concerned shall—

    (a)    as soon as practicable after the proposal for such extension, notify in writing her employer (or cause her employer to be so notified) of the proposed extension; and

    (b)    as soon as practicable after the date of confinement, confirm in writing to her employer the notification under paragraph (a) and specify the duration of the extension.

GENERAL NOTE

If the baby's late birth means that an employee has less than four weeks' leave remaining after the **CB.129** week in which her baby was born, this section provides that she may extend her maternity leave to ensure that she has a full four weeks off following the week of the birth.

## Commencement of maternity leave (early confinement)

**13.**—(1) Where, in relation to a pregnant employee, the date of confinement **CB.130** occurs in a week that is four weeks or more before the expected week of confinement, the employee shall, where the circumstances so require, be deemed to have complied with section 9(1)(a) if the notification required by that section is given in the period of 14 days commencing on the date of confinement.

(2) [Notwithstanding section 10(1), but subject to regulations under section 11, the minimum period of maternity leave for an employee referred to in subsection (1) shall be a period of not less than—

    (a)    [22] consecutive weeks, or

    (b)    [22] weeks part of which is postponed in accordance with section 14B,

as may be appropriate, commencing on whichever of the following is the earlier—

    (i)    the first day of maternity leave taken in accordance with section 10, or

    (ii)    the date of confinement.]

GENERAL NOTE
**CB.131**  If an employee's baby is born four weeks or more earlier than expected and before she has gone on maternity leave, her employer must be notified in writing within fourteen days of the birth. The employee will then be entitled to the full period of maternity leave from the date of the birth. Subsection (2) was substituted by virtue of s.4 of the Maternity Protection (Amendment) Act 2004 and subsequently amended by virtue of Art.5 of the Maternity Protection Act 1994 (Extension of Periods of Leave) Order 2006 (S.I. No. 51 of 2006).

## Entitlement to additional maternity leave

**CB.132**   **14.**—[(1) An employee who has taken maternity leave shall, if she so wishes, be entitled in accordance with this section to further leave from her employment, to be known (and referred to in this Act) as "additional maternity leave", for a maximum period of—

   (a)   [12] consecutive weeks commencing immediately after the end of her maternity leave, or

   (b)   [12] weeks, all or part of which is postponed in accordance with section 14B, commencing either in accordance with that section or immediately after the end of her maternity leave,

as may be appropriate.]

(2) An employee shall be entitled to additional maternity leave, whether or not the minimum period of maternity leave has been extended under section 12.

(3) [Subject to section 14B, entitlement to additional maternity leave] shall be subject to an employee having notified in writing her employer (or caused her employer to be so notified) in accordance with subsection (4) of her intention to take such leave.

(4) Notification under subsection (3) shall be given either at the same time as the relevant notification under section 9 or not later than four weeks before the date which would have been the employee's expected date of return to work under Part IV if she had not taken the additional maternity leave.

(5) A notification under this section may be revoked by a further notification in writing given by or on behalf of the employee concerned to her employer not later than four weeks before the date which would have been her expected date of return to work under Part IV if she had not taken the additional maternity leave.

(6) [The Minister may by order amend subsection (1) so as to extend the period mentioned in that subsection.]

GENERAL NOTE
**CB.133**   The amendments to subss.(1), (3) and (6) were effected by virtue of s.5 of the Maternity Protection (Amendment) Act 2004. The extension of additional maternity leave from eight to 12 weeks was effected by the Maternity Protection Act 1994 (Extension of Periods of Leave) Order 2006 (S.I. No. 51 of 2006).

## [Termination of additional maternity leave in event of sickness of mother

**CB.133A**   **14A.**—(1) If, at any time—

   (a)   during the last 4 weeks of maternity leave whether or not part of such leave is postponed under section 14B and where, in accordance with section 14(4), an employee has, or is deemed under section 14B(3) to have, notified her employer, or caused her employer to be notified, of her intention to take additional maternity leave, or

(b)    during the additional maternity leave whether or not such leave or part of it is postponed under section 14B,

an employee who is sick wishes to terminate the additional maternity leave, she may request in writing (or cause a written request to be submitted to) her employer to terminate the additional maternity leave.

(2) An employer who receives a request under subsection (1) may agree to terminate the additional maternity leave of the employee concerned and, if the employer does so, the additional maternity leave shall terminate on a date agreed by the employee and the employer that is not earlier than the date of the commencement of the employee's sickness and not later than the date on which the additional maternity leave would have ended in accordance with the notification given by the employee to the employer under section 14(4) or 14B(8), as the case may be.

(3) An employer who receives a request under subsection (1) shall notify

the employee concerned in writing of the employer's decision in relation to the request as soon as reasonably practicable following the receipt of it.

(4) Where the additional maternity leave of an employee is terminated under this section—

(a)     the absence from work of the employee due to sickness following such termination shall be treated in the same manner as any absence from work of the employee due to sickness, and

(b)     the employee shall not be entitled to the additional maternity leave or the part of it not taken by her at the date of such termination.

GENERAL NOTE

This section was inserted by virtue of s.6 of the Maternity Protection (Amendment) Act 2004 and **CB.133B** provides that, in the event of the employee's sickness, the employer may agree to terminate the period of additional maternity leave. Once terminated, however, the employee will not be entitled to take the remainder of the leave at a later date. It would appear that there is no right of appeal against an employer's refusal to agree to terminate the period of additional maternity leave, although any such refusal would give rise to a "trade dispute" to enable investigation by a Rights Commissioner or the Labour Court under the Industrial Relations Act 1969.

## Postponement of maternity leave or additional maternity leave in event of hospitalisation

**14B.**—(1) Subject to subsection (2), an employee who is on maternity leave or **CB.133C** is entitled to, or is on, additional maternity leave may, if the child in connection with whose birth she is on, or is entitled to, that leave (in this section referred to as "the child") is hospitalised, request in writing (or cause a written request to be submitted to) her employer to postpone—

(a)     part of the maternity leave,

(b)     part of the maternity leave and the additional maternity leave, or

(c)     the additional maternity leave or part of it,

as may be appropriate, in accordance with this section.

(2) An employee may make a request under paragraph (a) or (b) of subsection (1) to postpone part of her maternity leave with effect from a date she selects only if the period of maternity leave taken by her on that date is not less than 14 weeks and not less than 4 of those weeks are after the end of the week of confinement.

(3) Notwithstanding the fact that an employee who is on maternity leave has not in accordance with section 14(4) notified her employer in writing (or caused her employer to be so notified) of her intention to take additional maternity leave, she shall be deemed, for the purposes of making a request under paragraph (b) or (c) of subsection (1), to have complied with section 14(4).

(4) An employer who receives a request under subsection (1) may agree to postpone the leave concerned and, if the employer does so—

(a)     the employee concerned shall return to work on a date agreed by her and the employer that is not later than the date on which the leave concerned is due to end in accordance with the notification given, or deemed under subsection (3) to have been given, by the employee to the employer under section 9 or 14, as the case may be,

(b)     the leave concerned shall be postponed with effect from the date agreed under paragraph (a), and

C–61

(c)    the employee concerned shall be entitled to—
    (i)   the part of the maternity leave,
    (ii)  the part of the maternity leave and the additional maternity leave, or
    (iii) the additional maternity leave or the part of it,
    as the case may be, not taken by her by reason of the postponement (in this section referred to as "resumed leave") in accordance with regulations made under this section by the Minister to be taken in one continuous period commencing not later than 7 days after the discharge of the child from hospital.

(5) An employer who receives a request under subsection (1) shall notify the employee concerned in writing of the employer's decision in relation to the request as soon as reasonably practicable following the receipt of it.

(6) Where, following the postponement of leave under this section, an employee returns to work in accordance with subsection (4)(a) and during the period of the postponement she is absent from work due to sickness, the employee shall be deemed to commence resumed leave on the first day of such absence unless she notifies her employer in writing (or causes her employer to be so notified) as soon as reasonably practicable that she does not wish to commence such leave and, following such notification—

(a)    the absence from work of the employee due to sickness shall be treated in the same manner as any absence from work of the employee due to sickness, and

(b)    the employee shall not be entitled to the resumed leave.

(7) Without prejudice to the generality of subsection (4), regulations under this section may make provision in relation to either or both of the following matters:

(a)    the maximum period of postponement of leave under this section, and

(b)    the evidence to be furnished by an employee to her employer of the hospitalisation, and the discharge from hospital, of the child.

(8) Entitlement to resumed leave shall, subject to subsection (10), be subject to an employee having notified her employer in writing (or caused her employer to be so notified) as soon as reasonably practicable but not later than the day on which the leave begins of her intention to commence such leave.

(9) A notification under subsection (8) may be revoked by a further notification in writing given by or on behalf of the employee concerned to her employer within the period specified in that subsection for the giving of the notification concerned.

(10) An employer may, at the discretion of the employer, waive the right to receive a notification in accordance with subsection (8).

(11) Where an employee's leave is postponed under this section—

(a)    subject to paragraphs (b) and (c), the employee shall comply with subsection (1A), in lieu of subsection (1), of section 28,

(b)    the employee shall not, in relation to returning to work under subsection (4)(a), be required to comply with section 28, and

(c)    the employee shall, if deemed under subsection (6) to be on resumed leave, comply with subsection (1B), in lieu of subsection (1) or (1A), of section 28.]

GENERAL NOTE

This section was inserted by virtue of s.7 of the Maternity Protection (Amendment) Act 2004 and **CB.133D** provides that, in the event of the hospitalisation of the child, the employer may agree to postpone the maternity leave or additional maternity leave and allow the employee to return to work on an agreed date. The section provides that it will only be possible to postpone maternity leave where the employee has taken at least 14 weeks maternity leave, four of which are after the end of the week of the birth. Where the employer agrees to postponement, and where the employee has adhered to certain notification requirements, the employee will be entitled to take the postponed leave in one continuous block known as "resumed leave". This "resumed leave" must commence not later than seven days after the discharge of the child from hospital. The Maternity Protection (Postponement of Leave) Regulations 2004 (S.I. No. 655 of 2004) provide that the maximum period of postponement is six months and that the evidence to be furnished to an employer is:

(a)    a letter or other appropriate document from the hospital in which the child concerned is hospitalised confirming the hospitalisation, and

(b)    a letter or other appropriate document from the hospital concerned or the child's medical practitioner confirming that the child has been discharged from hospital and the date of that discharge.

It would appear that there is no right of appeal against an employer's refusal to postpone the leave, although any such refusal would give rise to a "trade dispute" to enable investigation by a Rights Commissioner or the Labour Court under the Industrial Relations Act 1969.

## Right to time off from work for ante-natal or post-natal care

**15.**—(1) For the purpose of receiving ante-natal or post-natal care or both, an **CB.134** employee shall be entitled to time off from her work, without loss of pay, in accordance with regulations made under this section by the Minister.

(2) Without prejudice to the generality of subsection (1), regulations under this section may make provision in relation to all or any of the following matters—

(a)    the amount of time off to which an employee shall be entitled under this section;

(b)    the terms or conditions relating to such time off;

(c)    the notice to be given in advance by an employee so entitled to her employer (including any circumstances in which such notice need not be given);

(d)    the evidence to be furnished by an employee so entitled to her employer of any appropriate medical or related appointment.

GENERAL NOTE

The relevant Regulations are the Maternity Protection (Time Off for Ante-Natal and Post-Natal **CB.135** Care) Regulations 1995 (S.I. No. 18 of 1995) which came into operation on January 30, 1995. Subject to an employee having complied with the notification requirements set out in Regulation 4, Regulation 3 provides that a pregnant employee who has a medical or related appointment "shall be entitled, without loss of pay, to take such time off from her work during her normal working time as is necessary to enable her to keep that appointment". This goes further than the Pregnant Workers Directive which, in Article 9, merely provides that the Member States are to take the necessary measures to ensure that pregnant workers are entitled to time off "without loss of pay" in order to attend "ante-natal examinations" if such examination had to take place during working hours.

## [Entitlement to time off from work to attend ante-natal classes

**15A.**—(1) Subject to subsection (3), a pregnant employee shall be entitled to **CB.135A** time off from her work, without loss of pay, in accordance with regulations made under this section by the Minister, for the purpose of attending one set of ante-natal classes (other than the last 3 classes in such a set) and those classes may be attended by her during one or more pregnancies.

(2) Subject to subsection (3), an expectant father of a child (if he is employed under a contract of employment) shall be entitled once only to time off from his work, without loss of pay, in accordance with regulations made under this section by the Minister, for the purpose of attending the last 2 ante-natal classes in a set of such classes attended by the expectant mother of their child before the birth of the child.

(3) Subsection (1) or (2) shall not apply—

(a)     to a member of the Defence Forces who is—

    (i)   on active service within the meaning of section 5 of the Defence Act 1954 or deemed to be on active service within the meaning of section 4(1) of the Defence (Amendment) (No. 2) Act 1960,

    (ii)  engaged in operational duties at sea,

    (iii) engaged in operations in aid of the civil power,

    (iv)  engaged in training that is directly associated with any of the activities referred to in subparagraphs (i), (ii) and (iii) of this paragraph, or

    (v)   engaged in any other duty outside the State,

(b)     if the Chief of Staff of the Defence Forces in exceptional circumstances so directs, to a member of the Defence Forces who is required to perform a duty which is, in the opinion of the Chief of Staff of the Defence Forces, of a special or urgent nature for so long as the member is performing the duty,

(c)     to a member of the Garda Síochána who is on the direction, or with the consent, of the Commissioner of the Garda Síochána serving outside the State performing duties of a police character or advising others on, or monitoring them in, the performance of such duties or any related duties for so long as the member is so serving, and

(d)     if the Commissioner of the Garda Síochána in exceptional circumstances so directs, to a member of the Garda Síochána who is required to perform a duty which is, in the opinion of the Commissioner of the Garda Síochána, of a special or urgent nature for so long as the member is performing the duty.

(2) Without prejudice to the generality of subsections (1) and (2), regulations under this section may make provision in relation to all or any of the following matters:

(a)     the amount of time off to be allowed for attendance at ante-natal classes;

(b)     the terms or conditions relating to such time off;

(c)     the notice to be given in advance by a pregnant employee or an expectant father entitled to time off under this section to her or his employer;

(d)     the evidence to be furnished by a pregnant employee or an expectant father so entitled to her or his employer of ante-natal classes that she or he is to attend.

GENERAL NOTE

This section was inserted by s.8 of the Maternity Protection (Amendment) Act 2004 and provides **CB.135B** that a pregnant employee is entitled to time off work, without loss of pay, for the purpose of attending one set of ante-natal classes, other than the last three classes in such a set (which, ordinarily, are attended in the final weeks of pregnancy while the employee is on maternity leave). Provision is also made for a once-off entitlement to an expectant father to time off work, without loss of pay, for the purpose of attending the last two ante-natal classes in a set of such classes attended by the expectant mother of the child. A limited exclusion is provided in the case of members of the Defence Forces, the Garda Síochána serving overseas or in other exceptional circumstances.

The Maternity Protection (Time off for Ante-Natal Classes) Regulations 2004 (S.I. No. 653 of 2004) provide that entitlement to time off under this section is subject to the employee having:

(a) notified her or his employer in writing of the dates and times of the classes, or the date and time of each class, to which the time off will relate as soon as practicable and in any event not later than two weeks before the date of the first class, or the class concerned, as the case may be, and

(b) produced for the employer's inspection if so requested an appropriate document indicating the dates and times of the classes or the date and time of the class concerned.

The Regulations also provide for the situation where the employee is unable to attend one full set of classes due to circumstances beyond her control, such as illness or miscarriage.

## Entitlement to time off from work or reduction of working hours for breastfeeding

**15B.**—(1) An employee who is breastfeeding shall be entitled, without loss of **CB.135C** pay, at the option of her employer to either—

(a) time off from her work for the purpose of breastfeeding in the workplace in accordance with regulations made under this section by the Minister where facilities for breastfeeding are provided in the workplace by her employer, or

(b) a reduction of her working hours in accordance with regulations made under this section by the Minister for the purpose of breastfeeding otherwise than in the workplace.

(2) An employer shall not be required to provide facilities for breastfeeding in the workplace if the provision of such facilities would give rise to a cost, other than a nominal cost, to the employer.

Without prejudice to the generality of subsection (1), regulations under this section may make provision in relation to all or any of the following matters:

(a) the amount of time off and the number and frequency of breastfeeding breaks to which an employee is entitled under paragraph (a) of that subsection;

(b) the reduction of working hours to which an employee is entitled under paragraph (b) of that subsection;

(c) the terms or conditions relating to time off under paragraph (a), or to a reduction of working hours under paragraph (b), of that subsection;

(d) the notice to be given in advance by an employee to her employer in relation to the proposed exercise by her of her entitlement under this section;

(e) the evidence to be furnished by such an employee to her employer in relation to the date of confinement.

(3) If an employee who has exercised her entitlement under subsection (1) ceases to breastfeed, she shall, at the earliest practical time, notify her employer in writing that she has so ceased.

(4) In this section, "breastfeeding", means breastfeeding a child or expres-

sing breast milk and feeding it to a child immediately or storing it for the purpose of feeding it to the child at a later time.]

GENERAL NOTE

**CB.135D**     This section was inserted by virtue of s.9 of the Maternity Protection (Amendment) Act 2004 and provides that an employee who is breastfeeding, and has informed her employer that she is so doing, shall be entitled, without loss of pay, to either breastfeeding breaks (where facilities for breastfeeding are provided in the workplace) or to a reduction in working hours. Employers will not be required to provide facilities for breastfeeding breaks in the workplace where the provision of such facilities would give rise to more than a nominal cost. The words "nominal cost" are not defined in the Act but the word "nominal" is defined in the *Concise Oxford Dictionary* as "1. existing in name only; not real or actual (*nominal and real prices; nominal rules*) 2. (of a sum of money, rent, *etc.*) virtually nothing; much below the actual value of a thing". The words were used in s.16 of the Employment Equality Act 1998 (before its amendment by the Equality Act 2004) and the cases suggest that the definition of "nominal" would not be the same for every employer. The term was interpreted in a relative sense; so, in *An Employee v A Local Authority* DEC–E2002-004, the Equality Officer took into account the fact that the respondent was "a large public sector organisation". See also *A Motor Company v A Worker* DEE6/2002.

The Maternity Protection (Protection of Mothers who are Breastfeeding) Regulations 2004 (S.I. No. 654 of 2004) set out the details of the general entitlement of employees under this section. The Regulations provide that an employee who is breastfeeding (and has so informed her employer) shall be entitled, without loss of pay, to take one hour off from her work each working day as a breastfeeding break which may be taken in the form of one break of 60 minutes, two breaks of 30 minutes each, three breaks of 20 minutes each or in such other manner as to number and duration of breaks as may be agreed by her and her employer. It should be noted that, because of the definition of "employee who is breastfeeding", these entitlements only apply in the first six months following confinement. This restriction has been criticised by the Irish Congress of Trade Unions ("Congress") who point out, that for those mothers who take their full maternity leave, breastfeeding at work will only be an issue for several weeks. Congress believes that breastfeeding breaks should apply for as long as the mother chooses and at least for one year. Congress have issued guidelines aimed at assisting union negotiators in ensuring adequate breastfeeding facilities in the workplace (see *Industrial Relations News* 38, October 7, 2004, pp.14–15). The guidelines set out what Congress regards as adequate facilities in the workplace, noting that although employers may opt not to provide these, those opting out must provide extra breaks for mothers to breastfeed or express milk elsewhere. The facilities sought include:

(i)     a private room in which women can breastfeed or express milk, which would be clean and hygienic, with a lockable door;

(ii)    a secure dedicated refrigerator for storing breast milk;

(iii)   a lockable storage cupboard/locker for storing and sterilising pumping equipment;

(iv)    comfortable chairs to use while expressing milk or breastfeeding;

(v)     a table to support the breast pump and any other equipment;

(vi)    a power point for mothers who use an electric breast pump;

(vii)   a sink for washing hands and equipment; and

(viii)  a changing mat and a refuse bin.

The guidelines stipulate that simply placing a chair in the ladies' toilet is "not acceptable".

## Entitlement of employed father to leave on death of mother

**CB.136**     **16.**—[(1) If a woman who has been delivered of a living child (in this section referred to as "the mother") dies at any time before the expiry of the [thirty-second] week following the week of her confinement, the father of the child (if he is employed under a contract of employment) shall be entitled in accordance with this section to leave from his employment for a period ending as follows—

(a)     if the mother dies before the expiry of the [twentieth] week following the week of her confinement, the period ends, subject to section 16B, at the end of that [twentieth] week, and

(b)     if the mother dies at any time after the expiry of that [twentieth] week, the period ends, subject to sections 16A and 16B, at the end of her [thirty-second] week following the week of her confinement.]

(2) Entitlement to leave under subsection (1) shall be subject to the father—

C–66

(a)     notifying his employer in writing (or causing his employer to be so notified) not later than the day on which his leave begins of the death of the mother, of his intention to take leave under subsection (1) and of the length of the leave to which he believes he is so entitled; and

(b)     if requested by his employer, causing his employer to be supplied, as soon as is reasonably practicable, with a copy of the death certificate made in respect of the mother and of the birth certificate in respect of the child.

[(3) Subject to section 16B, the period of leave under subsection (1) shall commence within 7 days of the mother's death; and in this section and sections 16A and 16B—

(a)     a period of such leave which ends as mentioned in paragraph (a) of subsection (1) is referred to as "subsection (1)(a) leave", and

(b)     a period of such leave which ends as mentioned in paragraph (b) of that subsection is referred to as "subsection (1)(b) leave".

(4) A father who has taken subsection (1)(a) leave shall, if he so wishes, be entitled to further leave from his employment for a maximum period of—

(a)     [12] consecutive weeks commencing immediately after the end of his subsection (1) (a) leave, or

(b)     [12] weeks, all or part of which is postponed in accordance with section 16B, commencing either in accordance with that section or immediately after the end of his subsection (1)(a) leave, as may be appropriate.]

(5) [Subject to section 16B, entitlement to further leave under subsection (4)] shall be subject to the father having notified in writing his employer (or caused his employer to be so notified) in accordance with subsection (6) of his intention to take such leave.

(6) Notification under subsection (5) shall be given either at the same time as the notification under subsection 2(a) or (if it is later) not later than four weeks before the date which would have been the father's expected date of return to work under Part IV if he had not taken the further leave under subsection (4).

(7) A notification under this section may be revoked by a further notification in writing given by or on behalf of the father to his employer—

(a)     if it relates to subsection (1)(a) leave or subsection (1)(b) leave, not later than the day on which the leave is due to begin; and

(b)     if it relates to leave under subsection (4), not later than the latest date on which, under subsection (6), the notification which is to be revoked could have been given.

(8) The Minister may by order, made with the consent of the Minister for [Social and Family Affairs] and with the consent of the Minister for Finance, amend subsections (1) and (4) so as to extend the periods mentioned in those subsections.

(9) Any reference in this section to the week of the mother's confinement is a reference to the week in which fell the date of her confinement.

GENERAL NOTE

This is a new provision, as amended by s.10 of the Maternity Protection (Amendment) Act 2004 **CB.137** and Art.7 of the Maternity Protection Act 1994 (Extension of Periods of Leave) Order 2006 (S.I. No. 51

C–67

of 2006), which entitles the father to leave if the mother dies within 32 weeks of the birth of the child. In such circumstances an employed father is entitled to leave for the balance of the 32 weeks' period after the mother's death. The period of leave must commence within seven days of the death of the mother.

The title of the Minister for Social Welfare was amended by virtue of the Social Welfare (Alteration of Name of Department and Title of Minister) Order 1997 (S.I. No. 307 of 1997) and the Social, Community and Family Affairs (Alteration of Name of Department and Title of Minister) Order 2002 (S.I. No. 310 of 2002).

## [Termination of leave in event of sickness of father

CB.137A  **16A.**—(1) If, at any time—

(a) during the last 4 weeks of subsection (1)(a) leave, whether or not such leave or part of it is postponed under section 16B and where, in accordance with section 16(6), a father has, or is deemed under section 16B(2) to have, notified his employer, or caused his employer to be notified, of his intention to take further leave under section 16(4), or

(b) during subsection (1)(b) leave or a period of further leave under section 16(4), whether or not such leave or a part of it is postponed under section 16B.

a father who is sick wishes to terminate his subsection (1)(b) leave or a period of further leave under section 16(4), as the case may be, he may request in writing (or cause a written request to be submitted to) his employer to terminate that leave.

(2) An employer who receives a request under subsection (1) may agree to terminate the leave concerned of the father concerned and, if the employer does so, the leave concerned shall terminate on a date agreed by the father and the employer that is not earlier than the date of the commencement of the father's sickness and not later than the date on which the leave concerned would have ended in accordance with the notification given by the father to the employer under subsection (2)(a) or (6) of section 16 or section 16B(7), as the case may be.

(3) An employer who receives a request under subsection (1) shall notify the father concerned in writing of the employer's decision in relation to the request as soon as reasonably practicable following the receipt of it.

(4) Where the leave of a father is terminated under this section—

(a) the absence from work of the father due to sickness following such termination shall be treated in the same manner as any absence from work of the father due to sickness, and

(b) the father shall not be entitled to the subsection (1)(b) leave or further leave under section 16(4), as the case may be, or the part of such leave not taken by him at the date of such termination.

GENERAL NOTE

CB.137B    This section was inserted by virtue of s.11 of the Maternity Protection (Amendment) Act 2004 and mirrors the provisions of s.14A (inserted by s.6 of the 2004 Act).

## Postponement of leave under section 16 in event of hospitalisation of child

CB.137C    **16B.**—(1) A father who is entitled to, or is on, leave under section 16 may, if the child in connection with whose birth he is entitled to, or is on, that leave (in this section referred to as "the child") is hospitalised, request in writing (or cause a written request to be submitted to) his employer to postpone—

(a)	his subsection (1)(a) leave or part of such leave,
(b)	his subsection (1)(a) leave or part of such leave and a period of further leave under section 16(4),
(c)	his subsection (1)(b) leave or a period of further leave under section 16(4), as the case may be, or part of such leave,

as may be appropriate, in accordance with this section.

(2) Notwithstanding the fact that a father who is on subsection (1)(a) leave has not in accordance with section 16(6) notified his employer in writing (or caused his employer to be so notified) of his intention to take further leave under section 16(4), he shall be deemed, for the purposes of making a request under paragraph (b) or (c) of subsection (1), to have complied with section 16(6).

(3) An employer who receives a request under subsection (1) may agree to postpone the leave concerned and, if the employer does so—

(a)	he father concerned shall continue to work, or return to work on a date agreed by him and the employer that is not later than the date on which the leave concerned is due to end in accordance with the notification given, or deemed under subsection (2) to have been given, by the father to the employer under section 16, as may be appropriate,
(b)	the leave concerned shall be postponed or postponed with effect from the date agreed under paragraph (a), as may be appropriate, and
(c)	the father concerned shall be entitled to—
    (i)	the subsection (1)(a) leave or the part of such leave,
    (ii)	the subsection (1)(a) leave or the part of such leave and the period of further leave under section 16(4),
    (iii)	the subsection (1)(b) leave or the period of further leave under section 16(4), as the case may be, or the part of such leave,
    as the case may be, not taken by him by reason of the postponement (in this section referred to as "resumed leave") in accordance with regulations made under this section by the Minister to be taken in one continuous period commencing not later than 7 days after the discharge of the child from hospital.

(4) An employer who receives a request under subsection (1) shall notify the father concerned in writing of the employer's decision in relation to the request as soon as reasonably practicable following the receipt of it.

(5) Where, following the postponement of leave under this section, a father returns to work in accordance with subsection (3)(a) and during the period of the postponement he is absent from work due to sickness, the father shall be deemed to commence resumed leave on the first day of such absence unless he notifies his employer in writing (or causes his employer to be so notified) as soon as reasonably practicable that he does not wish to commence such leave and, following such notification—

(a)	the absence from work of the father due to sickness shall be treated in the same manner as any absence from work of the father due to sickness, and
(b)	the father shall not be entitled to the resumed leave.

C–68/1

Irish Employment Legislation	R.12: April 2005

(6) Without prejudice to the generality of subsection (3), regulations under this section may make provision in relation to either or both of the following matters:

    (a)    the maximum period of postponement of leave under this section, and

    (b)    the evidence to be furnished by a father to his employer of the hospitalisation, and the discharge from hospital, of the child.

(7) Entitlement to resumed leave shall, subject to subsection (9), be subject to a father having notified his employer in writing (or causing his employer to be so notified) as soon as reasonably practicable but not later than the day on which the leave begins of his intention to commence such leave.

(8) A notification under subsection (7) may be revoked by a further notification in writing given by or on behalf of the father concerned to his employer within the period specified in that subsection for the giving of the notification concerned.

(9) An employer may, at the discretion of the employer, waive the right to receive a notification in accordance with subsection (7).

(10) Where a father's leave is postponed under this section—

    (a)    subject to paragraphs (b) and (c), the father shall comply with subsection (1A), in lieu of subsection (1), of section 28,

    (b)    the father shall not, in relation to returning to work under subsection (3)(a), be required to comply with section 28, and

    (c)    the father shall, if deemed under subsection (5) to be on resumed leave, comply with subsection (1B), in lieu of subsection (1) or (1A), of section 28.]

GENERAL NOTE

**CB.137D**    This section was inserted by virtue of s.12 of the Maternity Protection (Amendment) Act 2004 and mirrors the provisions of s.14B (inserted by s.7 of the 2004 Act). The relevant Regulations are the Maternity Protection (Postponement of Leave) Regulations 2004 (S.I. No. 655 of 2004), reproduced *infra* at CC.901, which provide that the maximum period of postponement is six months and further prescribe the evidence to be furnished to an employer.

PART III

LEAVE TO PROTECT HEALTH AND SAFETY OF PREGNANT EMPLOYEES, ETC.

## Employees to whom Part III applies

**CB.138**    **17.** (1) This Part applies to—

    (a)    pregnant employees;

    (b)    employees who have recently given birth; and

    (c)    employees who are breastfeeding.

GENERAL NOTE

**CB.139**    "pregnant employee" is defined in s.2(1) as "an employee who is pregnant and who has informed her employer of her condition".

"employee who has recently given birth" is defined in s.2(1) as meaning "at any time an employee whose date of confinement was not more than 14 weeks earlier and who has informed her employer of her condition".

"employee who is breast feeding" is defined in s.2(1) as "at any time an employee whose date of confinement was not more than 26 weeks earlier, who is breastfeeding and who has informed her employer of her condition".

## Leave on health and safety grounds

**18.**—(1) If, by regulations under the 1989 Act implementing the 1992 Direc- CB.140
tive, an employer is required to move an employee to whom this Part applies to
other work (whether as a result of a risk assessment or because the employee
cannot be required to perform night work), but—

    (a)  it is not technically or objectively feasible for the employer to move the
employee as required by the regulations, or

    (b)  such a move cannot reasonably be required on duly substantiated
grounds, or

    (c)  the other work to which the employer proposes to move the employee
is not suitable for her,

the employee shall be granted leave from her employment under this section.

(2) Where an employee is granted leave under this section, she shall be
entitled to receive, on request to her employer, a certificate, in such form as
may be determined by regulations—

    (a)  stating that she has been granted leave for whichever of the reasons in
paragraphs (a) to (c) of subsection (1) is appropriate in the circumstances and containing such supplementary information as the regulations may require; and

    (b)  specifying the date on which the leave began and its expected duration.

(3) For the purposes of subsection (1)(c), other work is suitable for an
employee if it is—

    (a)  of a kind which is suitable in relation to the employee concerned, as an
employee to whom this Part applies; and

    (b)  appropriate for the employee to do in all the circumstances.

(4) For the first 21 days of leave granted to an employee by an employer
under this section in any relevant period, the employee shall be entitled to
receive from the employer remuneration of an amount determined in accordance with regulations.

(5) Regulations under subsection (2) or subsection (4) shall be made by the
Minister after consultation with—

    (a)  the Minister for Finance;

    (b)  the Minister for [Social and Family Affairs]; and

    (c)  the Minister for [Enterprise, Trade and Employment].

(6) In subsection (4) "relevant period", in relation to an employee, means
the period beginning with her pregnancy and continuing beyond any confinement resulting from that pregnancy until she ceases to be an employee who has
recently given birth or, as the case may be, an employee who is breastfeeding.

(7) Regulations under subsection (4) may provide that such day or days as
may be determined under the regulations shall be left out of account in calculating the 21 days referred to in that subsection.

GENERAL NOTE

    Regulation 4 of the Safety, Health and Welfare at Work (Pregnant Employees etc.) Regulations CB.141
1994 (S.I. No. 218 of 2000), which give effect to Articles 4, 5, 6 and 7 of the Pregnant Workers
Directive, provides that it shall be the duty of every employer:

      "(a) to assess any risk to the safety or health of employees and any possible effect on the
pregnancy of, or breastfeeding by, employees, resulting from any activity at that employer's

C–68/3

place of work likely to involve a risk of exposure to any agent, process or working condition and, for that purpose, to determine the nature, degree and duration of any employee's exposure to any agent, process or working condition and to take the preventive and protective measures necessary to ensure the safety and health of such employees and to avoid any possible effect on such pregnancy or breastfeeding,

(b) without prejudice to paragraph (a) and the provisions of the Safety, Health and Welfare at Work (Chemical Agents) Regulations 1994 (S.I. No. 445 of 1994) and to the occupational exposure limits laid down in any approved code of practice referred to in the said Regulations to—

(i) assess any risk to safety or health likely to arise from exposure of a pregnant employee to an agent or working condition listed in Part A of Schedule 2, resulting from any activity at that employer's place of work, and to ensure that such employee is not required to perform duties for which the assessment reveals such risk,

(ii) assess any risk to safety or health likely to arise from exposure of any employee who is breastfeeding to an agent or working condition in Part B of Schedule 2, resulting from any activity at that employer's place of work and to ensure that such employee is not required to perform duties for which the assessment reveals such risk,

(c) where the risk assessment carried out under paragraphs (a) and (c) reveals a risk to an employee's safety or health, or any possible effect on the pregnancy or breastfeeding of an employee, and it is not practicable to ensure the safety or health of such employee through protective or preventive measures, to adjust temporarily the working conditions or the working hours (or both) of the employee concerned so that exposure to such risk is avoided,

(d) in cases in which the adjustment of working conditions or working hours (or both), referred to in paragraph (c), is not technically or objectively feasible (or both), or cannot reasonably be required on duly substantiated grounds, to take the measures necessary to provide the employee concerned with other work, which does not present a risk to the safety or health of, or any possible effect on the pregnancy or breastfeeding by, such employee."

**CB.142** The non-exhaustive list of agents, processes and working conditions in Schedule 1 include physical agents, such as noise, extremes of cold or heat and shocks, vibrations or movement, "where these are regarded as agents causing foetal lesions or likely to disrupt placental attachment (or both)"; biological and chemical agents; industrial processes listed in the First Schedule to the Safety, Health and Welfare at Work (Carcinogens) Regulations 1993 (S.I. No. 80 of 1993) and underground mining work.

**CB.143** Section 18 only comes into operation if an employer is required, by the 2000 Regulations, to move an employee to other work but (i) it is not technically or objectively feasible for the employer to move the employee or (ii) such a move cannot reasonably be required on duly substantiated grounds or (iii) the other work to which the employer proposes to move the employee is not suitable for her. In any of these three cases the employee is to be granted "health and safety leave". By virtue of s.52 of the Social Welfare (Consolidation) Act 2005 an employee who has been granted such leave is entitled to "health and safety benefit" which is paid at a basic weekly rate of €165.80, with appropriate increases for adult and child dependants, from the first day of the fourth week of an employee's certified absence from work on "health and safety leave". The entitlement ends when the employee becomes entitled to maternity benefit. Section 57 of the 2005 Act provides, however, that a woman shall be disqualified for receiving health and safety benefit during any period in which she engages in any occupation other than domestic activities in her own household.

**CB.144** For the first 21 days of the "health and safety leave", the remuneration which an employee is entitled to receive from the employer is "an amount equal to three times the employee's normal weekly pay": Regulation 3(1) of the Maternity Protection (Health and Safety Leave Remuneration) Regulations 1995 (S.I. No. 20 of 1995).

**CB.145** The form of the relevant certificate is determined by the Maternity Protection (Health and Safety Leave Certification) Regulations 1995 (S.I. No. 19 of 1995).

**CB.146** The titles of the Ministers in subs.(5) were amended by virtue of the Social Welfare (Alteration of Name of Department and Title of Minister) Order 1997 (S.I. No. 307 of 1997) and the Social, Community and Family Affairs (Alteration of Name of Department and Title of Minister) Order 2002 (S.I. No. 310 of 2002) and the Enterprise and Employment (Alteration of Name of Department and Title of Minister) Order 1997 (S.I. No. 305 of 1997).

## Ending of leave under section 18 where no change of circumstances

**CB.147** **19.**—(1) Subject to subsection (2) and section 20, leave granted to an employee under section 18 shall end—

(a) in the case of leave granted to a pregnant employee, immediately before her maternity leave begins; and

    (b)    in any other case, on the date on which she ceases to be an employee to whom this Part applies.

(2) Where an employee to whom leave is granted under section 18 is employed under a contract for a fixed term and that term expires before the day which, apart from this subsection, would be the day on which that leave would end, then—

    (a)    the last day of the leave so granted to her shall be the day on which the term expires; and

    (b)    nothing in this Part shall affect the termination of the employee's contract of employment on that day.

### Ending of leave under section 18 on change of circumstances

**20.**—(1) If an employee to whom leave has been granted under section 18 as   **CB.148** being an employee who is breastfeeding ceases breastfeeding, she shall, at the earliest practical time, notify her employer in writing that she has so ceased.

(2) Without prejudice to subsection (1), if, during a period of leave granted to an employee under section 18, the employee becomes aware that her condition is no longer such that she is vulnerable to the risk by virtue of which she was granted the leave, she shall at the earliest practical time notify her employer in writing that she is no longer at risk.

(3) Where an employer receives notification from an employee under subsection (1) or subsection (2), and has no reason to believe that, if the employee returned to work, she would be vulnerable to risk as an employee to whom this Part applies—

    (a)    the employer shall take all reasonable measures to enable the employee to return to work in the job which she held immediately before the start of her leave and shall then notify her in writing that she can resume work in that job; and

    (b)    the leave granted to the employee under section 18 shall end seven days after the notification under paragraph (a) is received by her or, if it is earlier, on the day she returns to work.

(4) If, during a period of leave granted to an employee under section 18, her employer—

    (a)    either takes whatever measures are necessary to ensure that she will no longer be exposed to any risk by virtue of which she was granted the leave or becomes able to move the employee as mentioned in section 18(1), and

    (b)    notifies the employee in writing that she can return to work without exposure to that risk or, as the case may be, that other work is available to her which is suitable for her as mentioned in section 18(3),

the leave granted to the employee under section 18 shall end seven days after the notification under paragraph (b) is received by her or, if it is earlier, on the day she returns to work or, as the case may be, takes up the other work.

PART IV

EMPLOYMENT PROTECTION

### Interpretation of Part IV

**CB.149**  **21.**—(1) In this part—

"natal care absence", in relation to an employee, means a period of absence from her work to which the employee is entitled in accordance with regulations under section 15; and

"protective leave" means—

(a)  maternity leave;

(b)  additional maternity leave;

(c)  leave to which a father is entitled under subsection (1) or subsection (4) of section 16; or

(d)  leave granted under section 18.

(2) Where protective leave of one description is immediately followed by protective leave of another description, the time on leave shall be treated for the purposes of this Part as one continuous period of protective leave.

[(3) Where—

(a)  maternity leave,

(b)  additional maternity leave, or

(c)  leave to which a father is entitled under subsection (1) or (4) of section 16,

or part of such leave is postponed in accordance with section 14B or 16B, as may be appropriate, the time (if any) on leave before such postponement and the time on leave after such postponement shall be treated for the purposes of this Part as separate periods of protective leave.]

GENERAL NOTE

**CB.149A**  Subsection (3) was inserted by virtue of s.13 of the Maternity Protection (Amendment) Act 2004 and incorporates the postponement provisions under ss.7 and 12 of that Act.

### Preservation or suspension of certain rights, etc. while on protective leave, etc.

**CB.150**  **22.**—(1) During a period of absence from work by an employee while on—

(a)  maternity leave,

(b)  subsection (1)(a) leave, as defined in section 16(3), or

(c)  leave granted under section 18,

and during a period of natal care absence, the employee shall be deemed to have been in the employment of the employer and, accordingly, while so absent the employee shall, subject to subsection (6) and section 24, be treated as if she [or he] had not been so absent; and such absence shall not affect any right (other than, except in the case of natal care absence, the employee's right to remuneration during such absence), whether conferred by statute, contract or otherwise, and related to the employee's employment.

[(2) In respect of a period of absence from work by an employee while on—

(a)  additional maternity leave,

(b)  subsection (1)(b) leave, within the meaning of section 16, or

(c)  further leave under section 16(4),

the employee shall be deemed to have been in the employment of the employer and accordingly, while so absent the employee shall, subject to section 24, be treated as if she or he had not been so absent; and such absence shall not affect any right or obligation (other than the employee's right to remuneration or superannuation benefits or any obligation to pay contributions in or in respect of the employment during such absence), whether conferred or imposed by statute, contract or otherwise, and related to the employee's employment.

(2A) In respect of a period of absence from work by an employee while—

(a)    attending ante-natal classes in accordance with section 15A, or

(b)    breastfeeding in accordance with section 15B,

the employee shall be deemed to have been in the employment of the employer and accordingly, while so absent the employee shall, subject to section 24, be treated as if she or he had not been so absent; and such absence shall not affect any right, whether conferred by statute, contract or otherwise, and related to the employee's employment.]

(3) Nothing in this section affects—

(a)    an employee's right to be offered suitable alternative employment under section 27; or

(b)    an employee's right to remuneration in accordance with section 18(4).

(4) A period of absence from work while on protective leave shall not be treated as part of any other leave (including sick leave or annual leave) to which the employee concerned is entitled.

(5) An employee shall be deemed not to be an employed contributor for the purposes of the Social Welfare (Consolidation) Act [2005], for any contribution week (within the meaning of that Act) in a period of absence from work on protective leave if the employee does not receive any reckonable earnings (within the meaning of that Act) in respect of that week.

(6) Where subsection (1) applies during a period of absence by an employee while she is on leave granted under section 18, nothing in this section shall entitle her to benefits under [section 21 of the Organisation of Working Time Act, 1997] in respect of a public holiday (within the meaning of that Act) falling during that period of absence.

GENERAL NOTE

This section, as amended by the Maternity Protection (Amendment) Act 2004, makes it clear that **CB.151** the maternity leave is unpaid. The employee, however, is entitled to receive "maternity benefit" pursuant to section 47 of the Social Welfare (Consolidation) Act 2005 (as amended by s.7 of the Social Welfare Act 2005). Maternity benefit is paid at a rate of €165.60 or 80 per cent of reckonable weekly earnings up to a maximum of €232.36, whichever is the greater: Social Welfare (Consolidated Payments Provisions) Regulations 1994 (S.I No. 417 of 1994 as amended by S.I. No. 146 of 1995, S.I. No. 249 of 1997, S.I. No. 184 of 1998, S.I. No. 164 of 1999, S.I. No. 122 of 2000, S.I. No. 99 of 2001, S.I. No. 650 of 2001, S.I. No. 631 of 2002, S.I. No.724 of 2003 and S.I. No. 850 of 2004), Articles 22 and 23. The contribution conditions for the payment of maternity benefit are set out in s.48 of the 2005 Act and provide essentially that the claimant must have qualifying contributions in respect of not less than 39 weeks in the period beginning with her entry into insurance and ending immediately before the first day for which maternity benefit is claimed (the relevant day) *and* qualifying or credited contributions in respect of not less than 39 weeks in the second last complete contribution year before the beginning of the benefit year in which the relevant day occurs or in a subsequent complete contribution year before the relevant day *or* qualifying contributions in respect of not less than 26 weeks in each of the second last and third last complete contribution years before the beginning of the benefit year in which the relevant day occurs. Regulation 10(1) of the Social Welfare (Consolidated

Payments Provisions) Regulations 1994 (S.I. No. 417 of 1994 as amended by S.I. No. 146 of 1995) entitles an officer of the Minister for Social and Family Affairs to require an employer to furnish to the Minister certification that the claimant is entitled to leave under the Act, the amount of the claimant's gross earnings and any other relevant particulars. Regulation 102 of the 1994 Regulations provides that the prescribed time for making a claim for maternity benefit is "the date on which, apart from satisfying the condition of making a claim, the claimant becomes entitled thereto". Regulation 104(d) provides that, where a person fails to make a claim for maternity benefit within the prescribed time, she will be disqualified for receiving payment:

"(i) where the claim is made before the end of the week of confinement, payment in respect of any period before the beginning of the week in which the claim is made,

(ii) where the claim is made after the end of the week of confinement, payment in respect of any period before the beginning of the 7th week before the week in which the claim is made not being earlier than the commencement of the week of confinement."

Sections 10 and 11 of the Social Welfare Act 1997 provided for the extension of the maternity benefit scheme to the self-employed with effect from June 9, 1997: see now ss.47 and 48 of the Social Welfare (Consolidation) Act 2005.

**CB.152** Article 11(3) of the Pregnant Workers Directive requires that workers on maternity leave receive an "adequate" allowance and para. (3) provides that an allowance:

"shall be deemed adequate if it guarantees income at least equivalent to that which the worker concerned would receive in the event of a break in her activities on grounds connected with her state of health, subject to any ceiling laid down under national legisla-tion."

It should be noted that the Council and the Commission entered a statement in the minutes of the 1608th meeting of the Council (Luxembourg, October 19, 1992) that the reference in Art.11(2)(b) and (3) to "state of health" was "not intended in any way to imply that pregnancy and childbirth be equated with sickness". See also the decision of the Northern Ireland Court of Appeal in *Gillespie v Northern Health and Social Services Board (No.2)* [1997] I.R.L.R. 410 that pregnancy cannot be compared with sickness and disability.

**CB.153** The word "remuneration" is not defined in the Act (other than for the purposes of s.32) but the Employment Appeals Tribunal was of the opinion, in *McGivern v Irish National Insurance Co. Ltd* P5/1982, that the following statement from *S&U Stores Ltd v Lee* [1969] 2 All E.R. 417 at 419 was "a generally satisfactory definition":

**CB.154** "Remuneration is not mere payment for work done but is what the doer expects to get as the result of the work he does in so far as what he expects to get is quantified in terms of money."

**CB.155** In Case C–342/93, *Gillespie v Northern Health and Social Services Board* [1996] E.C.R. I-475 the Court of Justice, as well as holding that the equal pay principle did not require that women should continue to receive full pay during maternity leave, ruled that a woman on maternity leave must receive a pay rise awarded before or during maternity leave. The principle of non-discrimination required that a woman who was still employed during maternity leave must, like any other worker, benefit from any pay rise, even if backdated. The Court said that to deny such an increase to a woman on maternity leave would discriminate against her since, had she not been pregnant, she would have received the pay rise.

**CB.156** The Employment Appeals Tribunal has ruled that employees are entitled to be paid for the public holidays which fall during maternity leave: *Forde v Des Gibney Ltd* P8/1985. In *Byrne v Memorex Media Products Ltd* P9/1986 the claimant submitted that absence due to maternity leave should be an exception when attendance for the purpose of the company's Performance Award Scheme was being assessed. The scheme provided a financial attendance bonus and the company argued that payments under the scheme were "remuneration". This argument was accepted by the Tribunal in rejecting the claimant's contention that absence whilst on maternity leave must be regarded as attendance for the scheme. Generally speaking the provision of a company car will be regarded as forming part of an employee's remuneration and the employer will not be obliged to allow her the use of the car during maternity leave: *McGivern v Irish National Insurance Co. Ltd* P5/1982.

The words in square brackets in subs.(6) have been inserted because of the repeal of the Holidays (Employees) Act 1973 by the Organisation of Working Time Act 1997.

## Voidance of certain purported terminations of employment, etc.

**CB.157** **23.**—Each of the following shall be void:

(a) any purported termination of an employee's employment while the employee is absent from work on protective leave;

(b) any purported termination of an employee's employment during a period of natal care absence;

[(bb) any purported termination of an employee's employment during a

C–68/8

R.14: April 2006

Irish Employment Legislation

period of absence from work to attend ante-natal classes in accordance with section 15A;

(bbb) any purported termination of an employee's employment during a period of absence from work for breastfeeding in accordance with section 15B;]

(c) any notice of termination of an employee's employment given while the employee is absent from work on protective leave and expiring subsequent to such a period of absence;

(d) any notice of termination of an employee's employment given during a period of natal care absence and expiring subsequent to such a period;

[(dd) any notice of termination of an employee's employment given during a period of absence from work to attend ante-natal classes in accordance with section 15A and expiring subsequent to such a period;

(ddd) any notice of termination of an employee's employment given during a period of absence from work for breastfeeding in accordance with section 15B and expiring subsequent to such a period;]

[(e) any purported suspension from an employee's employment imposed while the employee is absent from work on protective leave, during a period of natal care absence or during a period of absence from work to attend ante-natal classes in accordance with section 15A or for breastfeeding in accordance with section 15B.]

GENERAL NOTE

The difficulties for employers posed by this provision were noted by the Employment Appeals **CB.157A** Tribunal in *Toner v ESAT Telecommunications Ltd* UD135/2003. Paragraphs (bb), (bbb), (dd) and (ddd) were inserted, and para.(e) was substituted, by virtue of s.15 of the Maternity Protection (Amendment) Act 2004.

## Extension of certain notices of termination of employment or of certain suspensions

**24.**—Any notice of termination of employment given in respect of an **CB.158** employee or any suspension from employment imposed on an employee—

(a) before the receipt by the employee's employer of a notification under [section 9, 12, 14, 14B, 15, 15A, 15B, 16 or 16B] (or, where appropriate, under section 28), or

(b) before the production for the employer's inspection of a certificate under section 11, [and due to expire during the employee's absence from work on protective leave, during a period of natal care absence or during a period of absence from work to attend ante-natal classes in accordance with section 15A or for breastfeeding in accordance with section 15B shall be extended by the period of such absence].

GENERAL NOTE

The amendments to this section were effected by virtue of s.16 of the Maternity Protection **CB.158A** (Amendment) Act 2004.

**Provisions regarding periods of probation, training and apprenticeship**

CB.159    **25.**—(1) During an employee's absence from work while on protective leave, being an employee who, starting with the commencement of her employment with the employer—

(a)    is on probation in that employment, or

(b)    is undergoing training in relation to that employment, or

(c)    is employed under a contract of apprenticeship,

the probation, training or apprenticeship shall stand suspended during such absence and shall be completed by the employee on her [or his] return to work after such absence.

(2) The Minister may by regulations prescribe a period or periods of training in relation to which subsection (1) shall not apply.

GENERAL NOTE

CB.159A    The amendments to subs.(1) were effected by virtue of s.17 of the Maternity Protection (Amendment) Act 2004.

**General right to return to work on expiry of protective leave**

CB.160    **26.**—(1) Subject to this Part, on the expiry of a period during which an employee was absent from work while on protective leave, the employee shall be entitled to return to work—

(a)    with the employer with whom she [or he] was working immediately before the start of that period or, where during the employee's absence from work there was a change of ownership of the undertaking in which she [or he] was employed immediately before her [or his] absence, with the owner (in this Act referred to as "the successor") of the undertaking at the expiry of the period of absence,

(b)    in the job which the employee held immediately before the start of that period, and

(c)    under the contract of employment under which the employee was employed immediately before the start of that period, or, where a change of ownership such as is referred to in paragraph (a) has occurred, under a contract of employment with the successor which is identical to the contract under which the employee was employed immediately before the start of that period, [and (in either case) under terms or conditions—

(i)    not less favourable than those that would have been applicable to the employee, and

(ii)   that incorporate any improvement to the terms or conditions of employment to which the employee would have been entitled, if she or he had not been so absent from work].

(2) For the purposes of subsection (1)(b), where the job held by an employee immediately before the start of the period of her [or his] absence on protective leave was not the employee's normal or usual job, the employee shall be entitled to return to work, either in her [or his] normal or usual job or in that job as soon as is practicable without contravention by the employee or the employer of any provision of a statute or instrument made under statute.

(3) In this section "job", in relation to an employee, means the nature of the work which she [or he] is employed to do in accordance with her [or his]

contract of employment and the capacity and place in which she [or he] is so employed.

GENERAL NOTE
Entitlement to return to work is conditional on compliance with the notification requirements set **CB.161** out in s.28. Since resumption in the same job might not be practicable in every case provision is made in section 27 for the provision of suitable alternative work. The amendments to this section were effected by s.18 of the Maternity Protection (Amendment) Act 2004.

## Right to suitable alternative work in certain circumstances on return to work

**27.**—(1) Where an employee is entitled to return to work in accordance with **CB.162** section 26 but it is not reasonably practicable for the employer or the successor to permit the employee to return to work in accordance with that section, the employee shall, subject to this Part, be entitled to be offered by the employer, the successor or an associated employer suitable alternative work under a new contract of employment.

(2) Work under a new contract of employment constitutes suitable alternative work for the purposes of this Act if—

(a)    the work required to be done under the contract is of a kind which is suitable in relation to the employee concerned and appropriate for the employee to do in the circumstances; and

[(b)    the terms or conditions of the contract—

(i)    relating to the place where the work under it is required to be done, the capacity in which the employee concerned is to be employed and any other terms or conditions of employment are not less favourable to the employee than those of her or his contract of employment immediately before the start of the period of absence from work while on protective leave, and

(ii)    incorporate any improvement to the terms or conditions of employment to which the employee would have been entitled if she or she had not been so absent from work during that period.]

(3) For the purposes of this Act one employer shall be taken to be associated with another—

(a)    if one is a body corporate of which the other (whether directly or indirectly) has control; or

(b)    if both are bodies corporate of which a third person (whether directly or indirectly) has control.

Subsection (2) was amended by virtue of s.19 of the Maternity Protection (Amendment) Act 2004. **CB.163** In *Tighe v Travenol Laboratories (Ireland) Ltd* P14/1986 (reported at (1989) 8 J.I.S.L.L. 124) the Employment Appeals Tribunal said that the words "suitable in relation to the employee concerned" in what is now subsection (2)(a) should be construed in the same way as the Tribunal had construed similar words in section 15(2)(c) of the Redundancy Payments Act 1967. The words should be interpreted "subjectively from the employee's standpoint, including the general nature of the work which suited her and her domestic considerations". See also *Butler v Smurfit Ireland Ltd* P3/1988, *Savino v Gardner Merchant (Ireland) Ltd* P7/1990 and *McCormack v Brady* P30/1992.

## Notification of intention to return to work

**28.**—(1) [Subject to sections 14B(11) and 16B(10), entitlement to return to **CB.164** work] in accordance with section 26 or to be offered suitable alternative work under section 27 shall be subject to an employee who has been absent from work while on protective leave in accordance with this Act having, not later than four weeks before the date on which she [or he] expects to return to work, notified in writing (or caused to be so notified) the employer or, where the employee is aware of a change of ownership of the undertaking concerned, the successor, of her [or his] intention to return to work and of the date on which she [or he] expects to return to work.

[(1A) Entitlement to return to work in accordance with section 26 or to be offered suitable alternative work under section 27 shall be subject to an employee who has been absent from work on resumed leave within the meaning of section 14B or 16B, as the case may be, having notified in writing (or caused to be so notified) the employer or, where the employee is aware of a change of ownership of the undertaking concerned, the successor, of her or his intention to return to work and of the date on which she or he expects to return to work—

(a) if the period of resumed leave concerned is 4 weeks or less—

    (i) at the same time as the relevant notification is given by the employee under section 14B(8) or 16B(7), as the case may be, or

    (ii) if the employer waives the right to receive such notification, not later than the day on which the employee expects to return to work,

or

(b) if the period of resumed leave concerned is more than 4 weeks, not later than 4 weeks before the date on which the employee expects to return to work.

(1B) Entitlement to return to work in accordance with section 26 or to be offered suitable alternative work under section 27 shall be subject to an employee who has been absent from work and been deemed under subsection (6) of section 14B or subsection (5) of section 16B, as the case may be, to be on resumed leave within the meaning of whichever of those sections is appropriate having, not later than the date on which she or he expects to return to work, notified in writing (or caused to be so notified) the employer or, where the employee is aware of a change of ownership of the undertaking concerned, the successor, of her or his intention to return to work and of the date on which she or he expects to return to work.]

(2) Where, in the opinion of a rights commissioner or the Tribunal, there are reasonable grounds—

(a) for an employee's failure to give notification under subsection (1), [(1A) or (1B), as may be appropriate,] or

(b) for an employee giving such notification otherwise than within the specified time limits, the rights commissioner or the Tribunal, as the case may be, shall extend the time for giving the notification.

(3) In the absence of reasonable grounds—

(a) failure to give notification under subsection (1), [(1A) or (1B), as may be appropriate,] or

(b) the giving of such notification otherwise than within the specified time limits, are matters that may be taken into account by a rights commissioner, the Tribunal or the Circuit Court in determining the employee's rights under the 1977 Act, this Act or any other relevant enactment, so far as the remedies of re-instatement, re-engagement or compensation are concerned.

GENERAL NOTE

**CB.165**     This section, as amended by s.20 of the Maternity Protection (Amendment) Act 2004, replaces section 22 of the 1981 Act, the requirements of which were held to be mandatory: see *Ivory v Skiline Ltd* [1988] I.R. 399. This section now gives the Rights Commissioner or the Tribunal discretion to extend the time for giving notification in certain circumstances. The Employment Appeals Tribunal has specifically held that the fact that an employee was informed by her employer that he would not be taking her back at the end of her protective leave constitutes reasonable grounds for the employee's failure to give notification pursuant to this section within the specified time limits: see *Grennan v Carty* RP161/2004.

**CB.166**     Even where the employee has failed to notify the employer of her intention to return to work, she may have a contractual right to maternity leave: see *Scott v Yeates & Sons Opticians Ltd* [1992] E.L.R. 83. Alternatively the employer may be estopped by its conduct from raising the question of non compliance: see *Butler v Smurfit Ireland Ltd* P3/1988, *O'Brien v Anglo Irish Beef Processors (Cahir) Ltd* P6/1987 and *Morgan v Dunnes Stores (Cork) Ltd* UD 761/1987.

## Postponement of return to work

**CB.167**     **29.**—Where, because of an interruption or cessation of work at an employee's place of employment, existing on the date specified in a notification under section 28 given by the employee, it is unreasonable to expect the employee to return to work on the date specified in the notification, the employee may return to work instead when work resumes at the place of employment after the interruption or cessation, or as soon as reasonably practicable after such resumption.

GENERAL NOTE

**CB.168**     This section ensures that, where employees comply with the notification requirements under section 28, they will not lose their entitlements to resume work if, on the date specified for their return, they are precluded from doing so because, for instance, there is a strike at the place of work or production has temporarily ceased.

PART V

RESOLUTION OF DISPUTES

## Reference of disputes to which Part V applies

**CB.169**     **30.**—(1) Subject to subsection (2), this Part applies to any dispute between the employee and the relevant employer relating to any entitlement of the employee under Parts II to IV (or any matter arising out of or related to such an entitlement) other than—

(a)  a dispute relating to the dismissal of an employee; or

(b)  a dispute as to a matter which is within the competence of the Authority under the 1989 Act;

and in the following provisions of this Part "dispute" means one to which this Part applies.

(2) This Part does not apply where the employee is in employment as a member of the Defence Forces and, accordingly, in the following provisions of this Part, "employee" does not include an employee in such employment.

(3) In this Part "the relevant employer", in relation to an employee, means the employee's employer or, where appropriate, the successor or an associated employer.

(4) Either the employee or the relevant employer may refer a dispute to a rights commissioner.

(5) The Minister may make regulations for the purposes of this Part, and in this Part "prescribed" means prescribed by such regulations.

(6) In subsection (1)(a) "dismissal" has the same meaning as in the 1977 Act

C–70

except that, in applying that definition for the purposes of subsection (1)(a), the expressions "employer" and "contract of employment", where used in that definition, shall be given the same meanings as in this Act.

GENERAL NOTE

The relevant Regulations are the Maternity Protection (Disputes and Appeals) Regulations 1995 **CB.170** (S.I. No. 17 of 1995) and the Maternity Protection (Maximum Compensation) Regulations 1999 (S.I. No. 134 of 1999).

The word "dismissal" is defined in section 1(1) of the Unfair Dismissals Act 1977 as meaning:

"(a)   the termination by his employer of the employee's contract of employment with the employer, whether prior notice of the termination was or was not given to the employee,

(b)   the termination by the employee of his contract of employment with his employer, whether prior notice of the termination was or was not given to the employer, in circumstances in which, because of the conduct of the employer, the employee was or would have been entitled, or it was or would have been reasonable for the employee, to terminate the contract of employment without giving prior notice of the termination to the employer,or

(c)   the termination of a contract of employment for a fixed term without its being renewed under the same contract or, in the case of contract for a specified purpose (being a purpose of such a kind that the duration of the contract was limited but was, at the time of its making, incapable of precise ascertainment), the cesser of the purpose".

## Procedure for referral of disputes to rights commissioner

**31.**—(1) The referral of a dispute shall be initiated by the employee or the **CB.171** relevant employer giving a notice in writing, containing such particulars (if any) as may be prescribed, to a rights commissioner—

[(a)  within the period of 6 months from the date on which the employer is informed of the initial circumstances relevant to the dispute, that is to say—

(i)   that the employee is pregnant, has recently given birth or is breast-feeding,

(ii)   in the case of an employee who is the expectant father of a child, that the expectant mother of the child is pregnant, or

(iii)   in the case of an employee who is the father of a child that the child's mother has died, or]

(b)   if the rights commissioner is satisfied that exceptional circumstances prevented the giving of the notice within the period specified in paragraph (a), within such period, not exceeding 12 months from the date so specified, as the rights commissioner considers reasonable.

(2) As soon as may be after a rights commissioner has received a notice under subsection (1) from one party to the dispute, the rights commissioner shall give a copy of the notice to the other party.

(3) Proceedings on the reference of a dispute to a rights commissioner shall be conducted otherwise than in public.

(4) The rights commissioner shall hear the parties to the dispute and any evidence tendered by them.

(5) The rights commissioner shall furnish the Tribunal with a copy of each decision given by the rights commissioner under this Part.

GENERAL NOTE

The amendments to subs.(1)(a) were effected by virtue of s.21 of the Maternity Protection (Amend- **CB.172** ment) Act 2004. Regulation 3(1) of the Maternity Protection (Disputes and Appeals) Regulations 1995 (S.I. No. 17 of 1995) provides that a notice of dispute should specify:

(a) the name and address of the party referring the dispute;

(b) the name and address of the other party to the dispute; and

(c) particulars of the facts or contentions which the party referring the dispute will put forward at the hearing.

## Redress

CB.173    **32.** —(1) On the hearing of a dispute a rights commissioner or the Tribunal shall—

    (a)  in the case of a rights commissioner, make a decision in relation to the dispute, or

    (b)  in the case of the Tribunal, make a determination in relation to the dispute, and may give to the parties concerned such directions as the rights commissioner or the Tribunal, as the case may be, considers necessary or expedient for the resolution of the dispute.

(2) If a decision or determination under subsection (1) is in favour of the employee then, without prejudice to the power to give directions under that subsection, the rights commissioner or Tribunal may order such redress for the employee as the rights commissioner or Tribunal considers appropriate, either or both of the following—

    (a)  the grant of leave for such period as may be so specified;

    (b)  an award for compensation in favour of the employee to be paid by the relevant employer.

(3) Compensation under subsection (2)(b) shall be of such amount as the rights commissioner or Tribunal deems just and equitable having regard to all the circumstances of the case but shall not exceed 20 weeks' remuneration in respect of the employee's employment calculated in such manner as may be prescribed.

(4) In this section "remuneration" includes allowances in the nature of pay and benefits in lieu of or in addition to pay.

(5) The decision of a rights commissioner or determination of the Tribunal shall be in writing and shall be communicated to the parties by the rights commissioner or Tribunal, as the case may be.

GENERAL NOTE

CB.174    The relevant Regulations are the Maternity Protection (Maximum Compensation) Regulations 1999 (S.I. No. 134 of 1999) which prescribe the method for calculating maximum compensation for the purposes of redress under this Part of the Act. In awarding compensation, the rights commissioner and the Tribunal must make it clear whether the award is or is not "in respect of remuneration including arrears of remuneration", otherwise it may not be regarded as being exempt from income tax: see s.192A of the Taxes Consolidation Act 1997 (inserted by s.7 of the Finance Act 2004).

## Appeal from decision of rights commissioner

CB.175    **33.**—(1) A party concerned may appeal to the Tribunal from a decision of a rights commissioner in relation to a dispute and the Tribunal shall hear the parties and any evidence relevant to the appeal tendered by them and shall make a determination in relation to the appeal.

(2) An appeal under this section shall be initiated by a party by giving, within four weeks of the date on which the decision to which it relates was given to the parties concerned, a notice in writing to the Tribunal (containing such particulars (if any) as may be prescribed) and the Tribunal shall give a copy of the notice to the other party concerned as soon as may be after the receipt by it of the notice.

(3) A witness before the Tribunal on an appeal under this section shall be entitled to the same immunities and privileges as if the witness were a witness before the High Court.

(4) The Tribunal shall, on the hearing of an appeal under this section, have power to take evidence on oath and for that purpose may cause oaths to be administered to persons attending as witnesses at the hearing.

(5) Any person who, upon examination on oath authorised under subsection (4), wilfully and corruptly gives false evidence or wilfully and corruptly swears anything which is false, shall be guilty of an offence and, on conviction thereof, be liable to the penalties for wilful and corrupt perjury.

(6) The Tribunal may, by giving notice in that behalf in writing, require any

person to attend at such time and place as is specified in the notice, to give evidence in relation to any matter referred to the Tribunal under this section or to produce any documents in that person's possession, custody or control which relate to any such matter, and a person to whom such a notice has been given who—

(a)  fails without just cause to attend in accordance with the notice, or

(b)  having so attended, fails without just cause to give evidence or to produce any document to which the notice relates,

shall be guilty of an offence and liable on summary conviction thereof to a fine not exceeding £1,000 [€1,269.74].

(7) Proceedings for an offence under subsection (6) may be brought and prosecuted by the Minister.

(8) A document purporting to be signed by the chairman or vice-chairman of the Tribunal stating that—

(a)  a person named in the document was by a notice under subsection (6) required to attend before the Tribunal on a day and at a time and place specified in the document, to give evidence or produce a document,

(b)  a sitting of the Tribunal was held on that day and at that time and place, and

(c)  the person did not attend before the Tribunal in pursuance of the notice or, as the case may be, having so attended, refused to give evidence or refused or failed to produce the document,

shall, in a prosecution of the person for an offence under subsection (6), be sufficient evidence of the matters so stated unless the contrary is shown.

GENERAL NOTE

Regulation 3(1) of the Maternity Protection (Disputes and Appeals) Regulations 1995 (S.I. No. 17 **CB.176** of 1995) provides that a notice of appeal should specify:

(a) the name and address of the party bringing the appeal;

(b) the name and address of the other party to the appeal; and

(c) particulars of the facts or contentions which the party bringing the appeal will put forward at the hearing.

Regulation 4(1) empowers the chairman of the Tribunal to require a party to furnish "further particulars relating to the facts or contentions which that party will put forward at the hearing".

## [Burden of Proof

**33A.**—(1) In this section—                                            **CB.176A**

"discrimination" means—

(a)  a failure, which gives rise to a dispute, to comply with a provision of Parts II to IV, or

(b)  an unfair dismissal (within the meaning of the 1977 Act) of an employee resulting wholly or mainly from—

(i)   the employee's pregnancy, attendance at ante-natal classes, giving birth or breastfeeding or any matters connected therewith, or

(ii)  the exercise or proposed exercise by the employee of the right under this Act to any form of protective leave or natal care absence, within the meaning of Part IV, or to time off from work to attend ante- natal classes in accordance with section 15A (inserted by section 8 of the Maternity Protection (Amendment) Act 2004), or to time off from work or a reduction of working hours for breastfeeding in accordance with section 15B (inserted by section 9 of the Maternity Protection (Amendment) Act 2004);

"employee", in relation to proceedings under the 1977 Act, has the meaning assigned to it by that Act;

"indirect discrimination" shall be construed in accordance with section 22 (as

C–72/1

amended by Regulation 4(b) of the European Communities (Burden of Proof in Gender Discrimination Cases) Regulations 2001 (S.I. No. 337 of 2001)) of the Employment Equality Act 1998 insofar as that section relates to discrimination on the gender ground within the meaning of that Act;
"proceedings" means—

(a) any proceedings under this Part before—

  (i) a rights commissioner dealing with a dispute referred to the rights commissioner by an employee, or

  (ii) the Tribunal,

or

(b) any proceedings under the 1977 Act before a rights commissioner, the Tribunal or the Circuit Court in which a claim is made by an employee for redress under that Act for unfair dismissal on the grounds that the dismissal resulted wholly or mainly from—

  (i) the employee's pregnancy, attendance at ante-natal classes, giving birth or breastfeeding or any matters connected therewith, or

  (ii) the exercise or proposed exercise by the employee of the right under this Act to any form of protective leave or natal care absence, within the meaning of Part IV, or to time off from work to attend ante-natal classes in accordance with section 15A (inserted by section 8 of the Maternity Protection (Amendment) Act 2004), or to time off from work or a reduction of working hours for breastfeeding in accordance with section 15B (inserted by section 9 of the Maternity Protection (Amendment) Act 2004),

and includes any subsequent proceedings, including proceedings on appeal, arising from the claim.

(2) Where in any proceedings facts are established by an employee from which it may be presumed that there has been discrimination or indirect discrimination in relation to him or her, it shall be for the respondent to prove the contrary.

(3) This section is without prejudice to section 6(6) of the 1977 Act or any other enactment or rule of law in relation to the burden of proof in proceedings which may be more favourable to such an employee.

(4) Nothing in this section shall operate to reduce the existing level of protection for employees in relation to the burden of proof in proceedings.

(5) The European Communities (Burden of Proof in Gender Discrimination Cases) Regulations 2001 (S.I. No. 337 of 2001) are revoked insofar as they apply to proceedings (within the meaning of this section).]

GENERAL NOTE

**CB.176B**    This section was inserted by virtue of s.22 of the Maternity Protection (Amendment) Act 2004 and provides, in accordance with Council Directive 97/80/EC, that, once the employee establishes a *prima facie* case that there has been discrimination, the onus shifts to the employer to prove the contrary. The extent of the evidential burden, which an employee must discharge, was set out by the Labour Court in *Southern Health Board v Mitchell* [2001] E.L.R. 201. Section 6(6) of the Unfair Dismissals Act 1977 provides that, in determining whether a dismissal is an unfair dismissal, it shall be for the employer to show that there were substantial grounds in justifying the dismissal. It should be noted that s.22 of the Employment Equality Act 1998 has been further amended by s.13 of the Equality Act 2004 and that S.I. No. 337 of 2001 has been revoked by what is now s.85A(5) of the 1998 Act (inserted by s.36 of the Equality Act 2004).

## Appeal to High Court on point of law

**CB.177**    **34.** —(1) The Tribunal may refer a question of law arising in proceedings before it under this Part to the High Court for determination by it.

(2) A party to proceedings before the Tribunal under this Part may appeal to the High Court from a determination of the Tribunal on a point of law.

GENERAL NOTE

Although the Rules of the Superior Courts do not specifically provide for appeals under this Act, it **CB.178** is suggested that any such appeal be brought by special summons, by analogy with the procedure set out in R.S.C. 1986, Order 105. In the absence of any specific rule of court, any such appeal need only be brought within a reasonable time: *per* McCracken J. in his *ex tempore* ruling in *McGaley v Liebherr Container Cranes Ltd* (2001/234Sp) delivered on October 12, 2001.

The circumstances in which the High Court will overturn a decision of a specialist tribunal such as the Employment Appeals Tribunal have been considered in many cases: see for example, *Henry Denny & Sons (Ireland) Ltd v Minister for Social Welfare* [1998] 1 I.R. 34 and in particular the comments of Hamilton C.J. at 37. In considering whether to allow an appeal against a decision of such a tribunal, the High Court must consider whether that body based its decision on an identifiable error of law or on an unsustainable finding of fact. A decision cannot be challenged on the grounds of irrationality if there is any relevant material to support it: see further *Mulcahy v Waterford Leader Partnership Ltd* [2002] E.L.R. 12 (O'Sullivan J.) and *Thompson v Tesco Ireland Ltd* [2003] E.L.R. 21 (Lavan J.). In *National University of Ireland, Cork v Ahern* [2005] 2 I.R. 577, the Supreme Court held that, although findings of fact must be accepted by the High Court on appeal, that court could still examine the basis upon which those facts were found. The relevance or admissibility of the matters relied on in determining the facts were questions of law.

## Service of documents

**35.**—(1) Service of a notice or other document on any person for the purpose of **CB.179** or in relation to any proceedings under this Part may be effected by delivering it to the person to whom it relates or by sending a copy of the document by registered prepaid post in an envelope addressed to the person to be served at that person's last known residence or place of business in the State.

(2) In the case of a company to which the Companies Act 1963 applies such service may be effected by delivering the document to, or by sending a copy of the document by registered prepaid post in an envelope addressed to, the company at its registered office.

(3) In the case of a body corporate to which subsection (2) does not apply or any unincorporated body of persons, such service may be effected by sending a copy of the document by registered prepaid post in an envelope addressed to the body at any place in the State where that body conducts its business or in such other manner as an originating summons may be served on such a body under the Rules of the Superior Courts.

## Provisions relating to winding up and bankruptcy

**36.**—(1) There shall be included among the debts which, under section 285 of **CB.180** the Companies Act 1963, are, in the distribution of the assets of a company being wound up, to be paid in priority to all other debts, all compensation payable under this Part by the company to an employee, and that Act shall have effect accordingly, and formal proof of the debts to which priority is given under this subsection shall not be required except in cases where it may otherwise be provided by rules made under that Act.

(2) There shall be included among the debts which, under section 81 of the Bankruptcy Act 1988, are in the distribution of the property of a bankrupt or arranging debtor, to be paid in priority to all other debts, all compensation payable under this Part by the bankrupt or arranging debtor, as the case may be, to an employee, and that Act shall have effect accordingly, and formal

C–73

proof of the debts to which priority is given under this subsection shall not be required except in cases where it may otherwise be provided by general orders made under that Act.

### Enforcement of decisions and determinations

CB.181    **37.**—(1) A decision of a rights commissioner or a determination of the Tribunal in proceedings under this Part may provide that the decision or determination shall be carried out before a specified date.

(2) Where a decision of a rights commissioner or a determination of the Tribunal does not provide as mentioned in subsection (1), the decision or determination shall be deemed, for the purposes of this section, to provide that it shall be carried out within four weeks from the date on which it is communicated to the parties.

(3) If a party fails to carry out the terms of a decision of a rights commissioner or of a determination of the Tribunal in relation to a dispute within the period appropriate under subsection (1) or subsection (2), the Circuit Court shall, on application to it in that behalf by—

(a) the other party, or

(b) the Minister, if of the opinion that it is appropriate to make the application having regard to all the circumstances,without hearing the party in default or any evidence (other than in relation to the failure), make an order directing that party to carry out the decision or determination in accordance with its terms.

(4) In subsection (3), the reference to a decision of a rights commissioner or a determination of the Tribunal is a reference to such a decision or determination, as the case may be, in relation to which, at the expiration of the time for bringing an appeal against it, no such appeal has been brought or, if such an appeal has been brought, it has been abandoned; and references in this section to the date on which the decision or determination is communicated to the parties shall, in the case where such an appeal is abandoned, be construed as a reference to the date of the abandonment.

(5) In an order under this section providing for the payment of compensation, the Circuit Court may, if in all the circumstances it considers it appropriate to do so, direct the relevant employer to pay to the employee concerned interest on the compensation at the rate referred to in section 22 of the Courts Act, 1981, in respect of the whole or any part of the period beginning four weeks after the date on which the decision or determination concerned is communicated to the parties and ending on the date of the order.

(6) Proceedings under this section shall be heard in the county in which the relevant employer ordinarily resides or carries on any profession, business or occupation.

GENERAL NOTE

CB.182    Although the Circuit Court Rules do not specifically provide for applications to enforce decisions of a rights commissioner or determinations of the Tribunal, it is suggested that any such application be made by way of Motion on Notice, by analogy with the procedures set out in Order 57 of the Circuit Court Rules 2001 (S.I. No. 510 of 2001).

## Part VI

### Amendments and Application of Other Enactments

## Amendments relating to unfair dismissal

**38.** [...]                                                                    CB.183

General Note

   This section amends the Unfair Dismissals Act 1977 in a number of respects so as to ensure   **CB.184**
that its provisions comply with the requirements of Directive 92/85. Subsection (1) amends
section 2(1) of the 1977 Act which excludes employees with less than one year's service
from protection. In conjunction with subsection (5), which inserts a new subsection (2A) into
the 1977 Act, these amendments make it clear that the one year service requirement does not
apply to employees dismissed for pregnancy, giving birth or breastfeeding or any matters
connected therewith. Subsection (5) also makes it clear that employees on probation, training
or apprenticeships are not excluded from the scope of the Unfair Dismissals legislation if they
are dismissed for pregnancy etc. It also extends that protection to those employees who would
otherwise be excluded under the 1977 Act, such as employees employed by near relatives.

   Dismissal for pregnancy may also constitute discrimination contrary to the Employment   **CB.185**
Equality Act 1998: see *Webb v. EMO Air Cargo (UK) Ltd (No. 2)* [1996] 1 W.L.R. 1454 and,

C–74/1

more recently Case C–394/96, *Brown v Rentokil Ltd* [1998] E.C.R. I-4185. In this latter case the Court of Justice ruled that Articles 2(1) and 5(1) of the Equal Treatment Directive precluded dismissal of a female worker at any time during her pregnancy for absences due to incapacity for work caused by illness resulting from that pregnancy. See also the decision of the Northern Ireland Court of Appeal in *Stephenson v F.A.Wellworth & Co. Ltd* [1997] N.I. 93.

## Amendment of Schedule 3 to Redundancy Payments Act, 1967
**39.** [...]

CB.186

GENERAL NOTE

This section amends the Redundancy Payments Act 1967 and ensures the continuity of employment CB.187 of an employee who has taken protective leave or natal care absence for the purposes of the redundancy payments legislation.

## Provisions applying where employee not permitted to return to work
**40.** —(1) This section applies to an employee who, having duly complied with CB.188 section 28, is entitled under Part IV to return to work but is not permitted to do so by the relevant employer, as defined in section 30(3), and in this section, in relation to such an employee, "the expected date of return" means [the date notified under subsection (1), (1A) or (1B), as may be appropriate, of section 28] as the date on which the employee expected to return to work.

(2) For the purposes of the Redundancy Payments Acts, 1967 to [2003], an employee to whom this section applies who is also an employee to whom those Acts apply shall be deemed to have been dismissed by reason of redundancy, the date of dismissal being deemed to be the expected date of return.

(3) For the purposes of the Minimum Notice and Terms of Employment Act, 1973, the contract of employment of an employee to whom this section applies who is also an employee to whom that Act applies shall be deemed to have been terminated on the expected date of return.

(4) For the purposes of the 1977 Act—

(a) an employee to whom this section applies who is also an employee to whom that Act applies shall be deemed to have been dismissed on the expected date of return; and

(b) the dismissal shall be deemed to be an unfair dismissal unless, having regard to all the circumstances, there were substantial grounds justifying the dismissal.

GENERAL NOTE

This section provides that the date of termination of employment, in the case of employees where CB.189 employment has ceased during a period of protective leave or natal care absence, is the date on which the employee would have resumed work had the employment not ceased before the due date of resumption. Subsection (1) was amended by virtue of s.25 of the Maternity Protection (Amendment) Act 2004.

## Protection of employee's rights on insolvency of employer
**41.** [...]

CB.190

GENERAL NOTE

This section provides that, in the event of an employer's insolvency, compensatory awards made by CB.191 a rights commissioner or by the Tribunal can be paid out of the Social Insurance Fund pursuant to section 6 of the Protection of Employees (Employers' Insolvency) Act 1984.

C–75

# MATERNITY PROTECTION (AMENDMENT) ACT 2004

## (2004 No.28)

ARRANGEMENT OF SECTIONS

CB.192    An Act to amend and extend the Maternity Protection Act 1994, to amend the Redundancy Payments Act 1967 and the Unfair Dismissals Act 1977, to revoke in part and enact in respect of certain proceedings the European Communities (Burden of Proof in Gender Discrimination Cases) Regulations 2001 which gave effect to Council Directive 97/80/EC of 15 December 1997 on the burden of proof in cases of discrimination based on sex and to provide for related matters.

[19th July, 2004]

INTRODUCTION AND GENERAL NOTE

CB.193    The purpose of this Act is to give effect to the recommendations made by the Working Group on the Review and Improvement of the Maternity Protection Legislation which was set up in accordance with commitments in the Programme for Prosperity and Fairness. The Working Group's recommendation that maternity leave and additional maternity leave be increased to 18 weeks and eight weeks respectively was given immediate effect by the Maternity Protection Act 1994 (Extension of Periods of Leave) Order 2001 (S.I. No.29 of 2001) and that Order is revoked and re-enacted in this Act (see ss.2, 5, 10 and 26).

   The other principal provisions of this Act are for the reduction of the compulsory period of pre-confinement maternity leave from four weeks to two (s.3); for the termination (subject to the employer's agreement) of additional maternity leave in the event of sickness (s.6); for the postponement (subject to the employer's agreement) of maternity leave in the event of the child's hospitalisation (s.7); for expectant mothers to attend one set of ante-natal classes without loss of pay (s.8); for fathers to paid time-off (on a once-off basis) to attend the last two ante-natal classes (s.8); and for breastfeeding mothers, without loss of pay, to either breastfeeding breaks or a reduction in working hours (s.9).

CITATION

See s.27. **CB.194**

COMMENCEMENT

The Act, with the exception of s.24, came into operation on October 18, 2004: see S.I. No. 652 of **CB.195**
2004. Section 24 came into effect on April 10, 2005; see S.I. No. 131 of 2005.

STATUTORY INSTRUMENTS

Maternity Protection (Amendment) Act 2004 (Commencement) Order 2004 (S.I. No. 652 of 2004). **CB.196**
Maternity Protection (Amendment) Act 2004 (Commencement) Order 2005 (S.I. No. 131 of 2005).

PARLIAMENTARY DEBATES

**CB.197**

173 *Seanad Debates* Cols 331–357 (Second Stage).
174 *Seanad Debates* Cols 1598–1638 (Committee Stage).
174 *Seanad Debates* Cols 1925–1936 (Report and Final Stages).
580 *Dáil Debates* Cols 1095–1128 (Second Stage).
Select Committee on Justice, Equality, Defence and Women's Rights (29 SJEDWR 1, No. 32, May
18, 2004) Cols 955–975 (Committee Stage).
588 *Dáil Debates* Cols 1289–1318 (Report and Final Stages).
177 *Seanad Debates* Cols 1130–1134 (Report and Final Stages).

## Interpretation

1.—(1) In this Act— **CB.198**

"Minister" means the Minister for Justice, Equality and Law Reform;
"Principal Act" means the Maternity Protection Act 1994.

(2) A reference in this Act to any enactment shall be construed as a reference to that enactment as amended, adapted or extended by or under any other enactment including this Act.

## Entitlement to Maternity Leave

2. [Amending section 8 of the Principal Act] **CB.199**

## Amendment of section 10(1) of Principal Act

3. [...] **CB.200**

## Amendment of section 14 of Principal Act

5. [...] **CB.201**

## Termination of additional maternity leave in event of sickness of mother

6. [inserting section 14A into Principal Act] **CB.202**

## Postponement of maternity leave or additional maternity leave in event of hospitalisation of child

7. [inserting section 14B into Principal Act] **CB.203**

## Entitlement to time off work to attend ante-natal classes

8. [inserting section 15A into Principal Act] **CB.204**

C–77

**Entitlement to time off from work or reduction of working hours for breastfeeding**

CB.205    9. [inserting section 15B into Principal Act]

**Amendment of section 16 of Principal Act**

CB.206    10. [...]

**Termination of leave in event of sickness of father**

CB.207    11. [inserting section 16A into Principal Act]

**Postponement of leave under section 16 of Principal Act in event of hospitalisation of child**

CB.208    12. [inserting section 16B into Principal Act]

**Amendment of section 21 of Principal Act**

CB.209    13. [...]

**Amendment of section 22 of Principal Act**

CB.210    14. [...]

**Amendment of section 23 of Principal Act**

CB.211    15. [...]

**Amendment of section 24 of Principal Act**

CB.212    16. [...]

**Amendment of section 25 of Principal Act**

CB.213    17. [...]

**Amendment of section 26 of Principal Act**

CB.214    18. [...]

**Amendment of section 27(2) of Principal Act**

CB.215    19. [...]

**Amendment of section 28 of Principal Act**

CB.216    20. [...]

**Amendment of section 31(1) of Principal Act**

CB.217    21. [...]

**Burden of Proof**

CB.218    22. [inserting section 33A into Principal Act]

**Amendments relating to unfair dismissal**

CB.219    23. [Amending sections 2(2) and 6(2) of the Unfair Dismissals Act 1977 as amended]

**Amendments of Schedule 3 to Redundancy Payments Act 1967**

CB.220    24. [...]

GENERAL NOTE

This section, which provides that continuity of service is preserved when there are certain breaks in   **CB.221** service and also provides that certain breaks in service are reckonable in the calculation of the statutory lump sum redundancy payment, amends Sch. 3 to the Redundancy Payments Act 1967.

## Amendment of section 40(1) of the Principal Act

25. [...]    **CB.222**

## Revocation of Maternity Protection Act 1994 (Extension of Periods of Leave) Order 2001

26.  The Maternity Protection Act 1994 (Extension of Periods of Leave) Order   **CB.223** 2001 (S.I. No. 29 of 2001) is revoked.

## Short title, collective citation and commencement

27.—(1) This Act may be cited as the Maternity Protection (Amendment) Act   **CB.224** 2004.

(2) The Principal Act and this Act may be cited together as the Maternity Protection Acts 1994 and 2004.

(3) This Act shall come into operation on such day or days as the Minister may appoint by order or orders either generally or with reference to any particular purpose or provision and different days may be so appointed for different purposes or different provisions.

GENERAL NOTE

This Act, with the exception of s.24, came into operation on October 18, 2004: see S.I. No. 652 of   **CB.225** 2004. Section 24 came into operation on April 10, 2005: see S.I. No. 131 of 2005.

# SAFETY, HEALTH AND WELFARE AT WORK (PREGNANT EMPLOYEES ETC.) REGULATIONS, 2000

## (S.I. No. 218 of 2000)

## Citation and Commencement

**1.** These Regulations may be cited as the Safety, Health and Welfare at Work **CC.101** (Pregnant Employees etc) Regulations, 2000.

## Interpretation

**2.**—(1) In these Regulations: **CC.102**

"the Directive" means Council Directive 92/185/EEC of 19 October, 1992 on the introduction of measures to encourage improvements in the safety and health at work of pregnant workers and workers who have recently given birth or are breastfeeding;

"agent, process or working condition" includes an agent, process or working condition specified in Schedule 1;

"approved" means approved in writing for the time being by the Authority or conforming with a specification in writing by the Authority;

"employee" means a pregnant employee, an employee who is breastfeeding or an employee who has recently given birth;

"employee who is breastfeeding" means an employee who, having given birth not more than twenty six weeks previously, is breastfeeding;

"employee who has recently given birth" means an employee who gave birth not more than fourteen weeks preceding a material date;

"employer" means any employer of an employee;

"pregnant employee" means an employee who is pregnant;

"registered medical practitioner" means a person whose name is entered in the General Register of Medical Practitioners established under the Medical Practitioners Act, 1978 (No. 4 of 1978);

"the Principal Regulations" means the Safety, Health and Welfare at Work (General Application) Regulations, 1993 (S.I. No. 44 of 1993).

(2) A word or expression used in these Regulations which is also used in the Directive has, unless the context otherwise requires, the same meaning in these Regulations as it has in the Directive.

(3) In these Regulations a reference to a paragraph is to a paragraph in the Regulations in which the reference occurs, unless it is indicated that reference to some other Regulation is intended, and a reference to a Regulation or a Schedule is to a Regulation of, or a Schedule to these Regulations, unless it is indicated that reference to some other Regulation or Schedule is intended.

(4) Regulation 4(2) and Part II of the Principal Regulations shall apply to these Regulations.

(5) The provisions of Regulation 3 of the Principal Regulations shall not apply to the application of the provisions of these Regulations.

## Application

**3.** The provisions of these Regulations shall apply to an employee subject to her **CC.103** notifying her employer of her condition as soon as is practicable after it occurs and, at the time of the notification, giving to her employer or producing for her employer's inspection a medical or other appropriate certificate confirming her condition.

### General Duties of Employer

CC.104 **4.** Without prejudice to the provisions of Regulation 10 of the Principal Regulations it shall be the duty of every employer—

(a) to assess any risk to the safety or health of employees, and any possible effect on the pregnancy of, or breastfeeding by, employees, resulting from any activity at that employer's place of work likely to involve a risk of exposure to any agent, process or working condition and, for that purpose, to determine the nature, degree and duration of any employee's exposure to any agent, process or working condition and to take the preventive and protective measures necessary to ensure the safety and health of such employees and to avoid any possible effect on such pregnancy or breast-feeding,

(b) without prejudice to paragraph (a) and the provisions of the Safety, Health and Welfare at Work (Chemical Agents) Regulations, 1994 (S.I. No. 445 of 1994) and to the occupational exposure limits laid down in any approved code of practice referred to in the said Regulations to—

(i) assess any risk to safety or health likely to arise from exposure of a pregnant employee to an agent or working condition listed in Part A of Schedule 2, resulting from any activity at that employer's place of work, and to ensure that such employee is not required to perform duties for which the assessment reveals such risk,

(ii) assess any risk to safety or health likely to arise from exposure of an employee who is breastfeeding to an agent or working condition listed in Part B of Schedule 2, resulting from any activity at that employer's place of work and to ensure that such employee is not required to perform duties for which the assessment reveals such risk.

(c) where the risk assessment carried out under paragraphs (a) and (c) reveals a risk to an employee's safety or health; or any possible effect on the pregnancy or breastfeeding of an employee, and it is not practicable to ensure the safety, or health of such employee through protective or preventive measures, to adjust temporarily the working conditions or the working hours (or both) of the employee concerned so that exposure to such risk is avoided,

(d) in cases in which the adjustment of working conditions or working hours (or both), referred to in paragraph (c), is not technically or objectively feasible (or both), or cannot reasonably be required on duly substantiated grounds, to take the measures necessary to provide the employee concerned with other work, which does not present a risk to the safety or health of, or any possible effect on the pregnancy or breastfeeding by, such employee.

### Night work

CC.105 **5.**—(1) If a registered medical practitioner certifies that it is necessary for the safety or health of an employee that she should not be required to perform night work during pregnancy or for 14 weeks following childbirth the employer shall not oblige her to perform night work during that period.

(2) In a case to which paragraph (1) relates, the employer shall transfer the employee to daytime work or, where such transfer is not technically or objectively feasible on duly substantiated grounds or both, grant the employee leave or extend the period of maternity leave.

(3) In this Regulation "night work" means work in the period between the hours of 11 p.m. on any day and 6 a.m. on the next following day, where—

(a) the employee works at least three hours in the said period as a normal course, or

(b) at least 25 per cent of the employee's monthly working time is performed in the said period.

## Information

**6.** It shall be the duty of every employer, without prejudice to the provisions of **CC.106** Regulation 11 of the Principal Regulations, to take appropriate steps to ensure that employees or their safety representative (or both) are provided with information on

(a) the results of the assessment referred to in Regulation 4 and

(b) the measures to be taken concerning employees' safety and health pursuant to these Regulations.

## Revocation

**7.** The Safety, Health and Welfare at Work (Pregnant Employees Etc.) Regulations, 1994 (S.I. No. 446 of 1994) are revoked.

**Regulation 4**                    SCHEDULE I

NON-EXHAUSTIVE LIST OF AGENTS, PROCESSES AND WORKING CONDITIONS

### Part A

### Agents

1. *Physical Agents*

Physical agents where these are regarded as agents causing foetal lesions or likely to disrupt **CC.107** placental attachment (or both), and in particular:

(a) shocks, vibration or movement,

(b) handling of loads entailing risks, particularly of a dorsolumbar,

(c) noise,

(d) non-ionizing radiation,

(e) extremes of cold or heat,

(f) movements and postures, travelling, either inside or outside the place of work, mental and physical fatigue and other physical burdens connected with the activity of the employee.

2. *Biological Agents*

Biological agents of risk groups 2, 3 and 4 within the meaning of Regulation 2(1) of the Safety, **CC.108** Health and Welfare at Work (Biological Agents) Regulations, 1994 (S.I. No. 146 of 1994), insofar as it is known that these agents or the therapeutic measures necessitated by such agents endanger the health of pregnant employees and the unborn child but excluding those referred to in Schedule 2.

3. *Chemical Agents*

The following chemical agents insofar as it is known that they endanger the health of pregnant **CC.109** employees and the unborn child but excluding those referred to in Schedule 2:

(a) substances labelled R40, R45, R61, R63 and R64 under the European Communities (Classifications, Packaging, Labelling and Notification of Dangerous Substances) Regulations, 1994 (S.I. No. 77 of 1994),

(b) chemical agents listed in the First Schedule to the Safety, Health and Welfare at Work (Carcinogens) Regulations, 1993 (S.I. No. 80 of 1993),

(c) mercury and mercury derivatives,

(d) antimiotic drugs,

(e) carbon monoxide,

(f) chemical agents of known and dangerous percutaneous absorption.

### Part B

### Processes

Industrial processes listed in the First Schedule to the Safety, Health and Welfare at Work (Carci- **CC.110** nogens) Regulations, 1993 (S.I. No. 80 of 1993).

C–103

*Part C*

*Working conditions*

**CC.111**    Underground mining work.


SCHEDULE 2


LIST OF AGENTS, PROCESSES AND WORKING CONDITIONS

**Regulation 4**                    PART A

*Pregnant Employees*

**CC.112**    1. Agents
(a) *Physical Agents*
   Work in hyperbaric atmosphere, such as in pressurised enclosures and underwater diving.
(b) *Biological Agents*
   The following biological agents:
   Toxoplasma
   Rubella virus,
   unless the pregnant employees are proved to be adequately protected against such agents by immunisation.
(c) *Chemical Agents*
   Lead and lead derivatives insofar as these agents are capable of being absorbed by the human organism.
2. Working Conditions
Underground mining work.

*Part B*

*Employees who are Breastfeeding*

**CC.113**    1. Agents
*Chemical Agents*
Lead and lead derivatives insofar as these agents are capable of being absorbed by the human organism.
2. Working Conditions
Underground mining work.

GENERAL NOTE

**CC.114**    These Regulations now fully implement the occupational safety and health provisions of the Pregnant Workers Directive (Council Directive 92/85/EEC of 19 October 1992). Regulation 4(2) of the Principal Regulations provides that any duty imposed by these Regulations on an employer also applies in respect of the use by the employer of the services of a fixed-term employee or a temporary employee. Part H of the Principal Regulations contains the general safety and health provisions. Regulation 3 of the Principal Regulations exempts members of the Defence Forces when they are on active service; engaged in action in the course of operational duties or in operations in aid to the Civil Power; or engaged in training directly associated with any of the foregoing activities. A "group 2 biological agent" is one which can cause human disease and might be a hazard to employees, although it is unlikely to spread to the community and in respect of which there is usually effective prophylaxis or treatment available. A "group 3 biological agent" is one which can cause severe human disease and presents a serious hazard to employees and which may present a risk of spreading to the community, though there is usually effective prophylaxis or treatment available. A "group 4 biological agent" is one which can cause severe human disease and is a serious hazard to employees and which may present a high risk of spreading to the community—and in respect of which there is usually no effective prophylaxis or treatment available.
   The chemical agents and industrial processes listed in the First Schedule to the Safety, Health and Welfare at Work (Carcinogens) Regulations 1993 (S.I. No. 80 of 1993) are as follows:
   1. Manufacture of auramine.

C–104

2. Work involving exposure to aromatic polycylic hydrocarbons present in coal soot, tar, pitch, fumes or dust.
3. Work involving exposure to dusts, fumes and sprays produced during the roasting and electro-refining of cupro-nickel matters.
4. Strong acid process in the manufacture of isopropyl alcohol.

# MATERNITY PROTECTION (DISPUTES AND APPEALS) REGULATIONS, 1995

## (S.I. No. 17 of 1995)

**1.** These Regulations may be cited as the Maternity Protection (Disputes and Appeals) Regulations, 1995 and shall come into operation on the 30th day of January, 1995.  CC.201

**2.** In these Regulations—  CC.202

"the Act" means the Maternity Protection Act, 1994 (No. 34 of 1994);

"dispute" means a dispute to which Part V of the Act applies and "appeal" shall be construed accordingly;

"notice of appeal" means a notice under section 33(2) of the Act;

"notice of dispute" means a notice under section 31(1) of the Act;

"the Register" has the meaning given by Regulation 9(1);

"the Tribunal" means the Employment Appeals Tribunal.

**3.**—(1) A notice of dispute or notice of appeal shall specify—  CC.203

(a)  the name and address of the party referring the dispute or bringing the appeal;

(b)  the name and address of the other party to the dispute or appeal; and

(c)  particulars of the facts or contentions which the party referring the dispute or bringing the appeal will put forward at the hearing.

(2) A party to a dispute or appeal ("the respondent") who receives from a rights commissioner or the Tribunal a copy of a notice of dispute or notice of appeal shall, within 14 days of the receipt of that notice, or within such longer period as the rights commissioner or Tribunal may allow, by notice—

(a)  indicate to the rights commissioner or Tribunal whether one respondent intends to contest the dispute or appeal; and

(b)  if the respondent does so intend, specify the facts or contentions which the respondent will put forward at the hearing.

(3) If the respondent does not comply with paragraph (2), he shall be treated for the purposes of these Regulations as having given notice under that paragraph that he does not intend to contest the dispute or appeal in question.

(4) A mistake of a formal nature shall not operate to invalidate notice under this Regulation.

**4.**—(1) If, after receipt by the Tribunal of a relevant notice, that is to say,—  CC.204

(a)  a notice of appeal, or

(b)  a notice under Regulation 3(2) indicating an intention to contest the appeal,

it appears to the chairman of the Tribunal appropriate to do so, the secretary of the Tribunal may, by notice in writing given to the party from whom the relevant notice was received, require that party to furnish to the Tribunal further particulars relating to the facts or contentions which that party will put forward at the hearing.

(2) As soon as may be after the receipt by the Tribunal of further particulars furnished by a party to an appeal pursuant to a notice from the Tribunal under paragraph (1), the Tribunal shall send a copy of those further particulars to the other party concerned.

CC.205    **5.**—(1) The chairman of the Tribunal shall from time to time fix dates, times and places for hearings (including postponed and adjourned hearings); and the secretary to the Tribunal shall give notice thereof to all persons appearing to the chairman to be concerned.

(2) The hearing of an appeal by the Tribunal shall take place in public unless, at the request of either party to the appeal, the Tribunal decides to hear the appeal, or any part of it, in private.

(3) Subject to paragraph (4), any party to an appeal may appear and be heard in person or may be represented by counsel or a solicitor or by a representative of a trade union or an association of employers or, with the leave of the Tribunal, by any other person.

(4) Unless the Tribunal at its discretion otherwise directs, paragraph (3) does not apply to a party who has (or is treated as having) given notice under Regulation 3(2) that he does not intend to contest the appeal.

CC.206    **6.**—(1) A party to an appeal may—

(a)  make an opening statement;

(b)  call witnesses;

(c)  cross examine any witness called by the other party;

(d)  give evidence on the party's own behalf; and

(e)  address the Tribunal at the close of the evidence.

(2) The Tribunal may admit any duly authenticated written statement as prima facie evidence when ever it thinks it just and proper to do so.

(3) The Tribunal may postpone or adjourn the hearing of an appeal from time to time.

(4) If, after notice of a hearing has been duly given, either of the parties fails to appear at the hearing, the Tribunal, after considering all the evidence before it, may make a determination on the appeal or may adjourn the hearing to a later date.

CC.207    **7.**—(1) A determination of the Tribunal on an appeal may be taken by a majority of the members.

(2) A determination of the Tribunal on an appeal shall be recorded in a document signed by the chairman and sealed with the seal of the Tribunal.

CC.208    **8.** By notice in writing to the parties to a dispute or appeal, a rights commissioner or, as the case may be, the chairman of the Tribunal may correct any mistake (including an omission) of a verbal or formal nature in a decision or determination.

CC.209    **9.**—(1) The Tribunal shall maintain a register (in these Regulations referred to as "the Register") in which shall be entered particulars of every determination by the Tribunal under Part V of the Act.

(2) The Register may be inspected free of charge by any person during normal office hours.

(3) When the chairman of the Tribunal makes a correction in a determination pursuant to Regulation 8, particulars of the correction shall be entered in the Register.

(4) The Tribunal shall ensure that a copy of an entry in the Register is given to the parties to the determination concerned.

**10.**—(1) Subject to paragraph (2), neither a rights commissioner nor the Tribunal shall award costs against any party to a dispute or an appeal. CC.210

(2) If, on an appeal, the Tribunal is of the opinion that a party (including one who has not entered an appearance) has acted frivolously or vexatiously, the Tribunal may make an order that that party shall pay to the other party such sum in respect of travelling expenses and, subject to paragraph (3), any other costs reasonably incurred as the Tribunal considers just.

(3) Cost shall not be awarded in respect of attendance at the appeal by any party or any person representing a party by virtue of Regulation 5(3).

(4) Any amount ordered to be paid under this Regulation shall be recoverable as a simple contract debt.

**11.**—(1) Subject to paragraph (2), the Tribunal may, at its discretion, award to persons appearing before it and whose appearance is deemed essential by the Tribunal— CC.211

    (a)  travelling expenses and subsistence allowances in accordance with such scale as the Minister, with the consent of the Minister for Finance, may determine and

    (b)  such sum in respect of expenses for loss of remunerative time as the Tribunal considers reasonable.

(2) The Tribunal shall not make an award under paragraph (1) in respect of the attendance before it of—

    (a)  the appellant or the respondent; or

    (b)  any person representing a party by virtue of Regulation 5(3).

(3) Any sums awarded under paragraph (1) shall be paid out of the Social Insurance Fund.

**12.**—(1) Any notice required by these Regulations to be given to a rights commissioner shall be properly given if sent by registered post addressed to the Rights Commissioner, Labour Relations Commission, Dublin 4. CC.212

(2) Any notice required by these Regulations to be given to the Tribunal shall be properly given is sent by registered post addressed to the Employment Appeals Tribunal, Dublin 2.

GENERAL NOTE

These Regulations prescribe the procedures to be followed in relation to the hearing of disputes and appeals under the 1994 Act. It should he noted that a decision or a determination which does not state correctly the name of the employer concerned or and any other material particular may, on application to the rights commissioner or the Tribunal (as the case may be), be amended so as to state correctly the name of the employer or the other material particular: see section 39(2) of the Organisation of Working Time Act 1997. CC.213

# MATERNITY PROTECTION (TIME OFF FOR ANTE-NATAL AND POST-NATAL CARE) REGULATIONS 1995

(S.I. No. 18 of 1995)

**1.** These Regulations may be cited as the Maternity Protection (Time off for Ante-Natal and Post-Natal Care) Regulations 1995 and shall come into operation on the 30th day of January 1995. CC.301

**2.** In these Regulations— CC.302

    "the 1994 Act" means the Maternity Protection Act 1994 (No. 34 of 1994);

    "confined" has the meaning given by section [51] of the Social Welfare (Consolidation) Act [2005];

"employee" has the same meaning as in Part II of the 1994 Act;

"medical or related appointment" means, in relation to an employee, an appointment for the purpose of an examination or test to be undergone by the employee that is carried out by, under the supervision of, or at the direction of, a registered medical practitioner and that—

(a) in the case of ante-natal care, relates directly to an existing pregnancy of the employee; and

(b) in the case of post-natal care, is after a confinement of the employee and consequential on that confinement;

"normal working time", in relation to time taken off from work, does not include overtime in the case of an employee who, in the month ending on the day on which the time off from work is taken, has worked less than 20 hours of overtime.

**CC.303**  **3.** Subject to Regulation 4 of these Regulations, an employee who is pregnant and who has a medical or related appointment shall be entitled, without loss of pay, to take such time off from her work during her normal working time as is necessary to enable her to keep that appointment.

**CC.304**  **4.**—(1) Entitlement to time off from her work under Regulation 3 of these Regulations shall be subject to an employee's having—

(a) notified her employer in writing of the date and time of the appointment to which the time off from her work will relate as soon as practicable and in any event not later than two weeks before the date of the appointment, and

(b) produced for her employer's inspection, on request, an appointment card or other appropriate document—

(i) indicating the date and time of the appointment, and

(ii) confirming the pregnancy or specifying the expected week of confinement.

(2) Paragraph (1)(b) of this Regulation shall not apply where the employee's appointment is her first medical or related appointment in relation to the pregnancy to which the appointment relates.

(3) Where the circumstances are such that, in the case of a particular appointment,

(a) compliance by an employee with paragraph (1) of this Regulation is not possible, and

(b) non-compliance is not due to the neglect or default of the employee in relation to the arrangement of the appointment, she shall be deemed to have complied with the requirements of that paragraph if, not later than one week after the date of the appointment, she furnishes the employer with evidence of her having kept the appointment and an indication of the circumstances which occasioned the non-compliance.

**CC.305**  **5.** Subject to Regulation 6 of these Regulations, an employee who has been confined and who has a medical or related appointment during the period of 14 weeks immediately after the confinement shall be entitled, without loss of pay, to take such time off from her work during her normal working time as is necessary to enable her to keep that appointment.

**CC.306**  **6.**—(1) Entitlement to time off from her work under Regulation 5 of these Regulations shall be subject to an employee's having—

(a) notified her employer in writing of the date and time of the appointment to which the time off from her work will relate, as soon as practicable and in any event not later than two weeks before the date of the appointment; and

(b) produced for her employer's inspection, on request, an appointment card or other appropriate document indicating the date and time of the appointment and the date of her confinement.

(2) Where the circumstances are such that, in the case of a particular appointment,—

(a) compliance by the employee with paragraph (1) of this Regulation is not possible, and

(b) non-compliance is not due to the neglect or default of the employee in relation to the arrangement of the appointment,she shall be deemed to have complied with the requirements of that paragraph if, not later than one week after the date of the appointment in question, she furnishes her employer with evidence of her having kept the appointment and an indication of the circumstances which occasioned the non-compliance.

GENERAL NOTE

These Regulations set out details of the general entitlement of employees to time off from work for **CC.307** the purpose of ante-natal and post-natal care under section 15 of the 1994 Act.

Section 51(1)(a) of the Social Welfare (Consolidation) Act 2005 provides that "confinement" means labour resulting in the issue of a living child, or labour after 24 weeks of pregnancy resulting in the issue of a child whether alive or dead and that "confined" should be "read accordingly".

# MATERNITY PROTECTION (HEALTH AND SAFETY LEAVE CERTIFICATION) REGULATIONS, 1995

## (S.I. No. 19 of 1995)

**1.** These Regulations may be cited as the Maternity Protection (Health and **CC.401** Safety Leave Certification) Regulations, 1995 and shall come into operation on the 30th day of January 1995.

**2.** The Certificate which an employee is entitled to receive, on request to her **CC.402** employer, under section 18(2) of the Maternity Protection Act, 1994 shall be in the form set out in the Schedule to these Regulations ("the Scheduled form") or in a form substantially to the like effect which contains—

(a) the appropriate information referred to in the Scheduled form; and

(b) such certifications, declaration and undertaking as are required by the Scheduled form.

CC.403                                         **SCHEDULE**

**CERTIFICATE OF RISK, NON-FEASIBILITY OF PROVIDING OTHER WORK AND
GRANT OF LEAVE ON HEALTH AND SAFETY GROUNDS**

**Maternity Protection Act, 1994**

**I    EMPLOYEE DETAILS**

**Figures**                    **Letters**

Name: _____ [PPS] Number: | | | | | | | |  | | |

Employee's Occupation: _____

The employee named above has notified me that:

she is pregnant                            □ }
she has recently given birth               □ } **tick as appropriate**
she is breastfeeding                       □ }

Is employee employed under a fixed-term contract?   Yes □          No □

Day  Month  Year

If 'Yes', state date contract ends          |   |    |    |

**II    CERTIFICATION OF RISK**

Please complete either (a)—*workplace risk* or (b)—*nightwork risk*

**(a)** The following *risk(s)* to the employee named above has/have been identified arising from a risk assessment undertaken in accordance with Regulations under the Safety, Health and Welfare at Work Act, 1989.

List risk(s) _____
_____
_____

Specify the reasons why it is not possible to eliminate the risk(s):
_____
_____

**(b)** The employee named above is required to perform *nightwork* (*i.e.* work between the hours of 11 pm and 6 am where the employee normally works at least three hours in the said period or at least 25% of her monthly working time in that period) and the medical registered practitioner named below has certified that the performance of night work poses a risk to the employee's health/safety and furthermore it is not feasible to transfer the employee to daywork.

Name of medical registered practitioner: _____

**II    CERTIFICATION OF NON-FEASIBILITY OF OTHER WORK AND THE GRANTING OF LEAVE**

As a result of the risk(s) identified above and, arising from Regulations on Safety, Health and Welfare at Work (Pregnant Employees, etc.) [(S.I. No. 218 of 2000)] and the Maternity Protection Act, 1994 for the reason(s) indicated as applying below the employee has been granted leave on health and safety grounds because

(i)   it is not technically or objectively feasible to move the
      employee                                               □ }
(ii)  such a move cannot be required on duly substantiated
      grounds                                                □ } **tick as appropriate**
(iii) the other work proposed for the employee is not suitable
      for her                                                □ }

**IV    SUPPLEMENTARY INFORMATION**

**Date of commencement of leave on health and safety grounds**

Day  Month  Year

Date: | | | | |              Expected duration of leave (in weeks): _____

*Expected date* or *date* of confinement as appropriate

Day  Month  Year

| | | | |

Date of **last day of 21 days** health and safety leave
during which payment by employer applies

Day  Month  Year

| | | | |

**V    DECLARATION**

I/We declare that the details I/we have given above are true and complete.

I/We undertake to inform the Department of Social and Family Affairs
immediately in the event of notifing the employee to return to work where:

—the risk to the employee no longer exists
—other work becomes available for the employee

Signed by or on behalf of Employer:          Company's Name: _____

_____          Address: _____

Position: _____          _____

Date:  Day  Month  Year          _____

| | | | |              Employer's Registered Number: _____

Date .................... 19..........

Telephone Number:  ............          **EMPLOYER'S OFFICIAL STAMP**

C–111

# MATERNITY PROTECTION (HEALTH AND SAFETY LEAVE REMUNERATION) REGULATIONS, 1995

## (S.I. No. 20 of 1995)

CC.501  **1.** These Regulations may be cited as the Maternity Protection (Health and Safety Leave Remuneration) Regulations, 1995 and shall come into operation on the 30th day of January 1995.

CC.502  **2.** In these Regulations—

"the Act" means the Maternity Protection Act, 1994 (No. 34 of 1994);

"basis week", in relation to an employee to whom health and safety leave has been granted, means—

   (a)  if the employee's pay is calculated by reference to a week ending on a day other than a Saturday, the last such week ending before the first of her 21 days of health and safety leave, and

   (b)  in any other case, the week ending on the last Saturday before the first of those 21 days;

"employee" means an employee to whom Part III of the Act applies;

"fixed rate", in relation to an employee's pay, means a rate of pay which is (or is a combination of)—

   (a)  a fixed wage, salary, allowance or bonus for each week, month or any other fixed period; or

   (b)  a fixed hourly or other time rate for a set number of hours (or other period of time) per week, month or any other fixed period;

"health and safety leave" means leave granted under section 18 of the Act;

"normal weekly pay" shall be construed in accordance with Regulations 4 and 5.

CC.503  **3.**—(1) Subject to paragraph (2), the remuneration which an employee shall be entitled to receive from her employer for the 21 days of health and safety leave referred to in section 18(4) of the Act shall be an amount equal to three times the employee's normal weekly pay.(2)

If, in the case of any employee, the 21 days of health and safety leave are not consecutive, then—

   (a)  if, in those 21 days, there is a period of at least 14 consecutive days, the employee shall be entitled to receive—

      (i)  in respect of the first 14 of those days, an amount of remuneration equal to twice her normal weekly pay, and

      (ii)  in respect of each (if any) further day in that period, remuneration at the appropriate daily rate for that day;

   (b)  if, in those 21 days, there is a period of 7, but less than 14, consecutive days, the employee shall be entitled to receive—

      (i)  in respect of the first 7 of those days, an amount of remuneration equal to her normal weekly pay, and

      (ii)  in respect of each (if any) further day in that period, remuneration at the appropriate daily rate for that day; and

   (c)  if, in those 21 days, there is a period of not more than 6 consecutive days (including a period of a single day) the employee shall be entitled to receive remuneration at the appropriate daily rate in respect of each of the days in that period.

(3) In paragraph (2), "the appropriate daily rate", in relation to a prticular employee means—

   (a)  for any day, other than one falling within paragraph (b) , an amount equal to her normal weekly pay divided by the number of days which she works in a normal working week or, if she does not work a set number of days, divided by five; and

(b)  for any day (such as Sunday) on which the employee would not normally work, nil.

**4.**—(1) Subject to paragraph (3) and Regulation 5, the normal weekly pay of an employee— **CC.504**
   (a)  whose pay, exclusive of any overtime, is wholly at a fixed rate, and
   (b)  whose employment involves work each week and, subject to overtime and holidays, the same number of hours each week,
is an amount equal to her pay in respect of the basis week, less any amount attributable to overtime.

(2) For the purpose of paragraph (1), so much of any pay as is payable to the employee otherwise than specifically by reference to the basis week shall be apportioned to that week on a pro rata basis.

(3) If an employee to whom paragraph (1) applies was not in fact working for the employer during the basis week or worked less than her normal number of hours in the basis week, paragraphs (1) and (2) shall have effect as if, for any reference to the basis week there were substituted a reference to that week—
   (a)  during which the employee worked her normal number of hours for her employer; and
   (b)  which ends on the same day (in the calendar week) as the basis week; and
   (c)  which is the last such week before the beginning of the basis week.

(4) Subject to paragraph 5 and Regulation 5, the normal weekly pay of an employee to whom paragraph (1) does not apply is an amount equal to one twenty sixth of her total pay in respect of the 26 weeks ending with the basis week; but, in calculating those 26 weeks and the employee's pay in respect of them, there shall be left out of account—
   (a)  any week during which the employee would normally have been but was not in fact, working for her employer; and
   (b)  any pay attributable to overtime.

(5) If an employee whose normal weekly pay fails to be determined under paragraph (4) has worked for her employer for a smaller number of weeks than allows for the 26 weeks referred to in that paragraph, that paragraph shall have effect as if for any reference to 26 weeks there were substituted a reference to that smaller number of weeks, and the reference to one twenty-sixth shall be construed accordingly.

(6) In this Regulation "pay", in relation to an employee, means pay to which she is entitled under her contract of employment, exclusive of any additional amount which, or so much of any amount as, is attributable to—
   (a)  night work;
   (b)  shift work;
   (c)  working unsocial hours; or
   (d)  the employee having to be available on stand by or otherwise on call.

**5.** If it appears to a rights commissioner or the Tribunal that the circumstances **CC.505** of a particular employee are such that her normal weekly pay cannot be calculated in accordance with Regulation 4, her normal weekly pay shall be calculated in such manner as, in the opinion of the rights commissioner or Tribunal, most closely corresponds with one or other of the bases set out in Regulation 4.

GENERAL NOTE

   These Regulations determine the manner of calculation of the amount of remuneration which an **CC.506** employee is entitled to receive from her employer for the first 21 days of leave granted by the employer to protect her safety and health, whether as a result of a risk assessment or because the employee cannot be required to perform nightwork.

C–113

# MATERNITY PROTECTION (MAXIMUM COMPENSATION) REGULATIONS, 1999

## (S.I. No. 134 of 1999)

CC.601    **1.** These Regulations may be cited as the Maternity Protection (Maximum Compensation) Regulations, 1999, and shall come into operation on the 18th day of May, 1999.

CC.602    **2.**—(1) In these Regulations—

"the Act" means the Maternity Protection Act, 1994 (No. 34 of 1994);

"relevant date" means the date on which a notice referring a dispute to a rights commissioner is given under section 31(1) of the Act;

"dispute" means a dispute to which Part V of the Act applies;

"relevant employment", in relation to an employee, means the employment in respect of which the 20 weeks' remuneration referred to in section 32(3) of the Act falls to be calculated;

"week", in relation to an employee whose remuneration is calculated by reference to a week ending on a day other than a Saturday, means a week ending on that other day and, in relation to any other employee, means a week ending on a Saturday, and "weekly" shall be construed accordingly.

(2) In these Regulations—

(a) a reference to a Regulation is a reference to a Regulation of these Regulations so numbered, and

(b) a reference to a paragraph is a reference to the paragraph of the provision in which the reference occurs.

CC.603    **3.** Where, by a decision of a rights commissioner or a determination of the Employment Appeals Tribunal in relation to a dispute, redress proposed for the employee concerned is or includes an award of compensation under subsection (2)(b) of section 32 of the Act, the 20 weeks' remuneration referred to in subsection (3) of that section shall be calculated in accordance with these Regulations.

CC.604    **4.**—(1) In the case of an employee who, before the relevant date, was remunerated in respect of the relevant employment wholly at an hourly rate, fixed wage or salary (with or without a regular bonus or allowance which does not vary by reference to the amount of work done), a week's remuneration for the purposes of section 32(3) of the Act shall be—

(a) the earnings in respect of that employment in the latest week before the relevant date in which the employee worked the number of hours per week that on that date was normal for that employment, plus

(b) if the employee was normally required to work overtime in the relevant employment, the average weekly overtime earnings in the relevant employment, as determined in accordance with paragraph (2).

(2) For the purposes of paragraph (1)(b), the average weekly overtime earnings of an employee in the relevant employment shall be—

(a)  in case the employee was employed for the whole of the period of 26 weeks ending 13 weeks before the relevant date, her overtime earnings during that period divided by 26, or

(b)  in any other case, her overtime earnings during the number of complete weeks worked before the relevant date divided by that number.

(3) If, in respect of the employment referred to in paragraph (1)(a), the employee's earnings would, apart from this paragraph, include a regular bonus bonus or similar payment which, in whole or in part, does not relate to work done in that

week, only so much (if any) of the payment which relates to that week shall be taken into account in determining the employee's earnings.

**5.**—(1) This Regulation applies to an employee whose remuneration in respect CC.605 of the relevant employment before the relevant date—

    (a)   was wholly or partly at piece rates,

    (b)   included commission directly related to the work done,

    (c)   otherwise varied in relation to the amount of work done by the employee, or

    (d)   varied on account of payments appropriate to attendance on a shift cycle, on particular days of the week or at particular times of the day.

(2) In relation to an employee to whom this Regulation applies, a week's remuneration for the purposes of section 32(3) of the Act shall be—

    (a)   in case the employee was employed in the relevant employment for the whole of the period of 26 weeks ending 13 weeks before the relevant date, her earnings for the number of hours worked during that period divided by that number, or

    (b)   in any other case, her earnings during the number of complete weeks worked before the relevant date divided by the number of hours worked during those weeks,and multiplied in either case by the number of hours per week that on the relevant date was normal for that employment.

(3) The earnings referred to in paragraph (2)(a) shall be adjusted in respect of any variation in rates of pay which took effect during the period of 13 weeks before the relevant date.

(4) Where in any week within the period of 26 weeks, or complete weeks, referred to in paragraph (2) the employee's earnings would, apart from this paragraph, include a regular bonus or similar payment which, in whole or in part, does not relate to work done in that week, only so much (if any) of the payment which does relate to that week shall be taken into account for the purposes of paragraph (2) in determining those earnings.

(5) For the purposes of paragraph (2), any week worked in another employment shall be taken into account if it would not have operated, for the purposes of the First Schedule to the Minimum Notice and Terms of Employment Act, 1973 (No. 4 of 1973), to break the continuity of service of the employee concerned in the relevant employment.

**6.** In determining an employee's earnings for any period for the purposes of CC.606 these Regulations, no account shall be taken of any sums paid by way of recoupment of expenses incurred by the employee in the discharge of the duties of her employment.

**7.** For the purposes of Regulations 4(2)(a) and 5(2)(a), any week during which CC.607 an employee did not work shall be disregarded and the latest week before the period of 26 weeks mentioned in those provisions, as the case may be, or before a week taken into account under this Regulation, as may be appropriate, shall be taken into account instead of a week during which the employee did not work as aforesaid.

**8.** Where, in respect of the relevant employment, there is no number of hours CC.608 for which employees work in each week which is normal for that employment, the weekly remuneration of each such employee shall be taken, for the purposes of these Regulations, to be the average amount of the remuneration paid to each such employee in the 52 weeks, or such lesser number of weeks as may be appropriate, in each of which the employee was working in the employment immediately before the relevant date.

**9.** Where under these Regulations account is to be taken of remuneration paid CC.609 in a period which does not coincide with the periods for which the remuneration is calculated, the remuneration shall be apportioned in such manner as may be just.

**10.**—(1) Where, under a contract of employment, an employee is required to CC.610 work for more hours per week than the number of hours that is normal for the employment, the hours for which the employee is so required to work shall be taken, for the purposes of Regulations 4 and 5(2), to be, in the case of that employee, the number of hours per week that is normal for the employment.

(2) Where, under a contract of employment, an employee is entitled to additional remuneration for working more than a specified number of hours per week—

(a)   in a case where the employee is required under the said contract to work for more than the said specified number of hours per week, the number of hours per week for which the employee is so required to work shall, for the purposes of Regulations 4 and 5(2), be taken to be, in the case of that employee, the number of hours of work per week that is normal for the employment, or

(b)   in any other case, the specified number of hours shall be taken, for the purposes of those provisions, to be, in the case of that employee, the number of hours of work per week that is normal for the employment.

GENERAL NOTE

**CC.611**    These Regulations prescribe the method for calculating maximum compensation for the purposes of redress under Part V of the Act.

# MATERNITY PROTECTION (TIME OFF FOR ANTE-NATAL CLASSES) REGULATIONS 2004

## S.I. No. 653 of 2004

**1.** (1) These Regulations may be cited as the Maternity Protection (Time off CC.701 for Ante-Natal Classes) Regulations 2004.

(2) These Regulations shall come into operation on 18 October 2004.

**2.** In these Regulations "Principal Act" means Maternity Protection Act CC.702 1994 (No. 34 of 1994).

**3.** (1) Subject to Regulation 4 of these Regulations, a pregnant employee to CC.703 whom section 15A(1) of the Principal Act applies shall be entitled to such time off from her work, without loss of pay, as is necessary for the purpose of attending one set of ante-natal classes (other than the last 3 classes in such a set).

(2) Subject to Regulation 4 of these Regulations, an expectant father of a child to whom section 15A(2) of the Principal Act applies shall be entitled once only to such time off from his work, without loss of pay, as is necessary for the purpose of attending the last 2 ante-natal classes in a set of such classes attended by the expectant mother of their child before the birth of the child.

**4.** (1) Entitlement to time off from work shall be subject to a pregnant CC.704 employee to whom section 15A(1) of the Principal Act applies, or an expectant father of a child to whom section 15A(2) of the Principal Act applies, having—

(a) notified her or his employer in writing of the dates and times of the classes, or the date and time of each class, to which the time off will relate as soon as practicable and in any event not later than 2 weeks before the date of the first class, or the class concerned, as the case may be, and

(b) produced for her or his employer's inspection, if so requested by the employer, an appropriate document indicating the dates and times of the classes or the date and time of the class concerned.

(2) Where the circumstances are such that, in the case of a particular class, non-compliance by the pregnant employee or the expectant father with paragraph (1) of this Regulation is not due to her or his neglect or default in relation to attendance at the class, she or he shall be deemed to have complied with the requirements of that paragraph if, not later than 1 week after the date of the class concerned, she or he furnishes her or his employer with evidence of her or him having attended the class and an indication of the circumstances which occasioned the non-compliance.

**5.** Subject to Regulation 4 of these Regulations, if a pregnant employee to CC.705 whom section 15A(1) of the Principal Act applies is unable to attend one full set of ante-natal classes (other than the last 3 classes in such a set) during a pregnancy due to circumstances beyond her control, including miscarriage, the premature birth of the baby concerned or the illness of the employee, she shall be entitled during one or more subsequent pregnancies to such time off from her work, without loss of pay, as is necessary for her to attend the classes (other than the last 3 classes) in such a set not attended by her.

GENERAL NOTE

These Regulations set out the details of the general entitlement of employees to time off work CC.706 without loss of pay for the purpose of attending ante-natal classes.

C–117

# MATERNITY PROTECTION (PROTECTION OF MOTHERS WHO ARE BREASTFEEDING) REGULATIONS 2004

## (S.I. No. 654 of 2004)

**CC.801**   **1.** (1) These Regulations may be cited as the Maternity Protection (Protection of Mothers who are Breastfeeding) Regulations 2004.

(2) These Regulations shall come into operation on 18 October 2004.

**CC.802**   **2.** In these Regulations—

"employee who is breastfeeding" means at any time an employee whose date of confinement was not more than twenty-six weeks earlier, who is breastfeeding and who has informed her employer of her condition;

"part-time employee" has the meaning assigned to it by section 7 of the Protection of Employees (Part-Time Work) Act 2001 (No. 4 of 2001);

"Principal Act" means Maternity Protection Act 1994 (No.34 of 1994).

**CC.803**   **3.** (1) An employee who is breastfeeding and to whom subsection (1)(a) of section 15B of the Principal Act applies shall be entitled, without loss of pay, to take 1 hour off from her work each working day as a breastfeeding break which may be taken—

(a) in the form of—

(i)  one break of 60 minutes,

(ii)  two breaks of 30 minutes each,

(iii) three breaks of 20 minutes each, or

(b) in such other manner as to number and duration of breaks as may be agreed by her and her employer.

(2) An employee who is breastfeeding and to whom subsection (1)(b) of section 15B of the Principal Act applies shall be entitled, without loss of pay, to have her working hours reduced by 1 hour each working day and that reduction may comprise one period of 60 minutes, two periods of 30 minutes each, 3 periods of 20 minutes each or such other periods as may be agreed by her and her employer.

**CC.804**   **4.** Time off from work, or a reduction in working hours, for breastfeeding in accordance with subsections (1)(a) and (1)(b) respectively of section 15B of the Principal Act and these Regulations shall be calculated in a *pro rata* basis for a part-time employee who is breastfeeding.

**CC.805**   **5.** When an employee who is breastfeeding proposes to exercise her entitlement to time off from work or a reduction of working hours under subsection (1)(1) or (1)(b), as the case may be, of section 15B of the Principal Act, she shall—

(a) notify her employer in writing of the proposal as soon as reasonably practicable but not later than the latest date specified in subsection (1), (1A) or 1(B), as may be appropriate, of section 28 of the Principal Act for her to notify her employer under that section of her intention to return to work and of the date on which she expects to return to work, and

(b) furnish, if so requested by her employer, the birth certificate of the child concerned or any other document establishing the date of birth of the child.

C–118

These Regulations set out the details of the general entitlement of employees to either time off work    **CC.806**
without loss of pay to breastfeed in the workplace or a reduction in working hours for the purpose of
breastfeeding outside the workplace. Because of the definition of "employee who is breastfeeding",
these entitlements only apply in the first six months following confinement. This restriction has been
criticised by the Irish Congress of Trade Unions ("Congress") who point out that, for those mothers
who take their full maternity leave, breastfeeding at work will only be an issue for several weeks.
Congress believes that breastfeeding breaks should apply for as long as the mother chooses and at least
for one year. Congress have also issued guidelines aimed at assisting trade union negotiators in
ensuring adequate breastfeeding facilities in the workplace (see *Industrial Relations News* 38, October
7, 2004, pp.14–15). These guidelines set out what Congress regards as adequate facilities in the
workplace and include a private room with a secure dedicated refrigerator, in which women can
breastfeed or express milk. Simply placing a chair in the ladies' toilet is not regarded as being
acceptable.

# MATERNITY PROTECTION (POSTPONEMENT OF LEAVE) REGULATIONS 2004

## (S.I. No. 655 of 2004)

**1.** (1) These Regulations may be cited as the Maternity Protection (Post-    **CC.901**
ponement of Leave) Regulations 2004.

(2)  These Regulations shall come into operation on 18 October 2004.

**2.** In these Regulations "Principal Act" means Maternity Protection Act    **CC.902**
1994 (No. 34 of 1994).

**3.** The maximum period of postponement of leave under section 14B or    **CC.903**
16B of the Principal Act is 6 months.

**4.** The evidence to be furnished by an employee or an employed father to    **CC.904**
her or his employer, if so requested by the employer, for the purposes of
section 14B or 16B, as the case may be, of the Principal Act shall be—

(a)  a letter or other appropriate document from the hospital in which the
child concerned is hospitalised confirming the hospitalisation, and

(b)  a letter or other appropriate document from the hospital concerned or
the child's medical practitioner confirming that the child has been
discharged from hospital, and the date of that discharge.

These Regulations set out the details of the postponement of maternity leave and/or additional    **CC.905**
maternity leave in the event of the child's hospitalisation.

# MATERNITY PROTECTION ACT 1994 (EXTENSION OF PERIODS OF LEAVE) ORDER 2006

## (S.I. No. 51 of 2006)

**CC.1001**  **1.** This Order may be cited as the Maternity Protection Act 1994 (Extension of Periods of Leave) Order 2006.

**CC.1002**  **2.** (1) Subject to paragraphs (2) and (3) of this Article, this Order (other than Articles 8 to 11 thereof) comes into operation on 1 February 2006.

(2) (a) Articles 4 and 5 of this Order apply in respect of a pregnant employee who commences maternity leave at any time not less than 4 weeks after the date specified in paragraph (1) of this Article.

(b) Article 6 of this Order applies in respect of an employee who commences additional maternity leave at any time not less than 4 weeks after the date specified in paragraph (1) of this Article.

(c) Article 7(a) of this Order applies in respect of a man who commences leave from his employment under section 16(1) (as amended by section 10(a) of the Act of 2004) of the Act of 1994 at any time after the date specified in paragraph (1) of this Article.

(d) (i) Subject to clause (ii) of this subparagraph, Article 7(b) of this Order applies in respect of a man who commences leave from his employment under section 16(4) (as amended by section 10(b) of the Act of 2004) of the Act of 1994 at any time not less than 4 weeks after the date specified in paragraph (1) of this Article.

(ii) Article 7(b) of this Order applies in respect of a man who commences leave from his employment under subsection (1)(a) of section 16 (as amended by section 10 of the Act of 2004) of the Act of 1994 at any time after the date specified in paragraph (1) of this Article and who gives notification under subsection (5) of the said section 16 (as so amended) at the same time as he gives notification under subsection (2)(a) thereof.

(3) (a) Articles 4 to 7 of this Order do not apply in respect of an employee who—

(i) at any time prior to the relevant date, postpones the leave concerned in accordance with section 14B (inserted by section 7 of the Act of 2004) or 16B (inserted by section 12 of the Act of 2004), as the case may be, of the Act of 1994, and

(ii) by reason only of that postponement, resumes or commences the leave concerned after the relevant date.

(b) In this paragraph "the relevant date" means—

(i) 1 February 2006, in respect of leave from a man's employment under—

(I) subsection (1) of section 16 (as amended by section 10 of the Act of 2004) of the Act of 1994, or

(II) subsection (4) of the said section 16 (as so amended)

where he gives notification under subsection (5) of that section at the same time as he gives notification under subsection (2)(a) thereof, and

(ii) 1 March 2006, in respect of maternity leave, additional maternity leave or leave under subsection (4) of the said section 16 (as so amended) other than in a case falling under subclause (II) of clause (i) of this subparagraph.

(4) Subject to paragraphs (5) and (6) of this Article, Articles 8 to 11 of this Order come into operation on 1 February 2007.

(5) (a) Articles 8 and 9 of this Order apply in respect of a pregnant employee who commences maternity leave at any time not less than 4 weeks after the commencement of those Articles.

(b) Article 10 of this Order applies in respect of an employee who commences additional maternity leave at any time not less than 4 weeks after the commencement of that Article.

(c) Paragraph (a) of Article 11 of this Order applies in respect of a man who commences leave from his employment under section 16(1) (as amended by section 10(a) of the Act of 2004) of the Act of 1994 at any time after the commencement of that Article.

(d) (i) Subject to clause (ii) of this subparagraph, paragraph (b) of Article 11 of this Order applies in respect of a man who commences leave from his employment under section 16(4) (as amended by section 10(b) of the Act of 2004) of the Act of 1994 at any time not less than 4 weeks after the commencement of that Article.

(ii) Paragraph (b) of Article 11 of this Order applies in respect of a man who commences leave from his employment under subsection (1)(a) of section 16 (as amended by section 10 of the Act of 2004) of the Act of 1994 at any time after the commencement of that Article and who gives notification under subsection (5) of the said section 16 (as so amended) at the same time as he gives notification under subsection (2)(a) thereof.

(6) (a) Articles 8 to 11 of this Order do not apply in respect of an employee who—

(i) at any time prior to the relevant date, postpones the leave concerned in accordance with section 14B (inserted by section 7 of the Act of 2004) or 16B (inserted by section 12 of the Act of 2004), as the case may be, of the Act of 1994, and

(ii) by reason only of that postponement, resumes or commences the leave concerned after the relevant date.

(b) In this paragraph "the relevant date" means—

(i) 1 February 2007, in respect of leave from a man's employment under—

(I) subsection (1) of section 16 (as amended by section 10 of the Act of 2004) of the Act of 1994, or

(II) subsection (4) of the said section 16 (as so amended)

where he gives notification under subsection (5) of that section at the same time as he gives notification under subsection (2)(a) thereof, and

(ii) 1 March 2007, in respect of maternity leave, additional maternity leave or leave under subsection (4) of the said section 16 (as so amended) other than in a case falling under subclause (II) of clause (i) of this subparagraph.

**3.** In this Order— CC.1003

"Act of 1994" means the Maternity Protection Act 1994 (No. 34 of 1994);

"Act of 2004" means the Maternity Protection (Amendment) Act 2004 (No. 28 of 2004).

CC.1004  **4.** [Amending section 8 of the Act of 1994]

CC.1005  **5.** [Amending section 13 of the Act of 1994]

CC.1006  **6.** [Amending section 14 of the Act of 1994]

CC.1007  **7.** [Amending section 16 of the Act of 1994]

CC.1008  **8.** Subsection (1) of section 8 (as amended by section 2 of the Act of 2004) of the Act of 1994 is amended—

(a) in paragraph (a), by substituting "26 consecutive weeks" for "22 consecutive weeks", and

(b) in paragraph (b), by substituting "26 weeks" for "22 weeks".

CC.1009  **9.** Subsection (2) of section 13 (as amended by section 4 of the Act of 2004) of the Act of 1994 is amended—

(a) in paragraph (a), by substituting "26 consecutive weeks" for "22 consecutive weeks", and

(b) in paragraph (b), by substituting "26 weeks" for "22 weeks".

CC.1010  **10.** Subsection (1) of section 14 (as amended by section 5 of the Act of 2004) of the Act of 1994 is amended—

(a) in paragraph (a), by substituting "16 consecutive weeks" for "12 consecutive weeks", and

(b) in paragraph (b), by substituting "16 weeks" for "12 weeks".

CC.1011  **11.** Section 16 (as amended by section 10 of the Act of 2004) of the Act of 1994 is amended—

(a) in subsection (1), by substituting "fortieth week" for "thirty-second week" in each place where it occurs and substituting "twenty-fourth week" for "twentieth week" in each place where it occurs, and

(b) in subsection (4)—

(i) in paragraph (a), by substituting "16 consecutive weeks" for "12 consecutive weeks", and

(ii) in paragraph (b), by substituting "16 weeks" for "12 weeks".

GENERAL NOTE

CC.1012  This Order amends the Maternity Protection Act 1994 so as to bring into effect the increases in maternity leave announced in the context of Budget 2006. Women who commenced maternity leave on or after March 1, 2006 will now be entitled to 22 weeks maternity leave and 12 weeks additional maternity leave (up from 18 and 8 weeks respectively). Women who commence maternity leave on or after March 1, 2007 will then be entitled to 26 weeks maternity leave and 16 weeks additional maternity leave.

# ADOPTIVE LEAVE ACT 1995

## (1995 No. 2)

ARRANGEMENT OF SECTIONS

PART I

PRELIMINARY AND GENERAL

PART II

ADOPTIVE LEAVE

PART III

PROVISIONS RELATING TO EMPLOYMENT CONTRACTS

Part IV

Amendment or Application of Other Enactments

*Unfair Dismissals Act, 1977*

*Redundancy Payments Act, 1967*

*Minimum Notice and Terms of Employment Act, 1973*

Part V

Disputes Relating to Entitlement

Part VI

Miscellaneous And Transitional Provisions

**DB.101**     An Act to entitle female employees, and in certain circumstances male
             employees, to employment leave for the purpose of child adoption, to
             extend to them the protection against unfair dismissal conferred by the
             Unfair Dismissals Act, 1977, and to provide for connected matters.

                                                              [15th March, 1995]

Introduction and General Note

**DB.102**     This Act gives effect to one of the recommendations in the Report of the Second Commission on the
             Status of Women (January 1993, at para. 3.7.16). The initial proposal for the introduction of adoptive
             leave was made in the Minister for Finance's 1992 Budget Statement. Subsequently in 1993 the

Programme for Partnership Government gave a firm commitment to the introduction of legislation for adoptive leave. The Bill was introduced in the Seanad in 1993 but was extensively amended when the Committee Stage was taken in November 1994. The Act (as amended) now envisages a 20 week period of leave for adopting mothers (and adopting fathers in certain very limited circumstances) covered by a social welfare payment and an optional 12 weeks' additional leave which will not attract payment rising to 24 and 16 weeks respectively with effect from March 1, 2007: see S.I. No. 52 of 2006. The scheme is modelled on the existing arrangements under the Maternity Protection Act 1994 (as amended) for natural mothers (see the Minister for Equality and Law Reform at 448 *Dáil Debates* Col. 746).

Opposition attempts to amend the Bill to allow either the adopting father or the adopting mother take adoptive leave failed. The Minister for Equality and Law Reform took the stance that the attempt was not "valid" in the context of the present proposal (449 *Dáil Debates* Col. 1995). He also said that it was not "appropriate" to deal here with the question of leave for fathers (138 *Seanad Debates* Col. 408) and that he could not agree to grant leave to adopting fathers "in isolation from an evaluation of the merits of the proposal generally for working parents whether adopting or natural" (449 *Dáil Debates* Col. 1995).

The Court of Justice of the European Communities in Case 162/83, *Commission v Italy* [1983] E.C.R. 3273, held that the restriction, under Italian legislation, of adoptive leave to women was justified by the State's legitimate concern to assimilate as far as possible the condition of entry of the child into the adopting family to those of a newborn child in the family during the very delicate initial period. The difference in treatment between adopting mothers and fathers could not, therefore, be regarded as discrimination within the meaning of Council Directive 76/207 (the Equal Treatment Directive). This case was distinguished, however, by the Supreme Court in *Telecom Éireann v O'Grady* [1998] 3 I.R. 432.

Mr O'Grady's application for adoptive leave was refused by Telecom Éireann on the basis that such leave, which was provided for Telecom staff pursuant to public service circular No. 20/83, was available for female employees only. Mr O'Grady claimed that the scheme discriminated against him on grounds of sex contrary to the Employment Equality Act 1977. That issue was referred to the Labour Court who, in turn, referred the matter to an Equality Officer for investigation and recommendation. The Equality Officer concluded that Telecom Éireann had not discriminated against Mr O'Grady contrary to the provisions of the 1977 Act. On appeal, the Labour Court decided otherwise. In the High Court Murphy J. was of the opinion that Mr O'Grady's claim that Telecom Éireann had discriminated against him within the meaning of section 2 of the Employment Equality Act 1977 was "prima facie well founded" in that women employees could obtain adoptive leave whereas men "similarly employed were not entitled to any comparable right". The question was whether section 16 of the 1977 Act "as properly interpreted" would allow "this apparent discrimination". Section 16 provided: "Nothing in this Act shall make it unlawful for an employer to arrange for or provide special treatment to women in connection with pregnancy or childbirth." Murphy J. said that "in its ordinary context" the word "childbirth" did not extend to or include "adoption". Counsel for Telecom Éireann had argued, however, that a more extensive meaning should be given to the word "childbirth" and had submitted that, as the 1977 Act was the mechanism by which Ireland had chosen to perform its obligations under Article 189 of the Treaty of Rome as regards the implementation of Council Directive 76/207, the court should adopt a teleological or purposive interpretation of the word. In this context counsel referred to Article 2(3) of the Directive which provides that the Directive "shall be without prejudice to provisions concerning protection of women, particularly as regards pregnancy and maternity". Murphy J. accepted that, as a result of the decisions of the Court of Justice in cases such as *Commission v Italy*, a Member State could legitimately restrict the availability of adoptive leave to female employees. He noted, however, that the Oireachtas, in enacting section 16, could have chosen to permit an employer to arrange for or provide special treatment to women in connection with "pregnancy and maternity" or "pregnancy and motherhood" but it chose to restrict the concession or exemption to "pregnancy and childbirth". He accepted the argument made by Counsel on behalf of Mr O'Grady that the purpose of the Directive was to avoid discrimination and that that goal was better achieved by giving a non-extended meaning to the words of exemption contained in section 16. Accordingly he was not prepared to interpret the word "childbirth" so as to include adoption.

Murphy J.'s decision was upheld by the Supreme Court (Hamilton C.J., Keane and Barron JJ.) Hamilton C.J. said ([1998] 3 I.R. 432 at 447) that the provisions of section 16 of the 1977 Act were "quite clear and explicit and no matter what manner of interpretation is applied thereto are incapable of being interpreted as to include adoption". In their view the scheme was "clearly discriminatory against male persons". Consequently any voluntary or contractual scheme for adoptive leave cannot be confined to female employees: see further *Merriman v Eastern Health Board* EE10/1998 and *Doolan v Dublin Institute of Technology* DEE 8/1998. Keane J., however, accepted that some persons would find it "surprising" that employers who had undertaken a scheme of adoptive leave were under a legal

D–5

obligation to afford adoptive fathers a similar facility although they were not obliged, in the case of biological mothers, to afford the biological father such a facility. He pointed out that "impending legislation" would make it clear that the exemption permitted by Article 2.3 of the Directive would apply to adoptive as well as maternity leave. That legislation has now been enacted and section 26(1) of the Employment Equality Act 1998 provides that nothing in that Act shall make it unlawful for an employer to arrange for or provide treatment which confers benefits on women "in connection with pregnancy and maternity (including breastfeeding) or adoption".

The arrangements for civil servants are now set out in Department of Finance Circular 2/97, clause 4 of which provides that civil servants on adoptive leave will be given full pay, except where he or she has been appointed for a fixed term of less than 26 weeks. Moreover clause 10 provides that adoptive leave for fathers is only available if the adopting mother dies within 14 weeks of the day of placement. The Act was amended by the Adoptive Leave Act 2005.

CITATION

**DB.103**   See section 1(1).

COMMENCEMENT

**DB.104**   The Act came into operation on March 20, 1995: see S.I. No. 64 of 1995.

STATUTORY INSTRUMENTS

**DB.105**   Adoptive Leave Act 1995 (Commencement) Order 1995 (S.I. No. 64 of 1995).
Adoptive Leave (Referral of Disputes and Appeals) (Part V) Regulations 1995 (S.I. No. 195 of 1995).
Adoptive Leave (Calculation of Weekly Remuneration) Regulations 1995 (S.I. No. 196 of 1995).
Adoptive Leave Act 1995 (Extension of Periods of Leave) Order 2006 (S.I. No. 52 of 2006).

PARLIAMENTARY DEBATES

**DB.106**   138 *Seanad Debates* Cols 407–433 (Second Stage)
141 *Seanad Debates* Cols 766–797 (Committee Stage)
141 *Seanad Debates* Cols 797–831 (Committee Stage resumed, Report and Final Stages)
448 *Dáil Debates* Cols 745–791 (Second Stage)
449 *Dáil Debates* Cols 1989–2035 (Committee and Final Stages)
142 *Seanad Debates* Cols 753–764 (Report and Final Stages)

PART I

PRELIMINARY AND GENERAL

## Short title and commencement

**DB.107**   **1.**—(1) This Act may be cited as the Adoptive Leave Act, 1995.

(2) This Act shall come into operation on such day as the Minister shall by order appoint.

GENERAL NOTE

**DB.108**   The Act came into operation on March 20, 1995: Adoptive Leave Act 1995 (Commencement) Order 1995 (S.I. No. 64 of 1995). The amendments effected by the Adoptive Leave Act 2005 (with the exceptions of ss.9 and 10 of that Act) came into effect on November 28, 2005: see the Adoptive Leave Act 2005 (Commencement) Order 2005 (S.I. No. 724 of 2005). The amendments effected by ss.9 and 10 of the 2005 Act came into effect on January 30, 2006: see the Adoptive Leave Act 2005 (Commencement) Order 2006 (S.I. No. 16 of 2006). The collective citation is now the Adoptive Leave Acts 1995 and 2005.

## Interpretation

**DB.109**   **2.**—(1) In this Act, except where the context otherwise requires—

"the Act of 1967" means the Redundancy Payments Act, 1967;
"the Act of 1977" means the Unfair Dismissals Act, 1977;

D–6

["additional adoptive leave" has, subject to subsection (2A), the meaning assigned to it by section 8(1) or, as the case may be, section 10(1);

"adoptive leave" has, subject to subsection (2A), the meaning assigned to it by section 6(1), or, as the case may be, section 9(1);]

"adopting father" means a male employee in whose care a child has been placed or is to be placed with a view to the making of an adoption order, or to the effecting of a foreign adoption or following any such adoption, where the adopting mother has died;

"adopting mother" means a woman, including an employed adopting mother, in whose care a child (of whom she is not the natural mother) has been placed or is to be placed with a view to the making of an adoption order, or to the effecting of a foreign adoption or following any such adoption;

"adopting parent" means employed adopting mother, adopting father or sole male adopter;

"associated employer" shall be construed in accordance with section 19(3);

"certificate of placement" has the meaning assigned to it by section 13;

"contract of employment" means, subject to subsection (2)—

(a) a contract of service or apprenticeship, or

(b) any other contract whereby an individual agrees with a person, who is carrying on the business of an employment agency within the meaning of the Employment Agency Act, 1971, and is acting in the course of that business, to do or perform personally any work or service for another person (whether or not that other person is a party to the contract),

whether the contract is express or implied and if express, whether it is oral or in writing;

"day of placement" means—

(a) the day on which the child is placed physically in the care of the adopting parent with a view to the making of an adoption order, or

(b) the day on which the child is placed physically in the care of the adopting parent with a view to the effecting of a foreign adoption, or

(c) in the case of a foreign adoption, where the child has not previously been placed in the care of the adopting parent, the day on which the child has been so placed following the adoption;

"employed adopting mother" means a female employee in whose care a child (of whom she is not the natural mother) has been placed or is to be placed with a view to the making of an adoption order, or to the effecting of a foreign adoption or following any such adoption;

"employee", subject to subsection (2), means (except in Part IV) a person who has entered into or works under (or, where the employment has ceased, entered into or worked under) a contract of employment;

"employer", subject to subsection (2), means, in relation to an employee, the person with whom the employee has entered into, or for whom the employee works under (or, where the employment has ceased, entered into or worked under) a contract of employment;

D–7

"foreign adoption" has the meaning assigned to it by the Adoption Act,
1991;

[...]

"the Minister" means the [Minister for Justice, Equality and Law Reform];

"prescribed" means prescribed by order or regulation under this Act;

"registered adoption society" means a body of persons entered in the
Adoption Societies Register kept by An Bord Uchtála under Part IV
of the Adoption Act, 1952;

"sole male adopter" means a male employee who is not an adopting father
within the meaning of this Act and in whose sole care a child has been
placed or is to be placed with a view to the making of an adoption order,
or to the effecting of a foreign adoption or following any such adoption;

"the successor" has the meaning assigned to it by section 18;

"the Tribunal" means the Employment Appeals Tribunal.

(2) For the purposes of this Act—

(a) a person holding office under, or in the service of, the State (including a
member of the Garda Síochána or the Defence Forces) or otherwise as a
civil servant, within the meaning of the Civil Service Regulation Act,
1956, shall be deemed to be an employee employed by the State or
Government, as the case may be, under a contract of service;

(b) an officer or servant of a local authority, for the purposes of the Local
Government Act, 1941, a harbour authority, [the Health Service Execu-
tive] or a vocational education committee shall be deemed to be an
employee employed by the authority, [the Executive] or committee, as
the case may be, under a contract of service; and

(c) in relation to an employee whose contract of employment falls (or, where
the employment has ceased, fell) within paragraph (b) of the definition of
"contract of employment" in subsection (1), the person who is liable to
pay her wages shall be deemed to be her employer.

[(2A) In this Act, except where the context otherwise requires, references to a
period of adoptive leave or additional adoptive leave are references to—

(a) in case part of such leave is postponed under section 11C, the part already
taken or the part postponed, as appropriate, or

(b) in any other case, a continuous such period, whether or not so postponed.]

(3) In this Act, a reference to a Part or section is to a Part or section of this
Act, unless it is indicated that reference to some other enactment is intended.

(4) In this Act, a reference to a subsection or paragraph is to the subsection or
paragraph of the provision in which the reference occurs, unless it is indicated
that reference to some other provision is intended.

(5) In this Act, a reference to any enactment includes a reference to that
enactment as amended by any other enactment including this Act.

GENERAL NOTE

**DB.110**     "the Act of 1977": this Act was amended by the Unfair Dismissals (Amendment) Act 1993.
"additional adoptive leave": this definition was inserted by s.2 of the Adoptive Leave Act 2005.
"adoptive leave": this definition was inserted by s.2 of the Adoptive Leave Act 2005.
"contract of employment": as to whether a person is employed under a contract of service see
*Henry Denny & Sons (Ireland) Ltd v Minister for Social Welfare* [1998] 1 I.R. 34. The inclusion of a
specific reference to persons employed through employment agencies is similar to the provisions of

s.13 of the Unfair Dismissals (Amendment) Act 1993, s.1(1) of the Terms of Employment (Information) Act 1994 and s.2(1) of the Organisation of Working Time Act 1997. But note the decision of the Labour Court in *Rooney v Diageo Global Supply* [2004] E.L.R. 133 that an agency supplied worker was employed by the client under a contract of employment.

"foreign adoption": s.1 of the Adoption Act 1991 defines this as:

"an adoption of a child who at the date on which the adoption was effected was under the age of 18 years, which was effected outside the State by a person or persons under and in accordance with the law of the place where it was effected and in relation to which the following conditions are satisfied:

(a)  the consent to the adoption of every person whose consent to the adoption was, under the law of the place where the adoption was effected, required to be obtained or dispensed with was obtained or dispensed with under that law,

(b)  the adoption has essentially the same legal effect as respects the termination and creation of parental rights and duties with respect to the child in the place where it was effected as an adoption effected by an adoption order,

(c)  the law of the place where the adoption was effected required an enquiry to be carried out, as far as was practicable, into the adopters, the child and the parents or guardian,

(d)  the law of the place where the adoption was effected required the court or other authority or person by whom the adoption was effected, before doing so, to give due consideration to the interests and welfare of the child,

(e)  the adopters have not received, made or given or caused to be made or given any payment or other reward (other than any payment reasonably and properly made in connection with the making of the arrangements for the adoption) in consideration of the adoption or agreed to do so."

"the Minister": this definition was amended by virtue of s.2 of the Adoptive Leave Act 2005.

"sole male adopter": it may be noted that McMahon J. in *O'G v Attorney General* [1985] I.L.R.M. 61 at 64 said the view "that a woman by virtue of her sex has an innate capacity for parenthood which is denied to a man and the lack of which renders a man unsuitable as an adopter" was not supported by any medical evidence adduced before him. A "sole male adopter" will invariably be the father, or other male relative of the child, or a widower. The Adoption Act 1991, however, provides in s.10(2) that An Bord Uchtála has discretion to grant an adoption order regardless of the applicant's marital status "in the particular circumstances of the case" and s.10(4) permits applications from one spouse in circumstances where the consent of the other is unavailable following their separation.

Subsection (2) was amended by s.66 of the Health Act 2004 and subs.(2A) was inserted by s.2 of the Adoptive Leave Act 2005.

## Orders and regulations

**3.**—(1) An order or regulation under this Act may contain such consequential, supplementary and ancillary provisions as the Minister considers necessary or expedient.    DB.111

(2) The Minister may by order amend or revoke an order under this Act, including an order under this subsection.

(3) Where an order is proposed to be made under this Act, a draft of the order shall be laid before both Houses of the Oireachtas and the order shall not be made until a resolution approving of the draft has been passed by each such House.

(4) Before making an order or regulation under this Act, the Minister shall consult such organisations or other bodies of persons representative of employers and such organisations or other bodies of persons representative of trades unions or bodies analogous to trade unions as the Minister considers appropriate.

(5) Subsections (1) to (4) do not apply to an order under section 1(2).

(6) Every regulation made under this Act shall be laid before each House of the Oireachtas as soon as practicable after it is made and, if a resolution annulling the regulation is passed by either such House within the next 21 days on which the House has sat after the regulation is laid before it, the regulation shall

be annulled accordingly, but without prejudice to the validity of anything previously done under the regulation.

## Voidance or modification of certain provisions in agreements

DB.112    **4.**—(1) In this section "agreement" means an agreement, whether a contract of employment or not, and whether made before or after the commencement of this Act.

(2) A provision in an agreement shall be void in so far as it purports to exclude or limit the application of any provision of this Act or is inconsistent with any provision of this Act.

(3) A provision in an agreement which is or becomes less favourable in relation to an adopting parent than a similar or corresponding entitlement conferred on her by this Act shall be deemed to be so modified as to be not less favourable to her.

(4) Nothing in this or any other enactment shall be construed as prohibiting the inclusion in an agreement of a provision (subsequently referred to in this section as "the additional provision") in relation to adoption, in addition to those required by this Act, the effect of which would be to render the agreement more favourable to an adopting parent than it would be if it did not include the additional provision.

(5) The inclusion of the additional provision in an agreement shall not, by reason of the fact that it applies to an adopting parent only, confer any right under this or any other enactment on an employee who is not an adopting parent.

GENERAL NOTE

DB.113    This section ensures that persons cannot contract out of their obligations or entitlements under the Act but allows for the provision of arrangements that are more favourable than those provided in the Act.

## Expenses

DB.114    **5.**—Any expenses incurred in the administration of this Act shall, to such extent as may be sanctioned by the Minister for Finance, be paid out of moneys provided by the Oireachtas.

PART II

ADOPTIVE LEAVE

## Entitlement of employed adopting mother (or sole male adopter) to minimum period of adoptive leave

DB.115    [**6.**—(1) Subject to this Part, an employed adopting mother (or sole male adopter) shall be entitled to leave (to be known as "adoptive leave") from the employee's employment.

(2) Adoptive leave shall begin on the date of placement and be for a minimum period of [20] weeks.

(3) The minimum period may be extended by order made by the Minister with

the consent of the Minister for Social and Family Affairs and the Minister for Finance.]

GENERAL NOTE

This section was substituted by virtue of s.3 of the Adoptive Leave Act 2005. The minimum period **DB. 116** was extended, with effect from February 1, 2006, by Article 4 of S.I. No. 52 of 2006.

## Notification of employer

**7.**—(1) In the case of an adoption other than a foreign adoption, entitlement to **DB.117** the minimum period of adoptive leave shall be subject to an employed adopting mother (or sole male adopter)—

(a) having, as soon as is reasonably practicable but not later than 4 weeks before the expected day of placement, caused her employer to be notified in writing of her intention to take adoptive leave, and

(b) having, as soon as is reasonably practicable, caused her employer to be notified in writing of the expected day of placement, and

(c) causing her employer to be supplied with the certificate of placement as soon as is reasonably practicable but not later than 4 weeks after the day of placement.

(2) In the case of a foreign adoption, entitlement to the minimum period of adoptive leave shall be subject to an employed adopting mother (or sole male adopter)—

(a) having, as soon as is reasonably practicable but not later than 4 weeks before the expected day of placement, caused her employer to be notified in writing of her intention to take adoptive leave, and

(b) having, as soon as is reasonably practicable, caused her employer to be notified in writing of the expected day of placement, and

(c) (i) having caused her employer to be supplied with a copy of the declaration made pursuant to section 5(1)(iii)(II) of the Adoption Act, 1991, before the expected day of placement, if not already supplied, and

(ii) causing her employer to be supplied with particulars in writing of the placement as soon as is reasonably practicable after the day of placement.

(3) A notification under this section may be revoked by a further notification in writing by or on behalf of the employed adopting mother (or sole male adopter) to her employer.

(4) Where the day of placement is postponed, commencement of the period of adoptive leave shall also be postponed subject to the employed adopting mother (or sole male adopter) causing her employer to be notified of the expected new day of placement as soon as is reasonably practicable.

GENERAL NOTE

This section requires employees, who wish to avail of adoptive leave, to inform the employer of **DB.118** their intention to take the leave and of the expected date of placement. At least four weeks' written notice of intention to take leave is required and subs.(1)(c) requires that evidence of placement must be furnished within four weeks of the placement, except in the case of a foreign adoption where, because of the variety of arrangements that may exist in practice, evidence need only be furnished as soon as is reasonably practicable.

**Entitlement of employed adopting mother (or sole male adopter) to additional adoptive leave**

DB.119

**8.**—[(1) (a) Subject to this Part, an employed adopting mother (or sole male adopter) who is entitled to, or is on, adoptive leave shall, on request, be entitled to further leave (to be known as "additional adoptive leave") from the employee's employment.

(b) The additional adoptive leave shall commence immediately after the adoptive leave and be for a maximum period of [12] weeks.

(c) The maximum period may be extended by order made by the Minister.]

(2) Entitlement to additional adoptive leave, in a situation other than one to which subsection (5) applies, shall be subject to an employed adopting mother (or sole male adopter) having caused her employer to be notified in writing of her intention to take such leave.

(3) Notification under subsection (2) shall be given either at the same time as the relevant notification under section 7(1)(a) or (2)(a) or not later than 4 weeks before the date which would have been the expected date of her return to work if the employed adopting mother (or sole male adopter) had not taken the additional adoptive leave.

(4) A notification under subsection (2) may be revoked by a further notification in writing by or on behalf of the employed adopting mother (or sole male adopter) to her employer not later than 4 weeks before the date which would have been the expected date of her return to work if the employed adopting mother (or sole male adopter) had not taken the additional adoptive leave.

(5) In the case of a foreign adoption, where the employed adopting mother (or sole male adopter) requires a period of additional adoptive leave before the day of placement, for the purposes of familiarisation with the child who is to be adopted, some or all of the additional adoptive leave may be taken before the day of placement.

(6) Entitlement to additional adoptive leave under subsection (5) shall be subject to the employed adopting mother (or sole male adopter)—

(a) having caused her employer to be notified in writing not later than 4 weeks before the date on which she intends to take such leave, of the intended date of commencement of such additional adoptive leave, and

(b) having caused her employer to be supplied with a copy of the declaration made pursuant to section 5(1)(iii)(II) of the Adoption Act, 1991.

(7) A notification under subsection (6)(a) may be revoked by a further notification in writing by or on behalf of the employed adopting mother (or sole male adopter) to her employer.

(8) A period of additional adoptive leave under subsection (5) shall expire immediately before the day of placement.

GENERAL NOTE

DB.120    Subsection (1) was substituted by virtue of s.4 of the Adoptive Leave Act 2005. The maximum period was extended, with effect from February 1, 2006, by Article 4 of S.I. No. 52 of 2006.

DB.121    This section now allows an adopting mother (or sole male adopter) to take up to 12 consecutive weeks' additional adoptive leave, immediately following the 20 weeks' adoptive leave. Entitlement to such additional leave is conditional on the employer being informed in writing not later than four weeks before the expected date of return from adoptive leave. Subsection (5) provides, in the case of a foreign adoption, that, subject to certain notification requirements, some or all of the period of additional leave may be taken before the day of placement.

### Entitlement of adopting father to adoptive leave in certain circumstances

**9.**—[(1) (a) Where an adopting mother dies, the adopting father shall be entitled to leave (to be known as "adoptive leave") from his employment.    **DB.122**

(b)  The adoptive leave shall be for a period of—

    (i)  in case the adopting mother dies on or after the day of placement, [20] weeks less the period between the date of placement and the date of her death, or

    (ii)  in any other case, [20] weeks.

(c)  The period may be extended by order made by the Minister with the consent of the Minister for Social and Family Affairs and the Minister for Finance.]

(2) Entitlement to a period of leave under subsection (1) shall be subject to the adopting father—

(a)  (i)  having, as soon as is reasonably practicable before the commencement of the leave, caused his employer to be notified in writing of his intention to take such leave, or

    (ii)  in a case where the adopting mother died after the day of placement, causing her employer to be notified in writing of his intention to take such leave no later than the day on which he commences the leave,

    and

(b)  having, as soon as is reasonably practicable, caused his employer to be notified in writing of the day or expected day of placement, as may be appropriate, and

(c)  (i)  in the case of an adoption other than a foreign adoption, causing his employer to be supplied with the certificate of placement as soon as is reasonably practicable but not later than 4 weeks after the day of placement or 4 weeks after the commencement of the leave whichever is the later, or

    (ii)  in the case of a foreign adoption,

        (I)  causing his employer to be supplied with a copy of the declaration made pursuant to section 5(1)(iii)(II) of the Adoption Act 1991, as soon as is reasonably practicable but not later than 4 weeks after the commencement of the leave, and

        (II)  causing his employer to be supplied with particulars in writing of placement as soon as is reasonably practicable,

    and

(d)  causing, if requested, his employer to be supplied with a copy of the death certificate made in respect of the deceased adopting mother as soon as is reasonably practicable.

(3) The period of adoptive leave referred to in subsection (1) shall commence within 7 days of the death of the adopting mother or on the day of placement whichever is the later.

D–13

(4) A notification under this section may be revoked by a further notification in writing by or on behalf of the adopting father to his employer.

(5) Where the day of placement is postponed, commencement of the period of adoptive leave shall also be postponed subject to the adopting father causing his employer to be notified of the expected new day of placement as soon as is reasonably practicable.

GENERAL NOTE

**DB.123**    This section, as amended by s.5 of the Adoptive Leave Act 2005, entitles an adopting father to adoptive leave where the adopting mother has died, irrespective of whether the mother was herself eligible for adoptive leave. The notification requirements are similar to those laid down in s.7, except that the requirements in relation to the timing of the notification take account of the special circumstances of the case. The adopting father is entitled to the period, or remainder of the period, of adoptive leave to which the mother, had she been an employed adopting mother, would have been entitled had she still been alive.

## Entitlement of adopting father to additional adoptive leave in certain circumstances

**DB.124**    **10.**—[(1) (a) An employed adopting father who is entitled to, or is on, adoptive leave on the death of the adopting mother shall, on request, be entitled to further leave (to be known as "additional adoptive leave") from his employment.

(b)  The additional adoptive leave shall be for a period of—
    (i)   in case the adopting mother dies on or after the expiration of [20] weeks from the day of placement, [12] weeks less the period between the date of that expiration and the date of her death, or
    (ii)  in any other case, [12] weeks.
(c)  The period of additional adoptive leave may be extended by order made by the Minister.]

(2) Entitlement to a period of leave under subsection (1) shall be subject to an adopting father complying with section 9(2) as adapted by subsection (3).

(3) For the purposes of this section, references in section 9(2) to adoptive leave shall be construed as including references to additional adoptive leave and references therein to subsection (1) of that section shall be construed as including references to subsection (1) of this section.

(4) Where an adopting father has already complied with the provisions of section 9(2)(b), (c) and (d), it shall not be necessary for him to comply with those provisions as adapted by subsection (3) in order to satisfy the requirements of subsection (2).

(5) The period of additional adoptive leave referred to in subsection (1) shall commence within 7 days of the death of the adoptive mother or, where the adopting father was on adoptive leave, on the day immediately following the end of such leave.

(6) A notification under this section may be revoked by a further notification in writing by or on behalf of the adopting father to his employer.

GENERAL NOTE

**DB.125**    This section, as amended by s.6 of the Adoptive Leave Act 2005, entitles an adopting father to additional leave where the adopting mother has died. The notification requirements are similar to those laid down in s.8, except that the requirements in relation to the timing of the notification take account of the special circumstances of the case. As with s.9, the entitlement applies irrespective of whether the adopting mother was herself eligible for adoptive leave.

## Entitlement of adopting father to additional adoptive leave before day of placement in certain circumstances

**11.**—(1) In the case of a foreign adoption, where the adopting mother dies and the adopting father requires a period of additional adoptive leave before the day of placement, for the purposes of familiarisation with the child who is to be adopted, some or all of the additional adoptive leave under section 10 may be taken immediately before the day of placement. **DB.126**

(2) Entitlement to a period of leave under subsection (1) shall be subject to the adopting father—

(a) having, as soon as is reasonably practicable, caused his employer to be notified in writing of his intention to take such additional adoptive leave before the day of placement, and

(b) causing his employer to be supplied with a copy of the declaration made pursuant to section 5(1)(iii)(II) of the Adoption Act, 1991, as soon as is reasonably practicable but not later than 4 weeks after commencement of the leave, and

(c) causing, if requested, his employer to be supplied with a copy of the death certificate made in respect of the deceased adopting mother as soon as is reasonably practicable.

(3) The period of additional adoptive leave referred to in subsection (1) shall commence as soon as is reasonably practicable after the death of the adopting mother.

(4) A notification under this section may be revoked by a further notification in writing by or on behalf of the adopting father to his employer.

(5) Where the expected day of placement is postponed, commencement of the period of additional adoptive leave under this section shall also be postponed subject to the adopting father causing his employer to be notified of the expected new day of placement as soon as is reasonably practicable.

GENERAL NOTE

This section entitles an adopting father, in a case of foreign adoption where the adopting mother has died, to take some or all of the period of additional leave before the day of placement. As with ss.9 and 10, the entitlement applies irrespective of whether the mother herself was eligible for adoptive leave. **DB.127**

## Time off to attend certain pre-adoption classes and meetings

[**11A.** (1) Subject to subsections (2) and (3), an employee shall be entitled to time off from work, without loss of pay, to attend any pre-adoption classes and meetings which the employee is obliged to attend. **DB.127A**

(2) Subsection (1) shall not apply—

(a) to a member of the Defence Forces who is—

(i) on active service within the meaning of section 5 of the Defence Act 1954 or deemed to be on active service within the meaning of section 4(1) of the Defence (Amendment) (No. 2) Act 1960,

(ii) engaged in operational duties at sea,

(iii) engaged in operations in aid of the civil power,

D–15

> > (iv) engaged in training that is directly associated with any of the activities referred to in subparagraphs (i), (ii) and (iii) of this paragraph, or
> > (v) engaged in any other duty outside the State,
> (b) if the Chief of Staff of the Defence Forces in exceptional circumstances so directs, to a member of the Defence Forces who is required to perform a duty which is, in the opinion of the Chief of Staff of the Defence Forces, of a special or urgent nature for so long as the member is performing the duty,
> (c) to a member of the Garda Síochána who is on the direction, or with the consent, of the Commissioner of the Garda Síochána serving outside the State and performing duties of a police character or advising others on, or monitoring them in, the performance of such duties or any related duties for so long as the member is so serving, and
> (d) if the Commissioner of the Garda Síochána in exceptional circumstances so directs, to a member of the Garda Síochána who is required to perform a duty which is, in the opinion of the Commissioner of the Garda Síochána, of a special or urgent nature for so long as the member is performing the duty.

(3) (a) In this subsection "classes" refers to the pre-adoption classes and meetings mentioned in subsection (1).

> (b) The entitlement of an employee to time off under subsection (1) is subject to his or her having—
> > (i) notified the employer in writing of the dates and times of the classes concerned, or the date and time of each class, as soon as practicable but not later than 2 weeks before the date of the first class, or the class concerned, as the case may be, and
> > (ii) produced to the employer, on request, an appropriate document indicating the dates and times of the classes, or the date and time of the class, concerned.
> (c) Where the circumstances are such that, in the case of a particular class, non-compliance by the employee with paragraph (b) is not due to any neglect or default by the employee in relation to attendance at the class, the employee is deemed to have complied with the requirements of that paragraph if, not later than one week after the date of the class concerned, he or she provides the employer with evidence of the attendance and an indication of the circumstances which gave rise to the non-compliance.

(4) References in this section to pre-adoption classes and meetings are references to such classes and meeting held within the State.]

GENERAL NOTE

**DB. 127B**  This section, which provides an entitlement to paid time-off to attend necessary pre-adoption classes and meetings, was inserted by s.7 of the Adoptive Leave Act 2005.

## Termination of additional adoptive leave on sickness of adopting parent

**DB. 127C**  [**11B.**—(1) An adopting parent ("the employee")—

> (a) who is sick while on adoptive leave or while entitled to, or on, additional adoptive leave, and
> (b) who wishes to terminate the additional adoptive leave,

may request the employer in writing to terminate the additional adoptive leave or cause such a request to be made.

(2) If the employer agrees to terminate the leave, it shall terminate on a date agreed by the employee and the employer that is—

(a)  not earlier than the date on which the sickness began, and

(b)  not later than the date on which the leave would have ended in accordance with the notification of intention to take it given by the employee to the employer under this Part or section 41, as the case may be.

(3) The employer shall notify the employee of the decision on the request as soon as is reasonably practicable after its receipt.

(4) On the termination of the additional adoptive leave—

the absence from work of the employee owing to sickness after the termination shall be treated in the same way as any other absence from work of the employee owing to sickness, and

(b)  the employee shall cease to be entitled to any leave not by then taken.]

GENERAL NOTE

This section, which allows for the termination of additional adoptive leave, was inserted by s.8 of the Adoptive Leave Act 2005.  **DB.127D**

## Postponement of leave on hospitalisation of child

[**11C.**—(1) If—  **DB.127E**

(a)  an adopted child is in hospital, and

(b)  the child's adopting parent ("the employee") is entitled to, or is on, adoptive leave or additional adoptive leave,

the employee may request the employer in writing (or cause such a request to be made) to postpone in accordance with this section—

(i)  the whole of the adoptive leave and any additional adoptive leave,

(ii)  the part of the adoptive leave not by then taken and any additional adoptive leave, or

(iii) the whole of the additional adoptive leave or any part not by then taken, as appropriate.

(2) If the employer agrees to the request—

(a)  the employee shall continue to work or, as the case may be, shall return to work on a date agreed by the employee and employer that is not later than the date on which the leave concerned is due to end in accordance with the notification given under section 7 or (as the case may be) given or deemed under subsection (5) to have been given, under section 8(3),

(b)  the leave concerned shall be postponed or, as the case may be, postponed with effect from the date agreed under paragraph (a),

(c)  the employee shall be entitled in accordance with this section to the leave or the part of the leave not taken  by reason of the postponement (in this Act referred to as "postponed leave"), and

(d)  the postponed leave shall be taken as a continuous period beginning not later than 7 days after the child is discharged from hospital or such other date as may be agreed between the employer and the employee.

D–17

(3) The employer shall notify the employee concerned in writing of the decision on the request as soon as is reasonably practicable after its receipt.

(4) (a) Subject to subsection (6), entitlement to postponed leave shall be subject to the employee having notified the employer in writing (or having caused the employer to be so notified) of the employee's intention to take the leave.

(b) The notification shall be given by the employee as soon as is reasonably practicable after the employee becomes aware of the date of the child's discharge from hospital.

(c) The notification may be revoked by a further notification in writing given by or on behalf of the employee to the employer.

(5) Notwithstanding that an employee who is on adoptive leave has not caused the employer to be notified in accordance with section 8(3) of his or her intention to take additional adoptive leave, the employee shall be deemed, for the purposes of paragraph (ii) or (iii) of subsection (1), to have done so.

(6) An employer may waive the right to receive a notification in accordance with subsection (4).

(7) The employer may require the employee to supply evidence of the child's hospitalisation and discharge from hospital.]

GENERAL NOTE

**DB.127F**     This section was inserted by s.9 of the Adoptive Leave Act 2005.

## Absence from work owing to sickness while leave postponed

**DB.127G**     [**11D.**—(1) Where—

(a) an employee whose request to postpone leave has been agreed by the employer continues to work or as the case may be, returns to work in accordance with section 11C(2)(a), and

(b) is absent from work owing to sickness while the leave is postponed,

the employee shall be deemed to begin the postponed leave on the first day of the absence unless the employee notifies the employer in writing (or causes the employer to be so notified) as soon as is reasonably practicable that the employee does not wish to begin the postponed leave.

(2) On any such notification—

(a) the absence from work of the employee owing to sickness shall be treated in the same way as any other absence from work of the employee owing to sickness, and

(b) the employee shall cease to be entitled to the postponed leave].

GENERAL NOTE

**DB.127H**     This section was inserted by s.10 of the Adoptive Leave Act 2005.

## Placements of less than 20 weeks duration

**DB.128**     **12.**—[(1) Where the placement of a child with an adopting parent terminates before the expiration of the period of leave from the employment to which the adopting parent is entitled under this Part (other than as a result of the death of the child), the adopting parent shall notify the employer in writing (or cause the employer to be so notified) of the date of termination as soon as reasonably practicable but not later than 7 days after that date.]

(2) On receipt by her employer of a notification under subsection (1), the adopting parent shall be required to return to work on such date as is convenient to her employer but not later than the date on which the notified period of adoptive leave or, as the case may be, the notified period of additional adoptive leave expires.

(3) In the case of a foreign adoption, where an adopting parent takes additional adoptive leave before the day of placement and no placement takes place, she shall return to work on the day on which the notified period of such leave expires, at the latest, and shall cause her employer to be notified of the intended date of her return to work as soon as is reasonably practicable.

(4) In a case to which subsection (2) relates an employer shall give the adopting parent one week's notice of the day on which she is required to return to work.

(5) Where, in the opinion of a rights commissioner or the Tribunal, there are reasonable grounds for an adopting parent's failure to give a notice under this section or for an adopting parent giving it otherwise than within the time limits specified thereunder, the rights commissioner or Tribunal, as the case may be, shall extend the time for service of the said notice.

(6) In the absence of reasonable grounds, failure to give notice under this section or the giving of it otherwise than in the time limits specified thereunder are matters that may be taken into account by a rights commissioner, the Tribunal or Circuit Court in determining the adopting parent's rights under the Act of 1977, this Act or any other relevant enactment so far as the remedies of re-instatement, re-engagement or compensation are concerned.

GENERAL NOTE

This section, as amended by s.11 of the Adoptive Leave Act 2005, provides for the return to work **DB.129** of an adopting parent in circumstances where the placement terminates before the expiration of the period of leave to which the adopting parent is entitled. In such circumstances, the adopting parent must inform the employer that the placement has terminated "as soon as is reasonably practicable" but not later than seven days after the date of termination. The employer is obliged to give such employee notice (which does not have to be in writing) of at least one week of the day on which she is required to return to work.

## Certificate of placement to be issued

**13.**—(1) An adopting parent shall, if she so requests, be issued with a certi- **DB.130** ficate ("the certificate of placement") by—

(a) the health board which arranges the placing of the child with the adopting parent, or

(b) the registered adopting society which arranges the placing of the child with the adopting parent.

(2) The certificate of placement referred to in subsection (1) shall be issued, no later than 7 days from the date of receipt of the request, by the health board or registered adoption society, as may be appropriate.

(3) The certificate of placement referred to in subsection (1) shall state the following—

(a) the date on which it is issued,

(b)  the day of placement,

(c)  the sex and date of birth of the child,

(d)  the name and address of the adopting parent or parents,

and shall be signed by a person authorised to issue such a certificate on behalf of the issuing authority.

(4) The certificate of placement when being issued in accordance with subsection (1)(a) may be issued on behalf of the health board by its chief executive officer.

(5) In subsection (4) "chief executive officer" includes a person acting as deputy chief executive officer in accordance with section 13 of the Health Act, 1970.

(6) Where the placing of the child with the adopting parent or parents was arranged otherwise than by a health board or registered adoption society and an application for an adoption order has been received by An Bord Uchtála from an adopting parent or parents, An Bord Uchtála shall, on receipt of a request from an adopting parent for a certificate ("the certificate of placement"), issue the adopting parent with a certificate of placement.

(7) The certificate of placement referred to in subsection (6) shall be issued, no later than seven days from the date of receipt of the request, by An Bord Uchtála.

(8) The certificate of placement referred to in subsection (6) shall state the following—

(a)  the date on which it is issued,

(b)  the date of the application for an adoption order,

(c)  the day of placement as stated in the application,

(d)  the sex and date of birth of the child,

(e)  the name and address of the adopting parent or parents,

and shall be signed by an officer of An Bord Uchtála authorised to issue such a certificate in that behalf.

### Evidence as to certificate of placement

DB.131    **14.**—The certificate of placement or a copy thereof certified by the body which issued the certificate of placement to be a true copy shall, unless the contrary is proved, be evidence of the matters referred to therein in any proceedings arising out of or relating to the exercise or attempted exercise by an adopting parent of her rights under this Act.

PART III

PROVISIONS RELATING TO EMPLOYMENT CONTRACTS

### Preservation or suspension of certain rights, etc. while on adoptive leave

DB.132    [**15.**—(1) While absent from work on adoptive leave, an employee—

(a)  shall be deemed to have been in the employment of the employer, and

(b) shall, subject to subsection (6) and section 17, be treated as if the employee had not been so absent,

and the absence shall not affect any right of the employee related to the employment (other than the right to remuneration during the absence), whether conferred by statute, contract or otherwise.

(2) While absent from work on additional adoptive leave, an employee—

(a) shall be deemed to have been in the employment of the employer, and

(b) shall, subject to subsection (6) and section 17, be treated as if the employee had not been so absent,

and the absence shall not affect any right or obligation related to the employee's employment (other than the employee's right to remuneration or superannuation benefits or any obligation to pay contributions in or in respect of the employment during the absence), whether conferred or imposed by statute, contract or otherwise.

(3) While absent from work attending pre-adoption classes or meetings in accordance with section 11A, an employee—

(a) shall be deemed to be in the employment of the employer, and

(b) shall, subject to subsection (6) and section 17, be treated as if the employee had not been so absent,

and the absence shall not affect any right related to the employee's employment, whether conferred by statute, contract or otherwise.

(4) Nothing in this section shall affect the right of an employee to be offered suitable alternative employment under section 19.

(5) A period of absence of work in accordance with this Act shall not be treated as part of any other leave (including sick leave or annual leave) to which an employee is entitled.

(6) Where, on starting employment, an employee is on probation, is undergoing training in relation to it or is an apprentice, the probation, training or apprenticeship shall stand suspended during any absence from work in accordance with this Act and shall be completed by the employee on returning to work after the absence.

(7) An employee shall be deemed not to be an employed contributor for the purposes of the Social Welfare Acts for any contribution week (within the meaning of those Acts) while absent from work on adoptive leave or additional adoptive leave if the employee does not receive any reckonable earnings (within that meaning) in respect of that week.

(8) The Minister may by regulations prescribe a period or periods of training in relation to which subsection (6) shall not apply.]

GENERAL NOTE

This section, as substituted by s.12 of the Adoptive Leave Act 2005, makes it clear that the 20 weeks' leave is unpaid. The employee, however, is entitled to receive "adoptive benefit" pursuant to s.58 of the Social Welfare (Consolidation) Act 2005 (as amended by s.8 of the Social Welfare Act 2005). Adoptive benefit is paid at a rate of €165.60 or 80 per cent of reckonable weekly earnings up to a maximum of €232.36, whichever is the greater: Social Welfare (Consolidated Payments Provisions) Regulations 1994 (S.I. No. 417 of 1994 as amended by S.I. No. 146 of 1995, S.I. No. 249 of 1997, S.I. No. 184 of 1998, S.I. No. 164 of 1999, S.I. No. 122 of 2000, S.I. No. 99 of 2001, S.I. No. 650 of 2001, S.I. No. 631 of 2002, S.I. No. 724 of 2003 and S.I. No. 850 of 2004), Articles 22 and 23. The contribution conditions for the payment of adoptive benefit are set out in s.59 of the 2005 Act and

**DB.133**

D–21

provide essentially that the claimant must have qualifying contributions in respect of not less than 39 weeks in the period beginning with her entry into insurance and ending immediately before the first day for which adoptive benefit is claimed (the relevant day) *and* qualifying or credited contributions in respect of not less than 39 weeks in the second last complete contribution year before the beginning of the benefit year in which the relevant day occurs or in a subsequent complete contribution year before the relevant day *or* qualifying contributions in respect of not less than 26 weeks in each of the second last and third last complete contribution years before the beginning of the benefit year in which the relevant day occurs. Article 101 of the Social Welfare (Consolidated Payments Provisions) Regulations 1994 (S.I. No. 417 of 1994 as amended by S.I. Nos 94 and 146 of 1995) entitles an officer of the Minister for Social and Family Affairs to require an employer to furnish to the Minister certification that the claimant is entitled to leave under the Act, the amount of the claimant's gross earnings and any other relevant particulars. Article 102 of the 1994 Regulations (as amended) provides that the prescribed time for making a claim for adoptive benefit is the date on which, apart from satisfying the condition of making a claim, the claimant becomes entitled thereto. Where a person fails to make a claim within the prescribed time, she will be disqualified for receiving payment "in respect of any period before the date on which the claim is made". Sections 10 and 11 of the Social Welfare Act 1997 provided for the extension of the adoptive benefit scheme to the self employed with effect from June 9, 1997: see now ss.58 and 69 of the Social Welfare (Consolidation) Act 2005.

The word "remuneration" is not defined in the Act (other than for the purposes of section 33) but the Employment Appeals Tribunal was of the opinion, in *McGivern v Irish National Insurance Co. Ltd* P5/1982, that the following statement from *S&U Stores Ltd v Lee* [1969] 2 All E.R. 417, 419 was "a generally satisfactory definition":

> "Remuneration is not mere payment for work done but is what the doer expects to get as the result of the work he does in so far as what he expects to get is quantified in terms of money".

## Voidance of certain purported terminations of employment, etc.

DB.134    [**16.**—Each of the following shall be void:

(a)  any purported termination of or suspension from employment of an adopting parent while absent from work—

  (i)   on adoptive leave or additional adoptive leave, or

  (ii)  attending pre-adoption classes or meetings in accordance with section 11A;

(b)  any notice of termination of the employment of an adopting parent given during the parent's absence from work—

  (i)   on adoptive leave or additional adoptive leave, or

  (ii)  while attending pre-adoption classes or meetings in accordance with that section,

and expiring after the absence.]

GENERAL NOTE

DB.134A    This section was substituted by virtue of s.13 of the Adoptive Leave Act 2005.

## Extension of certain notices of termination of employment and certain suspensions

DB.135    [**17.**—(1) This section applies to—

(a)  a notice of termination of employment, or

(b)  a suspension from employment,

which is given to or imposed on an adopting parent before the adopting parent begins a period of leave under this Act and which is due to expire during the adopting parent's absence from work on that leave.

(2) Any notice of termination or any suspension to which this section applies shall be extended by the period of the absence concerned.

(3) References in subsection (1) to a period of leave under this Act include

references to a period of time off from work while attending pre-adoption classes or meetings in accordance with section 11A.]

GENERAL NOTE

This section was substituted by virtue of s.14 of the Adoptive Leave Act 2005.    **DB.135A**

## General right to return to work after adoptive leave or additional adoptive leave

[**18.**—(1) An adopting parent ("the employee") who is absent from work    **DB.136** while on adoptive leave or additional adoptive leave shall be entitled to return to work—

    (a)  either—

        (i)  with the employer with whom the employee was working immediately before the absence, or

        (ii)  if during the absence there was a change of ownership of the undertaking in which the employee was employed immediately before the absence, with the owner (in this Act referred to as "the successor") of the undertaking when the absence ended,

    (b)  in the job which the employee held immediately before the absence began, and

    (c)  under the contract of employment under which the employee was employed immediately before the absence began, or (as the case may be) under a contract of employment with the successor, which is identical to the contract under which the employee was employed immediately before the absence and (in either case) under terms or conditions—

        (i)  that are not less favourable than those that would have been applicable, and

        (ii)  that incorporate any improvements in the terms and conditions of employment to which the employee would have been entitled,

if the employee had not been so absent from work.

(2) For the purposes of subsection (1)(b), where the job held by the employee immediately before the absence was not the employee's normal or usual job, the employee shall be entitled to return to work, either in the normal or usual job or in the job so held, as soon as is practicable.

(3) In this section "job" means the nature of the work which the employee is employed to do in accordance with the employee's contract of employment and the capacity and place in which the employee is so employed.]

GENERAL NOTE

This section was substituted by s.15 of the Adoptive Leave Act 2005. Entitlement to return to work    **DB.137** is conditional in compliance with the notification requirements set out in s.20. Since resumption in the same job might not be practicable in every case provision is made in s.19 for suitable alternative work.

## Right to suitable alternative employment in certain circumstances on return to work

**19.**—(1) Where an adopting parent is entitled to return to work under section    **DB.138** 18 but it is not reasonably practicable for her employer or the successor to permit her to return to work in accordance with that section, she shall be entitled to be offered by her employer, the successor or an associated employer suitable alternative employment in accordance with a new contract of employment.

(2) The following provisions shall apply to a new contract of employment under this section—

(a) the work required to be done under it shall be of a kind which is suitable in relation to the employee concerned and appropriate for her to do, and

[(b) the terms and conditions of the contract—

(i) relating to the place where the work under it is required to be done, the capacity in which the employee concerned is to be employed and any other terms and conditions of employment are not less favourable to the employee than those of the employee's contract of employment immediately before the absence from work on adoptive leave or additional adoptive leave, and

(ii) incorporate any improvements in the terms or conditions of employment to which the employee would have been entitled if the employee had not been so absent from work during that period.]

(3) For the purposes of this section two employers shall be taken to be associated if one is a body corporate of which the other (whether directly or indirectly) has control or if both are bodies corporate of which a third person (whether directly or indirectly) has control and references hereafter in this Act to associated employer shall be construed accordingly.

GENERAL NOTE

**DB.138A**   Paragraph (6) of subs.(2) was substituted by virtue of s.16 of the Adoptive Leave Act 2005. The words "suitable in relation to the employee concerned" will be construed in the same way as the similar words in s.15(2)(c) of the Redundancy Payments Act 1967, *i.e.* subjectively from the employee's standpoint: see *Tighe v Travenol Laboratories Ltd* P14/1986 (a decision under the Maternity Protection of Employees Act 1981, reported at (1989) 8 J.I.S.L.L. 124).

### Notification of intention to return to work

**DB.139**   **20.**—[(1) An employee who is entitled to, or is on, adoptive leave or additional adoptive leave shall cause the employer (or, if aware of a change of ownership of the undertaking concerned, the successor) to be notified in writing of the employee's intention to return to work and of the date on which the employee expects to do so—

(a) where the leave is for a period of 4 weeks or less, at the same time as the employee notifies the employer of intention to take the leave,

(b) where the leave is for a period of more than 4 weeks—

(i) subject to subparagraph (ii), in case the leave is postponed leave, either—

(I) at the same time as the employee notifies the employer under section 11C(4) of intention to take the leave, or

(II) at least 4 weeks before the date of the expected return to work,

whichever is the later,

(ii) in case the employee is deemed under section 11D(1) to be on postponed leave, as soon as is reasonably practicable after the beginning of the absence from work of the employee owing to sickness but not later than the date on which the employee expects to return to work,

(iii) in any other case, not later than 4 weeks before the date on which the employee expects to return to work.]

(2) Where, in the opinion of a rights commissioner or the Tribunal, there are reasonable grounds for an adopting parent's failure to give the notice under subsection (1) or for an adopting parent giving it otherwise than in the time limits specified thereunder, the rights commissioner or Tribunal, as the case may be, shall extend the time for service of the said notice.

(3) In the absence of reasonable grounds, failure to give notice under subsection (1) or the giving of it otherwise than in the time limits specified thereunder are matters that may be taken into account by a rights commissioner, the Tribunal or Circuit Court in determining the adopting parent's rights under the Act of 1977, this Act or any other relevant enactment so far as the remedies of re-instatement, re-engagement or compensation are concerned.

(4) [...]

GENERAL NOTE

This section, as amended by s.17 of the Adoptive Leave Act 2005, requires an adopting parent to give to her or his employer, not later than four weeks before the expected date of return to work, written notification of the intention to return to work. The rights commissioner or the Tribunal has the discretion, however, to extend the time for giving notification in certain circumstances.   **DB.139A**

## Postponement of return to work

**21.**—Where, because of an interruption or cessation of work at her place of employment, existing on the date specified in a notification given under section 12(3) or 20 or on the date on which an adopting parent is required to return to work under section 12(2), as the case may be, it is unreasonable to expect an adopting parent to return to work on such date, she may return to work instead when work resumes at the place of employment after the interruption or cessation, or as soon as is reasonably practicable after such resumption.   **DB.140**

GENERAL NOTE

This section ensures that, where employees comply with the notification requirements under sections 12 or 20, they will not lose their entitlement to resume work if, on the date specified for their return, they are precluded from doing so because, for instance, there is a strike at the place of work or production has temporarily ceased.   **DB.140A**

PART IV

AMENDMENTS OR APPLICATION OF OTHER ENACTMENTS

*Unfair Dismissals Act 1977*

## Amendment of section 1 of Act of 1977

**22.** [...]   **DB.141**

## Amendment of section 2(2) of Act of 1977

**23.** [...]   **DB.141A**

## Amendment of section 6(2) of Act of 1977

**24.** [...]   **DB.141B**

D–25

**Amendment of section 6 of Act of 1977**

DB.141C     **25.** [...]

**Adopting parent not permitted to return to work**

DB.142     **26.**—(1) This section applies to an adopting parent within the meaning of section 1 of the Act of 1977 as amended by section 22 who, having complied with section 20, is entitled to return to work but is not permitted to do so by her employer, the successor or an associated employer.

(2) For the purposes of the Act of 1977, an adopting parent shall be deemed to have been dismissed on the date specified in the relevant notification under section 20(1), and the dismissal shall be deemed to be an unfair dismissal unless, having regard to all the circumstances, there were substantial grounds justifying the dismissal.

*Redundancy Payments Act 1967*

**Amendment of section 2 of Act of 1967**

DB.143     **27.** [...]

**Amendment of Schedule 3 to Act of 1967**

DB.143A     **28.** [...]

**Adopting parent not permitted to return to work**

DB.144     **29.**—(1) This section applies to an adopting parent within the meaning of section 2 of the Act of 1967 as amended by section 27 who, having complied with section 20, is entitled to return to work but is not permitted to do so by her employer, the successor or an associated employer.

(2) For the purposes of the Act of 1967, an adopting parent shall be deemed to have been dismissed by reason of redundancy, the date of dismissal being deemed to be the date specified in the relevant notification under section 20(1).

*Minimum Notice and Terms of Employment Act 1973*

**Adopting parent not permitted to return to work**

DB.145     **30.** —(1) This section applies to an adopting parent who, having complied with section 20(1), is entitled to return to work but is not permitted to do so by her employer, the successor or an associated employer and who is an employee to whom the Acts referred to in subsection (2) apply.

(2) For the purposes of the Minimum Notice and Terms of Employment Acts 1973 to [2001], the contract of employment of an adopting parent to whom this section applies shall be deemed to have been terminated on the date specified in the relevant notification under section 20(1).

## Definition

**31.** —In this Part "relevant employer" means the employer, successor or associated employer, as may be appropriate.                                    DB.146

## Disputes regarding entitlement under this Act

**32.** —(1) This Part does not apply to an adopting parent who is in employment as a member of the Defence Forces.                                    DB.147

(2) Any dispute other than—

(a)  a dispute relating to a dismissal, including a dismissal within the meaning of the Act of 1977 or, the termination of a contract of employment, or

(b)  a claim under Part IV of the Act of 1967 as extended by section 29, or

(c)  a dispute under section 11 of the Minimum Notice and Terms of Employment Act, 1973, as extended by section 30, between an adopting parent and the relevant employer, relating to the adopting parent's entitlements under this Act (or to any matter arising out of or related to such entitlements), may be referred by either party to the dispute to a rights commissioner.

(3) A rights commissioner shall hear the parties to a dispute under this Part and any evidence relevant to the dispute tendered by them.

(4) The Minister may make regulations for the purposes of this Part.

GENERAL NOTE

The relevant regulations are the Adoptive Leave (Referral of Disputes and Appeals) (Part V)    DB.147A
Regulations 1995 (S.I. No. 195 of 1995) and the Adoptive Leave (Calculation of Weekly Remuneration) Regulations 1995 (S.I. No. 196 of 1995).

## Redress

**33.** —(1) On the hearing of a dispute under this Part, a rights commissioner or the Tribunal shall—                                    DB.148

(a)  in the case of a rights commissioner, make a decision in relation to the dispute, or

(b)  in the case of the Tribunal, make a determination in relation to the dispute, and may give to the parties concerned such directions as the rights commissioner or the Tribunal, as the case may be, considers necessary or expedient for the resolution of the dispute.

(2) A decision or determination under subsection (1) shall, if the rights commissioner or Tribunal, as the case may be, considers it appropriate, include an award of compensation in favour of the adopting parent to be paid by the relevant employer.

(3) Compensation under this section shall be of such amount as the rights commissioner or Tribunal deems just and equitable having regard to all the circumstances of the case but shall not exceed 20 weeks' remuneration in respect of the adopting parent's employment calculated in accordance with regulations made under section 32.

(4) In this section "remuneration" includes allowances in the nature of pay and benefits in lieu of or in addition to pay.

(5) The decision of a rights commissioner or determination of the Tribunal shall be in writing and shall be communicated to the parties by the rights commissioner or Tribunal, as the case may be.

GENERAL NOTE

**DB.148A**   The relevant Regulations are the Adoptive Leave (Calculation of Weekly Remuneration) Regulations 1995 (S.I. No. 196 of 1995) which prescribe the method for calculating maximum compensation for the purposes of redress under this Part of the Act. In awarding compensation, the rights commissioner and the Tribunal must make it clear whether the award is or is not "in respect of remuneration including arrears of remuneration", otherwise it may not be regarded as being exempt from income tax: see s.192A of the Taxes Consolidation Act 1997 (inserted by s.7 of the Finance Act 2004).

## Referral of disputes to rights commissioner

**DB.149**   **34.** —(1) Referral of a dispute under this Part shall be initiated by giving a notice in writing, containing such particulars (if any) as may be prescribed, to a rights commissioner—

(a) (i) not later than six months from the day of placement or, in circumstances where no placement takes place, within the period of six months from the date on which the employer receives the first notification of the adopting parent's intention to take leave under this Act, whether it be adoptive leave or additional adoptive leave, or

(ii) in the case of an adopting father, not later than six months from the date on which the adopting mother died, or

(b) if the rights commissioner is satisfied that exceptional circumstances prevented the giving of the notice within the period aforesaid, then, within such period not exceeding 12 months from the date aforesaid as the rights commissioner considers reasonable, and a copy of the notice shall be given by the rights commissioner to the other party to the dispute as soon as may be after the receipt of the notice by the rights commissioner.

(2) Proceedings under this Part before a rights commissioner shall be conducted otherwise than in public.

(3) A rights commissioner shall furnish the Tribunal with a copy of a decision given under this Part.

GENERAL NOTE

**DB.149A**   Regulation 3(1) of the Adoptive Leave (Referral of Disputes and Appeals) (Part V) Regulations 1995 (S.I. No. 195 of 1995) provides that a notice of dispute should contain the following particulars:
 (a) the names, addresses and descriptions of the parties to the proceedings;
 (b) the grounds upon which the applicant's claim is based;
 (c) the day of placement, or, where there has been no placement, the date on which the employer received the first notification of the adopting parent's intention to take leave under the Act, or, in the case of an adopting father, the date on which the adopting mother died;
 (d) in the case the notice is not given within the appropriate period, the reasons for the delay; and
 (e) the weekly remuneration of the adopting parent.
 Regulation 7, however, provides that "a mistake of a formal nature" shall not operate to invalidate the notice of dispute.

## Appeal from decision of rights commissioner

**DB.150**   **35.**—(1) A party concerned may appeal to the Tribunal from a decision of a rights commissioner in relation to a dispute referred under this Part and the

Tribunal shall hear the parties and any evidence relevant to the appeal tendered by them and shall make a determination in relation to the appeal.

(2) An appeal under this section shall be initiated by a party by giving, within four weeks of the date on which the decision to which it relates was given to the parties concerned, a notice in writing to the Tribunal (containing such particulars (if any) as may be prescribed) and the Tribunal shall give a copy of the notice to the other party concerned as soon as may be after the receipt by it of the notice.

(3) A witness before the Tribunal on an appeal under this section shall be entitled to the same immunities and privileges as if the witness were a witness before the High Court.

(4) (a) The Tribunal shall, on the hearing of an appeal under this section, have power to take evidence on oath and for that purpose may cause to be administered oaths to persons attending as witnesses at such hearing.

(b)  Any person who, upon examination on oath authorised under this subsection, wilfully and corruptly gives false evidence or wilfully and corruptly swears anything which is false, shall be guilty of an offence and, upon being convicted thereof, shall be liable to the penalties for wilful and corrupt perjury.

(c)  The Tribunal may, by giving notice in that behalf in writing, require any person to attend at such time and place as is specified in the notice, to give evidence in relation to any matter referred to the Tribunal under this section or to produce any documents in that person's possession, custody or control which relate to any such matter.

(d)  A person to whom a notice under paragraph (c) has been given and who fails, without just cause, to attend in accordance with the notice or who, having so attended, refuses to give evidence or fails, without just cause, to produce any document to which the notice relates shall be guilty of an offence and shall be liable on summary conviction thereof to a fine not exceeding £1,000 [€1,269.74].

(5) Proceedings for an offence under paragraph (b) or (d) of subsection (4) may be brought and prosecuted by the Minister.

(6) A document purporting to be signed by the chairman or vice-chairman of the Tribunal stating that—

(a)  a person named in the document was, by a notice under subsection (4)(c), required to attend before the Tribunal on a day and at a time and place specified in the document, to give evidence or produce a document.

(b)  a sitting of the Tribunal was held on that day and at that time and place, and

(c)  the person did not attend before the Tribunal in pursuance of the notice or, as the case may be, having so attended, refused to give evidence or refused or failed to produce the document,

shall, in a prosecution of the person for an offence under subsection (4)(d), be sufficient evidence of the matters so stated, unless the contrary is shown.

GENERAL NOTE

Regulation 3(1) of the Adoptive Leave (Referral of Disputes and Appeals) (Part V) Regulations 1995 (S.I. No. 195 of 1995) provides that a notice of appeal should contain the following particulars: **DB.150A**
(a) the names, addresses and descriptions of the parties to the proceedings;
(b) the grounds of appeal;

(c) the weekly remuneration of the adopting parent; and

(d) the date on which the decision to which the appeal relates was made and the name of the rights commissioner who made it.

Regulation 7, however, provides that "a mistake of a formal nature" shall not operate to invalidate a notice of appeal.

Regulation 12 provides that a respondent in an appeal, who does not enter an appearance in accordance with Regulation 5, shall not be entitled to take part in or be present or represented at any proceedings before the Tribunal relating to the matter under appeal.

## Appeal to High Court on point of law

DB.151    **36.**—(1) The Tribunal may refer a question of law arising in proceedings before it under this Part to the High Court for determination by it.

(2) A party to proceedings before the Tribunal under this Part may appeal to the High Court from a determination of the Tribunal on a point of law.

GENERAL NOTE

DB.151A    Although the Rules of the Superior Courts do not specifically provide for appeals under this Act, it is suggested that any such appeal be brought by special summons, by analogy with the procedure set out in R.S.C. 1986, Order 105. In the absence of any specific rule of court, any such appeal need only be brought within a reasonable time: *per* McCracken J. in his *ex tempore* ruling in *McGaley v Liebherr Container Cranes Ltd* (2001/234Sp) delivered on October 12, 2001.

The circumstances in which the High Court will overturn a decision of a specialist tribunal such as the Employment Appeals Tribunal have been considered in many cases: see for example, *Henry Denny & Sons (Ireland) Ltd v Minister for Social Welfare* [1998] 1 I.R. 34 and in particular the comments of Hamilton C.J. at 37. In considering whether to allow an appeal against a decision of such a tribunal, the High Court must consider whether that body based its decision on an identifiable error of law or on an unsustainable finding of fact. A decision cannot be challenged on the grounds of irrationality if there is any relevant material to support it: see further *Mulcahy v Waterford Leader Partnership Ltd* [2002] E.L.R. 12 (O'Sullivan J.) and *Thompson v Tesco Ireland Ltd* [2003] E.L.R. 21 (Lavan J.). In *National University of Ireland, Cork v Ahern* [2005] 2 I.R. 577, the Supreme Court held that, although findings of fact must be accepted by the High Court on appeal, that court could still examine the basis upon which those facts were found. The relevance or admissibility of the matters relied on in determining the facts were questions of law.

## Service of documents

DB.152    **37.**—(1) Service of a notice or other document on any person for the purpose of or in relation to any proceedings under this Part may be effected by delivering it to the person to whom it relates or by sending a copy of the document by registered prepaid post in an envelope addressed to the person to be served at that person's last known residence or place of business in the State.

(2) In the case of a company to which the Companies Act 1963, applies such service may be effected by delivering the document to, or by sending a copy of the document by registered prepaid post in an envelope addressed to, the company at its registered office.

(3) In the case of a body corporate to which subsection (2) does not apply or any unincorporated body of persons, such service may be effected by sending a copy of the document by registered prepaid post in an envelope addressed to the body at any place in the State where that body conducts its business or in such other manner as an originating summons may be served on such a body under the Rules of the Superior Courts.

## Provisions relating to winding up and bankruptcy

DB.153    **38.**—(1) There shall be included among the debts which, under section 285 of the Companies Act 1963, are, in the distribution of the assets of a company being wound up, to be paid in priority to all other debts, all compensation payable under this Part by the company to an adopting parent, and that Act shall have effect accordingly, and formal proof of the debts to which priority is given under this subsection shall not be required except in cases where it may otherwise be provided by rules made under that Act.

(2) There shall be included among the debts which, under section 81 of the Bankruptcy Act, 1988, are, in the distribution of the property of a bankrupt or arranging debtor, to be paid in priority to all other debts, all compensation payable under this Part by the bankrupt or arranging debtor, as the case may be, to an adopting parent, and that Act shall have effect accordingly, and formal proof of the debts to which priority is given under this subsection shall not be required except in cases where it may otherwise be provided by general orders made under that Act.

## Enforcement of decision of rights commissioner and determination of Tribunal

**39.** (1) (a) A decision of a rights commissioner and a determination of the    **DB.154** Tribunal in proceedings under this Part may provide that the decision or determination shall be carried out before a specified date.

(b) Where a decision of a rights commissioner or a determination of the Tribunal does not so provide, it shall be deemed, for the purposes of this section, to provide that it shall be carried out within four weeks from the date on which it is communicated to the parties.

(2) (a) If a party fails to carry out the terms of a decision of a rights commissioner or determination of the Tribunal in relation to a dispute referred under this Part within the period as provided in accordance with subsection (1), the Circuit Court shall, on application to it in that behalf by—

(i)   the other party concerned, or

(ii)  the Minister, if of opinion that it is appropriate to make the application having regard to all the circumstances,

without hearing the party in default or any evidence (other than in relation to the failure), make an order directing the party in default to carry out the decision or determination in accordance with its terms.

(b) In paragraph (a), the reference to a decision of a rights commissioner or a determination of the Tribunal is a reference to such a decision or determination, as the case may be, in relation to which, at the expiration of the time for bringing an appeal against it, no such appeal has been brought or, if such an appeal has been brought, it has been abandoned and the reference to the date on which the decision or determination is communicated to the parties shall, in a case where such an appeal is abandoned, be construed as a reference to the date of such abandonment.

(3) The Circuit Court may, in an order under this section, if in all the circumstances it considers it appropriate to do so, in case the order relates to the payment of compensation, direct the relevant employer to pay to the adopting parent concerned interest on the compensation at the rate referred to in section 22 of the Courts Act, 1981, in respect of the whole or any part of the period beginning four weeks after the date on which the decision of a rights commis-

sioner or the determination of the Tribunal, as the case may be, is communicated to the parties and ending on the date of the order.

(4) Proceedings under this section shall be heard in the county in which the relevant employer ordinarily resides or carries on any profession, business or occupation.

GENERAL NOTE

**DB.154A**     The Circuit Court Rules (S.I. No. 510 of 2001) Order 57, rule 3 prescribe the procedures in respect of applications brought under this section. This provides that applications for enforcement shall be made by way of Motion on Notice. Save by "special leave" of the Court all applications under this section shall only be heard upon oral evidence and the Court "may make such Order as to costs as may be appropriate".

## Extension of Protection of Employees (Employers' Insolvency) Act, 1984

**DB.155**     **40.**—In section 6 of the Protection of Employees (Employers' Insolvency) Act, 1984—

(a)  the references in subparagraph (v) of subsection (2)(a) to a determination or order shall be construed as including references to a decision, determination or order under Part V, and

(b)  the references in subparagraph (i) of subsection (4)(c) to a determination shall be construed as including references to a decision or determination under Part V and the reference in clause (II) of the said subparagraph, to section 10(4) of the Act of 1977 shall be construed as including a reference to section 35 or 36, as may be appropriate.

GENERAL NOTE

**DB.155A**     This section provides that, in the event of an employer's insolvency, compensatory awards made by a rights commissioner or by the Employment Appeals Tribunal can be paid out of the Social Insurance Fund pursuant to the Protection of Employees (Employers' Insolvency) Act 1984.

PART VI

MISCELLANOUS AND TRANSITIONAL PROVISIONS

## Alternative notification procedure

**DB.156**     **41.**—(1) Where an adopting parent commences employment within a period of six weeks before the day of placement she shall, as soon as is reasonably practicable but not later than the day on which she commences adoptive leave, cause her employer to be notified in writing of her intention to take adoptive leave, and where such notification is given, the provisions of section 7(1)(a), 7(2)(a) or 9(2)(a)(i), as the case may be, shall not apply in respect of that period of leave.

(2) Where an adopting parent commences employment within a period of six weeks before the day of placement and wishes to take a period of additional adoptive leave before the day of placement under section 8(5) or section 11, as the case may be, the adopting parent shall, as soon as is reasonably practicable, but no later than the day on which she commences such leave, cause her employer to be notified in writing of her intention to take additional adoptive leave before the day of placement, and when such notification is given the provisions of section 8(6)(a) or 11(2)(a), as the case may be, shall not apply in respect of that period of leave.

(3) Where a child is to be placed with an adopting parent within the period of six weeks beginning on the commencement of this Act, the adopting parent shall, as soon as is reasonably practicable but not later than the day of placement, cause her employer to be notified in writing of her intention to take adoptive leave, and where such notification is given, the provisions of section 7(1)(a), 7(2)(a) or 9(2)(a)(i), as the case may be, shall not apply in respect of that period of leave.

(4) Where a child is to be placed with an adopting parent within the period of six weeks beginning on the commencement of this Act, and the adopting parent wishes to take a period of additional adoptive leave before the day of placement under section 8(5) or section 11, as the case may be, the adopting parent shall, as soon as is reasonably practicable, but no later than the day on which she commences such leave, cause her employer to be notified in writing of her intention to take additional adoptive leave before the day of placement, and when such notification is given the provisions of section 8(6)(a) or 11(2)(a), as the case may be, shall not apply in respect of that period of leave.

(5) An employer, who receives a notification under this section within two weeks of the notified day of commencement of the leave, may require the adopting parent to delay commencement of the leave, in respect of which the notification was given, for up to two weeks from the day on which the notification was received.

## Right to adoptive leave where child placed before commencement of Act

**42.** [...]                                                                          DB.157

GENERAL NOTE
These transitional provisions have been omitted as no longer being relevant.         DB.157A

## Right to additional adoptive leave where child placed before commencement of Act

**43.** [...]                                                                          DB.157B

GENERAL NOTE
These transitional provisions have been omitted as no longer being relevant.         DB.157C

## Notification of intention to return to work in respect of leave taken under sections 42 and 43

**44.** [...]                                                                          DB.157D

GENERAL NOTE
These transitional provisions have been omitted as no longer being relevant.         DB.157E

## Revocation

[**45.**—The Adoptive Leave Act 1995 (Extension of Periods of Leave) Order    DB.157F
2001 (S.I. No. 30 of 2001), as far as unrevoked, and the Adoptive Leave Act
1995 (Extension of Periods of Leave) Order 2004 (S.I. No. 667 of 2004) are
revoked.]

GENERAL NOTE
This section was inserted by s.21 of the Adoptive Leave Act 2005.                     DB.157G

# ADOPTIVE LEAVE ACT 2005

## (2005 No. 25)

ARRANGEMENT OF SECTIONS

**DB.160**    An Act to amend the Adoptive Leave Act 1995 and to provide for connected matters.

[*2nd November, 2005*]

GENERAL NOTE

**DB.161**    This Act amends the Adoptive Leave Act 1995 ("the 1995 Act") to implement some (but not all) of the recommendations of relevance to adoptive leave made by the Working Group on the Review and Improvement of the Maternity Protection Legislation. The recommendations of relevance to maternity leave were implemented by the Maternity Protection (Amendment) Act 2004.

The 1995 Act was introduced to provide an entitlement to periods of leave from employment for an adopting mother after the placement of a child into her care on an equivalent basis to the entitlement to leave available under the Maternity Protection Act 1994 to natural mothers. According to figures maintained by the Department of Social and Family Affairs there were 215 recipients of adoptive benefit in 2002, and 183 such recipients in 2003 (see 176 *Seanad Debates* Col. 1313).

The main changes to the 1995 Act are the provision of paid time-off to attend pre-adoption classes and meetings (s.7), provision for termination of additional adoptive leave in the event of the employee's illness (s.8), provision for an employee to split the period of adoptive leave and additional adoptive leave in the event of hospitalisation of the child (s.9), and provision that an employee's absence from work on additional adoptive leave will count for any employment rights associated with the employment (except remuneration) such as annual leave and seniority (s.12).

This Act also makes the necessary amendments to ss.2 and 6 of the Unfair Dismissals Act 1977 (ss.18 and 19) and to the Redundancy Payments Act 1967 (s.20).

CITATION

**DB.162**    Adoptive Leave Act 2005.

STATUTORY INSTRUMENTS

**DB.163**    Adoptive Leave Act 2005 (Commencement) Order 2005 (S.I. No. 724 of 2005).
Adoptive Leave Act 2005 (Commencement) Order 2006 (S.I. No. 16 of 2006).

Commencement

The Act, with the exception of ss.9 and 10, came into effect on November 28, 2005 (see S.I. No. 724   **DB.164** of 2005). Sections 9 and 10 came into effect on January 30, 2006 (see S.I. No. 16 of 2006).

PARLIAMENTARY DEBATES

176 *Seanad Debates* Cols 1239–1252 (Second Stage).   **DB.165**
176 *Seanad Debates* Cols 1253–1256 (Second Stage resumed).
176 *Seanad Debates* Cols 1301–1318 (Committee Stage).
176 *Seanad Debates* Cols 1467–1474 (Committee Stage resumed).
177 *Seanad Debates* Cols 13–18 (Report and Final Stages).
590 *Dáil Debates* Cols 54–86 (Second Stage).
Select Committee on Justice, Equality, Defence and Women's Rights (29 SJEDWR 1, No. 45 December 7, 2004) Cols 1443–1452 (Committee Stage).
606 *Dáil Debates* Cols 96–103 (Report Stage).
608 *Dáil Debates* Cols 130–142 (Report Stage resumed and Final Stage).
181 *Seanad* Cols 842–847 (Report and Final Stages).

Be it enacted by the Oireachtas as follows:

# Definitions
  **DB.165A**

1.—[…]
  **DB.166**

# Amendment of section 2 of Principal Act

2.—[…]
  **DB.167**

# Amendment of section 6 of Principal Act

3.—[…]
  **DB.168**

# Amendment of section 8 of Principal Act

4.—[…]
  **DB.169**

# Amendment of section 9 of Principal Act

5.—[…]
  **DB.170**

# Amendment of section 10 of Principal Act

6.—[…]
  **DB.171**

# New section 11A to Principal Act

7.—[…]
  **DB.172**

# New Section 11B to Principal Act

8.—[…]
  **DB.173**

# New Section 11C to Principal Act

9.—[…]
  **DB.174**

# New Section 11D to Principal Act

10.—[…]
  **DB.175**

# Amendment of section 12 of Principal Act

11.—[…]
  **DB.176**

**Amendment of section 15 of Principal Act**

DB.177    12.—[…]

**Amendment of section 16 of Principal Act**

DB.178    13.—[…]

**Amendment of section 17 of Principal Act**

DB.179    14.—[…]

**Amendment of section 18 of Principal Act**

DB.180    15.—[…]

**Amendment of section 19 of Principal Act**

DB.181    16.—[…]

**Amendment of section 20 of Principal Act**

DB.182    17.—[…]

**Amendment of section 23 of Principal Act**

DB.183    18.—[…]

**Amendment of section 24 of Principal Act**

DB.184    19.—[…]

**Substitution of section 28 of Principal Act**

DB.185    20.—[…]

**New section 45 to Principal Act**

DB.186    21.—[…]

**Short title, collective citation and commencement**

DB.188    22.—[…]

GENERAL NOTE

    The Act, with the exception of ss.9 and 10, was brought into operation with effect from November 28, 2005, by the Adoptive Leave Act 2005 (Commencement) Order 2005 (S.I. No. 724 of 2005). Sections 9 and 10 were brought into operation with effect from January 30, 2006 by the Adoptive Leave Act 2005 (Commencement) Order 2006 (S.I. No. 16 of 2006).

# CARER'S LEAVE ACT 2001

## (2001 No. 19)

ARRANGEMENT OF SECTIONS

### PART 1

PRELIMINARY AND GENERAL

### PART 2

CARER'S LEAVE

### PART 3

EMPLOYMENT RIGHTS

### PART 4

RESOLUTION OF DISPUTES

### PART 5

MISCELLANEOUS

D–37

25. Winding tip and bankruptcy.
26. Amendment of Act of 1967.
27. Amendment of Act of 1977.
28. Amendment of Organisation of Working Time Act 1997.
29. Amendment of National Minimum Wage Act 2000.
30. Extension of Protection of Employees (Employers' Insolvency) Act 1984.
31. Maintenance of records.
32. Inspectors.
33. Penalties, proceedings, etc.
34. Review of Act.

**DB.201**  An Act to provide for the temporary absence from employment of employees for the purpose of the provision of full-time care and attention to a person requiring it, to protect the employment rights of those employees during such absence, and for that purpose to amend certain enactments and to provide for related matters.

[2nd *July*, 2001]

GENERAL NOTE

**DB.202**  The purpose of this Act, as amended by section 48 of the Social Welfare Law Reform and Pensions Act 2006, is to confer a right on employees to take temporary leave from their employment for up to 104 weeks to look after persons in need of full-time care and attention. It is designed to complement the carer's benefit scheme introduced by the Minister for Social, Community and Family Affairs with effect from October 26, 2000: see Social Welfare (Consolidated Contributions and Insurability) (Amendment) (No. 1) (Carer's Benefit) Regulations 2000 (S.I. No. 338 of 2000) and the Social Welfare (Consolidated Payments Provisions) (Amendment) (No. 2) (Carer's) Regulations 2006 (S.I. No. 145 of 2006).

**DB.203**  Under these Regulations, an employee qualifies for carer's benefit (currently €180.70 per week plus dependant allowances) if he or she:
   (i) is 16 years of age, or over;
   (ii) satisfies the PRSI contribution conditions (156 contributions paid since entry into insurance of which 39 or more contributions must either have been paid in the governing contribution year or in the 12 months immediately before commencement of the benefit or, alternatively, of which 26 contributions must have been paid in the current governing contribution year and 26 contributions paid in the previous governing contribution year);
   (iii) has been in paid employment for the previous three-month period;
   (iv) leaves his or her employment to provide full-time care to a person who has been certified by a deciding officer or an appeals officer of the Department of Social and Family Affairs as being in need of full-time care and attention;
   (v) is not employed in self employment outside the "home" during the period of the receipt of the benefit;
   (vi) is living in the State; and
   (vii) is not living in a hospital, convalescent home or other similar institution.
An employee, who is entitled to carer's benefit, may engage in limited self-employment within the home or employment outside the home for up to ten hours a week and an income ceiling of €290 per week. He or she may also pursue an educational or training course for up to ten hours per week.

**DB.204**  The provisions of this Act entitle employees to carer's leave and protects their employment rights over the period of the absence. The leave may be taken by an employee who satisfies the conditions set down in the Act. Failure to qualify for carer's benefit by not having the necessary PRSI contributions does not prevent the employee availing of the leave. Although there is no minimum hours threshold, the employee must have been in the continuous employment of the employer from whose employment the leave is to be taken for at least 12 months before he or she can commence the leave. The 104-week leave entitlement may be taken as a continuous period or in separate unit periods, the aggregate duration of which does not exceed 104 weeks. Disputes are referable to a rights commissioner with a right of appeal to the Employment Appeals Tribunal, unless the dispute relates to whether the person in respect of whose care the leave is taken is a person in need of full-time care and attention. That matter is to be resolved pursuant to the Social Welfare legislation.

CITATION

**DB.205**  See section 1.

COMMENCEMENT
This Act came into operation on July 2, 2001.                           **DB.206**

PARLIAMENTARY DEBATES
*530 Dáil Debates* Cols. 47–54 (Second Stage)                          **DB.207**
530 *Dáil Debates* Cols. 91–133 (Second Stage resumed)
530 *Dáil Debates* Cols. 277–318 (Second Stage resumed)
533 *Dáil Debates* Cols. 320–336 (Second Stage resumed)
Select Committee on Enterprise and Small Business (ESB 4 No 5 April 11, 2001) Cols. 179–216
537 *Dáil Debates* Cols. 551–578 (Report Stage)
537 *Dáil Debates* Cols. 613–634 (Report Stage resumed and Final Stage)
167 *Seanad Debates* Cols. 380–411 (Second Stage)
167 *Seanad Debates* Cols. 602–608 (Committee and Remaining Stages)

Be it enacted by the Oireachtas as follows:

PART I

PRELIMINARY AND GENERAL

## Short title

**1.**—This Act may be cited as the Carer's Leave Act, 2001.            **DB.208**

## Interpretation

**2.**—(1) In this Act, unless the context otherwise requires—          **DB.209**

"Act of 1967" means the Redundancy Payments Act, 1967;

"Act of 1977" means the Unfair Dismissals Act, 1977;

"Act of [2005]" means the Social Welfare (Consolidation) Act, [2005]; [...];

"appeals officer" has the meaning assigned to it by the Act of 1993;

"associated employer" shall be construed in accordance with subsection (2);

"carer's leave" shall be construed in accordance with section 6;

"confirmation document" has the meaning assigned to it by section 10;

"continuous employment" shall be construed in accordance with section 7(6);

"contract of employment" means—

(a) a contract of service or apprenticeship, and

(b) any other contract whereby an individual agrees with another person, who is carrying on the business of an employment agency, within the meaning of the Employment Agency Act, 1971, and is acting in the course of that business, to do or perform personally any work or service for a third person (whether or not that third person is a party to the contract),

whether the contract is express or implied and, if express, whether it is oral or in writing;

"deciding officer" has the meaning assigned to it by the Act of [2005];

"dispute" shall be construed in accordance with section 17;

"employee" means a person of any age, who has entered into or works under (or, where the employment has ceased, entered into or worked

D–39

under) a contract of employment and references, in relation to an employer, to an employee shall be construed as references to an employee employed by that employer; and for the purposes of this Act, a person holding office under, or in the service of, the State (including a civil servant within the meaning of the Civil Service Regulation Act, 1956) shall be deemed to be an employee employed by the State or Government, as the case may be, and an officer or servant of a local authority for the purposes of the Local Government Act, 1941, or of a harbour authority, [the Health Service Executive] or vocational education committee shall be deemed to be an employee employed by the authority, [the Executive] or committee, as the case may be;

"employer" means, in relation to an employee—

(a)  the person with whom the employee has entered into or for whom the employee works under (or, where the employment has ceased, entered into or worked under) a contract of employment, subject to the qualification that the person who under a contract of employment referred to in paragraph (b) of the definition of "contract of employment" is liable to pay the wages of the individual concerned in respect of the work or service concerned shall be deemed to be the individual's employer, and

(b)  includes, where appropriate, the successor of the employer or an associated employer of the employer;

"full-time care and attention" shall be construed in accordance with section [99(2) of the Act of 2005];

"Minister" means the Minister for Enterprise, Trade and Employment;

"prescribed" means prescribed by regulations made by the Minister under this Act;

"relevant person" has the meaning assigned to it by section [99(1) of the Act of 2005];

"successor" has the meaning assigned to it by section 14(1)(a);

"Tribunal" means the Employment Appeals Tribunal.

(2) For the purposes of this Act, 2 employers shall be taken to be associated if one is a body corporate of which the other (whether directly or indirectly) has control or if both are bodies corporate of which a third person (whether directly or indirectly) has control and "associated employer" shall be construed accordingly.

(3) In this Act—

(a)  a reference to a Part or section is a reference to a Part or section of this Act, unless it is indicated that a reference to some other enactment is intended,

(b)  a reference to a subsection or paragraph is a reference to the subsection or paragraph of the provision in which the reference occurs, unless it is indicated that a reference to some other provision is intended, and

(c)  a reference to any enactment shall, unless the context otherwise requires, be construed as a reference to that enactment as amended or adapted by or under any subsequent enactment.

GENERAL NOTE

*"contract of employment"*

As to whether a person is employed under a contract of service see *Henry Denny & Sons (Ireland)* **DB.210** *Ltd v Minister for Social Welfare* [1998] 1 I.R. 34. The inclusion of a specific reference to persons employed through employment agencies is similar to the provisions of s.13 of the Unfair Dismissals (Amendment) Act 1993, s.1(1) of the Terms of Employment (Information) Act 1994, s.1(1) of the Protection of Young Persons (Employment) Act 1996, s.2(1) of the Organisation of Working Time Act 1997 and s.2(1) of the Parental Leave Act 1998. But note the decision of the Labour Court in *Rooney v Diageo Global Supply* [2004] E.L.R. 133, that an agency supplied worker was employed by the client under a contract of employment. The definition of "employee" was amended by s.66 of the Health Act 2004.

*"full-time care and attention"*

By virtue of s.99(2) of the Social Welfare (Consolidation) Act 2005, a relevant person shall be **DB.211** regarded as requiring full-time care and attention where:
"(a) the person has such a disability that he or she requires from another person
 (i) continual supervision and frequent assistance throughout the day in connection with normal bodily functions, or
 (ii) continual supervision in order to avoid danger to himself or herself, and
(b) the nature and extent of his or her disability has been certified in the prescribed manner by a medical practitioner".

*"relevant person"*

This term is defined by s.99(1) of the Social Welfare (Consolidation) Act 2005 as meaning: **DB.212** "a person who has such a disability that he or she requires full-time care and attention".

## Regulations

**3.**—(1) The Minister may— **DB.213**

(a) by regulations, provide for any matter referred to in this Act as prescribed or to be prescribed, and

(b) make regulations generally for the purpose of giving effect to this Act.

(2) Before making regulations under this Act, the Minister shall consult with the Minister for [Social and Family Affairs], any other Minister of the Government with whom, in his or her opinion, it is appropriate to consult and persons whom the Minister considers to be representative of employers and employees having regard to the regulations so made.

(3) Regulations under this Act may contain such consequential, supplementary and ancillary provisions as the Minister considers necessary or expedient.

(4) Every regulation under this Act shall be laid before each House of the Oireachtas as soon as may be after it is made and, if a resolution annulling the regulation is passed by either such House within the next 21 days on which the House has sat after the regulation is laid before it, the regulation shall be annulled accordingly, but without prejudice to the validity of anything previously done thereunder.

GENERAL NOTE

The title of the Minister in subs.(2) was amended by virtue of the Social, Community and Family **DB.213** Affairs (Alteration of Name of Department and Title of Minister) Order 2002 (S.I. No. 310 of 2002).

## Voidance or modification of certain provisions in agreements

**4.**—(1) A provision in any agreement shall be void in so far as it purports to **DB.214** exclude or limit the application of any provision of this Act or is inconsistent with any provision of this Act.

(2) A provision in any agreement which is or becomes less favourable in relation to an employee than a similar or corresponding entitlement conferred on the employee by this Act shall be deemed to be so modified as to be not less favourable.

(3) Nothing in this Act shall be construed as prohibiting the inclusion in an agreement of a provision more favourable to an employee than any provision in Parts 2 to 5.

(4) References in this section to an agreement are to any agreement, whether a contract of employment or not and whether made before or after the passing of this Act.

GENERAL NOTE

**DB.215**     This section ensures that person cannot agree to nullify or exclude the application of the provisions of the Act although it allows for the provision of arrangements more favourable than those herein provided.

## Expenses

**DB.216**     **5.**—Any expenses incurred by the Minister in the administration of this Act, shall, to such extent as may be sanctioned by the Minister for Finance, be paid out of monies provided by the Oireachtas.

PART 2

CARER'S LEAVE

## Entitlement to carer's leave

**DB.217**     **6.**—(1) Subject to this Act, an employee who has been employed for a period of 12 months continuous employment by the employer from whose employment the carer's leave is proposed to be taken shall be entitled to leave from the employment concerned (to be known and referred to in this Act as "carer's leave") for the purpose of providing full-time care and attention to a relevant person for a period not exceeding [104] weeks for each relevant person if—

(a)  the person in respect of whom the employee proposes to provide full-time care and attention is a relevant person,

(b)  the employee provides the employer concerned with a decision referred to in subsection (5), or, where appropriate, subsection (6),

(c)  during the period of carer's leave the employee provides full-time care and attention to the relevant person, and

(d)  during the period of carer's leave the employee does not engage in employment or self-employment other than employment or self-employment prescribed under section [100(3) of the Act of 2005].

(2) An employee shall give the employer a copy of the decision referred to in subsection (1)(b) as soon as he or she receives it and the employee shall not be entitled to carer's leave until the employer has been given the copy.

(3) An employee shall not be entitled to carer's leave for the purpose of providing full-time care and attention to a relevant person during the same period

D–42

in which another employee is absent from employment on carer's leave for the purpose of providing full-time care and attention to the same relevant person.

(4) An employee shall, subject to section 7(2), be entitled to a period of carer's leave for one relevant person at any one time.

(5) An employee who proposes to avail of carer's leave shall apply to the Minister for [Social and Family Affairs] for a decision by a deciding officer under the Act of [2005] that the person in respect of whom the employee proposes to avail of carer's leave in order to provide full-time care and attention is a relevant person for the purposes of Chapter [14 of Part 2 of the Act of 2005].

(6) A decision of a deciding officer under subsection (5) may be appealed under section [311 of the Act of 2005].

(7) For the avoidance of doubt it is declared that entitlement to carer's benefit under Chapter [14 of Part 2 of the Act of 2005] is not a condition for entitlement to carer's leave.

GENERAL NOTE

This section, as amended by section 48 of the Social Welfare Law Reform and Pensions Act 2006, defines the qualifying conditions for entitlement to carer's leave. An employee is entitled to carer's leave of 104 weeks in respect of any relevant person to enable him or her to provide full-time care and attention to that person. An employee must apply to the Minister for Social and Family Affairs for a decision on whether the person to be cared for is a "relevant person" for the purposes of this Act. An employee must provide the employer with a decision from a deciding officer (or an appeals officer) that the person in respect of whose care the leave is to be taken is a "relevant person" before the commencement of the leave. An employee must also have completed 12 months continuous employment before commencing carer's leave.

## Supplemental provisions to section 6

**7.** —(1) An employee shall, as soon as is practicable, notify his or her employer **DB.219** of any change in circumstances which affect the entitlement to carer's leave.

(2) Notwithstanding sections 6(4), 8(4) and 9(1) and subject to subsections (4) and (5), an employee may, while on carer's leave in respect of a relevant person, apply for carer's leave for another person if that person resides with the relevant person.

(3) An employee who wishes to apply for carer's leave for another person in the circumstances referred to in subsection (2) shall apply for carer's leave under section 6.

(4) Where an application referred to in subsection (3) is made and an employee who is on carer's leave in respect of a relevant person takes carer's leave in respect of a second relevant person—

(a) the period of carer's leave for the first-mentioned relevant person shall not exceed [104] weeks from its commencement, and

(b) the period of carer's leave for the second-mentioned relevant person shall commence on the date of the decision under section 6(5) or section 6(6) and shall not exceed [104] weeks from its commencement, and the total amount of weeks for such carer's leave shall not exceed [208] weeks.

(5) An employee who is on carer's leave in respect of a relevant person and who takes carer's leave in respect of a second relevant person shall not make

another application for carer's leave in the circumstances referred to in subsection (2).

(6) The First Schedule to the Minimum Notice and Terms of Employment Act 1973, shall apply for the purpose of ascertaining the period of service of an employee and whether that service has been continuous.

(7) Regulations made under section [100(3) the Act of 2005] shall apply to this Act with any necessary modifications.

GENERAL NOTE

**DB.220**    This section, as amended by section 48 of the Social Welfare Law Reform and Pensions Act 2006, requires an employee to satisfy his or her employer of any change of circumstances which affect his or her entitlement to carer's leave. The section also permits an employee to avail of leave for the care of a second relevant person while already on leave for the care of a relevant person, where the two relevant persons concerned reside together.

## Manner in which carer's leave may be taken

**DB.221**    **8.**—(1) The period of carer's leave from employment to which an employee is entitled shall not exceed [104] weeks for each relevant person and may, subject to subsections (2) and (3) and any regulations made under subsection (6), be taken in the form of—

(a)  one continuous period of [104] weeks for each relevant person, or

(b)  a number of periods, the aggregate duration of which does not exceed a total of [104] weeks from the date of the commencement of the carer's leave.

(2) An employer may refuse, on reasonable grounds, to permit an employee to take a period of carer's leave which is less than 13 weeks duration and where the employer so refuses he or she shall specify in writing to the employee the grounds for such refusal.

(3) An employee who has taken a period of carer's leave in accordance with subsection (1)(b) in respect of a relevant person, shall not be entitled to commence a further period of carer's leave in respect of the same relevant person, until a period of 6 weeks has elapsed since the termination of the previous period of carer's leave.

(4) Where an employee has taken carer's leave in respect of a relevant person and that period of carer's leave has terminated the employee shall not commence carer's leave in respect of another relevant person until a period of 6 months has elapsed since the termination of the previous period of carer's leave.

(5) Nothing in this Act shall be construed as prohibiting an agreement between an employer and employee in respect of carer's leave on terms which are more favourable to the employee than the entitlements of the employee under this Act.

(6) The Minister may make regulations in respect of the form in which carer's leave may be taken by any specified class or classes of employees in circumstances where carer's leave is to be taken in the form referred to in subsection (1)(b).

GENERAL NOTE

**DB.222**    This section, as amended by section 48 of the Social Welfare Law Reform and Pensions Act 2006, specifies that carer's leave in respect of any one relevant person may be taken in one continuous period of 104 weeks or in a number of periods, the aggregate duration of which does not exceed 104 weeks. An employer, on reasonable grounds notified to the employee in writing, may refuse to grant carer's leave for any period of less than 13 weeks. There must be a gap of at least six weeks between periods of carer's leave taken by an employee in respect of a relevant person.

The section also provides that an employee who has taken carer's leave in respect of a relevant person cannot commence a period of carer's leave in respect of another relevant person until a period of six months has elapsed from the date on which leave in respect of the first relevant person terminated.

## Notice of carer's leave

**9.** —(1) When an employee proposes to take carer's leave, the employee shall, **DB.223** not later than 6 weeks before the proposed commencement of the carer's leave, provide the employer with a notice in writing stating—

    (a) the proposal to take the carer's leave,

    (b) that an application referred to in section 6(5) or, where appropriate, section 6(6), has been made, and

    (c) the proposed date of commencement of the carer's leave and the form in which it is proposed to be taken.

(2) Where, in exceptional or emergency circumstances, it is not reasonably practicable to give notice in accordance with the period specified in subsection (1) the employee shall give that notice as soon as is reasonably practicable.

(3) An employee may revoke a notice of the proposal to take carer's leave given to the employer in accordance with subsection (1) or, where appropriate, subsection (2), by notice in writing given to the employer before the date of the confirmation document and where the notice of the proposal to take carer's leave is so revoked the employee shall not be entitled to take carer's leave at the time specified in the notice given in accordance with subsection (1) or, where appropriate, subsection (2).

(4) Notwithstanding subsection (1) where leave, purporting to be carer's leave, is taken by an employee who is entitled to carer's leave but who has not complied with subsection (1) or (2), the employer may, at his or her discretion and subject to subsection (8), treat that leave as carer's leave and this Act shall apply to that leave accordingly.

(5) An employer shall retain the documents given to him or her in accordance with subsection (1).

(6) An employee who is on carer's leave shall, not less than 4 weeks before the date on which that employee is due to return to his or her employment, give notice in writing to the employer of the intention to return to work.

(7) Subsection (6) shall not apply if the period of carer's leave is terminated in accordance with section 11(2).

(8) An employer may, when exercising his or her discretion under subsection (4), refuse to treat leave as carer's leave on reasonable grounds and where the employer so refuses he or she shall specify in writing the grounds for such refusal.

GENERAL NOTE

This section and section 10 regulate the procedures to be followed by an employee in giving notice **DB.224** of intention to avail of his or her entitlement to carer's leave. At least six weeks prior notice in writing is required, except in exceptional or emergency situations. The terms of the leave constitute a document to be known as a "confirmation document" which must be prepared and signed by the employer and employee not less than two weeks before the leave is due to commence. An employee must give at least four weeks' prior notice in writing of his or her intention to return to employment.

## Confirmation of carer's leave

**DB.225**    **10.** —(1) Where an employee has given his or her employer the decision referred to in section 6(1)(b), the employee and the employer shall, on a date that is not less than 2 weeks before the proposed commencement of the carer's leave concerned, prepare and sign a document (referred to in this Act as a "confirmation document") specifying the date of the commencement of the carer's leave, its duration and the form in which it will be taken.

(2) Subsection (1) shall apply to the taking of carer's leave in accordance with section 9(4) and the employee and the employer shall prepare and sign the confirmation document as soon as may be.

(3) An employer shall retain a confirmation document signed by him or her and shall give a copy of it to the employee concerned who shall retain it.

(4) A confirmation document, including any amendments to it made under section 12(1), shall be a notice for the purposes of section 31.

## Termination of carer's leave

**DB.226**    **11.** —(1) The period of carer's leave shall terminate—

(a) on the date of termination of the period of carer's leave specified in the confirmation document,

(b) on a date agreed between the employee and employer concerned,

(c) where the person in respect of whom the employee has taken carer's leave ceases to satisfy the conditions for a relevant person for the purposes of the Act,

(d) where the employee ceases to satisfy the conditions for the provision of full-time care and attention for the purposes of the Act,

(e) where a decision under subsection (2) is made, on the date specified in subsection (3), and

(f) where the relevant person dies during a period of carer's leave on the date earliest of the following dates—

(i) the date that is 6 weeks after the date of death, or

(ii) the date of termination of the period specified in the confirmation document.

(2) Where a deciding officer or an appeals officer makes a decision under section 18(4) or section 18(5) that—

(a) the person in respect of whom an employee proposed to take or has taken carer's leave did not or does not satisfy or no longer satisfies the requirements for a relevant person,

(b) the employee does not satisfy the conditions for providing full-time care and attention, or

(c) the employee is engaging or has engaged in employment or self-employment other than as prescribed under section [100(3) the Act of 2005],

the period of carer's leave shall terminate and the deciding officer or the appeals officer shall, as soon as practicable, notify the employer and the employee of that decision.

(3) The employer, following a notification referred to in subsection (2), shall, as

soon as practicable, give the employee a notice in writing specifying the date on which the employee is to return to his or her employment and that date shall be a date that is reasonable and practicable having regard to all the circumstances.

(4) Where carer's leave is terminated under subsection (2), the employee concerned shall return to his or her employment on the day specified in the notice under subsection (3) and any period between the date of the return to the employment and the date of the end of the period of the carer's leave that is specified in the confirmation document concerned, shall be deemed not to be carer's leave.

(5) An employer shall, when the employee returns to his or her employment, give a notice in writing to the Minister for [Social and Family Affairs] that the period of carer's leave has terminated, the employee has returned to work and the date of the return to employment.

(6) A person shall retain a notice under this section given to him or her and a copy of a notice under this section given by him or her.

(7) Notwithstanding section 24, the giving of a notice to an employee under this section shall be effected by delivering it to the employee or by sending a copy of it by prepaid registered letter in an envelope addressed to the employee at the last known residence of the employee or, where appropriate, the residence of the relevant person.

## Postponement, curtailment and variation of carer's leave by parties concerned

**12.** —(1) If, after the date of the confirmation document (whether or not the **DB.227** period of carer's leave to which it relates has commenced) the employer and the employee so agree—

(a) the carer's leave or part of it may be postponed to such time as may be so agreed between the parties,

(b) the period of carer's leave may be curtailed in a manner and to an extent as may be so agreed between the parties, or

(c) the form of the carer's leave may be varied in a manner as may be so agreed between the parties,

and the confirmation document shall be amended in accordance with such agreement.

(2) Where carer's leave is postponed, curtailed or varied the period of carer's leave that is not taken by reason of such postponement, curtailment or variation may, subject to section 6, be taken at another time.

GENERAL NOTE

This section provides for the postponement, curtailment and variation of the form in which carer's **DB.228** leave may be taken by agreement.

PART 3

EMPLOYMENT RIGHTS

## Protection of employment rights

**13.**—(1) An employee who is absent from work on carer's leave shall be **DB.229**

regarded as still working in the employment for all purposes relating to his or her employment and none of his or her rights or obligations related to the employment shall be affected by availing of carer's leave other than—

  (a)  the right to—

        (i)   remuneration,

        (ii)  annual leave, except as provided for in subsection (2),

        (iii) public holidays, except as provided for in subsection (3), and

        (iv)  superannuation benefits,

        and

  (b)  any obligation to pay contributions in, or in respect of, the employment.

  (2) Section 19 of the Organisation of Working Time Act, 1997, shall apply to the first 13 weeks of absence from work on carer's leave for each relevant person.

  (3) Section 21(1) of the Organisation of Working Time Act, 1997, shall apply to the first 13 weeks of absence from work on carer's leave for each relevant person and shall not apply to public holidays that occur after such period of absence from work.

  (4) Absence from employment while on carer's leave shall not be treated as part of any other leave from the employment (including sick leave, annual leave, adoptive leave, maternity leave, parental leave and force majeure leave) to which the employee concerned is entitled.

  (5) Where—

  (a)  an employee who is on probation in his or her employment or is undergoing training in relation to that employment or is employed under a contract of apprenticeship takes carer's leave, and

  (b)  his or her employer considers that the employee's absence from employment while on carer's leave would not be consistent with the continuance of the probation, training or apprenticeship,

the employer may require that the probation, training or apprenticeship be suspended during the period of the carer's leave and be completed by the employee at the end of that period.

GENERAL NOTE

**DB.230**    This section provides, in essence, that an employee on carer's leave will be treated as if he or she had not been absent from his or her employment so that all his or her employment rights, except the right to remuneration, annual leave and public holidays in excess of the initial period of 13 weeks of carer's leave, and superannuation benefits, will be unaffected during the leave. The word "remuneration" is not defined in the Act (other than for the purposes of s.21) but the Employment Appeals Tribunal was of the opinion, in *McGivern v Irish National Insurance Co Ltd* P5/1982, that the following statement from *S & U Stores Ltd v Lee* [1969] 2 All E.R. 417, 419 was "a generally satisfactory definition":

    "Remuneration is not mere payment for work done but is what the doer expects to get as the result of the work he does insofar as what he expects to get is quantified in terms of money".

## Return to work

**DB.231**    **14.**—(1) On the termination of carer's leave in accordance with this Act, the employee concerned shall be entitled to return to work—

  (a)  with the employer with whom he or she was working immediately before the start of the period or, where during the employee's absence from work there was or were a change or changes of ownership of the undertaking in which the employee was employed immediately before the absence, the owner on the expiration of the period ("the successor"),

(b) in the job that the employee held immediately before the commencement of the period, and

(c) under the contract of employment in respect of which the employee was employed immediately before the commencement of the period or, where a change of ownership such as is referred to in paragraph (a) has occurred, under a contract of employment with the successor, that is identical to the contract under which the employee was employed immediately before such commencement, and (in either case) under terms or conditions not less favourable to the employee than those that would have been applicable to him or her if he or she had not been so absent from work.

(2) For the purposes of subsection (1)(b), where the job held by an employee immediately before the commencement of a period of carer's leave to which he or she is entitled was not the employee's normal or usual job, the employee shall be entitled to return to work, either in that job or in his or her normal or usual job as soon as is practicable without contravention by the employee or the employer of any provision of a statute or provision made under statute.

(3) Where, because of an interruption or cessation of work at an employee's place of employment that exists at the time of the expiration of a period of carer's leave taken by the employee, it is unreasonable to expect the employee to return to work on such expiration, the employee may return to work instead when work resumes at the place of employment after the interruption or cessation, or as soon as reasonably practicable after such resumption.

GENERAL NOTE

This section provides an entitlement to return to work on the expiration of a period of carer's leave **DB.232** and is in terms similar to those of s.26 of the Maternity Protection Act 1994, s.18 of the Adoptive Leave Act 1995 and s.15 of the Parental Leave Act 1998.

## Right to alternative employment

**15.**—(1) Where an employee is entitled to return to work pursuant to section 14 **DB.233** but it is not reasonably practicable for the employer to permit the employee to return to work in accordance with that section, the employee shall be entitled to be offered by his or her employer suitable alternative employment under a new contract of employment.

(2) Work under a new contract of employment constitutes suitable alternative work for the purposes of this Act if—

(a) it is of a kind that is suitable in relation to the employee concerned and appropriate for the employee to do in the circumstances,

(b) the terms or conditions of the contract relating to the place where the work under it is required to be done, the capacity in which the employee concerned is to be employed and any other terms or conditions of employment are not substantially less favourable to the employee than those of his or her contract of employment immediately before the commencement of the period of absence from work while on carer's leave, and

(c) the continuity of service is preserved.

GENERAL NOTE

This section provides that, where it is not practicable to permit the employee to return to work in accordance with s.14, the employee is entitled to be offered suitable alternative employment. It is in terms similar to those of s.27 of the Maternity Protection Act 1994, s.19 of the Adoptive Leave Act 1995 and s.16 of the Parental Leave Act 1998.

## Protection of employees from penalisation

DB.235    **16.**—(1) An employer shall not penalise an employee for proposing to exercise or having exercised his or her entitlement to carer's leave.

(2) Penalisation of an employee includes—

(a) dismissal of the employee,

(b) unfair treatment of the employee, including selection for redundancy, and

(c) an unfavourable change in the conditions of employment of the employee.

(3) If a penalisation of an employee, in contravention of subsection (1), constitutes a dismissal of the employee, as referred to in subsection (2)(a) the employee may institute proceedings under the Unfair Dismissals Acts, 1977 to 2001, in respect of that dismissal and such dismissal may not be referred to a rights commissioner under Part 4.

(4) An employee who is entitled to return to work in the employment concerned in accordance with section 14 but is not permitted by his or her employer to do so—

(a) shall be deemed to have been dismissed on the date on which he or she was entitled to so return to work and the dismissal shall be deemed, for the purposes of the Unfair Dismissals Acts, 1977 to 2001, to have been an unfair dismissal unless, having regard to all the circumstances, there were substantial grounds justifying the dismissal, and

(b) shall be deemed for the purposes of the Redundancy Payments Acts, 1967 to [2003], to have had his or her contract of employment with his or her employer terminated on the date aforesaid.

PART 4

RESOLUTION OF DISPUTES

## Disputes

DB.236    **17.**—(1) This Part applies to any dispute between an employee and the employer relating to any entitlement of the employee under this Act (or any matter arising out of or related to such an entitlement) but does not apply to a dispute relating to—

(a) any matter arising out of sections 6(5) and 6(6),

(b) any matter arising out of paragraphs (a), (c) and (d) of section 6(1), and

(c) any matter arising out of section 18.

(2) Where, in a dispute, there is a decision of a deciding officer or an appeals officer that concerns a matter specified in paragraph (a), (b) or (c) of subsection

D–46/4

(1), the rights commissioner shall accept that decision as a final determination of that matter.

(3) A document purporting to be a decision of a deciding officer or an appeals officer and signed by that officer shall be sufficient evidence of the making of the decision and of its terms, without proof of the signature of that officer or of the official capacity of that officer.

(4) This Part does not apply to a member of the Defence Forces.

GENERAL NOTE

The Minister's explanation for the exclusion of the Defence Forces from this part of the Act was that they have their own statutory redress mechanisms under the Defence Act 1954 (see 167 *Seanad Debates* Col. 390). **DB.237**

## Reference by employer to Minister for [Social and Family Affairs] on certain issues

**18.**—(1) An employer who is of the opinion that— **DB.238**

(a) the person in respect of whom the employee proposes to take carer's leave is not or is no longer a relevant person, or

(b) the person in respect of whom carer's leave has been granted, and in respect of whom the employee is on carer's leave, is not or is no longer a relevant person,

shall notify the Minister for [Social and Family Affairs] of his or her opinion and the grounds for that opinion.

(2) An employer who is of the opinion that an employee who proposes to take, or is on, carer's leave does not satisfy the conditions for providing full-time care and attention to the relevant person shall notify the Minister for [Social and Family Affairs] of his or her opinion and the grounds for such opinion.

(3) An employer who is of the opinion that an employee who proposes to take, or is on, carer's leave is engaging or has engaged in employment or self-employment other than as prescribed under section [100(3) of the Act of 2005] shall notify the Minister for [Social and Family Affairs] of his or her opinion and the grounds for such opinion.

(4) On receipt of a notification under subsection (1), (2) or (3), the notification shall be referred to a deciding officer for a decision under the Act of [2005] as to whether—

(a) the person referred to in subsection (1) is a relevant person,

(b) the employee satisfies the conditions for providing full-time care and attention to the relevant person, or

(c) the employee is engaging or has engaged in employment or self-employment other than as prescribed under [100(3) of the Act of 2005],

for the purposes of Chapter [14 of Part 2 of the Act of 2005].

(5) A decision of a deciding officer under subsection (4) may be appealed under section [311 of the Act of 2005].

GENERAL NOTE

The title of the Minister was amended by virtue of the Social, Community and Family Affairs (Alteration of Name of Department and Title of Minister) Order 2002 (S.I. No. 310 of 2002). **DB.238A**

## Reference of disputes to rights commissioner

**19.**—(1) An employee may refer a dispute to a rights commissioner that the **DB.239**

employee's employer has contravened a provision of this Act in relation to the employee.

(2) A rights commissioner—

(a) shall hear the parties to a dispute and receive any relevant evidence tendered by either of them,

(b) shall give a decision on the dispute in writing, and may, in accordance with section 21, make provision for redress, and

(c) shall communicate the decision to the parties.

(3) An employee making a reference under subsection (1) shall give a notice in writing containing such particulars (if any) as may be prescribed to a rights commissioner within 6 months of the date of the contravention giving rise to the dispute.

(4) The rights commissioner shall give a copy of the notice referred to in subsection (3) to the employer.

(5) Proceedings before a rights commissioner under this section shall be conducted otherwise than in public.

(6) A rights commissioner shall furnish a copy of each decision made by him or her under this Part to the Tribunal.

(7) The Minister may by regulations provide for any matters relating to the proceedings under this section that the Minister considers appropriate.

(8) A rights commissioner may, if he or she considers it reasonable to do so having regard to all the circumstances, extend by a specified period (not exceeding a further period of 6 months) the period of time within which a notice under subsection (3) is required to be given.

GENERAL NOTE

**DB.240**     This section confers a right of redress, in the first instance, to a rights commissioner who is empowered to hear the parties and receive any relevant evidence tendered. The question of redress is governed by s.21. The claim must be referred not later than six months after the occurrence of the dispute.

## Appeal from decision of rights commissioner

**DB.241**     **20.**—(1) A party concerned may appeal to the Tribunal from a decision of a rights commissioner under section 19 and the Tribunal shall give the parties an opportunity to be heard by it and to present to it any evidence relevant to the appeal, and—

(a) shall make a determination in writing in relation to the appeal, affirming, varying or setting aside the decision,

(b) may, in accordance with section 21, make provision for redress, and

(c) shall communicate the determination to the parties.

(2) An appeal under this section shall be initiated by the party concerned giving, within 4 weeks of the date on which the decision to which it relates was communicated to the party, a notice in writing to the Tribunal containing such particulars (if any) as may be prescribed and stating the intention of the party concerned to appeal against the decision.

(3) A copy of a notice under subsection (2) shall be given by the Tribunal to the

other party concerned as soon as may be after the receipt of the notice by the Tribunal.

(4) A person whose evidence has been, is being, or is to be given before the Tribunal, or who produces or sends a document to the Tribunal pursuant to a notice under subsection (5) or who is required by such a notice to give evidence or produce a document to the Tribunal or to attend before the Tribunal and there to give evidence or produce a document, shall be entitled to the same privileges and immunities as if the person were a witness before the High Court.

(5) The Tribunal may, by giving notice in that behalf in writing, require any person to attend before the Tribunal on a date and at a time and place specified in the notice and to give evidence and to produce any document specified in the notice in his or her possession or power or to send to the Tribunal any document specified in the notice in his or her possession or power or require a person in attendance before the Tribunal to produce to the Tribunal any document in his or her possession or power specified in that requirement.

(6) Paragraphs (a) and (e) of section 39(17) of the Act of 1967 shall apply for the purposes of this section as they apply for the purposes of section 39 with the modification that "€3,000 (£2,362.69)" shall be substituted for "£150" and with any other necessary modifications.

(7) Proceedings for an offence under section 39(17) of the Act of 1967, as applied by this section, may be brought and prosecuted by the Minister.

(8) If a person gives false evidence before the Tribunal in proceedings under this section in such circumstances that, if the person had given the evidence before a court, the person would be guilty of perjury, the person shall be guilty of an offence and shall be liable on conviction on indictment to the penalties applying to perjury.

(9) The Tribunal may, if it considers it reasonable to do so having regard to all the circumstances, extend by a specified period (not exceeding a further period of 6 weeks) the period of time within which a notice under subsection (2) is required to be given.

GENERAL NOTE

This section provides that a decision of a rights commissioner may be appealed to the Employment **DB.242** Appeals Tribunal within four weeks of the date of the decision although that period can be extended for up to a further six weeks by the Tribunal.

## Redress

**21.**—(1) The rights commissioner or the Tribunal may order such redress for **DB.243** the party concerned as the rights commissioner or the Tribunal considers appropriate, having regard to all the circumstances and to the provisions of this Act, and accordingly may specify—

(a) the grant of carer's leave of such length to be taken at such time or times and in such manner as may be so specified,

(b) an award of compensation in favour of the employee concerned to be paid by the employer concerned, or

(c) a grant referred to in paragraph (a) and an award referred to in paragraph (b).

(2) Compensation under subsection (1)(b) shall be of such amount as the rights commissioner or the Tribunal deems just and equitable having regard to all the circumstances but shall not exceed 26 weeks remuneration in respect of the employee's employment calculated in such manner as may be prescribed.

(3) The decision of a rights commissioner or the determination of the Tribunal shall be in writing and shall be communicated to the parties by the rights commissioner or the Tribunal, as the case may be.

(4) Where appropriate, the confirmation document concerned shall be amended by the parties so as to accord with a decision, determination or direction under this section.

(5) In this section "remuneration" includes allowances in the nature of pay and benefits in lieu of or in addition to pay.

GENERAL NOTE

**DB.244**    This section empowers a rights commissioner and, on appeal, the Tribunal to order such redress as they consider appropriate including the granting of carer's leave of such length and at such time as may be specified and the award of compensation of up to 26 weeks remuneration. In awarding compensation, the rights commissioner and the Tribunal must make it clear whether the award is or is not "in respect of remuneration including arrears of remuneration", otherwise it may not be regarded as being exempt from income tax: see s.192A of the Taxes Consolidation Act 1997 (inserted by s.7 of the Finance Act 2004).

## Enforcement of decisions and determinations

**DB.245**    **22.**—(1) If a person fails or refuses to comply with a decision of a rights commissioner under section 19 or a determination of the Tribunal referred to in section 20 and in respect of which, at the expiration of the time for bringing an appeal against it, no such appeal has been brought, or if such an appeal has been brought, it has been abandoned—

(a)  the other party to the dispute, or

(b)  the Minister, if he or she is of the opinion that it is appropriate to do so having regard to all the circumstances,

may apply to the Circuit Court for an order directing that party to carry out the terms of the decision or determination.

(2) Where, in proceedings under subsection (1), the Circuit Court is satisfied that, owing to lapse of time, it would not be possible for one party to comply with an order under that subsection, the Circuit Court shall make an order providing for such redress as it considers appropriate having regard to the provisions of this Act and all the circumstances.

(3) In an order under this section providing for the payment of compensation, the Circuit Court may, if in all the circumstances it considers it appropriate to do so, direct the employer concerned to pay to the employee concerned interest on the compensation at the rate referred to in section 22 of the Courts Act, 1981, in respect of the whole or any part of the period beginning 4 weeks after the date on which the decision or determination concerned is communicated to the parties and ending on the date of the order.

(4) Proceedings under this section shall be heard in the county in which the

relevant employer ordinarily resides or carries on any profession, business or occupation.

GENERAL NOTE
This section provides that, if a party fails to carry out the terms of a rights commissioner decision or a Tribunal determination, the Circuit Court may make an order directing that it be carried out. The procedures governing applications for enforcement are set out in the Circuit Court Rules (Carer's Leave Act 2001) 2005 (S.I. No. 387 of 2005) reproduced *infra* at DC.601. **DB.246**

## Appeal to High Court on point of law

**23.**—(1) The Tribunal may refer a question of law arising in proceedings before it under this Part to the High Court for determination by it. **DB.247**

(2) A party to proceedings before the Tribunal under this Part may appeal to the High Court from a determination of the Tribunal on a point of law.

GENERAL NOTE
This section provides for a right of appeal, on a point of law only, to the High Court. Although the Rules of the Superior Courts 1986 (as amended) do not specifically provide for appeals under this Act, it is suggested that any such appeal be brought by special summons, by analogy with the procedure set out in R.S.C. 1986, Order 105. In the absence of any specific rule of court, any such appeal need only be brought within a reasonable time: *per* McCracken J. in his *ex tempore* ruling in *McGaley v Liebherr Container Cranes Ltd* (2001/234Sp) delivered on October 12, 2001. **DB.248**

The circumstances in which the High Court will overturn a decision of a specialist tribunal such as the Employment Appeals Tribunal have been considered in many cases: see for example, *Henry Denny & Sons (Ireland) Ltd v Minister for Social Welfare* [1998] 1 I.R. 34 and in particular the comments of Hamilton C.J. at 37. In considering whether to allow an appeal against a decision of such a tribunal, the High Court must consider whether that body based its decision on an identifiable error of law or on an unsustainable finding of fact. A decision cannot be challenged on the grounds of irrationality if there is any relevant material to support it: see further *Mulcahy v Waterford Leader Partnership Ltd* [2002] E.L.R. 12 (O'Sullivan J.) and *Thompson v Tesco Ireland Ltd* [2003] E.L.R. 21 (Lavan J.). In *National University of Ireland, Cork v Ahern* [2005] 2 I.R. 577, the Supreme Court held that, although findings of fact must be accepted by the High Court on appeal, that court could still examine the basis upon which those facts were found. The relevance or admissibility of the matters relied on in determining the facts were questions of law.

PART 5

MISCELLANEOUS

## Service of notices

**24.**—(1) A notice or other document under Part 4 shall be, subject to subsection (2), addressed to the person concerned by name, and may be served on or given to the person in one of the following ways— **DB.249**

   (a) by delivering it to the person,

   (b) by leaving it at the address at which the person ordinarily resides or, in a case in which an address for service has been furnished, at that address,

   (c) by sending it by post in a prepaid registered letter to the address at which the person ordinarily resides, or in a case in which an address for service has been furnished, to that address.

(2) For the purposes of this section, a company, within the meaning of the Companies Acts 1963 to [2005], shall be deemed to be ordinarily resident at its

registered office, and every other body corporate and every unincorporated body shall be deemed to be ordinarily resident at its principal office or place of business.

## Winding up and bankruptcy

DB.250     **25.**—(1) There shall be included among the debts that, under section 285 of the Companies Act 1963, are in the distribution of the assets of a company being wound up, to be paid in priority to all other debts, any compensation payable under this Act by the company to an employee, and that Act shall have effect accordingly, and formal proof of the debts to which priority is given under this subsection shall not be required except in cases where it may otherwise be provided by rules of court.

    (2) There shall be included among the debts that, under section 81 of the Bankruptcy Act 1988, are in the distribution of the property of a bankrupt or arranging debtor, to be paid in priority to all other debts, any compensation payable under this Act by the bankrupt or arranging debtor, as the case may be, to an employee, and that Act shall have effect accordingly, and formal proof of the debts to which priority is given under this subsection shall not be required except in cases where it may otherwise be provided by rules of court.

## Amendment of Act of 1967

DB.251     **26.**—[...]

## Amendment of Act of 1977

DB.252     **27.**—[...]

## Amendment of Organisation of Working Time Act 1977

DB.253     **28.**—[...]

## Amendment of National Minimum Wage Act 2000

DB.254     **29.**—[...]

## Extension of Protection of Employees (Employers' Insolvency) Act 1984

DB.255     **30.**—[...]

GENERAL NOTE

DB.256     This section allows any compensation awarded by a rights commissioner or the Tribunal to be paid out of the Social Insurance Fund in the event of an employer's insolvency.

## Maintenance of records

DB.257     **31.**—(1) An employer shall make a record of the carer's leave taken by his or her employees indicating the period of employment for each employee and the dates and times in respect of which each employee was on carer's leave.

(2) A record made under this section shall be retained by the employer concerned for a period of 8 years and, if the Minister prescribes the form of such records, the records shall be kept in the prescribed form.

(3) Notices, or copies of notices, required to be retained under this Act by a person shall be retained by that person for a period of 3 years.

(4) An employer who contravenes subsection (1) or (2) shall be guilty of an offence and shall be liable on summary conviction to a fine not exceeding €3,000 (£2,362.69).

GENERAL NOTE

This section imposes an obligation on employers in relation to the keeping of records and notices **DB.258** relating to carer's leave. Such records may be inspected by an inspector duly appointed under section 32.

## Inspectors

**32.**—(1) In this section "inspector" means a person appointed under subsection **DB.259** (2).

(2) The Minister may appoint in writing such and so many persons as the Minister sees fit to be inspectors for the purposes of this Act.

(3) An inspector may for the purposes of this Act do all or any of the following things—

(a) subject to the provisions of this section, enter at all reasonable times any premises or place where he or she has reasonable grounds for supposing that any employee is employed in work or from which he or she has reasonable grounds for supposing the activities that an employee is employed to carry on are directed or controlled (whether generally or as respect particular matters),

(b) make such examination or enquiry as may be necessary for ascertaining whether the provisions of this Act are complied with in respect of any employee employed in any such premises or place or any employee the activities aforesaid of whom are directed or controlled from any such premises or place,

(c) require the employer of any employee or the representative of such employer to produce to him or her any records which such employer is required to keep under section 31 and inspect and take copies of entries in such records (including in the case of information in a non-legible form a copy of or an extract from such information in a permanent legible form),

(d) require any person whom he or she has reasonable cause to believe to be or to have been an employee or the employer of any employee to furnish such information as the inspector may reasonably request,

(e) examine, with regard to any matters under this Act, any person whom he or she has reasonable cause to believe to be or to have been an employer or employee and require him or her to answer such questions (other than questions tending to incriminate him or her) as the inspector may put relative to those matters and to sign a declaration of the truth of the answers.

(4) An inspector shall not, other than with the consent of the occupier, enter a private dwelling (other than a part of the dwelling used as a place of work) unless he or she has obtained a warrant from the District Court under subsection (7) authorising such entry.

(5) Where an inspector in the exercise of his or her powers under this section is prevented from entering any premises an application may be made under subsection (7) authorising such entry.

D–47

(6) An inspector, where he or she considers it necessary to be so accompanied, may be accompanied by a member of the Garda Síochána when exercising any powers conferred on an inspector by this section.

(7) If a judge of the District Court is satisfied on the sworn information of an inspector that there are reasonable grounds for suspecting that information required by an inspector under this section is held on any premises or any part of any premises, the judge may issue a warrant authorising an inspector accompanied by other inspectors or a member of the Garda Síochána, at any time or times within one month from the date of issue of the warrant, on production, if so requested, of the warrant, to enter the premises (if need be by reasonable force) and exercise all or any of the powers conferred on an inspector under subsection (3).

(8) A person who—

(a) obstructs or impedes an inspector in the exercise of any of the powers conferred on an inspector under this section,

(b) refuses to produce any record which an inspector lawfully requires him or her to produce,

(c) produces or causes to be produced or knowingly allows to be produced, to an inspector, any record which is false or misleading in any material respect knowing it to be so false or misleading,

(d) gives to an inspector any information which is false or misleading in any material respect knowing it to be so false or misleading,

(e) fails or refuses to comply with any lawful requirement of an inspector under subsection (3), shall be guilty of an offence.

(9) Every inspector shall be furnished by the Minister with a certificate of his or her appointment and, on applying for admission to any premises or place for the purposes of this Act, shall, if requested by a person affected, produce the certificate or a copy of it to that person.

## Penalties, proceedings, etc.

DB.260    **33.**—(1) A person guilty of an offence under this Act shall be liable on summary conviction to a fine not exceeding €3,000 (£2,362.69).

(2) Where an offence under this Act is committed by a body corporate and is proved to have been committed with the consent or connivance of, or to be attributable to any neglect on the part of, a person being a director, manager, secretary or other officer of that body corporate, or a person who was purporting to act in that capacity, that person shall also be guilty of an offence and be liable to be proceeded against and punished as if he or she were guilty of the first-mentioned offence.

(3) Proceedings for an offence under sections 31 and 32 may be brought and prosecuted by the Minister.

(4) Notwithstanding section 10(4) of the Petty Sessions (Ireland) Act, 1851, proceedings for an offence under this Act may be instituted within 12 months from the date of the offence.

## Review of Act

DB.261    **34.**—The Minister shall, not earlier than 2 years and not later than 3 years after the commencement of this Act, after consultation with persons whom he or she considers to be representative of employers generally and persons whom he or she considers to be representative of employees generally, conduct a review of the operation of this Act and shall prepare a report in writing of the findings of the review and shall cause copies of the report to be laid before each House of the Oireachtas.

# ADOPTIVE LEAVE (REFERRAL OF DISPUTES AND APPEALS) (PART V) REGULATIONS, 1995

## (S.I. No. 195 of 1995)

**1.**—(1) These Regulations may be cited as the Adoptive Leave (Referral of  DC.101
Disputes and Appeals) (Part V) Regulations, 1995.

(2) These Regulations shall come into operation on the 20th day of July, 1995.

**2.**—(1) In these Regulations, except where the context otherwise requires—  DC.102

"the Act" means the Adoptive Leave Act, 1995 (No. 2 of 1995);

"appeal" means an appeal to the Tribunal under Part V of the Act;

"appellant" means a person who appeals to the Tribunal under Part V of the Act against a decision of a rights commissioner;

"applicant" means a person who refers a dispute to a rights commissioner under Part V of the Act;

"reference" means a dispute which is referred to a rights commissioner under Part V of the Act;

"regulations of 1979" means the Redundancy (Employment Appeals Tribunal) Regulations, 1979 (S.I. No. 114 of 1979); and

"respondent" means a party to a reference under Part V of the Act other than an applicant, or a party to an appeal under the said Part V, other than an appellant, as may be appropriate.

(2) In these Regulations, a reference to a Regulation is a reference to a Regulation of these Regulations, unless it is indicated that reference to some other Regulation is intended.

(3) In these Regulations, a reference to a paragraph or subparagraph is a reference to the paragraph or subparagraph of the provision in which the reference occurs, unless it is indicated that reference to some other provision is intended.

**3.**—(1) A notice under section 34 (1) or 35 (2) of the Act shall contain the  DC.103
following particulars:

   (a) the names, addresses and descriptions of the parties to the proceedings;

   (b) in the case of a reference, the grounds upon which the applicant's claim is based;

   (c) in the case of an appeal, the grounds of appeal;

   (d) in the case of a reference—

      (i) the day of placement, or

      (ii) where there has been no placement, the date on which the employer received the first notification of the adopting parent's intention to take leave under the Act, or

      (iii) in the case of an adopting father, the date on which the adopting mother died;

   (e) in case the notice is under section 34 (1) of the Act and is not given within the appropriate period specified in that section, the reasons for the delay,

   (f) the weekly remuneration of the adopting parent; and

   (g) in the case of an appeal, the date on which the decision to which the

D–51

appeal relates was made and the name of the rights commissioner who made it.

**DC.104** **4.**—(1) A reference or an appeal may be withdrawn by giving a notice in writing to the rights commissioner or the Tribunal, as may be appropriate, of the withdrawal of the reference or appeal.

(2) On receipt of a notice under paragraph (1) the rights commissioner or Tribunal, as the case may be, shall, as soon as is reasonably practicable thereafter, notify the respondent in writing of the withdrawal of the reference or appeal.

**DC.105** **5.**—(1) A respondent who receives notice of an appeal, shall, if she wishes to contest the appeal, or wishes to appear or be heard at the hearing thereof, enter an appearance to it by giving a notice of appearance in writing to the Tribunal within 14 days (or such longer period as the Tribunal may fix under paragraph (3)) of the receipt by her of a copy of the notice concerned under section 35 (2) of the Act.

(2) A notice of appearance under this Regulation shall contain a brief outline of the grounds upon which the matter under appeal will be contested.

(3) A respondent in an appeal may apply to the Tribunal by notice in writing for an extension of the period within which to enter an appearance stating the grounds for the application, and the Tribunal may extend the time within which to enter the said appearance by such period as the Tribunal considers appropriate, if satisfied that there are reasonable grounds for so doing.

**DC.106** **6.**—A copy of the notice of appearance shall be given by the Tribunal to the appellant as soon as may be after the receipt of the notice of appearance under Regulation 5 by the Tribunal.

**DC.107** **7.**—A mistake of a formal nature shall not operate to invalidate a notice given under section 34 (1) or 35 (2) of the Act.

**DC.108** **8.**—(1) The rights commissioner may request the parties in a reference to furnish him or her with particulars in relation to the dispute and may invite them to make submissions, either orally or in writing, in relation to the dispute.

(2) The rights commissioner may, if he or she considers it appropriate, convene an oral hearing at which he or she may put questions to the applicant and respondent and request the production of documents by them, in relation to the matters in dispute.

(3) Where a party in a reference falls or refuses without just cause, to attend an oral hearing convened under paragraph (2), the rights commissioner may proceed with the hearing in that party's absence.

(4) The rights commissioner may draw such inferences, as to him or her appear proper, from a failure or refusal by a party in a reference to comply with a request made under paragraph (1) or (2), or a failure or refusal by, such a party to answer a question put to her by the rights commissioner.

**DC.109** **9.**—A mistake (including an omission) of a verbal or formal nature, in a decision of a rights commissioner, may be corrected by a certificate signed by the rights commissioner.

**DC.110** **10.**—A mistake (including an omission) of a verbal or formal nature, in a determination of the Tribunal may be corrected by a certificate signed by the chairman of the Tribunal, or, if the determination concerned was made at a time when a vice-chairman was acting as chairman of the Tribunal, by the chairman of the Tribunal or such vice-chairman.

**11.**—(1) The Tribunal shall maintain a register to be known as the Register of   DC.111
Adoptive Leave Determinations (referred to subsequently in this Regulation as
Register") and shall cause to be entered therein particulars of every determination
by the Tribunal under Part V of the Act.

(2) The Register may be inspected free of charge by, any person during normal
office hours.

(3) Particulars of any correction made under Regulation 10 shall be entered in
the Register.

(4) The parties to an appeal shall be furnished with a copy of the entry in the
Register which relates to that appeal.

**12.**—A respondent in an appeal who does not enter an appearance in accor-   DC.112
dance with Regulation 5, shall not be entitled to take part in or be present or
represented at any proceedings before the Tribunal, relating to the matter under
appeal.

**13.**—(1)Where a notice is required, under the Act or these Regulations, to be   DC.113
served on a rights commissioner. the address for service of such notice shall be
"Rights Commissioner, Labour Relations Commission, Tom Johnson House,
Haddington Road, Dublin 4.".

(2) Where a notice is required, under the Act or these Regulations, to be served
on the Tribunal, the address for service of such notice shall be "The Secretary.
Employment Appeals Tribunal, Davitt House, 65A Adelaide Road, Dublin 2".

**14.**—Paragraphs 10 to 17(2), 19, 20, 20A (inserted by the regulations of 1979),   DC.114
23, 23A (inserted by the regulations of 1979) and 24 of the Redundancy (Redundancy Appeals Tribunal) Regulations, 1968 (S.I. No. 24 of 1968), shall, with any
necessary modifications (including, in the case of the said paragraphs 20 and 20A,
the modification that a sum awarded by the Tribunal under either of those paragraphs shall, in lieu of being paid out of the fund referred to therein, be paid by the
Minister for [Enterprise, Trade and Employment] with the consent of the Minister
for Finance), apply in relation to appeals under section 35 of the Act.

GENERAL NOTE

These Regulations prescribe the procedures to be followed in relation to the hearing of disputes and   DC.115
appeals under Part V of the 1995 Act. The title of the Minister in Regulation 14 was amended by virtue
of the Enterprise and Employment (Alteration of Name of Department and Title of Minister) Order
1997 (S.I. No. 305 of 1997). It should be noted that a decision or a determination which does not state
correctly the name of the employer concerned or any other material particular may, on application to
the rights commissioner or the Tribunal (as the case may be), be amended so as to state correctly the
name of the employer or the other material particular: see section 39(2) of the Organisation of Working
Time Act 1997.


# ADOPTIVE LEAVE (CALCULATION OF WEEKLY REMUNERATION) REGULATIONS, 1995


## (S.I. No. 196 of 1995)


**1.**—(1) These Regulations may be cited as the Adoptive Leave (Calculation of   DC.201
Weekly Remuneration) Regulations, 1995.

(2) These Regulations shall come into operation on the 20th day of July, 1995.

**2.**—(1) In these Regulations—   DC.202

"the Act", means the Adoptive Leave Act 1995 (No. 2 of 1995);

"relevant date" means the date on which the adopting parent commenced leave under the Act or, where she has not commenced leave under the Act, the date on which her employer first received notification of her intention to take leave under the Act;

"relevant employment", in relation to an employee. means the employment in respect of which the weekly. remuneration of the employee is calculated for the purposes of section 33 (3) of the Act;

"week", in relation to an employee whose remuneration is calculated by reference to a week ending on a day. other than a Saturday, means a week ending on that other day, and. in relation to any other employee, means a week ending on a Saturday, and "weekly" shall be construed accordingly.

DC.203    **3.**—(a) A week's remuneration of an employee in respect of an employment shall be calculated, for the purposes of section 33 (3) of the Act, in accordance with these Regulations.

(b)  Where, on the relevant date, an employee had less than 52 weeks' continuous service in the employment, a week's remuneration of the employee in respect of the employment shall be calculated, for the purposes of the said section 33 (3), in the manner that, in the opinion of the rights commissioner or the Tribunal, corresponds most closely to that specified in these Regulations.

DC.204    **4.**—In the case of an employee who is wholly remunerated in respect of the relevant employment at an hourly time rate or by a fixed wage or salary, and in the case of any other employee whose remuneration in respect of the relevant employment does not vary by reference to the amount of work done by her, her weekly remuneration in respect of the relevant employment shall be her earnings in respect of that employment (including any regular bonus or allowance which does not vary having regard to the amount of work done and any payment in kind) in the latest before the relevant date, in which she worked for the number of hours that was normal for the employment together with, if she was normally required to work overtime in the relevant employment, her average weekly overtime earnings in the relevant employment as determined in accordance with Regulation 5 of these Regulations.

DC.205    **5.**—For the purpose of Regulation 4 of these Regulations. the average weekly overtime earnings of an employee in the relevant employment shall be the amount obtained by dividing by 26 the total amount of her overtime earnings in that employment in the period of 26 weeks ending 13 weeks before the relevant date.

DC.206    **6.**—For the purpose of Regulations 5 and 7 (h) of these Regulations, any week during which the employee concerned did not work shall be disregarded and the latest week before the period of 26 weeks mentioned in the said Regulation 5 or 7 (b), as the case may be, of these Regulations or before a week taken into account under this Regulation, as may be appropriate, shall be taken into account instead of a week during which the employee did not work as aforesaid.

DC.207    **7.**—(a) In the case of an employee who is paid remuneration in respect of the relevant employment wholly or partly at piece rates, or whose remuneration includes commissions (being piece rates or commissions related directly to her output at work) or bonuses, and in the case of any other employee whose remuneration in respect of the relevant employment varies in relation to the amount of work done by her, her weekly remuneration shall be the amount obtained by dividing the amount of the remuneration to be taken into account in accordance with paragraph (b) of this Regulation by the number of hours worked in the period of 26 weeks mentioned in the said paragraph (b) and multiplying the resulting amount by the normal number of hours for which, on the relevant date, an employee in the relevant employment was required to work in each week.

(b) The remuneration to be taken into account for the purposes of paragraph (a) of this Regulation shall be the total remuneration paid to the employee concerned in respect of the employment concerned for all the hours worked by the employee in the employment in the period of 26 weeks that ended 13 weeks before the relevant date, adjusted in respect of any variation in the rate of pay which became operative during that 13 week period.

(c) For the purpose of paragraph (b) of this Regulation, any week worked in another employment shall be taken into account if it would not have operated, for the purposes of the First Schedule to the Minimum Notice and Terms of Employment Act, 1973 (No. 4 of 1973), to break the continuity of service of the employee concerned in the relevant employment.

**8.**—(1) Where, under her contract of employment, an employee is required to work for more hours than the number of hours that is normal for the employment, the hours for which she is so required to work shall be taken, for the purposes of Regulations 4 and 7 (b) of these Regulations, to be, in the case of that employee, the number of hours that is normal for the employment. **DC.208**

(2) Where, under her contract of employment, an employee is entitled to additional remuneration for working for more than a specified number of hours per week-

(a) in case the employee is required under the said contract to work for more than the said specified number of hours per week, the number of hours per week for which she is so required to work shall, for the purposes of Regulations 4 and 7 (b) of these Regulations, be taken to be, in her case, the number of hours of work per week that is normal for the employment, and

(b) in any other case, the specified number of hours shall be taken, for the purposes of the said Regulations 4 and 7 (b), to be, in the case of that employee, the number of hours of work per week that is normal for the employment.

**9.**—Where, in a particular week, an employee qualifies for a payment of a bonus, pay allowance or commission which relates to work the whole or part of which was not done in that particular week, the whole or the appropriate proportionate part of the payment, as the case may be, shall, for the purposes of Regulations 4 and 7 (b) of these Regulations, be disregarded in relation to that particular week and shall for those purposes, be taken into account in relation to any week in which any of the work was done. **DC.209**

**10.**—An employee who is normally employed on a shift cycle and whose remuneration in respect of the employment varies having regard to the particular shift on which she is employed, and an employee whose remuneration for working for the number of hours that is normal for the employment varies having regard to the days of the week or the times of the day on or at which she works, shall each be **DC.210**

D–55

taken, for the purposes of these Regulations, to be an employee who is paid wholly or partly by piece rates.

DC.211    **11.**—Where, in respect of the relevant employment, there is no number of hours for which employees work in each week that is normal for the employment, the weekly remuneration of each such employee shall be taken, for the purposes of these Regulations, to be the average amount of the remuneration paid to each such employee in the 52 weeks in each of which she was working in the employment immediately before the relevant date.

DC.212    **12.**—Where under these Regulations account is to be taken of remuneration paid in a period which does not coincide with the periods for which the remuneration is calculated, the remuneration shall be apportioned in such manner as may be just.

DC.213    **13.**—For the purposes of Regulations 4 and 7 of these Regulations, account shall not be taken of any sums paid to an employee by way of recoupment of expenses incurred by her in the discharge of the duties of her employment.

GENERAL NOTE

DC.214    These Regulations prescribe the method of calculating weekly remuneration for the purpose of redress in the form of compensation under Part V of the 1995 Act.


# CIRCUIT COURT RULES 2001

## (S.I. No. 510 of 2001)

### ORDER 57

### Rule 3 Adoptive Leave Act 1995

DC.351    **1.** In this Order "the Act" means the Adoptive Leave Act, 1995 (No. 2 of 1995), and "the Tribunal" means the Employment Appeals Tribunal and "Commissioner" means a rights commissioner and "the Minister" means the Minister for Justice, Equality and Law Reform.

DC.352    **2.** Applications for the enforcement of a decision of a Commissioner or determinations of the Tribunal, whether such application be made by the party in whose favour the decisions or determinations were made or by the Minister, shall, pursuant to section 39 of the Act, be made by way of Motion on Notice in accordance with Form 36C of the Schedule of Forms annexed hereto which shall set out the grounds upon which the plaintiff relies for the reliefs sought and shall have annexed thereto

(a) a certified copy of the decision of the Commissioner or a certified copy of the determination of the Tribunal, and

(b) a certified copy of the covering offer from the Commissioner or the Tribunal issued to the applicant with the aforementioned decision of the Commissioner or determination of the Tribunal;

(c) a copy Notice of Appeal, if applicable; and shall set out

D–56

(i)   all facts relevant to the alleged failure to carry out the decisions or determinations;

(ii)   whether or not an appeal has been brought from the decisions or determinations and,

if no such appeal has been brought, that the time for appeal has elapsed and, if such appeal has been brought, the date upon which Notice of Appeal was given and evidence of abandonment thereof.

**3.** Applications shall, in accordance with section 39(4) of the Act, be brought in the county where the relevant employer ordinarily resides or carries on any profession, business or occupation. **DC.353**

**4.** All applications shall be served no later than 10 days prior to the return date set out in the Motion either in accordance with the provisions as to service of Civil Bills and other documents contained in Order 11 of these Rules or by being delivered to or served upon the Solicitor who is on record before the Tribunal as acting for the person named as the defendant before the Court; and service of an application or any other document upon such Solicitor, or delivery of the same at his office, or sending the same to him by prepaid post to such office shall be deemed to be good service upon the party for whom such Solicitor acts upon the day when the same is so delivered or served, or upon which in the ordinary course of postage it would be delivered. The Motion shall be listed for mention only on the return date set out therein at which time a date for hearing shall be fixed by the Court. **DC.354**

**5.** Notice of every application shall be given to the Tribunal and the Commissioner. Such notice shall be effected before filing of the application by the delivery of a copy of the application at, or by sending the same by prepaid registered post to, the Office of the Secretary of the Tribunal or to the Rights Commissioner, Labour Relations Commission, as appropriate. **DC.355**

**6.** Save by special leave of the Court, all applications under section 39 of the Act shall only be heard upon oral evidence or as may be determined by the Court. **DC.356**

**7.** The Court may make such Order as to costs as may be appropriate including an Order measuring the costs. **DC.357**

**DC.358**

Form 36C

AN CHÚIRT CHUARDA

THE CIRCUIT COURT

CIRCUIT                                                                    COUNTY OF

IN THE MATTER OF THE ADOPTIVE LEAVE ACT, 1995

NOTICE OF MOTION FOR RELIEF UNDER SECTION 39 OF THE
ADOPTIVE LEAVE ACT, 1995

BETWEEN

.............................................................................................................. Plaintiff

AND

................................................................................................ Defendant

Take notice that application will be made to the Court on the or the next opportunity thereafter for the following reliefs:

[Here insert details of the relief sought by way of enforcement.]

And further take notice that the said application will be grounded upon:

1.  [here insert grounds upon which the Applicant is relying for the reliefs sought to include all facts relevant to the alleged failure to carry out the decisions or determinations and whether or not an appeal has been brought from the decisions or determinations and, if no such appeal has been brought, that the time for appeal has elapsed and, if such appeal has been brought, the date upon which Notice of Appeal was given and evidence of abandonment thereof.]

2.  [here insert basis of jurisdiction]

3.  [here insert name, address and description of the Plaintiff]

4.  [The following documents must be annexed to this Notice of Motion namely a certified copy of the original decision of the Commissioner or a certified copy of the original determination of the Tribunal; a certified copy of the covering letter from the Commissioner or the Tribunal issued to the Plaintiff with the aforementioned decision of the Commissioner or determination of the Tribunal; a copy Notice of Appeal, if applicable.]

Dated the            day of

Signed:   ....................................................
Plaintiff/Solicitor for the Plaintiff

To:      ...............................................................
The Defendant/Solicitor for the Defendant

And

To:      The Employment Appeals Tribunal/Rights Commissioner

And

To:      The County Registrar

GENERAL NOTE

**DC.359**     This rule prescribes Circuit Court procedures in respect of applications brought under section 39 of the 1995 Act for enforcement of decisions of a rights commissioner or determinations of the Employment Appeals Tribunal pursuant to the 1995 Act.

D–58 [NEXT PAGE D–61]

# CIRCUIT COURT RULES (CARER'S LEAVE ACT, 2001) 2005

## (S.I. No. 387 of 2005)

1. These Rules, which may be cited as the Circuit Court Rules (Carer's Leave DC.601 Act 2001), 2005, shall come into operation on the 4th day of August 2005.

2. The Orders referred to in these Rules shall be added to and construed DC.602 together with those Orders contained in the Circuit Court Rules, 2001, as amended.

ORDER 57 Rule 8 — Carer's Leave Act, 2001
(CARER'S LEAVE ACT, 2001) (No. 19 of 2001)

**Rule One**

1. In this Order "the Act" means the Carer's Leave Act, 2001 (No. 19 of 2001), and "the Tribunal" means the Employment Appeals Tribunal and "commissioner" means a rights commissioner and "the Minister" means the Minister for Enterprise, Trade and Employment.

**Rule Two**

2. All applications served or proceedings taken before these Rules shall have come into operation but which are in accordance with the existing Rules and practice of the Court shall have the same validity as application made or proceedings taken in accordance with these Rules.

**Rule Three**

3. Applications for the enforcement of decisions of a commissioner or determinations of the Tribunal, whether such application be made by the party in whose favour the decisions or determinations were made or by the Minister, shall, pursuant to section 22 of the Act, be made by way of Motion on Notice grounded upon Affidavit sworn by the party seeking enforcement of the decisions or determinations or, in the case of the Minister, by an appropriate officer duly authorised by the Minister, which said Affidavit shall exhibit

(a) a certified copy of the decision of the commissioner or a certified copy of the determination of the Tribunal and

(b) a certified copy of the covering letter from the commissioner or the Tribunal issued to the Applicant with the aforementioned decision of the commissioner or determination of the Tribunal;

(c) a copy Notice of Appeal, if applicable;

and shall set out

(i) all the facts relevant to the alleged failure to carry out the decisions or determinations;

(ii) whether or not an appeal has been brought from the decisions or determinations and, if no such appeal has been brought, that the time for appeal has elapsed and, if such appeal has been brought, the date upon which Notice of Appeal was given and evidence of abandonment thereof.

**Rule Four**

4. Applications shall, in accordance with section 22(4) of the Act, be brought in the County where the relevant employer ordinarily resides or carries on any profession, business or occupation.

**Rule Five**

5. Notice of every application shall be given to the employer or employers in question and to the Tribunal and the commissioner as appropriate by serving notice of the proceedings (including the Notice of Motion and grounding Affidavits, if any) no later than 10 days prior to the return date specified in the Notice of Motion, in the case of the employer or employers personally in accordance with the provisions of Order 11 of these Rules or by leaving a true copy of same at the employer's residence or place of business or by pre-paid registered post to the employer's residence or place of business and by the delivery of a copy of the application at, or by sending the same by pre-paid registered post to the Office of the Secretary of the Tribunal or to the commissioner, Labour Relations Commission, as appropriate.

**Rule Six**

6. Save by special leave of the Court, all applications under Section 22 of the Act shall be heard only upon Affidavit.

**Rule Seven**

7. The Court may make such Order as to costs as may be appropriate including an Order measuring the costs.

GENERAL NOTE

**DC.603** These rules prescribe Circuit Court procedures in respect of applications for the enforcement of Rights Commissioner decisions or Employment Appeals Tribunal determinations pursuant to s.22 of the 2001 Act.

# ADOPTIVE LEAVE ACT 1995 (EXTENSION OF PERIODS OF LEAVE) ORDER 2006

## (S.I. No. 52 of 2006)

**1.** This Order may be cited as the Adoptive Leave Act 1995 (Extension of Periods of Leave) Order 2006. **DC.701**

**2.** (1) Subject to paragraphs (2) and (3) of this Article, this Order (other than Articles 8 to 11 thereof) comes into operation on 1 February 2006. **DC.702**

(2) (a) Articles 4 and 5 of this Order apply in respect of an employed adopting mother or sole male adopter who commences adoptive leave or additional adoptive leave, as the case may be, at any time not less than 4 weeks after the date specified in paragraph (1) of this Article.

(b) Articles 6 and 7 of this Order apply in respect of an adopting father who commences adoptive leave or additional adoptive leave, as the case may be, at any time after the date specified in paragraph (1) of this Article.

(3) (a) Articles 4 to 7 of this Order do not apply in respect of an employee who—

(i) at any time prior to the relevant date, postpones the leave concerned in accordance with section 11C (inserted by section 9 of the Act of 2005) of the Act of 1995, and

(ii) by reason only of that postponement, resumes or commences the leave concerned after the relevant date.

(b) In this paragraph "the relevant date" means—

(i) 1 February 2006, in respect of an adopting father's adoptive leave or additional adoptive leave, and

(ii) 1 March 2006, in respect of an employed adopting mother or sole male adopter's adoptive leave or additional adoptive leave.

(4) Subject to paragraphs (5) and (6) of this Article, Articles 8 to 11 of this Order come into operation on 1 February 2007.

(5) (a) Articles 8 and 9 of this Order apply in respect of an employed adopting mother or sole male adopter who commences adoptive leave or additional adoptive leave, as the case may be, at any time not less than 4 weeks after the commencement of those Articles.

(b) Articles 10 and 11 of this Order apply in respect of an adopting father who commences adoptive leave or additional adoptive leave, as the case may be, at any time after the commencement of those Articles.

(6) (a) Articles 8 to 11 of this Order do not apply in respect of an employee who—

(i) at any time prior to the relevant date, postpones the leave concerned in accordance with section 11C (inserted by section 9 of the Act of 2005) of the Act of 1995, and

(ii) by reason only of that postponement, resumes or commences the leave concerned after the relevant date.

(b) In this paragraph "the relevant date" means—

(ii) 1 March 2007, in respect of an employed adopting mother or sole male adopter's adoptive leave or additional adoptive leave.

**3.** In this Order— **DC.703**

"Act of 1995" means the Adoptive Leave Act 1995 (No. 2 of 1995);

"Act of 2005" means the Adoptive Leave Act 2005 (No. 25 of 2005).

**DC.704**

**4.** The minimum period for the purposes of section 6 (as amended by section 3 of the Act of 2005) of the Act of 1995 is 20 weeks.

DC.705    **5.** The maximum period for the purposes of section 8(1) (as amended by section 4 of the Act of 2005) of the Act of 1995 is 12 weeks.

DC.706    **6.** The adoptive leave for the purposes of section 9(1) (as amended by section 5 of the Act of 2005) of the Act of 1995 shall be for a period of—

   (a) in case the adopting mother dies on or after the day of placement, 20 weeks less the period between the date of placement and the date of her death, or

   (b) in any other case, 20 weeks.

DC.707    **7.** The additional adoptive leave for the purposes of section 10(1) (as amended by section 6 of the Act of 2005) of the Act of 1995 shall be for a period of—

   (a) in case the adopting mother dies on or after the expiration of 20 weeks from the day of placement, 12 weeks less the period between the date of that expiration and the date of her death, or

   (b) in any other case, 12 weeks.

DC.708    **8.** The minimum period for the purposes of section 6 (as amended by section 3 of the Act of 2005) of the Act of 1995 is 24 weeks.

DC.709    **9.** The maximum period for the purposes of section 8(1) (as amended by section 4 of the Act of 2005) of the Act of 1995 is 16 weeks.

DC.710    **10.** The adoptive leave for the purposes of section 9(1) (as amended by section 5 of the Act of 2005) of the Act of 1995 shall be for a period of—

   (a) in case the adopting mother dies on or after the day of placement, 24 weeks less the period between the date of placement and the date of her death, or

   (b) in any other case, 24 weeks.

DC.711    **11.** The additional adoptive leave for the purposes of section 10(1) (as amended by section 6 of the Act of 2005) of the Act of 1995 shall be for a period of—

   (a) in case the adopting mother dies on or after the expiration of 24 weeks from the day of placement, 16 weeks less the period between the date of that expiration and the date of her death, or

   (b) in any other case, 16 weeks.

GENERAL NOTE

DC.712    This Order amends the Adoptive Leave Act 1995 so as to bring into effect the increases in adoptive leave announced in the context of Budget 2006. Adopting mothers or sole male adopters who commenced adoptive leave on or after March 1, 2006 will now be entitled to 20 weeks adoptive leave and 12 weeks additional adoptive leave (up from 16 and 8 weeks respectively). Adopting mothers or sole male adopters who commence adoptive leave on or after March 1, 2007 will be entitled to 24 weeks adoptive leave and 16 weeks additional adoptive leave.

# PARENTAL LEAVE ACT 1998

## (1998 No. 30)

ARRANGEMENT OF SECTIONS

PART I

PRELIMINARY AND GENERAL

PART II

PARENTAL LEAVE AND *FORCE MAJEURE* LEAVE

PART III

EMPLOYMENT RIGHTS

PART IV

RESOLUTION OF DISPUTES

E–51

PART V

MISCELLANEOUS

22A. Codes of practice.
23. Notices.
24. Winding up and bankruptcy.
25. Amendment of enactments.
26. Extension of Protection of Employees (Employers' Insolvency) Act 1984.
27 Records.
28. Review of Act.

**EB.101** An Act to implement Council Directive 96/34/EC of 3 June 1996 on the framework agreement on parental leave concluded by UNICE, CEEP and the ETUC, for that purpose to amend certain enactments and to provide for related matters.

[8th July, 1998]

INTRODUCTION AND GENERAL NOTE

**EB.102** The purpose of this Act is the transposition into Irish Law of Council Directive 96/34/EC of June 3, 1996 on the framework agreement on parental leave concluded by the three principal cross-industry organisations. The Act provides for an entitlement for men and women to avail of unpaid parental leave to enable them to take care of their young children. The Act also contains provision for limited paid leave for employees in family crises-to be known as *force majeure* leave.

A Directive on parental leave and leave for family reasons was first proposed by the European Commission in 1983. This draft directive was based on Article 100 of the Treaty and thus required unanimous approval in the Council of Ministers. This unanimity was not forthcoming, with the U.K. government being the main obstacle, and the proposal lay dormant until 1993 when a new text was drawn up under the Belgian Presidency. Following renewed debate in Council, a "broad consensus" was noted among the Member States' governments but adoption was not possible with the U.K. again being the principal opponent. The Social Policy Agreement annexed to the Treaty on European Union, however, provided a mechanism whereby proposals which had failed to gain approval in Council could be revived. Consequently in February 1995 the Commission initiated the first stage of consultation of the social partners, as provided for by Article 3(2) of the Agreement. This was the second time this procedure had been used, the first being the 1994 initiative which led to the European Works Council Directive (Directive 94/45/EC).

The first stage of consultation under the Agreement relates to the possible direction of Community action on this subject. Responses were received from 17 organisations which, according to the Commission's Explanatory Memorandum (COM (96) 26 final), revealed a consensus in favour of action of some sort. It was generally acknowledged that a Community initiative was needed but a number of responses recommended that the social partners play an active role in drafting and implementing principles in this area.Having considered these responses, the Commission began the second stage of consultation, as provided for in Article 3(3) of the Social Policy Agreement, in June 1995. On July 5, 1995, however the Union of Industrial and Employers' Confederations of Europe (UNICE), the European Centre of Enterprises with Public Participation (CEEP) and the European Trade Union Confederation (ETUC) sent a joint letter to the Commission requesting it, as provided for in Article 4 of the Social Policy Agreement, to suspend its legislative procedure while they commenced negotiations on a framework agreement. Formal talks began on July 12 and, after several months of negotiations, the three organisations concluded a draft agreement on parental leave in November 1995, which agreement was then ratified and formally signed on December 14, 1995.

Having concluded their first-ever Europe-wide agreement, the three organisations took up the option provided by Article 4(2) of the Social Policy Agreement of jointly requesting that the Commission submit the framework agreement to the Council for implementation.

**EB.103** The Commission, having concluded that the three organisations fulfilled the condition of representativeness and that none of the framework agreement's clauses were contrary to Community Law, proposed that the most suitable instrument for its application was a Council Directive. In addition, the Commission endorsed the aims of the framework agreement, seeing it as an important step in two respects. First it stressed the importance of parental leave for reconciling family and working life—and thus for equality of opportunity between men and women—and, secondly, it was important in the context of new and flexible ways of organising working time. The draft directive was adopted by the Council on June 3, 1996 and Member States (other than the U.K.) were given two years to implement

E–52

the Directive's provisions, although they could have a maximum of one more year if this was necessary "to take account of special difficulties". Directive 97/75/EC, however, extends the Directive to the U.K., where it was to be implemented by December 15, 1999.

In February 1998, the Department of Justice, Equality and Law Reform contacted the Commission seeking to delay transposition by six months—to December 3, 1998. According to the Minister (155 *Seanad Debates* Col. 1410), this approach was made because of an assessment of "the timeframe for enactment of the legislation and our knowledge of the potential difficulties for employers of having to implement the legislation immediately after the enactment of the Bill". Apparently the Commission acceded to this request.

At the time of the adoption of the Directive, Ireland, along with the U.K. and Luxembourg, were the only Member States not to have some kind of statutory parental leave. In seven-Sweden, Finland, Denmark, Belgium, Germany, Austria and Italy-some form of payment was provided. Apparently, however (see the Minister at 155 *Seanad Debates* Col. 1408), even in those jurisdictions where the leave is paid the take-up rate by men is extremely low, Sweden apart. So in Austria, for example, where workers opting for parental leave receive a monthly payment from the State of approximately €356, only 1.5 per cent of workers so opting are men (see EIRR 296, p. 3). In Luxembourg, parents taking parental leave receive a monthly payment of €272.68.

The framework agreement, which is made obligatory by the Directive, is important in a number of respects, not least of which is the identity of the participants in the social dialogue process. A number of organisations which do not consider themselves represented by UNICE, CEEP and the ETUC protested about their being excluded from negotiations which led to the signing of the framework agreement. Prominent amongst those were Euro Commerce (representing retail and wholesale employers), the Confederation Européene des Cadres (representing unionised managerial and professional staff not organised by ETUC affiliates) and the European Association of Craft, Small and Medium-Sized Enterprises (UEAPME). Indeed the last mentioned organisation sought the Directive's annulment pursuant to Article 173 of the Treaty alleging that Articles 2, 3(1) and 4 of the Social Policy Agreement had been breached.

In Case T–135/96, *Union Européene de l'Artisanat et des Petites et Moyennes Entreprises v.* **EB.104** *Council of the European Union* [1998] E.C.R. II–2335, the Court of First Instance ruled that the legal challenge was not valid. The Court held that, based on its representativeness, UEAPME had not shown that it was sufficiently distinctive from other social partner organisations which were not involved in negotiating the agreement. The Commission and the Council were therefore justified in considering that the representativeness of the agreement concluded by UNICE, CEEP and the ETUC was sufficient to form the basis of a Directive and that the involvement of UNICE and CEEP was sufficient to represent the interests of small and medium-sized firms.

Although the Directive sets certain minimum standards for parental leave, it affords substantial discretion to the Member States as to the components of its parental leave scheme. The key features of the scheme set out in the Act, as amended by the European Communities (Parental Leave) Regulations 2000 (S.I. No. 231 of 2000) and the Parental Leave (Amendment) Act 2006, are that:

(i)     the leave will apply to parents of children born or adopted on or after December 3, 1993;
(ii)    each parent will be entitled to a total of 14 weeks leave for such a child;
(iii)   the leave must be taken before a child is eight (16 in the case of a disabled child);
(iv)    the leave may be taken as a continuous block or in blocks of at least six weeks or, by agreement between employer and employee, in shorter blocks or by reduced working hours;
(v)     the leave is unpaid.

Research commissioned by the Working Group on the Review of the Parental Leave Act 1998 (on which see the annotation to section 28) showed that almost 7 per cent of employees were eligible for parental leave in 2001. 20 per cent of eligible employees were estimated to have taken parental leave (with the level of uptake being higher in the public sector) with the majority of those taking parental leave being women (84 per cent).

CITATION

See section 1.                                                                                                          **EB.105**

COMMENCEMENT

The Act came into operation on December 3, 1998: see section 1(2). The amendments effected by **EB.106** the Parental Leave (Amendment) Act 2006 came into operation on May 18, 2006.

STATUTORY INSTRUMENTS

Parental Leave (Notice of *Force Majeure* Leave) Regulations 1998 (S.I. No. 454 of 1998).     **EB.107**
Parental Leave (Disputes and Appeals) Regulations 1999 (S.I. No. 6 of 1999).
Parental Leave (Maximum Compensation) Regulations 1999 (S.I. No. 34 of 1999).

E–53

Parliamentary Debates

EB.108    155 *Seanad Debates* Cols. 1405–1440 (Second Stage).
        155 *Seanad Debates* Cols. 1496–1522 (Committee and Remaining Stages).
        493 *Dáil Debates* Cols. 26–35 (Second Stage).
        493 *Dáil Debates* Cols. 93–131 (Second Stage resumed).
        493 *Dáil Debates* Cols. 152–174 (Second Stage resumed).
        Select Committee on Justice, Equality and Women's Rights (JUS 1, No. 11, June 25, 1998)
    Cols. 307–348 (Committee Stage).
        493 *Dáil Debates* Cols. 526–542 (Report and Final Stages).
        156 *Seanad Debates* Cols. 531–539 (Report and Final Stages).

EB.109    Be it enacted by the Oireachtas as follows:

## PART I

### PRELIMINARY AND GENERAL

### Short title and commencement

EB.110    **1.**—(1) This Act may be cited as the Parental Leave Act 1998.

(2) This Act shall come into operation on the 3rd day of December, 1998.

GENERAL NOTE

EB.111    The Directive set a deadline of June 3, 1998 for its transposition into national law but the Government sought and obtained from the E.U. Commission a six month extension to December 3, 1998. The Bill was presented on June 4, 1998 in the Seanad and was signed by the President on July 8, 1998. The Minister said (155 *Seanad Debates* Col. 1410) that the interval would enable employer and worker organisations to inform their members about the implications of the Act; allow employers to put systems in place and to make any necessary modification to existing non-statutory leave schemes; allow secondary legislation to be put in place; facilitate Departments in making consequential changes; and generally permit the smooth introduction of the scheme (see also the Minister of State at the Department at 155 *Seanad Debates* Col. 1497). Although the Directive did not specify any form of retrospection, the Act now provides that parental leave will apply to parents of children born or adopted on or after December 3, 1993.

    The collective citation is now the Parental Leave Acts 1998 and 2006: see s.13(2) of the Parental Leave (Amendment) Act 2006.

### Interpretation

EB.112    **2.**—(1) In this Act—

    "adoption order" means an order under section 9 of the Adoption Act 1952;

    "confirmation document" has the meaning assigned to it by section 9;

    "contract of employment" means—

        (a)   a contract of service or apprenticeship, or

        (b)   any other contract whereby an individual agrees with another person, who is carrying on the business of an employment agency within the meaning of the Employment Agency Act 1971, and is acting in the course of that business, to do or perform personally any work or service for a third person (whether or not the third person is a party to the contract), whether the contract is express or implied and if express, whether it is oral or in writing;

    "date", in relation to a confirmation document, means the date on which it is signed by the parties thereto or the later of the dates on which it is so signed;

    "employee" means a person of any age who has entered into or works under (or, where the employment has ceased, entered into or worked under) a contract of employment, and references, in relation to an employer, to an

E–54

employee shall be construed as references to an employee employed by that employer; and for the purposes of this Act, a person holding office under, or in the service of, the State (including a member of the Garda Síochána or the Defence Forces or a civil servant within the meaning of the Civil Service Regulation Act, 1956) shall be deemed to be an employee employed by the head (within the meaning of the Freedom of Information Act, 1997), of the public body (within the meaning aforesaid) in which he or she is employed and an officer or servant of a local authority for the purposes of the Local Government Act, 1941, or of a harbour authority, [the Health Service Executive] or vocational education committee shall be deemed to be an employee employed by the authority, [the Executive] or committee, as the case may be;

"employer", in relation to an employee—

(a) means the person with whom the employee has entered into or for whom the employee works under (or, where the employment has ceased, entered into or worked under) a contract of employment, subject to the qualification that the person who under a contract of employment referred to in paragraph (b) of the definition of "contract of employment" is liable to pay the remuneration of the individual concerned in respect of the work or service concerned shall be deemed to be the individual's employer, and

(b) includes, where appropriate, the successor or an associated employer of the employer;

"*force majeure* leave" shall be construed in accordance with section 13(1);

"job", in relation to an employee, means the nature of the work that the employee is employed to do in accordance with his or her contract of employment and the capacity and place in which he or she is employed;

"the Minister" means the Minister for Justice, Equality and Law Reform;

"parental leave" shall be construed in accordance with section 6(1);

"prescribed" means prescribed by the Minister by regulations;

"successor", in relation to an employer, shall be construed in accordance with section 15(1);

"the Tribunal" means the Employment Appeals Tribunal.

(2) For the purposes of this Act, two employers shall be taken to be associated if one is a body corporate of which the other (whether directly or indirectly) has control or if both are bodies corporate of which a third person (whether directly or indirectly) has control and "associated employer" shall be construed accordingly.

(3) In this Act—

(a) a reference to a Part or section is a reference to a Part or section of this Act unless it is indicated that reference to some other provision is intended,

(b) a reference to a subsection, paragraph or subparagraph is a reference to a subsection, paragraph or subparagraph of the provision in which the reference occurs unless it is indicated that reference to some other provision is intended, and

(c) a reference to any enactment shall be construed as a reference to that enactment as amended, adapted or extended, whether before or after the passing of this Act, by or under any subsequent enactment.

(4) A word or expression used in this Act and also in Council Directive 96/34/EC of 3 June, 1996, shall have the same meaning in this Act as in that Directive.

GENERAL NOTE

**EB.113**    "contract of employment": as to whether a person is employed under a contract of service see *Henry Denny & Sons (Ireland) Ltd v Minister for Social Welfare* [1998] 1 I.R. 34. The inclusion of a specific reference to persons employed through employment agencies is similar to the provisions of section 13 of the Unfair Dismissals (Amendment) Act 1993, section 1(1) of the Terms of Employment (Information) Act 1994, section 1(1) of the Protection of Young Persons (Employment) Act 1996 and section 2(1) of the Organisation of Working Time Act 1997. But note the decision of the Labour Court in *Rooney v Diageo Global Supply* [2004] E.L.R. 133 that an agency supplied worker was employed by the client under a contract of employment. The definition of "employee" was amended by virtue of s.66 of the Health Act 2004.

## Regulations

**EB.114**    **3.**—(1) The Minister may—

(a) by regulations provide for any matter referred to in this Act as prescribed or to be prescribed, and

(b) make regulations generally for the purpose of giving effect to this Act and, if in any respect any difficulty arises during the period of two years after the commencement of this section in bringing into operation this Act, by regulations do anything which appears to be necessary or expedient for enabling this Act to have full effect.

(2) Before making a regulation under this Act, the Minister shall consult with persons whom he or she considers to be representative of employers generally and persons whom he or she considers to be representative of employees generally in relation to the regulation.

(3) A regulation under this Act may contain such consequential, supplementary and ancillary provisions as the Minister considers necessary or expedient.

(4) Every regulation under this Act shall be laid before each House of the Oireachtas as soon as may be after it is made and, if a resolution annulling the regulation is passed by either such House within the next 21 days on which that House has sat after the regulation is laid before it, the regulation shall be annulled accordingly, but without prejudice to anything previously done thereunder.

## Voidance or modification of certain provisions in agreements

**EB.115**    **4.**—(1) A provision in any agreement shall be void in so far as it purports to exclude or limit the application of any provision of this Act or is inconsistent with any provision of this Act.

(2) A provision in any agreement which is or becomes less favourable in relation to an employee than a similar or corresponding entitlement conferred on the employee by this Act shall be deemed to be so modified as to be not less favourable.

(3) Nothing in this Act shall be construed as prohibiting the inclusion in an agreement of a provision more favourable to an employee than any provision in Parts II to V.

(4) References in this section to an agreement are to any agreement, whether a contract of employment or not and whether made before or after the passing of this Act.

GENERAL NOTE

**EB.116**    This section seeks to ensure that persons cannot nullify or exclude the application of the provisions of the Act but it allows for the provision of arrangements between an employer and an employee that are more favourable than those provided for in the Act.

## Expenses

**EB.117**    **5.**—Any expenses incurred by the Minister or the Minister for Enterprise, Trade and Employment in the administration of this Act shall, to such extent as may be sanctioned by the Minister for Finance, be paid out of moneys provided by the Oireachtas.

PART II

PARENTAL LEAVE AND *FORCE MAJEURE* LEAVE

## Entitlement to parental leave

[**6.**—(1) Subject to this Act, an employee who is a relevant parent in respect of a child shall be entitled to leave from his or her employment, to be known and referred to in this Act as "parental leave" for a period of 14 working weeks to enable him or her to take care of the child.   **EB.118**

(2) Subject to sections 10(4) and 11(6), a period of parental leave shall end–

(a)  subject to paragraphs (b) and (c), not later than the day on which the child concerned attains the age of 8 years,

(b)  subject to paragraph (c), in the case of a child who—

   (i)   is the subject of an adoption order, and

   (ii)  has, on or before the date of the making of that order, attained the age of 6 years but not 8 years,

not later than the expiration of the period of 2 years beginning on that date, or

(c)  if the child concerned has a disability, not later than the day on which the child—

   (i)   attains the age of 16 years, or

   (ii)  ceases to have that disability or any other disability,

whichever first occurs.

(3) A period of parental leave shall not commence before a time when the employee concerned has completed one year's continuous employment with the employer from whose employment the leave is taken.

(4) Subject to this Act, an employee shall be entitled to parental leave in respect of each child of which he or she is a relevant parent.

(5) A person who is a relevant parent in more than one capacity in respect of a child shall not be entitled to parental leave in more than one such capacity in respect of the child.

(6) Where 2 of more relevant parents in respect of a child are entitled to parental leave in respect of the child, none of the parents shall be entitled to—

(a)  the parental leave of any other parent in respect of the child, or

(b)  transfer any part of the period of his or her parental leave to any other parent in respect of the child.

(7) Notwithstanding subsection (3), where an employee—

(a)  will not have completed one year's continuous employment with his or her employer on the latest day for commencing a period of parental leave having regard to subsection (2), but

(b)  has completed 3 months of such employment on the latest day for commencing a period of such leave provided for by this subsection,

the employee shall, subject to this Act, be entitled to parental leave for a period of one week for each month of continuous employment that he or she has completed with the employer at the time of the commencement of the leave.

(8) Where, before the relevant day, a person who is a relevant parent in respect of a child—

E–57

(a) has taken 14 weeks parental leave in respect of the child (and irrespective of whether the leave consisted of a continuous period or a number of periods), or

(b) has not taken 14 weeks parental leave in respect of the child (and irrespective of whether the person was prevented from taking all or any of the parental leave by the operation of subsection (3) of this section as in force before the relevant day),

then, on and after the relevant day—

(c) if paragraph (a) is applicable, nothing in this Act as amended by the relevant Act shall entitle the person to any further period of parental leave in respect of that child, and

(d) if paragraph (b) is applicable, this Act as amended by the relevant Act shall apply to so much of the 14 weeks of parental leave referred to in that paragraph as was not taken before the relevant day in respect of that child.

(9) In this section—

"adopting parent" means an adopting father, adopting mother or sole male adopter within the meaning of the definitions of "adopting father",

"adopting mother" and "sole male adopter" respectively in section 2 of the Adoptive Leave Act 1995 but as if, in each of those definitions, the words "or is to be placed" were omitted;

"adoptive parent", in relation to a child, means a person in whose favour an adoption order in respect of the child has been made and is in force;

"disability" in relation to a child means an enduring physical, sensory, mental health or intellectual impairment of the child such that the level of care required for the child is substantially more than the level of care that is generally required for children of the same age who do not have any such impairment;

"relevant Act" means the Parental Leave (Amendment) Act 2006;

"relevant day" means the day on which section 2 of the relevant Act comes into operation;

"relevant parent"; in relation to a child, means a person who is—

(a) the natural parent, the adoptive parent or the adopting parent in respect of the child, or

(b) acting *in loco parentis* to the child.]

GENERAL NOTE

**EB.119**     This section, as substituted by section 2 of the Parental Leave (Amendment) Act 2006, sets out the qualifying conditions for parental leave. An employee who is the natural, adopting or adoptive parent of a child or who is in *loco parentis* to that child, and who has completed one year's continuous employment is entitled to unpaid parental leave of 14 working weeks. As originally enacted the entitlement to parental leave only applied in respect of children born or adopted after June 3, 1996. However, following a complaint by the Irish Congress of Trade Unions, the European Commission issued a Reasoned Opinion dated April 3, 2000 to the effect that Ireland, by so restricting the right to parental leave, had not fully complied with its obligations under the Directive: but see the decision of the English High Court in *R. v Secretary of State for Trade and Industry, ex parte Trades Union Congress* [2000] I.R.L.R. 565 to refer this issue to the Court of Justice. The Commission's decision has now been endorsed by the Court of Justice: see Case C–519/03, *Commission v Luxembourg* [2005] 3 C.M.L.R. 1. The European Communities (Parental Leave) Regulations 2000 (S.I. No. 231 of 2000) gave effect to the decision of the Commission by providing that parents of children born or adopted between December 3, 1993 and June 2, 1996 will be entitled to parental leave and December 31, 2001 was set as the date by which such parents must use up that entitlement, notwithstanding that some of the children concerned would be over the age of five years by that date: reg.4 of the 2000 Regulations. For children born or adopted after June 3, 1996, the period of parental leave must end not later than the day on which the child attains the age of eight (16 in the case of a disabled child), although in the case of an

E–58

adopted child who is six or more but less than eight at the time of the adoption, the leave can be taken within two years of the adoption order.

Probably the key issue the Government had to consider was whether parental leave should be paid, either by the employer or by the Exchequer in the form of a social welfare payment, or unpaid. The Minister explained (155 *Seanad Debates* Col. 1408) why the Government had decided parental leave should be unpaid:

"To require employers to provide pay for the person who is absent on parental leave for 14 weeks, in addition to the cost of a replacement of that person, would not only be costly for individual employers but would be fundamentally damaging to Ireland's competitive position ... Were the Exchequer, on the other hand, to provide a benefit similar to maternity leave to all persons who took parental leave, the estimated cost would be £40 million a year in social welfare benefits alone".

The figures provided to the Working Group on the Review of the Parental Leave Act 1998 (on which see the annotation to s.28) indicated that, if parental leave were paid at the same rate as maternity benefit, it would cost €78.74m decreasing to €34.17m, if it were paid at the same rate as disability benefit.

Even though the leave is unpaid, nothing in the Act prevents an employer from paying for parental leave if the employer so wishes. Section 14 of the Act provides that employees on parental leave will be treated for the purposes of all other employment rights as if they remained at work. This means that time spent on parental leave will be counted as service for the purposes of promotions, increments, annual leave, etc. The Minister also indicated (155 *Seanad Debates* Col. 1409) that the Minister for Social, Community and Family Affairs would be introducing regulations to ensure that time spent on parental leave will be credited for social welfare purposes where necessary.

Another issue of concern would have been the maximum age of the child concerned. The Directive permitted this to be set anywhere between two and eight inclusive. Only Sweden and Denmark had an upper age limit of eight, while in Luxembourg, it is five, in Belgium it is four, in France and Germany it is three and in Austria it is two. The Minister (155 *Seanad Debates* Col. 1409) said that it had been decided to set the limit at five "by which age almost all children have started school". The Parental Leave (Amendment) Act 2006 extended the limit to eight years (16 in the case of a disabled child).

Efforts to amend subs.(7) so as to allow for the transfer of parental leave if the employer consented, failed with the Minister asserting that international experience had shown that, where transfers of leave was allowed, the traffic was invariably in one direction, from fathers to mothers. The purpose of parental leave, however, was to encourage the sharing of responsibilities between men and women (Select Committee, Col. 329).

Section 3 of the Parental Leave (Amendment) Act 2006, however, purported to permit the transfer of parental leave entitlements from one parent to the other where both were employed by the same employer. Because of a drafting error, however, this is not legally permissible (see General Note to s.3 of the 2006 Act, *infra* at EB.207).

Section 2(1) of the Adoptive Leave Act 1995 defines "adopting parent" as follows:

"adopting father" means "a male employee in whose care a child has been placed or is to be placed with a view to the making of an adoption order or to the effecting of a foreign adoption or following any such adoption, where the adopting mother has died";

"adopting mother" means "a woman, including an employed adopting mother, in whose care a child (of whom she is not the natural mother) has been placed or is to be placed with a view to the making of an adoption order, or to the effecting of a foreign adoption or following any such adoption";

"sole male adopter" means "a male employee who is not an adopting father within the meaning of this Act and in whose sole care a child has been placed or is to be placed with a view to the making of an adoption order, or to the effecting of a foreign adoption or following any such adoption".

As to the meaning of a "foreign adoption" see s.1 of the Adoption Act 1991, reproduced *supra* at DB.100.

Note also that the definition of "disability" differs from that contained in the Employment Equality Act 1998.

## Manner in which parental leave may be taken

**7.**—(1) Subject to this Act, parental leave may consist of—                    **EB.120**

(a)  a continuous period of 14 weeks,

[(aa) subject to subsection (1A), 2 separate periods—

    (i)  each consisting of not less than 6 weeks, and

    (ii)  not exceeding 14 weeks in total, or]

(b)  with the agreement of the employer or representatives of the employer and other employers and the employee or representatives of the employee and other employees, a number of periods each of which comprises—

E–59

(i) one or more days on which, but for the leave, the employee would be working in the employment concerned,

(ii) one or more hours during which, but for the leave, the employee would be working in the employment concerned, or

(iii) any combination of periods referred to in subparagraphs (i) and (ii).

[(1A) Subject to subsection (1B), where parental leave in respect of a child is taken by an employee pursuant to subsection (1)(aa), then in respect of that child the employee is not entitled to take the second period of parental leave unless not less than 10 weeks have elapsed since the first period of parental leave ended.

(IB) The employer concerned (or representatives of the employer and other employers) and the employee concerned (or representatives of the employee and other employees) may agree to a shorter period than the 10 weeks referred to in subsection (1A), either in a particular case or a class of cases.]

(2) (a) Parental leave taken by an employee pursuant to subsection (1)(b) shall be such that the number of hours during which, but for the leave, the employee would be working in the employment concerned equals—

(i) the number of hours during which the employee worked in the employment concerned in such continuous period of 14 weeks before the commencement of the leave as may be determined by the employee concerned and the employer, or

(ii) if the employee and the employer fail to determine a period for the purposes of subparagraph (i), 14 times the average number of hours per week during which the employee worked in the employment in each of the periods of 14 weeks ending immediately before the commencement of each week in which he or she takes any of the leave.

(b) In determining a period [referred to in paragraph (a) or (aa)], holidays (including public holidays) to which the employee concerned is entitled or days on which he or she is absent from work on sick leave, maternity leave, adoptive leave, or *force majeure* leave shall be excluded and a corresponding number of days immediately before the commencement of the period shall be included and time spent on parental leave by the employee shall be deemed to be time spent by him or her at work in the employment concerned.

(3) [Subject to subsection (3A), where] an employee is entitled to parental leave in respect of more than one child and the children concerned are not children of a multiple birth, the period of parental leave taken by him or her in any period of 12 months shall not, without the consent of the employer, exceed that provided for in subsection (1).

[(3A) Subsection (3) shall not apply to—

(a) any period of parental leave proposed to be taken by an employee—

(i) in respect of a child who has attained the age of 7 years before or on the date of commencement of this subsection, and

(ii) before the 1st anniversary of that date,

if the operation of section 6(2)(a) would prevent the employee from taking all or any part of that parental leave after that date, or

(b) any period of parental leave proposed to be taken by an employee—

(i) in respect of a child who has attained the age of 15 years before or on the date of commencement of this subsection, and

(ii) before the 1st anniversary of that date,

if the operation of section 6(2)(c) would prevent the employee from taking all or any part of that parental leave after that date.]

E–60

(4) (a) Where any holiday (other than a public holiday) to which an employee is entitled falls during a period of parental leave of the employee and on a day when (but for the leave and the holiday) the employee would be working in the employment concerned, the holiday shall be taken at such other time as may be determined by the employer concerned pursuant to section 20 of the Organisation of Working Time Act 1997.

  (b) Where any public holiday to which an employee is entitled falls during a period of parental leave of the employee and on a day when (but for the leave and the holiday) the employee would be working in the employment concerned, a day shall be added to the period of parental leave that the employee is entitled to take.

GENERAL NOTE

This section, as amended by s.4 of the Parental Leave (Amendment) Act 2006, specifies that **EB.121** parental leave may consist of a continuous period of 14 weeks or two separate periods each consisting of not less than six weeks. With the agreement of the employer and the employee (or their respective representatives), parental leave may also be taken in shorter blocks or by working reduced hours to the limit of 14 weeks. Subsection (2) sets out the formulae for calculating the parental leave entitlement of such employees. If the employer does not agree, then the employee has no entitlement to take leave otherwise than as provided for in this section: see the Employment Appeals Tribunal's determination in *O'Neill v. Dunnes Stores* [2000] E.L.R. 306. Subsection (4) provides that, whereas public holidays which fall during parental leave will be added to the end of parental leave, annual leave which accrues will be granted in accordance with s.20 of the Organisation of Working Time Act 1997 which provides that the time at which annual leave is granted is to be determined by the employer having regard to work requirements and subject to the employer taking into account, *inter alia*, the need for the employee to reconcile work and family responsibilities.

## Notice of parental leave

**8.**—(1) When an employee proposes to take parental leave, he or she shall, as **EB.122** soon as reasonably practicable but not later than 6 weeks before the commencement of the leave, give notice in writing of the proposal to his or her employer.

(2) A notice under subsection (1) shall specify the date of commencement of the parental leave concerned and its duration and the manner in which it is proposed to be taken and shall be signed by the employee concerned.

(3) Before the date of the confirmation document concerned, an employee may, by notice in writing signed by him or her and given to his or her employer, revoke a notice under subsection (1) given by him or her and, if the employee does so, he or she shall not be entitled to take parental leave at the time specified in the latter notice.

(4) Notwithstanding subsection (1), where leave purporting to be parental leave is taken by an employee who is entitled to parental leave but who has not complied with subsection (1) in relation to the leave, the employer may, at his or her discretion, treat the leave as parental leave and this Act shall apply accordingly.

(5) An employer shall retain a notice given to him or her under this section and shall give a copy of it to the employee concerned who shall retain it.

(6) [An employee who has given a notice to his or her employer under subsection (1) shall, if the employer so requests, furnish to the employer such evidence as the employer may reasonably require in relation to—

  (a) the date of birth of the child in respect of whom the parental leave is sought,

  (b) the employee being a relevant parent, within the meaning of section 6(9), of the child, and

  (c) if relevant, the disability, within the meaning of section 6(9), of the child.

(7) Where an employee proposes to take parental leave in respect of a child

pursuant to section 7(1)(aa), then the notice under subsection (1) required to be given by the employee shall, for the purposes of this Act, be treated as—

    (a) one such notice, if the employee complies with that requirement by giving one notice specifying the 2 periods of parental leave proposed to be taken, and

    (b) 2 such notices if the employee complies with that requirement by giving 2 notices each specifying one of the periods of parental leave proposed to be taken,

and the other provisions of this Act (including section 11) shall be construed accordingly.]

GENERAL NOTE

EB.123    This section, as amended by section 5 of the Parental Leave (Amendment) Act 2006, together with section 9, regulates the procedure to be followed by employees in giving notice of intention to avail of parental leave. At least six weeks advance notice is required from the employee, presumably so that the employer can make alternative arrangements for the performance of the employee's duties.

## Confirmation of parental leave

EB.124    **9.**—(1) Where an employee has given a notice under section 8(1) to his or her employer, they shall, not less than 4 weeks before the commencement of the parental leave concerned, prepare and sign a document (referred to in this Act as a "confirmation document") specifying the date of commencement of the leave, its duration and the manner in which it will be taken.

(2) Where leave is treated as parental leave pursuant to section 8(4), a confirmation document in relation to the leave shall be prepared and signed by the employer and the employee concerned as soon as may be.

(3) An employer shall retain a confirmation document signed by him or her and shall give a copy of it to the employee concerned who shall retain it.

GENERAL NOTE

EB.125    This section requires that, once the arrangements for the parental leave are agreed, they are to be embodied in a document to be known as a "confirmation document". This document should be prepared and signed by both employer and employee not less than four weeks before the leave is due to commence.

## Postponement, curtailment and variation of parental leave by parties concerned

EB.126    **10.**—(1) Subject to this Act, when a confirmation document has been prepared and signed in accordance with section 9, the employee concerned shall not be entitled to work in the employment concerned during the period of parental leave specified in the document.

[(2) Notwithstanding subsection (1), if, after the date of a confirmation document (whether or not the period of parental leave to which it relates has commenced)—

    (a) the employer concerned or his or her successor and the employee concerned so agree, the leave or part of it may be postponed to such time as may be so agreed upon, the period of such leave may be curtailed in such manner and to such extent as may be so agreed upon or the form of the leave may be varied in such manner as may be so agreed upon, and in such a case the confirmation document shall be amended accordingly, or

    (b) the employee concerned becomes sick such that the employee is unable to care for the child the subject of the parental leave to which the confirmation document relates, then the employee may, by notice in writing given to the employer concerned or his or her successor, as soon as is reasonably

E–62

practicable after becoming sick, and accompanied by the relevant evidence in respect of the sickness—

(i)   if the period of parental leave has not commenced, postpone the taking of the leave to such time as the employee is no longer sick, or

(ii)  if the period of parental leave has commenced, suspend the taking of the balance of the leave to such time as the employee is no longer sick,

and in such a case the confirmation document shall be deemed to be amended accordingly.]

(3) Where parental leave is curtailed under [subsection (2)(a)] or Part IV, the parental leave not taken by reason of the curtailment may be taken at such other time as may be agreed upon by the parties concerned.

[(4) If, solely because of the postponement or suspension under subsection (2)(b) of the taking of parental leave, or the taking of the balance of parental leave, as the case may be, the period of the parental leave ends by virtue of the operation of section 6(2), then the event which causes that period to so end shall be deemed, for the purposes of this Act, to have occurred after the end of that period.

(5) In subsection (2)(b), "relevant evidence" in relation to an employee, means—

(a)  a medical certificate—

(i)   stating that the employee named in the certificate is, by reason of the sickness specified in the certificate, unable to care for the child in the certificate, and

(ii)  signed by a registered medical practitioner within the meaning of section 2 of the Medical Practitioners Act 1978,

or

(b)  if the employee does not have a medical certificate referred to in paragraph (a) such evidence as the employer concerned or his or her successor may reasonably require in order to show that the employee is, by reason of sickness, unable to care for the child concerned.]

GENERAL NOTE

This section, as amended by section 6 of the Parental Leave (Amendment) Act 2006, provides that **EB.127** once a "confirmation document" has been signed, the employee is not entitled to work during the agreed period of parental leave. Both parties, however, can agree to postpone or curtail the leave after it has been confirmed or even commenced. Specific provision is also made for the case where the employee becomes sick.

## Postponement by employer of parental leave

**11.**—(1) Subject to this section, where an employee has given a notice under **EB.128** section 8(1) to his or her employer and the employer is satisfied that the taking of parental leave at the time specified in the notice would have a substantial adverse effect on the operation of his or her business, profession or occupation by reason of seasonal variations in the volume of the work concerned, the unavailability of a person to carry out the duties of the employee in the employment, the nature of those duties, the number of employees in the employment or the number thereof whose periods, or parts of whose periods, of parental leave will fall within the period specified in the said notice or any other relevant matters, the employer may, by notice in writing given to the employee not later than 4 weeks before the intended commencement of the leave, postpone the commencement of the leave to such time not later than 6 months after the date of commencement specified in the relevant notice under section 8(1) as may be agreed upon by the employer and the employee.

E–63

(2) Before giving a notice under this section to an employee, an employer shall consult with the employee in relation to the proposed postponement of parental leave.

(3) A notice under subsection (1) shall contain a statement in summary form of the grounds for the postponement of the commencement of the parental leave concerned.

(4) The commencement of parental leave in respect of a particular child may not be postponed more than once under this section unless a ground for the postponement is seasonal variation in the volume of the work concerned; and, where that is a ground for the postponement, such commencement in respect of a particular child may not be postponed more than twice.

(5) Subsection (1) does not apply to parental leave in relation to which a confirmation document has been signed by the parties concerned.

[(6) If, solely because of the postponement under this section of the commencement of parental leave, the period of the parental leave ends by virtue of the operation of section 6(2), then the event which caused that period to so end shall be deemed, for the purposes of this Act, to have occurred after the end of that period.

(6A) Where a notice under section 8(1) by an employee to his or her employer falls within section 8(7)(a) then, subject to any agreement between the employee and the employer, any postponement under this section of the commencement of parental leave must apply to both periods of proposed parental leave the subject of the notice.]

(7) An employer shall retain a copy of a notice under this section given by him or her to an employee of his or hers and the employee shall retain the notice.

(8) In this section, references to parental leave include references to a period of parental leave specified in section 7(1)(b).

GENERAL NOTE

**EB.129**   This section, as amended by section 7 of the Parental Leave (Amendment) Act 2006, permits an employer, if it is satisfied that the taking of the proposed parental leave would have a substantial adverse effect on the employer's business, to postpone the commencement of the parental leave for a period not exceeding six months. This facility cannot repeatedly be availed of by the employer and no postponement can take place unless the employee in question has been consulted.

## Abuse of parental leave

**EB.130**   **12.**—(1) The entitlement to parental leave is subject to the condition that it is used to take care of the child concerned.

(2) Where an employer has reasonable grounds for believing that an employee of his or hers who is on parental leave is not using the leave for the purpose of taking care of the child concerned, the employer may, by notice in writing given to the employee, terminate the leave and the notice shall contain a statement in summary form of the grounds for terminating the leave and shall specify the day (being a day not later than the date of the end of the period of the leave specified in the confirmation document concerned nor, subject to the foregoing requirement, earlier than 7 days after the date of the receipt by the employee concerned of the notice).

(3) Where parental leave is terminated under subsection (2), the employee concerned shall return to his or her employment on the day specified in the notice under that subsection concerned and any period between the date of such return and the date of the end of the period of the leave specified in the confirmation document concerned shall be deemed not to be parental leave.

(4) Where an employee gives his or her employer a notice under section 8(1)

and the employer has reasonable grounds for believing that the employee is not entitled to the parental leave concerned, the employer may, by notice in writing given to the employee, refuse to grant the leave to the employee and, if the employer does so, the employee shall not be entitled to take the parental leave concerned.

(5) A notice under subsection (4) shall contain a statement in summary form of the grounds for refusing to grant the parental leave concerned.

(6) Where an employer proposes to give a notice under subsection (2) or (4) to an employee of his or hers, the employer shall, before giving the notice, give notice in writing of the proposal to the employee and the notice shall contain a statement in summary form of the grounds for terminating, or, as the case may be, refusing to grant, the parental leave concerned and a statement that the employee may within 7 days of the receipt of the notice make representation to the employer in relation to the proposal; and any such representations made by an employee to an employer within the period aforesaid shall be considered by the employer before he or she decides whether to give a notice under subsection (2), or as the case may be, subsection (4) to the employee.

(7) A person shall retain a notice under this section given to him or her and a copy of a notice under this section given by him or her.

GENERAL NOTE

This section provides that it is a condition of parental leave that it is used to take care of the child **EB.131** concerned. If the employer believes that the parental leave is being abused, it can be terminated. The procedures to be followed, however, must be consistent with the requirements of natural justice, so the employee must be afforded one week in which to make representations about the termination of the leave and a further week's notice before he or she is required to return to work.

## Leave on grounds of *force majeure*

**13.**—(1) An employee shall be entitled to leave with pay from his or her **EB.132** employment, to be known and referred to in this Act as "*force majeure* leave", where, for urgent family reasons, owing to an injury to or the illness of a person specified in subsection (2), the immediate presence of the employee at the place where the person is, whether at his or her home or elsewhere, is indispensable.

(2) The persons referred to in subsection (1) are—

(a)  a person of whom the employee is the parent or adoptive parent,

(b)  the spouse of the employee or a person with whom the employee is living as husband or wife,

(c)  a person to whom the employee is in *loco parentis*,

(d)  a brother or sister of the employee,

(e)  a parent or grandparent of the employee, and

[(f)  a person other than one specified in any of paragraphs (a) to (e), who resides with the employee in a relationship of domestic dependency.

(2A) For the purposes of subsection (2)(f)—

(a)  a person who resides with an employee is taken to be in a relationship of domestic dependency with the employee if, in the event of injury or illness, one reasonably relies on the other to make arrangements for the provision of care, and

(b)  the sexual orientation of the persons concerned is immaterial.

(2B) Paragraph (b) of subsection (2A) is not to be taken to limit in any way the classes of persons in respect of whom the employee is entitled to *force majeure* leave by virtue of subsection (2)(f).]

(3) When an employee takes force majeure leave, he or she shall, as soon as reasonably practicable thereafter, by notice in the prescribed form given to his or

her employer, confirm that he or she has taken such leave and the notice shall specify the dates on which it was taken and contain a statement of the facts entitling the employee to *force majeure* leave.

(4) *Force majeure* leave shall consist of one or more days on which, but for the leave, the employee would be working in the employment concerned but shall not exceed 3 days in any period of 12 consecutive months or 5 days in any period of 36 consecutive months.

(5) A day on which an employee is absent from work on *force majeure* leave in an employment for part only of the period during which he or she is required to work in the employment on that day shall be deemed, for the purposes of subsection (4), to be one day of force majeure leave.

GENERAL NOTE

**EB.133**     This section provides for the entitlement of employees to limited leave with pay for family crises. Such leave is called *force majeure* leave and may be availed of in cases where a family member is ill or injured. The expression "*in loco parentis*" was considered by the Supreme Court in *Waters v Cruikshank* [1967] I.R. 378 who (in the context of a claim under the Fatal Injuries Act 1956) rejected the defendant's argument for a narrow definition of the phrase. The Court said that it did not require the assumption of a clear and definite obligation to financially provide for the person in question. The amendment effected by s.8 of the Parental Leave (Amendment) Act 2006 extends the entitlement in respect of persons, including same-sex partners, with whom employees have a relationship of domestic dependency.

**EB.134**     The maximum *force majeure* leave which may be availed of is three days in twelve consecutive months or five days in 36 consecutive months. An employee who takes *force majeure* leave is required to notify the employer as soon as reasonably practicable and within four weeks to supply to the employer a medical certificate containing particulars of the family member's injury or illness. The notice to be given under subsection (3) should be set out in the form in the Schedule to the Parental Leave (Notice of *Force Majeure* Leave) Regulations 1998 (S.I. No. 454 of 1998) or a form to like effect. The Act lays down no rules, specifying in the words of the directive, the "modalities of application" for this leave entitlement and the lack of guidance in interpreting the criteria for the grant thereof was commented upon by a rights commissioner in PL 32/99/CW. In the absence of "any objective rules" he could only apply what he described as "a reasonable subjective test" to the circumstances before him. The stipulation that the need must be "urgent" implies that, if the employee has sufficient advance notice, he or she should make alternative arrangements such as taking a day's holiday: see PL4/99/CW. Where an employee takes two or more consecutive day's leave, the statutory qualifications of "urgent", "immediate" and "indispensable" must be present on each of the succeeding days: see PL5/99/CW. This reasoning also underlies the determination of the Tribunal in *Quinn v J. Higgins Engineering Galway Ltd* [2000] E.L.R. 102. Here the claimant's wife and children fell ill, at a time when there was a meningitis scare in the locality. The claimant took two days off work to take them to a doctor and to mind them thereafter. The Tribunal found that the claimant's concerns were not unreasonable and that he had "no choice" but to stay off work in order to get medical assistance. Accordingly he was entitled to *force majeure* leave for the first day but not the second as, although they were ill, the doctor had advised that they were not suffering from meningitis. Extra consideration should be afforded to single parents: see PL 20/99/CW. For a full analysis of Rights Commissioner recommendations in 1999 see *Industrial Relations News* No. 8 (February 24, 2000) at pp. 22–24.

**EB.135**     In *Carey v Penn Racquet Sports Ltd* [2001] 3 I.R. 32, Carroll J. in the High Court emphasised that questions of urgency and indispensability should not be judged with hindsight. In this case the plaintiff was a single mother with an eight year old child. She had taken a day's leave to look after the child who had woken up with a rash on her legs. The company refused to grant *force majeure* leave because, following an examination by the plaintiff's General Practitioner, the child was diagnosed as having a rash which was not serious. The Tribunal, by a majority, upheld the company's decision but Carroll J. was of the opinion that the Tribunal had erred in law in so deciding.

     "The matter should have been looked at from the plaintiff's point of view at the time the decision was made not to go to work. Also, the plaintiff could not be assumed to have medical knowledge which she did not possess."

     In the later case of *McGaley v Liebherr Container Cranes Ltd* [2001] 3 I.R. 563, McCracken J. said that *Carey* was "clear authority" that the Tribunal, in judging whether the facts of a particular case came within s.13, must base its judgment on the facts "as they existed at the time of the circumstances which it is alleged gave use to the implementation of the section". He agreed with Carroll J. that it was

E–66

an "error of law" to view these circumstances with hindsight and to take into account the ultimate seriousness or otherwise of the illness. McCracken J., however, went on to hold that the question of whether the employee's immediate presence was or was not indispensable was a question of fact to be determined by the Tribunal looking at the circumstances that were known at the time the employee decided to stay at home.

Employers contend that it is difficult to develop a company policy on how to deal with such cases, as the criterion for *force majeure* leave is interpreted on a subjective "parental belief" basis. The Employment Appeals Tribunal, in *Dunnes Stores v Hallinan* PL3/2001, said it appreciated the needs of employers to be consistent in their response to such cases but commented that, as a result of *Carey*, each leave application could only be assessed on a case-by-case basis. It continued: "a policy approach to this issue could only be general in nature and therefore inappropriate for the individual circumstances of each case." Section 22A of the Act (as inserted by virtue of s.12 of the Parental Leave (Amendment) Act 2006), however, empowers the Equality Authority to draft a Code of Practice on this and other issues.

PART III

EMPLOYMENT RIGHTS

## Protection of employment rights

**14.**—(1) An employee shall, while on parental leave, be regarded for all **EB.136** purposes relating to his or her employment (other than his or her right to remuneration or superannuation benefits or any obligation to pay contributions in or in respect of the employment) as still working in the employment and none of his or her other rights relating to the employment shall be affected by the leave.

(2) Absence from employment while on parental leave shall not be treated as part of any other leave from employment (including sick leave, annual leave, adoptive leave, maternity leave and *force majeure* leave) to which the employee concerned is entitled.

(3) Where—

(a) an employee who is on probation in his or her employment or is undergoing training in relation to that employment or is employed under a contract of apprenticeship takes parental leave, and

(b) his or her employer considers that the employee's absence from employment while on parental leave would not be consistent with the continuance of the probation, training or apprenticeship, the employer may require that the probation, training or apprenticeship be suspended during the period of the parental leave and be completed by the employee at the end of that period.

(4) An employee shall, while on *force majeure* leave, be regarded for all purposes relating to his or her employment as still working in the employment concerned and none of his or her rights relating to the employment shall be affected by the leave.

(5) Absence from employment while on *force majeure* leave shall not be treated as part of any other leave from the employment (including sick leave, annual leave, adoptive leave, maternity leave and parental leave) to which the employee concerned is entitled.

GENERAL NOTE

This section addresses the employment position of an employee while absent on parental leave. It **EB.137** provides that:

(i) an employee on parental leave will be treated as if he or she had not been absent so that all his or her employment rights, except the right to remuneration and superannuation benefits, will be unaffected during the leave;

E–67

(ii)  periods of probation and apprenticeship may be suspended;

(iii)  periods of parental leave (and of *force majeure* leave) are not to be reckoned as any other type of leave.

The word "remuneration" is not defined in the Act (other than for the purposes of s.21) but the Employment Appeals Tribunal was of the opinion, in *McGivern v Irish National Insurance Co Ltd* P5/1982, that the following statement from *S & U Stores Ltd v Lee* [1969] 2 All E.R. 417, 419 was "a generally satisfactory definition":

> "Remuneration is not mere payment for work done but is what the doer expects to get as the result of the work he does insofar as what he expects to get is quantified in terms of money".

## Return to work

**EB.138**

**15.**—(1) On the expiration of a period of parental leave (being, in a case where parental leave has been terminated under section 12, the period specified in the confirmation document concerned) ("the period"), the employee concerned shall be entitled to return to work—

(a)  with the employer with whom he or she was working immediately before the start of the period or, where during the employee's absence from work there was or were a change or changes of ownership of the undertaking in which he or she was employed immediately before the absence, the owner on the expiration of the period ("the successor"),

(b)  in the job that the employee held immediately before the commencement of the period, and

[(c)  under the contract of employment under which the employee was employed immediately before the commencement of the period or, where a change of ownership such as is referred to in paragraph (a) has occurred, under a contract of employment with the successor that is identical to the contract under which the employee was employed immediately before such commencement, and (in either case) under terms or conditions—

(i)  not less favourable than those that would have been applicable to the employee, and

(iii)  that incorporate any improvement to the terms or conditions of employment to which the employee would have been entitled,

if he or she had not been so absent from work.]

(2) For the purposes of subsection (1)(b), where the job held by an employee immediately before the commencement of a period of parental leave to which he or she is entitled was not the employee's normal or usual job, he or she shall be entitled to return to work, either in his or her normal or usual job or in that job as soon as is practicable without contravention by the employee or the employer of any provision of a statute or provision made under statute.

(3) Where, because of an interruption or cessation of work at an employee's place of employment, existing on the expiration of a period of parental leave taken by the employee, it is unreasonable to expect the employee to return to work on such expiration, the employee may return to work instead when work resumes at the place of employment after the interruption or cessation, or as soon as reasonably practicable after such resumption.

GENERAL NOTE

**EB.139**     This section, as amended by section 9 of the Parental Leave (Amendment) Act 2006, provides an entitlement to return to work on the expiration of a period of parental leave and is similar to section 26 of the Maternity Protection Act 1994 and section 18 of the Adoptive Leave Act 1995 on which see CB.161 and DB.148 *supra* respectively.

E–68

## Right to alternative employment

**16.**—(1) Where an employee is entitled to return to work pursuant to section 15 **EB.140**
but it is not reasonably practicable for the employer to permit the employee to
return to work in accordance with that section, the employee shall be entitled to be
offered by his or her employer suitable alternative employment under a new
contract of employment.

(2) Work under a new contract of employment constitutes suitable alternative
work for the purposes of this Act if—

    (a)  it is of a kind that is suitable in relation to the employee concerned and
appropriate for the employee to do in the circumstances,

    [(b) the terms and conditions of the contract—

        (i)   relating to the place where the work under it is required to be done,
the capacity in which the employee concerned is to be employed and
any other terms or conditions of employment are not less favourable
to the employee than those of his or her contract of employment
immediately before the start of the period of absence from work
while on parental leave, and

        (ii)  incorporate any improvements to the terms or conditions of employ-
ment to which the employee would have been entitled if he or she had
not been so absent from work during that period,

and

    (c)  the continuity of service is preserved.]

GENERAL NOTE

    This section, as amended by section 10 of the Parental Leave (Amendment) Act 2006, provides **EB.141**
that, where it is not practicable to permit the employee to return to work in accordance with section 15,
the employee is entitled to be offered suitable alternative employment. It is in terms similar to those of
section 27 of the Maternity Protection Act 1994 and section 19 of the Adoptive Leave Act 1995. As to
the meaning of the words "suitable in selection to the employee concerned" see *Tighe v Travenol
Laboratories (Ireland) Ltd* P14/1986 (a decision under the Maternity Protection of Employees Act
1981), reported at (1989) 8 J.I.S.L.L. 124, where the Tribunal said that they should be interpreted
"subjectively, from the employee's standpoint, including the general nature of the work which suited
her and her domestic considerations."

## [Protection of employees from penalisation

**16A.**—(1) An employer shall not penalise an employee for proposing to exer- **EB.141A**
cise or having exercised his or her entitlement to parental leave or *force majeure*
leave.

(2) Penalisation of an employee includes—

    (a)  dismissal of the employee,

    (b)  unfair treatment of the employee, including selection for redundancy, and

    (c)  an unfavourable change in the conditions of employment of the employee.

(3) If a penalisation of an employee, in contravention of subsection (1), constitutes an dismissal of the employee, as referred to in subsection (2)(a), the
employee may institute proceedings under the Unfair Dismissals Acts 1977 to
2005 in respect of that dismissal and such dismissal may not be referred to a rights
commissioner under Part IV.

(4) An employee who is entitled to return to work in the employment concerned
in accordance with section 15 but is not permitted by his or her employer to do so–

    (a)  shall be deemed to have been dismissed on the date on which he or she was
entitled to so return to work and the dismissal shall be deemed, for the
purposes of the Unfair Dismissals Acts 1977 to 2005, to have been an

E–69

unfair dismissal unless, having regard to all the circumstances, there were substantial grounds justifying the dismissal, and

(b) shall be deemed for the purposes of the Redundancy Payments Acts 1967 to 2003, to have had his or her contract of employment with his or her employer terminated on the date aforesaid.]

GENERAL NOTE

This section was inserted by s.11 of the Parental Leave (Amendment) Act 2006.

PART IV

RESOLUTION OF DISPUTES

## "Dispute"

EB.142    **17.**—In this Part—

"dispute" shall be construed in accordance with section 18.

## Reference of disputes to rights commissioner

EB.143    **18.**—(1) This Part does not apply to a member of the Defence Forces.

(2) Any dispute or difference between an employee and his or her employer relating to the entitlements of the employee under this Act (or to any matter arising out of or related to those entitlements or otherwise arising under this Act) other than a dispute or difference—

(a) relating to a dismissal from employment, including a dismissal within the meaning of the Unfair Dismissals Acts 1977 to [2005],

(b) consisting of a question to which section 39(15) of the Redundancy Payments Act 1967, applies, or

(c) a dispute to which section 11 of the Minimum Notice and Terms of Employment Act 1973, applies,

may be referred by either of those parties to a rights commissioner, and in the subsequent provisions of this Part "dispute" means a dispute or difference which is or may be referred as aforesaid.

(3) A rights commissioner shall hear the parties to a dispute and receive any relevant evidence tendered by either of them.

(4) A reference under subsection (2) shall be made by giving to a rights commissioner a notice in writing containing such particulars (if any) as may be prescribed and a copy of the notice shall be given by the commissioner to the other party to the dispute.

(5) A notice under subsection (4) shall be given as soon as reasonably may be after the occurrence of the dispute concerned and in any event not later than 6 months after the occurrence of the dispute.

(6) Proceedings before a rights commissioner under this section shall be conducted otherwise than in public.

(7) A rights commissioner shall furnish a copy of each decision made by him or her under this Part to the Tribunal.

GENERAL NOTE

EB.144    This section confers a right of redress, in the first instance, to a rights commissioner who is empowered, in a dispute as to an employee's entitlement to parental leave, to hear the parties and receive any relevant evidence tendered. The question of redress is governed by section 21. The claim must be referred not later than six months after the occurrence of the dispute. The procedures to be followed in relation to the hearing of disputes are set out in the Parental Leave (Disputes and Appeals) Regulations 1999 (S.I. No. 6 of 1999).

E–70

## Appeal from decision of rights commissioner

**19.**—(1) A party concerned may appeal to the Tribunal from a decision or  **EB.145** direction of a rights commissioner under section 21 and the Tribunal shall receive any relevant evidence tendered by a party to the dispute.

(2) An appeal under this section shall be initiated by a party to the dispute concerned giving to the Tribunal, as soon as may be and in any event not later than 4 weeks from the date on which the decision was given to the party, a notice in writing to the Tribunal containing such particulars (if any) as may be prescribed and the Tribunal shall give a copy of the notice to the other party concerned as soon as may be after the receipt by it of the notice.

(3) A person whose evidence has been, is being or is to be given before the Tribunal, or who produces or sends a document to the Tribunal, pursuant to a notice under subsection (4) or who is required by such a notice to give evidence or produce a document to the Tribunal or to attend before the Tribunal and there to give evidence or produce a document shall be entitled to the same privileges and immunities as if the person were a witness before the High Court.

(4) The Tribunal may, by giving notice in that behalf in writing, require any person to attend before the Tribunal on a date and at a time and place specified in the notice and there to give evidence and to produce any document in his or her possession or power specified in the notice or to send to the Tribunal any document in his or her possession or power specified in the notice or require a person in attendance before the Tribunal pursuant to a notice under this subsection to produce to the Tribunal any document in his or her possession or power specified in the requirement.

(5) Paragraphs (a) and (e) of subsection (17) of section 39 of the Redundancy Payments Act, 1967, shall apply for the purposes of this section as it applies for the purposes of the said section 39 with the modification that "£1,500" (€1,904.61) shall be substituted for "£150" (€190.46) and with any other necessary modifications.

(6) Proceedings for an offence under the said subsection (17), as applied by this section, may be brought and prosecuted by the Minister.

(7) If a person gives false evidence before the Tribunal in proceedings under this section in such circumstances that, if the person had given the evidence before a court, the person would be guilty of perjury, the person shall be guilty of an offence and shall be liable on conviction on indictment thereof to the penalties applying to perjury.

GENERAL NOTE

This section provides that, where either party is dissatisfied with the rights commissioner's deci-  **EB.146** sion, it may be appealed to the Employment Appeals Tribunal. Section 39(17) of the Redundancy Payments Act 1967 empowers the Tribunal to take evidence on oath and to require persons to attend and produce documents. The procedures to be followed in relation to the hearing of disputes are set out in the Parental Leave (Disputes and Appeals) Regulations 1999 (S.I. No. 6 of 1999).

## Appeal to High Court on point of law

**20.**—(1) The Tribunal may refer a question of law arising in proceedings  **EB.147** before it under this Part to the High Court for determination by it.

(2) A party to proceedings before the Tribunal under this Part may appeal to the High Court from a determination of the Tribunal on a point of law.

GENERAL NOTE

This section provides for a right of appeal, on a point of law only, to the High Court. Although the  **EB.148** Rules of the Superior Courts do not specifically provide for appeals under this Act, it is suggested that any such appeal be brought by special summons, by analogy with the procedure set out in R.S.C. 1986, Order 105.

The circumstances in which the High Court will overturn a decision of a specialist tribunal such as the Employment Appeals Tribunal have been considered in many cases: see for example, *Henry Denny & Sons (Ireland) Ltd v Minister for Social Welfare* [1998] 1 I.R. 34 and in particular the comments of Hamilton C.J. at 37. In considering whether to allow an appeal against a decision of such a tribunal, the High Court must consider whether that body based its decision on an identifiable error of law or on an unsustainable finding of fact. A decision cannot be challenged on the grounds of irrationality if there is any relevant material to support it: see further *Mulcahy v Waterford Leader Partnership Ltd* [2002] E.L.R. 12 (O'Sullivan J.) and *Thompson v Tesco Ireland Ltd* [2003] E.L.R. 21 (Lavan J.). In *National University of Ireland, Cork v Ahern* [2005] 2 I.R. 577, the Supreme Court held that, although findings of fact must be accepted by the High Court on appeal, that court could still examine the basis upon which those facts were found. The relevance or admissibility of the matters relied on in determining the facts were questions of law.

## Redress

**EB.149**  **21.** (1) On the hearing of a dispute, a rights commissioner or the Tribunal shall—

  (a)  in the case of a rights commissioner, make a decision in relation to the dispute, or

  (b)  in the case of the Tribunal, make a determination in relation to the dispute,

and may, in the decision or determination, as the case may be, give to the parties concerned such directions as the rights commissioner or the Tribunal, as the case may be, considers necessary or expedient for the resolution of the dispute.

(2) Under subsection (1), the rights commissioner or the Tribunal may order such redress for the party concerned as the rights commissioner or the Tribunal, as the case may be, considers appropriate, having regard to all the circumstances and to the provisions of this Act, and specifies, including either or both of the following:

  (a)  the grant of parental leave of such length to be taken at such time or times and in such manner as may be so specified,

  (b)  an award of compensation in favour of the employee concerned to be paid by the employer concerned.

(3) Compensation under subsection (2)(b) shall be of such amount as the rights commissioner or the Tribunal deems just and equitable having regard to all the circumstances but shall not exceed 20 weeks' remuneration in respect of the employee's employment calculated in such manner as may be prescribed.

(4) The decision of a rights commissioner or the determination of the Tribunal shall be in writing and shall be communicated to the parties by the rights commissioner or the Tribunal, as the case may be.

(5) A rights commissioner or the Tribunal may, if the commissioner or the Tribunal considers it reasonable to do so, having regard to the illness or other incapacity of the employee concerned or any other circumstance direct that parental leave be taken at a time that does not accord with section 6(3).

(6) Without prejudice to the generality of subsections (1) and (2), where, on a reference under section 18(2) or an appeal under section 19(1), a rights commissioner or the Tribunal is satisfied that the taking of parental leave at the time specified in the notice under section 8(1) concerned would have a substantial adverse effect by reason of any of the matters specified in section 11(1), the commissioner or the Tribunal, as the case may be, may, if the commissioner or the Tribunal considers it reasonable to do so, direct that the commencement of the leave be postponed for a specified period (whether or not being the period specified in the relevant notice under section 11(1)).

(7) Without prejudice to the generality of subsections (1) and (2), where, on a

reference under section 18(2) or an appeal under section 19(1), a rights commissioner or the Tribunal considers that it is reasonable to do so because of a serious and substantial change in any circumstances affecting the employer or the employee, the commissioner or the Tribunal may direct that the period of parental leave concerned be curtailed or that its form be varied or its commencement postponed for a specified period or that parental leave not taken by reason of curtailment as aforesaid be taken at a specified time.

(8) Where appropriate, the confirmation document concerned shall be amended by the parties to it so as to accord with a decision, determination or direction under this section.

(9) In this section "remuneration" includes allowances in the nature of pay and benefits in lieu of or in addition to pay.

GENERAL NOTE

This section empowers a rights commissioner and, on appeal, the Tribunal to order such redress as **EB.150** they consider appropriate including the granting of the parental leave of such length and at such time as may be specified and the award of compensation of up to 20 weeks' remuneration. The method of calculating this 20 weeks' remuneration is set out in the Parental Leave (Maximum Compensation) Regulations 1999 (S.I. No. 34 of 1999). In *Dunnes Stores v Hallinan* PL3/2001, the claimant was denied *force majeure* leave and was awarded £150 (€190.46) by the Rights Commissioner. The Employment Appeals Tribunal, however, was persuaded that the just and equitable compensation was one day's pay and awarded £54 (€68.57). The Tribunal did add that it appreciated that a situation might arise in another case where, "because of the inconvenience to the employee or because of aggravating behaviour on the part of the employer, an award greater than the loss could be made". In awarding compensation, the rights commissioner and the Tribunal must make it clear whether the award is or is not "in respect of remuneration including arrears of remuneration", otherwise it may not be regarded as being exempt from income tax: see s.192A of the Taxes Consolidation Act 1997 (inserted by s.7 of the Finance Act 2004).

## Enforcement of decisions of rights commissioner and determinations of Tribunal

**22.**—(1) (a) If a person fails or refuses to comply with a decision of a rights **EB.151** commissioner under this Part ("a decision"), or a determination of the Tribunal under this Act ("a determination"), the Circuit Court shall, on application to it in that behalf by—

    (i)   the other party concerned, or

    (ii)  the Minister, if he or she is of opinion that it is appropriate to do so having regard to all the circumstances,

make an order directing that party to carry out the decision or determination in accordance with its terms.

  (b)  In paragraph (a), the reference to a decision or a determination is a reference to such a decision or determination, as the case may be, in relation to which, at the expiration of the time for bringing an appeal against it, no such appeal has been brought or, if such an appeal has been brought, it has been abandoned.

(2) Notwithstanding subsection (1), where, in proceedings under that subsection, the Circuit Court is satisfied that, owing to lapse of time, it would not be possible to comply with an order under that subsection, that Court shall make an order providing for such redress as it considers appropriate having regard to the provisions of this Act and all the circumstances.

(3) In an order under this section providing for the payment of compensation, the Circuit Court may, if in all the circumstances it considers it appropriate to do so, direct the employer concerned to pay to the employee concerned interest on the compensation at the rate referred to in section 22 of the Courts Act, 1981, in respect of the whole or any part of the period beginning 4 weeks after the date on

which the decision or determination concerned is communicated to the parties and ending on the date of the order.

(4) Proceedings under this section shall be heard in the county in which the relevant employer ordinarily resides or carries on any profession, business or occupation.

GENERAL NOTE

**EB.152**  This section provides that, if a party fails to carry out the terms of a rights commissioner decision or a Tribunal determination, the Circuit Court may make an order directing that it be carried out. The procedures governing applications for enforcement are set out in Order 57, rule 5 of the Circuit Court Rules 2001 (S.I. No. 510 of 2001).

PART V

MISCELLANEOUS

## [Codes of practice

**EB.152A**  **22A.**—(1) The Equality Authority may, or if requested to do so by the Minister shall, prepare for submission to the Minister a draft code of practice for the purposes of providing practical guidance as to the steps that may be taken for complying with one or more provisions of this Act.

(2) Before submitting a draft code of practice under subsection (1) to the Minister, the Equality Authority shall consult such other Minister of the Government or other person or body as the Equality Authority considers appropriate or as the Minister may direct.

(3) After a draft code of practice has been submitted under subsection (1), the Minister may by order declare that the draft—

(a)  is an approved code of practice for the purposes of this Act, or

(b)  as amended by the Minister after consultation with the Equality Authority, is an approved code of practice for the purposes of this Act,

and an order under this subsection shall set out the text of the approved code of practice to which it relates.

(4) In any proceedings under this Act before a court, the Employment Appeals Tribunal or a rights commissioner, an approved code of practice shall be admissible in evidence and, if any provision of the code appears to be relevant to any question arising in the proceedings, it shall be taken into account in determining that question.

(5) The Minister may, by order, after consultation with the Equality Authority, revoke or amend an approved code of practice.

(6) Every order made under subsection (3) or (5) shall be laid before each House of the Oireachtas as soon as practicable after it is made and, if a resolution annulling the order is passed by either such House within the next 21 days on which that House has sat after the order is laid before it, the order shall be annulled accordingly, but without prejudice to the validity of anything previously done thereunder.

(7) In this section, "Equality Authority" means the Equality Authority as construed in accordance with section 38(1) of the Employment Equality Act 1998.]

GENERAL NOTE

This section was inserted by s.12 of the Parental Leave (Amendment) Act 2006.

## Notices

**23.**—(1) The giving of a notice or other document to a person for the purposes  **EB.153** of proceedings under this Act may be effected by delivering it to the person or by sending a copy of it by registered prepaid post in an envelope addressed to the person at the person's last known residence or place of business.

(2) In the case of a company to which the Companies Act 1963, applies, such a document may be given by delivering it, or sending a copy of it by registered prepaid post in an envelope addressed to the company at its registered office.

(3) In the case of a body corporate to which subsection (2) does not apply or an unincorporated body of persons, such a document may be given by sending a copy of it to the body at any place in the State where it carries on business or in such other manner as an originating summons may be served on the body under rules of court.

(4) A rights commissioner may, if he or she considers it reasonable to do so having regard to all the circumstances, extend by a specified period (not exceeding 6 weeks) the period of time within which a notice under this Act (other than section 19(2)) is required to be given.

(5) The Tribunal may, if it considers it reasonable to do so having regard to all the circumstances, extend by a specified period the time within which a notice under section 19(2) is required to be given.

(6) Time may be extended under subsection (4) or (5) after the expiration of the period of time concerned.

## Winding up and bankruptcy

**24.**—(1) There shall be included among the debts that, under section 285 of the  **EB.154** Companies Act 1963, are in the distribution of the assets of a company being wound up, to be paid in priority to all other debts, any compensation payable under this Act by the company to an employee, and that Act shall have effect accordingly, and formal proof of the debts to which priority is given under this subsection shall not be required except in cases where it may otherwise be provided by rules of court.

(2) There shall be included among the debts that, under section 81 of the Bankruptcy Act 1988, are, in the distribution of the property of a bankrupt or arranging debtor, to be paid in priority to all other debts, any compensation payable under this Act by the bankrupt or arranging debtor, as the case may be, to an employee, and that Act shall have effect accordingly, and formal proof of the debts to which priority is given under this subsection shall not be required except in cases where it may otherwise be provided by rules of court.

## Amendment of enactments

**25.**—(1) [Amending paragraph 5(1) of Schedule 3 to the Redundancy  **EB.155** Payments Act 1967]

(2) [Amending the Unfair Dismissals Act 1977]

(3) An employee who is entitled to return to work in the employment concerned in accordance with section 15 but is not permitted by his or her employer to do so—

    (a) shall be deemed to have been dismissed on the date on which he or she was entitled to return to work as aforesaid and the dismissal shall be deemed, for the purposes of the Unfair Dismissals Acts 1977 to [2005], to have been an unfair dismissal unless, having regard to all the circumstances, there were substantial grounds justifying the dismissal,

    (b) shall be deemed for the purposes of the Redundancy Payments Acts 1967 to [2003], to have been dismissed by reason of redundancy on the date aforesaid, and

(c) shall be deemed for the purposes of the Minimum Notice and Terms of Employment Acts 1973 to [2005], to have had his or her contract of employment with his or her employer terminated on the date aforesaid.

(4) [Amending the Organisation of Working Time Act 1997]

(5) [Amending the Employment Equality Act 1998]

GENERAL NOTE

**EB.156**     This section ensures that other relevant enactments take account of the introduction of parental leave and *force majeure* leave. Consequently such periods of leave do not break continuity of employment for the purposes of the redundancy payments legislation and a dismissal for reasons connected with the exercise of rights under the Act is deemed to be an unfair dismissal.

## Extension of Protection of Employees (Employers' Insolvency) Act 1984

**EB.157**     **26.** [...]

GENERAL NOTE

**EB.158**     This section allows compensation awarded by a rights commissioner or the Tribunal to be paid out of the Social Insurance Fund in the event of the employer's insolvency.

## Records

**EB.159**     **27.**—(1) An employer shall make a record of the parental leave and *force majeure* leave taken by his or her employees showing the period of employment of each employee and the dates and times upon which each employee was on parental leave or *force majeure* leave.

(2) A record made under this section shall be retained by the employer concerned for a period of 8 years and, if the Minister specifies the form of such records (which he or she is hereby empowered to do), the record shall be in that form or a form to the like effect.

(3) Notices, or copies of notices, required by this Act to be retained by a person shall be retained by the person for a period of one year.

(4) An employer who contravenes subsection (1) or (2) of this section shall be guilty of an offence and shall be liable on summary conviction to a fine not exceeding £1,500 (€1,904.61).

(5) An inspector (within the meaning of the Organisation of Working Time Act 1997) may, for the purposes of this section, exercise any of the powers conferred on him or her by that Act.

(6) Proceedings for an offence under this section may be brought and prosecuted by the Minister.

GENERAL NOTE

**EB.160**     This section imposes an obligation on employers in relation to the keeping of records and notices relating to parental leave and force majeure leave. Such records may be inspected by an inspector duly appointed under the Organisation of Working Time Act 1997.

## Review of Act

**EB.161**     **28.**—The Minister shall, not earlier than 2 years and not later than 3 years after the commencement of this Act, after consultation with persons whom he or she considers to be representative of employers generally and persons whom he or she considers to be representative of employees generally, conduct a review of the operation of this Act and shall prepare a report in writing of the findings of the review and shall cause copies of the report to be laid before each House of the Oireachtas.

E–76

GENERAL NOTE

 The Report of the Working Group on the Review of the Parental Leave Act 1998 was published in **EB.162** April 2002 (Pn 11344). The Group, which comprised the social partners, relevant Government Departments and the Equality Authority, could not reach consensus on the principle of paid parental leave nor on the issue of paternity leave. The majority of the group recommended that the duration of parental leave should be increased by four weeks and that the maximum age of the child in respect of whom employees may avail of parental leave should be increased to eight. The group were unanimous in recommending that there should be a statutory right to take parental leave in some format other than a continuous block. The group were also unanimous in recommending that in the case of a child with a disability the maximum age of a child should be increased to 16. The agreed recommendations were implemented by the Parental Leave (Amendment) Act 2006.

# PARENTAL LEAVE (AMENDMENT) ACT 2006

## (2000 No. 13)

ARRANGEMENT OF SECTIONS

An Act to amend and extend the Parental Leave Act 1998.

[18th May, 2006]

INTRODUCTION AND GENERAL NOTE

**EB.201**    This Act amends the Parental Leave Act 1998 with effect from May 18, 2006, to give effect to the agreed recommendations of the social partners arising from the Report of the Working Group on the Review of the 1998 Act published in April 2002 (Pn 11344). The social partners had failed to reach a consensus on the principle of paid parental leave and paternity leave nor was there agreement on the extension of the parental leave period by a further four weeks. During the Bill's passage through the Seanad and the Dáil, any opposition attempts to introduce amendments which went beyond the consensus reached by the social partners were firmly resisted (see, for instance, Deputy Fahey — the Minister of State at the Department of Justice, Equality and Law Reform — at 179 *Seanad Debates* Col. 484 and 618 *Dáil Debates* Cols. 74–75).

The main provisions of the Act are (i) the raising of the maximum age of the eligible child to 8 years (16 in the case of a disabled child); (ii) the extension of parental leave entitlements to adopting parents and to persons acting in *loco parentis* in respect of an eligible child; (iii) the extension of the *force majeure* provisions to include persons in a relationship of domestic dependency (including same-sex partners); (iv) the entitlement to take the parental leave in separate blocks of at least six weeks; (v) the suspension of parental leave where the employee falls ill; and (vi) the provision for statutory Codes of Practice.

CITATION

**EB.202**    See section 13.

COMMENCEMENT

**EB.203**    May 18, 2006.

PARLIAMENTARY DEBATES

**EB.204**    179 *Seanad Debates* Cols. 169–213 (Second Stage)
179 *Seanad Debates* Cols. 481–508 (Committee Stage)
179 *Seanad Debates* Cols. 638–651 (Report and Final Stages)
608 *Dáil Debates* Cols. 420–429 (Second Stage)
608 *Dáil Debates* Cols. 1427–1460 (Second Stage resumed)
609 *Dáil Debates* Cols. 1675–1698 (Second Stage resumed)
Select Committee on Justice, Equality and Women's Rights (29 SJEDWR 1, No. 71, March 22, 2006) Cols. 2427–2451 (Committee Stage)
618 *Dáil Debates* Cols. 58–76 (Report and Final Stages)
183 *Seanad Debates* Cols. 1056–1060 (Report and Final Stages)

E–78

Be it enacted by the Oireachtas as follows:

## Interpretation

**1.**—(1) In this Act—                                                      EB.205

"Minister" means the Minister for Justice, Equality and Law Reform;

"Principal Act" means the Parental Leave Act 1998.

(2) A reference in this Act to any enactment shall be construed as a reference to that enactment as amended, adapted or extended by or under any other enactment including this Act.

## Entitlement to Parental Leave

**2.**—[Amending section 6 of the Principal Act]                             EB.206

## Amendment of section 6 of Principal Act

**3.**—Section 6 of the Principal Act is amendment in subsection (7) by—     EB.207

(a) inserting "and where they are both employed by the same employer" after "child" where it secondly occurs, and

(b) substituting "either parent" for "neither of the parents".

GENERAL NOTE

At Committee Stage in the Dáil an attempt was made to provide parents with some flexibility by allowing them to share their parental leave or a portion thereof (see Select Committee at Cols. 2439–2440). The Minister of State (Deputy Fahey) opposed the amendment but it was reworded and moved at Report Stage (see Deputy English at 618 *Dáil Debates* Cols. 66–67). The amendment was accepted by the Minister (618 *Dáil Debates* Col. 68). The amendment seeks to provide for the transfer of parental leave entitlements from one parent to the other where both are employed by the same employer. Because of a drafting error, however, this is not legally permissible. Section 2 of this Act amends s.6 of the 1998 Act by substituting an entirely new s.6, subs.(6) of which expressly prohibits the transfer of parental leave entitlements. This section purports to amend subs.(7) of s.6 of the 1998 Act (which originally prohibited the transfer of parental leave) by providing that either parent can take the parental leave, or a portion thereof, of the other parent "where they are employed by the same employer". That subsection, however, has been replaced by subs.(6) and subs.(7) now deals with those employees who have completed less than one year's service. It is unlikely that this obvious drafting error can be corrected under the guise of statutory interpretation in light of the Supreme Court decision in *State (Murphy) v Johnson* [1983] I.R. 245. Furthermore, clause 2(2) of the Framework Agreement annexed to Directive 96/34/EC provides that the right to parental leave should be granted, in principle, on a "non transferable basis".

## Amendment of section 7 of Principal Act

**4.**—[…]                                                                   EB.208

## Amendment of section 8 of Principal Act

**5.**—[…]                                                                   EB.209

## Amendment of section 10 of Principal Act

**6.**—[…]                                                                   EB.210

## Amendment of section 11 of Principal Act

**7.**—[…]                                                                   EB.211

## Amendment of section 13 of Principal Act

**8.**—[…]                                                                   EB.212

## Amendment of section 15 of Principal Act

EB.213    **9.**—[…]

## Amendment of section 16 of Principal Act

EB.214    **10.**—[…]

## Protection of employees from penalisation

EB.215    **11.**—[inserting section 16A in Principal Act]

## Codes of Practice

EB.216    **12.**—[inserting section 22A in Principal Act]

## Short title and collection citation

EB.217    **13.**—(1) This Act may be cited as the Parental Leave (Amendment) Act 2006.

(2) The Principal Act and this Act may be cited together as the Parental Leave Acts 1998 and 2006.

# PARENTAL LEAVE (NOTICE OF *FORCE MAJEURE* LEAVE) REGULATIONS, 1998

## (S.I. No. 454 of 1998)

**1.** These Regulations may be cited as the Parental Leave (Notice of *Force Majeure* Leave) Regulations, 1998, and shall come into operation on the 3rd day of December, 1998.  **EC.101**

**2.** The notice to be given by an employee to his or her employer under section 13(3) of the Parental Leave Act, 1998, shall be in the form set out in the Schedule to these Regulations (the "scheduled form") or in a form to the like effect containing the information and declaration referred to in the scheduled form.  **EC.102**

### SCHEDULE

### Parental Leave Act, 1998

### Notice to Employer of *Force Majeure* Leave

This form, or a form to the like effect containing the information and declaration referred to in this form, must be completed by an employee who takes *force majeure* leave as soon as reasonably practicable after the leave is taken.  **EC.103**

An employee is entitled to *force majeure* leave where for urgent family reasons, owing to an injury to or the illness of a person referred to in section 13(2) of the Act, the employee's immediate presence is indispensable at the place where the person is.

The persons referred to in section 13(2) of the Act are: child, adopted child or a person in relation to whom the employee is in *loco parentis*; spouse or person with whom the employee is living as husband or wife; brother or sister; parent or grandparent.

*Force majeure* leave must not exceed 3 working days in any period of 12 consecutive months or 5 working days in any period of 36 consecutive months.

In the event of any dispute or difference between an employer and employee in relation to *force majeure* leave the issue may be referred by either party to a rights commissioner.

Name of employee _____

|  | *Figures* |  | *Letters* |
|---|---|---|---|

RS1 Number

Name and address of employer _____
_____
_____

Name and address of
injured*/ill*person during
*force majeure* leave _____
_____
_____

Relationship to employee _____
Nature of injury*/illness* _____
Date(s) of *force majeure* leave _____

Irish Employment Legislation

I confirm that I have taken *force majeure* leave on the above mentioned dates because for urgent family reasons owing to the injury to*/illness of* the person specified above, my immediate presence at that person's address was indispensable.

### DECLARATION

I declare that the information given above is true and complete.

Signature of
employee _____

Date _____

*Delete as appropriate

GENERAL NOTE

EC.104     The Regulations prescribe the form of the notice to be given to an employer by an employee following the taking of *force majeure* leave.

## PARENTAL LEAVE (DISPUTES AND APPEALS) REGULATIONS, 1999

### (S.I. No. 6 of 1999)

EC.201     **1.** These Regulations may be cited as the Parental Leave (Disputes and Appeals) Regulations, 1999, and shall come into operation on the 20th day of January, 1999.

EC.202     **2.**—(1) In these Regulations—

"the Act" means the Parental Leave Act, 1998 (No. 30 of 1998);

"dispute" means a dispute to which Part IV of the Act applies and "appeal" shall be construed accordingly;

"notice of appeal" means a notice under section 19(2) of the Act;

"notice of dispute" means a notice under section 18(4) of the Act;

"the Tribunal" means the Employment Appeals Tribunal.

(2) In these Regulations—

(a) a reference to a Regulation is a reference to a Regulation of these Regulations, and

(b) a reference to a paragraph is a reference to the paragraph of the provision in which the reference occurs.

EC.203     **3.** A notice of dispute shall specify—

(a) the name and address of the party referring the dispute,

(b) the name and address of the other party to the dispute,

(c) the nature of the dispute,

(d) particulars of any facts or contentions which the party referring the dispute will put forward at the hearing,

(e) if the dispute relates to parental leave—

    (i) the date on which the applicant for the parental leave entered the employment in question,

    (ii)   the name of the child to whom the parental leave relates,

    (iii)  the date of the child's birth and, where appropriate, of the relevant adoption order,

    (iv)  the period of parental leave sought or granted,

    (v)   the date on which notice of parental leave was given,

    (vi)  where appropriate, the date of the document confirming parental leave,

    (vii) where appropriate, the date on which the parental leave terminated,

  (f)  if the dispute relates *force majeure* leave—

    (i)   the name and address of the injured or ill person concerned,

    (ii)   that person's relationship to the employee,

    (iii)  the nature of the injury or illness,

    (iv)  the period of *force majeure* leave taken.

**4.**—(1) A party to a dispute who receives from a rights commissioner a copy of the notice of dispute ("the respondent") shall, within 14 days of the receipt of the notice, or within such longer period as the rights commissioner may allow, by notice—   **EC.204**

  (a)  indicate to the rights commissioner whether the respondent intends to contest the dispute, and

  (b)  if the respondent does so intend, specify the facts or contentions which the respondent will put forward at the hearing.

(2) A copy of a notice by the respondent under *paragraph (1)* shall be given by the rights commissioner to the other party to the dispute as soon as practicable after its receipt.

**5.**—(1) The rights commissioner may request the parties to a dispute to furnish him or her with particulars in relation to the dispute and may invite them to make submissions, either orally or in writing, in relation to it.   **EC.205**

(2) The rights commissioner may, if he or she considers it appropriate, convene an oral hearing at which he or she may put questions to the parties, and request the production of documents by them, in relation to the matters in dispute.

(3) Where one of the parties fails or refuses, without just cause, to attend an oral hearing convened *under paragraph (2),* the rights commissioner may proceed with the hearing in *that party's absence.*

(4) The rights commissioner may draw such inferences, as to him or her appear proper, from a failure or refusal by a party to comply with a request under paragraph (1) or*(2)* or to answer a question put to the party by the rights commissioner.

**6.** A notice of appeal shall specify—   **EC.206**

  (a)  the name and address of the party bringing the appeal,

  (b)  the name and address of the other party to the appeal,

  (c)  the date on which the decision or direction to which the appeal relates was made and the name of the rights commissioner who made it,

  (d)  particulars of any facts or contentions which the party bringing the appeal will put forward at the hearing.

**7.**—(1) A party to an appeal who receives from the Tribunal a copy of the notice of appeal ("the respondent") and who wishes to contest the appeal, or to appear or be heard at the hearing thereof, shall enter an appearance to it by giving a notice of appearance in writing to the Tribunal within 14 days (or such longer period as the Tribunal may fix under *paragraph (3))* of the receipt by the party of a copy of the notice of appeal.   **EC.207**

(2) A notice of appearance shall contain a brief outline of the grounds upon which the matter under appeal will be contested.

(3) The respondent may apply to the Tribunal by notice in writing for an extension of the period within which to enter an appearance stating the grounds for the application, and the Tribunal may extend the time within which to enter an appearance by such period as the Tribunal considers appropriate, if satisfied that there are reasonable grounds for so doing.

(4) A copy of a notice of appearance shall be given by the Tribunal to the other party to the appeal as soon as practicable after its receipt.

(5) A respondent who does not enter an appearance shall not be entitled to take part in, or to be present or represented at, any proceedings before the Tribunal relating to the matter under appeal.

EC.208  **8.**—(1) If, after receipt by the Tribunal of a relevant notice, that is to say,—

(a)  a notice of appeal, or

(b)   a notice of appearance under *Regulation 7*,

it appears to the chairman of the Tribunal appropriate to do so, the secretary of the Tribunal may, by notice in writing given to the party from whom the relevant notice was received, require that party to furnish to the Tribunal further particulars relating to any facts or contentions which that party will put forward at the hearing.

(2) As soon as practicable after receipt of the further particulars required by the Tribunal under paragraph (1), the Tribunal shall send a copy of those particulars to the other party concerned.

EC.209  **9.**—(1) The chairman of the Tribunal shall from time to time fix dates, times and places for hearings (including postponed and adjourned hearings) and the secretary to the Tribunal shall give notice of the hearings to all persons appearing to the chairman to be concerned.

(2) The hearing of an appeal by the Tribunal shall take place in public unless, at the request of either party to the appeal, the Tribunal decides to hear the appeal, or any part of it, in private.

(3) Subject to *Regulation 7(5)*, any party to an appeal may appear and be heard in person or may be represented by counsel or a solicitor or by a representative of a trade union or of an association of employers or, with the leave of the Tribunal, by any other person.

EC.210  **10.**—(1) A party to an appeal may—

(a)  make an opening statement,
(b)  call witnesses,
(c)  cross-examine any witness called by the other party,
(d)  give evidence on the party's own behalf, and
(e)  address the Tribunal at the close of the evidence.

(2) The Tribunal may postpone or adjourn the hearing of an appeal from time to time.

(3) If, after notice of a hearing has been duly given, either of the parties fails to appear at the hearing, the Tribunal, after considering all the evidence before it, may make a determination on the appeal or may adjourn the hearing to a later date.

EC.211  **11.**—(1) A determination of the Tribunal on an appeal may be taken by a majority of the members.

(2) The determination shall be recorded in a document signed by the chairman and sealed with the seal of the Tribunal.

EC.212  **12.**—(1) The Tribunal shall maintain a register ("the Register") in which shall be entered particulars of every determination by the Tribunal under Part IV of the Act.

(2) The Register may be inspected free of charge by any person during normal office hours.

(3) When the chairman of the Tribunal makes a correction in a determination pursuant to *Regulation 16,* particulars of the correction shall be entered in the Register.

(4) The Tribunal shall ensure that a copy of an entry in the Register is given to the parties to the appeal concerned.

**13.**—(1) Subject to *paragraph (2),* the Tribunal may at its discretion award, out of the Social Insurance Fund, to persons appearing before it and whose appearance is deemed essential) by the Tribunal— **EC.213**

    (a) travelling expenses and subsistence allowances in accordance with such scale as the Minister for Justice, Equality and Law Reform, after consultation with the Minister for Enterprise, Trade and Employment and with the consent of the Minister for Finance, may determine, and

    (b) such sum in respect of expenses for loss of remunerative time as the Tribunal considers reasonable.

(2) The Tribunal shall not make an award under *paragraph (1)* in respect of the attendance before it of—

    (a) any party to the appeal, or

    (b) any person representing such a party by virtue of *Regulation 9(3).*

**14.**—(1) A reference or an appeal may be withdrawn by giving a notice in writing to the rights commissioner or, as the case may be, the Tribunal of the withdrawal of the reference or appeal. **EC.214**

(2) On receipt of a notice under *paragraph (1)* the rights commissioner or, as the case may be, the Tribunal shall, as soon as practicable, notify the other party to the reference or appeal in writing that it has been withdrawn.

**15.** The Tribunal may consider and decide— **EC.215**

    (a) any question duly referred to it for consideration and determination, and

    (b) any appeal duly made to it,notwithstanding the failure or neglect of any person to comply with any provision of these Regulations.

**16.** By notice in writing to the parties to a dispute or appeal, a rights commissioner or, as the case may be, the chairman of the Tribunal may correct any mistake (including an omission) of a verbal or formal nature in a decision or determination. **EC.216**

**17.**—(1) Subject to *paragraph (2),* neither a rights commissioner nor the Tribunal shall award costs against any party to a dispute or an appeal. **EC.217**

(2) If, on an appeal, the Tribunal is of the opinion that a party (including one who has not entered an appearance) has acted frivolously or vexatiously, the Tribunal may make an order that that party shall pay to the other party such sum in respect of travelling expenses and, subject to *paragraph (3),* any other costs reasonably incurred as the Tribunal considers just.

(3) Costs shall not be awarded in respect of attendance at the appeal by any party or any person representing a party by virtue of *Regulation 9(3).*

(4) Any amount ordered to be paid under this Regulation shall be recoverable as a simple contract debt.

**18.** A mistake of a formal nature in a notice required by these Regulations shall not operate to invalidate it. **EC.218**

EC.219    **19.**—(1) Any notice required by these Regulations to be given to a rights commissioner shall be properly given if sent by registered post addressed to the Rights Commissioner at the Office of the Labour Relations Commission.

(2) Any notice required by these Regulations to be given to the Tribunal shall be properly given if sent by registered post addressed to the Employment Appeals Tribunal.

GENERAL NOTE

EC.220    These Regulations prescribe the procedures to be followed in relation to the hearing of disputes and appeals by a rights commissioner or the Employment Appeals Tribunal under Part IV of the Act. They also provide for matters incidental to the hearing of such disputes and appeals such as the contents of notices of dispute and appeal, notification of decisions and determinations and the awarding of costs and expenses.

# PARENTAL LEAVE (MAXIMUM COMPENSATION) REGULATIONS 1999

## (S.I. No. 34 of 1999)

EC.301    **1.** These Regulations may be cited as the Parental Leave (Maximum Compensation) Regulations, 1999, and shall come into operation on the 10th day of February, 1999.

EC.302    **2.**—(1) In these Regulations—

"the Act" means the Parental Leave Act, 1998 (No. 30 of 1998);

"relevant date" means the date on which a notice referring a dispute to a rights commissioner is given under section 18(4) of the Act;

"dispute" means a dispute to which Part IV of the Act applies;

"relevant employment" in relation to an employee, means the employment in respect of which the 20 weeks' remuneration referred to in section 21(3) of the Act falls to be calculated;

"week", in relation to an employee whose remuneration is calculated by reference to a week ending on a day other than a Saturday, means a week ending on that other day and, in relation to any other employee, means a week ending on a Saturday, and "weekly" shall be construed accordingly.

(2) In these Regulations—

(a) a reference to a Regulation is a reference to a Regulation of these Regulations so numbered, and

(b) a reference to a paragraph is a reference to the paragraph of the provision in which the reference occurs.

EC.303    **3.** Where, by a decision of a rights commissioner or a determination of the Employment Appeals Tribunal in relation to a dispute, redress proposed for the employee concerned is or includes an award of compensation under subsection (2)(b) of section 21 of the Act, the 20 weeks' remuneration referred to in subsection (3) of that section shall be calculated in accordance with these Regulations.

EC.304    **4.**—(1) In the case of an employee who, before the relevant date, was remunerated in respect of the relevant employment wholly at an hourly rate, fixed wage or salary (with or without a regular bonus or allowance which does not vary by reference to the amount of work done), a week's remuneration for the purposes of section 21(3) of the Act shall be—

(a)  the earnings in respect of that employment in the latest week before the relevant date in which the employee worked the number of hours per week that on that date was normal for that employment. plus

(b)  if the employee was normally required to work overtime in the relevant employment, the average weekly overtime earnings in the relevant employment, as determined in accordance with *paragraph (2).*

(2) For the purposes of *paragraph (1)(b)*, the average weekly overtime earnings of an employee in the relevant employment shall be—

(a)  in case the employee was employed for the whole of the period of 26 weeks ending 13 weeks before the relevant date, his or her overtime earnings during that period divided by 26, or

(b)  in any other case, his or her overtime earnings during the number of complete weeks worked before the relevant date divided by that number.

(3) If, in respect of the employment referred to in *paragraph (1)(a),* the employee's earnings would, apart from this paragraph. include a regular bonus or similar payment which, in whole or in part, does not relate to work done in that week, only so much (if any) of the payment which relates to that week shall be taken into account in determining the employee's earnings.

**5.**—(1) This Regulation applies to an employee whose remuneration in respect    EC.305
of the relevant employment before the relevant date—

(a)  was wholly or partly at piece rates,

(b)  included commission directly related to the work done.

(c)  otherwise varied in relation to the amount of work done by the employee, or

(d)  varied on account of payments appropriate to attendance on a shift cycle, on particular days of the week or at particular times of the day.

(2) In relation to an employee to whom this Regulation applies, a week's remuneration for the purposes of section 21(3) of the Act shall be—

(a)  in case the employee was employed in the relevant employment for the whole of the period of 26 weeks ending 13 weeks before the relevant date, his or her earnings for the number of hours worked during that period divided by that number, or

(b)  in any other case, his or her earnings during the number of complete weeks worked before the relevant date divided by the number of hours worked during those weeks,and multiplied in either case by the number of hours per week that on the relevant date was normal for that employment.

(3) The earnings referred to in *paragraph (2)(a)* shall be adjusted in respect of any/variation in rates of pay which took effect during the period of 13 weeks before the relevant date.

(4) Where in any week within the period of 26 weeks, or complete weeks, referred to in *paragraph (2)* the employee's earnings would, apart from this paragraph, include a regular bonus or similar payment which, in whole or in part, does not relate to work done in that week, only so much (if any) of the payment which does relate to that week shall be taken into account for the purposes of *paragraph (2)* in determining those earnings.

(5) For the purposes of *paragraph (2),* any week worked in another employment shall be taken into account if it would not have operated, for the purposes of the First Schedule to the Minimum Notice and Terms of Employment Act, 1973 (No. 4 of 1973), to break the continuity of service of the employee concerned in the relevant employment.

EC.306　　**6.** In determining an employee's earnings for any period for the purposes of these Regulations, no account shall be taken of any sums paid by way of recoupment of expenses incurred by the employee in the discharge of the duties of his or her employment.

EC.307　　**7.** For the purposes of *Regulations 4(2)(a)* and *5(2)(a)*, any week during which an employee did not work shall be disregarded and the latest week before the period of 26 weeks mentioned in those provisions. as the case may be, or before a week taken into account under this Regulation, as may be appropriate, shall be taken into account instead of a week during which the employee did not work as aforesaid.

EC.308　　**8.** Where, in respect of the relevant employment, there is no number of hours for which employees work in each week which is normal for that employment, the weekly remuneration of each such employee shall be taken, for the purposes of these Regulations, to be the average amount of the remuneration paid to each such employee in the 52 weeks, or such lesser number of weeks as may be appropriate, in each of which the employee was working in the employment immediately before the relevant date.

EC.309　　**9.** Where under these Regulations account is to be taken of remuneration paid in a period which does not coincide with the periods for which the remuneration is calculated, the remuneration shall be apportioned in such manner as may be just.

EC.310　　**10.**—(1) Where, under a contract of employment. an employee is required to work for more hours per week than the number of hours that is normal for the employment, the hours for which the employee is so required to work shall be taken, for the purposes of *Regulations 4* and *5(2)*, to be, in the case of that employee, the number of hours per week that is normal for the employment.

　　(2) Where, under a contract of employment. an employee is entitled to additional remuneration for working more than a specified number of hours per week—

　　(a)　in a case where the employee is required under the said contract to work for more than the said specified number of hours per week, the number of hours per week for which the employee is so required to work shall, for the purposes of *Regulations 4* and *5(2)*, be taken to be, in the case of that employee, the number of hours of work per week that is normal for the employment, or

　　(b)　in any other case, the specified number of hours shall be taken, for the purposes of those provisions, to be, in the case of that employee, the number of hours of work per week that is normal for the employment.

GENERAL NOTE

EC.311　　These Regulations prescribe the method of calculating maximum compensation for the purposes of redress under Part IV of the Act.

E–108

# CIRCUIT COURT RULES 2001

## (S.I. No. 510 of 2001)

### Rule 5 Parental Leave Act 1998

**1.** In this Order "the Act" means the Parental Leave Act 1998 (No. 30 of 1998), **EC.451** and "the Tribunal" means the Employment Appeals Tribunal and "Commissioner" means a rights commissioner and "the Minister" means the Minister for Justice, Equality and Law Reform.

**2.** All applications served or proceedings taken before these Rules shall have **EC.452** come into operation but which are in accordance with the existing Rules and practice of the Court shall have the same validity as application made or proceedings taken in accordance with these Rules.

**3.** Applications for the enforcement of decisions of a Commissioner or deter- **EC.453** minations of the Tribunal, whether such application be made by the party in whose favour the decisions or determinations were made or by the Minister, shall, pursuant to section 22 of the Act, be made by way of Motion on Notice grounded upon Affidavit sworn by the party seeking enforcement of the decisions or determinations or, in the case of the Minister, by an appropriate officer duly authorised by the Minister, which said Affidavit shall exhibit

(a) a certified copy of the decision of the Commissioner or a certified copy of determination of the Tribunal and

(b) a certified copy of the covering letter from the Commissioner or the Tribunal issued to the Applicant with the aforementioned decision of the Commissioner or determination of the Tribunal;

(c) a copy Notice of Appeal, if applicable; and shall set out
  (i) all the facts relevant to the alleged failure to carry out the decisions or determinations;
  (ii) whether or not an appeal has been brought from the decisions or determinations and, if no such appeal has been brought, that the time for appeal has elapsed and, if such appeal has been brought, the date upon which Notice of Appeal was given and evidence of abandonment thereof.

**4.** Applications shall, in accordance with section 22(4) of the Act, be brought in **EC.454** the County where the relevant employee ordinarily resides or carries on any profession, business or occupation.

**5.** Notice of every application shall be given to the employer or employers in **EC.455** question and to the Tribunal and the Commissioner as appropriate by serving notice of the proceedings (including the Notice of Motion and grounding Affidavits, if any) no later than 10 days prior to the return date specified in the Notice of Motion, in the case of the employer or employers personally in accordance with the provisions of Order 10 of the Circuit Court Rules, 1950, as amended, or by leaving a true copy of same at the employer's residence or place of business or by pre-paid registered post to the employer's residence or place of business and by the delivery of a copy of the application at, or by sending the same by prepaid registered post to the Office of the Secretary of the Tribunal or to the Rights Commissioner, Labour Relations Commission, as appropriate.

**6.** Save by special leave of the Court, all applications under section 22 of the **EC.456** Act shall only be heard upon Affidavit.

EC.457    **7.** The Court may make such Order as to costs as may be appropriate.

GENERAL NOTE

EC.458    This rule prescribes Circuit Court procedures in respect of applications for the enforcement of rights commissioner decisions or Employment Appeals Tribunal determinations pursuant to section 22 of the 1998 Act. Given that the 1950 rules have been repealed, it is submitted that the reference in paragraph 5 to Order 10 should be read as a reference to Order 11 of the Circuit Court Rules 2001.

# EUROPEAN COMMUNITIES (PARENTAL LEAVE) REGULATIONS, 2000

## (S.I. No. 231 of 2000)

EC.501    **1.** These Regulations may be cited as the European Communities (Parental Leave) Regulations, 2000.

EC.502    **2.**—(1) In these Regulations—

"the Minister" means the Minister for Justice, Equality and Law Reform;

"the Principal Act" means the Parental Leave Act 1998 (No. 30 of 1998);

"the specified period" means the period beginning on 3 December 1993, and ending on 2 June, 1996.

(2) A word or expression that is used in these Regulations and is also used in the Principal Act has the same meaning in these Regulations as it has in that Act.

(3) In these Regulations, a reference to a Regulation is a reference to a Regulation of these Regulations unless it is indicated that reference to some other provision is intended.

EC.503    **3.**—(1) An employee who is the natural parent of a child born in the specified period is entitled to parental leave in respect of the child.

(2) An employee who is the adoptive parent of a child born on or after 3 December, 1993, and in whose case an adoption order was made during the specified period is entitled to parental leave in respect of the child.

(3) Section 6(2) of the Principal Act is repealed.

EC.504    **4.** A period of parental leave taken by virtue of Regulation 3 shall end not later than 31 December, 2001, and section 6(3) of the Principal Act shall not apply to such a period.

EC.505    **5.** Where—

(a) an employee to whom Regulation 3 applies changes his or her employment during the period of 12 months before the making of these Regulations, and

(b) the period of parental leave to which he or she is entitled in the new employment would have been longer if the change of employment had not occurred, then, for the purposes of subsections (4) and (8) of section 6 of the Principal Act, the periods of employment in the new employment and the previous employment or employments—

(i) shall be taken into account for the purpose of calculating entitlement to parental leave under Regulation 3, and

(ii) shall be regarded as one continuous period of employment.

EC.506    **6.** The references in section 7(3) of the Principal Act to parental leave do not include references to parental leave taken by virtue of Regulation 3.

EC.507    **7.** Where an employee is entitled to a period of parental leave in respect of more than one child and one at least of the entitlements is by virtue of Regulation 3—

    (a)  sections 10 and 11 of the Principal Act shall apply to each such period to which the employee is entitled, and

    (b)  if, by virtue of the postponement of a period under the said section 10 or 11 or of part of such a period under the said section 10 (being periods the entitlement to which is under Regulation 3), the period expires after 31 December, 2001, the period shall be deemed to have expired before that date.

**8.** A rights commissioner or the Tribunal may, if the commissioner or the EC.508 Tribunal considers it reasonable to do so, having regard to the illness or other incapacity of an employee entitled to parental leave by virtue of Regulation 3 or any other circumstance, direct that the leave be taken at a time that does not accord with Regulation 4.

GENERAL NOTE

    These regulations were made by the Minister on July 19, 2000, following the issue by the European EC.509 Commission of a Reasoned Opinion to the effect that Ireland, by restricting the right to parental leave to employees with children born or adopted on or after June 3, 1996 had not fully complied with its obligations under clause 2(1) of the Framework Agreement on Parental Leave annexed to Directive 96/34/EC. The impact of these Regulations is that parents of children born or adopted between December 3, 1993 and June 2, 1996 will be entitled to parental leave and December 31, 2001 is set as the date by which such parents must use up that entitlement.

# PROTECTION OF YOUNG PERSONS (EMPLOYMENT) ACT 1996

## (1996 No. 16)

ARRANGEMENT OF SECTIONS

An Act to revise and extend the law relating to the protection of young **FB.101** persons in employment and to enable effect to be given to Council Directive No. 94/33/EC of 22 June 1994 on the Protection of Young People at Work (other than Articles 6 and 7) and for those purposes to repeal the Protection of Young Persons (Employment) Act, 1977, and certain provisions of the Conditions of Employment Act, 1936, and to provide for related matters.

F–51

[26th June, 1996]

INTRODUCTION AND GENERAL NOTE

**FB.102**    This Act repeals the Protection of Young Persons (Employment) Act 1977 and certain provisions of the Conditions of Employment Act 1936 and gives effect to Council Directive 94/33/EC of June 22, 1994 on the Protection of Young People at Work, (except for Articles 6 and 7 which are now implemented under the Safety, Health and Welfare at Work (Children and Young Persons) Regulations 1998 (S.I. No. 504 of 1998)). The Act also satisfies Ireland's obligations under Article 32 of the U.N. Convention on the Rights of the Child (ratified in 1992) and continues to implement ILO Convention No. 79 on Night Work by Young People (ratified in 1946).

According to the Minister for State at the Department of Enterprise and Employment (Eithne Fitzgerald, T.D.) the legislation "aims to protect young people at a stage when they are moving from education into the field of work, from the home into independence and when they are combining work with education". It also sends a "very strong signal" that education comes first (147 *Seanad Debates* Col. 670).

Generally speaking the Act raises the minimum age for normal working from 15 to 16 years. Provision is made, however, for the employment of young workers by licence or regulation. Fourteen and 15 year olds are allowed to work during the school holidays and for a limited amount of time during term time. The avenue of redress under the Act is in the first instance to a Rights Commissioner and, on appeal, to the Employment Appeals Tribunal.

CITATION

**FB.103**    See section 29(1).

COMMENCEMENT

**FB.104**    The Act came into operation on January 2, 1997: see S.I. No. 371 of 1996.

STATUTORY INSTRUMENTS

**FB.105**    Protection of Young Persons (Employment) Act 1996 (Commencement) Order 1996 (S.I. No. 371 of 1996).

Protection of Young Persons (Employment) (Exclusion of Workers in the Fishing or Shipping Sectors) Regulations 1997 (S.I. No. 1 of 1997).

Protection of Young Persons (Employment of Close Relatives) Regulations 1997 (S.I. No. 2 of 1997).

Protection of Young Persons (Employment) (Prescribed Abstract) Regulations 1997 (S.I. No. 3 of 1997).

Protection of Young Persons (Employment) Act 1996 (Employment in Licensed Premises) Regulations 2001 (S.I. No. 350 of 2001).

Protection of Young Persons (Employment) Act 1996 (Bar Apprentices) Regulations 2001 (S.I. No. 351 of 2001).

PARLIAMENTARY DEBATES

**FB.106**    461 *Dáil Debates* Cols. 2031–2056 (Second Stage).

461 *Dáil Debates* Cols. 2149–2162 (Second Stage resumed).

461 *Dáil Debates* Cols. 2305–2326 (Second Stage resumed).

Select Committee on Enterprise and Economic Strategy E5, No. 5 Col. 211–236 (Committee Stage).

465 *Dáil Debates* Cols. 12–37 (Report and Final Stages).

147 *Seanad Debates* Cols. 670–734 (Second Stage).

147 *Seanad Debates* Cols. 1894–1940 (Committee Stage).

148 *Seanad Debates* Cols. 101–104 (Report and Final Stages).

**FB.107**    Be it enacted by the Oireachtas as follows:

## Interpretation

**FB.108**    **1.**—(1) In this Act—

"agreement" means a collective agreement, an employment regulation order or a registered employment agreement;

"break" means the interval during which a child or young person may not be
permitted under this Act to work;

["child" means a person who has not reached the age of 16 years;]

"collective agreement" means an agreement by or on behalf of an
employer on the one hand, and by or on behalf of a trade union or

trade unions representative of the employees to whom the agreement relates on the other hand;

"contract of employment" means—

(a) a contract of service or apprenticeship, and

(b) any other contract whereby an individual agrees with another person, who is carrying on the business of an employment agency within the meaning of the Employment Agency Act, 1971, and is acting in the course of that business, to do or perform personally any work or service for a third person (whether or not the third person is party to the contract),

whether the contract is express or implied or if express, whether it is oral or in writing;

"the Council Directive" means Council Directive No. 94/33/EC of 22 June 1994 on the protection of young people at work, the text of which, with the exception of Section II and the Annex thereto, is set out for convenience of reference in the First Schedule;

"day" means a period of 24 consecutive hours commencing at midnight;

"employee" means a child or a young person who has entered into or works under (or, where the employment has ceased, entered into or worked under) a contract of employment and references, in relation to an employer, to an employee shall be construed as references to an employee employed by that employer; and for the purposes of this Act, a person holding office under, or in the service of, the State (including a member of the Garda Síochána or the Defence Forces) or otherwise as a civil servant, within the meaning of the Civil Service Regulation Act, 1956, shall be deemed to be an employee employed by the State or Government, as the case may be, and an officer or servant of a local authority for the purposes of the Local Government Act, 1941, a harbour authority, a health board or a vocational education committee shall be deemed to be an employee employed by the authority, board or committee, as the case may be;

"employer" in relation to an employee, means the person with whom the employee has entered into or for whom the employee works under (or, where the employment has ceased, entered into or worked under) a contract of employment subject to the qualification that the person who under a contract of employment referred to in paragraph (b) of the definition of "contract of employment" is liable to pay the wages of the individual concerned in respect of the work or service concerned shall be deemed to be the individual's employer;

"employment regulation order" means an employment regulation order within the meaning of the Industrial Relations Acts, 1946 to [2004];

"hours of work" does not include periods of rest during which the employee is not required to be available for work;

"industrial work" means such work as the Minister may declare by order under section 2 to be industrial work for the purposes of this Act;

"inspector" means a person appointed by the Minister under section 22 to be an inspector for the purposes of this Act;

"light work" means all work which is not industrial work and which, on account of the inherent nature of the tasks which it involves and the particular conditions under which they are performed, is not likely to be harmful to the safety, health or development of children, and is not such as to be harmful to their attendance at school, their participation in vocational guidance or training programmes approved by the competent authority or their capacity to benefit from the instruction received;

"the Minister" means the Minister for [Enterprise, Trade and Employment];

"prescribed" means prescribed by regulations made by the Minister;

"registered employment agreement" means a registered employment agreement within the meaning of the Industrial Relations Acts, 1946 to [2004];

"representatives of employees" means such trade unions as are, in the opinion of the Minister, representative of the employees in relation to whom the expression is used, or where there is no such trade union, such persons as are, in the opinion of the Minister, representative of such employees;

"representatives of employers" means such associations as are, in the opinion of the Minister, representative of the employers in relation to whom the expression is used, or where there is no such association, such persons as are, in the opinion of the Minister, representative of such employers;

"rest period" means any period which is not working time;

[…]

"trade union" means a body entitled under the Trade Union Act, 1941, to carry on negotiations for the fixing of wages or other conditions of employment;

"the Tribunal" means the Employment Appeals Tribunal;

"week" means a period of 7 consecutive days;

"working time" means any period during which a person is at work, at the employer's disposal and carrying out his or her activity or duties;

["young person" means a person who has reached the age of 16 years but has not reached the age of 18 years].

(2) A word or expression that is used in this Act and is also used in the Council Directive has, unless the contrary intention appears, the meaning in this Act that it has in the Council Directive.

(3) In construing a provision of this Act, a court shall give to it a construction that will give effect to the Council Directive, and for this purpose a court shall have regard to the provisions of the Council Directive, including the preamble.

(4) In this Act a reference to a section or Schedule, is a reference to a section of, or Schedule to, this Act, unless there is an indication that a reference to any other enactment is intended.

(5) In this Act a reference to a subsection, paragraph or subparagraph is a reference to the subsection, paragraph or subparagraph of the provision in which the reference occurs, unless there is an indication that a reference to some other provision is intended.

GENERAL NOTE

**FB.109**     "child": this definition was substituted by virtue of s.31 of the Education (Welfare) Act 2000.

"collective agreement": this definition differs somewhat from the definition of "collective agreement" in s.1(1) of the Anti-Discrimination (Pay) Act 1974 which only covered agreements "relating to terms and conditions of employment" which are made "between parties who are or represent employers and parties who are or represent employees".

4"contract of employment": as to whether a person is employed under a contract of service see, most recently, *Henry Denny & Sons (Ireland) Ltd v Minister for Social Welfare* [1998] 1 I.R. 34. The inclusion of a specific reference to persons employed through employment agencies is similar to the provisions of s.13 of the Unfair Dismissals (Amendment) Act 1993 and s.1(1) of the Terms of Employment (Information) Act 1994. But note the decision of the Labour Court in *Rooney v Diageo Global Supply* [2004] E.L.R. 133 that an agency supplied worker was employed by the client under a contract of employment.

"the Council Directive": the Directive was published at [1994] O.J L216/12 and is reproduced at FA.101 supra.

"employment regulation order": these are orders made by the Labour Court following the formulation of proposals by a Joint Labour Committee, for the fixing of minimum rates of remuneration and for regulating the conditions of employment of workers covered by the committee. When such proposals are confirmed by the Labour Court they become statutory minimum remuneration and statutory conditions of employment and employers are bound under penalty to pay rates of wages and to grant conditions of employment not less favourable than those prescribed in the order. There are currently sixteen Joint Labour Committees.

"the Minister": this definition was amended by virtue of the Enterprise and Employment (Alteration of Name of Department and Title of Minister) Order 1997 (S.I. No. 305 of 1997).

"registered employment agreement": these are agreements which have been registered with the Labour Court and which, pursuant to s.30 of the Industrial Relations Act 1946, apply to every worker of the class, type or group to which the agreement is expressed to apply, and to his or her employer, notwithstanding that such worker or employer is not a party to the agreement.

"the school leaving age": this definition was deleted by virtue of s.31 of the Education (Welfare) Act 2000.

"trade union": s.6(1) of the Trade Union Act 1941 provides that it "shall not be lawful for any body of persons, not being an excepted body, to carry on negotiations for the fixing of wages or other conditions of employment unless such body is the holder of a negotiation licence." The term "excepted body" is defined in s.6(3) of the 1941 Act.

"young person": this definition was substituted by virtue of s.31 of the Education (Welfare) Act 2000.

## Industrial work

**2.**—(1) The Minister may by order declare any form of work to be industrial work for the purposes of this Act. **FB.110**

(2) The Minister may by order amend or revoke an order under this section including an order under this subsection.

## Prohibition on employment of children

**3.**—(1) Subject to this section and section 9, an employer shall not employ a child to do work. **FB.111**

(2) The Minister may, by licence, authorise in individual cases, the employment of a child in cultural, artistic, sports or advertising activities which are not likely to be harmful to the safety, health or development of the child and which are not likely to interfere with the child's attendance at school, vocational guidance or training programmes or capacity to benefit from the instruction received.

(3) The Minister may, by regulations, authorise the employment of children over the age of 13 years in cultural, artistic, sports or advertising activities which are not harmful to the safety, health or development of children and which are not likely to interfere with their attendance at school, vocational guidance or training programmes or capacity to benefit from the instruction received.

(4) An employer may employ a child who is over the age of 14 years to do light work during any period outside the school term:
Provided that—
  (a) the hours of work do not exceed 7 hours in any day or 35 hours in any week,
  (b) the work is not harmful to the safety, health and development of the child, and
  (c) during the period of the summer holidays, the child does not do any work for a period of at least 21 days.

(5) An employer may employ a child who is over the age of 15 years to do light work during school term time, provided that the hours of work do not exceed 8 hours in any week.

(6) Subject to subsection (7), an employer may employ a child who is over the age of 14 years and who is a full-time student at an institute of secondary education pursuant to any arrangements made or approved of by the Minister for [Education and Science] as part of a programme of work experience or educational programme:

Provided that the hours of work do not exceed 8 hours in any day or 40 hours in any week.

(7) The Minister may, after consultation with the Minister for [Education and Science] and such other interested parties as the Minister sees fit, by regulations, make exemptions from subsection (6) in relation to the hours of work of children participating in a work experience or training programme approved by the Minister for [Education and Science] under subsection (6).

(8) An employer may employ a child over the age of 15 years to participate in a training or work experience programme pursuant to arrangements made or approved of by the Minister or FÁS—the Employment and Training Authority, provided that the hours of work do not exceed 8 hours in any day or 40 hours in any week.

(9) Whenever the Minister grants a licence under subsection (2) or makes regulations under subsection (3) or (7), the Minister may attach to such licence or provide in such regulations such conditions as the Minister sees fit.

(10) An employer may retain in his or her employment any child of 15 years of age who was in his or her employment immediately before the commencement of this section:

Provided that the hours of work do not exceed 7 hours in any day or 35 hours in any week.

(11) An employer who contravenes subsection (1) shall be guilty of an offence.

GENERAL NOTE

**FB.112**  This section prohibits the employment of children under 16 years of age. It does allow children, however, to be employed in certain circumstances by licence or regulation. The employment of children in cultural, artistic, sports and advertising activities may be authorised by licence in individual cases and the employment of children over the age of 13 may also be authorised by regulation.

Subsection (4) provides that a child over the age of 14 may be employed to do light work outside of the school terms provided the hours of work do not exceed seven hours in any day or 35 hours in any week, the work is not harmful to the child's safety, health and development and, during the period of the summer holidays, the child does not do any work for a period of at least 21 days. The Minister said (147 *Seanad Debates* Col. 677) that it was important that a child had an adequate rest period during the summer holidays "so that the young person will go back to school refreshed and in a position to derive benefit from the next year's school work".

Subsection (9) provides that a child over the age of 15 may do light work during the school term time for up to eight hours per week.

The section does not apply to the employment of close relatives: see Protection of Young Persons (Employment of Close Relatives) Regulations 1997 (S.I. No. 2 of 1997). The title of the Minister for Education was amended by virtue of the Education (Alteration of Name of Department and Title of Minister) Order 1997 (S.I. No. 430 of 1997).

## Additional provisions in relation to employment of children

**FB.113**  **4.**—(1) An employer shall not employ any child on any work between 8 p.m. on any one day and 8 a.m. on the following day.

(2) Subject to subsection (3), an employer shall ensure that an employee who is a child receives a minimum rest period of 14 consecutive hours in each period of 24 hours.

(3) The minimum consecutive hours of rest in each period of 24 hours specified in subsection (2) may be interrupted by an employer in the case of a child employed on activities that do not extend beyond 2 hours in each day or are separated, exclusive of breaks, over the day, provided that, in each period of 24 hours, the child receives a minimum rest period of 14 hours.

(4) An employer shall ensure that an employee who is a child receives, in any period of 7 days, a minimum rest period of 2 days which shall as far as is practicable be consecutive.

(5) The minimum period of rest during each period of 7 days specified in subsection (4) may be interrupted by an employer in the case of a child employed on activities that do not extend beyond 2 hours in each day or are separated, exclusive of breaks, over the day, provided that, in each period of 7 days, the cumulative rest period is 2 days.

(6) The Minister may, by regulations, reduce the minimum period of rest specified in subsection (4) to 36 consecutive hours in respect of any class of employees or class of work where in the opinion of the Minister this is justified for technical or organisational reasons.

(7) Whenever the Minister makes regulations under subsection (6), the Minister may provide in such regulations such conditions as the Minister sees fit.

(8) An employer shall not permit a child employed by him or her to do for him or her any work for any period exceeding 4 hours without a break of at least 30 consecutive minutes.

(9) A child shall not be entitled to be paid in respect of the break specified in subsection (8).

(10) An employer who contravenes subsection (1), (2), (4) or (8) shall be guilty of an offence.

GENERAL NOTE

This section specifies additional provisions relating to the employment of children, where permitted **FB.114** by section 3, relating to night work, minimum rest periods and breaks.

## Duties of employer in relation to young persons and children

**5.**—(1) Subject to section 9, any employer who employs a young person or **FB.115** child to work for him or her shall—

(a) before employing the young person or child, require the production of a copy of the birth certificate of, or other satisfactory evidence of the age of, the young person or child, as the case may be,

(b) before employing a child, obtain the written permission of the parent or guardian of the child, and

(c) maintain a register, or other satisfactory record, containing, in relation to every young person or child employed by him or her, the following particulars—

  (i)   the full name of the young person or child,

  (ii)  the date of birth of the young person or child,

  (iii) the time the young person or child commences work each day,

  (iv)  the time the young person or child finishes work each day,

  (v)   the rate of wages or salary paid to the young person or child for his or her normal working hours each day, week, month or year, as the case may be, and

  (vi)  the total amount paid to each young person or child by way of wages or salary.

(2) An employer who fails to comply with the provisions of this section and the parent or guardian of a young person or child who aids or abets an employer in the contravention of this section shall be guilty of an offence.

F–57

**FB.116** This section does not apply to the employment of close relatives: see Protection of Young Persons (Employment of Close Relatives) Regulations 1997 (S.I. No. 2 of 1997).

## Employment of young persons

**FB.117** **6.**—(1) An employer shall not employ a young person on any work except where, subject to this section and sections 7, 8 and 9, the employer—

(a) does not require or permit the young person to work for more than 8 hours in any day or 40 hours in any week,

(b) does not require or permit the young person to work-

(i) between 10 p.m. on any one day and 6 a.m. on the following day, or

(ii) between 11 p.m. on any one day (provided the day is not before a school day during a school term where such young person is attending school) and 7 a.m. on the following day, where the Minister is satisfied, following consultation with such representatives of employers and representatives of employees as the Minister considers appropriate, that there are exceptional circumstances affecting a particular branch of activity or a particular area of work as may be prescribed,

(c) ensures that the young person receives a minimum rest period of 12 consecutive hours in each period of 24 hours,

(d) ensures that the young person receives in any period of 7 days a minimum rest period of 2 days which shall, as far as is practicable, be consecutive, and

(e) does not require or permit the young person to do for him or her any work for any period exceeding 4 hours without a break of at least 30 consecutive minutes.

(2) The minimum consecutive hours of rest in each period of 24 hours specified in subsection (1)(c) may be interrupted by an employer in the case of a young person employed on activities that do not extend beyond 2 hours in each day or are separated, exclusive of breaks, over the day provided that, in each period of 24 hours, the young person receives a minimum rest period of 12 hours.

(3) The minimum periods of rest during each period of 7 days specified in subsection (1)(d) may be interrupted by an employer in the case of a young person employed on activities that do not extend beyond 2 hours in each day or are separated, exclusive of breaks, over the day provided that, in each period of 7 days, the cumulative rest period is 2 days.

(4) The minimum periods of rest in each period of 24 hours and each period of 7 days specified in subsection (1)(c) and (d) shall not apply to a young person who is employed in the shipping or fishing sectors:

Provided that—

(a) there are objective grounds justifying the non-application of the provisions;

(b) such young persons receive appropriate compensatory rest times at some time during each period of 24 hours and each period of 7 days, and

(c) the trade union or representative of the young person is consulted.

(5) The limitations on hours of work and on night work specified in subsection (1)(a) and (b), and the minimum periods of rest specified in subsection (1)(c) and (d) shall not apply to young persons who are members of the Defence Forces when they are—

(a) on active service within the meaning of section 5 of the Defence Act, 1954, or deemed to be on active service, within the meaning of section 4(1) of the Defence (Amendment) (No. 2) Act, 1960;

(b) engaged in action in the course of operational duties at sea;

(c) engaged in operations in aid of the civil power; or

(d) engaged in training directly associated with any of the aforesaid activities;

Provided that such young persons are allowed equivalent compensatory rest times within 3 weeks of having ceased to engage in the aforesaid activities.

(6) A young person shall not be entitled to be paid in respect of the break specified in subsection (1)(e).

(7) An employer who contravenes subsection (1) shall be guilty of an offence.

GENERAL NOTE

This section specifies the circumstances in which an employer may employ a young person. It was **FB.118** amended at Report Stage in the Dáil so as to ensure that young people who are working may be allowed to work until 11 p.m. on days when they do not have school the next day. Under the 1977 Act young persons were not allowed to work after 10 p.m., a provision in respect of which there was "widespread breach" (see Select Committee Col. 223). Subsection (1)(a) does not apply to the employment of close relatives: see Protection of Young Persons (Employment of Close Relatives) Regulations 1997 (S.I. No. 2 of 1997). The minimum rest period provisions do not apply to young persons employed in the shipping or fishing sectors provided there are objective grounds for not complying with the provisions and provided that the young persons receive compensatory rest time and provided that the trade union or representative of the young person is consulted. See Protection of Young Persons (Employment) (Exclusion of Workers in the Fishing or Shipping Sectors) Regulations 1997 (S.I. No. 1 of 1997) which provide that an employer in these sectors may employ a young person in terms other than those specified in paragraph (a) or (b) of subsection (1) provided that any young person so employed is allowed compensatory rest time.

This section, and the subsequent sections, must now be read in the light of section 29 of the Education (Welfare) Act 2000, which requires the National Educational Welfare Board to establish and maintain "a register of young persons". By virtue of subsection (16), section 29 does not apply to a young person who is (a) registered at a recognised school; (b) is engaged or has completed a course of study within the meaning of the Regional Technical Colleges Act 1992; or (c) is engaged in or has completed a prescribed programme of education, training or instruction. Any young person, or child who would at the end of a school year cease to be child, may apply to the Board to be registered. The Board, having received an application and having consulted with the young person and his or her parents, must prepare a plan of assisting the applicant to avail of educational and training opportunities. Having done that, the Board issues a certificate of registration and subsection (9) provides that an employer "shall not employ a young person on any work unless the young person is the holder of a valid certificate, and the employer shall make and retain a copy of each such certificate". Subsection (10) goes on to provide that an employer "shall as soon as practicable but in any case not later than one month after the young person concerned has commenced employment with the employer so inform the Board by notice in writing, and the employer shall retain a copy of such notice". Employers who contravene subsection (9) or (10) are guilty of an offence and are liable on summary conviction to a fine not exceeding €1,904.61 or to imprisonment for a term not exceeding six months.

## Employment of young persons under licence

**7.**—(1) The Minister may, by licence, permit an individual employer to **FB.119** employ young persons on terms specified in the licence in lieu of any of those referred to in section 6(1) and may attach to the licence such conditions as the Minister sees fit:

Provided that the Minister is satisfied that—

(a) the terms of the licence are in compliance with the terms of the Directive,

(b) the health, welfare and safety of the employees affected will not be endangered, and

(c) compliance with one or more of the terms of section 6(1) would be impractical due to the seasonal nature of the work or the technical or organisational requirements of the work or for other substantial reasons.

(2) Before granting a licence under subsection (1), the Minister shall consult such representatives of employers and representatives of employees as the Minister considers appropriate.

## Employment of young persons under regulations

**FB.120**  **8.**—(1) The Minister may, by regulations, permit any group or category of employers to employ young persons on terms specified in the regulations in lieu of any of those referred to in section 6(1) and may include in the regulations such conditions as the Minister sees fit:

Provided that the Minister is satisfied that—

(a) the terms of the regulations are in compliance with the terms of the Directive,

(b) the health, welfare and safety of the employees affected will not be endangered, and

(c) compliance with one or more of the terms of section 6(1) would be impractical due to the seasonal nature of the work or the technical or organisational requirements of the work or for other substantial reasons.

(2) Before making regulations under subsection (1), the Minister shall—

(a) consult such representatives of employers and representatives of employees as the Minister considers appropriate, and

(b) publish in such manner as the Minister thinks fit notice of the Minister's intention to do so and give persons desiring to make representations in relation to the proposed regulations a period of 21 days to do so.

GENERAL NOTE

**FB.121**  The Protection of Young Persons (Employment) (Exclusion of Workers in the Fishing or Shipping Sectors) Regulations 1997 (S.I. No. 1 of 1997) provide that an employer in the fishing or shipping sectors may employ a young person in either of these sectors on terms other than those specified in paragraph (a) or (b) of section 6(1) provided that any young person so employed who is assigned to work between the hours of 10 p.m. in any one day and 6 a.m. on the following day is allowed equivalent compensatory rest time: see also the Protection of Young Persons (Employment) Act 1996 (Employment in Licensed Premises) Regulations 2001 (S.I. No. 350 of 2001) and the Protection of Young Persons (Employment) Act 1996 (Bar Apprentices) Regulations 2001 (S.I. No. 351 of 2001). These regulations concern 16 and 17 year olds who are employed to carry out general duties or as an apprentice in a full-time capacity in a licensed premises.

## Exclusion from or modification of certain provisions of Act by regulations in relation to employment of close relatives

**FB.122**  **9.**—(1) Sections 3, 5, 6, 10 and 11 shall apply to the employment of close relatives subject to any exclusion or modification of the application of any or all of those sections or any provisions thereof as may be prescribed:

Provided that the Minister is satisfied that—

(a) the regulations are in compliance with the terms of the Directive, and

(b) the health, welfare and safety of the employees affected will not be endangered.

(2) In this section "close relative" means an employee who is employed—

(a) by his or her spouse, father, mother, grandfather, grandmother, stepfather, stepmother, brother, sister, half-brother or half-sister, and

(b) (i) in a private dwelling house or on a farm, in or on which both the employee and employer reside, or

(ii) in a family undertaking on work which is not industrial work.

GENERAL NOTE

This section was inserted at Report Stage in the Dáil. Under the 1977 Act the position was that, **FB.123** under the Protection of Young Persons (Employment) (Exclusion of Close Relatives) Regulations 1977 (S.I. No. 303 of 1977), the provisions on minimum age for employment, the duties of an employer, normal and maximum working hours, overtime pay and vocational training did not apply to the employment of close relatives. See now Protection of Young Persons (Employment of Close Relatives) Regulations 1997 (S.I. No. 2 of 1997).

## Prohibition on double employment

**10.**—(1) Subject to section 9, an employer shall not permit an employee **FB.124** to do for him or her any form of work on any day on which the employee has done any form of work for any other employer, except where the aggregate of the periods for which the employee does work for such employers on that day does not exceed the period for which such employee could lawfully be employed to do work for one employer on that day.

(2) Whenever an employer employs an employee in contravention of this section, the employer shall be guilty of an offence and the employee, if he or she is a young person, shall also be guilty of an offence.

(3) The parent or guardian of an employee who aids or abets an employer in the contravention of this section shall be guilty of an offence.

F–60/1

(4) Whenever an employer is prosecuted for an offence under this section it shall be a defence for him or her to prove either that he or she did not know, or could not by reasonable enquiry have known, that the employee had done work for any other employer on the day in respect of which the prosecution is brought or that he or she did not know, or could not by reasonable enquiry have known, that the aggregate of the periods for which the employee did work on that day exceeded the period for which he or she could lawfully be employed to do work for one employer on that day.

GENERAL NOTE

This section, which re-enacts section 16 of the 1977 Act, prohibits double employment and **FB.125** both the employer and the employee are liable to be prosecuted. It would seem to follow from the majority decision of the former Supreme Court in *Martin v. Galbraith Ltd* [1942] I.R. 37 that the employee would not be able to sue for the wages due under the second contract (see Murnaghan J. at 54).

## Time spent on vocational training

**11.**—Subject to section 9, any time spent, with the consent of his or her **FB.126** employer, by an employee who is a young person working under a combined work/training scheme or an in-plant work experience scheme shall be deemed to be working time for the purposes of section 6.

GENERAL NOTE

This section re-enacts section 19 of the 1977 Act. It does not apply to the employment of close **FB.127** relatives: see Protection of Young Persons (Employment of Close Relatives) Regulations 1997 (S.I. No. 2 of 1997).

## Display of abstract of Act

**12.**—(1) Every employer shall display at the principal entrances to the **FB.128** premises where any of his or her employees work, and in such other places as an inspector may require, in such a position that it may be easily read by employees so employed, the prescribed abstract of this Act.

(2) An employer who fails to comply with the provisions of this section shall be guilty of an offence.

GENERAL NOTE

The prescribed abstract should be in the form specified in the Schedule to the Protection of Young **FB.129** Persons (Employment) (Prescribed Abstract) Regulations 1997 (S.I. No. 3 of 1997).

## Preservation of existing rates of pay and conditions of employment

**13.**—Where, in order to comply with the provisions of this Act, the hours of **FB.130** work prevailing immediately before the commencement of this Act in regard to all employees or any particular employee employed in any particular form of work are reduced or are otherwise altered, the following provisions shall have effect, that is to say—

    (a) the rate of salary, wages or other reward payable to any such employee immediately before the commencement of this Act and the repeal of the Protection of Young Persons (Employment) Act, 1977, in regard to normal working hours (within the meaning of section 7 of that Act) shall not be reduced or be otherwise altered to the detriment of such employee merely because of the said reduction or alteration in the hours of work of such employee;

    (b) the said reduction or alteration of hours shall not terminate or prejudicially affect the contract of service under which such employee is so employed immediately before the commencement of this Act, and

F–61

every such contract shall continue in force after such commencement with such modifications only as may be necessary in order to comply with this Act;

(c) every agreement which is in force immediately before the commencement of this Act and regulates or restricts the rate of salary, wages or other reward payable to any such employee shall continue in force after such commencement notwithstanding the said reduction or alteration of hours of work but with the modification that every rate of salary, wages or other reward which is fixed by such agreement and every restriction on any rate of salary, wages or other reward contained in such agreement shall remain unchanged in amount;

(d) every minimum rate of salary, wage or other reward fixed by statute or under statutory authority which is in force immediately before the commencement of this Act shall, if and so far as it is applicable to any such employee, continue after such commencement in force and unchanged in amount notwithstanding the said reduction or alteration of hours of work.

GENERAL NOTE

**FB.131**    This section preserves existing pay and conditions of employment where, in order to comply with the provisions of the Act, the hours of work are reduced or altered.

## Emergency as defence

**FB.132**    **14.**—(1) It shall be a defence to any proceedings taken against any employer for a breach of any of the provisions of this Act in relation to an employee who is a young person if such employer shows to the satisfaction of the court before which such proceedings are brought that any act occasioning such breach was rendered necessary or reasonably proper by the actual occurrence or the threat or reasonable anticipation of fire, flood, storm, violence, a breakdown of plant or machinery or any other emergency;

Provided that—

(a) the work is of a temporary nature and has to be performed immediately,

(b) adult workers are not available,

(c) the young person is allowed equivalent compensatory rest time within 3 weeks of the date of occurrence of the breach concerned, and

(d) the young person is paid at the rate of time plus a quarter for any time worked as a result of the emergency.

(2) A certificate signed by or on behalf of any Minister of the Government that an act done by or in relation to any young person employed by that Minister was rendered necessary by an emergency shall be evidence that such act was so rendered necessary.

## Employer records

**FB.133**    **15.**—(1) An employer shall keep, at the place where a young person or child is employed, such records as are necessary to show whether the provisions of this Act are being complied with in relation to his or her employees and such records shall be retained by the employer for at least 3 years.

(2) In any case where—

(a) there is a dispute between an employer and employee, or

(b) there is a prosecution for an offence under this Act, and the records required to be kept by an employer under subsection (1) are not available, the onus of proving that the provisions of this Act have been complied with shall lie on the employer.

(3) An employer who contravenes subsection (1) shall be guilty of an offence.

GENERAL NOTE

This obligation to keep records, if the young person or child is employed by the employer at two or more places, is to be construed as an obligation "to keep the said records at the place from which the activities that the young person or child is employed to carry on are principally directed or controlled": Organisation of Working Time Act 1997, section 36(3).  **FB.134**

## Recovery of money due to employee

**16.**—(1) Any sum of money due to an employee from his or her employer under any provision of this Act shall be recoverable by the employee from his or her employer as a simple contract debt in a court of competent jurisdiction.  **FB.135**

(2) Proceedings for the recovery of any sum due by an employer to an employee under any provision of this Act may be instituted and maintained on behalf of the employee by his or her trade union or parent or guardian.

(3) Whenever in a prosecution for an offence under this Act, it appears that a sum of money is due by an employer to an employee, and the employer is convicted of that offence, a court may, if it is satisfied that the employer is liable to pay to his or her employee a sum of money, order, in addition to any penalty which it may impose pursuant to this Act, that the employer pay any such sum of money to the employee.

GENERAL NOTE

This section re-enacts section 18 of the 1977 Act.  **FB.136**

## Refusal by child or young person to co-operate with employer in breaching Act

**17.** An employer shall not penalise an employee for having in good faith opposed by lawful means an act which is unlawful under this Act.  **FB.137**

## Complaints to rights commissioner

**18.**—(1) The parent or guardian of a child or young person may present a complaint to a rights commissioner that the employer of the child or young person has contravened section 13 or 17 in relation to the child or young person.  **FB.138**

(2) Where a complaint under subsection (1) is made, the rights commissioner shall give the parties an opportunity to be heard by the commissioner and to present to the commissioner any evidence relevant to the complaint, shall give a recommendation in writing in relation to it and shall communicate the recommendation to the parties.

(3) A recommendation of a rights commissioner under subsection (2) shall do one or more of the following—

(a) declare that the complaint was or, as the case may be, was not well founded,

(b) order the employer to take a specific course of action,

(c) order the employer to pay to the employee compensation of such amount (if any) as is just and equitable having regard to all the circumstances,and the references in the foregoing paragraphs to an employer shall be construed, in a case where ownership of the business of the employer changes after a contravention to which the complaint relates, as references to the person who, by virtue of the change, becomes entitled to such ownership.

F–63

(4) A rights commissioner shall not entertain a complaint under this section unless it is presented to him within the period of 6 months beginning on the date of the contravention to which the complaint relates or (in a case where the rights commissioner is satisfied that exceptional circumstances prevented the presentation of the complaint within the period aforesaid) such further period not exceeding 6 months as the rights commissioner considers reasonable.

(5) (a) A complaint shall be presented by giving notice thereof in writing to a rights commissioner and the notice shall contain such particulars and be in such form as may be specified from time to time by the Minister.

(b) A copy of a notice under paragraph (a) shall be given to the other party concerned by the rights commissioner concerned.

(6) Proceedings under this section before a rights commissioner shall be conducted otherwise than in public.

(7) A rights commissioner shall furnish the Tribunal with a copy of any recommendation given by the commissioner under subsection (2).

(8) The Minister may by regulations—

(a) provide for any matters relating to proceedings under this section that the Minister considers appropriate, and

(b) amend paragraph (c) of subsection (3) so as to vary the maximum amount of the compensation provided for in that paragraph, and this section shall have effect in accordance with the provisions of any regulations under this paragraph for the time being in force.

GENERAL NOTE

**FB.139** Although the employee's trade union is permitted to institute and maintain civil proceedings pursuant to s.16(2), to apply to the District Court to enforce a Tribunal determination pursuant to s.20(1)(a)(ii) and to prosecute certain offences pursuant to s.24(2), a trade union is not specifically empowered to present a complaint to a rights commissioner under this section. In awarding compensation, the rights commissioner and the Tribunal must make it clear whether the award is or is not "in respect of remuneration including arrears of remuneration", otherwise it may not be regarded as being exempt from income tax: see s.192A of the Taxes Consolidation Act 1997 (inserted by s.7 of the Finance Act 2004).

## Appeals from and enforcement of recommendations of rights commissioner

**FB.140** **19.**—(1) A party concerned may appeal to the Tribunal from a recommendation of a rights commissioner under section 18 and, if the party does so, the Tribunal shall give the parties an opportunity to be heard by it and to present to it any evidence relevant to the appeal, shall make a determination in writing in relation to the appeal affirming, varying or setting aside the recommendation and shall communicate the determination to the parties.

(2) (a) Subject to any regulations made under subsection (3)(g), an appeal under this section shall be initiated by the party concerned giving, within 6 weeks of the date on which the recommendation to which it relates was communicated to the party, a notice in writing to the Tribunal containing such particulars (if any) as may be specified in regulations under subsection (3) and stating the intention of the party concerned to appeal against the recommendation.

(b) A copy of a notice under paragraph (a) shall be given by the Tribunal to the other party concerned as soon as may be after the receipt of the notice by the Tribunal.

(3) The Minister may by regulations provide for all or any of the following matters in relation to proceedings under this Act before the Tribunal and for anything consequential thereon or incidental or ancillary thereto—

(a) the procedure in relation to all matters concerning the initiation and the hearing by the Tribunal of appeals under this section,

(b) the times and places of hearings of such appeals,

(c) the representation of the parties to such appeals,

(d) the publication and notification of determinations of the Tribunal,

(e) the particulars to be contained in a notice under subsection (2),

(f) the award by the Tribunal of costs and expenses in relation to such appeals and the payment thereof,

(g) the extension by the Tribunal of the time for initiating such appeals.

(4) (a) The Minister may, at the request of the Tribunal, refer a question of law arising in proceedings before it to the High Court for determination by it and the determination of the High Court shall be final and conclusive.

(b) A party to proceedings before the Tribunal may appeal to the High Court from a determination of the Tribunal on a point of law and the determination of the High Court shall be final and conclusive.

(5) (a) The Tribunal shall, on the hearing of any matter referred to it under this section, have power to take evidence on oath and for that purpose may cause to be administered oaths to persons attending as witnesses at such hearing.

(b) Any person who, upon examination on oath authorised under this subsection, wilfully gives false evidence or wilfully swears anything which is false, being convicted thereof, shall be liable to the penalties for perjury.

(c) The Tribunal may, by giving notice in that behalf in writing to any person, require such person to attend at such time and place as is specified in the notice to give evidence in relation to any matter referred to the Tribunal under this section or to produce any documents in his or her possession, custody or control which relate to any such matter.

(d) A notice under paragraph (c) may be given either by delivering it to the person to whom it relates or by sending it by post in a prepaid registered letter addressed to such person at the address at which he or she ordinarily resides.

(e) A person to whom a notice under paragraph (c) has been given and who refuses or wilfully neglects to attend in accordance with the notice or having so attended, refuses to give evidence or refuses or wilfully fails to produce any document to which the notice relates shall be guilty of an offence.

(6) (a) Where a recommendation of a rights commissioner in relation to a complaint under this Act has not been carried out by the employer concerned in accordance with its terms, the time for bringing an appeal against the recommendation has expired and no such appeal has been brought, the employee concerned may bring the complaint before the Tribunal and the Tribunal shall, without hearing the employer concerned, other than in relation to the matters aforesaid or any evidence other than in relation to such matters, make a determination to the like effect as the recommendation.

(b) The bringing of a complaint before the Tribunal by virtue of this subsection shall be effected by giving to the Tribunal a notice in writing containing such particulars (if any) as may be specified in regulations made for the purposes of subsection (3).

GENERAL NOTE

**FB.141**     This section provides that either party may appeal to the Employment Appeals Tribunal from a recommendation of the rights commissioner under section 18. Subsection (4) provides for a further appeal on a point of law only to the High Court and also enables the Tribunal to request the Minister to refer a question of law to the High Court. Although the Rules of the Superior Courts do not specifically provide for appeals under this Act, it is suggested that any such appeal be brought by special summons by analogy with the procedure set out in R.S.C. 1986, Order 105. In the absence of any specific rule of court, any such appeal need only be brought within a reasonable time: *per* McCracken J. in his *ex tempore* ruling in *McGaley v Liebherr Container Cranes Ltd* (2001/234Sp) delivered on October 12, 2001. No Regulations have yet been promulgated prescribing the procedures to be followed in relation to the submission and hearing of appeals and complaints before the Tribunal.

The circumstances in which the High Court will overturn a decision of a specialist tribunal such as the Employment Appeals Tribunal have been considered in many cases: see for example, *Henry Denny & Sons (Ireland) Ltd v Minister for Social Welfare* [1998] 1 I.R. 34 and in particular the comments of Hamilton C.J. at 37. In considering whether to allow an appeal against a decision of such a tribunal, the High Court must consider whether that body based its decision on an identifiable error of law or on an unsustainable finding of fact. A decision cannot be challenged on the grounds of irrationality if there is any relevant material to support it: see further *Mulcahy v Waterford Leader Partnership Ltd* [2002] E.L.R. 12 (O'Sullivan J.) and *Thompson v Tesco Ireland Ltd* [2003] E.L.R. 21 (Lavan J.). In *National University of Ireland, Cork v Ahern* [2005] 2 I.R. 577, the Supreme Court held that, although findings of fact must be accepted by the High Court on appeal, that court could still examine the basis upon which those facts were found. The relevance or admissibility of the matters relied on in determining the facts were questions of law.

## Enforcement of determination of Tribunal

**FB.142**     **20.**—(1) (a) If an employer fails to carry out in accordance with its terms a determination of the Tribunal in relation to a complaint under section 18 within 6 weeks from the date on which the determination is communicated to the parties, the District Court shall, on application to it in that behalf by—

(i)   the parent or guardian of the child or young person concerned,

(ii)  the trade union of the young person concerned, or

(iii) the Minister, if the Minister considers it appropriate to make the application having regard to all the circumstances,

without hearing the employer concerned, other than in relation to the matters aforesaid or any evidence other than in relation to such matters, make an order directing the employer to carry out the determination in accordance with its terms.

(b) In paragraph (a) the reference to a determination of the Tribunal is a reference to such a determination in relation to which, at the expiration of the time for bringing an appeal against it, no such appeal has been brought, or if such an appeal has been brought it has been abandoned and the reference to the date on which the determination is communicated to the parties shall, in a case where such an appeal is abandoned, be construed as a reference to the date of such abandonment.

(2) The District Court may, in an order under this section, if in all the circumstances it considers it appropriate to do so, where the order relates to the payment of compensation, direct the employer concerned to pay to the employee concerned interest on the compensation at the rate referred to in

F–66

section 22 of the Courts Act, 1981, in respect of the whole or any part of the period beginning 6 weeks after the date on which the determination of the Tribunal is communicated to the parties and ending on the date of the order.

(3) Proceedings under this section shall be heard by the judge assigned to the district court district in which the employer concerned ordinarily resides or carries on any profession, business or occupation.

GENERAL NOTE

This section provides for enforcement of Tribunal determinations by giving the Minister, the **FB.143** employee's trade union or the employee concerned the power to apply to the District Court for an order directing the employer to implement the determination. The District Court is also empowered by subsection (2) to award interest on any compensation awarded. Although the District Court Rules do not specifically provide for applications to enforce Tribunal determinations, it is suggested that any such application be made by a suitably adapted notice to that set out in Sch.1 to the District Court (Terms of Employment Information) Rules 2003 (S.I. No. 409 of 2003) reproduced *supra* at AC. 501.

## Evidence of failure to attend before or give evidence or produce documents to Tribunal

**21.** A document purporting to be signed by the chairman or a vice-chairman of **FB.144** the Tribunal stating that—

(a)  a person named in the document was, by a notice under paragraph (c) of section 19(5) required to attend before the Tribunal on a day and at a time and place specified in the document, to give evidence or produce a document,

(b)  a sitting of the Tribunal was held on that day and at that time and place, and

(c)  the person did not attend before the Tribunal in pursuance of the notice or, as the case may be, having so attended, refused to give evidence or refused or failed to produce the document,

shall, in a prosecution of the person under paragraph (e) of that section, be evidence of the matters so stated without further proof.

### Powers of inspectors

**22.**—(1) The Minister may appoint in writing such and so many persons as the Minister sees fit to be inspectors for the purposes of this Act.  **FB.145**

(2) An inspector may for the purposes of this Act do all or any of the following things—

(a)  subject to the provisions of this section, enter at all reasonable times any premises or place where he or she has reasonable grounds for supposing that any employee is employed in work [or from which he or she has reasonable grounds for supposing the activities that an employee is employed to carry on are directed or controlled (whether generally or as respects particular matters)],

(b)  make such examination or enquiry as may be necessary for ascertaining whether the provisions of this Act are complied with in respect of any employee employed in any such premises or place [or any employee the activities aforesaid of whom are directed or controlled from any such premises or place],

(c)  require the employer of any employee or the representative of such employer to produce to him or her any records which such employer is required to keep and inspect and take copies of entries in such records (including in the case of information in a non-legible form a copy of or an extract from such information in a permanent legible form),

(d)  require any person whom he or she has reasonable cause to believe to be or to have been an employee or the employer of any employee to furnish such information as the inspector may reasonably request,

(e)  examine with regard to any matters under this Act any person whom he or she has reasonable cause to believe to be or to have been an employer or employee and require him or her to answer such questions (other than questions tending to incriminate him or her) as the inspector may put relative to those matters and to sign a declaration of the truth of the answers.

(3) An inspector shall not, other than with the consent of the occupier, enter a private dwelling (other than a part of the dwelling used as a place of work) unless he or she has obtained a warrant from the District Court under subsection (6) authorising such entry.

(4) Where an inspector in the exercise of his or her powers under this section is prevented from entering any premises an application may be made under subsection (6) authorising such entry.

(5) An inspector appointed under this section, where he or she considers it necessary, may be accompanied by a member of the Garda SÚochÃna when performing any powers conferred on an inspector by this Act.

(6) If a judge of the District Court is satisfied on the sworn information of an inspector that there are reasonable grounds for suspecting that there is information required by an inspector under this section held on any premises

F–67

or any part of any premises, the judge may issue a warrant authorising an inspector accompanied by other inspectors or a member of the Garda Síochána, at any time or times within one month from the date of issue of the warrant, on production, if so requested, of the warrant, to enter the premises (if need be by reasonable force) and exercise all or any of the powers conferred on an inspector under subsection (2).

(7) A person who—

(a) obstructs or impedes an inspector in the exercise of any of the powers conferred on an inspector under this section,

(b) refuses to produce any record which an inspector lawfully requires him or her to produce,

(c) produces or causes to be produced or knowingly allows to be produced, to an inspector, any record which if false in any material respect knowing it to be false,

(d) gives to an inspector any information which is false or misleading, or

(e) wilfully fails or refuses to comply with any lawful requirement of an inspector under subsection (2), shall be guilty of an offence.

(8) Every inspector shall be furnished by the Minister with a certificate of his or her appointment and, on applying for admission to any premises or place for the purposes of this Act, shall, if requested by a person affected, produce the certificate or a copy thereof to that person.

GENERAL NOTE

FB.146  The words in square brackets in paragraphs (a) and (b) of subsection (2) were inserted by virtue of section 36(4) of the Organisation of Working Time Act 1997.

## Offences by bodies corporate

FB.147  **23.**—(1) Where an offence under this Act is committed by a body corporate or by a person acting on behalf of a body corporate and is proved to have been so committed with the consent, connivance or approval of, or to have been facilitated by any neglect on the part of any director, manager, secretary or any other officer of such body or a person who was purporting to act in any such capacity, such person shall also be guilty of an offence and shall be liable to be proceeded against and punished as if he or she were guilty of the first-mentioned offence.

(2) Any summons or other document required to be served for the purpose or in the course of proceedings on a body corporate may be served by leaving it at or sending it by post to the registered office of that body or, if there is in the State no such office, by leaving it at or sending it by post to that body at any place in the State at which it conducts its business.

GENERAL NOTE

FB.148  This section re-enacts section 22 of the 1977 Act.

## Prosecutions

FB.149  **24.**—(1) An offence under this Act may be prosecuted summarily by the Minister.

(2) An offence, other than an offence under section 19 or 22, may be prosecuted summarily by the trade union of which the employee is a member.

(3) Notwithstanding section 10(4) of the Petty Sessions (Ireland) Act, 1851, summary proceedings for an offence under this Act may be instituted within 12 months from the date of the offence.

## Penalties

**25.**—(1) A person guilty of an offence under this Act shall be liable on summary conviction to a fine not exceeding £1,500 [€1,904.61]. **FB.150**

(2) Where a person after conviction for an offence under this Act continues to contravene the provision concerned, the person shall be guilty of an offence on every day on which the contravention continues and for each such offence shall be liable to a fine on summary conviction not exceeding £250 [€317.43].

## Repeals

**26.**—The enactments *specified* in column (2) of the *Second Schedule* are hereby repealed to the extent specified in column (3) of that Schedule. **FB.151**

## Expenses

**27.**—The expenses incurred by the Minister in the administration of this Act shall, to such extent as may be sanctioned by the Minister for Finance, be paid out of monies provided by the Oireachtas. **FB.152**

## Regulations

**28.**—(1) The Minister may make regulations for prescribing any matter referred to in this Act as prescribed. **FB.153**

(2) A draft of every order proposed to be made under section 2 and of every regulation proposed to be made under this Act shall be laid before each House of the Oireachtas and the order or regulation, as the case may be, shall not be made until a resolution approving of the draft has been passed by each such House.

## Short title and commencement

**29.**—(1) This Act may be cited as the Protection of Young Persons (Employment) Act, 1996. **FB.154**

(2) This Act shall come into operation on such day as the Minister may appoint by order.

GENERAL NOTE

The Act came into operation on January 2, 1997: see Protection of Young Persons (Employment) Act 1996 (Commencement) Order 1996 (S.I. No. 371 of 1996). **FB.155**

First Schedule

Council Directive 94/33/EC of 22 June 1994

**FB.156**
(See para. FA.101, above.)

Second Schedule

**FB.157**
Enactments Repealed

| Number and Year (1) | Short title (2) | Extent of Repeal (3) |
|---|---|---|
| 1936, No. 2 | Conditions of Employment Act, 1936 | Sections 15, 41(1)(b), 45, 47 and 49(7). |
| 1977, No. 9 | Protection of Young Persons (Employment) Act, 1977 | The whole Act. |

F–70

## PROTECTION OF YOUNG PERSONS (EMPLOYMENT) (EXCLUSION OF WORKERS IN THE FISHING OR SHIPPING SECTORS) REGULATIONS, 1997

### (S.I. No. 1 of 1997)

**1.** These Regulations may be cited as the Protection of Young Persons (Employment) (Exclusion of Workers in the Fishing or Shipping Sectors) Regulations, 1997.   **FC.101**

**2.** An employer in the fishing or shipping sectors may employ a young person employed in either of those sectors on terms other than those specified in paragraph (a) or (b) of section 6(1) of the Protection of Young Persons (Employment) Act, 1996 (No. 16 of 1996):   **FC.102**

Provided that any young person so employed who is assigned to work between the hours of 10 p.m. in any one day and 6 a.m. on the following day is allowed equivalent compensatory rest time.

GENERAL NOTE

These Regulations modify certain provisions of the 1996 Act in regard to their application to young persons employed in the fishing or shipping sectors.   **FC.103**

## PROTECTION OF YOUNG PERSONS (EMPLOYMENT OF CLOSE RELATIVES) REGULATIONS, 1997

### (S.I. No. 2 of 1997)

**1.** These Regulations may be cited as the Protection of Young Persons (Employment of Close Relatives) Regulations, 1997.   **FC.201**

**2.** It is hereby prescribed that sections 3, 5, 6(1)(a) and 11 of the Protection of Young Persons (Employment) Act, 1996 (No. 16 of 1996), shall not apply to the employment of close relatives.   **FC.202**

GENERAL NOTE

These regulations modify certain provisions of the 1996 Act in regard to their application to close relatives.   **FC.203**

## PROTECTION OF YOUNG PERSONS (EMPLOYMENT) (PRESCRIBED ABSTRACT) REGULATIONS, 1997

### (S.I. No. 3 of 1997)

**1.** These Regulations may be cited as the Protection of Young Persons (Employment) (Prescribed Abstract) Regulations, 1997.   **FC.301**

**2.** It is hereby prescribed that the abstract of the Protection of Young Persons (Employment) Act, 1996 (No. 16 of 1996), shall be in the form specified in the Schedule to these Regulations.   **FC.302**

SCHEDULE

ABSTRACT
OF
PROTECTION OF YOUNG PERSONS (EMPLOYMENT) ACT 1996

SUMMARY OF MAIN RULES ON EMPLOYING PEOPLE UNDER 18

AGE LIMITS

**FC.303**    For a regular job, the general minimum age is 16. Employers can take on 14 and 15 year olds on light work:

- part-time during the school term (over 15 years only)

- as part of an approved work experience or educational programme

- during the school holidays, provided there is a minimum three week break from work in the summer.

Any child under 16 may be employed in film, theatre, sports or advertising under licence.

MAXIMUM HOURS OF WORK PER WEEK

**FC.304**    Under 18s may not be employed for more than 40 hours a week or 8 hours a day, except in a genuine emergency. The maximum weekly working hours for 14 and 15 year olds are:

| Age | 14 | 15 |
|---|---|---|
| Term-time | Nil | 8 hours |
| Holiday work | 35 hours | 35 hours |
| Work experience | 40 hours | 40 hours |

EARLY MORNING AND NIGHT WORK

**FC.305**  The hours permitted are:

| Age | Under 16s | 16 and 17s |
|---|---|---|
| Early morning | after 8 am | after 6 am |
| Night work | | |
|    – with school next morning | up to 8 pm | up to 10 pm |
|    – no school next morning | up to 8 pm | up to 11 pm (and not |
|    – *e.g. holidays, weekends* | | before 7 am next morning) |

REST BREAKS

| **FC.306** | Under 16s | 16 and 17s |
|---|---|---|
| 30 minutes break after working | 4 hours | 4½ hours |
| Every 24 hours | 14 hours off | 12 hours off |
| Every 7 days | 2 days off | 2 days off |

EXCEPTIONS

**FC.307**    The full provisions of the Act do not apply to:

- employment of close relatives
- employment in fishing, shipping, or the Defence Forces.

DUTIES OF EMPLOYERS

Employers must:                                                                    **FC.308**
See a copy of the birth certificate and, before employing someone under 16, must get the written permission of the parent or guardian.
Keep a register containing the following particulars of each person under 18 employed:
- full name
- date of birth
- time work begins each day
- time work finishes each day
- rate of wages or salary paid per day, week, month or year, as appropriate
- total amount of wages or salary paid to each person.

COMPLAINTS

Complaints about breaches of the Act may be made in confidence to the Employment Rights **FC.309** Section, Department of Enterprise, Trade and Employment, Davitt House, 65A Adelaide Road, Dublin 2, phone (01) 6614444. The Department's Inspectors have powers to go into places of work, question employers and employees and examine records.
Parents may refer certain breaches of the Act to a Rights Commissioner.

PENALTIES

Offenders could face fines of up to £1,500 [€1,904.61], and an extra £250 [€317.43] a day for a **FC.310** continuing offence.
*This gives a brief outline of the law and is not a legal interpretation. If you want further information, You can contact the Information Unit, Department of Enterprise, Trade and Employment, Davitt House, 65A Adelaide Road, Dublin 2, phone (01) 6614444 or read the more detailed Guide to the Act.*

GENERAL NOTE

These Regulations set out the abstract of the 1996 Act which an employer of employees under 18 **FC.311** years of age must display at the principal entrances to the work premises. By virtue of the Terms of Employment (Information) Act 1994 (Section 3(6)) Order 1997 (S.I. No. 4 of 1997) an employer of a child or young person within the meaning of the 1996 Act must give or cause to be given, not less than one month after employment commences, a copy of this abstract.

# SAFETY, HEALTH AND WELFARE AT WORK (CHILDREN AND YOUNG PERSONS) REGULATIONS, 1998

## (S.I. No. 504 of 1998)

## Citation and Commencement
**1.**—(1) These Regulations may be cited as the Safety, Health and Welfare at **FC.401** Work (Children and Young Persons) Regulations, 1998.

(2) These Regulations shall come into operation on the 18th day of December, 1998.

## Interpretation
**2.** —(1) In these Regulations—                                              **FC.402**
"child" means a person who is under 16 years of age or the school leaving age whichever is the higher;
"the Council Directive" means Council Directive No. 94/33/EC of 22 June 1994 on the protection of young people at work;" night work" means—

(a) in the case of a child, any work between 8 p.m. on any one day and 8 a.m. on the following day,

(b) in the case of a young person, the hours mentioned in paragraph (b) of section 6 (1) of the Protection of Young Persons (Employment) Act, 1996 (No. 16 of 1996), as qualified by that section and sections 7 and 8 thereof;

"the Regulations of 1993" means the Safety, Health and Welfare at Work (General Application) Regulations, 1993 (S.I. No. 44 of 1993);

"risk assessment" means the assessment of a risk referred to in Regulation 3(a);

"the school leaving age" means the age at which the School Attendance Act, 1926, ceases to apply or in lieu thereof any age set down by or under any enactment, passed and in operation after the passing of the Protection of Young Persons (Employment) Act, 1996 (No. 16 of 1996) as the minimum age at which compulsory full-time schooling ends;

"young person" means a person who has reached 16 years of age or the school-leaving age (whichever is higher) but is less than 18 years of age.

(2) A word or expression used in these Regulations which is also used in the Council Directive has, unless the context otherwise requires, the same meaning in these Regulations as it has in the Council Directive.

(3) In these Regulations, unless otherwise indicated—

(a) a reference to a Regulation is to a Regulation of these Regulations,

(b) a reference to a Schedule is to a Schedule to these Regulations, and

(c) a reference to a paragraph or a subparagraph is to a paragraph or a subparagraph of the Regulation in which the reference occurs.

## Duties of Employer

FC.403    **3.** It shall be the duty of every employer:—

(a) without prejudice to the provisions of Regulation 10 of the Regulations of 1993, to assess any risk to the safety or health of a child or young person and any specific risk to their safety, health and development arising from—

    (i) his or her lack of experience, absence of awareness of existing or potential risks or lack of maturity,

    (ii) any work activity likely to involve a risk of harmful exposure to the physical, biological and chemical agents specified in Part I of the Schedule, and

    (iii) the processes and work specified in Part II of the Schedule and to take the preventive and protective measures necessary;

(b) to carry out a risk assessment before employing a child or young person and whenever there is a major change in the place of work which could affect the safety or health of such child or young person;

(c) when carrying out a risk assessment to take account of the following—

    (i) the fitting-out and the layout of the place of work and of the work-station,

    (ii) the nature, degree and exposure to any physical, chemical or biological agent at the place of work,

    (iii) the form, range and use of work equipment, in particular agents, machines, apparatus and devices, and the way in which they are handled,

      (iv) the arrangement of work processes and of work operations at the place of work and of the way in which these may be organised in combination for the purposes of carrying out work, and

      (v) the training, instruction and level of supervision provided to a child or young person at the place of work;

(d) where a risk assessment reveals that. the work involved is work which-

      (i) is beyond the physical or psychological capacity of the child or young person concerned,

      (ii) involves harmful exposure to agents which are toxic, carcinogenic, cause heritable genetic damage, or harm to the unborn child or which in any other way chronically affects human health,

      (iii) involves harmful exposure to radiation,

      (iv) involves the risk of accidents which it may be assumed cannot be recognised or avoided by a child or young person owing to insufficient attention to safety or lack of experience or training, or

      (v) presents a risk to health from exposure to extreme heat or cold and to noise or vibration,

not to employ such child or young person at such work;

(e) in taking the protective and preventive measures in accordance with paragraph (a) and as regards planning for and implementing measures to monitor and protect the safety and health of a child or young person, to take account of Regulation 8 of the Regulations of 1993;

(f) without prejudice to the provisions of Regulation 11 of the Regulations of 1993, to inform a child or young person of any risk identified in accordance with paragraph (a) and of the preventive and protective measures taken and, in the case of a child, to inform the parent or guardian of such child of such risk and such preventive and protective measures;

(g) where a risk assessment reveals a risk to safety or health or to the physical or mental development of a child or young person, to make available health surveillance in accordance with Regulation 15 of the Regulations of 1993;

(h) to make available to a child or young person a free assessment of his or her health and capabilities before assignment to night work and at regular intervals thereafter;

(i) to inform a child or young person of the result of any health surveillance or health assessment carried out in accordance with paragraphs (g) or (h) and, in the case of a child, to inform the parent or guardian of such child of the results of any health surveillance or health assessment.

**Regulation 3**                                                SCHEDULE

NON-EXHAUSTIVE GUIDE LIST OF AGENTS, PROCESSES AND WORK

PART I

AGENTS

**FC.404**                                                  *1. Physical Agents*

(a)  Ionizing radiation;
(b)  Work in a high-pressure atmosphere such as in pressurized containers or diving;

*2. Biological agents*

(a)  Biological agents of risk groups 3 and 4 within the meaning of Regulation 2(1) of the Safety, Health and Welfare at Work (Biological Agents) Regulations, 1994, (S.I. No. 146 of 1994);

*3.  Chemical agents*

(a)  Substances and preparations classified under the European Communities (Classification, Packaging, Labelling and Notification of Dangerous Substances) Regulations, 1994, (S.I. No. 77 of 1994) as toxic (T), very toxic (Tx), corrosive (C) or explosive (E);
(b)  Substances and preparations classified under the European Communities (Classification, Packaging, Labelling and Notification of Dangerous Substances) Regulations, 1994, (S.I. No. 77 of 1994), and the European Communities (Classification, Packaging and Labelling of Dangerous Preparations) Regulations, 1992, (S.I. No. 393 of 1992), as harmful (Xn) and with one or more of the following risk phrases:
   —danger of very serious irreversible effects (R39)
   —possible risk of irreversible effects (R40)
   —may cause sensitization by inhalation (R42)
   —may cause sensitization by skin contact (R43)
   —may cause cancer (R45)
   —may cause heritable genetic damage (R46)
   —danger of serious damage to health by prolonged exposure (R48) may impair fertility (R60)
   —may cause harm to the unborn child (R61);
(c)  Substances and preparations classified under the European Communities (Classification, Packaging, Labelling and Notification of Dangerous Substances) Regulations, 1994, (S.I. No. 77 of 1994), and the European Communities (Classification, Packaging and Labelling of Dangerous Preparations) Regulations, 1992, (S.I. No. 393 of 1992), as irritant (Xi) and with one or more of the following risk phrases:
   —highly flammable (R12)
   —may cause sensitization by inhalation (R42)
   —may cause sensitization by skin contact (R43)
(d)  Substances and preparations referred to in the Safety, Health and Welfare at Work (Carcinogens) Regulations, 1993, (S.I. No. 80 of 1993);
(c)  Lead and compounds thereof, in as much as the agents in question are absorbable by the human organisms;
(f)  Asbestos.

PART II

PROCESSES AND WORK

**FC.405**  1. Processes at work referred to in the Safety, Health and Welfare at Work (Carcinogens) Regulations, 1993, (S.I. No. 80 of 1993).
2. Manufacture and handling of devices, fireworks or other objects containing explosives.

F–106

3. Work with dangerous, fierce or poisonous animals.

4. Animal slaughtering on an industrial scale.

5. Work involving the handling of equipment for the production, storage or application of compressed, liquefied or dissolved gases.

6. Work with vats, tanks, reservoirs or carboys containing chemical agents referred to in item 3 of Part 1 to this Schedule.

7. Work involving a risk of structural collapse.

8. Work involving high-voltage electrical hazards.

9. Work the pace of which is determined by machinery and involving payment by results.

GENERAL NOTE

The purpose of these Regulations is to implement the health and safety aspects of Council Directive 94/33/EEC on the protection of young people at work. It should be noted that the definitions of "child" and "young person" in the 1996 Act were amended by the Education (Welfare) Act 2000 so that they now mean "a person who has not reached the age of 16 years" and "a person who has reached the age of 16 years but has not reached the age of 18 years" respectively. It should also be noted that the School Attendance Act 1926 has been repealed by the 2000 Act and the school leaving age is now 16. **FC.406/A**

# PROTECTION OF YOUNG PERSONS (EMPLOYMENT) ACT, 1996 (EMPLOYMENT IN LICENSED PREMISES) REGULATIONS, 2001

## (S.I. No. 350 of 2001)

**1.** These Regulations may be cited as the Protection of Young Persons **FC.501** (Employment) Act, 1996 (Employment in Licensed Premises) Regulations, 2001.

**2.** In these Regulations— **FC.502**

"general duties" does not include supplying intoxicating liquor from behind the bar counter in licensed premises or supplying it for consumption off those premises

"licensed premises" means premises—

(a) to which a licence (within the meaning of the Licensing Acts, 1833 to [2004]) is attached, and

(b) the whole or any part of which is used to sell food or intoxicating liquor or both for consumption thereon.

**3.** A person who employs a young person to carry out general duties in a **FC.503** licensed premises—

(a) may require the young person to work up to 11 p.m. on any one day, where—

(i) the day is not a day immediately preceding a school day during a school term where the young person is attending school, and

(ii) the young person is not required or permitted to commence work until 7 a.m. on the following day,

and

(b) shall have regard to the Code of Practice concerning the Employment of Young Persons in Licensed Premises, the terms of which are set out in the Schedule hereto.

SCHEDULE

CODE OF PRACTICE CONCERNING THE EMPLOYMENT OF YOUNG PERSONS
IN LICENSED PREMISES

**Introduction**

**FC.504**    The main purpose of this Code of Practice is to set out for the guidance of employers and employees the duties and responsibilities (including statutory obligations) in relation to the employment of young persons on general duties in licensed premises.

This Code of Practice covers 16 and 17 year olds, including all second level students (excluding bar apprentices in the licensed trade) who are employed at any time in licensed premises be it summer, other holidays or part-time work.

Meetings and consultations were held for the purposes of the preparation of this Code between representatives of (a) The Irish Congress of Trade Unions, (b) The Irish Hotels Federation, (c) The Licensed Vintners Association, (d) Mandate, (e) The National Parents Council post primary, (f) The Restaurants Association of Ireland and (g) The Vintners Federation of Ireland, who are all party to this Code.

For the purposes of this Code;

"licensed premises" means premises—

(a) to which a licence (within the meaning of the Licensing Acts, 1833 to [2004]) is attached, and

(b) the whole or any part of which is used to sell food or intoxicating liquor or both for consumption thereon.

"general duties" does not include supplying intoxicating liquor from behind the bar counter in licensed premises or supplying it for consumption off those premises.

To ensure that some of these employees, who may be interested in careers in the industry, are encouraged to consider such long term options, it is important that their work experience is positive and that they receive on-going training.

It is also important that the purpose, function and terms of this Code are known and understood by management, employees, trade unions and parents.

Employers who are party to this Code, shall not discriminate against any young person who seeks his/her entitlements under employment legislation or otherwise or the benefit of this Code.

GENERAL PRINCIPLES

**1. Provision of Written Terms and Conditions of Employment**

Section 3 of the Terms of Employment (Information) Act, 1994, provides that an employer must provide a written statement of terms of employment to those employees who are at least 1 month in employment, within two months of commencement of employment. Notwithstanding this, these provisions will be complied with by employers covered by this Code on commencement of employment of all young persons in their employment, and shall include such information as is required by the Act, including the rate of pay for the job and starting and finishing times.

Regulations made under section 11 of the 1994 Act require an employer to produce to an employee, who is a young person, a copy of an abstract of the Protection of Young Persons (Employment) Act, 1996, within a month of commencement of employment. Employers will ensure that this will be complied with.

In accordance with Regulations made under the Act, employers shall ensure that the Abstract of the Protection of Young Persons (Employment) Act, 1996, is on display in a prominent position.

Employers shall also ensure that the provisions of the Protection of Young Persons (Employment) Act, 1996, are complied with in relation to the employment of the young persons, with particular regard to hours of work, breaks and finishing times.

Employers shall further ensure that the provisions of the Organisation of Working Time Act, 1997, are complied with, with particular regard to annual leave entitlement, public holiday entitlement and payment of Sunday premium.

Employers shall ensure that the provision of sections 29 and 30 of the Education (Welfare) Act, 2000, are complied with. These sections, in summary, provide that a 16 or 17 year old, other than a person who is a registered student or who is engaged in or has completed a prescribed programme of education, training or instruction, may not be employed by an

F–108

employer unless the person is the holder of a certificate issued by the National Educational Welfare Board. The Act imposes on the Board a duty to provide for the continuing education and training of such young persons.

## 2. Rates of Pay

(i)    The rate of pay will be a matter for local agreement, whether made collectively or otherwise, having taken into account the provisions of the National Minimum Wage Act, 2000.

(ii)   Section 4 of the Payment of Wages Act, 1991, provides that every employer must arrange that a written statement of wages be given to every employee with every payment of wages. Employers shall ensure that all young persons employed are given such written statements of wages and deductions.

## 3. Induction Training

On commencement of employment, the young person shall receive appropriate training on all aspects of his/her employment. This process shall include the supply of written copies of-

(i)    this Code of Practice;

(ii)   the statement of the terms of the employment;

(iii)  a summary of the provisions of the Protection of Young Persons (Employment) Act, 1996; and

(iv)  a copy of any relevant Collective Agreement or Employment Regulation Order.

## 4. Study Time

Provision should be made for students with impending examinations. These should allow for study leave and leave to sit the exams, without having to work excessive hours in the period approaching the exams. Employers shall ensure that a student's job is protected in the event of his/her returning to work following study/exam leave.

Employees are required to give at least 4 weeks' notice of such leave.

## 5. Continuing Education and Training

Provision should also be made for young persons who, while they are not registered as full-time students in a school or other education institution, are engaged in education and training programmes. These should allow for reasonable flexibility in the number of working hours and the time of such work as the demands of any education or training programme require.

## 6. Right to Representation

In the event of the employee having a difficulty with any aspect of his/her contract of employment, the employer recognises the right of the employee to trade union representation.

## 7. Health and Safety

Employers shall ensure that the risk assessments in the Safety Statement required under the Safety, Health and Welfare at Work Act, [2005] should take account of the particular needs of young persons in employment, with particular regard to the Safety, Health & Welfare at Work (Children and Young Persons) Regulations, 1998.

## 8. Bullying, Sexual Harassment and Equality Issues

Explanations on these matters and details of internal grievance procedures shall be given in the training session.

## 9. Requirement to Work Beyond Grade

Employers shall specify in the terms of employment, the types of work that young persons may be asked to perform and prevent abuses by employers such as requiring the young person to perform tasks appropriate to other grades.

## 10. Consent of Parent or Guardian

Before employing the young person, the employer shall obtain the written permission of the parent or guardian of the young person.

In accordance with the Protection of Young Persons (Employment) Act, 1996, before employing the young person, the employer shall require the production of a copy of the birth certificate of, or other satisfactory evidence of age of the young person.

F–109

Obtaining the consent of a parent or guardian should also include consultation with the employer on arrangements to get the employee home after work.

## 11. Review of Code of Practice

The Code of Practice may be reviewed after six months in operation.

## 12. Signatories to the Code of Practice

I hereby agree to the Terms of the Code of Practice as set out above.

| | |
|---|---|
| (Sd.) Thomas A. Wall | Irish Congress of Trade Unions |
| (Sd.) John Power | Irish Hotels Federation |
| (Sd.) Frank Fell | Licensed Vintners Association |
| (Sd.) John Douglas | Mandate |
| (Sd.) Marie Danaswamy | National Parents Council post primary |
| (Sd.) Henry O'Neill | Restaurants Association of Ireland |
| (Sd.) Tadg O'Sullivan | Vintners Federation of Ireland |

Signed in the presence of Mr Tom Kitt T.D., Minister for Labour, Trade and Consumer Affairs, this 24th day of July, 2001.

Detach here (This part is to be retained by the Employee)
Code of Practice-Employment of Young Persons in Licensed Premises I have read and understand the Code of Practice and agree to adhere to its contents.

Date

Parental or Guardian consent

I agree to the employment of.................................with the above employer.

.............................................................
Signature of either parent or guardian

...................
Date

Detach here (This part is to be retained by the Employer)
Code of Practice-Employment of Young Persons in Licensed Premises I have read and understand the Code of Practice and agree to adhere to its contents.

Employee.............................................

Employer.............................................

Date ......................................................
Parental or Guardian consent

I agree to the employment of.................................with the above employer.

.............................................................
Signature of either parent or guardian

.......................
Date

GENERAL NOTE

These Regulations concern young persons (16 and 17 year olds) employed to carry out general  FC.505
duties in a licensed premises and provide that the young person may be required to work up to 11
p.m. in such premises on a day, which is not a day immediately preceding a school day, during a
school term where the young person is attending school. The Regulations also provide that, in
such circumstances, the young person may not commence work before 7 a.m. on the following
day.

These Regulations also provide that the employer of a young person employed to carry out
general duties in a licensed premises shall have regard to the Code of Practice concerning the
Employment of Young Persons in Licensed Premises, the terms of which are set out in the
Schedule to the Regulations.


# PROTECTION OF YOUNG PERSONS (EMPLOYMENT) ACT, 1996 (BAR APPRENTICES) REGULATIONS, 2001

## (S.I. No.351 of 2001)

**1.** These Regulations may be cited as the Protection of Young Persons  FC.601
(Employment) Act, 1996 (Bar Apprentices) Regulations, 2001.

**2.** In these Regulations—  FC.602

"licensed premises" means premises to which a licence (within the meaning
   of section 2 of the Intoxicating Liquor Act, 2000 (No. 17 of 2000)), is
   attached.

**3.** A person who employs a young person in a full time capacity as an appren-  FC.603
tice in a licensed premises may require the young person to work up to midnight
on any one day, where the young person

(a)  will not be required or permitted to commence work until 8 a.m. on the
     following day, and
(b)  is supervised by an adult.

GENERAL NOTE

These Regulations provide that a young person (a 16 or 17 year old), employed as an  FC.604
apprentice in a full-time capacity in a licensed premises, may be required to work up to
midnight on any one day and not before 8 a.m. on the following day provided that the
young person is supervised by an adult.

# PAYMENT OF WAGES ACT 1991

(1991 No. 25)

ARRANGEMENT OF SECTIONS

SECT.

ENACTMENTS REPEALED

An Act to Provide Further Protection for Employees in Relation to the Payment **GA.101** of Wages, to Facilitate the Payment of Wages Otherwise than in Cash, for that Purpose to Repeal the Truck Acts, 1831 to 1896, and Related Enactments and to Provide for Connected Matters.

[July 23, 1991]

GENERAL NOTE

According to the Minister for Labour (129 *Seanad Debates* Col. 77), the purpose of this Act was to **GA.102** repeal the Truck Acts and put in place new provisions for the payment of wages "which will meet current and future requirements." The Truck Acts outlawed the "truck system," which was the name given to a set of closely related arrangements whereby some form of consumption was tied to the employment contract. As Hilton, *The Truck System* (1960), explains (at p. 1):

"Until the late eighteenth or early nineteenth century, its most common form appears to have been payment of wages in goods, usually groceries, but occasionally cloth or the product of the employer's own firm. Alternatively, the employee was paid in tickets redeemable in goods at a store owned by his employer, or by a private shop-keeper who granted the employer a rebate on the employee's purchases. In the nineteenth century the truck system consisted mainly of compulsion to deal with the employer's grocery shop at risk of reprimand or discharge."

Many explanations have been offered for the development of such a system. For the Webbs **GA.103** (*Industrial Democracy* (1902) pp. 317–318) it was a method of circumventing a standard rate of wages set by collective bargaining. For Francis Walker (*The Wages Problem* (1877) pp. 343–344) it it was a monopsonistic device, a method of restricting labourers to their employers through debt. Others (see references in Hilton, *op. cit.*, p. 6, n. 3) interpreted the truck system as the outgrowth of a chronically inadequate supply of coins or of insufficient or imperfectly developed credit facilities. Hilton, however, concluded (*op. cit.* p. 40) that no single explanation of the truck system was sufficient but had no doubt that Alfred Marshall (*Principles of Economics* (1890) p. 580) was correct in describing it as a device for employers "getting back by underhand ways part of the wages which they nominally paid away." Marshall (*op. cit.* p. 581) in fact ranked the truck system with the old s.9

G–3

poor-law and unhealthful conditions of juvenile labour, as the chief cause of degradation of labourers in the early nineteenth century. It was a major cause of dissension and it is noteworthy that most of the eighteenth century British Combination Acts (e.g. Weavers' Combination Act 1726 (12 Geo. 1, c. 34), the provisions of which were extended to many other trades in 1749 by 22 Geo. II, c. 27) also prohibited masters from paying wages "by way of truck" (see Orth, *Combination and Conspiracy* (1991) pp. 11–19).

**GA.104**   Although in Britain anti-truck legislation dates back to 1465 (4 Edw. IV, c. 1), it was not dealt with in this jurisdiction until 1743 under an Act (17 Geo. II, c. 8) passed by the pre-Union Irish Parliament. Section 6 of this Act made it an offence, punishable by a £10 fine, for "any person or persons, concerned in employing any artificer, workman, servants or labourers, in any of the trades or manufactures of this Kingdom" to pay any such person their wages or any part thereof "either in goods or by way of truck, or in any other manner than in ready money." In 1831 the various British Acts prohibiting the truck system were repealed and a general prohibition of payment of wages otherwise than in the "current coin of the realm" was enacted (1 & 2 Will. IV, c. 37). The 1831 Act, largely through the efforts of O'Connell (see Hilton *op. cit.* p. 111), did not apply to Ireland and its provisions were only extended to this jurisdiction by the Truck (Amendment) Act 1887 (50 & 51 Vic., c. 46), by which time the system had virtually passed out of existence. In 1896 (59 & 60 Vic., c. 44) the related problem of arbitrary and excessive industrial fines and shop fees was brought within the scope of the legislation. See further, Greer and Nicholson *The Factory Acts in Ireland 1802-1914* (2002) pp.191–226.

**GA.105**   Employers had long regarded the provisions of the Truck Acts as being totally unsuited to the needs of modern employments and as a major barrier to the more widespread use of non-cash methods of wage payments. This was because payment by cheque was not regarded as payment in the current coin of the realm: see the unreported judgment of Hutton J. in the Chancery Division of the High Court of Justice in Northern Ireland in *Tipping v. Warne Surgical Products Ltd* (May 21, 1986). The Payment of Wages Act 1979 sought to address this issue by permitting employers to pay wages otherwise than in cash where the employees so agreed. The 1979 Act, however, stopped short of a fundamental review of the Truck Acts and allowed for unilateral rescission of an agreement on payment of wages by non-cash means. Employers continued to press for repeal of the Truck Acts (see FUE Bulletin, July 1987) and in November 1987 the Department of Labour issued a *Discussion Document* which, *inter alia*, examined the options for repeal of the Truck Acts and for new legislation governing the payment of wages. The views of all the interests concerned were sought and as part of the Programme for Economic and Social Progress the Minister for Labour undertook to finalise legislation which would facilitate the move towards cashless pay.

**GA.106**   The motivation for this Act stems from a variety of inter-related concerns (see 409 *Dáil Debates* Cols. 1246–1247). A survey in *European Industrial Relations Review* No. 161 (June 1987) had revealed that Ireland was very much behind its major trading partners and competitors in changing over to non-cash methods of wage payment. The high incidence of cash payments suggested to the Minister that many employers had yet to exploit the advantages offered by new technology and there were the inevitable security problems arising from armed robberies of payroll cash. For the Minister such a high level of cash wages clearly could not "but affect the cost competitiveness of business both here in Ireland and abroad." Additionally, the application of the legislation to all employees—the Truck Acts only applied to those engaged in manual labour—would "help to lessen some of the class distinctions in employment" (129 *Seanad Debates* Col. 105).

**GA.107**   Three basic rights are enshrined in this Act (and it should be noted that there are no qualifying periods of service or minimum hours thresholds):

(1) the right of every employee to a readily negotiable mode of wage payment;
(2) the right of every employee to protection against unlawful deductions;
(3) the right of every employee to a written statement of wages and any deductions therefrom.

**GA.108**   This Act, however, does not impose a mode of wage payment other than cash on an employee who has been entitled up to now to wages in cash, nor is the right removed to revert to payment in cash by unilaterally altering arrangements and agreements entered into under the 1979 Act. The transitional arrangements, which are contained in section 3, are intended to allow an employee currently paid in cash to continue to be so paid until such time as an alternative method is agreed with the employer. The Minister said (409 *Dáil Debates* Col. 1252) that he had examined the case against these transitional arrangements but was disinclined to accept it because of the "serious industrial relations and other difficulties" inherent in an approach based on compulsion. Another contentious issue was whether employees should have a right to time off for cashing cheques but the Minister indicated (129 *Seanad Debates* Col. 79) that this was an issue best left for discussion and arrangement between employers and employees at local level.

G–4

CITATION

See section 14.  **GA.109**

COMMENCEMENT

Signed by the President on July 23, 1991 and came into operation on January 1, 1992: see **GA.110**
S.I. No. 350 of 1991.

STATUTORY INSTRUMENTS

Payment of Wages Act 1991 (Commencement) Order 1991 (S.I. No. 350 of 1991).  **GA.111**
Payment of Wages (Appeals) Regulations 1991 (S.I. No. 351 of 1991).

PARLIAMENTARY DEBATES

129 *Seanad Debates* Cols. 73–111 (Second Stage)  **GA.112**
129 *Seanad Debates* Cols. 111–112 (Committee and Final Stages)
409 *Dáil Debates* Cols. 1245–1262 (Second Stage)
409 *Dáil Debates* Cols. 2196–220 (Second Stage resumed)
410 *Dáil Debates* Cols. 783–819 (Committee and Final Stages)
129 *Seanad Debates* Cols. 1651–1663 (Report and Final Stages)

Be it Enacted by the Oireachtas as Follows:  **GA.113**

# Interpretation

**1.**—(1) In this Act—  **GA.114**
"cash" means cash that is legal tender;
"contract of employment" means—
   (a)   a contract of service or of apprenticeship, and
   (b)   any other contract whereby an individual agrees with another person
         to do or perform personally any work or service for a third person
         (whether or not the third person is a party to the contract) whose status
         by virtue of the contract is not that of a client or customer of
         any profession or business undertaking carried on by the individual, and
         the person who is liable to pay the wages of the individual in respect
         of the work or service shall be deemed for the purposes of this Act to
         be his employer,
   whether the contract is express or implied and if express, whether it is oral
   or in writing;
"employee" means a person who has entered into or works under (or,
   where the employment has ceased, entered into or worked under) a
   contract of employment and references, in relation to an employer, to
   an employee shall be construed as references to an employee employed
   by that employer; and for the purpose of this definition, a person
   holding office under, or in the service of, the State (including a
   member of the Garda Síochána or the Defence Forces) or otherwise
   as a civil servant, within the meaning of the Civil Service Regulation
   Act, 1956, shall be deemed to be an employee employed by the State
   or the Government, as the case may be, and an officer or servant of a
   local authority for the purposes of the Local Government Act, 1941, a
   harbour authority, [the Health Service Executive] or a vocational
   education committee shall be deemed to be an employee employed
   by the authority, [Executive] or committee, as the case may be;
"employer", in relation to an employee, means the person with whom the
   employee has entered into or for whom the employee works under (or,
   where the employment has ceased, entered into or worked under) a
   contract of employment;
"the Minister" means the Minister for [Enterprise, Trade, and Employment];
"strike" and "industrial action" have the meanings assigned to them by the
   Industrial Relations Act, 1990;

"the Tribunal" means the Employment Appeals Tribunal;

"wages", in relation to an employee, means any sums payable to the employee by the employer in connection with his employment, including—

    (a)  any fee, bonus or commission, or any holiday, sick or maternity pay, or any other emolument, referable to his employment, whether payable under his contract of employment or otherwise, and

    (b)  any sum payable to the employee upon the termination by the employer of his contract of employment without his having given to the employee the appropriate prior notice of the termination, being a sum paid in lieu of the giving of such notice:

Provided however that the following payments shall not be regarded as wages for the purposes of this definition:

        (i)  any payment in respect of expenses incurred by the employee in carrying out his employment,

        (ii)  any payment by way of a pension, allowance or gratuity in connection with the death, or the retirement or resignation from his employment, of the employee or as compensation for loss of office,

        (iii)  any payment referable to the employee's redundancy,

        (iv)  any payment to the employee otherwise than in his capacity as an employee,

        (v)  any payment in kind or benefit in kind.

(2) Except in section 5(5)(f), a reference in this Act to an employer receiving a payment from an employee is a reference to his receiving such a payment in his capacity as the employee's employer.

(3) In this Act, a reference to a section is a reference to a section of this Act, unless it is indicated that reference to some other enactment is intended.

(4) In this Act, a reference to a subsection, paragraph or subparagraph is a reference to a subsection, paragraph or subparagraph of the provision in which the reference occurs, unless it is indicated that reference to some other provision is intended.

GENERAL NOTE

**GA.115**    "cash": this includes both notes and coins. By virtue of Council Regulation (EC) No. 974/98 of May 3, 1998 ([1998] O.J. L139/1) the currency of the State, with effect from January 1, 2002, is the euro. The notes come in denominations of 5, 10, 20, 50, 100, 200 and 500 euro and the coins come in denominations of 1 and 2 euro and 1, 2, 5, 10, 20 and 50 cent. By virtue of s.8 of the Decimal Currency Act 1969, as amended by s.127 of the Central Bank Act 1989, coins are not legal tender for an amount in excess of twenty times the face value of the coin.

    "contract of employment": this definition is much wider than that contained in the Unfair Dismissals Act 1977 in that it specifically includes persons who would be regarded as being employed under a contract for services. Excepted are cases where the status of the party for whom the services are being performed is that of a client or customer of any profession or business undertaking carried on by the individual.

    "employee": this definition, as amended by virtue of s.66 of the Health Act 2004, makes it clear that all persons employed by or under the State, not just those standing designated under s.17 of the Industrial Relations Act 1969, are included. The definition, however, does not provide that, in the case of the death of the employee concerned, it should extend to the employee's personal representative. *Quaere* whether a claim under the 1991 Act comes within the ambit of s.7 of the Civil Liability Act 1961 which makes provision for the survival of actions which are vested in the deceased for the benefit of his or her estate.

**GA.116**    "the Minister": this definition was amended by virtue of the Labour (Transfer of Departmental Administration and Ministerial Functions) Order 1993 (S.I. No. 18 of 1993), the Industry and Commerce (Alteration of Name of Department and Title of Minister) Order 1993 (S.I. No. 19 of 1993) and the Enterprise and Employment (Alteration of Name of Department and Title of Minister) Order 1997 (S.I. No. 305 of 1997).

G–6

"strike": this is defined in s.8 of the Industrial Relations Act 1990 as meaning:

"a cessation of work by any number or body of workers acting in combination or a concerted **GA.117** refusal or a refusal under a common understanding of any number of workers to continue to work for their employer done as a means of compelling their employer, or to aid other workers in compelling their employer, to accept or not to accept terms or conditions of or affecting employment."

"industrial action": this is defined in s.8 of the Industrial Relations Act 1990 as meaning:

"any action which affects, or is likely to affect, the terms or conditions, whether express or implied, of a contract and which is taken by any number or body of workers acting in combination or under a common understanding as a means of compelling their employer, or to aid other workers in compelling their employer, to accept or not to accept terms or conditions of or affecting employment".

"the Tribunal": the Employment Appeals Tribunal was established under section 39 of the Redun- **GA.118** dancy Payments Act 1967 and was originally known as the Redundancy Appeals Tribunal. Its name was changed by s.18 of the Unfair Dismissals Act 1977. It deals with disputes arising under the Redundancy Payments Acts 1967–2003, the Minimum Notice and Terms of Employment Acts 1973–2001, the Unfair Dismissals Acts 1977–2001 and the Protection of Employees (Employers' Insolvency) Act 1984. It also has appellate jurisdiction under the Terms of Employment (Information) Act 1994, the Maternity Protection Acts 1994 and 2004, the Adoptive Leave Act 1995, the Protection of Young Persons (Employment) Act 1996, the Parental Leave Act 1998 and the Carer's Leave Act 2001. The Tribunal, which is an independent body bound to act judicially, consists of a Chairman, 31 vice-Chairmen and a panel of 72 other members (36 nominated by the Irish Congress of Trade Unions and 36 by organisations representative of employers). The Tribunal sits in divisions, each consisting of either the Chairman or a vice-Chairman and two other members, drawn from each side of the panel.

"wages": In *Sullivan v Department of Education* [1998] E.L.R. 217 the Tribunal took the word **GA.119** "payable" to mean "properly payable", consequently it was not simply a matter of what may have been paid from the outset but all sums to which an employee is properly entitled. This definition also makes it clear that payments in lieu of notice are "wages"-"such payments are moneys which the employee would have earned as wages had he worked out his notice" (per the Minister for Labour at 410 *Dáil Debates* Col. 786). In Britain there had been conflicting EAT decisions as to whether "pay in lieu of notice" fell within the definition of "wages" in the Wages Act 1986 (see *Foster Wheeler (London) Ltd v Jackson* [1990] I.C.R. 757; *Delaney v Staples* [1990] I.R.L.R. 86; *Kournavous v J.R Masterton (Demolition) Ltd* [1990] I.C.R. 387; *Janstorp International (UK) Ltd v Allen* [1990] I.R.L.R. 417) and in *Delaney v Staples* [1992] 1 A.C. 687 the House of Lords finally ruled that a claim could not be brought under the Wages Act 1986 (see now the Employment Rights Act 1996) to an Industrial Tribunal in respect of a failure to pay wages in lieu of notice. Were the English EAT decision in *Kent Management Services v Butterfield* [1992] I.R.L.R. 394 to be followed in this jurisdiction, the absence of a contractual obligation to pay would not be fatal to a claim in respect of deductions under the Act. Here the company commissions were defined as discretionary and *ex gratia* and as not constituting a contractual arrangement with the employees concerned. The anticipation of both parties, however, was that commission which had been earned would be paid. Withholding commission due on fees which the company had already received was, therefore, an unlawful deduction from wages. The expression "payment in respect of expenses incurred by the employee in carrying out his employment" in the similarly worded s.7(2)(b) of the Wages Act 1986 was considered by the English EAT in *London Borough of Southwark v O'Brien* [1996] I.R.L.R. 420. For a payment to be "in respect of expenses" it was not necessary to show that what was paid was a reimbursement of the precise amount expended by the employee. "In respect of" meant "referring to" or "relating to" or "concerning in a general way". Payment of a mileage allowance did not cease to be in respect of expenses merely because it was found to be generous. Consequently, notwithstanding the profit element in the allowance, it was a payment in respect of expenses, not "wages", and thus the withholding of the allowance could not be a deduction made unlawful by the Act.

## Modes of payment of wages

**2.** —(1) Wages may be paid by and only by one or more of the following **GA.120** modes:

(a) a cheque, draft or other bill of exchange within the meaning of the Bills of Exchange Act, 1882,

(b) a document issued by a person who maintains an account with the Central Bank of Ireland or a holder of a licence under section 9 of the Central Bank Act 1971, which, though not such a bill of exchange as aforesaid, is intended to enable a person to obtain payment from that bank or that holder of the amount specified in the document,

(c) a draft payable on demand drawn by a holder of such a licence as aforesaid upon himself whether payable at the head office or some other office bank to which the licence relates,

(d) a postal, money or paying order, or a warrant, or any other like document, issued by or drawn on An Post or a document issued by an officer of a Minister of the Government that is intended to enable a person to obtain payment from that Minister of the Government of the sum specified in the document,

(e) a document issued by a person who maintains an account with a trustee savings bank within the meaning of the Trustee Savings Bank Act 1989, that is intended to enable a person to obtain payment from the bank of the sum specified in the document,

(f) a credit transfer or another mode of payment whereby an amount is credited to an account specified by the employee concerned.

(g) cash,

(h) any other mode of payment standing specified for the time being by regulations made by the Minister after consultation with the Minister for Finance.

(2) Where wages fall to be paid to an employee by a mode other than cash at a time when, owing to a strike or other industrial action affecting a financial institution, cash, is not readily available to the employee, the employer concerned shall, if the employee consents, pay the wages by another mode (other than cash) specified in subsection (1) and, if the employee does not so consent, pay them in cash.

(3) An employer who pays wages to an employee otherwise than by a mode specified in subsection (1) or contravenes subsection (2) shall be guilty of an offence and shall be liable on summary conviction to a fine not exceeding £1,000 [€1,269.74].

GENERAL NOTE

**GA.121**    This section requires every employer to pay wages by one of the modes listed herein. All the recognised means of paying money are covered and, since "rapid future change in this area is to be anticipated because of advances in electronic data processing," the Minister is given power to add additional modes of wage payment "if and when new methods of money transfer are developed and gain public acceptance" (*per* the Minister for Labour at 129 *Seanad Debates* Col. 79).

Under the Bills of Exchange Act 1882 a cheque is defined in s.73 as "a bill of exchange drawn on a banker payable on demand" and a bill of exchange is itself defined in s.3(1) as "an unconditional order in writing, addressed by one person to another, signed by the person giving it, requiring the person to whom it is addressed to pay on demand or at a fixed or determinable future time a sum certain in money to or to the order of a specified person, or to bearer." A bill of exchange is sometimes referred to as a "draft," but in commercial usage the term "draft" is ordinarily used to denote an unaccepted bill (see *Chalmers and Guest on Bills of Exchange* (14th ed., 1991), p. 1991). Since a banker's draft is drawn by a banker upon itself it is neither a bill nor a cheque and it is therefore dealt with separately in paragraph (c). The Minister also assured Deputies (see 410 *Dáil Debates* Col. 792) that paragraph (f) was sufficiently broad to encompass the lodgement of wage payments to a credit union as well as to a building society.

## Repeal of Truck Acts, 1831 to 1896 and related enactments

**GA.122**    **3.** —(1) The enactments specified in column (2) of the Schedule to this Act are hereby repealed to the extent specified in column (3) of that Schedule.

(2) Notwithstanding any provision of this Act—

(a) where, immediately before the commencement of this Act, an employee's wages were being paid to him in cash, the employer shall, while the employee is in the employment concerned, continue to pay those wages to him in cash unless any other mode of payment specified in section 2 is agreed upon by the employer or an organisation representative of employers (of which the employer is a member) and the employee or an organisation representative of employees (of which the employee is a member), and

(b) where, immediately before such commencement, an employee's wages were being paid to him, pursuant to section 3 of the Payment of Wages Act, 1979, by an instrument or mode of payment to which that section applied, then, if after such commencement, the agreement or other arrangement authorising payment of the wages by the instrument or mode aforesaid is terminated in a manner specified in that section, the employer shall pay those wages to him in cash unless any other mode of payment specified in section 2 is agreed upon as aforesaid.

(3) An employer who contravenes subsection (2) shall be guilty of an offence and shall be liable on summary conviction to a fine not exceeding £1,000 [€1,269.74].

GENERAL NOTE

This section repeals the Truck Acts but also provides transitional arrangements for employees **GA.123** currently paid in cash and for manual workers who have agreed to non-cash wages under the Payment of Wages Act 1979. The Minister (410 *Dáil Debates* Col. 806) made it clear that he was not prepared to countenance a move to non-cash methods of payment that was based on compulsion. He said that many employees, in accordance with agreements made with their employers under s.3 of the Payment of Wages Act 1979, have been and are being paid wages by a method other than cash. "At present under such arrangements those employees have a right to revert to cash payment of wages at the end of the period of such agreement or, when there is no specific termination date for the agreement, at any time by giving the employer four week's notice of the wish to revert to cash payment of wages" (*ibid.* Col. 805). The purpose of subs.(2)(b) is to guarantee for employees arrangements for reversion to cash payment similar to those that they accepted at the time they agreed to non-cash payment of wages under the 1979 Act.

An amendment to insert the words "in writing" after the words "agreed upon" in subs.(2)(a) was put and declared lost after the Minister said (*ibid.* Col. 804) that he was disposed to the view that the parties to the agreement were those "best qualified to decide whether agreement should be oral or in writing." He did not intend to "impose the level of formality involved in drawing up a written agreement in every instance."

## Statements of wages and deductions from wages

**4.** —(1) An employer shall give or cause to be given to an employee a state- **GA.124** ment in writing specifying clearly the gross amount of the wages payable to the employee and the nature and amount of any deduction therefrom and the employer shall take such reasonable steps as are necessary to ensure that both the matter to which the statement relates and the statement are treated confidentially by the employer and his agents and by any other employees.

(2) A statement under this section shall be given to the employee concerned—

(a) if the relevant payment is made by a mode specified in section 2 (1) (f), as soon as may be thereafter,

(b) if the payment is made by a mode of payment specified in regulations under section 2 (1) (h), at such time as may be specified in the regulations,

G–9

(c) if the payment is made by any other mode of payment, at the time of the payment.

(3) Where a statement under this section contains an error or omission, the statement shall be regarded as complying with the provisions of this section if it is shown that the error or omission was made by way of a clerical mistake or was otherwise made accidentally and in good faith.

(4) An employer who contravenes subsection (1) or (2) shall be guilty of an offence and shall be liable on summary conviction to a fine not exceeding £1,000 [€1,269.74].

GENERAL NOTE

**GA.125**    This section imposes on employers an obligation to give to each employee a written statement of wages and deductions. The statement must be given to the employee at the time of wage payment, except in the case of payment by credit transfer, when the statement should be given as soon as possible thereafter. The Minister said (129 *Seanad Debates* Col. 80) that the exception for credit transfer was necessary due to the nature of the technology:

"The employer is unlikely to know the time of the credit transfer in advance. Indeed, computerised credit transfers are often transacted electronically outside normal business hours when off-peak electricity is available."

Subsection (1) was amended at Committee Stage to place beyond doubt the intention of the section- "that a pay statement will clearly and specifically identify the gross amount of the wages as well as the nature and amount of each deduction" (see the Minister for Labour at 129 *Seanad Debates* Col. 1652).

## Regulation of certain deductions made and payments received by employers

**GA.126**    **5.** —(1) An employer shall not make a deduction from the wages of an employee (or receive any payment from an employee) unless—

(a) the deduction (or payment) is required or authorised to be made by virtue of any statute or any instrument made under statute,

(b) the deduction (or payment) is required or authorised to be made by virtue of a term of the employee's contract of employment included in the contract before, and in force at the time of, the deduction or payment, or

(c) in the case of a deduction, the employee has given his prior consent in writing to it.

(2) An employer shall not make a deduction from the wages of an employee in respect of—

(a) any act or omission of the employee, or

(b) any goods or services supplied to or provided for the employee by the employer the supply or provision of which is necessary to the employment,

unless—

(i) the deduction is required or authorised to be made by virtue of a term (whether express or implied and, if express, whether oral or in writing) of the contract of employment made between the employer and the employee, and

(ii) the deduction is of an amount that is fair and reasonable having regard to all the circumstances (including the amount of the wages of the employee), and

(iii) before the time of the act or omission or the provision of the goods or services, the employee has been furnished with—

(I) in case the term referred to in subparagraph (i) is in writing, a copy thereof,

(II) in any other case, notice in writing of the existence and effect of the term, and

(iv) in case the deduction is in respect of an act or omission of the employee, the employee has been furnished, at least one week before the making of the deduction, with particulars in writing of the act or omission and the amount of the deduction, and

G–10/1

    (v)  in case the deduction is in respect of compensation for loss or damage sustained by the employer as a result of an act or omission of the employee, the deduction is of an amount not exceeding the amount of the loss or the cost of the damage, and

    (vi)  in case the deduction is in respect of goods or services supplied or provided as aforesaid, the deduction is of an amount not exceeding the cost to the employer of the goods or services, and

    (vii) the deduction or, if the total amount payable to the employer by the employee in respect of the act or omission or the goods or services is to be so paid by means of more than one deduction from the wages of the employee, the first such deduction is made not later than 6 months after the act or omission becomes known to the employer or, as the case may be, after the provision of the goods or services.

(3) (a) An employer shall not receive a payment from an employee in respect of a matter referred to in subsection (2) unless, if the payment were a deduction, it would comply with that subsection.

  (b)  Where an employer receives a payment in accordance with paragraph (a) he shall forthwith give a receipt for the payment to the employee.

(4) A term of a contract of employment or other agreement whereby goods or services are supplied to or provided for an employee be an employer in consideration of the making of a deduction by the employer from the wages of the employee or the making of a payment to the employer by the employee shall not be enforceable by the employer unless the supply or provision and the deduction or payment complies with subsection (2).

(5) Nothing in this section applies to—

  (a)  a deduction made by an employer from the wages of an employee, or any payment received from an employee by an employer, where—

    (i)  the purpose of the deduction or payment is the reimbursement of the employer in respect of—

    (I)   any overpayment of wages, or

    (II)  any overpayment in respect of expenses incurred by the employee in carrying out his employment,

       made (for any reason) by the employer to the employee, and

    (ii)  the amount of the deduction or payment does not exceed the amount of the overpayment,

    or

  (b)  a deduction made by an employer from the wages of an employee, or any payment received from an employee by an employer, in consequence of any disciplinary proceedings if those proceedings were held by virtue of a statutory provision, or

  (c)  a deduction made by an employer from the wages of an employee in pursuance of a requirement imposed on the employer by virtue of any statutory provision to deduct and pay to a public authority, being a Minister of the Government, the Revenue Commissioners or a local authority for the purposes of the Local Government Act, 1941, amounts determined by that authority as being due to it from the employee, if the deduction is made in accordance with the relevant determination of that authority, or

  (d)  a deduction made by an employer from the wages of an employee in pursuance of any arrangements—

(i) which are in accordance with a term of a contract made between the employer and the employee to whose inclusion in the contract the employee has given his prior consent in writing, or

(ii) to which the employee has otherwise given his prior consent in writing,

and under which the employer deducts and pays to a third person amounts, being amounts in relation to which he has received a notice in writing from that person stating that they are amounts due to him from the employee, if the deduction is made in accordance with the notice and the amount thereof is paid to the third person not later than the date on which it is required by the notice to be so paid, or

(e) a deduction made by an employer from the wages of an employee, or any payment received from an employee by his employer, where the employee has taken part in a strike or other industrial action and the deduction is made or the payment has been required by the employer on account of the employee's having taken part in that strike or other industrial action, or

(f) a deduction made by an employer from the wages of an employee with his prior consent in writing, or any payment received from an employee by an employer, where the purpose of the deduction or payment is the satisfaction (whether wholly or in part) of an order of a court or tribunal requiring the payment of any amount by the employee to the employer, or

(g) a deduction made by an employer from the wages of an employee where the purpose of the deduction is the satisfaction (whether wholly or in part) of an order of a court or tribunal requiring the payment of any amount by the employer to the court or tribunal or a third party out of the wages of the employee.

(6) Where—

(a) the total amount of any wages that are paid on any occasion by an employer to an employee is less than the total amount of wages that is properly payable by him to the employee on that occasion (after making any deductions therefrom that fall to be made and are in accordance with this Act), or

(b) none of the wages that are properly payable to an employee by an employer on any occasion (after making any such deductions as aforesaid) are paid to the employee,then, except in so far as the deficiency or non-payment is attributable to an error of computation, the amount of the deficiency or non-payment shall be treated as a deduction made by the employer from the wages of the employee on the occasion.

GENERAL NOTE

**GA.127**     This section is concerned with "deductions" from an employee's wages. The section also precludes an employer from paying wages in full without deduction but then receiving a payment from the employee. Essentially the section prohibits an employer from making a deduction or receiving any payment unless the deduction or payment is required by statute, such as PAYE and PRSI; it is authorised by a term in the contract of employment, such as a pension contribution; or it is a deduction to which the employee has consented in writing, such as a trade union subscription under a "check off" system. According to the English EAT in *Potter v. Hunt Contracts Ltd* [1992] I.R.L.R.108, when considering the similarly worded provisions of section 1(1) of the Wages Act 1986, to fulfil the condition in paragraph (c) of subsection (1) there must be a document which clearly states that the deduction is to be made from the employee's wages. It must also make clear that the employee agrees to the deduction being made from that source. Where there is contractual authority for the type of deduction made, it is submitted that the rights commissioners (see section 6) are entitled to embark on a factual enquiry to discover whether the sum deducted actually fell within the contractual provisions: see *Fairfield v. Skinner* [1992] I.C.R 836. In *Ryanair Ltd v Downey* PW6/2006, the Employment Appeals Tribunal held that the fact that a clause in the employee's contract provided for a deduction did not of itself justify the deduction. For the deduction to be lawful, the employer must comply with the relevant provisions of subs.(2), in that case the giving of one week's notice before making the deduction and complying with the requirement that the amount of the deduction be fair and reasonable.

All other deductions are prohibited save those specified in subsection (5), such as deduc-**GA.128** tions or payments the purpose of which is the reimbursement of the employer in respect

of any over payment of wages or expenses or deductions or payments arising from the employee's taking part in a strike or other industrial action (on which see *Beaumont Hospital v McNally* PN29/ 1996). The section also contains further restrictions which apply to two particular categories of deduction. The first is where the deduction is made in respect of either goods or services supplied by the employer which are necessary to the employment. The Minister (129 *Seanad Debates* Col. 80) gave as examples the employee's contribution towards the purchase or cleaning of work clothes or the supply of transport to work by the employer. The second is where the deduction is made in respect of any act or omission of the employee. In both respects the deduction is only permitted if all the conditions specified in subs.(2) are satisfied and in particular that the deduction is of an amount that is "fair and reasonable having regard to all the circumstances (including the amount of the wages of the employee)": for an example of a deduction not being found "fair and reasonable" see *Riley v Joseph Frisby Ltd* [1982] I.R.L.R. 479.

Paragraph (vi) of subs.(2) was amended at Committee Stage to allow for collection by the employer of second and subsequent installments of a particular deduction over a long duration. It does require, however, that the first installment of the deduction must be made by the employer within the six month period provided for. The Minister said (129 *Seanad Debates* Col. 1653) that the purpose of the amendment was to allow employees to have deductions spread over a long period so as to keep the weekly deductions from wages at a minimum.

In relation to subs.(5)(a) the English EAT in *Home Office v Ayres* [1992] I.C.R 175, when considering **GA.129** the similarly worded provisions of s.1(5)(a) of the Wages Act 1986, has held that an employer is only allowed to make a deduction from wages in respect of an overpayment where the deduction is a lawful deduction and the reimbursement is of monies to which the employer is lawfully entitled. If the reasoning in this case were to be applied in this jurisdiction it should follow that the word "lawful" must be read into each of the paragraphs (a)–(g) inclusive. It was for this reason, however, that the English EAT decided not to follow the *Ayres* decision in *Sunderland Polytechnic v Evans* [1993] I.C.R. 392; see also, *SIP (Industrial Products) v Swinn* [1994] I.R.L.R. 323. It should be noted that the *Evans* decision turned on the fact that there had been clear statements by responsible ministers during the passage of the Wages Act through Parliament which made it plain that there was no intention to give industrial tribunals jurisdiction to determine whether a deduction from wages by reason of industrial action was contractually authorised. No such statements were made in either the Dáil or the Seanad.

This issue has been further considered in *Gill v Ford Motor Co Ltd.* and *Wong v BAE Systems Operations Ltd.*, both reported at [2004] I.R.L.R. 840. In the former, the claimants had their pay for a particular shift stopped because of their alleged involvement in industrial action which had brought the assembly line to a halt. The claimants denied being involved. In the latter, the claimants received deductions from their wages in connection with what the employer considered to have been an over-payment of bonus the previous month. In both cases, their claims to an employment tribunal were dismissed on the basis that the British equivalent of subs.(5)(a) and (c) applied. On appeal, Beatson J., giving the judgment of the English EAT, said that the tribunals had been wrong to refuse to make findings of fact to determine whether they had jurisdiction. The "jurisdictional facts" were, in the former, whether the claimants had taken part in industrial action and, in the latter, whether there had been an overpayment of wages. It was only when those facts had been established, could a tribunal look at the employer's motivation for the deduction. He added that investigating the "jurisdictional facts" need not involve investigating whether the particular deduction was contractually authorised.

In relation to subs.(5)(g) the Minister said (129 *Seanad Debates* Col. 1054) that it was the intention to exclude these deductions from the complaints procedure because any complaint which an employee might have about the level or frequency of an attachment of earnings order would be appropriate only to the court that made the order. He emphasised, however, that these deductions were only excluded if the employer deducted the amount required of him by the order. If he deducted a higher amount the provisions of the Act would apply and an aggrieved employee would have a right of complaint under s.6.

Another question, and one that had given rise to a conflict of opinion in Britain, was whether non- **GA.130** payment of "wages" was a "deduction." In *Delaney v Staples* [1991] 2 Q.B. 47, the claimant had been summarily dismissed and at the time of dismissal was owed £55.00 in commission and holiday pay. These payments were never made and she presented a complaint under the Wages Act 1986 (which, in similar but not identical terms, prohibited deductions from wages). The English EAT held that non-payment was not a "deduction" and therefore the Industrial Tribunal had no jurisdiction to make an award for non-payment of wages (see also *Barlit v Whittle* [1990] I.R.L.R. 79, and *Alsop v Star Vehicle Contracts* [1990] I.R.L.R. 83.) The Court of Appeal, however, preferred the views expressed in *Greg May (Carpet Fitters and Contractors) v Dring* [1990] I.R.L.R. 19 and *Kournavous v J.R Masterton (Demolition)* [1990] I.C.R. 387, and held that the tribunal could entertain "any claim by an employee that his employer failed to pay him at the appropriate time the full amount of the wages, as defined, which he ought then to have been paid." This reasoning would seem to apply a fortiori to this Act given the specific wording of subs.(6)(b). Indeed it is difficult to discern any underlying policy reason

G–13

why a distinction should be drawn between the underpaid and the non-paid. To say to the latter that he or she has to go to the District Court hardly seems sensible and would give rise to undesirable practical consequences. So, in *Morgan v West Glamorgan County Council* [1995] I.R.L.R. 68, a reduction in an employee's salary consequent upon a demotion for disciplinary reasons which the employer wrongly thought that it was entitled to impose was held to be a "deduction" even though the employee might have had a claim for damages for breach of contract. Similarly, in *International Packaging Corporation (UK) Ltd v Balfour* [2003] I.R.L.R. 11, a reduction in the applicant's pay following the unilateral introduction of short-time working was held to amount to an unauthorised deduction from wages. The Employment Appeal Tribunal sitting in Scotland were of the opinion that a reduction in working hours was plainly a variation of a contract of employment and unless expressly catered for within the contract, or allowed by implication within the terms of the contract, any actual deduction of wages, even if related to hours worked, was not authorised by statute and could only be achieved by agreement. Conversely in *Hussman Manufacturing Ltd v Weir* [1998] I.R.L.R. 288, where the employer had the right under the contract of employment to change an employee's working hours, the consequent reduction in income did not amount to a deduction from wages. See also *Sullivan v Department of Education* [1998] E.L.R. 217 where the Employment Appeal Tribunal held that, if employees do not receive from the outset what is "properly payable" to them, then this could amount to a deduction within the meaning of the Act. The importance of establishing what remuneration was "properly payable" was emphasised by Finnegan P. in *Dunnes Stores (Cornelscourt) Ltd v Lacey*, unreported, High Court, December 9, 2005.

If this interpretation is correct it means that the rights commissioners have been conferred with jurisdiction to deal with all complaints concerning non-payment of wages, which term is defined in s.2 as "any sums payable to the employee by the employer in connection with his employment" including holiday pay, as well as deductions therefrom.

## Complaints by employees in relation to contraventions of section 5 by their employers

GA.131    **6.** —(1) An employee may present a complaint to a rights commissioner that his employer has contravened section 5 in relation to him and, if he does so, the commissioner shall give the parties an opportunity to be heard by him and to present to him any evidence relevant to the complaint, shall give a decision in writing in relation to it and shall communicate the decision to the parties.

(2) Where a rights commissioner decides, as respects a complaint under this section in relation to a deduction made by an employer from the wages of an employee or the receipt from an employee by an employer of a payment, that the complaint is well-founded in regard to the whole or a part of the deduction or payment, the commissioner shall order the employer to pay to the employee compensation of such amount (if any) as he thinks reasonable in the circumstances not exceeding—

(a)  the net amount of the wages (after the making of any lawful deduction therefrom) that—

(i)   in case the complaint related to a deduction, would have been paid to the employee in respect of the week immediately preceding the date of the deduction if the deduction had not been made, or

(ii)  in case the complaint related to a payment, were paid to the employee in respect of the week immediately preceding the date of payment,

or

(b)  if the amount of the deduction or payment is greater than the amount referred to in paragraph (a), twice the former amount.

(3) (a) A rights commissioner shall not give a decision under this section in relation to a deduction or payment referred to in subsection (2) at any time after the commencement of the hearing of proceedings in a court brought by the employee concerned in respect of the deduction or payment.

(b) An employee shall not be entitled to recover any amount in proceedings in a court in respect of such a deduction or payment as aforesaid at any time after a rights commissioner has given a decision under this section in relation to the deduction or payment.

(4) A rights commissioner shall not entertain a complaint under this section unless it is presented to him within the period of 6 months beginning on the date of the contravention to which the complaint relates or (in a case where the rights commissioner is satisfied that exceptional circumstances prevented the presentation of the complaint within the period aforesaid) such further period not exceeding 6 months as the rights commissioner considers reasonable.

(5) (a) A complaint shall be presented by giving notice thereof in writing to a rights commissioner and the notice shall contain such particulars and be in such form as may be specified from time to time by the Minister.

(b) A copy of a notice under paragraph (a) shall be given to the other party concerned by the rights commissioner concerned.

(6) Proceedings under this section before a rights commissioner shall be conducted in public unless, and to the extent that, the commissioner, on application to him in that behalf by a party to the proceedings, decides otherwise.

(7) A rights commissioner shall furnish the Tribunal with a copy of any decision given by him under subsection (1).

(8) The Minister may by regulations provide for any matters relating to proceedings under this section that he considers appropriate.

GENERAL NOTE

This section provides for a complaints procedure for employees who have been subject to **GA.132** unlawful deductions. The right of complaint in the first instance is to a rights commissioner with a right of appeal (see s.7) to the Employment Appeals Tribunal. The office of rights commissioner was first created by the Industrial Relations Act 1969. At present there are eight commissioners whose function under the 1969 Act is to investigate trade disputes which are not connected with rates of pay, hours of work or annual holidays of a body of workers. They also have certain functions under the Unfair Dismissals Acts 1977–2001, the Terms of Employment (Information) Act 1994, the Maternity Protection Acts 1994 and 2004, the Adoptive Leave Acts 1995 and 2005, the Protection of Young Persons (Employment) Act 1996, the Organisation of Working Time Act 1997, the Parental Leave Act 1998, the National Minimum Wage Act 2000, the Carer's Leave Act 2001, the Protection of Employees (Part-Time Work) Act 2001, the Protection of Employees (Fixed-Term Work) Act 2003 and the Safety, Health and Welfare at Work Act 2005. By virtue of s.35(1) of the Industrial Relations Act 1990, rights commissioners operate as a service of the Labour Relations Commission. On the role of the rights commissioner see Kelly "The Rights Commissioner: Conciliator, Mediator or Arbitrator" in *Industrial Relations in Ireland: Contemporary Issues and Developments* (Department of Industrial Relations UCD, 1989) and Walker "An Analysis of Referrals and Results of Disputes and Claims to Four Rights Commissioners" (1986) 5 J.I.S.L.L. 67.

## Appeal from decision of rights commissioner

**7.**—(1) A party concerned may appeal to the Tribunal from a decision of a **GA.133** rights commissioner under section 6 and, if he does so, the Tribunal shall give the parties an opportunity to be heard by it and to present to it any evidence relevant to the appeal, shall make a determination in writing in relation to the appeal affirming, varying or setting aside the decision and shall communicate the determination to the parties.

(2) An appeal under this section shall be initiated by a party by his giving, within 6 weeks of the date on which the decision to which it relates was communicated to him—

> (a) a notice in writing to the Tribunal containing such particulars (if any) as may be specified in regulations under subsection (3) and stating the intention of the party concerned to appeal against the decision, and
>
> (b) a copy of the notice to the other party concerned.

(3) The Minister may by regulations provide for all or any of the following matters in relation to proceedings before the Tribunal and for anything consequential thereon or incidental or ancillary thereto:

> (a) the procedure in relation to all matters concerning the initiation and the hearing by the Tribunal of appeals under this section,
>
> (b) the times and places of hearings of such appeals,
>
> (c) the representation of the parties to such appeals,
>
> (d) the publication and notification of determinations of the Tribunal,
>
> (e) the particulars to be contained in a notice under subsection (2),
>
> (f) the award by the Tribunal of costs and expenses in relation to such appeals and the payment thereof,
>
> (g) the extension by the Tribunal of the time for initiating such appeals.

(4) (a) The Minister may, at the request of the Tribunal, refer a question of law arising in proceedings before it to the High Court for determination by it and the determination of the High Court shall be final and conclusive.

> (b) A party to proceedings before the Tribunal may appeal to the High Court from a determination of the Tribunal on a point of law and the determination of the High Court shall be final and conclusive.

(5) Section 39(17) of the Redundancy Payments Act, 1967, shall apply in relation to proceedings before the Tribunal under this Act as it applies to matters referred to it under that section.

GENERAL NOTE

**GA.134**  This section provides for an appeals procedure, first to the Employment Appeals Tribunal and then on a point of law only to the High Court, whose decision is "final and conclusive." Although the Rules of the Superior Courts do not specifically provide for appeals under this Act, it is suggested that any such appeal be brought by special summons, by analogy with the procedure set out in RSC 1986, Order 105. In the absence of any specific rule of court, any such appeal need only be brought within a reasonable time: *per* McCracken J. in his *ex tempore* ruling in *McGaley v Liebherr Container Cranes Ltd* (2001/234 Sp) delivered on October 12, 2001. The Tribunal has held that subs.(2), by the use of the word "shall", contains a mandatory requirement of service on the other party concerned within the six week period: see *Shahid Sultan v Nasem* [2001] E.L.R. 302, *Marrinan v ESAT Telecommunications Ltd* PW64/2001, *Garrigan v Irish Prison Service* PW11/2003 and *The Garda Commissioner v Galvin* PW31/2005. The use of the word "his" before the word "giving" suggests that there is also a requirement that the party personally serve the copy on the other party and that it is not sufficient that service is effected by the Tribunal: see *Riehn v Royale* PW21/2005. It is also submitted that, following *Walsh v H.R. Holfeld Hydraulics Ltd*, Circuit Court, April 25, 1985 (reproduced in Madden and Kerr, *Unfair Dismissal: Cases and Commentary* (1st ed., 1990), p. 26), time begins to run from the date the written determination is communicated to the party concerned and not from the date when the decision is verbally communicated to the parties.

The Payment of Wages (Appeals) Regulations 1991 (S.I. No. 351 of 1991) provide, in reg.2, that a notice under subs.(2) in relation to an appeal shall contain:

> (a) the names, addresses and descriptions of the parties to the proceedings to which the appeal relates,
>
> (b) the date of the decision to which the appeal relates and the name of the rights commissioner who made the decision, and

(c) a brief outline of the grounds of appeal.

The circumstances in which the High Court will overturn a decision of a specialist tribunal such as the Employment Appeals Tribunal have been considered in many cases: see for example, *Henry Denny & Sons (Ireland) Ltd v Minister for Social Welfare* [1998] 1 I.R. 34, and in particular the comments of Hamilton C.J. at 37. In considering whether to allow an appeal against a decision of such a tribunal, the High Court must consider whether that body based its decision on an identifiable error of law or on an unsustainable finding of fact. A decision cannot be challenged on the grounds of irrationality if there is any relevant material to support it: see further, *Mulcahy v Waterford Leader Partnership Ltd* [2002] E.L.R. 12 (O'Sullivan J.) and *Thompson v Tesco Ireland Ltd* [2003] E.L.R. 21 (Lavan J.). In *National University of Ireland, Cork v Ahern* [2005] 2 I.R. 577, the Supreme Court held that, although findings of fact must be accepted by the High Court on appeal, that court could still examine the basis upon which those facts were found. The relevance or admissibility of the matters relied on in determining the facts was a question of law.

Regulation 5(1) provides that, if a party receives a copy of a notice of appeal under subs.(2), he **GA.135** shall, if he intends to contest the appeal or be heard by the Tribunal at the hearing of the appeal, enter an appearance to the appeal by giving a notice of appearance (in a form specified by the Minister) within 14 days or such longer period as the Tribunal may fix under para.(3) of reg.5. Interestingly the Regulations do not specify, as do the Unfair Dismissals (Claims and Appeals) Regulations 1977 (S.I. No. 286 of 1977), that the application to extend the time for entering a notice of appearance must be made before the expiration of the 14-day period. Nor do the Regulations specifically provide that a party to an appeal who does not enter an appearance shall not be entitled to take part in or be present or represented at any proceedings before the Tribunal in relation to the appeal. That the Tribunal undoubtedly has a discretion to decide to allow such party to be heard is clear, however, from the Supreme Court's decision in *Halal Meat Packers (Ballyhaunis) Ltd. v Employment Appeals Tribunal* [1990] I.L.R.M. 293.

Section 39(17) of the Redundancy Payments Act 1967 provides that the Tribunal shall have power to take evidence on oath and for that purpose may cause to be administered oaths to persons attending as witnesses. It also empowers the Tribunal to require a person to attend to give evidence or to produce documents in his possession, custody or control.

## Enforcement of decisions of rights commissioner and determinations of Tribunal

**8.**—(1) A decision of a rights commissioner, or a determination of the Tribunal, **GA.136** made in proceedings under this Act may be enforced as if it were an order of the Circuit Court made in civil proceedings by the judge of the Circuit Court for the place wherein the person in whose favour the decision or determination was made ordinarily resides.

(2) (a) A decision of a rights commissioner, and a determination of the Tribunal, in proceedings under this Act may provide that the decision or determination shall be carried out before a specified date.

G–16/1

(b) Where a decision of a rights commissioner or a determination of the Tribunal does not so provide, it shall be deemed, for the purposes of this section, to provide that it shall be carried out within 6 weeks from the date on which it is communicated to the parties concerned.

GENERAL NOTE

This section provides for the enforcement of a decision of a rights commissioner or a determination **GA.137** of the Tribunal as if it were an order of the Circuit Court. The procedures governing applications for enforcement are set out in Order 57, rule 2 of the Circuit Court Rules 2001 (S.I. No. 510 of 2001).

## Powers of authorised officers

**9.**—(1) In this section "authorised officer" means a person appointed by the **GA.138** Minister to be an authorised officer for the purposes of this Act.

(2) An authorised officer may, for the purposes of this Act, on production, if so requested by any person affected, of his authorisation and, where appropriate, of a certificate under subsection (3)—
(a) enter at all reasonable times any premises or place where he reasonably believes that an employee is employed,
(b) make therein any inspection or enquiry that he reasonably considers to be necessary for the purpose of ascertaining whether this Act is being complied with,
(c) require any person in the premises or at the place to give to him such information as he may reasonably require for the purposes of his functions under this Act,
(d) inspect and take copies of, or of extracts from, any records (whether in manual or other form) or books or other documents found on the premises or at the place.

(3) the powers conferred by subsection (2) shall not be exercised in respect of a dwelling unless the Minister (or an officer of the Minister authorised by the Minister in that behalf) certifies in writing that he has reasonable grounds for believing that an offence under this Act in relation to an employee employed in the dwelling has been committed by the employer.

(4) A person who obstructs or impedes an authorised officer in the exercise of a power or, without reasonable excuse, does not comply with a requirement under this section or who, in purported compliance with such a requirement gives to an authorised officer information that he knows to be false or misleading in a material particular shall be guilty of an offence and shall be liable on summary conviction to a fine not exceeding £1,000 [€1,269.74].

GENERAL NOTE

This section empowers the Minister to appoint "authorised officers" for the purpose of ensuring **GA.139** compliance with the terms of the Act. The powers conferred on such authorised officers are similar to those provided in other employment protection legislation.

## Provisions in relation to offences

**10.**—(1) Proceedings for an offence under this Act may be brought and prose- **GA.140** cuted by the Minister.

(2) Notwithstanding section 10 (4) of the Petty Sessions (Ireland) Act,

1851, proceedings for an offence under this Act may be instituted within 12 months from the date of the offence.

(3) Where an offence under this Act is committed by a body corporate and is proved to have been so committed with the consent or connivance of or to be attributable to any neglect on the part of any person, being a director, manager, secretary or other officer of the body corporate, or a person who was purporting to act in any such capacity, that person, as well as the body corporate, shall be guilty of an offence and shall be liable to be proceeded against and punished as if he were guilty of the first-mentioned offence.

GENERAL NOTE

GA.141    This section allows the Minister to prosecute offences arising under the Act.

### Voidance of certain provisions in agreements

GA.142    **11.** A provision in an agreement (whether a contract of employment or not and whether made before or after the commencement of this Act) shall be void in so far as it purports to preclude or limit the application of, or is inconsistent with, any provision of this Act.

GENERAL NOTE

GA.143    This section renders void any agreement which "purports to preclude or limit the application of, or is inconsistent with, any provision of the Act." The meaning of the identically worded section 13 of the Unfair Dismissals Act 1977 was considered by the Tribunal in *Gaffney v. Fannin Ltd* UD1/1989 (reproduced in Madden and Kerr, *Unfair Dismissal: Cases and Commentary* (2nd ed., 1996), p. 28). Here an agreement to accept a sum of money in full and final settlement of termination of employment, which sum was expressly stated to be inclusive of entitlements under, *inter alia*, the 1977 Act, was held to neither exclude nor limit the application of the Act nor to be inconsistent with it. Note that Judge Buckley in the Circuit Court has held that the doctrine of "informed consent" applies to section 13: *Hurley v. Royal Yacht Club* [1997] E.L.R. 225.

### Laying of regulations before Houses of Oireachtas

GA.144    **12.** Every regulation made under this Act shall be laid before each House of the Oireachtas as soon as may be after it is made and, if a resolution annulling the regulation is passed by either such House within the next 21 days on which that House has sat after the regulation is laid before it, the regulation shall be annulled accordingly but without prejudice to the validity of anything previously done thereunder.

### Expenses of Minister

GA.145    **13.** The expenses incurred by the Minister in the administration of this Act shall, to such extent as may be sanctioned by the Minister for Finance, be paid out of moneys provided by the Oireachtas.

### Short title and commencement

GA.146    **14.**—(1) This Act may be cited as the Payment of Wages Act, 1991.

(2) This Act shall come into operation on such day as the Minister may appoint by order.

GENERAL NOTE

GA.147    By virtue of the Payment of Wages Act 1991 (Commencement) Order 1991 (S.I. No. 350 of 1991) the Act came into operation on January 1, 1992.

SCHEDULE

(Section 3)

ENACTMENTS REPEALED                                                GA.148

| Session and Chapter or Number & Year (1) | Short title (2) | Extent of Repeal (3) |
|---|---|---|
| 17 Geo. 2, c. 8 | Truck Act, 1743 | Sections 6 and 7 |
| 12 Will. 4, c. 37 | Truck Act, 1831 | The whole Act |
| 9 Vict., c. 2 | County Works (Ireland) Act, 1846 | Section 20 |
| 37 & 38 Vict., c. 48 | Hosiery Manufacture (Wages) Act, 1874 | The whole Act |
| 50 & 51 Vict., c. 46 | Truck Amendment Act, 1887 | The whole Act |
| 59 & 60 Vict., c. 44 | Truck Act, 1896 | The whole Act |
| No. 40 of 1979 | Payment of Wages Act, 1979 | The whole Act. |

G–19

# NATIONAL MINIMUM WAGE ACT 2000

## (2000 No. 5)

ARRANGEMENT OF SECTIONS

PART 1

PRELIMINARY

PART 2

WORKING HOURS AND PAY REFERENCE PERIOD

PART 3

NATIONAL MINIMUM HOURLY RATE OF PAY

*Declaration and Review of National Minimum Hourly Rate of Pay*

*Entitlement of Employee to Payment and Sub-minimum Rates*

*Calculation of Minimum Hourly Rate of Pay*

G–21

SCHEDULE

**GA.201** An Act to provide for the determination, declaration and review of a national minimum hourly rate of pay for employees, the entitlement of employees to remuneration for employment at a rate not less than or calculated by reference to that national minimum hourly rate, the calculation of employees' entitlements, the settlement of disputes relating to such entitlements, the enforcement and recovery of wages, the imposition of penalties for breaches of this Act, the amendment of the Terms of Employment (Information) Act, 1984, the Organisation of Working Time Act, 1997, and the Protection of Employees (Employers' Insolvency) Act, 1984, and for related purposes.

[31st March, 2000]

INTRODUCTION AND GENERAL NOTE

**GA.202**     The purpose of this Act is to provide the legislative framework for the introduction of a national minimum hourly rate of pay. It seeks to ensure that employees, to whom the Act applies, are paid by their employer for their working hours at an hourly rate of pay that, on average, is not less than the prescribed minimum hourly rate of pay.

    Ireland was the last of the Western economies to introduce a legal national minimum wage or equivalent, although there has been legal minimum wage machinery in those sectors of the economy originally covered by Trade Boards and, since 1946, Joint Labour Committees pursuant to the provisions of Part IV of the Industrial Relations Act 1946 as amended by the Industrial Relations Act 1990.

    In the United Kingdom the National Minimum Wage Act gained the "royal assent" on July 31, 1998 and came into effect on April 1, 1999 (see, generally, Simpson "A Milestone in the Legal Regulation of Pay: The National Minimum Wage Act 1998" (1999) 28 I.L.J.1 and "The National Minimum Wage Five Years On: Reflections on Some General Issues" (2004) 33 I.L.J. 22). The U.K. legislation set the minimum hourly rate of pay initially at £3.60, increasing to £4.10 on October 1, 2001, £4.20 in October 1, 2002, to £4.50 in October 1, 2003, to £4.85 on October 1, 2004 and to £5.05 (currently €7.39) on October 1, 2005. In this jurisdiction the minimum hourly rate was initially set at £4.40 (or €5.59), although the rate was increased to £4.70 (€5.97) from July 1, 2001 and to £5 (€6.35) from October 1, 2002. From February 1, 2004 the rate was increased to €7.00 and from May 1, 2005 to €7.65.

**GA.203**     On July 18, 1997 the Government appointed the National Minimum Wage Commission under the chairmanship of Evelyn Owens, the then Chairman of the Labour Court. Its terms of reference included an examination of the range of possible mechanisms for determining and implementing minimum wages and advice on the best way to implement a national minimum hourly wage "having regard to the level and extent of low pay in the economy". The Report of the Commission was published on April 5, 1998 and it recommended a target date of April 1, 2000 for implementation and an initial rate set at around at two-thirds of median earnings (then €5.59) which took into account employment, overall economic conditions and competitiveness.

    Following submission of the Report, the Government established an Inter-Departmental Group representative of the Departments of the Taoiseach; Finance; Enterprise, Trade and Employment; Social, Community and Family Affairs; Health and Children; Tourism, Sport and Recreation; and Education and Science to assist in formulating proposals and a plan of action. The Group undertook "a technical assessment of the consequential implications and effects resulting from the implementation of the Commission's recommendations". It suggested alternatives to the Commission's proposals "only where major concerns—economic and social—were identified arising from their implementation". The Group's *Final Report* was published in May 1999.

**GA.204**     Despite trade union calls for an initial rate of £5 (€6.35), the Government decided that it should be set at £4.40 (€5.59) or around 52 per cent of median earnings at the time of its introduction. Projections by the Economic and Social Research Institute, set out in the Inter-Departmental Group's *Final Report*, suggest that this rate would benefit 13.5 per cent of the workforce (or some 163,000 workers) and add 1.6 per cent to the national wage bill. It was also estimated that the direct cost implications for the Exchequer, as an employer, would be approximately £2 million (€2.54 million) a year, outside of the health sector, where the cost implications could be as much as £12 million (€15.24 million) a year. For a detailed analysis of the Act, see Smith "Legislating Against Low Pay" (2000) 18 I.L.T. (n.s.) 222 and 234.

G–22

CITATION

See section 1(1).                                                            **GA.205**

COMMENCEMENT

The Act came into operation on April 1, 2000: see S.I. No. 96 of 2000.       **GA.206**

STATUTORY INSTRUMENTS

National Minimum Wage Act 2000 (National Minimum Hourly Rate of Pay) Order 2000 (S.I. No.  **GA.207**
95 of 2000).

National Minimum Wage Act 2000 (Commencement) Order 2000 (S.I. No. 96 of 2000).

National Minimum Wage Act 2000 (Prescribed Courses of Study or Training) Regulations 2000
(S.I. No. 99 of 2000).

National Minimum Wage Act 2000 (National Minimum Hourly Rate of Pay) (No. 2) Order 2000
(S.I. No. 201 of 2000).

National Minimum Wage Act 2000 (National Minimum Hourly Rate of Pay) Order 2003 (S.I. No.
250 of 2003).

National Minimum Wage Act 2000 (National Minimum Hourly Rate of Pay) Order 2005 (S.I. No.
203 of 2005).

PARLIAMENTARY DEBATES

515 *Dáil Debates* Cols 969–1010 (Second Stage)                              **GA.208**

515 *Dáil Debates* Cols 1178–1225 (Second Stage resumed)

Select Committee on Enterprise and Small Business (ESB 3, No. 9, March 7, 2000) Cols 343–408
(Committee Stage)

Select Committee on Enterprise and Small Business (ESB 3, No. 10, March 8, 2000) Cols 411–468
(Committee Stage resumed)

Select Committee on Enterprise and Small Business (ESB 3, No. 11, March 22, 2000) Cols 471–
536 (Committee Stage resumed)

Select Committee on Enterprise and Small Business (ESB 3, No. 12, March 23, 2000) Cols 539–
568 (Committee Stage resumed)

516 *Dáil Debates* Cols 1338–1368 (Report Stage)516 *Dáil Debates* Cols 1395-1398 (Report Stage
resumed and Final Stage)

162 *Seanad Debates* Cols 1266–1327 (Second Stage)

162 *Seanad Debates* Cols 1367–1400 (Committee, Report and Final Stages)

Be it enacted by the Oireachtas as follows:                                 **GA.209**

## PART I

### PRELIMINARY

## Short title and commencement

**1.** —(1) This Act may be cited as the National Minimum Wage Act, 2000.    **GA.210**

(2) This Act shall come into operation on such day or days as, by order or
orders made by the Minister under this section, may be fixed therefor, either
generally or with reference to a particular purpose or provision, and different
days may be so fixed for different purposes and different provisions.

GENERAL NOTE

By virtue of the National Minimum Wage Act 2000 (Commencement) Order 2000 (S.I. No. 96 of  **GA.211**
2000), April 1, 2000 was appointed as the day on which the Act came into operation.

## Interpretation

**2.** —(1) In this Act, unless the context otherwise requires—            **GA.212**

"contract of employment" means—

(*a*) a contract of service or apprenticeship, or

(*b*) any other contract whereby an individual agrees with another person to do or perform personally any work or service for that person or a third person (whether or not the third person is a party to the contract),

whether the contract is express or implied and, if express, whether or not it is in writing;

"employee" means a person of any age who has entered into, or works or has worked under, a contract of employment;

"employer", in relation to an employee, means the person with whom the employee has entered into, or for whom the employee works or has worked under, a contract of employment, and includes a transferee of an undertaking referred to in section 46;

"functions" includes powers and duties;

"inspector" means a person appointed under section 33(1) as an inspector;

"Minister" means the Minister for Enterprise, Trade and Employment;

"national minimum hourly rate of pay" means the rate of pay declared by order of the Minister under section 11;

"pay" means all amounts of payment, and any benefit-in-kind specified in Part 1 of the Schedule, made or allowed by an employer to an employee in respect of the employee's employment;

"pay reference period", in relation to an employee, means the period selected under section 10 by his or her employer;

"premium" means any amount in excess of basic pay payable to an employee in respect of his or her work;

"prescribed" means prescribed by regulations made under this Act by the Minister;

"working hours" has the meaning assigned to it by section 8.

(2) A reference in this Act to an employee of an employer shall be construed as as reference to an employee employed by that employer or to whom the employer is liable to pay wages and for that purpose a person holding office under, or in the service of, the State (including a civil servant within the meaning of the Civil Service Regulation Act, 1956) shall be deemed to be an employee employed by the State or the Government and an officer or servant of a local authority for the purposes of the Local Government Act, 1941, or of a harbour authority, [the Health Service Executive] or vocational education committee, shall be deemed to be an employee employed by the respective authority, [Executive] or committee.

(3) In this Act—

(*a*) a reference to any other enactment shall, expect to the extent that the context otherwise requires, be construed as a reference to that enactment as amended by or under any other enactments, including this Act,

(*b*) a reference to a section or Part is a reference to a section or Part of this Act, unless it is indicated that reference to some other enactment is intended,

(*c*) a reference to a subsection, paragraph or subparagraph is a reference to a subsection, paragraph or subparagraph of the provision in which the

G–24

reference occurs, unless it is indicated that a reference to some other provision is intended, and

(*d*) a reference to the Schedule is a reference to the Schedule to this Act.

GENERAL NOTE

"contract of employment" : as to whether a person is employed under a contract of service see **GA.213** *Henry Denny & Sons (Ireland) Ltd v Minister for Social Welfare* [1998] 1 I.R. 34. Subsection (2) was amended by virtue of s.66 of the Health Act 2004.

## Regulations

**3.**—(1) The Minister may make regulations prescribing such matters as may be   GA.214
prescribed under this Act by the Minister, and may make such other regulations as
are necessary or expedient for the purpose of giving effect to this Act.

(2) Regulations made under this section may contain such incidental,
supplementary and consequential provisions as appear to the Minister to be
necessary.

GENERAL NOTE

In exercise of her powers under this section, the Minister has made the National Minimum Wage   GA.215
Act 2000 (Prescribed Courses of Study or Training) Regulations 2000 (S.I. No. 99 of 2000).

## Laying of orders and regulations before Houses of Oireachtas

**4.**--Every order (other than an order made under section 1(2)) or regulation   GA.216
made by the Minister under this Act shall be laid before each House of the
Oireachtas as soon as practicable after it is made and, if a resolution annulling
the order or regulation is passed by either House within the next subsequent 21
days on which that House has sat after the order or regulation is laid before it, the
order or regulation shall be annulled accordingly, but without prejudice to the
validity of anything previously done under the order or regulation.

## Non-application of Act

**5.**—This Act does not apply to the remuneration of a person who is—   GA.217

    (*a*) the spouse, father, mother, grandfather, grandmother, step-father, step-
        mother, son, daughter, step-son, step-daughter, grandson, grand-daugh-
        ter, brother, sister, half-brother or half-sister of an employer, employed
        by the employer, or

    (*b*) an apprentice within the meaning of or under the Industrial Training
        Act, 1967, or the Labour Services Act, 1987.

## Expenses of Minister

**6.**—Any expenses incurred by the Minister in the administration of this Act   GA.218
shall, to such extent as may be approved of by the Minister for Finance, be paid
out of moneys provided by the Oireachtas.

## Provisions in agreement or legislation to pay less than national minimum hourly rate of pay are void

**7.**—(1) A provision in a contract of employment (whether made or entered into   GA.219
before or after the commencement of this section) is void in so far as it purports to
exclude or limit the operation of any provision of this Act.

(2) A contract or agreement or an enactment in force immediately before
the commencement of this section that provides for the entitlement to pay for
an employee less favourable than that to be provided in accordance with this
Act is hereby modified to that extent necessary to provide that the employee's
entitlement after the commencement of this section shall be not less favourable than that to be provided in accordance with this Act.

(3) Nothing in this section shall prevent the inclusion in a contract of
employment of a provision more favourable to an employee than an entitlement in accordance with this Act.

GENERAL NOTE

**GA.220**   The scope of the equivalent in other legislation of subsection (1)—such as section 13 of the Unfair Dismissals Act 1977—has generally been considered in the context of a claimant purportedly having signed an agreement settling or compromising any claims he or she might have under the relevant legislation: see *Hurley v. Royal Yacht Club* [1997] E.L.R. 235 and *Fitzgerald v. Pat the Baker* [1999] E.L.R. 227.

Subsection (2) modifies all existing contracts of employment, collective agreements or legislative provisions which provide for less favourable remuneration than is conferred by this Act.

PART 2

WORKING HOURS AND PAY REFERENCE PERIOD

## Working hours of employee for pay reference period

**GA.221**   **8.**—(1) For the purpose of determining under this Act whether an employee is being paid not less than the minimum hourly rate of pay to which he or she is entitled in accordance with this Act, but subject to section 9, "working hours", in relation to an employee in a pay reference period, means—

(*a*) the hours (including a part of an hour) of work of the employee as determined in accordance with—

(i)   his or her contract of employment,

(ii)   any collective agreement that relates to the employee,

(iii)   any Registered Employment Agreement that relates to the employee,

(iv)   any Employment Regulation Order that relates to the employee,

(v)   any statement provided by the employee's employer to the employee in accordance with section 3(1) of the Terms of Employment (Information) Act, 1994,

(vi)   any notification by the employee's employer to the employee under section 17 of the Organisation of Working Time Act, 1997,

(vii)   section 18 of the Organisation of Working Time Act, 1997, or

(viii) any other agreement made between the employee and his or her employer or their representatives that includes a provision in relation to hours or work,

or

(*b*) the total hours during which the employee carries out or performs the activities of his or her work at the employee's place of employment or is required by his or her employer to be available for work there and is paid as if the employee is carrying out or performing the activities of his or her work.whichever, in any case, is the greater number of hours of work.

(2) "Working hours" under this section shall include—

(*a*) overtime,

(*b*) time spent travelling on official business, and

(*c*) time spent on training or on a training course or course of study authorised by the employer, within the workplace or elsewhere, during normal working hours,but shall not include—

(i)   time spent on standby or on call at a place other than a place of work or training provided by or on behalf of the employer for whom the employee is on standby or on call,

G–26

(ii) [time spent absent from work on annual leave, sick leave, protective leave, adoptive leave, parental leave, carer's leave under the Carer's Leave Act 2001, while laid off, on strike or on "lock-out", or time for which the employee is paid in lieu of notice, or]

(iii) time spent on travelling between an employee's place of residence and place of work and back.

GENERAL NOTE

This section sets out the sources from which an employee's working hours must be determined in a **GA.222** pay reference period. Significantly the concept of "working hours" does not include time spent on standby or on call nor time spent absent from work, *inter alia*, while on strike or on lockout, although neither term is defined. This reflects the principle that the law guarantees a minimum level of pay for employees only in respect of times when they are working. Subsection (2)(ii) was substituted by virtue of s.29 of the Carer's Leave Act 2001.

## Certain employees to provide record of working hours to employer

**9.**—(1) Where an employee's working hours are assessed as provided in **GA.223** section 8(1)(b) but are not normally controlled by his or her employer, the following shall apply:

(a) the employee shall keep a written record of his or her working hours during every day he or she is employed during a pay reference period;

(b) the employee shall give the record to his or her employer as soon as reasonably practicable after the end of the pay reference period;

(c) if the employee fails to comply with paragraph (b), the working hours of the employee shall be calculated in accordance with section 8(1)(a) and the employer shall notify the employee of that circumstance as soon as possible after the expiration of the period, but in any case not later than at the time of receipt by the employee of his or her pay for the working hours concerned.

(2) Subsection (1) does not apply to an employee whose average hourly rate of pay for the working hours concerned is likely to be not less than 150 per cent, or such other percentage as may be prescribed, of the national minimum hourly rate of pay.

(3) An employee who provides his or her employer with information in a record of working hours under this section that the employee knows to be false or misleading in a material respect shall be guilty of an offence and shall be liable on summary conviction to a fine not exceeding £1,500 (€1,904.61).

GENERAL NOTE

This section obliges an employee, whose hours of work are not controlled or supervised by his or **GA.224** her employer, to keep a written record of working hours for each day that the employee works and further obliges such an employee to submit this record to his or her employer after the end of the pay reference period. This obligation, however, only applies to employees whose average hourly rate of pay is likely to be not less than 150 per cent of the national minimum wage rate of pay (*i.e.* €9.52).

## Pay reference period

**10.**—An employer shall select as a pay reference period for the purposes of this **GA.225** Act a period not exceeding one calendar month.

GENERAL NOTE

This section prescribes that the maximum period of a pay reference period is to be one calendar **GA.226** month.

## PART 3

### *Declaration and Review of National Minimum Hourly Rate of Pay:*

## National Minimum Hourly Rate of Pay

**GA.227**   **11.**—(1)  The Minister shall, by order, after taking into account the impact the proposed rate may have on employment, the overall economic conditions in the State and national competitiveness, declare a national minimum hourly rate of pay for the purposes of this Act.

(2) A national minimum hourly rate of pay may include an allowance for board with lodgings, board only or lodgings only at such rates as the Minister may specify in the order under subsection (1).

(3) Subject to sections 12 and 13, the Minister may, by order and after taking into account the matters referred to in subsection (1), amend or revoke an order made under this section, including an order made under this subsection.

GENERAL NOTE

**GA.228**    In exercise of her powers under this section, the Minister made the National Minimum Wage Act 2000 (National Minimum Hourly Rate of Pay) (No. 2) Order 2000 (S.I. No. 201 of 2000) which prescribed a national minimum hourly rate of pay of £4.70 (€5.97) on and from July 1, 2001 increasing to €6.35 from October 1, 2002. On and from February 1, 2004 the rate increased to €7.00: National Minimum Wage Act 2000 (National Minimum Hourly Rate of Pay) Order 2003 (S.I. No. 250 of 2003). On and from May 1, 2005 the rate increased to €7.65: National Minimum Wage Act 2000 (National Minimum Hourly Rate of Pay) Order 2005 (S.I. No. 203 of 2005). The National Minimum Wage Act 2000 (National Minimum Hourly Rate of Pay) Order 2000 (S.I. No. 95 of 2000) provides that the national minimum hourly rate of pay may include the following allowances:

    (i)   for full board and lodgings, £42.63 (€54.13) per week or £6.09 (€7.73) per day;

    (ii)  for full board only, £25.31 (€32.14) per week or £3.62 (€4.60) per day;

    (iii) for lodgings only, £17.21 (€21.85) per week or £2.47 (€3.14) per day.

These rates are based on the notional values used by the Joint Labour Committee for the Hotel Industry outside Dublin and Dun Laoghaire.

## National economic agreement recommending national minimum hourly rate of pay

**GA.229**   **12.**—(1) The Minister shall, from time to time in accordance with this section or section 13, review the national minimum hourly rate of pay.

(2) Where in the opinion of the Minister there is in existence or proposed a relevant agreement ("national economic agreement") among economic and social interests in the State which includes a recommendation in relation to the national minimum hourly rate of pay of employees for the duration of the agreement, the Minister shall, within 3 months after being advised of the recommendation, and taking into account the matters referred to in section 11(1)—

    (a)  accept or vary the recommendation and declare the national minimum hourly rate of pay under section 11 accordingly or amend the order, or

    (b)  reject the recommendation.

(3) If the Minister varies or rejects a recommendation under subsection (2), the Minister shall, as soon as practicable, make a statement to the Oireachtas giving his or her reasons for that variation or rejection.

GENERAL NOTE

**GA.230**    The *Programme for Prosperity and Fairness* recommended that the original rate of £4.40 (€5.59) be increased to £4.70 (€5.97) from July 1, 2001 and to £5 (€6.35) from October 1, 2002. See now the National Minimum Wage Act 2000 (National Minimum Hourly Rate of Pay) (No. 2) Order 2000 (S.I. No. 201 of 2000) and the National Minimum Wage Act 2000 (National Minimum Hourly Rate of Pay) Order 2003 (S.I. No. 250 of 2003). The latter Order increased the rate to €7.00 from February 1, 2004. Under the current agreement—*Sustaining Progress*—it was provided that the Labour Court be asked to

                                        Irish Employment Legislation

review the rate with effect from May 1, 2005. The Court has now advocated that the rate should be increased to €7.65 which was effected by the National Minimum Wage Act 2000 (National Minimum Hourly Rate of Pay) Order 2005 (S.I. No. 203 of 2005).

## Labour Court may recommend national minimum hourly rate of pay where no national economic agreement

**13.**—(1) Any organisation claiming to be substantially representative of GA.231 employees or employers in the State may apply to the Minister for his or her opinion as to whether a relevant national economic agreement exists for the purpose of section 12.

(2) Where in the opinion of the Minister there is no relevant national economic agreement as referred to in section 12 or, if there is such an agreement, it makes no recommendaton in relation to the national minimum hourly rate of pay of employees that should obtain for the duration of the agreement, the Minister shall, in writing, advise the applicant accordingly.

(3) Any organisation which the Labour Court is satisfied is substantially representative of employees or employers in the State may separately or jointly, not earlier than 12 months after the Minister has last declared a national minimum hourly rate of pay of employees under section 11, request the Labour Court to examine the national minimum hourly rate of pay of employees and make a recommendation to the Minister.

(4) The Labour Court in undertaking an examination as the result of an application under subsection (3), shall consult with such persons, including representatives of employers and employees in the private sector and public sector of the economy, as it thinks appropriate and if it is satisfied that general agreement is reached between the parties as to the appropriate hourly rate of pay of employees, recommend in writing to the Minister that rate accordingly.

(5) If, after the consultations referred to in subsection (4), the Labour Court is satisfied that general agreement between the parties cannot be reached, it may still make a recommendation to the Minister, but in doing so it shall have regard to the following matters:

(a) the movement in earnings of employees since the Minister last declared the national minimum hourly rate of pay under section 11 or amended the order;

(b) relevant exchange rate movement;

(c) the likely impact of any proposed change on-

(i) the level of unemployment and whether it is increasing or decreasing.

(ii) the level of employment and whether it is increasing or decreasing,

(iii) inflation in the economy, and

(iv) national competitiveness.

(6) The procedures of the Labour Court in relation to an application or hearing under this section shall be as determined by the Labour Court.

(7) The Minister shall, within 3 months after receiving a recommendation of the Labour Court under subsection (4) or (5), and after taking into account the matters referred to in section 11(1), accept or vary the recommendation and declare the national minimum hourly rate of pay under section 11 accordingly, amend the order or reject the recommendation.

(8) If the Minister varies or rejects a recommendation under subsection (7), the Minister shall as soon as practicable make a statement to the Oireachtas giving his or her reasons for the variation or rejection.

GA.232     This section provides for an alternative method to review the national minimum hourly rate of pay, where there is no national economic agreement or where such agreement contains no recommendation in relation to the national minimum hourly rate of pay, and gives the Labour Court important new functions.

## *Entitlement of Employee to Payment and Sub-minimum Rates*

### Entitlement to minimum hourly rate of pay

GA.233     **14.**—Subject to sections 17 and 18—

(a)  an employee who has attained the aged of 18 years shall, subject to sections 15, 16 and 41, be remunerated by his or her employer in respect of the employee's working hours in any pay reference period, at an hourly rate of pay that on average is not less than the national minimum hourly rate or pay, and

(b)  an employee who has not attained the age of 18 years shall be remunerated by his or her employer in respect of the employee's working hours in any pay reference period, at an hourly rate of pay that on average is not less than 70 per cent of the national minimum hourly rate of pay.

GENERAL NOTE

GA.234     This section entitles an employee, who is 18 years of age and over, to be paid by his or her employer at an hourly rate of pay that, on average, is not less than the national minimum hourly rate unless s.15 (job entrant), s.16 (trainee rates) or s.41 (employer in financial difficulty) applies in respect of that employee.

The section also provides that an employee under the age of 18 years is to be paid at an hourly rate of pay that, on average, is not less than 70 per cent of the national minimum hourly rate (*i.e.* €5.36). In the United Kingdom, 18–21 year-olds are entitled to a "development rate" of £4.25 (currently €6.21) per hour while those aged 16 and 17 are entitled to £3 (currently €4.38) per hour.

### Rates of pay during first 2 years of employment after entering employment after, or attaining, age of 18 years

GA.235     **15.**—(1) Subject to subsection (2) and sections 16, 17 and 18, a person who—

(a)  enters employment for the first time after attaining the age of 18 years, or

(b)  having entered into employment before attaining the age of 18 years continues in employment on attaining that age,

shall be remunerated by his or her employer in respect of his or her working hours in any pay reference period at an hourly rate of pay that on average is not less than—

(i)  in the case of an employee commencing employment for the first time after attaining the age of 18 years—

(I)  in his or her first year after having commenced employment, 80 per cent, and

(II)  in his or her second year after having commenced employment, 90 per cent.

(ii)  in the case of an employee having entered into employment before attaining the age of 18 years and continuing in employment on attaining that age—

(I)  in his or her first year after having attained the age of 18 years, 80 per cent, and

(II)  in his or her second year after having attained that age, 90 per cent, of the national minimum hourly rate of pay, notwithstanding that the employee, if he or she has changed his or her employer during the relevant period, may have been remunerated at a higher rate by the previous employer.

(2) In calculating a period of employment for the purpose of subsection (1), any period of employment during which the employee had not attained the age of 18 years shall be ignored.

(3) An employer shall not be liable in a dispute with an employee to whom this section applies as to the applicable rate of pay for the employee if the employer took reasonable steps to obtain detailed information about the employee's employment with any previous employer and paid the employee at an hourly rate in accordance with the information and this section.

(4) This section applies to an employee in circumstances described in subsection (1)(a) or (b) whether he or she entered employment, or continued in employment on attaining the age of 18 years, before or after the commencement of this section, but the employee's entitlement to remuneration as provided for in subsection (1) shall be only in respect of any period remaining after the commencement of this section of the employee's first and/or second year after so entering employment for the first time or, as the case may be, so attaining the age of 18 years and continuing in employment.

GENERAL NOTE

This section applies sub-minimum rates to an employee who enters employment for the first time **GA.236** after attaining the age of 18 years or, if in employment under the age of 18, who continues in employment on attaining that age. The employee is to be paid at an hourly rate of pay that, on average, is not less than:

(a) 80 per cent of the national minimum hourly rate of pay in the first year (*i.e.* €6.12) and

(b) 90 per cent of the national minimum hourly rate of pay in the second year (*i.e.* €6.89).

## Trainee rates

**16.**—(1) Subject to subsection (3) and sections 17 and 18, where an employee **GA.237** who has attained the age of 18 years undergoes a course of study or training authorised by the employer within the workplace or elsewhere during normal working hours, such courses or training to be prescribed in regulations made by the Minister, the employee shall be remunerated by his or her employer in respect of his or her working hours in any pay reference period at a rate of pay that on average is not less than the following percentages of the national minimun hourly rate of pay:

(a) in respect of the first one-third period (but not exceeding 12 months) of the total study or training period, 75 per cent;

(b) in respect of the second one-third period (but not exceeding 12 months) of the total study or training period, 80 per cent;

(c) in respect of the third one-third period (but not exceeding 12 months) of the total study or training period, 90 per cent.

(2) For the purpose of subsection (1), where a one-third period exceeds 12 months, the next subsequent one-third period shall be deemed to commence on the expiration of the previous period of 12 months.

(3) This section extends to an employee who is undergoing a course of study or training authorised by his or her employer which is subsequently prescribed for the purposes of subsection (1) and who—

(a) had not attained the age of 18 years at the time of the prescribing of the course of study or training, or

(b) had attained the age of 18 years at the time of the commencement of the course of study or training (whether or not he or she commenced that course before or after the commencement of this section), and the date by reference to which the one-third periods of the total study or training period shall be calculated for the purposes of subsection (1) as so extended is the date (before or after the commencement of this section) on which the employee's period of study or training actually commenced, but the employee shall be entitled to remuneration at the relevant percentage of the national minimum hourly rate of pay, as provided for in subsection (1), only in respect of that part of such one-third period or periods remaining after the date on which—

(i) this section commenced,

(ii) the course of study or training was or is prescribed, or

(iii) the employee attained or attains the age of 18 years,whichever is the later date.

(4) Subsection (1) does not apply to an employee who has already undertaken, before or after the commencement of this section, a course of study or training that is similar in purpose or content, while employed by the same or a different employer.

GENERAL NOTE

GA.238      This section applies sub-minimum rates to an employee who undergoes a prescribed course of study or training authorised by the employer. Such an employee is to be paid at an hourly rate of pay that, on average, in not less than:

(a) 75 per cent of the national minimum hourly rate of pay in the first period of the course (*i.e.* €5.74);

(b) 80 per cent of the national minimum hourly rate of pay in the second period (*i.e.* €6.12); and

(c) 90 per cent of the national minimum hourly rate of pay in the third period (*i.e.* €6.89).

The National Minimum Wage Act 2000 (Prescribed Courses of Study or Training) Regulations 2000 (S.I. No. 99 of 2000) set out the criteria that must be satisfied before this section applies. The employee's participation in the course must be directed or approved by the employer. The course must last for at least three months and any fees concerned must be paid by the employer. More importantly, the course must enable the acquisition of skills and/or knowledge expected to enhance the employee's work performance at the end of the course.

## Pro-rata entitlement to minimum hourly rate of pay for less than full hour

GA.239      **17.**—The rate of pay that a person is entitled to in accordance with this Part shall be calculated pro-rata in respect of any time that is less than a full hour.

*Calculation of Minimum Hourly Rate of Pay*

## Calculations for purpose of this Part

GA.240      **18.**—(1) Nothing in this Part prevents the deduction from any pay to which an employee is entitled in accordance with this Act, or the payment by an employee to an employer, of any amount permitted in accordance with section 5 of the Payment of Wages Act, 1991, or any other enactment or instrument made under an enactment.

(2) No such deductions shall be made or payment allowed for in calculating the hourly rate of pay of an employee for the purpose of determining under this Act whether the employee is being paid not less than the minimum hourly rate of pay to which he or she is entitled in accordance with this Act.

GENERAL NOTE

GA.241      This section permits an employer to continue to make lawful and authorised deductions from the pay of an employee in accordance with section 5 of the Payment of Wages Act 1991. However, in determining if an employee has been paid not less than his or her entitlement under this Act, no such deduction may be taken into account.

## Reckonable and non-reckonable pay components in calculating average hourly rate of pay

**19.**—(1) Subject to section 18, all the pay of an employee in a specific pay reference period shall be included in calculating the employee's average hourly rate of pay in that period for the purposes of determining under this Act whether an employee is being paid not less than the minumum hourly rate of pay to which he or she is entitled in that period.

(2) Any payments or benefits-in-kind listed in Part 2 of the Schedule are not included as pay of any employee for the purposes of subsection (1).

(3) The Minister may, by regulation, add an item to, delete an item from, or otherwise amend, the Schedule but only after consultation with such representatives of employers and employees in the State as the Minister considers appropriate.

(4) An employer shall not, for the purposes of this Act, change a payment or benefit-in-kind listed as a non-reckonable component of pay as set out in Part 2 of the Schedule so that its status becomes that of a reckonable component of pay as set out in Part 1 of the Schedule.

(5) For the purposes of this section, the amount, if any, that shall be allowed for board with lodgings, board only, and lodging only in calculating the hourly rate of pay of an employee in a pay reference period shall be the amount declared as such under section 11.

GA.242

GENERAL NOTE

This section and the Schedule to which it refers set out what components of an employee's pay are reckonable and non-reckonable when calculating if an employee has been paid at least the minimum hourly rate of pay to which he or she is entitled. The Schedule, as originally drafted, reflected the recommendation of the Inter-Departmental Group that all gross payments should be considered to be reckonable including all premium payments. Following the expression of opposition, backbench and trade union concerns, the Schedule was amended at Committee and Report Stage in the Dáil to exclude service pay, weekend and public holiday premiums, unsociable hours premiums, tips or gratuities paid throught the payroll and allowances for special or additional duties including those of a post of responsibility (such as a keyholder allowance). Whereas tips or gratuities are excluded, the amount of any "service charge" distributed to an employee through the payroll is included as a reckonable component.

GA.243

## Method of calculating employee's average hourly rate of pay

**20.**—For the purpose of determining under this Act whether an employee is being paid not less than the minimum hourly rate of pay to which he or she is entitled under this Act in a pay reference period, the gross remuneration of the employee calculated in accordance with section 19 shall be divided by the total working hours of the employee in the pay reference period calculated under section 8.

GA.244

GENERAL NOTE

This section prescribes the calculation to be undertaken to determine if an employee is being paid not less than his or her minimum entitlement to pay in accordance with the Act.

GA.245

## Payment of amount owed to employee on termination of employment

**21.**—To avoid doubt, where the employment of an employee is terminated, the employee shall be paid at not less than the minimum hourly rate of pay to which he or she is entitled in accordance with this Act in respect of the period commencing on the beginning of the pay reference period in which his or her employment was terminated and ending on the date of that termination.

GA.246

GENERAL NOTE

This section ensures that, in the event of an employee's employment being terminated, the employee is to be paid for his or her working hours, from the beginning of the last pay reference

GA.247

period to the date of the termination of employment, at not less than the employee's entitlement to pay in accordance with the Act.

PART 4

RECORDS AND STATEMENT OF AVERAGE HOURLY EARNINGS

## Records

GA.248    **22.**—(1) An employer shall keep, at the premises or place where his or her employee works or, if the employee works at 2 or more premises or places, the premises or place from which the activities that the employee is employed to carry on are principally directed or controlled, such records as are necessary to show whether this Act is being complied with in relation to the employee and, subject to section 23(5), those records shall be retained by the employer for at least 3 years from the date of their making.

(2) An employer who, without reasonable cause, fails to comply with subsection (1) shall be guilty of an offence and be liable on summary conviction to a fine not exceeding £1,500 [ 1,904.61].

(3) Without prejudice to subsection (2), where an employer fails to keep records under subsection (1) in respect of his or her compliance with a particular provision of this Act in relation to an employee, the onus of proving, in proceedings before a rights commissioner or the Labour Court, that the provision was complied with lies on the employer.

NOTE

GA. 248A    The importance of maintaining records is highlighted by the Labour Court's decision in *Mansion House Ltd v Izquierdo* MWD3/2004.

## Employee entitled to statement of average hourly rate of pay for pay reference period

GA.249    **23.**—(1) Subject to subsection (2), an employee may request from his or her employer a written statement of the employee's average hourly rate of pay for any pay reference period (other than the employee's current pay reference period) falling within the 12 month period immediately preceding the request.

(2) An employee shall not make a request under subsection (1) in respect of any pay reference period during which the hourly rate of pay of the employee was on average not less than 150 per cent calculated in accordance with section 20, or such other percentage as may be prescribed, of the national minimum hourly rate of pay or where the request would be frivolous or vexatious.

(3) A request under subsection (1) shall be in writing and identify the pay reference period or periods to which it relates.

(4) The employer shall, within 4 weeks after receiving the employee's request, give to the employee a statement in writing setting out in relation to the pay reference period or periods—

(a) details of reckonable pay components (including the value of all forms of remuneration) paid or allowed to the employee in accordance with Part 1 of the Schedule,

(b) the working hours of the employee calculated in accordance with section 8,

(c) the average hourly pay (including the value of forms of remuneration other than cash payments) actually paid or allowed to the employee, as determined in accordance with section 20, and

(d) the minimum hourly rate of pay to which the employee is entitled in accordance with this Act.

G–34

(5) A statement under subsection (4) shall be signed and dated by or on behalf of the employer and a copy shall be kept by the employer for a period of 15 months beginning on the date on which the statment was given by the employee.

(6) An employer who, without reasonable excuse, fails to comply with this section or a request under this section, or who provides false or misleading information to an employee in a statement under subsection (4) knowing it to be false or misleading, shall be guilty of an offence and be liable on summary conviction to a fine not exceeding £1,500 [ 1,904.61].

GENERAL NOTE

This section entitles an employee to request from his or her employer a written statement of the employee's average hourly rate of pay during any pay reference period falling within the 12 month period immediately preceding the request. The employer is required to reply to any such request within four weeks of receiving it. The Minister (see 515 *Dáil Debates* Col. 975) described this section as having been designed "to provide a structure that allows any potential dispute to be resolved speedily between an employee and an employer".

GA.250

PART 5

DISPUTES ABOUT ENTITLEMENT AND ENFORCEMENT

*Hearing of Disputes*

## Disputes about entitlement to minimum hourly rate of pay

**24.**—(1) Without prejudice to any other action that might be brought against an employer under this Act or otherwise, but subject to subsection (2), if an employee and his or her employer cannot agree on the appropriate entitlement of the employee to pay in accordance with this Act resulting in an alleged under-payment to the employee, the employee or the employer, or the representative of either of them with their respective consent, may, by notice in writing containing such particulars, if any, as may be prescribed, refer the dispute to a rights commissioner for the rights commissioner's decision.

GA.251

(2) A dispute cannot be referred to or dealt with by a rights commissioner—

(a) unless the employee—
   (i) has obtained under section 23 a statement of his or her average hourly rate of pay in respect of the relevant pay reference period, or
   (ii) having requested the statement, has not been provided with it within the time limited by that section for the employer to supply the information,

   and a period of 6 months (or such longer period, not exceeding 12 months, as the rights commissioner may allow) has not elapsed since that statement was obtained or time elapsed, as the case may be,

or

(b) where, in respect of the same alleged under-payment, the employer is or has been—
   (i) the subject of investigation by an inspector under section 33 or 34, or
   (ii) prosecuted for an offence under section 35.

(3) As soon as practicable after a dispute is referred to him or her, the rights commissioner shall give to the other party to the dispute a copy of the notice of referral.

(4) An inspector shall advise a rights commissioner, on request by the rights commissioner, as to whether the inspector has investigated or is investigating an alleged under-payment the subject of the dispute.

G–35

(5) A rights commissioner shall hear the parties to a dispute and any evidence relevant to the dispute offered by them, and otherwise inform himself or herself about the dispute in such manner as prescribed or, if not manner is prescribed, then as the rights commissioner thinks appropriate.

(6) The Minister may, by regulation, prescribe such matters relating to proceedings of the rights commissioner under this section as the Minister thinks appropriate.

(7) The hearing of a dispute shall not be open to the public.

GENERAL NOTE

GA.252     This section provides that an employee, who has complied with s.23, or an employer may refer a dispute to a rights commissioner for a hearing. In *Mansion House Ltd v Izquierdo* MWD3/2004, the Labour Court held that, where a claimant had failed to request a statement in accordance with s.23(1) of the Act, the "appropriate course of action" was for the Rights Commissioner to decline jurisdiction without prejudice to the claimant's right to re-enter the same complaint having complied with the said subsection. It was the Labour Court's view that a decision dismissing the claim on its merits on the basis of non-compliance with s.23(1) was neither "appropriate nor is it warranted by any provision of the Act".

## Prohibition of reduction in hours or work of an employee without a concomitant reduction in duties or amount of work

GA.253     **25.**—(1) Where an employee alleges that he or she is being prejudiced by a reduction in his or her hours of work without a concomitant reduction in duties or amount of work, because of an increased liablity of the employer resulting from the passing of this Act or the declaration of a national minimum hourly rate of pay, and the employer, within 2 weeks of being so requested by the employee or the employee's representative with the employee's consent, does not restore the employee's working hours to those obtaining immediately before the reduction, the employer and employee shall, for the purposes of section 24(1), be deemed not to be able to agree on the appropriate entitlement of the employee to pay in accordance with this Act resulting in an alleged underpayment to the employee, and sections 24 to 32 (except section 24(2)), with the necessary modifications, shall apply accordingly.

(2) A dispute cannot be referred to a rights commissioner under subsection (1) if a period of 6 months (or such longer period not exceeding 12 months, as the rights commissioner may allow) has elapsed since the employee's hours of work were reduced or alleged to be reduced.

(3) In proceedings under this section in respect of an allegation under subsection (1), the onus lies with the employer to prove that any reduction in hours of work was not for the purpose of avoiding the alleged increased liability referred to in subsection (1).

GENERAL NOTE

GA.254     This section prohibits an employer from reducing an employee's hours of work without a corresponding reduction in the amount of work which that employee is required to do. Without such a provision some employers might have reduced an employee's weekly hours while paying the same weekly wage. This would have had the effect of increasing the employee's nominal hourly rate but leaving the employee with the same weekly wage for doing the same amount of work.

## Decision of rights commissioner

GA.255     **26.**—(1) The rights commissioner shall, as soon as practicable after hearing a dispute, come to a decision on the dispute, advise the parties, in writing, of the decision and give to the Labour Court a copy of that decision.

(2) A decision of the rights commissioner may—

(a) include an award of—

(i) arrears, being the difference between any amount paid or allowed by the employer to the employee for pay and the

G–36

minimum amount the employee was entitled to be paid or allowed in accordance with this Act in respect of the period to which the dispute relates, and

    (ii)  reasonable expenses of the employee in connection with the dispute.

  (b)  require an employer to remedy, within a specified time (not being later than 6 weeks after the date the decision was communicated to the employer) or in a specific manner, any matter, including the payment of any amount, in respect of which the employer is in breach of this Act,

as the rights commissioner considers appropriate.

(3) A rights commissioner shall maintain a register of all decisions made by him or her under this section and shall make the register available for inspection by members of the public during normal office hours.

GENERAL NOTE

This section provides that the decision of a rights commissioner, if the employee's case is upheld, **GA.256** may award redress of arrears of pay owing to the employee in accordance with the Act. The rights commissioner may also award reasonable expenses to a successful employee.

## Appeal against rights commissioner's decision

**27.**—(1) A party to a dispute who is aggrieved by a decision of a rights **GA.257** commissioner under section 26 may, within 6 weeks of the date on which the decision was communicated to the party under section 26(1), by written notice of appeal containing such particulars, if any, as may be determined by the Labour Court, appeal to the Labour Court against the decision.

(2) As soon as practicable after receiving a notice of appeal, the Labour Court shall give to the other party to the dispute a copy of the notice.

(3) An appeal under this section shall be in the nature of a rehearing and proceedings in the appeal shall be conducted in such manner as the Labour Court thinks appropriate.

GENERAL NOTE

This section provides for an appeal to the Labour Court against a decision of a rights commissioner. **GA.258** The appeal must be lodged with the Court within six weeks of the decision being communicated to the party aggrieved.

## Power of Labour Court in relation to evidence

**28.**—(1) The Labour Court, in the hearing of an appeal under section 27, may **GA.259** take evidence on oath or affirmation and for that purpose may cause to be administered oaths to persons attending as witnesses at the hearing.

(2) A person who, on examination on oath or affirmation authorised under this section, wilfully and corruptly gives false evidence or wilfully and corruptly swears anything which is false, shall be guilty of an offence and shall be liable on summary conviction to a fine not exceeding £1,500 [€1,904.61].

The Labour Court may, by notice in writing to a person, require the pers(3) on to attend at such time and place as is specified in the notice to give evidence in relation to the hearing of an appeal or to produce any documents in his or her possession, custody or control which relate to the matter of the hearing.

(4) A person to whom a notice under subsection (3) has been given who refuses or wilfully neglects to attend in accordance with the notice or who, having so attended, refuses to give evidence or refuses or wilfully fails to produce any document to which the notice relates shall be guilty of an offence and shall be liable on summary conviction to a fine not exceeding £1,500 [€1,904.61].

(5) A document purporting to be signed by the chairperson of the Labour Court and stating that—

(a) a person named in the document was, by notice under subsection (3), required to attend before the Labour Court on a day and at a time and place specified in the document, to give evidence or produce a document,

(b) a sitting of the Labour Court was held on that day and at that time and place, and

(c) the person did not attend before the Labour Court in pursuance of the notice or, having so attended, refused to give evidence or refused or failed to produce the document,

shall, in a prosecution for an offence under subsection (4), be evidence of the matters stated, without further proof.

(6) A witness in a hearing of an appeal before the Labour Court has the same privileges and immunities as a witness before the High Court.

## Determination of Labour Court on appeal

GA.260    **29.**—(1) The Labour Court shall, as soon as practicable after hearing an appeal under section 27, determine the appeal by confirming the decision of the rights commissioner or substituting for that decision any decision of its own that the rights commissioner could have made on the hearing of the dispute.

(2) As soon as practicable after determining an appeal under subsection (1), the Labour Court shall give to the parties to the appeal a copy of the determination.

## Referral or appeal to High Court on question of law

GA.261    **30.**—(1) The Minister may, at the request of the Labour Court, refer to the High Court for determination a question of law arising in an appeal under section 27.

(2) A party to an appeal under section 27 may appeal to the High Court from a determination of the Labour Court but only on a question of law.

GENERAL NOTE

GA.262    This section provides for an appeal to the High Court on a question of law only. Although the Rules of the Superior Courts do not specifically provide for appeals under this Act, it is suggested that any such appeal be brought either by special summons or by notice of motion, by analogy with the procedures set out in R.S.C. 1986, Orders 105 and 106 respectively. In the absence of any specific rule of court, any such appeal need only be brought within a reasonable time: *per* McCracken J. in his *ex tempore* ruling in *McGaley v Liebherr Container Cranes Ltd* (2001/234Sp) delivered on October 12, 2001.

The circumstances in which the High Court will overturn a decision of a specialist tribunal such as the Labour Court have been considered in many cases: see for example, *Henry Denny & Sons (Ireland) Ltd v Minister for Social Welfare* [1998] 1 I.R. 34 and in particular the comments of Hamilton C.J. at 37. In considering whether to allow an appeal against a decision of such a tribunal, the High Court must consider whether that body based its decision on an identifiable error of law or on an unsustainable finding of fact. A decision cannot be challenged on the grounds of irrationality if there is any relevant material to support it: see further *Mulcahy v Waterford Leader Partnership Ltd* [2002] E.L.R. 12 (O'Sullivan J.) and *Thompson v Tesco Ireland Ltd* [2003] E.L.R. 21 (Lavan J.). In *National University of Ireland, Cork v Ahern* [2005] 2 I.R. 577, the Supreme Court held that, although findings of fact must be accepted by the High Court on appeal, that court could still examine the basis upon which those facts were found. The relevance or admissibility of the matters relied on in determining the facts were questions of law.

## Referral of decision of rights commissioner to Labour Court for determination

GA.263    **31.**—(1) Where a decision of a rights commissioner in relation to a dispute under this Act has not been fully complied with by the employer concerned and the time for bringing an appeal against the decision has expired and no such appeal has been brought or if such an appeal has been brought it has been abandoned, the employee concerned may bring the dispute before the Labour Court and the Labour Court shall, without hearing the employer concerned or any evidence (other than in relation to the matters aforesaid), make a determination to the like effect as the decision of the rights commissioner.

(2) The bringing of a dispute before the Labour Court under subsection (1) shall be effected by giving to it a notice in writing containing such particulars, if any, as may be determined by the Labour Court.

GENERAL NOTE

This section provides for the enforcement of rights commissioner decisions which have not been **GA.264** implemented by the employer.

## Enforcement of determination of Labour Court

**32.**—(1) A determination of the Labour Court in proceedings under this Act **GA.265** may provide that any matter, including the payment of any amount, in respect of which the employer is in breach of this Act, shall be remedied within a specified time or in a specified manner.

(2) Where a determination of the Labour Court does not specify a date by which a matter in respect of which an employer is in breach of this Act shall be remedied, the determination shall be deemed, for the purposes of this section, to provide that it shall be remedied within 6 weeks from the date on which the determination is communicated to the parties.

(3) If an employer fails to remedy a matter in respect of which he or she is in breach of this Act within the period provided under subsection (1) or (2), the Circuit Court shall, on application to it in that behalf—

(a) by the employee concerned,

(b) with the consent of the employee, by a trade union which holds a negotiation licence under the Trade Union Act, 1941, of which the employee is a member, or

(c) by the Minister, if the Minister considers it appropriate to make the application having regard to all the circumstances,

without hearing the employer or any evidence (other than in relation to the matters aforesaid), make an order directing the employer to remedy the matter within the time specified or deemed to be specified in, and in accordance with the terms of, the determination.

(4) The reference in subsection (3) to a determination of the Labour Court is a reference to such a determination in relation to which, at the expiration of the time for bringing an appeal, if any, against it, no such appeal has been brought, or if such an appeal has been brought it has been abandoned, and the reference in subsection (2) to the date on which the determination is communicated to the parties shall, in a case where an appeal is abandoned, be construed as a reference to the date of such abandonment.

(5) The Circuit Court may, in an order under this section, if in all the circumstances it considers it appropriate to do so, where the order relates to arrears of pay, direct the employer concerned to pay to the employee concerned interest on the arrears at the rate referred to in section 22 of the Courts Act, 1981, in respect of the whole or any part of the period beginning 6 weeks after the date on which the determination of the Labour Court is communicated to the parties and ending on the date of the order.

(6) An application under this section to the Circuit Court shall be made to the judge of the Circuit Court for the circuit in which the employer concerned ordinarily resides or carries out any profession, business or occupation.

(7) In proceedings under this section every document purporting to be issued by

the Labour Court and sealed with its official seal, is to be received in evidence without further proof.

GENERAL NOTE

GA.266    This section provides for the enforcement of Labour Court determinations which have not been implemented by the employer. It provides that the determination can be enforced by the employee, the employee's trade union or the Minister in the Circuit Court without the employer or any evidence, other than in relation to non-implementation, being heard. Although the Circuit Court Rules do not specifically provide for applications to enforce such determinations of the Labour Court, it is suggested that any such application be made by way of Motion on Notice, by analogy with the procedure set out in Order 57 of the Circuit Court Rules 2001.

## *Inspectors and Inspections*

### Inspectors and their powers

GA.267    **33.**—(1) The Minister may, in writing, appoint as many persons as the Minister thinks appropriate to be inspectors for the purposes of this Act.

(2) Subject to this section, an inspector may do all or any of the following things for the purposes of this Act—

(a) enter at all reasonable times any premises or place where the inspector believes on reasonable grounds that—

(i)  an employee is employed in work; or

(ii)  the work that an employee is employed to do is directed or controlled,

(b) make such examination or enquiry as may be necessary for ascertaining whether this Act is being complied with in respect of an employee employed in those premises or that place or an employee whose work is directed or controlled from the premises or place,

(c) require the employer of an employee, or the representative of the employer, to produce to the inspector any records the employer is required to keep and inspect and take copies of entries in the records (including in the case of information in a non-legible form a copy of or an extract from that information in a permanent legible form),

(d) require any person the inspector believes on reasonable grounds to be or to have been an employee or the employer of an employee to furnish such information as the inspector may reasonably request,

(e) examine with regard to any matters under this Act any person the inspector has reasonable cause to beleive to be or to have been an employer or employee and require the person to answer such questions (other than questions tending to incriminate the person) as the inspector may put relative to those matters and to sign a declaration of the truth of the answers.

(3) An inspector shall not, except with the consent of the occupier, enter a private dwelling (other than a part of the dwelling used as a place of work) unless he or she has obtained a warrant from the District Court under subsection (6) authorising the entry.

(4) Where an inspector in attempting to exercise his or her powers under this section is prevented from entering any premises, he or she may apply under subsection (6) for a warrant authorising the entry.

(5) An inspector, where he or she considers it necessary to be so accompanied,

may be accompanied by a member of the Garda Síochána when exercising a power conferred on an inspector by this section.

(6) If a judge of the District Court is satisfied on the sworn information of an inspector that there are reasonable grounds for suspecting that information required by an inspector under this section is held on any premises or any part of premises, the judge may issue a warrant authorising an inspector accompanied by other inspectors or a member of the Garda Síochána, at any time or times within one month from the date of issue of the warrant, on production, if so requested, of the warrant, to enter the premises (if need be by the use of reasonable force) and exercise all or any of the powers conferred on an inspector under subsection (2).

(7) A person who—

(a) obstructs or impedes an inspector in the exercise of any of the powers conferred on an inspector under this section,

(b) refuses to produce a record which an inspector lawfully requires the person to produce,

(c) produces or causes to be produced, or knowingly allows to be produced, to an inspector, a record which is false or misleading in a material respect, knowing it to be false or misleading,

(d) gives to an inspector information which is false or misleading in a material respect knowing it to be false or misleading, or

(e) fails or refuses to comply with a lawful requirement of an inspector under subsection (2),

shall be guilty of an offence.

(8) Every inspector shall be furnished by the Minister with a certificate of his or her appointment and, on applying for admission to any premises or place for the purposes of this Act, shall, if requested by a person affected, produce a certificate or a copy of the certificate to that person.

GENERAL NOTE

GA.268 The *Explanatory and Financial Memorandum* accompanying the Bill indicated that increased staffing resources, including seven Labour Inspectors, would be assigned to the Labour Inspectorate to carry out national minimum wage-related enforcement responsibilities. According to a report in Industrial Relations News (IRN 29, July 27, 2000), half of the resources in the Labour Inspectorate are to concentrate on enforcing the national minimum wage. Eight of the 17 inspectors have been newly recruited and these are to focus on the minimum wage until the end of 2000, after which it will become part of the standard labour law compliance audit by all inspectors. The High Court has ruled that there is nothing in either the express powers or the purposes for which those powers are conferred which enables them to be construed as including any incidental or consequential power to prepare a report intended for publication of the results of an investigation into alleged breaches by an employer of its obligations under the 2000 Act: *Gama Endustri Tesisleri Imalat Montaj AS v Minister for Enterprise, Trade and Employment*, unreported, High Court, June 14, 2005. Finlay Geoghegan J., however, went on to hold that an inspector must have an implicit or consequential power to pass to the Minister and persons concerned with the civil enforcement procedures information, documents or evidence gathered pursuant to the Inspector's express statutory powers for the purposes of those persons enforcing the obligations imposed by the Act on employers either by way of civil procedures or by prosecuting alleged offences.

## Investigation of allegation or matter by inspector

GA.269 **34.**—(1) Where an employee alleges that his or her employer has failed to remunerate the employee to an extent required in accordance with this Act, the employee or the employee's representative with the consent of the employee, may request an inspector to investigate the allegation.

(2) An inspector may, on the request or on behalf of an employee under subsection (1), or of the inspector's own motion if the inspector believes that an under-payment of pay to an employee has been made, investigate the allegation or matter and, where the investigation is on the request or behalf of an employee, advise the employee of the outcome of the investigation.

(3) Subject to subsection (5), an inspector shall, on the request for advice under section 39 by the Minister, investigate the matter on which the advice is sought and advise the Minister accordingly.

(4) Where after investigating an allegation or matter under this section an inspector is satisfied that an offence under this Act has been committed, or when so requested by the Minister, the inspector shall furnish a report on his or her investigation to the Minister.

(5) An inspector shall not investigate an allegation or matter—

(a) in relation to a dispute which has been referred to a rights commissioner under section 24 (and shall cease any investigation he or she has commenced on becoming aware of any such referral); or

(b) involving payments made or alleged entitlements arising more than 3 years before the date of the inspection or proposed inspection.

(6) A rights commissioner shall, at the request of an inspector, inform the inspector as to whether a particular dispute has been referred to the rights commissioner under section 24.

GENERAL NOTE

**GA.270**   This section provides for an alternative mechanism open to employees to ensure that their employer complies with the provision of the Act. An employee, instead of referring a dispute to a rights commissioner, may refer a complaint to an inspector appointed under section 33.

OFFENCES AND ENFORCEMENT

### Offence to refuse or fail to pay minimum hourly rate of pay

**GA.271**   **35.**—(1) An employer who refuses or fails to remunerate an employee for each working hour or part of a working hour in any pay reference period at an hourly rate of pay that on average is not less than the employee's entitlement to the minimum hourly rate of pay in accordance with this Act shall be guilty of an offence.

(2) Where the employer charged is found guilty of an offence under this section, evidence may be given of any like contravention on the part of the employer in respect of any period during the 3 years immediately preceding the date of the offence.

(3) In proceedings against a person under subsection (1), it shall lie with the person to prove that he or she has paid or allowed pay of not less than the amount he or she was required to pay or allow in accordance with this Act.

### Prohibition of victimisation of employee by employer

**GA.272**   **36.**—(1) An employer shall not cause any action prejudicial to an employee for the employee having—

(a) exercised or having proposed to exercise a right under this Act,

(b) in good faith opposed or proposed to oppose by lawful means an act which is unlawful under this Act, or

(c) become, or in future will or might become, entitled in accordance with this Act to remuneration at an hourly rate of pay that on average is not less than the national minimum rate of pay, or a particular percentage of that rate of pay.

(2) Dismissal of an employee in contravention of subsection (1) shall be deemed to be an unfair dismissal of the employee within the meaning and for the purposes of section 6(1) of the Unfair Dismissals Acts 1977 to [2005] (but without prejudice to sections 2 to 5 of the Unfair Dismissals Act 1977, except that it is not necessary for the employee to have at least one year's continuous service with the employer [...] and those Acts, with the necessary modifications, shall apply accordingly.

(3) Where an employee alleges he or she has suffered an action prejudicial to the employee in contravention of subsection (1) and the employer, within 2 weeks of being so requested by the employee or the employee's representative with the employee's consent, does not restore the employee to conditions of employment he or she enjoyed immediately before suffering the alleged prejudicial action, the employer and the employee shall, for the purposes of section 24(1), be deemed not to be able to agree on the appropriate entitlement of the employee to pay in accordance with this Act, resulting in an alleged underpayment to the employee, and sections 24 to 32 (except section 24(2)), with the necessary modifications, shall apply accordingly.

(4) A dispute cannot be referred to a rights commissioner in pursuance of subsection (3) if a period of 6 months (or such longer period not exceeding 12 months, as the rights commissioner may allow) has elapsed since the employer's alleged prejudicial action referred to in subsection (1).

GENEARL NOTE

The words in square brackets have been deleted consequent upon the repeal of the Worker Protection (Regular Part-Time Employees) Act 1991 by the Protection of Employees (Part-Time Work) Act 2001.

## Penalties and proceedings

**37.**—(1) A person guilty of an offence under this Act for which no penalty, GA.273 other than under this section, is provided shall be liable-

(a) on summary conviction, to a fine not exceeding £1,500 [€1,904.61] or, at the discretion of the court, to imprisonment for a term not exceeding 6 months, or to both the fine and the imprisonment, or

(b) on conviction on indictment, to a fine not exceeding £10,000 [€12,697.38] or, at the discretion of the court, to imprisonment for a term not exceeding 3 years, or both the fine and the imprisonment.

(2) If the offence of which a person was convicted is continued after conviction, the person shall be guilty of a further offence on every day on which the act or omission constituting the offence continues, and for each such further offences the person shall be liable on summary conviction to a fine not exceeding £200 [€253.95] or on conviction on indictment to a fine not exceeding £1,000 [€1,269.74].

(3) Where an offence under this Act is committed by a body corporate or by a person acting on behalf of a body corporate and is proved to have been so committed with the consent, connivance or approval of, or to have been attributable to any neglect on the part of, a person who, when the offence was committed, was a director, manager, secretary or other similar officer of the body corporate or a person who was purporting to act in any such capacity, that person (as well as the body corporate) shall be guilty of an offence and be liable to be proceeded against and punished as if guilty of the offence committed by the body corporate.

(4) Proceedings in relation to a summary offence under this Act may be prosecuted by the Minister.

(5) Notwithstanding section 10(4) of the Petty Sessions (Ireland) Act, 1851, proceedings for an offence under this Act may be instituted within 12 months from the date of the discovery of the offence.

## Defence for employer in proceedings

**38.**—It shall be a defence in proceedings for an offence under this Act by an GA.274 employer if the employer proves that he or she exercised due diligence and took reasonable precautions to ensure that this Act and any relevant regulations made under it were complied with by the employer and any person under his or her control.

## Civil proceedings

GA.275 **39.**—(1) Where an employer has not paid to an employee an amount of pay to which the employee is entitled in accordance with this Act and, in respect of that amount no dispute has been referred to a rights commissioner under section 24 or allegation referred to an inspector under section 34 for investigation, and, in the opinion of the Minister, it is not reasonable in the circumstances to expect the employee, or the representative of the employee with the employee's consent, to either refer a dispute or allegation, or to institute civil proceedings for the recovery of the amount, the Minister may request an inspector to advise the Minister whether or not, in the inspector's opinion, civil proceedings should be insituted by the Minister on behalf and in the name of the employee.

(2) After considering the advice of an inspector requested under subsection (1), the Minister may, in his or her absolute discretion, institute or refrain from instituting civil proceedings in the name of the employee for the recover of the amount.

(3) In proceedings under subsection (2) the employee shall not be liable for costs but the court before which the proceedings are brought may order that any costs that might otherwise have been awarded against the employee shall be paid by the Minister.

(4) The power given by subsection (2) shall not be in derogation of any right of an employee to insitute civil proceedings on the employee's own behalf.

## Employee's entitlements not affected by conditions of contract of employment contravening certain Acts

GA.276 **40.**—(1) Where a term or condition of the contract of employment concerned contravenes the Taxes Consolidation Act, 1997, or the Social Welfare Acts, the employee concerned shall, notwithstanding the contravention, be entitled to redress under this Act for any under-payment of an amount of pay to which he or she would otherwise be entitled under this Act.

(2) Where, in proceedings under this Act, it is shown that a term or condition of a contract of employment contravenes the Taxes Consolidation Act, 1997, or the Social Welfare Acts, the rights commissioner, the Labour Court, an inspector or the Circuit Court, as the case may be, shall notify the Revenue Commissioners or the Minister for [Social and Family Affairs], as may be appropriate, of the matter.

GENERAL NOTE

The title of the Minister in subsection (2) was amended by virtue of the Social, Community and Family Affairs (Alteration of Name of Department and Title of Minister) Order 2002 (S.I. No. 310 of 2002).

## PART 6

### MISCELLANEOUS

## Employer in financial difficulty

GA.277 **41.**—(1) The Labour Court may, in accordance with this section, exempt an employer from the obligation to pay an employee or number of employees entitlements otherwise payable to them in accordance with section 14, not being entitlements to which section 14(b), 15 or 16 apply.

(2) An exemption under subsection (1) shall be for a period not exceeding one

year and not less than 3 months, and while it remains in force the employer accordingly need not so comply.

(3) The Labour Court shall not exempt an employer under subsection (1) if the employer has previously ever been granted an exemption under that subsection.

(4) An employer or employer's representative with the employer's consent may, in the manner and form approved by the Labour Court, apply to the Labour Court for an exemption under subsection (1).

(5) On receiving an application under subsection (4) the Labour Court shall convene a hearing of parties to the application and shall give its decision on the application in writing to the parties.

(6) Before granting an exemption under subsection (1), the Labour Court must be satisfied that—

   (a)  where the employer employs more than one employee—
      (i)   the employer has entered into an agreement with the majority of the employees or the representative of the majority of the employees, or
      (ii)  there is a collective agreement covering the majority of the employees in respect of whom the exemption is sought,

   whereby the employees or their representative consent to—
      (I)   the employer making the application, and
      (II)  abide by any decision on the application that the Labour Court may make,

   (b)  where the employer makes an application in respect of a single employee, the employer has entered into an agreement with the employee or the representative of the employee whereby the employee or his or her representative consents to the employer making the application and to abide by any decision on the application that the Labour Court may make, and that, in either case, the employer cannot pay an entitlement under section 14 to an employee to whom the agreement relates due to the employer not having the ability to pay or being unlikely to be able to pay, to the extent that, if the employer were compelled to pay—
      (i)  the employee would be likely to be laid-off employment with the employer, or
      (ii) the employee's employment would be likely to be terminated.

(7) A decision of the Labour Court to exempt an employer under subsection (1) shall specify—

   (*a*)  the names and employment positions occupied by employees to whom the exemption applies;
   (*b*)  the duration of the exemption; and
   (*c*)  the average hourly rate of pay to be paid to the employee or employees during the period of the exemption, and the employee or employees shall be entitled to be paid at not less than that rate accordingly.

(8) Where during the period of an exemption under this section a new employee replaces an employee to whom the exemption relates, the employer may pay the new employee the hourly rate of pay specified by the Labour Court in respect of the former employee and shall, as soon as practicable, notify the Labour Court in writing of the employment and the new employee.

(9) The Labour Court shall establish its own procedures for the hearing of applications, and in relation to incidental matters to be dealt with, under this section.

(10) The Labour Court shall maintain a register of all decisions under this section and shall make the register available for examination by members of the public at such place and reasonable times as it thinks fit.

(11) No appeal shall lie from a decision of the Labour Court under this section except to the High Court on a question of law.

(12) For the purposes of calculating an employee's entitlement to a redundancy payment under the Redundancy Payments Acts 1967 to [2003], any exemption under this section shall be ignored and the calculation made as if the employee had been paid the national minimum hourly rate of pay to which he or she was otherwise entitled under this Act, for the period of the exemption.

(13) A payment in lieu of notice to an employee in accordance with the Minimum Notice and Terms of Employment Acts 1973 to [2005], shall not have regard to any exemption under this section and the payment in lieu of notice shall be made to the employee as if the employee had been paid the national minimum hourly rate of pay to which he or she was otherwise entitled under this Act, for the period of the exemption.

(14) A payment from the Social Insurance Fund in accordance with section 6(2)(*a*)(i) of the Protection of Employees (Employers' Insolvency) Acts 1984 to [2004], shall not have regard to any exemption under this section and any such payment shall be made to the employee as if the employee had been paid the minimum hourly rate of pay to which he or she was otherwise entitled under this Act, for the period of the exemption.

GENERAL NOTE

GA.278    This section permits the Labour Court to grant an employer a temporary exemption from paying the national minimum hourly rate of pay to an employee or to a number of employees. Before granting any such exemption, the court must be satisfied that the employer is unable to pay; that the employer would likely lay off or dismiss the employees concerned; and that the majority of employees affected have consented.

Insofar as this section provides for an appeal on a point of law to the High Court, see the General Note to s.30 of this Act at GA.262 *supra*.

## Act not to derogate from certain provisions of or under Industrial Relations Acts 1946 to [2004]

GA.279    **42.**—The provisions of this Act are in addition to and not in derogation of the Industrial Relations Acts 1946 to [2004], or—

(*a*) Employment Regulations Orders, and the enforcement of such Orders, made under those Acts, or

(*b*) Registered Employment Agreements, and the enforcement of such Agreements, on the register under those Acts on the commencement of this section.except that where a minimum hourly rate of pay in accordance with this Act is a greater amount than the minimum rate of pay prescribed under an Employment Agreement, the employee's entitlement to pay in accordance with this Act shall prevail.

## Repercussive claims

GA.280    **43.**—(1) The Labour Relations Commission or the Labour Court shall not recommend in favour of or endorse a claim or a part of a claim for the improvement in the pay of an employee who has access to any of its services if in the view of the Labour Relations Commission or the Labour Court, as the case may be, the claim or part of the claim is based on the restoration of a pay differential between the employee and another employee who has secured or is to secure an increase in pay as the result of the passing of this Act.

(2) The Labour Court shall not by Employment Regulation Order give effect to a proposal which could be submitted to it by a Joint Labour Committee under section 42 of the Industrial Relations Act, 1946, or section 48 of the Industrial Relations Act, 1990, if, in the view of the Labour Court, the proposal is based on or partly on the restoration of a pay differential between an employee and another employee who has secured or is to secure an increase in pay as the result of the passing of this Act.

(3) The Labour Court shall not register an employment agreement under section 27 of the Industrial Relations Act, 1946, or vary such an agreement under section 28 of that Act if, in the view of the Labour Court, the agreement or variation, or part of the agreement or variation, is based on or partly on the restoration of a pay differential between an employee and another employee who has secured or is to secure an increase in pay as the result of the passing of this Act.

(4) No conciliation or arbitration scheme in the public sector shall recommend in favour or endorse a claim or a part of a claim for the improvement in the pay of an employee who is subject to the scheme if the claim or part of the claim is based on the restoration of a pay differential between the employee and another employee who has secured or is to secure an increase in pay as the result of the passing of this Act.

GENERAL NOTE

This section provides that the Labour Relations Commission and the Labour Court or a Conciliation **GA.281** and Arbitration Scheme in the public sector may not recommend in favour of a claim which is based on the restoration of a pay differential between an employee and another employee who has secured or is to secure an improvement in pay arising from the provisions of the Act.

## Amendment of section 3 of Terms of Employment (Information) Act, 1994

**44.**—[...]                                                                                          **GA.282**

## Amendment of section 39 of Organisation of Working Time Act, 1997

**45.**—[...]                                                                                          **GA.283**

## Change of ownership of business

**46.**—Without prejudice to the generality of the [European Communities **GA.284** (Protection of Employees on Transfer of Undertakings) Regulations, 2003 (S.I. No. 131 of 2003)], on the transfer of an undertaking within the meaning of those regulations the transferee shall become liable to an employee in the undertaking to whom this Act applies in respect of any matter under this Act, in the same manner and to the same extent as the transferor immediately before the transfer, as if the transferee had originally entered into the relevant contract of employment or other agreement with the employee.

GENERAL NOTE

The 2003 Regulations which repeal and re-enact S.I. Nos 306 of 1980 and 487 of 2000, purport to **GA.285** implement Council Directive 2001/23/EC, the purpose of which is to ensure that, in any transfer of a business or undertaking or part thereof, the employment of the existing workers is preserved or, if their employment terminates by reason of the transfer, that their rights arising out of that termination are effectively safeguarded. For a detailed analysis of the previous Regulations and the earlier Directives see Byrne, *Transfer of Undertakings* (Blackhall Publishing, 1999) and McMullen, *Business Transfers and Employee Rights* (3rd ed, Butterworths, 1998).

## Extension of Protection of Employees (Employers' Insolvency) Act, 1984

**47.**—[...]                                                                                          **GA.286**

## Service of documents

**48.**—(1) The service of a notice or other document on a person for the purpose **GA.287** of or in relation to a proceeding under this Act may be effected by delivering it to the person or by sending a copy by prepaid registered post in an envelope addressed to the person at his or her last known residence or place of business in the State.

(2) In the case of a company to which the Companies Act, 1963, applies, service may be effected by delivering the document to, or by sending it by registered prepaid post in an envelope addressed to the company at its registered office.

(3) In the case of a body corporate to which subsection (2) does not apply or an unincorporated body of persons, the service may be effected by sending a copy of the notice or other document by registered prepaid post in an envelope addressed to the body at any place in the State where the body conducts its business or in such other manner as an originating summons may be served on such a body under the Rules of the Superior Courts.

## Provisions relating to winding-up and bankruptcy

**GA.288**    **49.**—(1) There shall be included among the debts which, under section 285 of the Companies Act, 1963, are, in the distribution of the assets of a company being wound-up, to be paid in priority to all other debts, all arrears of pay payable under this Act by a company to an employee, and that Act shall have effect accordingly.

(2) There shall be included among the debts which, under section 81 of the Bankruptcy Act, 1988, are, in the distribution of the property of a bankrupt or arranging debtor, to be paid in priority to all other debts, all arrears of pay payable under this Act by the bankrupt or arranging debtor.

(3) Formal proof of the debts to which priority is given under subsection (1) or (2) shall not be required except in cases where it may otherwise be provided by rules or general orders made under the respective Act.

## Recovery of money due to employee

**GA.289**    **50.**—(1) Without prejudice to section 39, any amount of money due to an employee from his or her employer under or in accordance with this Act shall be recoverable by the employee as a simple contract debt in a court of competent jurisdiction and action for its recovery may be instituted and maintained on behalf of the employee by the employee's trade union, if the employee is a member.

(2) Where in a prosecution for an offence under this Act it appears to a court that money is due by an employer to an employee, and the employer is convicted of that offence, the court may, if it is satisfied that the employer is liable to pay to his or her employee an amount of money, order, in addition to any penalty which it may impose pursuant to this Act, that the employer pay the amount to the employee.

SECTION 19                                    SCHEDULE

RECKONABLE AND NON-RECKONABLE PAY COMPONENTS IN CALCULATING AVERAGE
HOURLY RATE OF PAY

PART 1 — RECKONABLE COMPONENTS

**GA.290**    1. Basic salary.
2. Shift premium.
3. Piece and incentive rates, commission and bonuses, which are productivity related.
4. The monetary value of board with lodgings or board only or lodgings only, not exceeding the amount, if any, prescribed for the purposes of this item.
5. The amount of any service charge distributed to the employee through the payroll.
6. Any payments under section 18 of the Organisation of Working Time Act, 1997 (zero hour protection).
7. Any amount in respect of any of the above items advanced in a previous pay reference period that relates to the specific pay reference period.

G–48

8. Any amount in respect of any of the above items earned in the specific pay reference period and paid in the next pay reference period or, where section 9(1)(b) applies, paid in the pay reference period in which the record of working hours is received or due to be received by the employer or the pay reference period immediately after that.

## PART 2 — NON-RECKONABLE COMPONENTS

**GA.291**

1. Overtime premium.
2. Call-out premium.
3. Service pay.
4. Unsocial hours premium.
5. Any amount distributed to the employee of tips or gratuities paid into a central fund managed by the employer and paid through the payroll.
6. Public holiday premium, Saturday premium and Sunday premium, where any such holidays or days are worked.
7. Allowances for special or additional duties including those of a post of responsibility.
8. Any payment of expenses incurred by the employee in carrying out his or her employment, including travel allowance, subsistence allowance, tool allowance and clothing allowance.
9. On-call or standby allowance.
10. Any payments for or in relation to a period of absence of the employee from the workplace, such as sick pay, holiday pay, payment for health and safety leave under the Maternity Protection Act, 1994, or pay in lieu of notice, but not including a payment under section 18 of the Organisation of Working Time Act, 1997 (zero hour protection).
11. Any payment by way of an allowance or gratuity in connecton with the retirement or resignation of the employee or as compensation for loss of office.
12. Pension contributions paid by the employer on behalf of the employee.
13. Any payment referable to the employee's redundancy.
14. Any advance of a payment referred to in Part 1 of this Schedule in the specific pay reference period relating to a subsequent pay reference period.
15. Any payment-in-kind or benefit-in-kind, except board with lodgings, lodgings only or board only.
16. Any payment to the employee otherwise than in his or her capacity as an employee.
17. Any payment representing compensation for the employee, such as for injury or loss of tools and equipment.
18. An amount of any award under a staff suggestion scheme.
19. Any loan by the employer to the employee, other than an advance payment referred to in paragraph 7 in Part 1 of this Schedule.

# CIRCUIT COURT RULES 2001

## (S.I. No. 510 of 2001)

### ORDER 57

### Rule 2 Payment of Wages Act 1991

**1.** In this Order "the Act" means the Payment of Wages Act 1991 (No. 25 of 1991), and "the Tribunal" means the Employment Appeals Tribunal and "Commissioner" means a rights commissioner. **GC.151**

**2.** Applications for the enforcement of decisions of a Commissioner or deter- **GC.152** minations of the Tribunal shall, pursuant to section 8 of the Act, be made by way of Motion on Notice in accordance with Form 36B of the Schedule of Forms annexed hereto which shall set out the grounds upon which the applicant relies for the reliefs sought and shall have annexed thereto:

  (a) a certified copy of the original decision of the Commissioner or the original determination of the Tribunal, and

  (b) a certified copy of the original letter from the Commissioner or the Tribunal notifying the applicant of the making of the said decision or determination.

**3.** Applications shall be brought in the County where the person in whose **GC.153** favour the decision or determination was made, ordinarily resides.

**4.** All applications shall be served no later than 10 days prior to the return date **GC.154** set out in the Motion either in accordance with the provisions as to service of Civil Bills and other documents contained in Order 11 of these Rules or by being delivered to or served upon the Solicitor who is on record before the Tribunal as acting for the person named as the defendant before the Court; and service of an application or any other document upon such Solicitor, or delivery of the same at his office, or sending the same to him by prepaid post to such office shall be deemed to be good service upon the party for whom such Solicitor acts upon the day when the same is so delivered or served, or upon which in the ordinary course of postage it would be delivered. The Motion shall be listed for mention only on the return date set out therein at which time a date for hearing shall be fixed by the Court.

**5.** Notice of every application shall be given to the Tribunal and the Commis- **GC.155** sioner. Such notice shall be effected by the delivery of a copy of the application at, or by sending same by prepaid registered post to, the Office of the Secretary of the Tribunal or the Office of the Secretary of the Labour Relations Commission, as appropriate.

**6.** Save by special leave of the Court, all applications under Section 8 of the Act **GC.156** shall be heard upon oral evidence or as may be determined by the Court.

**7.** The Court may make such Order as to costs as may be appropriate. **GC.157**

**8.** The Secretary of the Tribunal and the Secretary of the Labour Relations **GC.158** Commission shall have the right of access to all the information contained on the file kept in the Office of the County Registrar in respect of each application and shall be entitled upon request to receive copy of any written Judgment delivered by the Judge relating thereto.

GC.159

# FORM 36B

## AN CHÚIRT CHUARDA

## THE CIRCUIT COURT

CIRCUIT                                         COUNTY OF

## IN THE MATTER OF THE PAYMENT OF WAGES ACT, 1991

## NOTICE OF MOTION FOR RELIEF UNDER SECTION 8 OF THE PAYMENT OF WAGES ACT, 1991

BETWEEN

............................ Plaintiff

AND

............................ Defendant


Take Notice that application will be made to the Court on the or the next opportunity thereafter for the following reliefs:
[Here insert details of the relief sought by way of enforcement.]


And further take notice that the said application will be grounded upon:
1. [here insert grounds upon which the Applicant is relying for the reliefs sought]

2. [here insert basis of jurisdiction]

3. [here insert name, address and description of the Plaintiff]

4. [The following documents must be annexed to this Notice of Motion namely a certified copy of the original decision of the Commissioner or a certified copy of the original determination of the Tribunal; a certified copy of the original letter from the Commissioner or the Tribunal notifying the Plaintiff of the making of the said decision or determination.]

Dated the ............. day of .............

SIGNED ...................................
Plaintiff/Solicitor for the Plaintiff

The Defendant/Solicitor for the Defendant

And

To:   The Employment Appeals Tribunal/Rights Commissioner

And

To:   The County Registrar


GENERAL NOTE

GC.160    This rule prescribes Circuit Court procedures in respect of applications brought under section 8 of the 1991 Act (see above, para. GA.137).

# PAYMENT OF WAGES (APPEALS) REGULATIONS, 1991

## (S.I. No. 351 of 1991)

**1.**—(1) These Regulations may be cited as the Payment of Wages (Appeals) GC.201 Regulations, 1991.

(2) These Regulations shall come into operation on the 1st day of January, 1992.

**2.** In these regulations— GC.202

"the Act" means the Payment of Wages Act, 1991 (No. 25 of 1991);

"appeal" means an appeal under section 7 of the Act;

"the Minister" means the Minister for [Enterprise, Trade and Employment];

"the Tribunal" means the Employment Appeals Tribunal.

**3.** A notice under section 1(2) in relation to an appeal shall contain— GC.203

(a) the names, addresses and descriptions of the parties to the proceedings to which the appeal relates,

(b) the date of the decision to which the appeal relates, and the name of the rights commissioner who made the decision, and

(c) a brief outline of the grounds of the appeal.

**4.** An appeal may be withdrawn by giving a notification in writing signifying GC.204 such withdrawal to the Tribunal.

**5.**—(1) If a party to proceedings under the Act before a rights commissioner GC.205 receives a copy of a notice of appeal under section 7(2) of the Act in relation to the proceedings, he shall, if he intends to contest the appeal or to be heard by the Tribunal at the hearing of the appeal, enter an appearance to the appeal by giving a notice of appearance to the Tribunal within 14 days (or such longer period as the Tribunal may fix under paragraph (3) of this Regulation).

(2) A notice of appearance under this Regulation shall be in a form specified by the Minister and shall contain a brief outline of the grounds on which the appeal concerned will be contested by the person entering the appearance.

(3) A party to an appeal may apply to the Tribunal, by notice in writing given to the Tribunal and containing a brief outline of the grounds for the application, for an extension of the time specified in paragraph (1) of this Regulation for entering an appearance to the appeal and the Tribunal may, if it is satisfied that there are reasonable grounds for doing so, extend the time aforesaid by such period as it considers appropriate.

**6.** On receipt by the Tribunal of a notice of appearance under Regulation 5 of GC.206 these Regulations or a notification under Regulation 4 of these Regulations, the Tribunal shall cause a copy of the notice or notification, as the case may be, to be given to the other party concerned.

**7.** An error (including an omission) of a formal nature in a determination of the GC.207 Tribunal may be corrected—

(a) in any case, by the chairman of the Tribunal, and

(b) in a case in which the determination concerned was made at a time when a vice-chairman was acting as chairman of the Tribunal, by the vice-chairman,by a certificate signed by him.

**8.**—(1) The Tribunal shall maintain a register, to be known as the Register of GC.208 Payment of Wages Determinations (referred to subsequently in this Regulation as

G–53

"the Register") and shall cause to be entered in the Register a complete record of every determination of the Tribunal under section 7 of the Act.

(2) The Register may be inspected free of charge by any person during normal office hours.

(3) Particulars of any correction made under Regulation 7 of these Regulations shall be entered in the Register.

(4) A copy of an entry in the Register shall be sent to the parties concerned.

**GC.209**   **9.**—(1) A notice under these Regulations or paragraph (a) of section 7(2) of the Act may be given by sending it by registered post addressed to the Secretary, Employment Appeals Tribunal, Davitt House, 65A Adelaide Road, Dublin 2, and a notice under these Regulations or a document under paragraph (b) of the said section 7(2) may be given to any other person by sending it by registered post addressed to the person—

(a)   in case his address is specified correctly in a notice referred to in Regulation 5 of these Regulations, at that address, and

(b)   in any other case—

(i)    if the person is a company (within the meaning of the Companies Act, 1963), at its registered office,

(ii)   if the person is not a company (within the meaning aforesaid) at the place where the person resides or carries on a profession, business or occupation.

(2) Any such notice or notification aforesaid that is given to a person authorised to receive it by the person to whom it is required by the Act or by these Regulations to be given shall be deemed to have been given to the latter person.

**GC.210**   **10.** Regulations 10 to 17 (2), 19, 20, 20A (inserted by the Redundancy (Employment Appeals Tribunal) Regulations, 1979 (S.I. No. 114 of 1979)), 23, 23A (inserted by the Redundancy (Employment Appeals Tribunal) Regulations, 1979) and 24 of the Redundancy (Redundancy Appeals Tribunal) Regulations, 1968 (S.I. No. 24 of 1968), shall, with any necessary modifications (and, in the case of the said Regulations 20 and 20A, with the modification that a sum awarded by the Tribunal under either of those Regulations shall, in lieu of being paid out of the Fund referred to therein, be paid by the Minister for [Enterprise, Trade and Employment] with the consent of the Minister for Finance) apply in relation to appeals and proceedings in relation to such appeals as they apply in relation to appeals provided for by section 39 of the Redundancy Payments Act, 1967 (No. 21 of 1967), and proceedings in relation to such appeals.

GENERAL NOTE

**GC.211**   These regulations prescribe the procedures to be followed in relation to the submission and hearing of appeals before the Employment Appeals Tribunal under the 1991 Act. The definition of the Minister was amended by virtue of the Labour (Transfer of Departmental Administration and Ministerial Functions) Order 1993 (S.I. No. 18 of 1993), the Industry and Commerce (Alteration of Name of Department and Title of Minister) Order 1993 (S.I. No. 19 of 1993) and the Enterprise and Employment (Alteration of Name of Department and Title of Minister) Order 1997 (S.I. No. 305 of 1997). It should be noted that a determination which does not state correctly the name of the employer concerned or any other material particular may, on application to the Tribunal, be amended so as to state correctly the name of the employer or other material particular: see section 39(2) of the Organisation of Working Time Act 1997.

# NATIONAL MINIMUM WAGE (NATIONAL MINIMUM HOURLY RATE OF PAY) ORDER 2000

## (S.I. No. 95 of 2000)

**1.** This Order may be cited as the National Minimum Wage Act, 2000 (National  GC.301
Minimum Hourly Rate of Pay) Order, 2000.

**2.** [...]  GC.302

**3.**—(1) The national minimum hourly rate of pay may include the following  GC.303
allowances:

(i)   for full board and lodgings, £42.63 [€54.13] per week or £6.09 [€7.73 per day;

(ii)  for full board only, £25.31 [€32.14] per week or £3.62 [€4.60] per day;

(iii) for lodgings only, £17.21 [€21.85] per week or £2.47 [€3.14] per day.

(2) In this article "day" means a day on which the full board and lodgings, full
board only or lodgings only, as the case may be, is or are provided by an employer
to an employee.

GENERAL NOTE

This Order set the national minimum hourly rate of pay at £4.40 (€5.59) and also sets out the  GC.304
monetary allowances for board and/or lodgings which may be included by an employer in calculating
the national minimum hourly rate of pay for an employee. By virtue of the National Minimum Wage
Act 2000 (National Minimum Hourly Rate of Pay) (No. 2) Order 2000 (S.I. No. 201 of 2000), Article 2
stood revoked on July 1, 2001 and, as and from that date, the national hourly rate of pay was £4.70
(€5.97). The (No. 2) Order further provided that on and from October 1, 2002, the national minimum
hourly rate of pay would be £5.00 (€6.35). By virtue of the National Minimum Wage Act 2000
(National Minimum Hourly Rate of Pay) Order 2003 (S.I. No. 250 of 2003), the rate increased to
€7 per hour as and from February 1, 2004 and, by virtue of the National Minimum Wage Act 2000
(National Minimum Hourly Rate of Pay) Order 2005 (S.I. No. 203 of 2005), to €7.65 as and from May
1, 2005.

# NATIONAL MINIMUM WAGE ACT 2000 (PRESCRIBED COURSES OF STUDY OR TRAINING) REGULATIONS 2000

## (S.I. No. 99 of 2000)

### Citation

**1.** These regulations may be cited as the National Minimum Wage Act 2000  GC.401
(Prescribed Courses of Study or Training) Regulations 2000.

### Definitions

**2.** In these regulations, in relation to a course of study or training—  GC.402

"approach" means the training methods and techniques, and how the learning
will be delivered;

"assessment and certification procedure" means how the course is to be
assessed for certification purposes and identifies the certifying body or
the arrangements concerning written confirmation of the employee's
completion of the course identifying the level of employee attainment
against the objectives, which must include provision for the employee's
signature;

"directed study or training" means planned and structured study or training which is insulated from immediate operational job pressures and can be delivered inside or outside the workplace;

"duration" means the total time allocated to the course in terms of hours per week and number of weeks; the duration of all main elements including workplace training and directed training, as appropriate, and the assessment time should be clearly shown;

"objectives" means the expected performance to be demonstrated by the employee at the end of the overall period of the course; that is, what the employee will be able to do on completion of the course in terms of knowledge, practical and personal skills to be demonstrated:

"outline plan" means the content of each module of the course which should state the titles, sequence of delivery, and time (in days/weeks/months) of each module;

"purpose" includes the rationale for the course, describing what it is expected to achieve and the expected outcomes of the training in terms of trainee opportunities;

"record system" means the types of records to be kept for the purposes of—

(a) planning and implementing the study or training;

(b) showing progress against the training objective;

(c) administration;

"title" means the name of the course

"workplace training" means planned and structured study or training carried out under normal job pressures.

### Prescribed courses of study or training

GC.403   3. A course of study or training that satisfies the following criteria is a prescribed course of study or training for the purposes of section 16 of the National Minimum Wage Act, 2000:

(1) The employee's participation in the course is directed or approved by the employer.

(2) The duration of the course is for a minimum period of 3 calendar months.

(3) Subject to paragraph (4), the course takes place during the normal working hours of the employee.

(4) The course involves at least 10% of directed study or training, which may be within or outside of normal working hours.

(5) Any fees concerned with the employee's participation in the course directed by the employer, are paid by the employer.

(6) The course—

(a) enables the acquisition of skills and/or knowledge expected to enhance the work performance of the employee at the end of the course,

(b) includes directed study or training,

(c) includes workplace training,

(d) involves supervision of the employee during workplace training,

(e) includes a system of recording progress and results, which must provide for the retention of the employer for 3 years after the end of the employee's participation in the course at the premises or place where the employer works or, if the employee works at 2 or more premises or places, the premises or place from which the activities of the employee are principally directed or controlled,

(f)   include an assessment and certification procedure or written confirmation of the employee's completion of the course identifying the level of employee attainment against the objectives, which must include the employee's signature.

(7) The course is the subject of a pre-existing written document or documents detailing the following information:

(a)   its title and purpose,

(b)   its objectives,

(c)   an outline plan of duration and approach,

(d)   the record system to apply,

(e)   the assessment and certification procedure,

(f)   advice given by the employer of any facilities, including any time-off, to be given to the employee during the period of the employee's participation in the course to enable the employee to successfully complete the course, and any changes to the employee's working arrangements during the period of the employee's participation in the course.

GENERAL NOTE

These Regulations prescribe the criteria a course of study or training must satisfy in order that an **GC.404** employee, undergoing such a course, shall be paid in accordance with section 16(1) of the Act.

# NATIONAL MINIMUM WAGE ACT 2000 (NATIONAL MINIMUM HOURLY RATE OF PAY) ORDER 2005

## (S.I. No. 203 of 2005)

**1.** This Order may be cited as the National Minimum Wage Act 2000 (National **GC.601** Minimum Hourly Rate of Pay) Order 2005.

**2.** On May 1 the National Minimum Wage Act 2000 (National Minimum Hourly Rate of Pay) Order 2003 (S.I. No. 250 of 2003) shall stand revoked.

**3.** On and from May 1, 2005 the national minimum hourly rate of pay is €7.65.

GENERAL NOTE

This Order increases the national minimum hourly rate of pay to €7.65 on and from May 1, 2005. **GC.602**

# PROTECTION OF EMPLOYEES (PART-TIME WORK) ACT, 2001

## (No. 45 of 2001)

ARRANGEMENT OF SECTIONS

PART 1

PRELIMINARY AND GENERAL

An Act to provide for the implementation of Directive 97/81/EC of 15 **HB.201** December, 1997, of the Council of the European Communities concerning the framework agreement on part-time work concluded by UNICE, CEEP and the ETUC [O.J. No. L14, 20.1.1998, p. 9], to clarify the effect certain enactments relating to employees have in cases where the employee concerned is a posted worker (within the meaning of Directive 96/71/ EC of the European Parliament and of the Council of 16 December, 1996, Concerning the Posting of Workers in the Framework of the Provi-

H–61

sion of Services [O.J. No. L018, 21.1.1997, p. 1]) or otherwise has an employment relationship in the State, to amend section 14(2) of the Protection of Employment Act, 1977, and to provide for related matters.

[*15th December, 2001*]

INTRODUCTION AND GENERAL NOTE

**HB.202**    The purpose of this Act is the transposition into Irish law of Council Directive 97/81/EC of December 15, 1997 concerning the framework agreement on part-time work concluded by the general cross-industry organisations at European level. The Act seeks to provide for the removal of discrimination against part-time workers and replaces, in its entirety, the Worker Protection (Regular Part-Time Employees) Act 1991.

Part-time working is not a recent phenomenon but recent decades have seen the growth of its importance as a proportion of the workforce (17 per cent in 1997), its spread through a wide range of industries and occupations and the fact that it is no longer limited to marginal groups seeking a supplementary income: see Drew, *Who Needs Flexibility? Part-Time Working-The Irish Experience* (Employment Equality Agency, 1991).

One major consequence of working part-time was the non-availability of important employment protection statutes, such as the Unfair Dismissals Act 1977, because of the 18 hours a week threshold stipulated therein. Such workers were also, in the main, excluded from the protection of the social welfare system: on this see generally Whyte, "Part-Time Workers under Labour and Social Welfare Law" (1989) 11 D.U.L.J. (*n.s.*) 24.

In 1991, two steps were taken to ameliorate the situation. Full insurance cover was extended to part-time workers by the Social Welfare (Employment of Inconsiderable Extent) (No. 2) Regulations 1991 (S.I. No. 72 of 1991 as amended by S.I. No. 76 of 1994). Under these Regulations part-time workers are fully insurable, provided they earn a minimum of €31.74 (£25) per week. Secondly, the Worker Protection (Regular Part-Time Employees) Act 1991 provided that "regular part-time employees" (defined as employees who were normally expected to work not less than 8 hours per week and had so worked for not less than 13 continuous weeks) enjoyed the same protection under the redundancy, minimum notice, worker participation, unfair dismissal, maternity, employers' insolvency and holidays legislation as did full-time employees. On the 1991 Act see Ryan, "Hours Thresholds after the 1991 Part-Time Workers Act" (1991) 13 D.U.L.J. (*n.s.*) 55 and Barrett, "Part-Time Workers Cross a New Threshold" (1990–93) 9 J.I.S.L.L. 1.

Following the failure of various attempts to address the issue at European level, the European Commission decided to utilise the procedure agreed under the Treaty on European Union which then excluded the United Kingdom: see Jeffery, (1998) 27 I.L.J. 193. A "framework agreement" between the Union of Industrial and Employers' Confederations of Europe (UNICE), the European Trade Union Confederation (ETUC) and the European Centre of Enterprises with Public Participation (CEEP) was concluded on June 6, 1997 and this agreement was adopted as Directive 97/81/EC on December 15, 1997. It was subsequently extended to the United Kingdom by Directive 98/29/EC: [1998] O.J. L131/10.

The stated purpose of the framework agreement on part-time work is (i) to provide for the removal of discrimination against part-time workers and to improve the quality of part-time work and (ii) to facilitate the development of part-time work on a voluntary basis and to contribute to the flexible organisation of working time in a manner which takes into account the needs of employers and workers (clause 1). Clause 4 of the agreement sets out the principle of non-discrimination, namely that, in respect of employment and conditions, part-time workers should not be treated in a less favourable manner than comparable full-time workers solely because they work part-time unless the different treatment is justified on objective grounds. Clause 5(2) provides that a worker's refusal to transfer from full-time to part-time work or vice versa should not constitute a valid reason for termination of employment without prejudice to termination for other reasons such as may arise from the operational requirements of the establishment concerned.

CITATION

**HB.203**    See section 1.

COMMENCEMENT

**HB.204**    The Act came into operation on December 20, 2001: see S.I. No. 636 of 2001.

STATUTORY INSTRUMENTS

Protection of Employees (Part-Time Work) Act 2001 (Commencement) Order 2001 (S.I. No. 636 **HB.205** of 2001).

PARLIAMENTARY DEBATES

530 *Dáil Debates* Cols 716–748 (Second Stage).  **HB.206**

530 *Dáil Debates* Cols 788–822 (Second Stage resumed).

Select Committee on Enterprise and Small Business (ESB4, No. 10, October 3, 2001) Cols 331–364 (Committee Stage).

542 *Dáil Debates* Cols 680–688 (Report Stage).

542 *Dáil Debates* Cols 1451–1462 (Report Stage resumed).

544 *Dáil Debates* Cols 1031–1034 (Report Stage resumed and Final Stage).

168 *Seanad Debates* Cols 1024-1056 (Second Stage).

168 *Seanad Debates* Cols 1233–1246 (Committee and Remaining Stages).

Be it enacted by the Oireachtas as follows:—

PART I

PRELIMINARY AND GENERAL

## Short title, collective citation and construction

**1.** —(1) This Act may be cited as the Protection of Employees (Part-Time **HB.207** Work) Act, 2001.

(2) In so far as it relates to the Minimum Notice and Terms of Employment Acts, 1973 and 1984, this Act and those Acts shall be construed together as one and may be cited together as the Minimum Notice and Terms of Employment Acts, 1973 to 2001.

(3) In so far as it relates to the Protection of Employees (Employers' Insolvency) Acts, 1984 and 1990, this Act and those Acts shall be construed together as one and may be cited together as the Protection of Employees (Employers' Insolvency) Acts, 1984 to 2001.

(4) In so far as it relates to the Redundancy Payments Acts, 1967 to 1990, this Act and those Acts shall be construed together as one and may be cited together as the Redundancy Payments Acts, 1967 to 2001.

(5) In so far as it relates to the Terms of Employment (Information) Act, 1994, this Act and that Act shall be construed together as one and may be cited together as the Terms of Employment (Information) Acts, 1994 and 2001.

(6) In so far as it relates to the Unfair Dismissals Acts, 1977 to 1993, this Act and those Acts shall be construed together as one and may be cited together as the Unfair Dismissals Acts, 1977 to 2001.

(7) In so far as it relates to the Worker Participation (State Enterprises) Acts, 1977 to 1993, this Act and those Acts shall be construed together as one and may be cited together as the Worker Participation (State Enterprises) Acts, 1977 to 2001.

GENERAL NOTE

By virtue of s.16(3) of the Industrial Relations (Miscellaneous Provisions) Act 2004, the collective citation of the Employers' Insolvency legislation is now the Protection of Employees (Employers' Insolvency) Acts 1984 to 2004. By virtue of s.17(3) of the Redundancy Payments Act 2003, the collective citation of the Redundancy Payments legislation is now the Redundancy Payments Acts 1967 to 2003.

## Commencement

**2.** —This Act shall come into operation on such day or days as the Minister **HB.208**

H–63

may appoint by order or orders either generally or with reference to any particular purpose or provision and different days may be so appointed for different purposes or different provisions.

GENERAL NOTE

**HB.209**    By virtue of the Protection of Employees (Part-Time Work) Act 2001 (Commencement) Order 2001 (S.I. No. 636 of 2001), December 20, 2001 was appointed as the day on which the Act came into operation.

## Interpretation (generally)

**HB.210**    **3.** —(1) In this Act, unless the context otherwise requires—

"collective agreement" means an agreement by or on behalf of an employer on the one hand, and by or on behalf of a body or bodies representative of the employees to whom the agreement relates on the other hand;

"conditions of employment" includes conditions in respect of remuneration and matters related thereto (and, in relation to any pension scheme or arrangement, includes conditions for membership of the scheme or arrangement and entitlement to rights thereunder and conditions related to the making of contributions to the scheme or arrangement);

"contract of employment" means—

(a)  a contract of service or apprenticeship, and

(b)  any other contract whereby an individual agrees with another person, who is carrying on the business of an employment agency within the meaning of the Employment Agency Act, 1971, and is acting in the course of that business, to do or perform personally any work or service for a third person (whether or not the third person is a party to the contract),

whether the contract is express or implied and, if express, whether it is oral or in writing;

"employee" means a person of any age who has entered into or works under (or, where the employment has ceased, entered into or worked under) a contract of employment and references, in relation to an employer, to an employee shall be construed as references to an employee employed by that employer; and for the purposes of this Act, a person holding office under, or in the service of, the State (including a civil servant within the meaning of the Civil Service Regulation Act, 1956) shall be deemed to be an employee employed by the State or Government, as the case may be, and an officer or servant of a local authority for the purposes of the Local Government Act, 1941, or of a harbour authority, [the Health Service Executive] or vocational education committee shall be deemed to be an employee employed by the authority, [Executive] or committee, as the case may be;

"employer" means, in relation to an employee, the person with whom the employee has entered into or for whom the employee works under (or, where the employment has ceased, entered into or worked under) a contract of employment, subject to the qualification that the person who under a contract of employment referred to in paragraph (b) of the definition of "contract of employment" is liable to pay the wages of the individual concerned in respect of the work or service concerned shall be deemed to be the individual's employer;

"Framework Agreement" means the Framework Agreement on part-time work concluded by UNICE, CEEP and the ETUC annexed to Directive 97/81/EC of 15 December, 1997 of the Council of the European Communities;

"Minister" means the Minister for Enterprise, Trade and Employment;

"prescribed" means prescribed by regulations made by the Minister under this Act;

H–64

"relevant enactment" means—

(a) the Carer's Leave Act, 2001,

(b) the Minimum Notice and Terms of Employment Acts, 1973 and 1984,

(c) the Protection of Employees (Employers' Insolvency) Acts, 1984 and 1990,

(d) the Redundancy Payments Acts, 1967 to 1990,

(e) the Terms of Employment (Information) Act, 1994,

(f) the Unfair Dismissals Acts, 1977 to 1993, or

(g) the Worker Participation (State Enterprises) Acts, 1977 to 1993;
    "remuneration", in relation to an employee, includes—

(a) any consideration, whether in cash or in kind, which the employee receives, directly or indirectly, from the employer in respect of the employment, and

(b) any amounts the employee will be entitled to receive on foot of any pension scheme or arrangement.

(2) In this Act—

(a) a reference to a Part or section is a reference to a Part or section of this Act unless it is indicated that reference to some other enactment is intended,

(b) a reference to a subsection, paragraph or subparagraph is a reference to the subsection, paragraph or subparagraph of the provision in which the reference occurs, unless it is indicated that reference to some other provision is intended, and

(c) a reference to any enactment shall be construed as a reference to that enactment as amended, adapted or extended by or under any subsequent enactment (including this Act).

GENERAL NOTE

"collective agreement": this definition is identical to that in s.2(1) of the Organisation of Working **HB.211** Time Act 1997.

"contract of employment": as to whether a person is employed under a contract of service see *Henry Denny & Sons (Ireland) Ltd v Minister for Social Welfare* [1998] 1 I.R. 34. The inclusion of a specific reference to persons employed through employment agencies is similar to the provisions of s.13 of the Unfair Dismissals (Amendment) Act 1993, s.1(1) of the Terms of Employment (Information) Act 1994, section 1(1) of the Protection of Young Persons (Employment) Act 1996, s.2(1) of the Organisation of Working Time Act 1997, s.2(1) of the Parental Leave Act 1998 and s.2(1) of the Carer's Leave Act 2001. But note the decision of the Labour Court in *Rooney v Diageo Global Supply* [2004] E.L.R. 133, that an agency supplied worker was employed by the client under a contract of employment.

"employee": this definition was amended by s.66 of the Health Act 2004.

"remuneration": this definition covers all benefits based on the wage or salary received by the employee. In construing the similar definition in the equal pay legislation (see para. LB.114 *infra)* the Labour Court has held that it is broad enough to include travel allowances, bonus payments, provision of a car, redundancy lump sum payments, hire purchase loans and sick pay.

## Regulations and orders

**4.**—(1) The Minister may make regulations prescribing any matter or thing **HB.212** which is referred to in this Act as prescribed or to be prescribed or for the purpose of enabling any provision of this Act to have full effect.

(2) Regulations under this Act may make different provisions in relation to different classes of employees or employers, different areas or otherwise by reference to the different circumstances of the matter.

(3) A regulation or order under this Act may contain such incidental, supple-

H–65

mentary and consequential provisions as appear to the Minister to be necessary or expedient.

(4) The Minister may by order amend or revoke an order under this Act (including an order under this subsection).

(5) A regulation or order under this Act (other than an order under section 2) shall be laid before each House of the Oireachtas as soon as may be after it is made and, if a resolution annulling that regulation or order is passed by either such House within the next 21 days on which that House has sat after the regulation or order is laid before it, the regulation or order shall be annulled accordingly, but without prejudice to the validity of anything previously done thereunder.

## Repeal

**HB.213**  **5.** The Worker Protection (Regular Part-Time Employees) Act, 1991, is repealed.

## Expenses

**HB.214**  **6.** The expenses incurred by the Minister in the administration of this Act shall, to such extent as may be sanctioned by the Minister for Finance, be paid out of moneys provided by the Oireachtas.

PART 2

PART-TIME WORK AND THE RIGHTS OF PART-TIME EMPLOYEES

## Interpretation (Part 2)

**HB.215**  **7.**—(1) In this Part—

"agency worker" means an employee whose contract of employment is of the kind mentioned in paragraph (b) of the definition of "contract of employment" in section 3;

"associated employer" shall be construed in accordance with subsection (5);

"comparable employee" shall be construed in accordance with subsection (2);

"full-time employee" means an employee who is not a part-time employee;

"normal hours of work" means, in relation to an employee, the average number of hours worked by the employee each day during a reference period;

"part-time employee" means an employee whose normal hours of work are less than the normal hours of work of an employee who is a comparable employee in relation to him or her;

"reference period" means a period which complies with the following conditions:

(a) the period is of not less than 7 days nor more than 12 months duration,

(b) the period is the same period by reference to which the normal hours of work of the other employee referred to in the definition of "part-time employee" in this section is determined, and

(c) the number of hours worked by the employee concerned in the period constitutes the normal number of hours worked by the employee in a period of that duration;

"relevant part-time employee" shall be construed in accordance with subsection (2).

H–66

(2) For the purposes of this Part, an employee is a comparable employee in relation to the employee firstly mentioned in the definition of "part-time employee" in this section (the "relevant part-time employee") if—

    (a) the employee and the relevant part-time employee are employed by the same employer or associated employers and one of the conditions referred to in subsection (3) is satisfied in respect of those employees,

    (b) in case paragraph (a) does not apply (including a case where the relevant part-time employee is the sole employee of the employer), the employee is specified in a collective agreement, being an agreement that for the time being has effect in relation to the relevant part-time employee, to be a type of employee who is to be regarded for the purposes of this Part as a comparable employee in relation to the relevant part-time employee, or

    (c) in case neither paragraph (a) nor (b) applies, the employee is employed in the same industry or sector of employment as the relevant part-time employee is employed in and one of the conditions referred to in subsection (3) is satisfied in respect of those employees,

and references in this Part to a comparable full-time employee in relation to a part-time employee shall be construed accordingly.

(3) The following are the conditions mentioned in subsection (2)—

    (a) both of the employees concerned perform the same work under the same or similar conditions or each is interchangeable with the other in relation to the work,

    (b) the work performed by one of the employees concerned is of the same or a similar nature to that performed by the other and any differences between the work performed or the conditions under which it is performed by each, either are of small importance in relation to the work as a whole or occur with such irregularity as not to be significant, and

    (c) the work performed by the relevant part-time employee is equal or greater in value to the work performed by the other employee concerned, having regard to such matters as skill, physical or mental requirements, responsibility and working conditions.

(4) If the relevant part-time employee is an agency worker then the application of subsection (3) shall not result in any employee, other than another agency worker, being regarded, for the purposes of this Part, as a comparable employee in relation to him or her (and likewise, if the relevant part-time employee is a non-agency worker, the application of that subsection shall not result in an agency worker being regarded, for the purposes of this Part, as a comparable employee in relation to the relevant part-time employee).

(5) For the purposes of this Part, 2 employers shall be taken to be associated if one is a body corporate of which the other (whether directly or indirectly) has control or if both are bodies corporate of which a third person (whether directly or indirectly) has control.

GENERAL NOTE

    Subsection (3) is drafted in terms similar to the definition of "like work" in s.7 of the Employment **HB.216** Equality Act 1998. Unlike the position under that Act however, in the absence of a comparable full-time employee in the employment where the part-time employee is employed, the comparator may be drawn from the same industry or sector of employment. As regards "agency workers", they can only compare themselves to comparable employees who are also agency workers. Opposition attempts to provide that a part-time "agency worker" could compare himself or herself with a full-time employee were resisted: see 542 *Dáil Debates* Cols. 1451–1461. See, however, *Rooney v Diageo Global Supply* [2004] E.L.R. 133, where the claimant, who was a registered general nurse supplied to the respondent by a licensed employment agency and paid by the agency, was found by the Labour Court to be employed by the respondent under a contract of employment.

## Application of relevant enactments

HB.217 **8.** Each relevant enactment shall apply to a part-time employee in the same manner, and subject to the like exceptions not inconsistent with this section, as it applies, other than by virtue of this Act, to an employee to whom that enactment relates.

## Conditions of employment for part-time employees

HB.218 **9.**—(1) Subject to subsections (2) and (4) and section 11(2), a part-time employee shall not, in respect of his or her conditions of employment, be treated in a less favourable manner than a comparable full-time employee.

(2) Without prejudice to section 11(2), if treating a part-time employee, in respect of a particular condition of employment, in a less favourable manner than a comparable full-time employee can be justified on objective grounds then that employee may, notwithstanding subsection (1), be so treated.

(3) Nothing in subsection (2) shall be construed as affecting the application of a relevant enactment, by virtue of section 8, to a part-time employee.

(4) Subsection (1) shall, in so far, but only in so far, as it relates to any pension scheme or arrangement, not apply to a part-time employee whose normal hours of work constitute less than 20 per cent of the normal hours of work of a comparable full-time employee.

(5) For the avoidance of doubt, the reference in this section to a comparable full-time employee is a reference to such an employee either of the opposite sex to the part-time employee concerned or of the same sex as him or her.

GENERAL NOTE

HB.219 This section, which gives effect to clause 4(1) of the Framework Agreement, provides, in general terms, that a part-time employee shall not be treated less favourably than a comparable full-time employee in respect of his or her conditions of employment. Subsection (2) provides that a part-time employee may, in respect of a particular condition of employment, be treated less favourably than a comparable full-time employee if that treatment can be justified on "objective grounds". Such grounds must be based on considerations other than the status of the employee as a part-timer and the less favourable treatment must be for the purpose of achieving a legitimate objective of the employer and must be necessary for that purpose. In *Curry v Boxmore Plastics Ltd* PTD5/2003, the Labour Court held that a condition of employment whereby part-time employees do not receive overtime until they have completed the standard number of hours under which a comparable full-time employee would be entitled to claim overtime is not unfavourable treatment and is thus not discriminatory. In *Abbott Ireland Ltd v SIPTU* PTD3/2004 the union claimed that part-time workers were entitled to rest breaks on a pro-rata basis with full-time employees and that part-time employees working between 4 p.m. and midnight were entitled to shift premium payments on a pro-rata basis with comparable full-time employees. Both claims were successful with the Labour Court holding as follows:

> "The purpose of this Act is to prevent part-time employees being less favourably treated than comparable full-time employees. In this case, the full-time employees receive a thirty minute break during their four hour shift. The fact that the break given to full-time employees is in line with their entitlements under the Organisation of Working Time Act cannot be used as objective justification for the less favourable treatment of part-time employees. Indeed the Act is quite clear in what must be justified is not the more favourable treatment of full-time employees, but the less favourable treatment of part-time employees…
> If the part-time employee works the same hours as a full-time employee and the full-time employee receives an unsocial shift premium for those hours then the part-time employee is also entitled to that premium unless there are objective grounds for its non-payment."

In *Ennis v Department of Justice, Equality and Law Reform* PTD1/2004, the Labour Court upheld a complaint that paying part-time traffic wardens, who worked 50 per cent of the hours of full-time wardens, only 50 per cent of the travel allowance constituted a contravention of this section. Subsection (4) provides that a part-time employee who normally works less than 20 per cent of the normal hours of work of a comparable full-time employee may be treated less favourably in relation to pensions.

## Proportionate provision of certain conditions of employment

**10.**—(1) The extent to which any condition of employment referred to in subsection (2) is provided to a part-time employee for the purposes of complying with section 9(1) shall be related to the proportion which the normal hours of work of that employee bears to the normal hours of work of the comparable full-time employee concerned. **HB.220**

(2) The condition of employment mentioned in subsection (1) is a condition of employment the amount of the benefit of which (in case the condition is of a monetary nature) or the scope of the benefit of which (in any other case) is dependent on the number of hours worked by the employee.

(3) For the avoidance of doubt, neither this section nor any other provision of this Act affects the operation of Part III of the Organisation of Working Time Act, 1997.

GENERAL NOTE

This section provides that a benefit accorded to a part-time employee shall be on the basis of the principle of *pro rata temporis*. In *Department of Education and Science v Gallagher* PTD7/2004, the Labour Court said that subs.(2) must be construed in harmony with clause 4(2) of the Framework Agreement which provides that the principle of non-discrimination could be satisfied by applying conditions of employment pro rata where appropriate. This, the Court said, recognised that the pro rata principle was not of universal application. Accordingly, the Court felt that the type of benefits contemplated by subs.(2) were "connected to those which by their nature are appropriately dependent on the number of hours worked by the employee". Under the Organisation of Working Time Act 1997 a part-time employee's annual leave entitlement is 8 per cent of the hours worked in a leave year subject to a maximum of four working weeks annual leave. **HB.221**

## Part-time employees who work on a casual basis

**11.**—(1) This section applies to a part-time employee who— **HB.222**

(a) works on a casual basis, and

(b) does not fall within a class of employee prescribed under subsection (7).

(2) Notwithstanding section 9(1), a part-time employee to whom this section applies may, if such less favourable treatment can be justified on objective grounds, be treated, in respect of a particular condition of employment, in a less favourable manner than a comparable full-time employee.

(3) Nothing in subsection (2) shall be construed as affecting the application of a relevant enactment, by virtue of section 8, to a part-time employee.

(4) For the purposes of this section, a part-time employee shall, at a particular time, be regarded as working on a casual basis if—

(a) at that time—

(i) he or she has been in the continuous service of the employer for a period of less than 13 weeks, and

(ii) that period of service and any previous period of service by him or her with the employer are not of such a nature as could reasonably be regarded as regular or seasonal employment,

or

(b) by virtue of his or her fulfilling, at that time, conditions specified in an approved collective agreement that has effect in relation to him or her,

H–69

he or she is regarded for the purposes of that agreement as working on such a basis.

(5) In subsection (4)(b), "approved collective agreement" means a collective agreement that stands approved of by the Labour Court under the Schedule to this Act.

(6) For the purposes of subsection (4)(a), the service of an employee in his or her employment shall be deemed to be continuous unless that service is terminated by—

(a) the dismissal of him or her by the employer, or

(b) the employee voluntarily leaving his or her employment.

(7) The Minister shall from time to time cause to be reviewed, in such manner as he or she determines, the operation of this section in relation to part-time employees and may, following such a review, subject to subsection (9), prescribe a class or classes of such employee to be a class or classes of employee to whom this section shall not apply.

(8) In determining the manner in which such a review shall be carried out, the Minister shall consult with such organisations representative of employers, such organisations representative of employees, and such other bodies as the Minister considers appropriate and, before making regulations under this section, the Minister shall consult with such organisations and bodies in relation to the terms of the proposed regulations.

(9) The Minister shall not make regulations under this section unless the results of the review concerned referred to in subsection (7), in the Minister's opinion, show that there cannot, in ordinary circumstances, be objective grounds for treating the class or classes of employees to whom the regulations relate in a less favourable manner than a comparable full-time employee.

General Note

**HB.223**    This section provides that a part-time employee who works on a casual basis may be treated less favourably than a comparable full-time employee if objective grounds exist to justify such less favourable treatment. By virtue of s.12, however, what may not be considered as an objective ground in relation to a part-time employee may be considered an objective ground in relation to a casual part-time employee.

By the end of 2003, the Labour Court had approved one collective agreement, the parties to which were the three teaching unions (INTO, ASTI and TUI), the Department of Education and Science, the Joint Managerial Body Secretariat of Secondary Schools, the Association of Community and Comprehensive Schools, the Irish Vocational Education Association and the Catholic Primary Schools Managers' Association. The agreement sets out the terms and conditions relating to an estimated 5,500 part-time teachers working on a casual basis.

## Objective grounds for less favourable treatment

**HB.224**    **12.**—(1) A ground shall not be regarded as an objective ground for the purposes of any provision of this Part unless it is based on considerations other than the status of the employee concerned as a part-time employee and the less favourable treatment which it involves for that employee is for the purpose of achieving a legitimate objective of the employer and such treatment is appropriate and necessary for that purpose.

(2) For the avoidance of doubt, a ground which does not constitute an objective ground for the purposes of section 9(2) may be capable of constituting an objective ground for the purposes of section 11(2).

## Review of obstacles to the performance of part-time work

**HB.225**    **13.**—(1) The Commission may, and at the request of the Minister shall, study every industry and sector of employment for the purposes of identifying obstacles that may exist in that industry or sector to persons being able to perform part-time work in that industry or sector and make recommendations as to how any such obstacles so identified could be eliminated.

(2) The Commission shall report to the Minister in relation to any study and recommendations made by it under subsection (1) (whether that study and those recommendations have been made of its own volition or not) and shall publish, in such manner as it thinks appropriate, that study and those recommendations.

(3) Any such publication may include such practical guidance for the industries and sectors of employment concerned with regard to the steps that may be taken to implement the recommendations of the Commission as the Commission thinks appropriate.

(4) In formulating recommendations under subsection (1), the Commission shall invite such organisations representative of employers, such organisations representative of employees, and such other bodies as the Commission considers appropriate, to make submissions, whether orally or in writing, to it in relation to the proposed recommendations, and shall have regard to any submissions made to it, in response to the invitation, by such organisations or bodies.

(5) The Commission shall, after consultation with organisations and bodies of the kind referred to in subsection (4), determine the extent to which the preparation of a code of practice under this subsection with respect to the steps that could be taken by employers for the purposes of Clause 5.3 of the Framework Agreement would, in its opinion, be of practical benefit to employees and employers and may, if in its opinion the preparation of such code would be of sufficient practical benefit to those persons, prepare and publish such a code accordingly.

(6) The Commission may, after consultation with the organisations and bodies referred to in subsection (5), amend or revoke, or replace with another code of practice thereunder, a code of practice under subsection (5); the Commission shall publish any such replacement code or, as appropriate, publish notice of the making of any such amendment and its nature or any such revocation, as the case may be.

(7) In this section—
"Commission" means the Labour Relations Commission;
"obstacles" includes obstacles arising by virtue of the operation of any enactment and the following of any practice;
"part-time work" means work which, if it were performed, would result in the person performing it being regarded as a part-time employee for the purposes of this Act.

GENERAL NOTE

The Labour Relations Commission has prepared a code of practice on access to part-time working **HB.225A** which has been implemented by the Industrial Relations Act 1990 (Code of Practice on Access to Part-Time Working) (Declaration) Order 2006 (S.I. No. 8 of 2006). The Code of Practice recognises the importance of developing access to part-time work as a strategic response to growing demands for modern, flexible work-organisation and seeks, *inter alia*, to provide the development of policies and procedures to assist employers and employees and their representatives, to improve access to part-time work for those who wish to work on a part-time basis. As to the status of such a Code of Practice, see s.42(4) of the Industrial Relations Act 1990 which provides that it shall be admissible in evidence in any proceedings before a court, the Labour Court, the Labour Relations Commission, the Employment Appeals Tribunal or the Equality Tribunal and any provision of the code which appears to the body concerned to be relevant to any question arising in the proceedings shall be taken into account in determining that question.

## Voidance of certain provisions

**14.** Save as expressly provided otherwise in this Act, a provision in an agree- **HB.226** ment (whether a contract of employment or not and whether made before or after the commencement of the provision concerned of this Act) shall be void in so far as it purports to exclude or limit the application of, or is inconsistent with, any provision of this Act.

GENERAL NOTE

HB.227    This section ensures that a person cannot agree to nullify or exclude the application of the Act. It is in terms similar to those of s.13 of the Unfair Dismissals Act 1977 and s.11 of the Payment of Wages Act 1991.

## Prohibition of penalisation of employee by employer

HB.228    **15.**—(1) An employer shall not penalise an employee—

(a) for invoking any right of the employee to be treated, in respect of the employee's conditions of employment, in the manner provided for by this Part, or

(b) for having in good faith opposed by lawful means an act which is unlawful under this Act, or

(c) for refusing to accede to a request by the employer to transfer from performing—

(i)    full-time work to performing part-time work, or

(ii)   part-time work to performing full-time work,

or

(d) for giving evidence in any proceedings under this Act or giving notice of his or her intention to do so or to do any other thing referred to in paragraph (a), (b) or (c).

(2) For the purposes of this section, an employee is penalised if he or she—

(a) is dismissed, suffers any unfavourable change in his or her conditions of employment or any unfair treatment (including selection for redundancy), or

(b) is the subject of any other action prejudicial to his or her employment,

but, where any such action with regard to the employee is in respect of the matter referred to in subsection (1)(c), that action shall not constitute a penalisation of the employee if both of the following conditions are complied with—

(i)    having regard to all the circumstances, there were substantial grounds both to justify the employer's making the request concerned and the employer's taking that action consequent on the employee's refusal, and

(ii)   the taking of that action is in accordance with the employee's contract of employment and the provisions of any other enactment of the kind to which section 20(2) applies.

(3) If a penalisation of an employee, in contravention of subsection (1), constitutes a dismissal of the employee within the meaning of the Unfair Dismissals Acts, 1977 to 2001, relief may not be granted to the employee in respect of that penalisation both under this Part and under those Acts.

(4) In this section—

"full-time work" means work which, if it were performed, would result in the person performing it being regarded as a full-time employee for the purposes of this Act;

"part-time work" has the same meaning as it has in section 13.

GENERAL NOTE

HB.229    Although this section prohibits an employer from penalising an employee for having done certain things, it specifically provides that the employer shall not be considered to have penalised an employee in relation to a request to transfer from full-time to part-time work or vice versa if certain conditions are met. These conditions are that (i) the employer must have substantial grounds both to justify the making of the request and for taking any action consequent on the employee's refusal, and (ii) the taking of the

H–72

action is in accordance with the employee's contract of employment and the provisions of the employment rights legislation.

## Complaints to rights commissioner

**16.**—(1) An employee or any trade union of which the employee is a member, **HB.230** with the consent of the employee, may present a complaint to a rights commissioner that the employee's employer has contravened section 9 or 15 in relation to the employee and, if the employee or such a trade union does so, the commissioner shall give the parties an opportunity to be heard by the commissioner and to present to the commissioner any evidence relevant to the complaint, shall give a decision in writing in relation to it and shall communicate the decision to the parties.

H–72/1

(2) A decision of a rights commissioner under subsection (1) shall do one or more of the following—

(a) declare that the complaint was or, as the case may be, was not well founded,

(b) require the employer to comply with the relevant provision,

(c) require the employer to pay to the employee compensation of such amount (if any) as is just and equitable having regard to all the circumstances, but not exceeding 2 years remuneration in respect of the employee's employment,

and the references in the foregoing paragraphs to an employer shall be construed, in a case where ownership of the business of the employer changes after the contravention to which the complaint relates occurred, as references to the person who, by virtue of the change, becomes entitled to such ownership.

(3) A rights commissioner shall not entertain a complaint under this section if it is presented to the commissioner after the expiration of the period of 6 months beginning on the date of the contravention to which the complaint relates or the date of termination of the contract of employment concerned, whichever is the earlier.

(4) Notwithstanding subsection (3), a rights commissioner may entertain a complaint under this section presented to him or her after the expiration of the period referred to in subsection (3) (but not later than 12 months after such expiration) if he or she is satisfied that the failure to present the complaint within that period was due to reasonable cause.

(5) A complaint shall be presented by giving notice of it in writing to a rights commissioner and the notice shall contain such particulars and be in such form as may be specified from time to time by the Minister.

(6) A copy of a notice under subsection (5) shall be given to the other party concerned by the rights commissioner concerned.

(7) Proceedings under this section before a rights commissioner shall be conducted otherwise than in public.

(8) A rights commissioner shall furnish the Labour Court with a copy of each decision given by the commissioner under subsection (1).

(9) The Minister may by regulations provide for any matters relating to proceedings under this section that the Minister considers appropriate.

GENERAL NOTE

This section provides that a complaint may be referred in the first instance to a rights commissioner **HB.231** who may, if the complaint is upheld, award compensation subject to a limit of two years remuneration. In awarding compensation, the rights commissioner and the Labour Court on appeal must make it clear whether the award is or is not "in respect of remuneration including arrears of remuneration", otherwise it may not be regarded as being exempt from income tax: see s.192A of the Taxes Consolidation Act 1997 (inserted by s.7 of the Finance Act 2004). Such complaints must be made within six months of the date of contravention of s.9 or 15, as the case may be, although this period may be extended by a further 12 months if the failure to refer the case within six months was due to "reasonable cause".

The power to extend the time-limit was fully considered by the Labour Court in *Cementation Skanska v Carroll* DWT38/2003, where the Court held that, in considering if "reasonable cause" existed, it was for the claimant to show that there were reasons which both explain the delay and afford an excuse for it. The Court continued:

"The explanation must be reasonable, that is to say it must make sense, be agreeable to reason and not be irrational or absurd. In the context in which the expression 'reasonable cause' appears in statute it suggests an objective standard but it must be applied to the facts and circumstances known to the claimant at the material time."

The length of the delay was also to be taken into account along with the possible prejudice to the employer.

Given that the Act enshrines the principle of "non-discrimination", it might have been more appropriate to provide that complaints be referred to the Director of the Equality Tribunal whose Equality Officers are familiar with this concept from cases under the Employment Equality Acts 1998 and 2004 and are empowered to fully investigate such complaints.

## Appeals from and enforcement of decisions of rights commissioner

**HB.232**

**17.**—(1) A party concerned may appeal to the Labour Court from a decision of a rights commissioner under section 16 and, if the party does so, the Labour Court shall give the parties an opportunity to be heard by it and to present to it any evidence relevant to the appeal, shall make a determination in writing in relation to the appeal affirming, varying or setting aside the decision and shall communicate the determination to the parties.

(2) An appeal under this section shall be initiated by the party concerned giving, within 6 weeks of the date on which the decision to which it relates was communicated to the party, a notice in writing to the Labour Court containing such particulars as are determined by the Labour Court under subsection (4) and stating the intention of the party concerned to appeal against the decision.

(3) A copy of a notice under subsection (2) shall be given by the Labour Court to the other party concerned as soon as may be after the receipt of the notice by the Labour Court.

(4) The following matters, or the procedures to be followed in relation to them, shall be determined by the Labour Court, namely—

   (a)  the procedure in relation to all matters concerning the initiation and the hearing by the Labour Court of appeals under this section,

   (b)  the times and places of hearings of such appeals,

   (c)  the representation of the parties to such appeals,

   (d)  the publication and notification of determinations of the Labour Court,

   (e)  the particulars to be contained in a notice under subsection (2), and

   (f)  any matters consequential on, or incidental to, the foregoing matters.

(5) The Minister may, at the request of the Labour Court, refer a question of law arising in proceedings before it under this section to the High Court for determination by the High Court and the determination of that Court shall be final and conclusive.

(6) A party to proceedings before the Labour Court under this section may appeal to the High Court from a determination of the Labour Court on a point of law and the determination of the High Court shall be final and conclusive.

(7) Section 39(17) of the Redundancy Payments Act, 1967, shall apply in relation to proceedings before the Labour Court under this Part as it applies to matters referred to the Employment Appeals Tribunal under that section with—

   (a)  the substitution in that provision of references to the Labour Court for references to the Tribunal,

   (b)  the deletion in paragraph (d) of that provision of "registered", and

   (c)  the substitution in paragraph (e) of that provision of "a fine not exceeding €1,900" for "a fine not exceeding twenty pounds [€25.39]".

(8) Where a decision of a rights commissioner in relation to a complaint under this Act has not been carried out by the employer concerned in accordance with its terms, the time for bringing an appeal against the decision has expired and no such appeal has been brought, [the employee concerned may bring the complaint] before the Labour Court and the Labour Court shall, without hearing the employer

concerned or any evidence (other than in relation to the matters aforesaid) make a determination to the like effect as the decision.

(9) The bringing of a complaint before the Labour Court under subsection (8) shall be effected by giving to the Labour Court a notice in writing containing such particulars (if any) as may be determined by the Labour Court.

(10) The Labour Court shall publish, in such manner as it thinks fit, particulars of any determination made by it under paragraphs (a),(b),(c),(e) and (f) of subsection (4) (not being a determination as respects a particular appeal under this section) and subsection (9).

GENERAL NOTE

This section provides that a decision of a rights commissioner may be appealed to the Labour Court **HB.233** within six weeks of the date of the decision. In *Bus Eireann v SIPTU* PTD8/2004, the Labour Court held that the reference in this section to a decision of a Rights Commissioner under s.16 could only be a reference to "a complete or final decision which determines whether or not there has been an infringement of the Act". The Labour Court was satisfied that the decision which the company sought to appeal was merely a ruling on one issue in the case and consequently did not have the character of a decision under s.16. Nevertheless, the Court did recognise that there would be "limited circumstances in which a preliminary point should be determined separately from other issues arising in a case". The Court indicated that this "normally" would only be done "where it could lead to considerable savings in both time and expense" and where the point was "a question of pure law where no evidence is needed and where no further information is required".

There is a further right of appeal on a point of law only to the High Court. Although the Rules of the Superior Courts 1986 (as amended) do not specifically provide for appeals under this Act, it is suggested that any such appeal be brought either by special summons or by notice of motion, by analogy with the procedures set out in R.S.C. 1986, Orders 105 and 106 respectively. In the absence of any specific rule of court, any such appeal need only be brought within a reasonable time: *per* McCracken J. in his *ex tempore* ruling in *McGaley v Liebherr Container Cranes Ltd* (2001/234 Sp) delivered on October 12, 2001.

The circumstances in which the High Court will overturn a decision of a specialist tribunal such as the Labour Court have been considered in many cases: see for example, *Henry Denny & Sons (Ireland) Ltd v Minister for Social Welfare* [1998] 1 I.R. 34 and in particular the comments of Hamilton C.J. at 37. In considering whether to allow an appeal against a decision of such a tribunal, the High Court must consider whether that body based its decision on an identifiable error of law or on an unsustainable finding of fact. A decision cannot be challenged on the grounds of irrationality if there is any relevant material to support it: see further *Mulcahy v Waterford Leader Partnership Ltd* [2002] E.L.R. 12 (O'Sullivan J.) and *Thompson v Tesco Ireland Ltd* [2003] E.L.R. 21 (Lavan J.). In *National University of Ireland, Cork v Ahern* [2005] 2 I.R. 577, the Supreme Court held that, although findings of fact must be accepted by the High Court on appeal, that court could still examine the basis upon which those facts were found. The relevance or admissibility of the matters relied on in determining the facts were questions of law.

Where a decision of a rights commissioner has not been carried out by the employer, and an appeal has not been brought, the employee may refer the complaint to the Labour Court and the Court, without hearing any evidence, shall make a determination to the like effect as the decision of the rights commissioner.

The words in square brackets in subs.(8) were substituted by virtue of s.19(3) of the Protection of Employees (Fixed-Term Work) Act 2003.

## Enforcement of determinations of Labour Court

**18.**—(1) If an employer fails to carry out in accordance with its terms a **HB.234** determination of the Labour Court in relation to a complaint under section 16 within 6 weeks from the date on which the determination is communicated to the parties, the Circuit Court shall, on application to it in that behalf by—

(a)   the employee concerned,

(b)   with the consent of the employee, any trade union of which the employee is a member, or

(c)   the Minister, if the Minister considers it appropriate to make the application having regard to all the circumstances,

H–75

without hearing the employer or any evidence (other than in relation to the matters aforesaid), make an order directing the employer to carry out the determination in accordance with its terms.

(2) The reference in subsection (1) to a determination of the Labour Court is a reference to such a determination in relation to which, at the expiration of the time for bringing an appeal against it, no such appeal has been brought or, if such an appeal has been brought it has been abandoned and the references to the date on which the determination is communicated to the parties shall, in a case where such an appeal is abandoned, be construed as references to the date of such abandonment.

(3) The Circuit Court may, in an order under this section, if in all the circumstances it considers it appropriate to do so, where the order relates to the payment of compensation, direct the employer concerned to pay to the employee concerned interest on the compensation at the rate referred to in section 22 of the Courts Act, 1981, in respect of the whole or any part of the period beginning 6 weeks after the date on which the determination of the Labour Court is communicated to the parties and ending on the date of the order.

(4) An application under this section to the Circuit Court shall be made to the judge of the Circuit Court for the circuit in which the employer concerned ordinarily resides or carries on any profession, business or occupation.

GENERAL NOTE

**HB.235**     This section provides that the Labour Court's determination can be enforced by the employee, the employee's trade union or the Minister in the Circuit Court without the employer or any evidence, other than in relation to non-implementation, being heard. The procedures governing applications for enforcement are set out in Order 57 Rule 7 of the Circuit Court Rules 2001 as inserted by S.I. No. 721 of 2004 (reproduced *infra* at HC.101).

## Non-application of sections 16 to 18

**HB.236**     **19.**—Sections 16 to 18 shall not apply to a member of the Defence Forces.

PART 3

MISCELLANEOUS

## Clarification of effect of certain enactments in relation to posted workers and others having an employment relationship in the State

**HB.237**     **20.** [...]

## Amendment of section 14(2) of Protection of Employment Act 1977

**HB.238**     **21.** [...]

SCHEDULE

APPROVAL OF COLLECTIVE AGREEMENTS FOR PURPOSES OF SECTION 11(4)

**HB.239**     1. In this Schedule, "collective agreement" means a collective agreement referred to in section 11(5).

**HB.240**     2.—(1) On an application being made in that behalf by any of the parties thereto, the Labour Court may, subject to the provisions of this Schedule, approve of a collective agreement.

(2) On receipt of an application under this paragraph, the Labour Court shall consult such representatives of employees and employers as it considers to have an interest in the matters to which the collective agreement, the subject of the application, relates.

H–76

(3) The Labour Court shall not approve of a collective agreement unless the following conditions are fulfilled as respects that agreement, namely—

(a) the Labour Court is satisfied that it is appropriate to approve of the agreement having regard to Clause 2.2 of the Framework Agreement,

(b) the agreement has been concluded in a manner usually employed in determining the pay or other conditions of employment of employees in the employment concerned,

(c) the body which negotiated the agreement on behalf of the employees concerned is the holder of a negotiation licence under the Trade Union Act, 1941, or is an excepted body within the meaning of that Act which is sufficiently representative of the employees concerned,

(d) the agreement is in such form as appears to the Labour Court to be suitable for the purposes of the agreement being approved of under this section.

(4) Where the Labour Court is not satisfied that the condition referred to in clause (a) or (d) of subparagraph (3) is fulfilled in relation to a collective agreement, the subject of an application under this paragraph (but is satisfied that the other conditions referred to in subparagraph (3) are fulfilled in relation to the agreement), it may request the parties to the agreement to vary the agreement in such manner as will result in the said condition being fulfilled and if those parties agree so to vary the agreement and vary it, accordingly, the Labour Court shall approve of the agreement as so varied.

3. Where a collective agreement which has been approved of under this Schedule is subsequently **HB.241** varied by the parties thereto, any of the said parties may apply to the Labour Court to have the agreement, as so varied, approved of by the Labour Court under this Schedule and the provisions of this Schedule shall apply to such an application as they apply to an application under paragraph 2.

4. The Labour Court may withdraw its approval of a collective agreement under this Schedule **HB.242** where it is satisfied that there are substantial grounds for so doing.

5. The Labour Court shall determine the procedures to be followed by a person in making an **HB.243** application under paragraph 2 or 3, by the Labour Court in considering any such application or otherwise performing any of its functions under this Schedule and by persons generally in relation to matters falling to be dealt with under this Schedule.

6. The Labour Court shall publish, in such manner as it thinks fit, particulars of the procedures **HB.244** referred to in paragraph 5.

7. The Labour Court shall establish and maintain a register of collective agreements standing **HB.245** approved of by it under this Schedule and such a register shall be made available for inspection by members of the public at all reasonable times.

# PROTECTION OF EMPLOYEES (FIXED-TERM WORK) ACT 2003

## (2003 No. 29)

ARRANGEMENT OF SECTIONS

PART 1

PRELIMINARY AND GENERAL

PART 2

FIXED-TERM WORK AND RIGHTS OF FIXED-TERM EMPLOYEES

PART 3

ENFORCEMENT

PART 4

EXCLUSIONS AND OTHER PROVISIONS

An Act to provide for the implementation of Directive No. 1999/70/EC of **HB.301** 28 June 1999, of the Council of the European Communities concerning the framework agreement on fixed-term work concluded by ETUC, UNICE and CEEP, to amend the Employment Agency Act 1971, the Organisation of Working Time Act 1997 and the Protection of Employees (Part-Time Work) Act 2001 and to provide for related matters.

[*14th July*, 2003]

INTRODUCTION AND GENERAL NOTE

The main purpose of the Act is the transposition into Irish law of Council Directive 1999/70/EC **HB.302** concerning the Framework Agreement on Fixed-Term Work concluded by the general cross-industry

H–77

organisations at European level. Consequently, the Act provides for the improvement of the quality of fixed-term work by ensuring the application of the principle of non-discrimination to fixed-term workers; in other words such workers may not be treated less favourably than comparable permanent workers. It also establishes a framework to prevent abuse arising from the use of successive fixed-terms employment contracts. In this regard, account must also be taken of the relevant provisions of s.2(2) of the Unfair Dismissals Act 1977 (as amended) (on which see para.JB.115 *infra*). Although the Central Statistics Office (CSO) does not have figures for this category of "atypical employment", the Minister of State at the Department of Enterprise, Trade and Employment estimated that there were 70,000 fixed term contract workers (or 4 per cent of the total workforce) (see 569 *Dáil Debates* Col. 1031). The Minister added *(ibid.)* that the CSO has been requested, as part of its review of the Quarterly National Household Survey 2003–2006, to include in its questionnaire a series of questions to ascertain the numbers of, and trends in relation to, such workers.

The Directive required implementation by July 10, 2001, but because the Act provides that the principle of non-discrimination applies to pay and pension entitlements, opposition attempts to apply its operation retrospectively were resisted.

CUITATION

**HB.303**    See section 1.

COMMENCEMENT

**HB.304**    The Act came into operation on July 14, 2003.

PARLIAMENTARY DEBATES

**HB.305**    173 *Seanad Debates* Cols. 495–519 Second Stage).
173 *Seanad Debates* Cols. 606–623 (Committee Stage).
173 *Seanad Debates* Cols. 784–787 (Report and Final Stages).
569 *Dáil Debates* Cols. 1029–1045 (Second Stage).
569 *Dáil Debates* Cols. 1073–1080 (Second Stage resumed).
569 *Dáil Debates* Cols. 1118–1152 (Second Stage resumed).
570 *Dáil Debates* Cols. 640–678 (Committee and Remaining Stages).
173 *Seanad Debates* Cols. 1765–1771 (Report and Final Stages).

Be it enacted by the Oireachtas as follows:

PART I

PRELIMINARY AND GENERAL

## Short title

**HB.306**    1.—This Act may be cited as the Protection of Employees (Fixed-Term Work) Act 2003.

## Interpretation

**HB.307**    2.—(1) In this Act, unless the context otherwise requires—

"Act of 2001" means the Protection of Employees (Part-Time Work) Act 2001;

"associated employer" shall be read in accordance with subsection (2);

"collective agreement" means an agreement by or on behalf of an employer on the one hand, and by or on behalf of a body or bodies representative of the employees to whom the agreement relates on the other hand;

"comparable permanent employee" shall be read in accordance with section 5;

"conditions of employment" includes conditions in respect of remuneration and matters relating thereto (and, in relation to any pension scheme or arrangement, includes conditions for membership of the scheme or arrangement and entitlement to rights thereunder and conditions related to the making of contributions to the scheme or arrangement);

"contract of employment" means a contract of service whether express or implied and, if express, whether oral or in writing but shall not include a contract whereby

H–78

an individual agrees with another person, who is carrying on the business of an employment agency within the meaning of the Employment Agency Act 1971 and is acting in the course of that business, to do or perform personally any work or service for a third person (whether or not the third person is a party to the contract);

"employee" means a person of any age, who has entered into or works under (or, where the employment has ceased, entered into or worked under) a contract of employment and references, in relation to an employer, to an employee shall be construed as references to an employee employed by that employer and, for the purposes of this Act, a person holding office under, or in the service of, the State (including a civil servant within the meaning of the Civil Service Regulation Act 1956) shall be deemed to be an employee employed by the State or Government, as the case may be, and an officer or servant of a local authority, a harbour authority, the [Health Service Executive] or vocational education committee shall be deemed to be an employee employed by the authority, [Executive] or vocational education committee, as the case may be;

"employer" means, in relation to an employee, the person with whom the employee has entered into or for whom the employee works under (or, where the employment has ceased, entered into or worked under) a contract of employment;

"fixed-term employee" means a person having a contract of employment entered into directly with an employer where the end of the contract of employment concerned is determined by an objective condition such as arriving at a specific date, completing a specific task or the occurrence of a specific event but does not include—

    (*a*) employees in initial vocational training relationships or apprenticeship schemes, or

    (*b*) employees with a contract of employment which has been concluded within the framework of a specific public or publicly-supported training, integration or vocational retraining programme;

"Framework Agreement" means the Framework Agreement on fixed-term work concluded by ETUC, UNICE and CEEP annexed to Directive No. 1999/70/EC of 28 June 1999 of the Council of the European Communities;

"local authority" means a county council, a city council or a town council for the purposes of the Local Government Act 2001;

"Minister" means the Minister for Enterprise, Trade and Employment;

"permanent employee" means an employee who is not a fixed-term employee;

"prescribed" means prescribed by regulations made by the Minister under this Act;

"relevant fixed-term employee" shall be read in accordance with section 5;

"remuneration", in relation to an employee, means—

    (*a*) any consideration, whether in cash or in kind, which the employee receives, directly or indirectly, from the employer in respect of the employment, and

    (*b*) any amounts the employee will be entitled to receive on foot of any pension scheme or arrangement;

"renewal" includes extension and cognate words shall be read accordingly;

"year" means any period of 52 weeks.

    (2) Employers are deemed to be associated if—

    (*a*) one is a body corporate of which the other (whether directly or indirectly) has control, or

    (*b*) both are bodies corporate of which a third person (whether directly or indirectly) has control.

    (3) A word or expression that is used in this Act and is also used in the

Framework Agreement has, unless the contrary intention appears, the same meaning in this Act as it has in the Framework Agreement.

(4) In this Act—

(*a*) a reference to a Part or section is a reference to a Part or section of this Act unless it is indicated that reference to some other enactment is intended,

(*b*) a reference to a subsection, paragraph or subparagraph is a reference to the subsection, paragraph or subparagraph of the provision in which the reference occurs, unless it is indicated that reference to some other provision is intended, and

(*c*) a reference to any enactment shall be construed as a reference to that enactment as amended, adapted or extended by or under any subsequent enactment (including this Act).

GENERAL NOTE

**HB.308** "collective agreement": this definition is identical to that in s.2(1) of the Organisation of Working Time Act 1997 and s.3(1) of the Protection of Employees (Part-time Work) Act 2001.

"contract of employment": as to whether a person is employed under a contract of service, see *Henry Denny & Sons (Ireland) Ltd v Minister for Social Welfare* [1998] 1 I.R. 34. Unlike previous legislation, persons employed through employment agencies are expressly excluded from the scope of the Act. Agency workers who are employed under a contract of employment with the employment agency, as in *O'Brien v Eglinton Personnel Group Ltd* UD 818/1992 (reproduced in Madden and Kerr, *Unfair Dismissal: Cases and Commentary* (2nd ed., 1996), p.49), are covered by the Act as the agency would be the employer: see the Minister of State at 569 *Dáil Debates* Cols. 1035–1036. Equally it should be noted that the definition of "contract of employment" does not include a contract of apprenticeship: see *ESB Networks v Kingham* FTD8/2005.

"employee": this definition was amended by s.66 of the Health Act 2004.

"fixed-term employee": in *Allen v National Australia Group Europe Ltd* [2004] I.R.L.R. 847, the English Employment Appeals Tribunal has confirmed that the ability of the parties to bring a contract for a fixed term to an end at an earlier date by the giving of notice did not make the contract anything other than a fixed-term contract. The definition also makes it clear that persons engaged on an apprenticeship scheme are not to be regarded as fixed-term employees. Consequently, a person's entry into apprenticeship will not constitute a renewal of any prior fixed term contracts within the meaning of s.9(1) of the Act: see *ESB Networks v Kingham* FTD8/2005.

"remuneration": this definition covers all benefits based on the wage or salary received by the employee. In construing the similar definition in the equal pay legislation (see para.LB.114 *infra*), the Labour Court has held that it is broad enough to include travel allowances, bonus payments, provision of a car, redundancy lump sum payment, hire purchase loans and sick pay.

## Regulations and orders

**HB.309** **3.**—(1) The Minister may make regulations prescribing any matter or thing which is referred to in this Act as prescribed or to be prescribed or for the purpose of enabling any provision of this Act to have full effect.

(2) Regulations under this Act may make different provisions in relation to different classes of employees or employers, different areas or otherwise by reference to the different circumstances of the matter.

(3) A regulation or order under this Act may contain such incidental, supplementary and consequential provisions as the Minister considers necessary or expedient.

(4) The Minister may by order amend or revoke an order under this Act (including an order under this subsection).

(5) A regulation or order under this Act shall be laid before each House of the Oireachtas as soon as may be after it is made and, if a resolution annulling the regulation or order is passed by either such House within the next 21 days on which that House has sat after the regulation or order is laid before it, the regulation or order shall be annulled accordingly, but without prejudice to the validity of any thing previously done under the regulation or order.

## Expenses

**4.**—Expenses incurred by the Minister in the administration of this Act shall, to **HB.310** such extent as may be sanctioned by the Minister for Finance, be paid out of monies provided by the Oireachtas.

PART 2

FIXED-TERM WORK AND RIGHTS OF FIXED-TERM EMPLOYEES

## Comparable permanent employee

**5.**—(1) For the purposes of this Part, an employee is a comparable permanent **HB.311** employee in relation to a fixed-term employee if—

(*a*) the permanent employee and the relevant fixed-term employee are employed by the same employer or associated employers and one of the conditions referred to in subsection (2) is satisfied in respect of those employees,

(*b*) in case paragraph (*a*) does not apply (including a case where the relevant fixed-term employee is the sole employee of the employer), the permanent employee is specified in a collective agreement, being an agreement that for the time being has effect in relation to the relevant fixed-term employee, to be a type of employee who is to be regarded for the purposes of this Part as a comparable permanent employee in relation to the relevant fixed-term employee, or

(*c*) in case neither paragraph (*a*) nor (*b*) applies, the employee is employed in the same industry or sector of employment as the relevant fixed-term employee and one of the conditions referred to in subsection (2) is satisfied in respect of those employees,

and references in this Part to a comparable permanent employee in relation to a fixed-term employee shall be read accordingly.

(2) The following are the conditions mentioned in subsection (1)—

(*a*) both of the employees concerned perform the same work under the same or similar conditions or each is inter-changeable with the other in relation to the work,

(*b*) the work performed by one of the employees concerned is of the same or a similar nature to that performed by the other and any differences between the work performed or the conditions under which it is performed by each, either are of small importance in relation to the work as a whole or occur with such irregularity as not to be significant, and

(*c*) the work performed by the relevant fixed-term employee is equal or greater in value to the work performed by the other employee concerned, having regard to such matters as skill, physical or mental requirements, responsibility and working conditions.

GENERAL NOTE

Subsection (2) is drafted in terms similar to the definition of "like work" in s.7 of the Employment **HB.312** Equality Act 1998. Unlike the position under that Act, however, in the absence of a comparable permanent employee in the employment where the fixed-term employee is employed, a comparator may be drawn from the same industry or sector of employment.

## Conditions of employment for fixed-term employees

**6.**—(1) Subject to subsections (2) and (5), a fixed-term employee shall not, in **HB.313** respect of his or her conditions of employment, be treated in a less favourable manner than a comparable permanent employee.

(2) If treating a fixed-term employee, in respect of a particular condition of

H–81

employment, in a less favourable manner than a comparable permanent employee can be justified on objective grounds then that employee may, notwithstanding subsection (1),be so treated.

(3) A period of service qualification relating to a particular condition of employment shall be the same for a fixed-term employee as for a comparable permanent employee except where a different length of service qualification is justified on objective grounds.

(4) For the avoidance of doubt, the reference in this section to a comparable permanent employee is a reference to such an employee either of the opposite sex to the fixed-term employee concerned or of the same sex as him or her.

(5) Subsection (1) shall, in so far, but only in so far, as it relates to any pension scheme or arrangement, not apply to a fixed-term employee whose normal hours of work constitute less than 20 per cent of the normal hours of work of a comparable permanent employee.

(6) The extent to which any condition of employment referred to in subsection (7) is provided to a fixed-term employee for the purpose of complying with subsection (1) shall be related to the proportion which the normal hours of work of that employee bears to the normal hours of work of the comparable permanent employee concerned.

(7) The condition of employment mentioned in subsection (6) is a condition of employment the amount of benefit of which (in case the condition is of a monetary nature) or the scope of the benefit of which (in any other case) is dependent on the number of hours worked by an employee.

(8) For the avoidance of doubt, neither this section nor any other provision of this Act affects the operation of Part III of the Organisation of Working Time Act 1997.

GENERAL NOTE

**HB.314**      This section provides, in general terms, that a fixed-term employee shall not be treated less favourably than a comparable permanent employee in respect of his or her conditions of employment. Subsection (2) provides that a fixed-term employee may, in respect of particular conditions of employment, be treated less favourably than a comparable permanent employee if that treatment can be justified on "objective grounds" (on which see General Note to s.7). Subsection (5) provides that a fixed-term employee who normally works less than 20 per cent of the normal hours of work of a comparable permanent employee may be treated less favourably in relation to pensions and is in terms identical to those of s.9(4) of the Protection of Employees (Part-Time Work) Act 2001.

The Labour Court has held, in *Health Service Executive v Prasad* FTD2/2006, that the non-renewal of a fixed-term contract was not in itself capable of constituting less favourable treatment for the purposes of this section. The Court said that neither the Directive nor this Act required "that a fixed-term contract of employment must be renewed unless the employer can show that the requirement for the work being performed by the fixed-term employee has ceased". See, to similar effect, the decision of the English Court of Appeal in *Department for Work and Pensions v Webley* [2005] I.R.L.R. 288.

## Objective grounds for less favourable treatment

**HB.315**      **7.**—(1) A ground shall not be regarded as an objective ground for the purposes of any provision of this Part unless it is based on considerations other than the status of the employee concerned as a fixed-term employee and the less favourable treatment which it involves for that employee (which treatment may include the renewal of a fixed-term employee's contract for a further fixed term) is for the purpose of achieving a legitimate objective of the employer and such treatment is appropriate and necessary for that purpose.

(2) Where, as regards any term of his or her contract, a fixed-term employee is treated by his or her employer in a less favourable manner than a comparable

permanent employee, the treatment in question shall (for the purposes of section 6(2)) be regarded as justified on objective grounds, if the terms of the fixed-term employee's contract of employment, taken as a whole, are at least as favourable as the terms of the comparable permanent employee's contract of employment.

GENERAL NOTE

This section makes it clear that the objective grounds referred to in ss.6(2) and (3), 8 and 9(4) must **HB.316** be based on considerations other than the status of the employee as a fixed-term worker. The less favourable treatment must be for the purpose of achieving a legitimate objective of the employer and must be appropriate and necessary for that purpose. In *Health Service Executive v Prasad* FTD2/2006, the Labour Court said that the second limb of subs.(1), which provides that the grounds relied upon must be justified as being for the purpose of achieving a legitimate objective of the employer and that such treatment must be appropriate and necessary for that purpose, was a restatement of the "three tier test for objective justification in indirect discrimination cases" formulated by the Court of Justice in Case 170/84, *Bilka Kaufhaus* [1986] E.C.R. 1607. This test is now set out in s.22(1)(a) of the Employment Equality Act 1998 and the various elements of the test were analysed by the Labour Court in detail in *Inoue v NBK Designs Ltd* [2003] E.L.R. 98.

## Written statements of employer

**8.**—(1) Where an employee is employed on a fixed-term contract the fixed- **HB.317** term employee shall be informed in writing as soon as practicable by the employer of the objective condition determining the contract whether it is—

(a)  arriving at a specific date,

(b)  completing a specific task, or

(c)  the occurrence of a specific event.

(2) Where an employer proposes to renew a fixed-term contract, the fixed-term employee shall be informed in writing by the employer of the objective grounds justifying the renewal of the fixed-term contract and the failure to offer a contract of indefinite duration, at the latest by the date of the renewal.

(3) A written statement under subsection (1) or (2) is admissible as evidence in any proceedings under this Act.

(4) If it appears to a rights commissioner or the Labour Court in any proceedings under this Act—

(a)  that an employer omitted to provide a written statement, or

(b)  that a written statement is evasive or equivocal,

the rights commissioner or the Labour Court may draw any inference he or she or it consider just and equitable in the circumstances.

## Successive fixed-term contracts

**9.**—(1) Subject to subsection (4), where on or after the passing of this Act a **HB.318** fixed-term employee completes or has completed his or her third year of continuous employment with his or her employer or associated employer, his or her fixed-term contract may be renewed by that employer on only one occasion and any such renewal shall be for a fixed term of no longer than one year.

(2) Subject to subsection (4), where after the passing of this Act a fixed-term employee is employed by his or her employer or associated employer on two or more continuous fixed-term contracts and the date of the first such contract is subsequent to the date on which this Act is passed, the aggregate duration of such contracts shall not exceed 4 years.

(3) Where any term of a fixed-term contract purports to contravene subsection (1) or (2) that term shall have no effect and the contract concerned shall be deemed to be a contract of indefinite duration.

(4) Subsections (1) to (3) shall not apply to the renewal of a contract of employment for a fixed term where there are objective grounds justifying such a renewal.

(5) The First Schedule to the Minimum Notice and Terms of Employment Acts 1973 to [2005] shall apply for the purpose of ascertaining the period of service of an employee and whether that service has been continuous.

NOTE

**HB. 318A**   The term "contract of indefinite duration" is not defined in the Act but it has been judicially defined as meaning no more than a contract terminable upon the giving of reasonable notice: see *Walsh v Dublin Health Authority* (1964) 98 I.L.T.R. 82 and *Sheehy v Ryan* [2004] E.L.R. 87. In *Health Service Executive v Khan* FTD4/2006, the Labour Court ruled that the contract of indefinite duration to which a fixed term employee might become entitled by operation of subs.(3) "is identical in its terms, including any express or implied terms as to training and qualifications, as the fixed term contract from which it was derived". In other words the only term of the preceding contract which is rendered void and severed was that relating to its expiry by effluxion of time. See also *State Laboratory v McArdle* FTD3/2006 (currently under appeal to High Court).

## Information on employment and training opportunities

**HB.319**   **10.**—(1) An employer shall inform a fixed-term employee in relation to vacancies which become available to ensure that he or she shall have the same opportunity to secure a permanent position as other employees.

(2) The information referred to in subsection (1) may be provided by means of a general announcement at a suitable place in the undertaking or establishment.

(3) As far as practicable, an employer shall facilitate access by a fixed-term employee to appropriate training opportunities to enhance his or her skills, career development and occupational mobility.

GENERAL NOTE

The ambit of subs.(1) was considered by the Labour Court in *Aer Lingus v IMPACT* [2005] E.L.R. 261. The Labour Court concluded that, although fixed-term employees had the right to receive information concerning vacancies for which they were qualified to apply, the subsection did not restrict the right of an employer to determine what those qualifications were to be. In *Scoil Iosagain v Henderson* [2005] E.L.R. 271, the Labour Court held that this section required that information on relevant vacancies "be imparted personally to fixed-term employees or that a notice be placed in the workplace". Merely placing an advertisement in a newspaper did not meet the requirements of the Act.

## Information and consultation

**HB.320**   **11.**—(1) Fixed-term employees shall be taken into account when calculating the threshold above which employees' representatives bodies may be constituted in an undertaking in accordance with section 4 of the Transnational Information and Consultation of Employees Act 1996.

(2) As far as practicable, employers shall consider providing information to employees' representatives about fixed-term work in the undertaking.

## Voidance of certain provisions

**HB.321**   **12.**—Save as expressly provided otherwise in this Act, a provision in an agreement (whether a contract of employment or not and whether made before or after the commencement of the provision concerned of this Act) shall be void insofar as it purports to exclude or limit the application of, or is inconsistent with, any provision of the Act.

GENERAL NOTE

**HB.322**   This section ensures that a person cannot agree to nullify or exclude the application of the Act. It is in terms similar to those of s.13 of the Unfair Dismissals Act 1977, s.11 of the Payment of Wages Act 1991 and s.14 of the Protection of Employees (Part-Time Work) Act 2001.

## Prohibition of penalisation of employee by employer

**13.**—(1) An employer shall not penalise an employee—

  (a)  for invoking any right of the employee to be treated, in respect of the employee's conditions of employment, in the manner provided for by this Part,

  (b)  for having in good faith opposed by lawful means an act which is unlawful under this Act,

  (c)  for giving evidence in any proceeding under this Act or for giving notice of his or her intention to do so or to do any other thing referred to in paragraph (a) or (b),or

  (d)  by dismissing the employee from his or her employment if the dismissal is wholly or partly for or connected with the purpose of the avoidance of a fixed-term contract being deemed to be a contract of indefinite duration under section 9(3).

(2) For the purposes of this section, an employee is penalised if he or she—

       

(*a*) is dismissed or suffers any unfavourable change in his or her conditions of employment or any unfair treatment (including selection for redundancy), or

(*b*) is the subject of any other action prejudicial to his or her employment.

PART 3

ENFORCEMENT

## Complaints to rights commissioner

**14.**—(1) An employee or any trade union of which the employee is a member, **HB.324** with the consent of the employee, may present a complaint to a rights commissioner that the employee's employer has contravened any provision of this Act in relation to the employee and, if the employee or such a trade union does so, the commissioner shall—

(*a*) give the parties an opportunity to be heard by the commissioner and to present to the commissioner any evidence relevant to the complaint,

(*b*) give a written decision in relation to the complaint, and

(*c*) communicate the decision to the parties concerned.

(2) A decision of a rights commissioner under subsection (1) shall do one or more of the following:

(*a*) declare whether the complaint was or was not well founded;

(*b*) require the employer to comply with the relevant provision;

(*c*) require the employer to re-instate or re-engage the employee (including on a contract of indefinite duration);

(*d*) require the employer to pay to the employee compensation of such amount (if any) as is just and equitable having regard to all the circumstances, but not exceeding 2 years remuneration in respect of the employee's employment;

and references in paragraphs (*a*) to (*d*) to an employer shall be read in a case where ownership of the business of the employer changes after the contravention to which the complaint relates occurred, as references to the person who, by virtue of the change, becomes entitled to such ownership.

(3) A rights commissioner shall not entertain a complaint under this section if it is presented to the commissioner after the expiration of the period of 6 months beginning on the date of the contravention to which the complaint relates or the date of termination of the contract of employment concerned, whichever is the earlier.

(4) Notwithstanding subsection (3), a rights commissioner may entertain a complaint under this section presented to him or her after the expiration of the period referred to in subsection (3) (but not later than 12 months after the end of that period) if he or she is satisfied that the failure to present the complaint within that period was due to reasonable cause.

(5) A complaint shall be presented by giving notice of it in writing to a rights commissioner and the notice shall contain such particulars and be in such form as may be specified from time to time by the Minister.

(6) A copy of a notice under subsection (5) shall be given to the other party concerned by the rights commissioner.

(7) Proceedings under this section before a rights commissioner shall be conducted otherwise than in public.

(8) A rights commissioner shall furnish the Labour Court with a copy of each decision given by the commissioner under subsection (1).

(9) The Minister may by regulations provide for any matters relating to proceedings under this section that the Minister considers appropriate.

GENERAL NOTE

**HB.325**    This section provides that a complaint may be referred in the first instance to a rights commissioner who may, if the complaint is upheld, award compensation subject to a limit of two years remuneration. In awarding compensation, the rights commissioner and the Labour Court on appeal must make it clear whether the award is or is not "in respect of remuneration including arrears of remuneration", otherwise it may not be regarded as being exempt from income tax: see s.192A of the Taxes Consolidation Act 1997 (inserted by s.7 of the Finance Act 2004). Such complaints must be made within six months of the date of contravention, although this period may be extended by a further 12 months if the failure to refer the case within six months was due to "reasonable cause". The power to extend the time-limit was fully considered by the Labour Court in *Cementation Skanska v Carroll* DWT38/2003, where the Court held that, in considering if "reasonable cause" existed, it was for the claimant to show that there were reasons which both explain the delay and afford an excuse for it. The Court continued:

> "The explanation must be reasonable, that is to say it must make sense, be agreeable to reason and not be irrational or absurd. In the context in which the expression 'reasonable cause' appears in statute it suggests an objective standard but it must be applied to the facts and circumstances known to the claimant at the material time."

The length of the delay was also to be taken into account along with the possible prejudice to the employer.

## Appeal from decision of rights commissioner

**HB.326**    **15.**—(1) A party concerned may appeal to the Labour Court from a decision of a rights commissioner under section 14 and, if the party does so, the Labour Court shall—

(*a*)   give the parties an opportunity to be heard by it and to present to it any evidence relevant to the appeal,

(*b*)   make a written determination in relation to the appeal affirming, varying or setting aside the decision, and

(*c*)   communicate the determination to the parties.

(2) An appeal under this section shall be initiated by the party concerned giving, within 6 weeks of the date on which the decision to which it relates was communicated to the party, a written notice to the Labour Court containing any particulars that are determined by the Labour Court under subsection (4) and stating the intention of the party concerned to appeal against the decision.

(3) A copy of a notice under subsection (2) shall be given by the Labour Court to the other party concerned as soon as practicable after the receipt of the notice by the Labour Court.

(4) The following matters, or the procedures to be followed in relation to them, shall be determined by the Labour Court, namely—

(*a*)   the procedure in relation to all matters concerning the initiation and the hearing by the Labour Court of appeals under this section,

(*b*)   the times and places of hearings of those appeals,

(*c*)   the representation of the parties to those appeals,

(*d*)   the publication and notification of determinations of the Labour Court,

(*e*)   the particulars to be contained in a notice under subsection (2), and

(*f*)   any matters consequential on, or incidental to, the foregoing matters.

(5) The Minister may, at the request of the Labour Court, refer a question of law arising in proceedings before it under this section to the High Court for

determination by the High Court and the determination of that Court shall be final and conclusive.

(6) A party to proceedings before the Labour Court under this section may appeal to the High Court from a determination of the Labour Court on a point of law and the determination of the High Court shall be final and conclusive.

(7) Section 39(17) of the Redundancy Payments Act 1967 shall apply in relation to proceedings before the Labour Court under this Part as it applies to matters referred to the Employment Appeals Tribunal under that section with—

(*a*) the substitution in that provision of references to the Labour Court for references to the Tribunal,

(*b*) the deletion in paragraph (*d*) of that provision of "registered", and

(*c*) the substitution in paragraph (*e*) of that provision of "a fine not exceeding €2,000" for "a fine not exceeding twenty pounds".

(8) Where a decision of a rights commissioner in relation to a complaint under this Act has not been carried out by the employer concerned in accordance with its terms, the time for bringing an appeal against the decision has expired and no such appeal has been brought, the employee concerned may bring the complaint before the Labour Court and the Labour Court shall, without hearing the employer concerned or any evidence (other than in relation to the matters aforesaid), make a determination to the like effect as the decision.

(9) The bringing of a complaint before the Labour Court under subsection (8) shall be effected by giving to the Labour Court a notice in writing containing such particulars (if any) as may be determined by the Labour Court.

(10) The Labour Court shall publish, in the manner it thinks fit, particulars of any determination made by it under paragraphs (*a*), (*b*), (*c*), (*e*) and (*f*) of subsection (4) (not being a determination as respects a particular appeal under this section) and subsection (9).

GENERAL NOTE

This section provides that a decision of a rights commissioner may be appealed to the Labour Court **HB.327** within six weeks of the date of the decision. In *Bus Eireann v SIPTU* PTD 8/2004, the Labour Court held that the reference to a decision of a Rights Commissioner in s.16 of the Protection of Employees (Part-Time Work) Act 2001 could only be a reference to "a complete or final decision". A decision to extend the time for "reasonable cause" was merely a ruling on one issue arising in the case (see the discussion at para HB.233 *supra*). There is a further right of appeal on a point of law only to the High Court. Although the Rules of the Superior Courts 1986, as amended, do not specifically provide for appeals under this Act, it is suggested that any such appeal be brought either by special summons or by notice of motion, by analogy with the procedures set out in R.S.C. 1986, Orders 105 and 106 respectively. In the absence of any specific rule of court, any such appeal need only be brought within a reasonable time: *per* McCracken J. in his *ex tempore* ruling in *McGaley v Liebherr Container Cranes Ltd* (2001/234 Sp) delivered on October 12, 2001. The circumstances in which the High Court will overturn a decision of a specialist tribunal such as the Labour Court have been considered in many cases: see, for example, *Henry Denny & Sons (Ireland) Ltd v Minister for Social Welfare* [1998] 1 I.R. 34, and in particular the comments of Hamilton C.J. at 37. In considering whether to allow an appeal against a decision of such a tribunal, the High Court must consider whether that body based its decision on an identifiable error of law or on an unsustainable finding of fact. A decision cannot be challenged on the grounds of irrationality if there is any relevant material to support it: see further, *Mulcahy v Waterford Leader Partnership Ltd* [2002] E.L.R. 12 (O'Sullivan J.) and *Thompson v Tesco Ireland Ltd* [2003] E.L.R. 21 (Lavan J.). In *National University of Ireland, Cork v Ahern* [2005] 2 I.R. 577, the Supreme Court held that, although findings of fact must be accepted by the High Court on appeal, that court could still examine the basis upon which those facts were found. The relevance or admissibility of the matters relied on in determining the facts were questions of law.

Where a decision of a rights commissioner has not been carried out by the employer and an appeal has not been brought, the employee may refer the complaint to the Labour Court and the Court, without hearing any evidence, shall make a determination to the like effect as the decision of the rights commissioner.

## Enforcement of determinations of Labour Court

HB.328    **16.**—(1) If an employer fails to carry out in accordance with its terms a determination of the Labour Court in relation to a complaint under section 14 within 6 weeks from the date on which the determination is communicated to the parties, the Circuit Court shall, on application to it in that behalf by—

(*a*)  the employee concerned,

(*b*)  with the consent of the employee, any trade union of which the employee is a member, or

(*c*)  the Minister, if the Minister considers it appropriate to make the application having regard to all the circumstances,

without hearing the employer or any evidence (other than in relation to the matters aforesaid) make an order directing the employer to carry out the determination in accordance with its terms.

(2) The reference in subsection (1) to a determination of the Labour Court is a reference to such a determination in relation to which, at the expiration of the time for bringing an appeal against it, no such appeal has been brought, or if such an appeal has been brought it has been abandoned and the references to the date on which the determination is communicated to the parties shall, in a case where such an appeal is abandoned, be read as a reference to the date of that abandonment.

(3) The Circuit Court may, in an order under this section, if in all the circumstances it considers it appropriate to do so, where the order relates to the payment of compensation, direct the employer concerned to pay to the employee concerned interest on the compensation at the rate referred to in section 22 of the Courts Act 1981 in respect of the whole or any part of the period beginning 6 weeks after the date on which the determination of the Labour Court is communicated to the parties and ending on the date of the order.

(4) An application under this section to the Circuit Court shall be made to the judge of the Circuit Court for the circuit in which the employer concerned ordinarily resides or carries on any profession, business or occupation.

GENERAL NOTE

HB.329    This section provides that the Labour Court's determination can be enforced by the employee, the employee's trade union or the Minister, in the Circuit Court without the employer or any evidence, other than in relation to non-implementation, being heard. The procedures governing applications for enforcement will presumably be similar to those set out in Ord.57 of the Circuit Court Rules 2001.

PART 4

EXCLUSIONS AND OTHER PROVISIONS

## Exclusion of certain types of contracts

HB.330    **17.**—This Act shall not apply to a contract where the employee is—

(*a*)  a member of the Defence Forces,

(*b*)  a trainee within the meaning of the Garda Síochána (Admissions and Appointments) Regulations 1988 (S.I. No. 164 of 1988), or

(*c*)  a nurse in training within the meaning of Parts III and IV of the Nurses Act 1985.

GENERAL NOTE

HB.331    Paragraph (c) excludes nurses in training from the scope of the Act in accordance with clause 2(2)(a) of the Framework Agreement, which provides that the Member States may provide that the agreement does not apply, *inter alia*, to initial vocational training relationships and apprenticeship schemes. Apparently the Department of Health and Children requested that nurses in training be specifically excluded "for the avoidance of doubt": see the Minister of State at the Department of Enterprise, Trade and Employment at 173 *Seanad Debates* Cols. 621–622.

**Limitation on relief**

**18.**—(1) If penalisation of an employee, in contravention of section 13(1),  **HB.332**
constitutes a dismissal of the employee within the meaning of the Unfair Dismissals Acts 1977 to 2001, relief may not be granted to the employee in respect of that
penalisation both under Part 3 and under those Acts.

(2) An individual who is a fixed-term employee under this Act and a part-time
employee under the Act of 2001 may obtain relief arising from the same circumstances under either, but not both, this Act or under Part 2 of the Act of 2001.

**Amendment of Employment Agency Act 1971, Organisation of Working
Time Act 1997 and Protection of Employees (Part-Time Work) Act 2001**

(1) [Amending the Employment Agency Act 1971].  **HB.333**
(2) [Amending the Organisation of Working Time Act 1997].
(3) [Amending the Protection of Employees (Part-Time Work) Act 2001].

GENERAL NOTE

This section raises the fines provided for in section 10(1) of the Employment Agency Act 1971 and  **HB.334**
amends both the Organisation of Working Time Act 1997 and the Protection of Employees (Part-Time
Work) Act 2001 by removing the six week time-limit applicable to referrals of a rights commissioner's
decision to the Labour Court.

# CIRCUIT COURT RULES (PROTECTION OF EMPLOYEES (PART-TIME WORK) ACT, 2001), 2004

## (S.I. No. 721 of 2004)

**HC.101**   1. These Rules, which may be cited as the Circuit Court Rules (Protection of Employees (Part-Time Work) Act, 2001), 2004, shall come into operation on the 17th day of December 2004.

**HC.102**   2. The Orders referred to in these Rules shall be added to and construed together with those Orders contained in the Circuit Court Rules, 2001, as amended.

ORDER 57 Rule 7 — Protection of Employees (Part-Time Work) Act, 2001
(PROTECTION OF EMPLOYEES (PART-TIME WORK) ACT, 2001)
(No. 45 of 2001)

### Rule One

1.   In this Order "the Act" means the Protection of Employees (Part-Time Work) Act, 2001 (No. 45 of 2001), "a determination of the Labour Court" shall be interpreted having regard to the provisions of Section 18(2) of the Act and "the Minister" means the Minister for Enterprise, Trade and Employment.

### Rule Two

2.   All applications under Section 18 of the Act by way of claim for enforcement of determinations of the Labour Court by the Minister or by the employee concerned or, with the consent of the employee, by any trade union of which the employee is a member shall be made by way of Motion on Notice in accordance with Form 1 annexed hereto with such amendments as are appropriate which shall set out the grounds on which the Applicant relies for the reliefs sought and which shall have annexed thereto the original determination of the Labour Court or a certified copy of same, certified by the plaintiff employee or his trade union or on behalf of the Minister as being a true copy of the determination received from the Labour Court and sought to be enforced and shall state the date on which the determination of the Labour Court was communicated to the Applicant.

### Rule Three

3.   Applications shall be brought in the County which the employer concerned ordinarily resides or carries on any profession, business or occupation.

### Rule Four

4.   Notice of every application shall be given to the employer or employers in question and to the Labour Court by serving notice of the proceedings (including the Notice of Motion and grounding Affidavits, if any), no later than 10 days prior to the return date specified in the Notice of Motion, in the case of the employer or employers, personally in accordance with the provisions of Order 11 of these Rules, or by leaving a true copy of same at the employer's residence or place of business or by pre-paid registered post to the employer's residence or place of business and, in the case of the Labour Court, by leaving a true copy of same at the Labour Court.

### Rule Five

5.   Save by special leave of the Court, all applications under Section 18 of the Act shall be heard upon oral evidence or as may be determined by the Court.

**Rule Six**

6.  The Court may make such Order as to costs as may be appropriate including an Order measuring the costs.

FORM 1

AN CHÚIRT CHUARDA

THE CIRCUIT COURT

CIRCUIT                                    COUNTY OF

IN THE MATTER OF THE PROTECTION OF EMPLOYEES (PART-TIME WORK) ACT, 2001

NOTICE OF MOTION FOR RELIEF UNDER SECTION 18 OF THE PROTECTION OF EMPLOYEES (PART-TIME WORK) ACT, 2001

BETWEEN

Plaintiff

AND

Defendant

TAKE NOTICE that application will be made to the Court on the                or the next opportunity thereafter for the following reliefs:

[Here insert details of the relief sought by way of enforcement.]

AND FURTHER TAKE NOTICE that the said application will be grounded upon:

1.      [Here insert grounds upon which the Applicant is relying for the reliefs sought to include all facts relevant to the alleged failure to carry out the decisions or determinations and whether or not an appeal has been brought from the decisions or determinations and, if no such appeal has been brought, that the time for appeal has elapsed and, if such an appeal has been brought, the date upon which the Notice of Appeal was given and evidence of abandonment thereof.]

2.      [Here insert basis of jurisdiction.]

3.      [Here insert name, address and description of the Plaintiff.]

4.      [Here insert the date on which the determination of the Labour Court was communicated to the Applicant.]

5.      [The following documents must be annexed to this Notice of Motion namely the original determination of the Labour Court or a certified copy of same, certified by the Applicant employee or his trade union or on behalf of the Minister as being a true copy of the determination received from the Labour Court and sought to be enforced.]

Dated this      day of      20      .

H–92

Signed: Plaintiff/Solicitor for the Plaintiff

To:

Defendant/Solicitor for the Defendant

And
To: The Labour Court
And
To: The County Registrar

GENERAL NOTE

These rules prescribe Circuit Court procedures in respect of applications for the enforcement of **HC.104**
Labour Court determinations pursuant to s.8 of the 2001 Act.

The Labour Relations Commission

Tom Johnson House
Haddington Road
Dublin 4

Telephone 01 613 6700
Fax 01 613 6701
E-mail: info@lrc.ie
Website: www.lrc.ie
LoCall (outside 01 area): 1890 220227

| APPLICATION TO RIGHTS COMMISSIONER |
| --- |
| MATERNITY PROTECTION ACT 1994 |

(PLEASE USE BLOCK CAPITALS)

NAME:_____

NAME OF COMPANY/
EMPLOYER: _____

ADDRESS: _____

ADDRESS: _____

_____

_____

_____

_____

TEL NO: _____

TEL NO: _____

NAME AND ADDRESS OF YOUR REPRESENTATIVE (IF ANY) _____
_____

EMPLOYMENT DETAILS

EMPLOYMENT BEGAN: __/__/__

EMPLOYMENT ENDED: __/__/__ [if applicable]

Pay (including benefits and regular overtime) per week: €_____GROSS
€_____TAKE HOME

MY DISPUTE IS THAT:

_____
_____
_____
_____
_____

SIGNATURE:_____ DATE:_____

PLEASE NOTE THAT A COPY OF THIS FORM WILL BE FORWARDED TO YOUR
EMPLOYER.

Maurice Cashell *(Chairman)*
Liam Downey
Josephine Feehily
Peter McLoone
Breege O'Donoghue
Brendan McGinty
Tom Wall

Kieran Mulvey *(Chief Executive)*

O–53

*Irish Employment Legislation*

**The Labour Relations Commission**

Tom Johnson House
Haddington Road
Dublin 4

Telephone 01 613 6700
Fax 01 613 6701
E-mail: info@lrc.ie
Website: www.lrc.ie
LoCall (outside 01 area): 1890 220227

**APPLICATION TO RIGHTS COMMISSIONER**

**THE PROTECTION OF YOUNG PERSONS (EMPLOYMENT) ACT, 1996**

(PLEASE USE BLOCK CAPITALS)

NAME: _____

NAME OF COMPANY
OR EMPLOYER: _____
(FULL LEGAL NAME, IF IN DOUBT CONSULT
YOUR P60 OR P45)

ADDRESS: _____

ADDRESS: _____

_____

_____

_____

_____

TEL NO: _____

TEL NO: _____

NAME AND ADDRESS OF YOUR REPRESENTATIVE (IF ANY) _____

I WISH TO MAKE A COMPLAINT TO A RIGHTS COMMISSIONER THAT MY EMPLOYER CONTRAVENED THE ABOVE ACT IN RELATION TO A <u>OR</u> B BELOW.

(PLEASE COMPLETE APPROPRIATE SECTION)

(A)  <u>SECTION 13</u> (PRESERVATION OF EXISTING RATES OF PAY AND CONDITIONS)

IN WHAT WAY HAS YOUR EMPLOYER BEEN IN BREACH OF THIS SECTION?

_____
_____
_____
_____

(B)  <u>SECTION 17</u> (REFUSAL TO CO-OPERATE WITH THE EMPLOYER IN BREACHING THE ACT)

IN WHAT WAY HAS YOUR EMPLOYER BEEN IN BREACH OF THIS SECTION?

_____
_____
_____
_____

EMPLOYEES SIGNATURE: _____    DATE: _____

PLEASE NOTE THAT A COPY OF THIS FORM WILL BE FORWARDED TO YOUR EMPLOYER.

Maurice Cashell *(Chairman)*
Liam Downey
Josephine Feehily
Peter McLoone
Breege O'Donoghue
Brendan McGinty
Tom Wall

Kieran Mulvey *(Chief Executive)*

Labour Relations Commission Forms

 **The Labour Relations Commission**

Tom Johnson House
Haddington Road
Dublin 4

Telephone 01 613 6700
Fax 01 613 6701
E-mail: info@lrc.ie
Website: www.lrc.ie
LoCall (outside 01 area): 1890 220227

## APPLICATION TO RIGHTS COMMISSIONER

## NATIONAL MINIMUM WAGE ACT, 2000

(PLEASE USE BLOCK CAPITALS)

NAME: _____

NAME OF COMPANY/
EMPLOYER: _____

ADDRESS: _____

ADDRESS: _____

_____

_____

_____

_____

TEL NO: _____

TEL NO: _____

DATE OF BIRTH (IF UNDER 21): _____

NAME AND ADDRESS OF YOUR REPRESENTATIVE (IF ANY): _____
_____

DATE ON WHICH THIS EMPLOYMENT BEGAN: _____

PAY PER HOUR PER WEEK:
PAY INCLUDING BENEFITS AND REGULAR OVERTIME PER WEEK

€ _____ PER HOUR
€ _____ GROSS
€ _____ TAKE HOME

WHAT IS YOUR PAY REFERENCE PERIOD (Section 10) ? _____

HAVE YOU REQUESTED FROM YOU EMPLOYER A WRITTEN STATEMENT OF YOUR AVERAGE HOURLY
RATE OF PAY FOR ANY "PAY REFERENCE PERIOD"? YES      NO

IF YES WHEN? _____ { SECTION 23(4) }

HAVE YOU REQUESTED AN "INSPECTOR" TO INVESTIGATE YOUR DISPUTE? (SECTION 34) YES      NO

MY DISPUTE IS THAT:

_____

_____

_____

EMPLOYEE'S SIGNATURE: _____      DATE: _____

**PLEASE NOTE THAT A COPY OF THIS FORM WILL BE FORWARDED TO YOUR
EMPLOYER.**

Maurice Cashell *(Chairman)*
Liam Downey
Josephine Feehily
Peter McLoone
Breege O'Donoghue
Brendan McGinty
Tom Wall

Kieran Mulvey *(Chief Executive)*

O–57

The Labour Relations Commission

Tom Johnson House
Haddington Road
Dublin 4

Telephone 01 613 6700
Fax 01 613 6701
E-mail: info@lrc.ie
Website: www.lrc.ie
LoCall (outside 01 area): 1890 220;

---

## APPLICATION TO RIGHTS COMMISSIONER
### Protection Of Employees (Part-Time Work) Act, 2001

**(PLEASE USE BLOCK CAPITALS)**

**Name:** _____

**Name of Company/Employer:** _____
(Full Legal Name, if in doubt consult your P60 or
P45)

**Address:** _____
_____
_____

**Address:** _____
_____
_____

**Telephone No:** _____

**Telephone:** _____

**Name & Address of your
Representative, if any:**

I wish to make a complaint to a Rights Commissioner that my employer has contravened
the above Act.
The grounds for my complaint are as follows:

_____
_____
_____
_____

If you consider that you are being treated in a less favourable manner than a comparable
full-time employee, who is that comparable full-time employee? _____

Does the comparable employee work for your employer?   Yes/No (delete as appropriate)

If the comparable employee does not work for your employer, what is the name and
address of the employer of that employee?

**Employee's signature:** _____

**Date:** _____
Please note that a copy of this form will be forwarded to your employer.

R:9 September 2003

*Irish Employment Legislation*

**The Labour Relations Commission**

Tom Johnson House
Haddington Road
Dublin 4

Telephone 01 613 6700
Fax 01 613 6701
E-mail: info@lrc.ie
Website: www.lrc.ie
LoCall (outside 01 area): 1890 220227

---

### NOTICE OF COMPLAINT TO A RIGHTS COMMISSIONER UNDER

### ADOPTIVE LEAVE ACT, 1995

(PLEASE USE BLOCK CAPITALS)

NAME: _____

NAME OF COMPANY/
EMPLOYER _____
(FULL LEGAL NAME IF IN DOUBT CONSULT YOUR
P45 OR P60)

ADDRESS:_____

ADDRESS: _____

_____

_____

_____

_____

TEL NO: _____

TEL NO: _____

NAME AND ADDRESS OF REPRESENTATIVE (IF ANY)_____
_____

DATE ON WHICH EMPLOYMENT BEGAN:          _/_/_

(A) MY DISPUTE RELATES TO ADOPTIVE LEAVE (PART II OF THE ACT) AND IS AS
FOLLOWS:_____
_____
_____
_____
_____

(B) MY DISPUTE RELATES TO THE PROVISIONS OF MY EMPLOYMENT CONTRACT
(PART III OF THE ACT) AND IS AS FOLLOWS:_____
_____
_____
_____
_____

SIGNATURE: _____          DATE: _____

PLEASE NOTE THAT A COPY OF THIS FORM WILL BE FORWARDED TO YOUR
EMPLOYER.

Maurice Cashell *(Chairman)*
Liam Downey
Josephine Feehily
Peter McLoone
Breege O'Donoghue
Brendan McGinty
Tom Wall

Kieran Mulvey *(Chief Executive)*

O–61

**The Labour Relations Commission**

Tom Johnson House
Haddington Road
Dublin 4

Telephone 01 613 6700
Fax 01 613 6701
E-mail: info@lrc.ie
Website: www.lrc.ie
LoCall (outside 01 area): 1890 220227

---

**NOTICE OF COMPLAINT TO RIGHTS COMMISSIONER**

**ORGANISATION OF WORKING TIME ACT, 1997**

(PLEASE USE BLOCK CAPITALS)

NAME: _____     NAME OF COMPANY/ EMPLOYER: _____

ADDRESS: _____     ADDRESS: _____

TEL NO: _____     TEL NO: _____

I WISH TO PRESENT A COMPLAINT TO A RIGHTS COMMISSIONER THAT MY EMPLOYER CONTRAVENED THE ABOVE ACT IN RELATION TO A OR B OR C BELOW. (PLEASE COMPLETE APPROPRIATE SECTION).

*N.B. YOUR EMPLOYER SHOULD BE MADE AWARE OF THE CLAIM PRIOR TO MAKING THIS COMPLAINT TO A RIGHTS COMMISSIONER.*

(A)   REST PERIODS AND SUNDAY WORK (SECTIONS 6(1) and 6(2) and 11 TO 14 OF THE ACT)
MY COMPLAINT IS THAT:_____

(B)   MINIMUM AND MAXIMUM WORKING HOURS (SECTIONS 15 TO 18 OF THE ACT)
MY COMPLAINT IS THAT:_____

(C)   HOLIDAYS (SECTIONS 19 TO 23 OF THE ACT)
MY COMPLAINT IS THAT:_____

(D)   OTHER (FOR EXAMPLE, SECTION 26 ON PARAGRAPH 1 OF THE FIFTH SCHEDULE OF THE ACT)
MY COMPLAINT IS THAT:_____

SIGNATURE: _____     DATE: _____

PLEASE NOTE A COPY OF THIS FORM WILL BE FORWARDED TO YOUR EMPLOYER

Maurice Cashell *(Chairman)*
Liam Downey
Josephine Feehily
Peter McLoone
Breege O'Donoghue
Brendan McGinty
Tom Wall

Kieran Mulvey *(Chief Executive)*

**The Labour Relations Commission**

Tom Johnson House
Haddington Road
Dublin 4

Telephone 01 613 6700
Fax 01 613 6701
E-mail: info@lrc.ie
Website: www.lrc.ie
LoCall (outside 01 area): 1890 220227

---

**NOTICE OF COMPLAINT TO RIGHTS COMMISSIONER**

**PARENTAL LEAVE ACT, 1998**

(PLEASE USE BLOCK CAPITALS)

NAME: _____     NAME OF COMPANY/
                                 EMPLOYER: _____
ADDRESS: _____   ADDRESS: _____

_____            _____

_____            _____

TEL NO: _____    TEL NO: _____

I WISH TO PRESENT A DISPUTE TO A RIGHTS COMMISSIONER THAT MY EMPLOYER CONTRAVENED THE ABOVE ACT.

*N.B. IS YOUR EMPLOYER AWARE THAT YOU ARE BRINGING THIS DISPUTE TO A RIGHTS COMMISSIONER.?*

1) WHEN DID YOU JOIN THE ORGANISATION _____

2) NAME OF THE CHILD TO WHOM THIS DISPUTE RELATES _____

3) DATE OF CHILD'S BIRTH _____ (THIS ACT DOES NOT APPLY TO CHILDREN BORN BEFORE 3RD JUNE 1996, OR TO THOSE WHO HAVE NOW REACHED 5 YEARS OF AGE)

PLEASE ENCLOSE A COPY OF THE CHILD'S BIRTH CERTIFICATE

4) WHAT PERIOD OF PARENTAL LEAVE DID YOU SEEK? _____
   ( SECTION 7 OF THE ACT)

5) DID YOU GIVE WRITTEN NOTICE TO YOUR EMPLOYER AND WAS IT ACCEPTED?
   (SECTION8, (1) TO (5) OF THE ACT)_____

6) DID YOU RECEIVE A "CONFIRMATION DOCUMENT" FROM YOUR EMPLOYER?
   (SECTION 9, (1) TO (3)_____

7) WAS YOUR PARENTAL LEAVE TERMINATED?_____

8) MY DISPUTE (UNDER SECTIONS 7 TO 9) IS THAT: _____
_____
_____
_____

9) (SECTION 13, FORCE MAJEURE LEAVE)
   MY DISPUTE IS THAT:
_____
_____
_____

PLEASE ENCLOSE COPIES OF ALL THE NOTICES GIVEN TO, AND RECEIVED FROM, YOUR EMPLOYER IN RELATION TO THIS DISPUTE (DO NOT SEND THE ORIGINALS)

SIGNATURE:_____     DATE:_____

PLEASE NOTE A COPY OF THIS FORM WILL BE FORWARDED TO YOUR EMPLOYER

**In accordance with Statutory Instrument No 6 of 1999, Regulations entitled "Parental Leave (Disputes and Appeals) Regulations 1999" paragraph 4, employers are obliged to provide a notice of appearance within 14 days of receipt of this notice.**

Maurice Cashell *(Chairman)*
Liam Downey
Josephine Feehily
Peter McLoone
Breege O'Donoghue
Brendan McGinty
Tom Wall

Kieran Mulvey *(Chief Executive)*

**The Labour Relations Commission**

Tom Johnson House
Haddington Road
Dublin 4

Telephone 01 613 6700
Fax 01 613 6701
E-mail: info@lrc.ie
Website: www.lrc.ie
LoCall (outside 01 area): 1890 220227

---

**NOTICE OF COMPLAINT TO RIGHTS COMMISSIONER**
**PAYMENT OF WAGES ACT 1991**

NAME: _____

NAME OF COMPANY OR EMPLOYER: _____
FULL LEGAL NAME, IF IN DOUBT
CONSULT YOUR P60 OR P45)

ADDRESS: _____

ADDRESS: _____

_____

_____

_____

_____

TEL NO: _____

TEL NO: _____

I wish to present a complaint to a Rights Commissioner that my employer contravened the above Act in relation to A **OR** B below.
(Please complete appropriate section).

N.B.: Your employer should be made aware of the claim prior to making this complaint to a Rights Commissioner.

(A) **DEDUCTION FROM PAY**

DATE OF DEDUCTION ____

AMOUNT OF DEDUCTION € _____

DID YOU RECEIVE NOTICE
INTENT TO MAKE THE DEDUCTION

WHAT WAS THE REASON FOR THE
DEDUCTION? please specify

YES          NO

_____

IF YES HOW MUCH NOTICE?

_____

_____

**OR**

(B) **ARE YOU MAKING A CLAIM FOR
NON PAYMENT OF**

DATE PAYMENT SHOULD
HAVE BEEN RECEIVED

(Please calculate monies due)

____ / ____ / ____

1.    WAGES/PAY          AMOUNT € _____
2.    MINIMUM NOTICE     AMOUNT € _____
3.    HOLIDAY PAY        AMOUNT € _____
4.    OTHER              AMOUNT € _____
If 4 please specify _____

TOTAL AMOUNT € _____

SIGNATURE: _____

DATE: _____

O–67

**The Labour Relations Commission**

Tom Johnson House
Haddington Road
Dublin 4

Telephone 01 613 6700
Fax 01 613 6701
E-mail: info@lrc.ie
Website: www.lrc.ie
LoCall (outside 01 area): 1890 220227

---

### NOTICE OF COMPLAINT TO A RIGHTS COMMISSIONER UNDER

### THE TERMS OF EMPLOYMENT (INFORMATION) ACT, 1994

(PLEASE USE BLOCK CAPITALS)

NAME: _____     NAME OF COMPANY/
EMPLOYER _____
(FULL LEGAL NAME IF IN DOUBT CONSULT YOUR
P45 OR P60)

ADDRESS:_____     ADDRESS: _____

_____          _____

_____          _____

TEL NO: _____     TEL NO: _____

NAME AND ADDRESS OF REPRESENTATIVE (IF ANY) _____
_____

DATE ON WHICH EMPLOYMENT BEGAN:          _/_/_

DATE ON WHICH YOU REQUESTED STATEMENT:     _/_/_

(A)     HOW HAS YOUR EMPLOYER FAILED TO COMPLY WITH THE REQUIREMENT
TO GIVE YOU A WRITTEN STATEMENT? _____
_____
_____
_____

(B)     MY COMPLAINT IS THAT CHANGES WERE MADE TO MY WRITTEN
STATEMENT WITHOUT NOTIFICATION (SECTION 5). PLEASE DESCRIBE YOUR
COMPLAINT. _____
_____
_____
_____

SIGNATURE: _____     DATE: _____

PLEASE NOTE THAT A COPY OF THIS FORM WILL BE FORWARDED TO YOUR
EMPLOYER.

Maurice Cashell *(Chairman)*
Liam Downey
Josephine Feehily
Peter McLoone
Breege O'Donoghue
Brendan McGinty
Tom Wall

Kieran Mulvey *(Chief Executive)*